Close Encounters

with the

Pilot's Grim Reaper

By: Lou Martin

Lt.Col. USAF (ret.)

Author: Lt.Col. Louis J. Martin (1966)

Third Edition (2008)

Order this book online at www.trafford.com
or email orders@trafford.com

Most Trafford titles are also available at major online book retailers.

Print information available on the last page.

ISBN: 978-1-4120-9229-6 (sc)

Trafford rev. 08/12/2016

North America & international
toll-free: 1 888 232 4444 (USA & Canada)
fax: 812 355 4082

Dedication

This book is dedicated to my many aviation colleagues who fell victim to the *Pilot's Grim Reaper* and were not allowed to join me in becoming a member of the living, "Old Pilot's Band of Brothers," able to spin wild tales, (mostly true) of exciting days of old. I have fond memories of each and every one of them. I also wish to extend appreciation to my wife Chieko, who never complained about the hours I spent sitting in front of my computer.

Notes

This is a nonfiction book. A few liberties were taken in the sequencing of events, but they all happened and are accurately portrayed to the best of my recollection. The use of pseudonyms, when referring to a few colleagues, was employed and when this occurs it will be noted by the symbol *(N)* the first time the name appears, but it represents an actual person. The reader will find other instances where I have elected to omit a name entirely, but my personal records contain accurate names and dates to support the persons portrayed. The reader may find a few references to aviation terminology not explained in the text. When this occurs, please refer to the abbreviated glossary. Some quotations may not be "verbatim," since they occurred 50 years ago, but I can assure the reader that the jest of the discussions are retained and truthful in context. The reader should also be advised that there was no "ghost writer" all 232,680 words were those of the author.

Contact
Author may be contacted at: pilotlou@aol.com
Tel: 952-891-1250 or 612-309-1825.

Acknowledgment

The material presented in this book was derived from my personal memory of my flying experiences, references to the remarks section of my Senior Pilot's Flight Log Book, my Official Air Force Pilot's Individual Flight Record, my wifes's diary and reams of personal documents I accumulated and saved during the past 60 years. However, information relating to various aircraft specifications and some dates and locations were obtained through Internet research. Utilizing this public source of information makes it impossible to acknowledge specific contributors. But other reference sources were useful in confirming and refreshing my own personal recollection of a myriad of subjects, they were: the United States Air Forces in Europe History book; the 317th Troop Carrier Wing Yearbook; the Everyday Japanese workbook; the common usage German Dictionary; The German Berlitz Traveler's Guide; the Air Force Magazine; the First Air Force Magazine; the *Pegasus* Magazine; the *F-100 Super Sabre* by Charles L. Weidinger; the Warbirds International Magazine; the Minnesota *Flyer* Magazine; the Minnesota Aviation Hall of Fame; the Air Force Historical Studies Office; the Jet Qualification Course Outline; the Air Training Command T-33 Student Study Guide; the Air Training Command T-33A Aircrew Checklist; the Continental Air Command Safety of Flight Checklist; *Flying the T-33* by Col. John Fulton; *Taming a Taildragger* by Bill Kelly; the Dover AFB, Delaware Air Museum; Cal Taylor's article, C-133 Down; Major Burnett's reports of a C-133 incident on November 12, 1963 and Mike Huttner's use of several pages of a C-119G Dash-1. Special thanks goes to my longtime friend and aviation colleague, Dorothy (Dottie) Bassett, for the hours she spent in reviewing my draft manuscript and for her comments and recommendations. Dottie worked for Northwest Airlines for 33 years as the Manager of Pilot and Aircraft Publications Compliance and the editor of the airline's *OnCourse* Magazine. I was fortunate to have had the honor of working with her.

The design of the front and back covers was the authors. However, the Grim Reaper Image on the front cover was reproduced with the permission of Mobtown Enterprises, 2620 West Fletcher St., Chicago, IL. 60618. The blue sky, filled with white clouds, was from a photograph taken by the author.

Contents

Illustrations depicted on the book covers, inside page one and in photo section Following Page 239.

The front cover portrays the author's Air Force Command pilot wings, the U.S. Flag that covered his brother Dan's coffin (a WW II U.S. Air Corps veteran), and an illustration of the Grim Reaper. The back cover illustrates a C-133, F-100, C-119 and the author next to the Grumman *Wildcat* fighter he flew to Newton, Iowa in 1995. The inside front cover contains a photo of author as a Lt.Col. in 1966 and his Japan Domestic Airline's pilot wings.

Photos 1 - 7 represent the author's early life from 1929 to 1947.

Photo   8 is the Martin family assemblage in 1968.

Photos 9 - 14 represents the author's early flying career.

Photos 15 - 23 represents the author and his son in pilot training.

Photos 24 - 35 depicts the author's life as a young Air Force pilot.

Photos 36 and 37 are of the author's 1952 MG-TD and 1950 Buick.

Photos 38 and 39 reflects a C-119 *Boxcar* in action in Germany.

Photos 40 and 41 are of the author's marriage in Germany in 1951 and flying school classmates in Greenville, SC in 1953.

Photos 42 - 47 are of the C-47, C-45, T-33, F-100, T-39 and C-123.

Photo   48 is the author in Bangkok, Thailand in 1962.

Photos 49 is of General Wallace presenting C-133 Aircraft Commander Certificate to the author in 1965.

Photos 50 & 51 are of a C-133 at Dover AFB and author in Vietnam.

Photo   52 is wreckage of C-133 that ditched in the Pacific Ocean.

Photo   53 is Albatross (Gooney Bird) on Midway Island.

Photos 54 - 59 relate to flying with Japan Domestic Airlines.

Photos 60 and 61 are of author's daughter Lynn and son Michael.

Photos 62 - 69 relate to life in Iran from 1976 to 1979.

Photo   70 is of author and friends enjoying skiing in Austria in 1995.

Photos 71 and 72 are of author and his wife Chieko enjoying life.

Photo   73 is Planes of Fame Air Museum Chief Pilot Kermit LaQuey.

Photo   74 is of the author enjoying last flight in F-100F in 1993.

Photos 75 - 77 are aircraft the author flew with Planes of Fame Air Museum in Eden Prairie, Minnesota.

Photo   78 is the Bob Pond racer in Mojave, CA in April 1991.

Photo   79 is author on *Wildcat* fighter he flew with Planes of Fame.

Photos 80 and 81 are of author touting his book *Wings Over Persia.*

Introduction

In *Close Encounters with the Pilot's Grim Reaper* (PGR), I hope to provide the reader with a documented account in an autobiographical format of in-flight close calls or near disasters I personally experienced in 60 years and 19,000 hours of flying, plus encounters, some fatal, of aviation colleagues. In addition, I will include interesting anecdotes of a young boy aspiring to become a pilot; and after reaching that goal, recollections of 22 years as an Air Force pilot, nearly five years as a captain for Japan Domestic Airlines, three years as a charter pilot in Iran and nearly 19 years as a pilot inspector and supervisor with the FAA.

It has been said that old pilots, who have devoted their lives to waltzing with the angels, while steering clear of the Grim Reaper, have achieved this eminence through a combination of good luck and skill. I am in full agreement with this rationale, as I obtained my Private Pilot's Certificate at age 17 and 62 years later still flying without ever experiencing a serious incident or accident. However, I'm not sure what percentage of this achievement was due to skill and what percentage attributable to Lady Luck. Perhaps a fifty/fifty ratio would be a valid speculation.

Looking back over my years of flying 65 hp Piper *Cubs*, high speed single engine jets, 275,000-pound four-engine transports, corporate aircraft and World War II restored warbirds, I can recall many life-threatening episodes, in both peace and war, that could have resulted in an early end to my exciting flying career.

Although each episode was unique, there were some aircraft that developed repetitive systemic problems before corrective actions were taken, or I was able to move on to a different type of aircraft and left the problem for other pilots to solve, or endure. Unfortunately, many of my colleagues were not as lucky, or did not possess the skill required to avoid the PGR's scathing scythe and are now residing in pilot's Valhalla.

I devote a separate chapter to each aircraft that provided the "Close Encounter" I consider worthy of note. In contrast, there were aircraft that I flew, which by reputation should have provided excitement and a "Close Encounter," that were as gentle as kittens. (It's possible these non events were due to good luck, or the *Saint Christopher Medal* I wore around my neck, next to my military dog tags.) An example would be the B-25

Mitchell Bomber, which I flew in advanced Air Force pilot training. I feel extremely fortunate that in all my years of flying my number of landings equal my number of takeoffs.

I learned a great deal from each incident, or emergency I encountered, and developed a feeling of confidence in being able to handle any and all situations the PGR threw at me, with his goal of preventing me from becoming an "old and bold pilot." Strange as it may sound, if I would fly for a period of several months, without experiencing an emergency or life-threatening event, I found myself looking forward to the next in-flight uncertainty. There is an old axiom which states, "Flying is 98% boredom and 2% sheer terror." In keeping with this philosophy, I felt that occasional emergencies were necessary to test my skill as a pilot, confirm that my good luck was still holding, making sure *Saint Christopher* hadn't gone out on strike, interrupting the boredom, and meeting the challenge of surviving another experience unscathed. I was surprised how quickly I adapted to a resilience in meeting potential danger! I believe my level of anxiety decreased with each successive crisis! Apparently, my trust in my own expertise and a natural feeling that it can't happen to me, allowed accepting risk as a normal component of being a pilot.

Since my flying experiences go back many years, there was never a question that I wouldn't be exposed to in-flight emergencies, or mechanical problems, before I gained sufficient experience to move to the left seat, as Pilot In Command. This early experience exposed me to engine fires, electrical problems, mechanical failures, flying through thunderstorms, etc., while observing how former WW II combat pilots calmly, and professionally, solved these problems. No matter what the crisis, they would state that it was nothing compared to flying through clouds of "flak" or being shot at by swarms of "enemy fighters." I felt very fortunate to have been exposed to this type of "hands-on-training," which was not available to the next generation of pilots.

There are some corporate and airline pilots flying today that have never experienced an actual in-flight emergency. The reliability of modern day aircraft (which is a tribute to how far aviation has advanced) is so dependable that the only emergencies many pilots experience is in a realistic aircraft visual simulator. We can be proud of this dependability achievement, but I have witnessed examples of younger pilots, when confronted with an real in-flight emergency, develop what I call "Buck Fever in the Cockpit," and exhibit a disbelief in recognizing that they are actually experiencing a genuine crisis. Because of this disrespect to the reality at hand, some pilots are slow to react in correcting the problem. However, once they experience one or more authentic emergencies, and come through the test unscathed, they become more confident pilots. Fortunately, or unfortunately, many airline pilots will reach the new mandatory retirement age of 65 without ever being exposed to an actual in-flight emergency. This was never a problem during my early years of flying, as in-flight emergencies were an accepted risk and not an uncommon occurrence.

I also provide a short description of each type aircraft presented, which I hope will provide ample datum for the reader to join me in the cockpit and together, we will stay one step ahead of the PGR as he swings his long freshly-honed, razor-sharp scythe in our direction.

My message for new pilots just starting their aviation careers is to encourage them to remember that there is no substitute for good common sense. One of the greatest tools the Grim Reaper has working for him is complacency. Know your limitations and don't become distracted. Never allow your brain to slide into a "screen-saver mode," as flying can, and does, become routine. When you accompany this with the excellent reliability of modern day aircraft, complacency is the pilot's biggest adversary. Approximately 60% of aircraft accidents are attributed to pilot error. Surprisingly, this cause factor has remained nearly constant for the past 50 years. (I'm sure this statistic has the PGR smiling with joy as he scans the sky for potential victims. Remember he is a slow but patient predator, just waiting for you to make a mistake.)

Throughout this book I sometimes refer to Close Encounters, and fatal accidents experienced by former aviation (non-pilot) friends and colleagues. I did this not only to emphasize that individuals other than pilots were potential Grim Reaper targets, but to pay homage to those who did not escape his stealthy scythe. He casts a net so wide that it is difficult to know whom it might ensnare. From the early days of aviation to the present, there is a certain amount of potential danger associated with pursuing a career in aviation. Perhaps this exposure to possible danger is what attracts many adventurous young men and women to follow it as a calling.

Many aircraft types I have flown are not described in this book, since they did not provide the excitement deserving of discussion or attract the PGR. However, a complete catalogue of the types I have flown are:

Single Engine: Taylorcraft BC-12. Aeronca 11-AC *Chief*, 7-AC *Champ* and *Citabra*. Piper J3 *Cub*, PA-28R *Arrow*, PA-32/300 *Cherokee Six*, PA-28 140 *Cherokee*, PA-22 *Tri-Pacer*, and PA-38 *Tomahawk*. Ercoupe 415C. Luscombe 8F *Silvaire*. Rockwell Aero Commander 100 *Lark*. Cessna 150 *Commuter*, 172 *Skyhawk* and 182 RG *Skylane*. *Lake Amphibian LA4-200 *Buccaneer*. Fairchild PT-19 *Cornell*. North American T-6 *Texan* and F-100 *Super Saber*. Beechcraft T-34 *Mentor*, F-33A, V-35B and A-36 *Bonanza*. Mooney M-20B. De-Havilland DH-82A *Tiger Moth*. Lockheed T-33 *Shooting Star*. Grumman FM-2 *Wildcat*. Boeing PT-17 *Kadet*. Homebuilt Open-air Breezy.

Twin Engine: *Douglas B-26 *Invader*, DC-9 and C-47 *Skytrain*. North American B-25 *Mitchell* and NA-265 *Saber Liner*. Beechcraft C-45 *Expediter*, BE-58 *Baron* and *Super King Air* 300. Fairchild C-82 *Packet*, C-119 *Boxcar*, FH-227 *Friendship* and *Metro III turboprop. Dassault Falcon DA-20. Paris Jet MS-760. Japanese Nihon YS-11 Turboprop. Fokker F-27 *Friendship*. Rockwell Turbo Commander NA-690A. Piper PA-44 *Seminole* and PA-34 *Seneca* II. *Gloster *Meteor* Twin Jet.

Three Engine: Boeing 727 *Trijet*.

Four Engine: *Boeing B-17 *Flying Fortress*, *B-29 *Super Fortress* and B-747 *Jumbo Jet*. Douglas C-54 *Skymaster* and C-133 *Cargomaster*.

Gliders: Schweizer SGS-2-33. Schleicher ASK-21, Ka-7 and Ka-8. PZL Bielsko Puchacz 50-3 Owl and SZD 51-1 Junior. Stamer Lippisch Schulgleiter SG-38 Boat and Schneider Baby Grunau. Tainan Mita III. (Glider flights were launched utilizing both aero and winch tow).

Note: Aircraft types identified with an (*) indicates aircraft that I was not qualified to fly as Pilot In Command (PIC), but did perform familiarization takeoffs and landings under the supervision of a qualified instructor pilot.

The Author

Lou Martin was born and raised in Ladysmith, a small Midwest farming town in Northern Wisconsin. He was the ninth of ten children of hard-working German, Scottish, Irish parents, and lived through the worst years of the worldwide economic depression of the 1930s. The hardship of the times imbued a sense of independence, confidence, and a will to succeed, no matter what the odds. This characteristic was sustained throughout his childhood and adult life. (See Photos No. 1, 2, and 8.)

His formative teenage years were during a time of a more genteel period in American society: A time when movie theater ushers escorted patrons to their seats with flashlights. A time when boys were not allowed to wear blue jeans, or baseball caps on backwards, and girls were not allowed to wear slacks in school. A time when teachers and students danced to the same music, and a time when radio stations (there was no TV) and movies were free from vulgarity, sexual promiscuity and rudeness. When maturing into puberty, his interest in the female anatomy was satisfied discreetly and innocently. Today's teenagers can satisfy this "natural curiosity" by viewing virtual pornography on the Internet. This cultured upbringing, (which was the norm for the times) developed a character that produced a respect for his fellow man and provided the foundation for a successful career.

He was 13 years old when the Japanese attacked Pearl Harbor on December 7, 1941, but along with other young boys his age contributed to America's victory to the extent possible. He collected scrap metal, delivered Western Union telegrams, assisted local farmers, worked as a railroad laborer, and in a defense plant in Chicago, Illinois.

His stint as a Western Union delivery boy was during the troubling war year of 1942, and recalls delivering telegrams to family members, informing them that their sons were killed, missing or prisoners of war. In 1943 he volunteered to support farmers in harvesting their crops, because most older men were in the military. During the summer of 1944, he worked ten hours, six days a week, as a Soo Line railroad worker (Gandy Dancer), "shoulder-to-shoulder" with adult muscular rugged laborers. He recounts how mature Gandy Dancers took great pleasure in introducing him, and his young colleagues, to the pleasures of drink and attempts in enticing them to visit bordellos. He admits to enjoying the former, but passed on the latter. (See photos 6 and 7.) When the war with Japan ended in August 1945, he was working in Detroit Michigan and recalls the unprecedented victory celebrations with clarity.

His first airplane ride was in a 65 hp Luscombe *Silvaire* at age 12, obtained his Private Pilot's Certificate at age 17, and for the next 62 years continued his dream of flying. After graduating from high school in 1947, he worked as an apprentice photographer and engaged in commercial flying by performing aerial mapping flights in a Piper *Cub*.

Three years after the end of World War II, the U.S. Air Force was again recruiting young men for pilot training. However, acceptance for the Aviation Cadet Program required a minimum of two years of college. With only a high school education, it appeared he would not be able to meet the basic education requirements and fulfill a boyhood dream.

However, an Army recruiting sergeant told him that the Air Force was accepting young men for pilot training if they could pass a written exam on Theories and Mechanics of flying, a two-year college equivalency knowledge of Algebra, Trigonometry, Geometry, Physics, U.S. History, Geography, English Composition and Grammar, be in perfect physical condition and be approved by a board of commissioned Air Force pilots.

Along with 11 other young potential Aviation Cadet candidates from the Midwest, he reported to Chanute AFB in June 1948 to compete in qualification testing. Only four of the 12 examined were accepted, with only two graduating as 2nd.Lts. and Air Force pilots 15 months later.

After graduating from pilot training in September 1949, he spent the next 21 years as a military pilot. His active service included six years in Germany, three years in Japan, and five years flying combat cargo support missions in Vietnam, where he was credited with 169 combat flight hours. His Air Force flying ranged from piloting large four-engine transports to single-engine jets.

Years attending night school allowed him to achieve a secondary goal of obtaining a college education and he graduated from the University of Maryland with a Bachelor of Science degree. He retired from the Air Force in 1970 with the rank of lieutenant colonel.

After leaving the Air Force Colonel Martin flew as a captain and Chief Pilot for Japan Domestic Airlines from 1970 to 1975. His job in Japan was unique in that he lived in Yokohama and flew a Japanese YS-11 turboprop with Japanese copilots and Japanese flight attendants. His years with Japan Airlines included flying with senior Japanese captains who had participated in the December 7, 1941 bombing of Pearl Harbor, and former members of inactive Kamikaze squadrons. When in Japan, he met, and later married, a Japanese senior flight attendant.

From 1976 to 1979 he flew as a captain for an air charter company in Tehran, Iran. In this capacity he traveled throughout the Middle East, and was in Karachi, Pakistan during the demonstrations preceding the overthrow of Prime Minister Zulfikar Ali Bhutto. He was in Iran during the Revolution that overthrew the Shah, but when his life was in danger made a hasty exit. His Iranian experiences are graphically summarized in his book, *Wings Over Persia,* which was rated the Best Aviation Writing by a Minnesotan by the Minnesota Aviation Hall of Fame for 2004.

In 1980, he accepted a position with the Federal Aviation Administration as an Air Carrier Pilot Inspector. His first FAA assignment was in Valley Stream, New York, where he supervised new startup airlines.

In 1983, he transferred to the Minneapolis, Minnesota FAA office with duties as a DC-9, B-727 and B-747 pilot examiner. He held the position of Chief FAA Inspector for Northwest Airlines for nine years.

From 1992 to 1996, he was attached to the U.S. Consulate Office in Frankfurt, Germany, where he served as the Operations Unit Supervisor for the FAA European International Field Office. In this position, he worked closely with foreign aviation authorities, including two trips to Moscow to assist Russian airlines in operating DC-10s and B-757s.

To round out his vast aviation experience, he became an active warbird pilot with the Planes of Fame Air Museum (East), where at the young age of 62 he checked out in the nimble single-seat Grumman FM-2 *Wildcat* fighter, an aircraft he built models of when he was 12-years-old.

Lou Martin retired from professional flying in January 1999, with a total of 19,000 accident-free flight hours. However, he still flies his privately owned single-engine Cessna to fly-ins and airshows throughout the Midwest. He holds an FAA Flight Instructor's and Flight Engineer's Certificate, is type rated in nine different aircraft, possesses Airline Transport Pilot Certificates with the United States, Japan and Iran. He is a member of the Soaring Society of America, the Commemorative Air Force, the Air Force Association, the American Legion, the 8th Air Force Historical Society, the Ntional Rifle Association, the Military Officer's Association of America, and the Experimental Aircraft Association, during their annual convention (Air Venture 2005 and 2006), he was interviewed for inclusion in EAA's *Timeless Voices of Aviation Oral History Program.*

Chapter One --- Aeronca Champ and Piper Cub

I pride myself in having an excellent memory, but I cannot recall a time when I wasn't interested in airplanes and someday becoming a pilot. As a boy, I would spend hours staring at the formation of majestic cumulous summer clouds, while fantasizing that I was flying like an eagle amongst these gigantic bubbling fruits of nature. I admired the freedom birds enjoyed, especially night hawks who would snatch their nightly meal by diving through swarms of fat summer mosquitoes. These magnificent birds would hover at around 200 feet and, at the right moment, dive down at "full throttle," with their beaks wide open and scoop up a mouthful of unsuspecting flying insects. When they pulled out of their high speed dive their wing tip feathers would flutter, producing a loud buzzing sound. I imagined myself riding on their backs, performing dive after dive, and pulling out just before hitting the ground. I knew that someday I would join them in soaring amongst the clouds! When the 1935 movie, *West Point of the Air,* starring Wallace Beery and Robert Young, came out, I sat through it several times, because as a seven-year-old I could attend the theater free and took full advantage of the opportunity. I later purchased the "Big Little Book" printing of the story and it became my primary reader for several years. (See Photo No. 5.)

The movie, West Point of the Air was a fictional story of a young West Point Academy graduate (Robert Young) who attended flight training at Randolph Air Force Base, Texas, under the tutelage of his crusty sergeant father (Wallace Beery). The movie contained scenes of pre-World War II aircraft and excited my fantasies of someday being stationed at Randolph AFB myself.

Another form of satisfying a youthful craving for flying was in joining crowds of curious locals, mesmerized by young barnstorming pilots flying open cockpit biplanes, during our county fair. Several early-thirties airplanes would land in a nearby farmer's field and fly brave passengers for two dollars per head. These aviation heroes, dressed in riding breeches and high lace-up boots, would sleep under the wings of their

13

aircraft and send young boys, like myself, on errands to fetch sandwiches and gasoline. Following one such task, which involved dragging 60-pound cans of gas in a wagon, the pilot allowed me to sit in the cockpit of his aircraft. (I considered this form of compensation excessive and he almost had to wrench me out of the aircraft when it came time to start flying paying passengers.) I never tired of listening to the loud bark of these nine cylinder round engines, making full power short-field takeoffs.

Excitement was something I fancied, even at a very young age. One method of fulfilling this appetite was through a homemade rope and pulley ride. My brother Hank and I tied 150 feet of strong hemp rope to a tree branch and the other end to the edge of our garage, about 125 feet away. I figured that by climbing the tree and hanging from the pulley as it sped down the slope of the rope, it would provide sufficient speed to satisfy my zest for adventure.

I volunteered to be the first to test our new "thrill ride" and after climbing 30 feet up the tree, I grabbed a hold of the pulley and let gravity take over. I was impressed in how quickly I picked up speed and fantasized that I was Tarzan swinging through the jungle and heading home to Jane. However, I didn't have long to dwell on such fantasy, as I was approaching the edge of the garage and still traveling quite fast. To keep from smacking into its side, and incurring broken bones, I let go and tumbled, end-over-end, in the grass. To alleviate the danger of crashing into a hard surface, we tied an old mattress to the side of the garage. However, riding the rope the full length resulted in such a jolt, when smacking into the mattress, that we would let go just before reaching the end of the line.

The rope slide was very popular with neighborhood kids and we began charging them five cents a ride, but in spite of its popularity, our exciting venture was short lived. Angry parents complained to our mother that their kids were coming home with black and blue bruises and afraid that broken bones would soon follow, if they continued patronizing our growing business. We declared "bankruptcy" and took down the rope!

Another area that intrigued me was the marvel of internal combustion gasoline engines. In the late 1930s, more and more farmers were acquiring electricity, making their gasoline-powered washing machines obsolete. Consequently, two-stroke, air-cooled Maytag engines could be purchased at a bargain price. In 1940 (at age 12) I purchased a 1/2 hp two-cylinder model for five dollars. I had a local mechanic fabricate a 12-inch aluminum grooved pulley, which I attached to the rear wheel spokes of my bicycle. I then bolted the engine to a "jury-rigged" mount over the rear wheel and ran an auto fan belt from the engine to the pulley. My clutch arrangement was an over-center belt tightening hinge.

When the project was complete, I proceeded to the top of a nearby hill, followed by a small group of admirers and skeptics. I decided to make the first run from the top of a hill, as I felt that a gravity boost would be required to obtain sufficient speed to provide an exciting ride and impress my gathering fans. I started the engine, adjusted the carburetor to "full throttle," and since the engine was not equipped with a muffler, its roaring bark could be heard throughout the neighborhood. As the tempo of excitement increased and the engine, because of tremendous vibration, looked like it might break free from its fragile mount, I decided it was time to launch. I hopped on the bike, began peddling with all my might and tightened the tension on the fan belt.

Propelled by rapid peddling and the power assist from the roaring engine, I quickly attained critical speed. Houses were racing by and the wind was whistling through my curly red hair. The bicycle began shaking violently and I thought that my first test run was going to end with a trip to the hospital or the morgue. Steering the vibrating handlebar with one hand, I reached back and released the tension on the fan belt. However, the engine, still running at full-throttle, and now unloaded, was emitting a load roaring bark and still shaking violently, but the noise and vibration were not my immediate problem. I was still traveling faster, on a wobbling bike, than I had ever gone before and the rear wheel coaster brake was screeching from the strong reverse pressure I was applying to the pedals.

I finally came to a stop, shut off the roaring smoking engine and stood next to my contrivance while savoring the thrilling ride. The crowd of admirers caught up with me, were very excited over the show and wanted me to do it again. I decided not to make any further test runs, feeling major modifications were needed. I continued peddling around the neighborhood with an engine roar that seemed incongruous to the speed I was making. My frequent excursions drew curious looks from people walking on the sidewalk, traveling almost as fast as I was on my homemade motorbike. Finally, the weight of the engine and severe vibration was too much for my tired old bike, and the whole contraption came crashing down in the middle of the street. I considered this adventure over and traded the Maytag engine for a Red Ryder BB gun.

In February 1941, my dream of flying in a real airplane became a reality. A young pilot was barnstorming passengers during our Winter Carnival in his ski-equipped Luscombe *Silvaire*. His runway was the frozen, snow-covered Flambeau River, and I spent the better part of a cold February day watching him fly excited passengers around the local area. During a short break from his busy schedule, he shut down the engine and climbed out from the cockpit for a well deserved break.

I bravely walked up to him and said, "Hey mister, how much do you charge for an airplane ride?"

He replied, "Two dollars for a quick flight around the city!"

With the sincerity of a 12-year-old, I reached into my pants pocket, where I kept my paper route money, pulled out a dollar bill and said, "I would like to buy half an airplane ride sir!"

He chuckled and said with an air of authority, "I don't give half airplane rides, kid!"

His rejection of my serious business proposition was very disappointing and I walked away with my head bowed. Interrupting my retreat he called out, "Wait a minute, kid. Do you know where you can get me a hamburger and a hot cup of coffee?" Rejuvenated by his question, I said, "Yes sir, I could fetch them for you in a matter of minutes." He handed me a dollar bill and said that if I was back in ten minutes, he would take me up for half an airplane ride!

Spirited on by the expectation of actually flying in a real airplane, I ran to the nearest restaurant with the speed of an Olympic sprint runner, and was back just as my pilot friend was taxiing in from another "full-paying" passenger flight.

I handed him his still-warm lunch, along with his change. Obviously pleased, he said with a wink, "Well done kid, hop in." When seated, I noted that I was too short to see over the nose of the aircraft, or out the side window, without rising up. Nevertheless, I was in a real airplane and didn't want to complain. The sound of the throbbing engine, along with the acceleration of the takeoff and a light-headed feeling of becoming airborne, created a passion for flying greater than I felt possible. The pilot made a quick circle of the city and we were back on the snow-covered frozen river before I could appreciate the full impact of my new adventure.

I was so excited that I ran home and talked my mother into loaning me a dollar out of her household budget. Refinanced, I ran back to the river and said to the Luscombe pilot, "I would like to buy another half airplane ride." He responded with a hardy laugh and sent me off on another hamburger and coffee errand. When I returned, he told me to wait a few minutes and he would take me up for another half airplane ride.

After his last full-paying passenger for the day deplaned, he motioned for me to come forward, but had me wait before climbing into the cockpit. As I stood in the cold propeller blast, he moved the seat forward and pulled out two seat cushions from the baggage compartment area. He positioned one on the seat and the other one against the backrest. As I sat in the cockpit this time, my feet reached the rudder pedals and I could see over the nose and out the side window.

After takeoff he told me to put my right hand on the control stick and my feet on the rudder pedals. He guided me through a few gentle turns and a few minutes later told me to look at his hands and feet, which he had removed from the controls! I was actually flying the airplane myself! I think he enjoyed seeing me in such rapture, as much as I enjoyed the experience myself. We circled around Ladysmith while admiring the orange setting winter sun, the city lights coming on one-by-one and viewing my house from the air. We landed back on the river in the last remaining light of the day and I helped him secure his airplane for the night. As I shook his hand good-bye, I thanked him for the happiest moment of my young life. I never saw this generous pilot again and often wondered what became of him. But since he was a CAB Certified pilot in early 1941, and being in his early twenties, I like to think that he became a famous World War II fighter pilot. He was certainly a hero to me!

Flying homemade kites was a favorite pastime in the windy spring months and my brother Hank and I were always striving to make bigger kites to outshine the competition of other neighborhood kids. In the spring of 1941, we had the bright idea of beating the opposition by not only constructing a bigger kite, but by sending up a live animal as a passenger. We built a six-foot high beauty, obtained some extra strong string and made several successful test flights. We then fabricated a small compartment from wooden produce boxes, and attached it to the center section of the kite. We equipped the box with a trap door that would be triggered from a pull on a string. In the compartment we placed a 12-pound rock that was fastened to a parachute made from the cloth of an old beach umbrella. Several preliminary test flights were made and each time we pulled the trap door release, the rock fell free, the parachute opened, and the rock floated gently back to earth. We were now ready for the real thing!

Across the open grassy field we spotted a large black and white cat snoozing in the warm spring sun. We picked up the accommodating feline (figured its weight to be about 12 pounds) and asked it if it would like to volunteer as a "Kitetronaut." The cat seemed to say "yes" as it responded with a loud purr. With a small group of fellow kite flyers looking on, we strapped our furry friend into the parachute harness, pushed it reluctantly into the compartment, and fastened the trap door shut.

Accompanied by a gentle breeze we launched the kite, with our volunteer "Kitetronaut" announcing its excitement through loud meows. The meows grew fainter as the kite gained altitude, but stopped completely when it began swaying back and forth. When the kite stabilized at around 200 feet, we pulled the compartment door release string, and to our delight, and I'm sure to our volunteer, all systems worked like a charm. The "Kitetronaut" came tumbling out, the parachute unfurled, blossomed fully, and our feline friend, with its four legs fully extended and announcing its excitement through loud screeching meows, began its gentle float back to earth. Unfortunately, due to winds that we hadn't compensated for, it landed on the roof of a nearby garage. We climbed up on the roof, congratulated our volunteer for a successful mission and released it from the harness. When free, it quickly scampered away never to be seen again. Following this trial run word apparently spread throughout the feline world to avoid boys flying kites as we never saw another cat in the area when flying our kites.

When we sent a cat aloft in a kite it was not our intent to impart any form of animal cruelty. Our entire family loved animals and pets were a part of our life. Our experiment was observed by a passing adult, who reported what he saw to our mother. She gave us holy hell for what we did and made us promise never to do it again. Our only excuse was that we became totally immersed in the project and did not fully evaluate what we were doing to the poor unsuspecting cat. We were very happy that no harm came to it.

When the U.S. became an active partner in WW II most healthy young men either joined the military or filled critical jobs in defense plants. This left many job vacancies on the home front which were then filled by teenagers. For example in 1943, at age 15, I spent my summer vacation working full time for a Coast To Coast hardware store and assisted farmers in harvesting their crops in the evening.

This manpower shortage was also addressed in an unexpected unique way. A group of German POWs captured in North Africa were sent to Ladysmith to assist in the processing of peas and beans at the Stockley

Van Camp Cannery. When the train transporting the POWs arrived a group of spectators gathered to catch a glimpse of Hitler's elite soldiers. I attended their arrival with my mother who spoke fluent German and when the prisoners were assembled she spoke to several of them (in German) inquiring as to their home town in Germany. (She was hoping to learn if any of them came from the same area where her father was born.)

Her oral engagement with the POWs generated a ground swell of "boos and hisses" from the gathered crowd along with calls of "traitor." These inconsiderate insults brought tears to my mother's eyes. I handed her my handkerchief, took her arm and walked her back home. During the POWs stay in Ladysmith I would ride my bicycle to their compound and attempt to communicate with them and was impressed in how friendly they and their military guards were in attempting to answer my youthful questions.

In late May 1945, Bob Burke, a high school classmate, and I rode the Soo Line passenger train to Chicago to seek employment in a defense plant. Jobs were plentiful and after securing a room in a boarding house we were working in a tool and die factory. To maximize our income we took a nighttime job with the Union Railway Station in downtown Chicago. Our job at the railway station was transferring checked passenger luggage from one train to another, utilizing electric tractors and baggage carts. There were times when I would be pulling a string of carts in an isolated underground area, with no one else in sight.

One night I pulled up next to a railroad baggage car in a remote section of the underground station to transfer a load of suitcases and foot lockers. As I slid open the baggage car door, I came across a scene that I wasn't supposed to see. Inside was a gang of tough-looking young hoodlums, breaking open and stealing items from checked luggage. (In early June 1945, most of the footlockers and suitcases belonged to servicemen returning from overseas and contained war memorabilia like cameras, coins, pistols and other valuable keepsakes.) The thieves I surprised had a stack of loot sitting in a pile next to them.

I started sliding the door toward the closed position, but one of the hoods held it open while the rest jumped out and surrounded me. One member of the gang, with tattoos running up and down both arms, who seemed to be the leader, asked me if I wanted to join them. When I said I wasn't interested, he pulled out a long switchblade knife, opened it, and said, "You're either with us or against us. What's it going to be?" I figured that unless I wanted my guts cut open I would have to say, "I'm with you."

However, as I was about to acquiesce to their demands, a big burly cop came walking toward us, whistling and swinging his big "billy club." The gang of hoodlums scattered and I jumped on my electric cart and went looking for my buddy, Bob Burke. When I found him I told him what had happened and we went directly to the office and told the foreman that we were quitting, and to send any unpaid wages to our Wisconsin address. (We didn't want to have our checks sent to our boarding house in Chicago, least some of the gang members try to look us up.)

The next day I made an anonymous call to the Chicago Police Department, informing them about a gang of crooks breaking into servicemen's checked baggage in the Union Station. A couple days later, I read in the *Chicago Times* that police had arrested a group of thieves who had been stealing from servicemen's bags in the downtown Union Railroad Station. (One person can make a difference.)

Soon after this scary event, I moved to Detroit, Michigan to work for my brother George, and accept his offer of giving me flying lessons. My first solo flight, after only seven hours of dual instruction, was on Saturday, July 21, 1945. This memorable event was in a 65 hp BC-12, side-by-side, Taylorcraft, at Triangle Airport, a small grass field near Plymouth.

The Taylorcraft is similar to a Piper J-3 Cub, except that the pilots sit side-by-side, instead of in tandem. It was developed over several years, starting in 1939, with just a 40 hp. engine. A version called the L-2 was used in great numbers by the military during WW II and became a popular postwar light plane. To fill a need for training glider pilots, a limited number of L-2s had their engines removed and were converted into three-place gliders and designated TG-6. It has a wingspan of 36 feet, a top speed of 105 mph, a gross weight of 1200 lbs. and a maximum ceiling of 14,400 feet. A new aircraft in 1940 sold for around $1,600, (equal to $21,000 today). (See Photos 9 and 10.)

Following my first solo, I almost lived at the airport and passed my private pilot's flight check 41 days later on Friday, August 31, 1945. Obtaining a Private Pilot's Certificate at age 17 was a fortunate milestone that I hadn't counted on when I decided to spend my high school summer vacation working for my brother in Detroit, who operated a photographic studio and put me to work as a "door-to-door" salesman. He was 36-years-old, and not eligible for the military draft, but wishing to

20

contribute to the war effort joined a Civilian Air Patrol Squadron (CAP), as a captain and flight instructor, flying his privately owned Taylorcraft. It was in this capacity that he became my personal flight instructor and mentor and provided me with the opportunity of obtaining a pilot's license. I was indeed fortunate to have such a generous brother, as the flight instruction and use of his aircraft was at no cost to me. George devoted many weekends and evenings in giving me free instruction and guidance in ensuring I returned home and to high school with a Private Pilot's Certificate. (See Photos 9, 10, 11 and 12.)

It was in Michigan where I experienced my first encounter with the Pilot's Grim Reaper (PGR), but not when flying, but riding a horse. I had accompanied my brother George and his wife Aurelie on a visit to her family farm near Ypsilanti. While the adults were inside visiting, two young men about my age were giving me a tour of their homestead. During the tour I attempted to regale them regarding my exploits as a pilot, which I'm sure presented an image of a "smart-ass-kid" from the city. They opened a door to a horse stall, and standing inside was a huge snorting black stallion with sinister looking staring eyes, a big wet nose, and long pointed quivering ears. (He was the perfect image of the bronco, that "nobody could ride," and immortalized in the popular cowboy ballad, *Strawberry Roan.)* My recalcitrant hosts asked me if my many talents included horseback riding. In a contemptuous voice, I said that they did! Hearing this they asked me if I would like to ride Old Blackie. After receiving an enthusiastic "yes," they led him, reluctantly, outside.

Standing "mountain high" was a gigantic black horse that was obviously unhappy in being dragged out into the bright sunlight. (I was starting to have second thoughts about my pretentious commitment to ride him, but my youthful arrogance wouldn't allow me to back out.) They threw a Western Style saddle on his shivering body and inserted a bit between snorting lips from a protruding lower jaw. I was then handed the reins with a, "He's all yours! Good luck."

I placed my left foot in a stirrup, coiled my hand around the reins and threw my 170 pound, 17-year-old frame in the saddle. When Old Blackie felt my weight on his back, it triggered an explosion and he began bucking with all the energy he could muster in attempting to throw me off. I gripped the saddle horn with all my strength and hung on accompanied with the "hoots and hollers" of my friends safely on the ground. Through sheer determination I was able to stay in the saddle although at times it seemed like I was sitting on nothing but empty space. Old Blackie, frustrated in not being able to send me flying, started heaving big sighs, reared up on his hind legs, came back down on all four and jumped up again like his legs were made of rubber. But I managed, somehow, to stay on his back.

Suddenly, as some horses will do, he decided that if he couldn't throw me off he would roll on the ground. He started a roll to the right, next to a horse drawn spike-toothed cultivator with exposed rows of sharp steel agitating teeth. I instinctively realized that if I remained in the saddle I would be impaled on several of these steel prongs! I removed my right foot from a stirrup, placed it on top of the saddle, and in concert with Blackie's rolling centrifugal force, and a hard push from my leg, propelled myself over the top of the cultivator. After picking myself up I was able to see what a Close Encounter I had avoided, as one of the steel spikes, intended for me, was lodged into the side of the saddle and Old Blackie was whining, snorting and kicking in attempting to break free.

The farmer, hearing all the commotion, came running outside and berated his kids who had talked me into riding Old Blackie. He said that he was an extremely dangerous horse and would throw any rider, except himself, who tried to ride him. When I told him about how long I had stayed on his back he was amazed and said that if I wanted to stick around perhaps he would allow me to ride him again. I thanked him for the offer, but said I would stick to flying airplanes!

When not flying, I enjoyed exploring downtown Detroit and only once did I experience a problem in wandering around the city by myself. After leaving a movie theater at around 9:30 p.m. I was walking along a deserted street toward a streetcar stop. A young male (perhaps in his mid-twenties), walked up and started fondling my shoulders, and when I attempted to push him away he became more aggressive in his sensuous gestures. I started to walk faster, but he matched my increased gait, step-by-step. I then started to run, as if my football coach was cheering me on, with my amorous admirer in close pursuit. Being only 17-years-old and in good shape, I figured I could outrun him and cut across Lafayette Park in a whir of speed. When I reached the opposite side, completely out of breath, I spotted a police officer walking his beat and saddled up next to him. In a suspicious tone of voice, he asked me why I had been running. When I told him that someone was chasing me, he looked around, saw no one, shrugged his shoulders, and walked on. (He most likely thought that my story was just a kid's fantasy.) I boarded a waiting streetcar and rode it north to Dearborn Avenue and my brother's apartment. When I told him about the incident, he wasn't surprised and advised me not to walk the downtown streets by myself at night. He said, "Stick with the crowds Louie, and you'll be safe!"

In less than 60 days from my first flight lesson, I logged 57 flight hours, completed all the requirements for a Private Pilot's Certificate and passed a 45 minute flight check administered by Mr. L.R. Buckler, a Civil Aeronautics Flight Inspector from Lansing, (In my judgment, I was the hottest pilot in all of Michigan, maybe even the entire country.)

On September 2, 1945, accompanied by my brother, I flew his Taylorcraft to Ladysmith, Wisconsin, eager to begin my junior year in high school and display my pilot's license to my classmates. I was disappointed when many of them didn't seem impressed, and even accused me of producing a false document intended to impress the girls. (I won't deny that I had hoped to impress the girls, but felt a sense of disappointment in my hard-won accomplishment being questioned.) However, the local Rusk County airport operator accepted my certificate as valid and after a local checkout in a 65 hp J-3 Piper *Cub* by Clayton Biller, a former B-24 WW II combat pilot, I was authorized to demonstrate to my classmate doubters, the prowess of a 17-year-old hot pilot.

At the time I could rent a J-3 *Cub*, or Aeronca *Champ*, for six dollars an hour (equal to $70 today) and took many of my high school classmates up for their first airplane ride. My method for generating flight hours was to solicit two male colleagues to pay three dollars each for a 30-minute flight. However, wishing to impress admiring females, I took them up for free. I was especially proud of being able to expose my high school "heart throb," Erna Lou Jones, to her first airplane ride. I had an intense crush on her, which was affecting my schoolwork, but with a typical 17-year-old naiveté, I didn't think anyone else noticed me walking around with my head in the clouds like a love sick simpleton.

Fortunately, my obsession did not go unnoticed by my high school history teacher, Walt Pearson. Mr. Pearson was popular with the students and substituted as our football coach when the regular coach was in the Navy. (If it wasn't for Mr. Pearson we would not have been able to field a team in 1944 and 1945.) One warm spring day in 1946 Mr. Pearson said that he would like to speak with me after class. After closing his door, he shocked me by coming right out and stating, "Louie, I have been watching you, and have noted that you are allowing your schoolwork to go downhill. I feel that you are going through a teenage-crush over Erna Lou Jones, and if you don't learn how to control it, your schoolwork will suffer, which would be a big disappointment to me!" (See Photos 3 and 4.)

His direct approach was a shock and I wondered how he knew. But he was right-on and it was exactly what I needed. (I don't think teachers today would take the time to counsel troubled teenagers.) Erna dumped me the following summer for Bob Stingle, a Navy sailor returning from the war. Unfortunately the wonderful man she married died in 1987, at age 61. Erna and I remain friends and I sometimes see her when I visit Ladysmith. However, this blow to my male ego didn't last long and I soon started dating another high school classmate. She was great fun and we succumbed to youthful passions and entered the world of consensual adult entertainment with the zest expected of two healthy 18-year olds.

In 1948, my last summer in Ladysmith, I started dating Mary, another high school classmate. She was 19-years-old, very beautiful, and a Northland Mardi Gras Beauty Queen. We would visit local bars followed by spreading out a blanket on a point of land overlooking the Flambeau River, known as the *Sister's Farm*. Disregarding voracious mosquitoes, we enjoyed many rapturous nights under the stars while engaging in youthful calisthenics. Following each session we would be covered with mosquito bites, especially my exposed buttocks, the most prominent target for our incessant buzzing intruders. Mary married a high school colleague who was unfortunately killed in August 1953 flying an F-80 jet fighter. I met Mary in Germany in 1955, when she was teaching in a U.S. Army dependents school, and we renewed our fondness for each other in her apartment. It was great to refresh old friendships without being eaten by hungry Northern Wisconsin mosquitoes. Mary is also deceased but has left me with many pleasant memories.

In 1997, during my 50th high school reunion, several of my classmates still remembered that they had experienced their first airplane ride with me as their pilot. Equally interesting was that several of my female classmates informed me that local mothers had told their daughters that they didn't want them flying with that 17-year-old pilot, Louie Martin. However, they added that they didn't heed their mother's warning and accepted a free exciting flight over the Northern Wisconsin countryside with Hot pilot Martin.

In November 1945, I started working in a local hamburger joint, after school and on weekends. The restaurant was the former teenage club known as the *Buzz Bowl*, but was now being operated as a restaurant by a likable 37-year-old man by the name of George Hunt. George had moved to Ladysmith from Milwaukee, but was no stranger to the area as he had married a local girl by the name of Blanch Paradise. George was thrilled when he learned that I held a Private Pilot's Certificate and when business was slow he would tell his wife to mind the store while he and Louie went flying. George would pay for the aircraft, while still paying me 60 cents an hour for working in his restaurant. (A deal I couldn't pass up.) One Saturday afternoon in February 1946, business was slow and George decided we should head for the airport to fly one of Hal Doughty's newly acquired 65 hp Aeronca *Champs* on skis. (See Photo No. 13.)

Hal was a former World War II P-40 and P-47 pilot, who had shot down 4 1/2 Japanese aircraft. After the war he returned home and operated a small airport south of Ladysmith. He had taken out a GI loan and purchased two new Aeronca 7ACs for about $2,000 each, (equal to $20,000 today). The Aeronca Champ was a popular U.S. Army liaison aircraft during the war with the military designation of L-3. To relieve a critical shortage of glider trainers, a number of L-3s had their engines removed and were converted into gliders for the training of glider pilots. The converted L-3 had a bulbous nose and designated TG-5. When the war ended, the Aeronca Aircraft Company concentrated on producing a light aircraft for the civilian market and introduced the 7AC. It has a max. weight of 1,220 lbs, a max. speed of 129 mph, a cruising speed of 80 mph, holds 13 gallons of fuel, and a takeoff ground roll of 224 feet.

Going flying, instead of flipping hamburgers, sounded like a great idea as it was a beautiful clear winter day and the ground was covered with a foot of new snow. We called the airport and Hal told us he would have an aircraft preheated and ready to go by the time we arrived. After driving through freshly plowed roads, with three-foot-high snow banks, we pulled into the airport parking lot one hour later.

Hal pointed to a shiny new yellow Aeronca *Champ*, all warmed up and awaiting us on the snow-covered field. After wading through knee-high deep snow, George climbed into the rear seat and I climbed into the pilot's front seat. Hal shouted "contact" and hand propped the 65 hp Continental engine. The four cylinders sprang to life on the first pull and a few minutes later we were taxiing out for takeoff. The airport was covered with about one foot of undisturbed fresh virgin powder snow and the only visible tracks were from our skis and the dragging tail wheel. After an engine run-up check, I advanced the power to "full-throttle," and the cold temperature made for a short "heart-throbbing" takeoff with powder snow billowing out from each side of the aircraft and a "rooster-tail" snow cloud raising up from the rear. As we became airborne I thought, "What a great day to fly!"

After circling the city of Ladysmith and observing snow plows clearing roads and shop owners shoveling their sidewalks, I sought out a more adventurous outlet for our one hour of pollution-free winter flying. I flew north and when over the frozen Flambeau River dropped down to five to ten feet above the snow-covered surface. I flew over the meandering river for a few miles and noted that the perception of speed and height, when flying close to the flat undisturbed snow, was deceptive. As we continued following the river, the aircraft dipped lower than I had planned and the aircraft's skis sliced into the thick coating of powder snow. Contact with the snow was as smooth as silk and when disturbed by the rapid movement of the skis and the air blast from the propeller produced billowing white snow clouds on both sides of the aircraft and against the side windows, plus portions fanning up over the top of the aircraft. George and I were thrilled in discovering a unique maneuver that would make our winter flight more thrilling than just boring holes in the sky.

I continued flying up the river at around 100 mph, while occasionally dipping low enough for the skis to make contact with the snow. I noted that if I allowed the skis to settle deeper into the surface, the snow cloud was more pronounced and produced louder shouts of joy from George in the back seat. After a few more dips into the snow, I turned around to observe George's facial expressions of excitement in our risky adventure.

I had diverted my attention, for just two or three seconds, before again directing my focus to our direction of flight. Directly in front of us were thick high tension electric cables, marked with large round orange plastic balls. My heart skipped several beats, but fortunately my young alert brain was still functional. The wires arched across the river, drooping down to approximately 20 feet above the ice. I intuitively knew that I couldn't climb above them so I pushed the stick rapidly forward and bounced off the ice underneath the center section of the cables. The extra firm contact created a snow cloud greater than any we had produced earlier and a large snow cloud temporarily engulfed the entire aircraft. George gave out with a shout of joviality while stating, "That was the best one yet, Louie. Do it again." He hadn't seen the wires we had just flown under and didn't know how close he came to ending his life wrapped around high tension cables in Northern Wisconsin.

With my heart in my throat, I realized how lucky we were to be alive and climbed to 1,000 feet and headed back toward the airport. George inquired as to where we were going. I told him, "We are heading back home as our flight for this day was over." He didn't understand, reminding me that our one-hour rental agreement wasn't up. I told him I would explain later when we were on the ground. George never told his wife how close she came to having to run the restaurant as a widow. George and I flew together many times following this incident, but left skimming over the snow-covered river to the crows and eagles.

That same winter one of my high school friends, Pete Peavey, requested to go flying in a ski equipped J-3 Piper *Cub*. He stipulated a two-place tandem seat aircraft, with side entrance doors that could be opened in-flight, since opening the doors would allow him to take unobstructed photos of his family's lake-side cabin. He stated that they had aerial pictures of it in the summer, but thought it would be neat to have one taken during the winter.

The Piper J-3 Cub was introduced in 1938, powered by a 40 hp engine, and sold for $1,300 ($16,000 in today's dollars). Engine power was soon raised to 50 hp and to 65 hp by 1940. When the U.S. became involved in WW II, sales were spurred by the formation of the, Civilian Pilot Training Program (CPT). During the war a new aircraft, known as the Grasshopper L-4, was produced every 20 minutes. A number of L-4s also had their engines removed and were converted into glider trainers, with the designation of TG-8. When production ended in 1947, 14,125 Piper Cubs had been built. The Piper Cub is an excellent basic pilot trainer and a delightful sport plane to fly. A new Piper Cub in 1947 sold for around $2,600, (equal to $23,400 today). (See Photo No. 14.)

We took off on an intensely cold January day and flew a direct course to his cabin 40 miles away. I opened the upper and lower side doors and circled while Pete took pictures. With the doors open the frigid air entering the cockpit produced uncomfortably cold conditions. I was somewhat sheltered in the front seat, but my picture-taking friend in the rear seat was exposed to the full blast of the arctic air. After two circles, Pete said that he had enough pictures, and through shivering lips, said it was time to close the side panels and head for the airport.

I reached down and closed the lower panel, but when I attempted to close the upper panel it broke loose. As it separated from the aircraft it swung upwards, sliced a large gash in the fabric on the underside of the right wing and smashed into the right horizontal stabilizer. The aircraft began to vibrate and entered a series of up-and-down oscillations. Attempting to determine the reason for the controllability problems, I noted that the right horizontal stabilizer had been deformed from the impact with the departing upper panel.

The vibrations and oscillations subsided when I reduced the airspeed, and at slower speeds the aircraft was flyable. I concluded that I should be able to make it back home without difficulty, but it would be a slow and cold flight. I was fairly comfortable in the front seat, but Pete was being buffeted by the full force of frigid air coming in through the missing side panel. He unfastened his seat belt and leaned over my shoulders, to avoid the cold blast to his face, but his lower body was still exposed.

It required about 40 minutes to reach the airport and after landing my rear-seat photographer friend was so numb that I had to help him out of the aircraft. Hal Doughty (the airport operator) initially seemed more concerned about his aircraft than he was about my frozen passenger and asked me to indicate on a map where the door had separated.

It took my high school friend 30 minutes to stop shivering and I had to caution him several times not to sit on the hot kerosene space heater in the airport office. The missing door was never found and Hal finally absolved me of any responsibility for the damage to his aircraft.

The following spring a Ladysmith businessman, Lester (Soapy) Grooms, experienced a Close Encounter when taking off in his Aeronca *Champ* in a strong crosswind. He was blown off-course toward a cement silo and instead of banking to avoid it, he panicked and attempted to climb over it, but didn't gain sufficient altitude and smacked directly into it. Fortunately, he was not killed but spent a lot of time in a hospital mending broken bones and in a dental office replacing missing teeth. Lester acquired his nickname "Soapy" by cleaning bath tubs in a local barbershop in the 1920s. This experience made him a much wiser pilot, and he died peacefully at age 93, on November 25, 2005. (This was a perfect example of what I refer to as "Buck Fever in the Cockpit.." I discuss this growing phenomenon further on pages seven and 359.)

Chapter Two --- T-6 Texan and T-34 Mentor

On Tuesday, October 5, 1948, I was sworn in as an Air Force Aviation Cadet in Eau Claire, Wisconsin. The next day I was on a bus for Minneapolis, Minnesota followed by a steam locomotive train to Waco, Texas. Three young colleagues, also from Wisconsin, who were destined for basic military training at Lackland AFB, Texas, accompanied me.

When boarding the train we were joined by several other young men, also heading for basic training. Once underway we congregated in the club car to exchange names, home towns and reasons for joining the Air Force. Early in the exchange, it became clear that I was the only Aviation Cadet, while the rest were heading for indoctrination as enlisted men.

Once they learned that I was an Aviation Cadet, I became the brunt of friendly ribbing, because, if plans materialized, one year later I would be a commissioned officer and an Air Force pilot, while my traveling companions would be "buck privates."

Approaching Kansas City, an African American porter came to the club car and inquired as to who was Mr. Martin. When I raised my hand, he said, "Your Pullman berth is ready Mr. Martin." My new-found friends seemed surprised and asked the porter, "Is there a Pullman berth for us?" "No sir," the porter responded, "just for Mr. Martin as his ticket states Aviation Cadet." I bid my friends goodnight and retreated to my squeaky clean, white-sheeted sleeping compartment. As I was lullabied to sleep by the "click, clack, click" of the train wheels, I thanked my guardian angel that I was heading for pilot training, not basic training as an enlisted man.

The first thing that caught my attention when I stepped off the train in Waco was that the drinking fountains and rest rooms were marked, **"Colored"** or **"White."** After riding a bus to Waco AFB, I was greeted by a group of upper-class cadets who barked out military commands, had my hair cut to a length of 1/4 inch, and was issued a set of green fatigues. My first assigned duty was picking up horse and cattle droppings left by ranchers who had been using the base for grazing livestock after it was deactivated at the end of World War II. This seemed like a demeaning task for a future Air Force pilot and I was glad my train buddies couldn't see me performing duties like a common criminal. But the cleanup detail was soon history and I spent the next three weeks learning how to march and absorb the strict discipline required of new Aviation Cadets. On October 28, 1948, I met my flight instructor, Captain Ray Meador, and experienced my first flight in a T-6 *Texan,* a 30 minute back seat orientation ride. It was a big change from flying the Aeronca *Champ.*

The T-6 Texan is a two-place advanced trainer, built by North American Aviation and has the flight characteristics of a fighter. It is not an easy airplane to master and was an excellent advanced trainer for future fighter pilots. (There is a saying among pilots that states, "When you master the T-6, you are ready to fly the F-51 Mustang, the F-47 Thunderbolt, or other high powered fighters.") It is powered by a 550 or 600 hp engine, is fully aerobatic, has a cruise speed of 145 mph and a maximum speed of 205. (However, Dick Sykes, in 1983, set a speed record at Reno, Nevada, of 226 mph.) The Texan was affectionately known as the "Pilot Maker" because of its role in training pilots for combat. During WW II more than 16,000 T-6s were built, with an estimated 500 still flying and others being restored. Due to its high relative engine power, speed and complexity, it was not considered suitable as a primary trainer. However, in 1948, the Air Force had thousands of them in storage and since the country was not at war, a high washout (failure) rate for initial student pilots was not considered a problem. It was phased out of regular Air Force service in 1958. However, more than 500 T-6s are still flown by warbird enthusiasts, and several were modified to resemble Japanese Mitsubishi Zero fighters, or Kate torpedo bombers for the movie, Tora-Tora-Tora. These Japanese replicas are very popular at air shows and put on a very realistic simulated Pearl Harbor Attack, through daring low level flyovers, roaring engines and loud realistic pyrotechnic explosions. (See Photo No. 19.)

Because I held a Private Pilot's Certificate, and had 120 flight hours, I quickly learned to master the T-6 and on December 4, 1948, I was the first cadet in my squadron to solo. (I thought my self-proclaimed reputation as a "Hot Pilot" was still the name of the game.)

Air Training Command Headquarters decided that all pilot flight schools would close for two weeks during the 1948 Christmas Holiday season. I arranged with a flight instructor to share in driving expenses to our respective homes in Wisconsin, returning to Texas ten days later. His home was in Bloomer, just a short drive from my home in Ladysmith.

Taking turns in driving, we drove straight through, covering the 1,200 miles in 24 hours. Following Christmas vacation, we headed back to Texas on December 31, with his wife joining us. By the time we reached Kansas, it was my turn at the wheel, and I was driving in freezing rain and restricted visibility on Highway 35 South (which at the time was still a two-lane road). The instructor's wife was sound asleep in the back seat, while her husband was dozing in the front passenger's seat. Because of the dangerous road conditions I was driving well below the speed limit, while listening to the 1949 New Year's Eve celebrations on the radio. As the slick road formed a slight decline, the car started sliding sideways and then did two complete 360 degree spins. One of the spins occurred between two cars going in the opposite direction, but without colliding with either one. Luckily, when the car stopped spinning, we were still in the right lane and still heading south. Neither the flight instructor nor his wife woke up during this frightening event, so they had no idea of how close they came to possible serious injury or death. (I never told either of them about the event.)

The instructor dropped me off in front of my barracks on Saturday afternoon, January 1, 1949. The barracks were empty, so I thought that my colleagues had not yet returned from vacation or were in Waco celebrating the new year. After a shower and a change of clothes, I took a bus downtown to see if I could find some of them to exchange Christmas Holiday stories. I went to a bar that Aviation Cadets frequently visited, but none of my classmates were there. Feeling somewhat tired, I decided I would have a beer and take a bus back to the base and get some rest.

A young man who I didn't know took a bar stool next to me and struck up a conversation. He asked if I was an Aviation Cadet. When I told him that I was, he said that he had wanted to become a pilot, but failed the color-blind eye exam. He seemed like a nice guy, especially when he bought me a beer. When I got up to leave he asked how I was getting back to the base. I told him, "By bus!" He said that he lived near the base and would be happy to drop me off, and on the way we could stop for a hamburger. "That sounds like a good plan," I said, "let's do it."

After our snack we got back into his car, but instead of driving in the direction of the air base he began driving in the opposite direction. When I asked him where he was going, he said that he wanted to show me his apartment before he dropped me off. He then started explaining, in graphic detail, how we could enjoy sexual pleasures in his apartment.

31

When I told him that I wasn't interested and to stop the car and let me out, he suggested I reconsider. In an obvious gesture of intimidation, to force me to rethink my decision, he opened his jacket and displayed a chrome-plated revolver in a shoulder holster.

With one eye on the pistol, and the other eye focused on the changing traffic light signal up ahead, I told him that perhaps I could spend an hour or so with him if he would drive me to the base afterwards. I noticed a smile of satisfaction appear on his face and an overall relaxation in his commanding demeanor. The traffic light was changing from green, to orange, and turned red before we reached the intersection. As he began to slow down, I slowly slid my hand unto the door release handle and when the car came to a stop, I opened the door and was gone in a flash, before he had a chance to react. Fearing that I might hear pistol shots aimed in my direction, I stayed low during my escape. A couple cars back I found an empty taxi, jumped in, and told the driver to take me to Waco Air Force Base. My Christmas vacation was over and I was eager to get back to flying T-6s where I would feel safe. Days later in the company of my classmates I visited the same bar, but my aggressive gay friend never showed up. It was probably fortunate that I didn't find him, because I may have gotten into a lot of trouble in attempting to settle scores.

This was not my last unsolicited proposition by a gay man. In 1979 (at age 51) I was flying space available on an Air Force C-141 from Scott AFB, Illinois, to Travis AFB, California. When after the seat belt sign was turned off, a man about my age sat down in an empty seat next to me and inquired if I was traveling alone and if I would be staying in Travis. When I told him that I was, he suggested that we get together and started running his hand up and down my leg. I Immediately changed seats and told him that if he continued to harass me I would report him to the male military flight steward. He left me alone, but somehow obtained my BOQ telephone number in Travis, and offered to take me out for dinner. I asked him for his room number, which he provided, and reported it to the Military Police. I never heard from him again! (I'm sure the action I took in 1979 would not be considered PC today, and I would be the one in trouble. Times have certainly changed!)

After acquiring approximately 75 flight hours in the T-6, I and several other Aviation Cadets were sitting in the cadet club and boasting about our individual skills as pilots, when the discussion turned to, "Is it possible to do an outside loop in the T-6?"

An outside loop is a maneuver that imposes negative gravity forces, versus the positive forces produced in an inside 360 degree loop.

The doubters of being able to perform this type of maneuver in a T-6 stressed that since the Pratt & Whitney Wasp engine had a float type carburetor and was not equipped with an inverted oil system, negative gravitational forces would cause the engine to become starved of fuel and oil and flounder. If this occurred, there would be insufficient power, or airspeed, to successfully complete the maneuver. I and a few other future 20-year-old fighter aces thought that if the outside loop was initiated with sufficient speed, you would be able to complete it, even after the engine quit, and before the lack of oil could damage the engine. The discussion ensued for some time when I announced that I was scheduled for a solo flight the next day and would attempt an outside loop and report back on my success, or failure.

The following morning I climbed to 8,000 feet, in a clear blue Texas sky, and after performing a few clearing turns (to check for the presence of other aircraft), I figured it was time to test my theory that with a high enough entry speed, I could perform an outside loop.

I pushed the throttle and prop control to maximum continuous power and put the aircraft into a dive. At around 250 mph, I pushed forward on the stick to complete the front portion of the loop and felt blood rushing from the lower portion of my body into my upper torso and brain, and began to experience typical "Red-Out Sensations." My vision blurred and I felt that if there was a safety valve on the top of my head, it would open and relieve the ever-building blood pressure on my expanding brain.

The last thing I remember, before losing consciousness, was the aircraft starting to bottom out, inverted, after completing the first half of the outside loop. A few seconds later, my vision began to clear and I noted that the aircraft was in a screaming high-speed dive. My body was shaking uncontrollably, my head felt like it was about to explode and I felt the urge to vomit. To arrest the high-speed dive, I placed the throttle in idle, pulled back on the control stick, slid open the canopy, and discharged my government-issued breakfast of bacon and eggs.

My head began to clear and with nothing more in my stomach, I felt a little better. My brain, now functioning on a proper level of oxygenated rich blood, alerted me to the fact that I had other problems. The engine appeared to have quit and was backfiring violently, and each backfire emitted puffs of smoke and explosions from the exhaust pipe. I thought maybe the aircraft was on fire!

In preparation for bailing out, I unfastened my seat belt and shoulder harness and pulled the engine fuel mixture control to off (just like my instructor had trained me to do). I then started to raise up from my seat to bail out, but when I did, I noticed that the engine backfiring had stopped, along with the large puffs of black smoke from the exhaust pipe.

I lowered myself back into the cockpit, established control of the aircraft, and slowly moved the fuel mixture control to the on position. The engine came back to life and sounded perfectly normal. I flew around close to the airport with the canopy open to clear my head while hoping that an instructor had not observed a smoking T-6 and reported it to the control tower. Hearing nothing on the radio regarding a T-6 in distress, I returned to the airport and made an uneventful smooth "three-point" landing.

When I taxied into my parking spot, I noticed a young crew chief gazing up at the right side of the aircraft and shaking his head. When the propeller came to a stop he climbed up on the wing while stating, "What happened, Mr. Martin? The right side of the aircraft is all black." I asked him if he could see any damage. He said, "No, just black soot marks." I told him what had happened and that I was afraid that an instructor might see the black streaks, and if they did, I would be in all kinds of trouble. His response, "Don't worry. I will have it all cleaned off in a few minutes." I tried to slip him five bucks for his trouble, but he refused to take it stating, "Hell, you cadets are only making $75.00 a month just like us peons and we all have to stick together."

I walked to the operations building, lugging my unused parachute, while feeling lucky that I had not tested it's operation. Back in the barracks that night I reported on my fiasco to my cadet colleagues, while telling them not to try an outside loop in a T-6. During the discussion we concluded that the engine backfires and puffs of black smoke were the result of an engine starved of fuel. Apparently the high negative "G forces" caused the carburetor float valve to temporarily stick at the top of the fuel chamber (cutting off normal fuel flow), but small amounts of fuel were still being sucked into the carburetor venturi, but only enough to produce intermittent backfires. The black smoke was the result of the wind milling engine sucking oil into the cylinders between the backfires. The next day I noticed a T-6 sitting on the ramp with a freshly polished right side, but no one bothered to ask why this particular aircraft had it's right side freshly polished, while the remainder of the aircraft was still quite dirty.

As I and my colleagues gained more experience in the nimble T-6 *Texan*, we envisioned ourselves as future fighter pilots, ready to do battle with our enemies. But in the spring of 1949 the U.S. was not engaged in a shooting war, so we would have to be content with testing our superior pilotage skills against each other. One exciting activity we employed, to prove we were destined for great aerial feats, was to meet in the sky at an obscure location over the Texas prairie and engage in tail chasing around well formed cumulus clouds.

When scheduled for a solo flight, I would check the flight schedule to see if one or more of my classmates were also flying solo. I noted that two colleagues were flying without an instructor and in a secluded corner of the briefing room we agreed to meet over a given area, at a certain time, and engage in simulated aerial dogfights. I knew that they would arrive at the rendezvous point early, so as to get a jump on them when they came into view, I decided to beat them to the punch and immediately after takeoff flew directly to the selected location.

It was a beautiful spring Texas day, with broken cumulous clouds extending from about 5,000 to 8,000 feet. I climbed above the clouds and kept myself hidden from view by skirting the cloud tops, while scanning the area below for my unsuspecting classmates. After about 30 minutes of waltzing with Mother Nature's white puffy clouds, I spied my two colleagues chasing each other around the clouds, 2,000 feet below. I positioned myself above and behind them, and at the right moment entered a steep dive at around 260 mph. Neither of my fellow combatants observed me diving on them and as I fell into a trail position, I gave out with, "rat-a-tat-tat, got-ya," on the radio. Surprised by my unseen attack they both executed a hard rolling maneuver hoping to lose me by skirting the edges of the clouds. For the next few minutes we were yanking and banking and nearly blacking out from pulling high G forces, while attempting to get on each other's ass.

Rounding one large cloud I misjudged my distance from it, and momentarily flew through a ragged edge. The cloud let me know that I wasn't welcome by buffeting my aircraft with sharp bouts of turbulence. A couple seconds later, I was back in clear skies, but had lost sight of the two aircraft I was chasing. Not wishing to admit failure, I started a search for my lost prey by skirting around the clouds in the area where I thought they should be.

Suddenly, as I was circumventing one large cumulus cloud in a clockwise direction, my two adversaries appeared directly in front and flying in the opposite direction. They were on a direct collision course with my aircraft, and to avoid colliding I executed a sharp 90 degree bank to the right, while my colleagues executed a hard bank in the opposite direction. With a closure rate of over 400 mph we missed each other by only a few feet. In the split second that it took us to pass, I could see tire tread marks on the retracted gear of the second aircraft.

My hard right bank prevented a collision, but I now found myself smack in the middle of a large summertime Texas cumulus cloud, that was rejecting my presence by kicking my aircraft around in severe turbulence. However, a more menacing problem was that I no longer had visual contact with the ground and was ill prepared to fly by reference to instruments alone. My instrument training at this point was limited and as a standard procedure, when performing aerobatics, I had caged (locked) my artificial horizon and directional gyroscope, which would be essential when flying on instruments.

I experienced an immediate onset of vertigo and literally didn't know which way was up. Not wishing to stall the aircraft, and ending up in a tailspin, I knew that I must keep the airspeed relatively high and wings level. I also knew (from my frightening experience in attempting to do an outside loop) that I must maintain a positive G-force to keep the engine operating. Realizing that by reducing power the aircraft would be forced to descend, I throttled back to almost idle while attempting to keep the airspeed above 150 mph. I was completely disorientated and opened the canopy in case it became necessary to bail out.

With the altimeter unwinding, I thought I was in a steep descending spiral, but because of the effects of vertigo, I wasn't sure. I felt that if the aircraft held together, I should soon pop out at the base of the clouds. (Ironically, in spite of the harrowing experience, I thought it strange that the excitement of the event was stronger than any sense of fear, and it occurred to me that I most likely would not find my attacking buddies, and consequently, lose the day's aerial duel.)

As suddenly as it began, my uncomfortable "Tango" with Mother Nature came to an abrupt end, when I broke out underneath the clouds in an inverted nose-down spiral. My distorted senses were telling my brain that I was in an upright spiral, but visual observations with the ground proved my senses wrong. (Due to the effects of extreme vertigo, It took several seconds before my visual acumen was in synchronization with what my brain was telling me.) Fighting false senses, I recovered from my unusual attitude by executing a high speed "Split-S" (half loop) maneuver, closed the canopy, and headed for home base. That night in the cadet club, my two combative friends and I had a wonderful time reliving our cloud chase over Texas. They were curious about my experience of flying into a fully developed cumulus Texas cloud. I told them it was a "piece of cake" and they should try it themselves. Their response, "No thanks."

On another occasion, I was planning a rendezvous with a classmate for some tail chasing and when I arrived at the agreed location, I circled around for about 15 minutes at 7,000 feet, but couldn't locate his aircraft. However, after rounding a large puffy cloud I saw a T-6 flying about 2,000 feet below and assumed it was my adversary. I shoved the nose of my aircraft into a pursuit dive and as I flashed past my unsuspecting victim I executed a beautiful barrel roll to kill of excess airspeed. I then throttled back to join-up on his right wing.

As I drew close to what I thought was my colleague's aircraft, my heart almost stopped. The T-6 I had just bounced was being flown by an instructor in the front seat and a student in the back seat practicing instrument flying, under a white canvas instrument hood. I didn't recognize the instructor, but I did note that he stared directly at me, took out a clipboard, and made a notation. I thought my Air Force career was over and flew back to Waco with a heavy heart. After parking my T-6 (which I prayed wouldn't be the last time), I walked to the flight operations building, stowed my parachute and went looking for my instructor.

Checking the flight schedule, I noted that he was flying, but should be landing shortly. Sometime later, Captain Meader entered the flight operations center and went into the flight instructor's room (off limits to cadets). I waited for him to emerge, and when he did, he saw me standing off to one side with a "whipped-dog" look. He motioned for me to follow him to a quiet corner and proceeded to chew me out in a manner that I hadn't been exposed to before. He said, "Mr. Martin, you did a very stupid thing today when you dove on an instructor working with a student under an instrument hood." "Yes sir," I said, "it was a very stupid act and I don't know what got in to me. What bothers me most is that I may have embarrassed you, since you have taught me to exercise better judgment. I apologize for letting you down." (I was hoping this humble approach would sway his better angels.)

Captain Meader then said, "Mr. Martin, what you did was wrong, and it could have resulted in you being washed-out. But fortunately, the instructor you attacked is a personal friend of mine and I persuaded him not to make an official report. So I'm telling you, be careful, as you have the makings of a good Air Force pilot and I don't want to see you washed out! Do you understand what I'm saying?" With a stern look, I said, "Yes sir, it won't happen again." I snapped him a smart salute and the subject never came up again.

A fellow Aviation Cadet from my barracks was not as lucky and became a PGR victim early in his flying career. He was in the back seat of a T-6, that was lined up on the runway in preparation for an instrument takeoff (ITO). He had the canvas instrument training hood covering his cockpit and was going through his checklist before advancing the throttle for takeoff. Another T-6, also with an instructor in the front seat and an instrument student in the rear seat, lined up on the runway directly behind them. The student in the second aircraft reported to his instructor that he was ready for takeoff, and the instructor, assuming the first aircraft had already taken off, gave his student permission for an ITO. The cadet held the brakes, advanced the power to 20 inches of manifold pressure and started to roll. However, the aircraft in front of them had not yet started its takeoff, and the left wing of their aircraft struck the empennage of the first T-6, causing its nose to swing into the rear cockpit. Its rotating propeller, acting like a giant shredder, chewed up the rear cockpit, and my classmate, before coming to a stop just short of the instructor in the front cockpit. I'm sure my classmate never knew what hit him, as his upper torso and head was shredded into a thousand pieces.

The primary cause of this accident was that the flight instructor in the second T-6 mistakenly assumed that the first aircraft had taken off and the runway in front of him was clear. However, as in most accidents, it was not this simple. Two T-6s taxied out for hooded-instrument takeoffs, each with an instructor in the front cockpit and an Aviation Cadet in the rear seat. The control tower was off the air because of a power shutdown, and there was no power for the Aldis signal lamp. An officer in a runway control truck was filling in for the tower, but radio conversation was cluttered with pilots making radio checks. The first T-6 swung onto the runway and rolled ahead about 200 feet, to make room behind them for aircraft crossing the runway. Seeing the first T-6 moving down the runway, the instructor in the second aircraft pulled onto the runway in preparation for takeoff. Assuming that the first T-6 had already taken off he gave his student permission to start his own takeoff roll.

Contributing factors were: one, the T-6, being a "tail-wheel" aircraft has a visual blind-spot directly ahead of its nose when on the ground. This is the reason "tail-dragger pilots" swerve from side-to-side (fishtail) when taxiing; two, both flight instructors were administering instrument training to their students, who were occupying the rear cockpits, with the canvas instrument hoods in place, (the purpose of the hood is to prevent the student from seeing outside the aircraft); three, both cadets were preparing to make an ITO. This training maneuver requires a lengthy verbal dialogue, on the interphone, between the instructor and student which tends to interfere with incoming radio communications; four, tail-wheel aircraft, when holding on the runway, should stop at an angle sufficient to see clearly ahead before commencing their own takeoff. If any of these safety concerns had been properly addressed, my classmate would not have been thrust into an early encounter with the PGR. (See Photo No. 18.)

My last personal Close Encounter in the T-6 *Texan* involved a dumb move intended to surprise my roommate, Archie Dulley. Archie had been encountering problems relating to rudder and aileron coordination and to help overcome this deficiency, I sat up with him, after lights out, holding two books to simulate rudder pedals while he used a toilet plunger to simulate an aircraft control stick. We worked on his "hands-and-feet" coordination problem until he could move both in perfect coordination. Because of this temporary setback, he was slow to solo and behind the rest of us in accomplishing required flight training maneuvers. He was a serious pilot, although a little slow, and not prone to stretching the envelope on solo flights like many other cadets.

I was scheduled for a solo aerobatics flight and noted that Archie was scheduled to fly solo to our auxiliary field, Prairie Hill, for supervised landings. I walked to my assigned aircraft, performed a preflight, and with an 18-year-old crew chief assisting me, strapped into the cockpit. With the whine from the electric inertia starter and puffs of smoke belching out from the exhaust, I brought the nine cylinders of the 550 hp Wasp engine to life. Hearing, and feeling, this big round engine spring to life always produced a heart-throbbing rush of excitement and I realized how fortunate I was to enjoy such an exhilarating life, at taxpayers' expense.

Taxiing out for takeoff I observed a long line of T-6s waiting for departure clearance and fell in line behind them. As I did I noted that I was positioned directly behind my roommate, Archie Dulley. He had not seen me and as the line of aircraft slowly moved forward, I positioned my *Texan* in such a way, that if he turned around he would not recognize who was following him.

Fifteen seconds after Archie took off, I was climbing out (still unobserved) behind him. He leveled off at 3,500 feet and set up a course for Prairie Hill. I continued my climb to 7,000 feet, while keeping the sun at my back so as to hide my position.

I closed the canopy, tightened my lap belt and shoulder harness, set the engine power to maximum continuous and started a pursuit dive on Archie's aircraft. I was diving at an airspeed of around 260 mph, which gave me a speed advantage over Archie of around 110 mph. When about 500 feet above him, and closing fast, I rolled inverted and passed over the top of his aircraft by about 200 feet. I observed a startled look on Archie's face as I flashed over him upside down. As soon as I was safely clear of his aircraft, I started a "Split-S" maneuver, but quickly realized that I was too low, and too fast, to recover in a half loop. I rolled the aircraft upright, reduced power and pulled out straight ahead in a 4-G pull-up.

With my aircraft once again heading skyward, I heard several calls on the radio stating, "T-6 diving on Prairie Hill, what is your call sign?" This call was repeated several times. (For the second time, as an Aviation Cadet, I felt a real sense of fear. It wasn't a fear of an early encounter with the PGR, but a fear of being washed out, because of another stupid careless act.) I kept the engine power at maximum continuous and wanted to get as far away from Prairie Hill as possible. When about 50 miles out, and flying in an opposite direction, I called the control tower and requested practice radio steers. (My intent was to get myself on a tape recording, proving that I was no where near Prairie Hill Airport earlier.)

After landing I went to the barracks, took a shower, and was changing into my Class A uniform in preparation for evening mess when Archie walked in. He was quite excited and started telling me about the stupid S.O.B. that passed over him inverted as he was approaching Prairie Hill. I asked him if he knew who performed such a stupid act. He said, "No, but his instructor and the operations officer are attempting to find out, and when they do his ass is toast." I agreed with Archie's sense of indignation, and told him that I sure hope they catch that stupid idiot!

The next day as we assembled in the briefing room, Captain Beck (the operations officer) called the group to attention. In a loud authoritative voice barked, "I want the cadet who dove on Mr. Dulley over Prairie Hill Airport yesterday to step forward." Even though my stomach was turning knots, I knew that if he was asking for the guilty pilot to step forward, he didn't know who it was. He repeated this command as the assembled cadets, including myself, looked around to see who would step forward, but no one did! Captain Beck left the room, with a grimaced grunt, stating he would find the guilty S.O.B. and when he did his ass would be history. (Lucky for me he never found the S.O.B.) (See Photos 15 and 17.)

Archie and I remained good friends and following graduation from pilot training, I intended to let him know who it was who dove on him inverted over Prairie Hill, but I never got the chance. Unfortunately he was killed flying an F-80 Shooting Star jet fighter during the Korean War.

My next Close Encounter with the PGR in a single-engine trainer was in a 225 hp Beechcraft T-34A *Mentor.*

The T-34 has a wing span of 33 feet, a maximum weight of 2,900 lbs, a maximum speed of 188 mph and a range of 770 miles. It replaced the T-6 Texan as the primary Air Force trainer in 1956. The Mentor, with its low power and tricycle landing gear, possesses excellent and forgiving handling characteristics and provided the practical experience student pilots needed to move up to bigger and faster aircraft, without exposing them to the high washout rate experienced in the T-6. The T-34 trainer was based on the successful civilian Beechcraft Bonanza, but provided tandem seating and a military style cockpit with a stick control. A total of 1,300 Mentors were built and when retired from active service, many were transferred to the Civil Air Patrol and Air Force Aero Clubs. More than 120 remain in service with civilian pilots. (See Photo No. 76.)

In 1958 I was stationed at the Niagara Falls, New York, Municipal Airport, as a C-119 flight instructor. The Air Force Fighter Interceptor Squadron, flying F-86Ds, operated an aero club utilizing a Cessna 172 and a C-150, but when the T-34 *Mentor* was dropped from active service, they acquired four, almost-new, *aircraft*. The only restriction that accompanied these aircraft was that they could not be transferred to civilian registration and that they be maintained in an airworthy condition at no expense to the Air Force. I was a member of this club and with the introduction of the *Mentor* my services as an experienced military propeller aircraft flight instructor were in high demand.

Our T-34s were extremely popular with active Air Force members and a fun aircraft to fly. One problem we encountered was in controlling the aerial fantasies of "aspiring-fighter-pilots" amongst our low-time (non-military) private pilots. I and several pilots from the fighter squadron formed an impromptu aerial demonstration team and would fly to regional airports and put on a modest airshow by performing loops, rolls, Cuban eights, and low level high speed passes. Our only charge for these demonstrations of aerial skill was a free breakfast and a full tank of gas.

I and two other T-34 hot pilots had performed our airshow and were preparing to land from a military style 360 degree overhead approach. (I was leading the formation, so would be the first aircraft to land.) On final approach I noted puddles of standing water on the sod runway, but didn't think it would cause a problem, so I continued my approach.

I touched down in a splash of water and held the nose off as long as possible. During the landing roll-out I could hear water splashing off the aircraft and thought about executing a go-around, but unfortunately decided against it. After lowering the nose I felt, and heard, a snapping sound followed by the nose of the aircraft dropping sufficiently to allow the propeller to strike the wet runway. The final portion of the landing roll-out was accentuated by mud and water breaking over the top of the aircraft. I quickly placed the fuel mixture control and the ignition switch to off and as the aircraft came to a stop a small crowd of "admirers" came running out to greet the embarrassed pilot. Since there was no apparent danger of fire, I switched on the radio and advised my two buddies, still airborne, not to attempt a landing and return to Niagara Falls, which they did.

A quick examination of the nose gear assembly revealed the problem. The T-34 was designed for hard-surfaced runways and was never intended for operations on wet, grassy fields covered with mud. The nose wheel tire is covered by a close-fitting fender and mud from the wet field quickly became impacted in this narrow space and acted as a nose wheel brake. This sudden deceleration put a strain on the small hollow strut, causing it to shear, just above the nose wheel assembly. Contact with the ground had also bent about one inch of both propeller tips.

I and several club members who had flown to the airport in our C-172 lifted the damaged nose wheel onto a small auto trailer and moved it inside a nearby hangar. We removed the bent propeller and decided to remove the sheared-off nose wheel strut for transport back to our home base in the C-172. Nobody knew the proper procedure for removing a damaged strut assembly, but a clutter of fingers were loosening and tugging at anything that looked like it should come loose. Suddenly, accompanied by a loud explosion, the jagged steel strut shot out from its housing, like it had been fired from a cannon. It whistled past my face so close that it struck the visor of my baseball cap, sending it flying. It then bounced off the concrete floor before coming to rest in a far corner of the hangar. (No one had thought about releasing the high pressure nitrogen charge contained in the strut housing before attempting to remove it.) Had I been leaning just an inch or so further forward, the ejected jagged strut would have taken off my entire face or possibly my head! It was so close that I felt a rush of air as it flew past in a blur. (An Encounter with the PGR too close for comfort!)

After arriving back in Niagara Falls, I loaded the damaged propeller in another T-34 by positioning it across the front and back cockpits and secured it with strands of rope. The damaged prop reached well into the front cockpit, requiring me to sandwich myself into the front seat and fly with my head tilted to the left all the way to Detroit, Michigan, where, hopefully, it could be repaired. I developed a stiff neck from this unusual position, but didn't complain as I felt a sense of responsibility for bending it when landing in a puddle of water and soft ground.

The propeller repair shop x-rayed it for cracks, trimmed off an inch at each tip, and declared it serviceable. While I waited for it to be repaired I had lunch with my brothers George and Dan and took each of them up for a flight in the T-34. They were thrilled in being able to fly in an airplane capable of mild aerobatics, and I especially enjoyed flying my older brother George, as he was my initial flight instructor and responsible for me obtaining a Private Pilot's Certificate 13 years earlier.

When the repair to the propeller was complete, I tied it down between the cockpits. However, for the return flight I arranged it so I had to crook my head in the opposite direction, so as to balance out my stiff neck problem. It seemed to do the trick, as when I landed in Niagara Falls, I was able to hold my head up straight.

We reinstalled the "squared-off" prop, and a new nose wheel strut, on our crippled Beechcraft *Mentor* and had it back in the air a few days later. I believe we had the only "clipped Prop" T-34 flying and it seemed to develop slightly more RPM on takeoff and a little more speed in cruise!

Chapter Three --- Douglas C-54 Skymaster

After completing basic pilot training in June 1949, I transferred to Barksdale AFB, Shreveport, Louisiana, for advanced training in the North American B-25 *Mitchell* bomber. I had indicated a preference for the North American F-51 *Mustang* fighter, but wasn't disappointed in being assigned to fly America's most famous airplane of WW II. The B-25 was the type aircraft flown by General Jimmy Doolittle's group of volunteers during their surprise bombing raid on Japan on April 18, 1942. It also saw extensive action in both the Pacific and European war zones. More than 9,800 *Mitchell* bombers were built, and following the end of hostilities, the U.S. Air Force employed hundreds as advanced multi-engine trainers and military executive transports. My first flight in this famous fast medium bomber was on Friday, June 24, 1949. I was immediately impressed by its exhilarating performance when compared to the T-6 *Texan*. Following 12 hours of dual instruction, I and a fellow 21-one-year-old student pilot were cleared to fly it by ourselves. (See Photo No. 20.)

The B-25 is powered by two Wright 1,700 hp engines, and absence its wartime configuration of five crew members, steel armor plating, guns and ammunition and 5,000 lbs. of bombs, it flew like a twin-engine fighter. It has a cruising speed of 230 mph and climbs like a homesick angel.

As an Aviation Cadet at Barksdale AFB, I was not held to the strict military discipline required at Waco, or at other advanced pilot training bases. Barksdale was the home of the first Air Force jet bomber squadron flying the North American B-45 *Tornado*, and this unique unit far outweighed any interest in our small cadet detachment. In addition, our class was the last Aviation Cadet group to be trained at Barksdale, so our tactical officers were devoting most of their time in preparing for their forthcoming move to Lubbock, Texas. Discipline was so lax that some cadets even discontinued making their beds, but I never went that far as I didn't wish to expose myself to unwarranted demerits. To allow time for our cadet detachment to relocate, we flew most Saturdays and completed all training requirements two weeks earlier than our classmates at other bases, but were not allowed to graduate until our entire class had completed training. I spent the last two weeks as an Aviation Cadet dressed in fatigues, loading moving vans and policing the area.

Shreveport, Louisiana was a military-friendly town and I savored the pleasure of being able to walk into a bar and order a drink after turning twenty-one. One Sunday, when attending services in the base chapel, the Priest announced that servicemen were invited to attend a picnic sponsored by a downtown Catholic Church. What caught my attention was his statement that there would be free food and beer, so several of us took a bus downtown, assembled in the front of a local church, and were transported by friendly parishioners to the picnic site.

There was plenty of food and beer, but what captured my eye was a beautiful young "Southern Belle" dressed in tight-fitting pedal pushers and sitting cross-legged on a table in the club house. She was obviously enjoying the attention young men were devoting to her warm smile, long flowing blond hair and bubbling personality. Working my way through the crowd I struck up a conversation, learned that her name was Carolyn Carroll, and before anyone else could beat me to the punch, I invited her to our cadet club dance the following Saturday evening. When accepting my invitation, she asked if I had a car. I told her no, but if she could find another girl to accompany us, I would find somebody who does. She said that this would be no problem, so we exchanged telephone numbers.

I talked a buddy, who owned a 1946 red Ford convertible, into accepting a blind date and the following week Carolyn and I were slow dancing to a Glenn Miller style big band in the patio of our spacious cadet club. Carolyn and I hit it off right from the start and soon fell in love. Whenever I could get away from the base I would take a bus downtown, pick her up at her house, and attend a movie, grab a sandwich or just walk the streets in her neighborhood. Since I was a Yankee from Northern Wisconsin, her father didn't take a liking to me, but at least he recognized that I had met his youngest daughter at a church picnic. (I wasn't batting a thousand, but I wasn't all bad either.) When I would ring her door bell, he would open it without saying hello, and call out in a loud Southern drawl, **"Carolyn, your Yankee boy friend is here!"**

Carolyn and I talked about marriage after I graduated from pilot training and commissioned a second lieutenant, but I wasn't sure I wanted to take the plunge so early in life. What finally saved me from popping the question was when she decided she could not take time away from her studies at Louisiana State University to attend my graduation ceremony and pin on my silver Air Force pilot wings. At the time my feelings were bruised, but in hindsight I feel my guardian angel was looking over me and saying, "Live a little first lieutenant." After 118 hours in the *Mitchell*, and a 27-ship graduation formation flyby, I was commissioned a second lieutenant and designated an Air Force pilot on September 29, 1949, with a salary of $336 per month, equal to $2,930 today. (See Photo No. 21.)

Following a two-week vacation in my hometown of Ladysmith, Wisconsin, I reported to Camp Kilmer, New Jersey for further transport by military troop ship to West Germany. I spent ten days at Camp Kilmer, with the only assigned duty of making daily checks of the bulletin board. I and several of my colleagues took in the sights of New York City, attended Broadway shows and just enjoyed walking the streets, while being mesmerized by the lights and activity of Times Square.

Camp Kilmer was activated in 1942 and was named after Joyce Kilmer, a soldier-poet of WW I. It is located near New Brunswick, 22 miles from New York City and is presently a U.S. Army Reserve Base.

One day, when several of us were enjoying a beer at the Camp Kilmer Officers' Club bar, an Army warrant officer with a chest full of military ribbons, inquired if we were awaiting shipment to Germany. When we replied in the affirmative, he told us that he had just returned from a three-year tour in Germany and that we were in for a great assignment. Moving to a bar stool next to me, he said, in a subdued voice, "How many cigarettes are you and your buddies shipping to Germany as unaccompanied hold baggage, lieutenant?" Not understanding the thrust of his question I replied by stating, "We are mostly nonsmokers and are not planning on shipping any cigarettes." With a screwed-up facial expression that implied disappointment in my response, he added, "You don't understand the reason I'm asking lieutenant." He then went on to explain that in Germany, cigarettes that cost ten cents a pack in the military post exchange (PX) bring one dollars worth of German marks on the black market. He further explained that we could fit three cases of Pall Malls (108 cartons, or 1,080 packs) in a military-style foot locker, and that the cost for 108 cartons, in the local PX, would be $108.00, plus about ten dollars for a footlocker. His benevolent recommendation continued, "After stacking the cigarettes into the footlocker, you can take it to the Army transportation office for shipment as unaccompanied hold baggage, and when in Germany, your footlocker load of smokes should be worth approximately $1,080" (equal to $8,738 today).

Armed with this unexpected bit of good advice, five new 2nd lieutenants rushed over to the PX, purchased five foot lockers and 15 cases of Pall Mall cigarettes. After filling the footlockers with our precious booty we commandeered a military truck to take us to the base transportation office, where we requested that our footlockers be "steel banded" and forwarded to us in Germany. We then returned to the Officers' Club bar to resume our beer-drinking session, while hoping that we hadn't committed ourselves to a one-way trip to the Fort Leavenworth Military Prison!

After a ten-day crossing of the North Atlantic on the U.S.N.S. troop ship *Henry Gibbons*, 20 eager young "Shave Tails" (second lieutenants) disembarked in the Northern German port city of Bremerhaven. The ocean crossing, on this relatively small ship, launched in November 1942, was crammed with 2,000 troops. It was scrapped in 1983 which was 20 years overdue. The next day we traveled by train to the ancient city of Marburg, located in what was then the British Military Zone of Occupation.

Marburg experienced little damage during the allied bombing raids, so the U.S. Army utilized an intact former German Army military base as a staging area for incoming Air Force and Army personnel. After arriving we were told that we could expect to be there for seven to ten days, while the Air Force Headquarters in Wiesbaden determined our final assignment. While awaiting disposition, we were free to explore the local area as long as we checked the bulletin board each morning for information relating to our next assignment. We were instructed that since Germany was under military occupation it was mandatory that when in public places, and on military installations, we wear our uniforms. The only exception was when participating in athletic events or sleeping.

These uniform requirements were rigidly enforced. Class B Uniforms (shirt and trousers) were allowed until 1700 hours (5 p.m.). After 1700, Class A Uniforms (blouse and tie) were required. There were times when we would be lounging in a bar, in Class B Uniforms, close to the bewitching hour of 5 p.m., when Military Policemen (MPs) would come by and politely advise us that we would soon be out of uniform. We would quickly "chug-a-lug" our beers and head for our rooms to change. (Apparently the type of underwear or pajamas we wore was optional, but as a dumb second lieutenant I didn't feel it prudent to ask.)

47

This was my first trip to Germany and I found walking the streets of Marburg and visiting centuries-old churches and castles extremely educational and interesting. I especially enjoyed the many taverns (Gasthaus) which served delicious food and strong German beer.

I and several of my colleagues were engaged in a beer-drinking session in a Gasthaus one evening, when a young German man came up and introduced himself in a combination of broken English and German. I returned his greeting in my "me Tarzan, you Jane" style German I had learned from my mother. Struggling to communicate with each other I soon learned that he was 23-years-old (two years my senior) and a former German Luffwaffe fighter pilot. He informed me that he had graduated from pilot training in the spring of 1945 and was on his way to join a FW-190 fighter squadron when the war ended.

The cultural and national barrier that we initially experienced soon disappeared in direct proportion to the amount of beer we drank. As we swapped stories about our military training as pilots, we learned that we were both second lieutenants, and due to our young age had missed fighting each other in combat by only a couple of years, and soon developed a pilot's mutual feeling of camaraderie. He said that it was fortunate that he didn't see combat, as his father was killed on the Russian front, and had he also been killed, it would have been a real hardship for his mother. He complimented me on my smart-looking blue Air Force uniform, but thought the Luftwaffe pilot's uniform was more distinctive. I acknowledged that the German uniform was quite natty, but I had only seen it in pictures. Eager to satisfy my interest, he invited me to accompany him to his apartment, which he shared with his mother and a German shepherd, where he would show me his Luftwaffe pilot's uniform and some pictures of him undergoing pilot training.

His two-bedroom apartment was small, but very clean, and as we entered he introduced me to his mother who was sitting in a rocking chair knitting. After opening a couple bottles of beer he went to a clothes closet and brought out his Luftwaffe pilot's uniform, along with a smart-looking garrison cap and shiny black, knee-high, riding boots. I admitted that it was a very attractive uniform and noting that we were about the same size, suggested that I put on his German uniform and he put on my Air Force uniform. He thought this was a grand idea and a few minutes later, I was dressed in his Luftwaffe uniform, along with a swastika arm band, riding breaches and black boots. I had to admit that it was a fine looking uniform! My German friend seemed equally impressed in the simplicity of my Air Force blue uniform, minus leather belts and a swastika arm band.

We had great fun saluting each other while continuing to consume several bottles of strong beer and singing "off-key" to 70 rpm recordings of German military ballads. His mother, not impressed in our youthful antics, continued knitting without saying a word. I told my friend that I wished my American pilot colleagues could see me in a German uniform and suggested we proceed to the Gasthaus, with him wearing my U.S. Air Force uniform and I wearing his German Luftwaffe uniform. He thought this was a good idea and we staggered toward the front door.

We hadn't taken more than two or three steps, before his mother rose up from her chair, and in a loud voice shouted, **"Nein, Nein"** (No, No). She pointed us back into the apartment and opened two more bottles of beer. I don't know how many more beers I drank, but sometime later I fell asleep on a sofa.

Hours later, I awoke in a stupor when I felt the need to relieve myself. The lights in the apartment had been dimmed and my comrade's mother had apparently gone to bed. Through blurry, bloodshot eyes, and a throbbing hangover, I noted that I was dressed in a German pilot's uniform. Initially, I didn't comprehend what I was seeing. It was like an episode right out of the TV show *Twilight Zone*. I looked over at my sleeping German friend, dressed in my Air Force uniform, which only added to my mental state of confusion. After relieving myself (by opening a fly with buttons instead of a zipper), I poked my German friend awake, and we exchanged uniforms. Properly dressed, I walked on wobbly legs to my temporary quarters in an old German barracks and went to bed.

I'm still grateful to my German pilot colleague's mother for stopping us from returning to the Gasthaus, with me in a German Luftwaffe pilot's uniform and my Nazi friend in my Air Force officer's uniform. Had I performed this foolish, "spur-of-the-moment" act I'm sure the Military Police would have been called and my military career would have ended right there! (I wouldn't even had been able to pickup my footlocker load of black market cigarettes.) I don't think the U.S. Military authorities would have taken too kindly to a drunk Air Force second lieutenant, drinking beer in a German Gasthaus, dressed in a German officer's uniform with a Nazi Swastika arm band prominently displayed!

After more than a week of enjoying the wonders of Marburg, I was eager to find out what the Air Force Headquarters at Wiesbaden's Camp Lindsey had in mind regarding my final assignment. In November 1949 the number of Air Force officers stationed in Germany was 2,421. Aircraft assigned, were B-17s, B-26s, C-47s, C-54s. C-82s, F-47s, F-80s, L-5s, RB-26s, T-6s and T-33s. Since I graduated from pilot training as a multi-engine pilot, I didn't have much hope of being assigned to a fighter squadron, but rumors were that most new pilots would be assigned to a RB-26 unit, and the possibility of being able to fly this fast light bomber was very exciting. However, all 20 multi-engine pilot graduates were issued orders to report to the 61st Troop Carrier Wing at Rhein Main Air Base, Frankfurt, Germany. We were told that they would determine our final assignment, which would be flying C-47s, C-54s or C-82s.

On Thursday, November 10th, twenty "Shave-tails" reported for duty at Rhein Main, Air Base, where we were informed that the base was preparing to celebrate a four-day holiday (Armistice Day), and we should obtain a room in the BOQ and use the time off in getting acquainted with the area. (On June 1, 1954 the U.S. changed the name to Veterans Day.)

Rhein Main Air Base was located near Frankfurt, Germany, and played a significant historical role for both Germany and the U.S. In 1909 Count Von Zeppelin used the area for launching his lighter-than-air dirigibles, but by 1936 the airport became an important commercial base for airplanes operating from the northern section, while rigid airships operated from the southern portion. The Hindenburg airship departed Rhein Main for its ill-fated flight to Lake Hurst, New Jersey, in May 1936. In 1940, the remaining rigid airships, and their huge hangars, were demolished, and the base became an important German Luftwaffe fighter base and was heavily bombed by the allies. In 1945 The U.S. occupied the base, cleared off the rubble and built new runways and support facilities. Initially the U.S. planned on using it for B-29s, but it soon became a primary transport base and known as the Gateway to Europe. It was a primary base for the round-the-clock Berlin Airlift from June 1948 to September 1949, and a major hub for Operation Desert Shield and Desert Storm in 1991. Rhein-Main Air Base was turned over to total German control on December 30, 2005, and the 120 former Air Force buildings will be demolished to make way for a third terminal capable of accommodating cargo aircraft and the Super Airbus Jumbo A380.

I was assigned a steel cot in a room of a former German Luftwaffle BOQ, which I would share with a captain and two first lieutenants. As I was unpacking my duffel bag my senior roommate, an Air Force captain, informed me that as the junior officer it would be my duty to keep the "potbelly stove," sitting in a sandbox in the center of the room, stoked with coal. He added, "When I get up at 7 a.m. I want the room toasty warm."

Several of us bought a handful of German marks and headed for Frankfurt to see the sights. The city was heavily bombed during the war and most of it was still a mess, but there were a sufficient number of Gasthauses and young friendly frauleins eager to accept our money and make us feel welcome.

On November 15th, we assembled in Colonel "Red" Foreman's office to learn of our final assignment. Col. Foreman was a highly-decorated WW II B-17 combat pilot and a very pleasant officer. He issued a warm welcome, while stating that although we were classmates, we would be assigned to different squadrons. Ten of us would remain at Rhein Main to fly C-54s, while ten would be assigned to Wiesbaden to fly C-82s. I was one of the pilots assigned to the ill-famed C-82 and Col. Foreman obviously sensed our disappointment. He attempted to soothe our concerns by informing us that being assigned to C-82s was not all bad, as we would be billeted in private rooms in Wiesbaden hotels, and initially fly C-54s, since the C-82s were temporarily grounded and that Wiesbaden was a great place to be stationed, as it incurred little bomb damage during the war. Realizing that there was nothing we could do about it anyway, we thanked him for his consideration, saluted and picked up our orders for Wiesbaden Air Base, referred to as "Y-80." (See Photo No. 24.)

The reason, I was disappointed in being assigned to fly the Fairchild C-82 Packet, was that it not only enjoyed a questionable reputation, but was presently grounded for safety reasons, and no one knew when the grounding order would be lifted. Secondly, when I was in basic pilot training in Waco Texas, a C-82 had visited the base and I and several other cadets examined it with considerable curiosity. It was our unanimous opinion that it was the one aircraft that we didn't wish to fly after graduation. I guess I should have kept my thoughts to myself, because apparently, someone was listening. I will discuss the C-82 in greater detail in the next chapter. (See Photos 26, 27, and 28.)

I was assigned a large spacious hotel room with a balcony on the third floor of the *Bellevue Hotel* in downtown Wiesbaden. The hotel was located on Wilhelmstrasse, a prominent street boarding a beautiful well-manicured spacious park. (It was certainly better than firing a potbelly stove in a drafty Rhein Main BOQ room shared with three other officers.)

Of the ten new second lieutenants ordered to Wiesbaden, five were assigned to the 10th Troop Carrier Squadron, and I and four others were assigned to the 12th Squadron. Each squadron was equipped with 18 C-82s, but since they were temporarily grounded we would initially be flying the Douglas C-54 *Skymaster.*

The C-54 was the first four-engine transport to enter military service, and the Air Force accepted a total of 1,164 from 1942 to 1947. Its maximum load capacity is 28,000 lbs of cargo, or 49 passengers. It is powered by four Pratt & Whitney R-2000 engines of 1,450 hp each, giving it a cruising speed of 190 mph and a maximum speed of 275. During the 1948/49 Berlin Airlift many of the C-54s that the military possessed were pressed into service to supply the isolated city of Berlin with the means of surviving the Soviet Union's blockade. (See photo No. 29.)

The crew complement in the C-54, for flights within Europe, was usually a pilot, copilot, and a crew chief. Occasionally a third pilot would be added, who would sit in the jump seat to assist in some cockpit functions. My checkout in the C-54 consisted of a supervised exterior preflight inspection, a reading of the checklist to an instructor pilot and three takeoffs and landings from the right seat. Following a two-hour flight I was a qualified *Skymaster* copilot. This brief "check-out" program may seem inadequate by today's standards, but in 1949 the main function of a copilot was to sit in the right seat, make radio calls, keep his mouth shut, don't ask too many questions and compliment the pilot on his smooth landings (true or not). If he bounced a landing, you would state, "You really handled that stiff crosswind well, Captain."

Another responsibility of the copilot was to sign out a box of 30 VHF radio transmitter crystals from the communications center. Early VHF radios only had about 12 pre-set frequencies installed and when flying from country to country we would be instructed to switch to a specific frequency, peculiar to that area, which was not installed. The copilot's duty was to select this frequency from a box of plug-in crystals, insert it into the transmitter and dial in the same frequency in the receiver, and then make a note of the new frequency, in pencil, on the frequency card on the pilot's pedestal. When the flight was over I would return the intact crystal box to our communications center. (This same procedure for copilots installing discrete transmitter crystals was also required in C-82s which are discussed in the following chapter.)

Although the Berlin Airlift officially ended on September 30, 1949, C-54s were still flying support flights to this war ravaged city, but not the frequency of the past year. Many of the Aircraft Commanders who had flown the Berlin Airlift were an interesting group as they had been recalled to active duty from the reserves. They reported for duty in a mixture of uniforms and some had gained so much weight that they had difficulty in buttoning their uniform blouses, without taking in a deep breath. If that didn't work they just left them unbuttoned. Others were highly professional B-17 or B-24 combat veterans, who took great pride in being able to serve their country once again. Their personal appearance reflected this pride, and they displayed an eagerness to assist inexperienced young copilots, like myself, in becoming productive pilots.

I flew several trips to Berlin with one of the more relaxed captains who was always accompanied with his large German shepherd named, Brutis. The dog slept in his hotel room, traveled with him in his 1941 Plymouth sedan, and had full run of his C-54 on all flights. I politely refused to ride with him in his car, least I become covered with dog hair.

Brutis was always hungry and en route to Berlin my "pet-loving" Aircraft Commander would share his lunch with him, while I attempted to keep him from drooling into mine. If the cargo compartment was empty, Brutis would be entertained by his master throwing a tennis ball to the rear of the cargo compartment, which would be quickly fetched by his 80-pound mascot. With the wet ball clamped between large "shark-like" teeth, Brutis would return to the cockpit, with his wagging tail spreading out the smell of his farts, and drop the wet ball in his master's hand, who would throw it back to the rear of the aircraft. This activity would go on for an hour or more, while I monitored the autopilot and attempted to keep my left sleeve dry, by avoiding Brutis' never-ending supply of drool.

One particular flight with Brutis and his master stands out and reflects the casual attitude of the times. Following a flight from Berlin, we had landed at Rhein Main Air Base and were taxiing into the parking ramp. As we approached the terminal my dog-loving captain said, "I recognize the German ground handler waving us in for parking. He loves dogs and has developed a fondness for Brutis. Let's surprise him with a good joke." After making this statement, he jumped out of the pilot's left seat and directed me to continue steering the aircraft using differential braking. At first I didn't comprehend what he had in mind, but his humorous plot was soon apparent. He directed Brutis to jump up into the pilot's left seat, placed a headset on his shaggy head and opened the pilot's sliding window. As we approached our parking spot, I thought the German ground handler was going to have a heart attack. He looked up at the captain's open window and there was Brutis, wearing a headset, poking his head outside and barking loudly!

My one Close Encounter in a C-54, occurred on a flight from Rhein Main to Berlin in December 1949. The Aircraft Commander was Captain Benson who had flown 30 B-17 combat missions over Germany in WW II. He remained on active duty after the war, had a chest full of ribbons, but didn't seem extremely tolerant in enhancing the learning curve of dumb second lieutenants. On this particular flight, a classmate (who was also a dumb second lieutenant) was flying in the right seat. I was occupying the jump seat and directed to accomplish minor tasks, like adjusting engine power settings and operating the carburetor fuel mixture controls. Our takeoff weight was close to the maximum of 73,000 pounds, which would press the capability of the aircraft to remain airborne in the event of an engine failure during the critical takeoff phase. (A failure of two engines could easily result in a crash.) The takeoff was routine and after becoming airborne Captain Benson directed me to place the fuel mixture control levers to "auto-lean" (halfway between full rich and cutoff).

The mixture control levers on a C-54 are shafts of smooth steel, with round plastic knobs on each end. (However, the control levers for engines 1 and 2, on this aircraft, were missing the plastic knobs.) To move them into "auto-lean" it was necessary to first pull them outward, to release a spring held detent, and then move them into the desired position. However, with the knobs missing, offsetting the tension would be difficult.

I had placed the mixture control levers for engines 3 and 4 into the "auto-lean" position, but was having difficulty in moving the bare steel shafts for engines 1 and 2. My difficulty in moving them was twofold: first, the absence of the plastic knobs made it difficult to obtain a firm grip; secondly, I was wearing thick leather gloves. While I was struggling in

54

overpowering the spring held detents, Captain Benson was losing patience with what he considered another dumb second lieutenant in not being able to follow orders. His patience ran out at about the same time that I was finally able to release the mixture controls from their spring-held position. He reached down and slapped my gloved hands while stating, **"I said place the mixtures into auto lean!"** His slapping of my hands, caused the fuel mixture controls for engines 1 and 2 to go to the full shutoff position, resulting in the immediate loss of two engines on the left side of the aircraft!

When engines 1 and 2 failed, we were climbing through 700 feet at an airspeed of 150 knots. This sudden loss of two engines caused our heavily-loaded aircraft to abruptly yaw to the left, lose airspeed and go into a steep descending left bank. Captain Benson pushed the nose over to increase the airspeed and regain control, while shoving all four throttles to the full power position. (Which naturally had no effect on the two left engines.) At the same time, several eager hands reached for the mixture controls for engines 1 and 2, with the intent of placing them back into the fuel-on position. But before my startled colleagues could react I placed them back on myself.

The engines, with a tremendous roar, came back to life! (When the fuel supply for engines 1 and 2 was abruptly cut, the constant speed propellers automatically went to a near flat pitch, high speed position, so when fuel was restored, without retarding the propeller control levers, the engines roared into a momentary over-speed condition of well over 3,000 rpm.) Captain Benson rolled the wings level and pulled the aircraft out of it's dive at about three hundred feet above the ground. (For a few brief, but hectic seconds, I felt that the Pilot's Grim Reaper figured he was going to welcome a few more errant aviators into his black kingdom.)

As we resumed a normal climb attitude, our male flight steward, alarmed by the sudden maneuver and strange noises, came to the cockpit to inquire if everything was OK. As I swabbed my brow of sweat, I assured him that everything was fine and that we had just flown through a bit of turbulence and not to worry. Shaking his head in disbelief he returned to the cabin. Captain Benson never accepted my explanation that it was not my fault that he had lost two engines immediately after takeoff and was more convinced then ever that second lieutenants should not be allowed to fly airplanes! However, I later flew with him on a flight to Rome, Italy, and everything seemed to have been forgiven.

Chapter Four --- Fairchild C-82 Packet

Wiesbaden, Germany is a city of considerable charm. It is reported to have one of the most famous mineral spas in Europe, dating back to the days of the Roman Empire. The city escaped the mass bombing raids that nearly destroyed other German cities, thereby making it a prime location to be stationed. According to reports, the city was only bombed once by an errant RAF Lancaster whose crew thought they were bombing Frankfurt. The stated reason for not designating Wiesbaden as a primary target was that it provided no significant military aid to the German military, but the real reason was that the U.S. Army Air Corps planned on establishing their headquarters in this exquisite city after the war.

As a 21-year-old second lieutenant, I felt very fortunate to be posted to such a tranquil area of post-war WW II occupied Germany. The city of Mainz, just across the Rhine River, was 85% destroyed and was still in a complete state of rubble. (See Photos No. 30 and 31.)

The U.S. Army Air Corps, after occupying the city, requisitioned all former German military installations, many large office buildings, most major hotels, cabarets, night clubs and large sections of civilian housing areas to accommodate the needs of the American military occupation forces and their families. The *Palast, Rose* and *Schwarzer Bock* hotels, all five-star and located in the center of the city, were designated officer hotels. Each contained an eloquent restaurant, a fully-stocked bar, and lavish guest rooms. The *Scala, a* famous German night club, was designated a downtown Officers' Club. A former Luftwaffe hotel known as the *Neroburg,* located on the foot hills of the Taunus Mountains, was declared a senior officer's facility. It provided excellent entertainment, a first class restaurant, a large swimming pool and a beautiful panoramic view of the city from its wide verandah. The famous *Kurhaus*, a large Gothic style building which contained a stately casino, concert hall, a posh restaurant and an outdoor cafe, was converted into a military "Special Service Club." It was a favorite meeting and recreation center for military personnel throughout the Wiesbaden area. The Air Force hung a huge sign over the Roman style pillars which read **Eagle Club.**

Just a few miles north of Wiesbaden is the *Kronberg Castle*. This elaborate former palace of the eldest daughter of Queen Victoria of England survived the war intact and was requisitioned by the U.S. Army and converted into a stylish 80-room officers' hotel and club. The rooms were reserved for field-grade officers, but the fabulous bar and restaurant were open to all officer ranks. Adjacent to the castle grounds was an 18-hole golf course and a stable of well-bred horses, which we could ride for one dollar per hour (Equivalent to $8.00 today.)

The Kronberg Castle was in the news in 1946, when the female club officer, and her U.S. Army colonel boyfriend, were charged with the theft of jewels and heirlooms worth more than $1.5 million (equal to $15 million today). Both were court-martialed, dismissed from the Army, and sent to prison, but most of the stolen jewels were never recovered.

In addition to horseback riding at the *Kronberg Castle*, I could ride robust horses at the former German officers riding stables in *Camp Lindsey*. My favorite mount was a white stallion by the name of Blitzen (lightning). Few visitors to the stable showed an interest in riding this spirited mount, so I usually had him to myself. Most of my riding excursions were very enjoyable, but there were two riding jaunts that I was very lucky not to have experienced the same misfortune that happened to Christopher Reeves, when he was thrown from a horse and suffered serious spinal cord injury in 1995. I was number 12 in a line of horses, on a simulated fox hunt, and racing at full gallop across a meadow south of Wiesbaden. The horses and riders in front of me had all successfully jumped across a small creek and I raised up in the stirrups of my small English-style saddle in preparation for Blitzen to make the jump as well. However, at the last second he balked and decided that the jump was not for him! He thrust out his two front legs, like ramrods, and I went flying through the air like Superman, (minus a flowing red cape). I hit the ground and rolled end-over-end in the tall grass. When I stopped tumbling, I laid flat on the ground for a few minutes, catching my breath, and taking stock of my physical condition. Other than a busted ego and a few bruises I appeared OK. Blitzen, however, considered my upset a non-event, as he was nonchalantly drinking from the creek. With a slight limp, I waded across the shallow stream, grabbed his hanging reins, jumped up on his back, and said, "You S.O.B Blitzen, you're going to jump the creek, or you're headed for a glue factory." I kicked him in his ribs with my spurs, ran him back about 30 feet, spurred him again, and shouted, "Giddyup you bastard!" In a spirited gallop he leaped the creek and I soon caught up with the rest of the riders.

My next Close Encounter on horseback occurred about a month later also when riding Blitzen. We were approaching the home stretch, and racing down a gravel road in a full gallop. We had about a half mile to go before the road made a gradual turn back to the stables, but as we raced past a foot path through the woods, Blitzen decided he was going to take a short cut without seeking my permission. He made an abrupt, 90-degree turn, and once again I made like Superman and went flying through the air. But this time, I landed on a hard dirt road and my tumbling "end-over-end" was in loose gravel. My clothes were torn and I incurred bruises and abrasions, but fortunately no broken bones or permanent injuries. Blitzen, now free of his rider, continued his run for the stables, which I reached some time later limping and cussing. I don't know who was looking after me during these potentially dangerous falls, but whoever it was, I'm eternally grateful!

Another popular facility liberated from the Germans was a former Army and Luftwaffe small arms training site. It contained numerous handgun and rifle ranges and intact support buildings. The entire area was converted into the Wiesbaden Rod and Gun Club, and was the finest such facility in the American Military Zone of Occupation. In addition to converting one of the buildings into a large club house, the U.S. Army Air Corps added skeet ranges and a champion 18-hole golf course.

When the war in Europe ended, the American military had millions of unused rounds of small arms ammunition and shipped in tons of 12-gauge shotgun shells for target practice on the skeet ranges. Rated officers (pilots and navigators) were required to shoot a certain number of rounds of skeet each month (with the theory that it would improve their aerial gunnery skills), but this requirement was not rigidly enforced. Therefore, those of us who enjoyed shooting had more free shotgun ammunition than we had time to shoot. In addition, officers could check out .30 caliber M-1 *Garand* rifles and carbines, .45 caliber Colt pistols, and Thompson submachine guns, along with cases of free ammunition.

A favorite target with the submachine gun was for two or three of us to form a line abreast, throw out empty ammunition cans, and see who could bounce them out the furthest, with one continuous blast from our automatic weapons. We would continue this noisy pastime until we created so much smoke that we couldn't see what we were shooting at.

We would then visit the skeet ranges and shoot Browning semiautomatic 12-gauge shotguns until our shoulders were sore. (We would pay our German trap pullers 25 cents for each round of skeet.)

M-1 rifles were also available for use in "Wild Boar" hunts. We would employ a German Jager Meister (hunting master), who would hire a number of beaters. The Jager Meister would position us in strategic locations, send the beaters to the far side of a wooded area, and when everyone was ready, blow his melodic-sounding brass horn. This would be the signal for the beaters to start walking in our direction, while shouting and beating on tin cans. They would invariably flush out one or more wild pigs, which would be running scared in our direction. We would then shoot at them with volleys of .30 caliber slugs (some of which would hit the pigs). We would then have the Jager Meister dress them out, and take their carcasses back to our base, where a sergeant from Texas (a master in barbecuing) would arrange a weekend beer bust and pig roast.

During one of my visits to the Rod and Gun Club, I purchased a German Diana pellet air pistol. It had a ten-inch rifled steel barrel, shot a 4.5-mm lead pellet, was extremely accurate and ideal for target practicing. I hung a sheet of plywood on the wall in my hotel room and we had great fun in drinking beer and shooting at small targets, sometimes even igniting the head of wooden matches. One night, one of my colleagues made some humorous sarcastic comments about German men of military age walking nonchalantly on the sidewalk in front of our hotel. Carrying the pellet gun, he walked out onto the third floor balcony and started plinking at the derrieres of unsuspecting Germans. Initially it seemed like great sport and several were eager to take their turn until I grabbed the pistol and put a stop to it. I don't know how many Germans were forced to jump from a unseen sting to their ass, but it was several. (I believe my young colleagues, in their alcohol-induced exuberance and frivolity, felt they were just plinking former Nazis, so what's the big deal?)

However, I knew that if anything came of this sudden burst of youthful stupidity, I would be held responsible as the pellet gun was owned by me. I'm fortunate to have put a quick end to this idiotic behavior, because the next day, when I was flying, a couple MPs came snooping around the hotel looking for whoever it was that was plinking Germans with a pellet gun! They didn't find the culprit, and since there was no more target practicing on German rear ends, the inquiry was dropped. (Another close call in ending my military career before it really got started.)

There were more lavish places to patronize than time would allow. Almost all German restaurants and clubs of any size entertained customers with tuxedo-clad musicians playing a violin, an accordion, or a piano, and all officer and enlisted men's clubs employed full-time bands. This, along with cheap beer and young German frauleins, willing to provide consensual adult dalliances for a pack of cigarettes (10 cents), gave me cause to give thanks to the "God-of-pleasure," upon awakening each morning in my downtown Wiesbaden hotel room.

However, there were some cautionary preventive measures that were necessary when indulging in this seemingly inexhaustible and inexpensive libidinous supermarket. We were advised that sexually transmitted diseases were numerous and as a preventative measure we were required to view a training film on Venereal Diseases (VD) every six months. The film was in color, extremely graphic and nothing you would wish to view on a full stomach. But, by exercising reasonable caution, my colleagues and I were able to avoid contracting any of the common diseases. But Pubic Lice (Crabs) were a constant concern and sometimes caused an unexpected and troublesome problem.

I was confronted with these little "blood-sucking buggers" just once, but once was enough! I resorted to the "word-of-mouth" remedy of saturating my pubic hair area with cigarette lighter fluid, followed by a hot bath. It worked like a charm, but during the initial treatment phase it was advisable to refrain from smoking and avoiding open flames!

This easy access to the company of German frauleins made it difficult to develop meaningful relationships with single American girls during the early days of the military occupation. Fraternization restrictions prohibited taking German dates to U.S. facilities, or American-sponsored events. Single American female dependents and military nurses were somewhat reluctant to date young American bachelors, thinking that they may be dating a guy who had been sleeping with a German girl the night before and would expect the same cooperative repartee from them. I believe this diffidence to dating by American girls or engaging in consensual adult merriment was a combination of a different cultural upbringing, not wishing to compete with sexually active European women, and a fear (mostly unfounded) of contracting VD from some careless American serviceman. This attitude changed with the end of the military occupation in May 1955 and with the improvement in the German economy. In fact, in later years, many Americans dated and married German girls who were woven into the American community without difficulty.

In the fall of 1950 I was attending a party at the Rhein Main Officers' Club, when one of the attendees was Molly Cannon, a popular 19-year-old daughter of the USAFE Commander, Lt.Gen. John K. Cannon (three-star). I was in the process of opening a bottle of champagne, and just as the metal covered cork was about to pop, Molly leaned over my shoulder to see what I was doing. Unfortunately, her curiosity coincided with the cork shooting out from the bottle, at terrific speed, and hit her nose with a dull squashing thud. Her nose started gushing blood, dilated with flowing tears, while she did her best in holding back muffled sobs. Being a perfect gentleman, I handed her my handkerchief, which was soon soaked with blood, while someone obtained ice cubes.

With cotton stuffed in both nostrils of her swollen bulbous blood red nose, I drove her home, but didn't think it advisable to see her to her door or seek a goodnight kiss. I expected to be called in for an "ass chewing" by General Cannon, but Molly was a good trooper and never told her father who popped her with a champagne cork, thank God!

Before leaving the subject of easy access to German feminine companionship, I don't want to leave the reader with the impression that the majority of German women, during the early years of the military occupation, were "free and easy." Most were decent young ladies, struggling to feed themselves and their families in a country ravaged by a brutal war and often supporting a widowed mother, whose husband had been killed during the conflict. However, it seemed only natural that we tended to exploit their relaxed approach to sensual pleasures, while at the same time helping their economy to recover. Most of us felt it was our duty, as an American Air Force officer, to help out where we could! However, one custom practiced by German women, that I never became comfortable with, was their reluctance to shave their armpits. This custom was especially unpleasant during the summer months when a raised arm, by an otherwise attractive fraulein, disclosed a black ball of fur, not unlike a bushy "bird's nest."

I was able to support this "carefree-life-style" in a lavish fashion, by bartering my share of rationed cigarettes, coffee, tea and chocolate candy bars on the black market, in exchange for German marks. My monthly allowance of rationed goods brought in approximately 500 marks ($1,000 at today's rate). However, my seemingly inexhaustible supply of black market merchandise got a tremendous boost when I was informed that my foot locker load of cigarettes had arrived. Everything was intact and I now had a cache of cigarettes worth 4,320 marks (nearly $8,800 today) in my hoarded nest egg.

At first I felt uneasy about selling my rationed items on the black market, but soon learned that it was an accepted practice to trade one's individual rationed goods without fear of being charged with violating military law. In fact, the general belief was that, in an inauspicious way, it actually helped the struggling German economy. Armed with this accepted doctrine, I was more than willing to help the Germans by indulging in all the pleasures I had time and money to enjoy.

Another enterprise many of us engaged in was the selling, on the black market, of U.S. dollars. To control currency speculation in a country undergoing postwar turmoil, military script was used in the American Occupation Zone of Germany. However, flight crew members traveling outside Germany were authorized to purchase a limited amount of dollars. I would sometimes sell a few I didn't need on the street for a good profit. Military script was issued in paper denominations of 5, 10, 25, and 50 cents, and in dollar amounts of 1, 5, and 10. To prevent speculation, and hoarding by Germans, a new issue would be introduced every year or so. The announcement of a new edition was always made public around midnight on a Saturday, and outdated script would have to be exchanged for the new issue within the next 48 hours. This surprise conversion always created a rush by German bar owners and pleasure house operators in trying to get rid of their old script at almost any price. They would congregate around military bases in the hopes of soliciting GI's help in exchanging their soon-to-be-worthless currency. However, military personnel had to be extremely careful in attempting to exchange large amounts of old script, as any suspicious behavior would be reported to the Office of Special Investigation (OSI). (I personally never engaged in military script speculation as the risks were too high.)

I was exchanging U.S. dollars for marks with a young German man in Wiesbaden one night and as I was about to hand him five ten-dollar bills he snatched them out of my hand and took off running down a narrow dark street. Realizing that I had just been screwed, I chased after him with the energy and spirit of a pissed-off 21-year-old second lieutenant.

I pursued him through back alleys, over sections of bombed-out buildings and was eagerly contemplating how I was going to beat the shit out of him and recover my money. However, as he rounded a corner I came upon an unfolding riot between about 20 Germans and a lesser number of American GIs. My concerns quickly switched from recouping my lost dollars to not becoming a part of a fracas that I was sure would draw the attention of the U.S. Military and German police. I sought refuge in the dark doorway of a small camera shop as the sound of the approaching police cars could be heard. Peering through a window I spied a middle-age German observing the melee from the safety of his closed shop. Through sign language I pleaded with him to open his door and allow me to seek refuge inside. Apparently he noted that I was not taking part in the on-going fist fights, and was an American officer. Hence he opened the door and allowed me to quickly slither inside.

From the safety of his shop I observed German and American military police break up the fight, arresting several participants while others scattered. When peace was restored I thanked my thoughtful German merchant for allowing me to escape a potential problem and in appreciation purchased a Zeiss Ikon black-and-white roll film camera with a folding bellows, which is now a museum piece.

When I reported for duty with the 12th Troop Carrier Squadron (TCS) at Wiesbaden Air Base, I was delighted to discover that the "carefree-life-style" practiced in postwar German cities was also being observed on the military base. My squadron shared a three-story, school-like building, (formally used by a Luftwaffe fighter squadron) with the 10th TCS, also equipped with C-82s. My flight leader was an affable WW II combat veteran by the name of Captain Pete Reed. Pete went out of his way in making me feel that I was a welcomed addition to the squadron and stated, "I will have you checked out in the C-82 *Packet* in no time at all Lieutenant Martin." He also exerted a personal effort in attempting to dispel the disappointment most new pilots felt in being assigned to fly such an ugly, under-powered aircraft. He gave a good "pep rally" style speech, but I never really learned to love the C-82!

The C-82 Packet was the first large capacity cargo aircraft designed to be loaded from trucks at ground level. It first flew in 1944 and when production ceased in 1948, 223 had been built. It was designed in 1942 to support the planned invasion of Japan in 1945 and 1946 under Operations "Downfall" and "Olympic." However, since this planned invasion never occurred, the Army Air Corps utilized it as a Tactical Troop Transport, which included the air-dropping of paratroopers and military equipment. It could carry 42 fully-armed troops, or 34 stretchers, and was equipped to tow gliders. To provide heat for wing and tail anti-icing, and the aircraft interior, hot engine exhaust was routed through heat-exchangers. Cold "ram air," passing through these exchangers, was heated and then directed to the aircraft interior, or anti-icing sections, through electrical actuated flapper valves, controlled by a switch in the cockpit. This method of providing heated air was a constant irritant for aircrew and passengers alike as the controlling mechanisms would often fail, producing either full heat, full cold, or nothing. This "rube-goldberg" system required the installation of several carbon monoxide detectors in the cabin and cockpit, which would occasionally start beeping false alarms. Five C-82s saw service during the Berlin Airlift for transporting bulky cargo that could not be carried in the Douglas C-54 or C-47. It was powered by two Pratt & Whitney R-2800 engines, of 2,100 hp each, carried 2,600 gallons of fuel (giving it tremendous range) and had a cruising speed of 162 mph. (See Photos 26, 27, and 28.)

Quite often the heating system controller would fail, with full heat being directed to the cockpit. When this occurred we would strip down to our underwear in attempting to keep cool. However, there were other times when the system would be delivering full cold air and we would dress like Eskimos to try to keep warm. I flew a U.S. Army colonel and a group of officers to Oslo, Norway one cold winter day, and when en route the heating system controller failed, resulting in full heat being directed to the cockpit, but full cold air to the cargo compartment. The colonel came to the cockpit, to complain about the frigid temperature in the cabin, and saw the flight crew in their underwear and basking in an overly warm environment. He assumed I was intentionally stealing heat from the cabin so as to keep the cockpit nice and warm. He wrote a "stinging complaint letter," regarding my callous disregard for the Army's comfort, and sent it through channels to my wing commander. In the report he added that several passenger seats in the cabin were missing safety belts, so the crew chief (I wasn't aware of this) secured the passengers using greasy strands of rope! It was easy for me to explain the heat problem, but I had to promise that I would no longer secure passengers, especially officers, with dirty rope. If the heating system failed, when flying in icing conditions, we would don oxygen masks, engage the engine superchargers and climb to 18 or 20 thousand feet, to get above the icing level.

Our operations officer, Major John E. VanDuyn, another WW II combat veteran stressed that every officer was required to be present for a daily 8 a.m. roll call, where they would be advised of the day's flight or training schedule, and If not scheduled would be free to spend the day as they wished, but no drinking before 1700 hours (5 p.m.).

Captain Reed led me up a winding spiral staircase to a third floor loft which contained a game room equipped with a green felt-covered card table. Pilots and navigators were sitting around the smoky table (almost everybody smoked in those days) engaging in a serious game of "table stakes" poker. Wagering was being conducted in a combination of military scrip, U.S. dollars and German marks. Being a lover of poker I displayed an interest, but Captain Reed cautioned me to use discretion when playing cards with my senior fellow officers, as most were WW II combat veterans and would have no mercy on an underpaid second lieutenant. I could see by the serious approach my new squadron colleagues were devoting to the game that this was sound advice.

After completing a two-week ground school course, including the proper method of tying knots in rope when securing cargo (not passengers) and a few short instructional flights, I was qualified to fly the Fairchild *Packet* as Pilot in Command (PIC), with an equally inexperienced 2nd Lt. in the right seat and a young crew chief in the jump seat. The C-82 was an easy airplane to fly and had the largest cockpit of any airplane I had seen. The pilot's seats were so far apart that even with outstretched arms we could only touch fingers. The cockpit was so wide that separate sets of throttles, propellers, and fuel mixture controls, were installed.

To gain experience in the aircraft I would be scheduled to fly four-hour local training flights with the mission objective left up to me or my colleague. In addition to flying practice approaches at various airports, I never tired of flying low level sight-seeing flights over the Rhine River. Leveling off at around 500 feet, I would follow the river from Wiesbaden north towards Koblenz, which would take me over the historical Rhine River Cities of Biebrich, Rudesheim, St. Goarshausem, and other unique towns and castles that had escaped destruction during the war, and basked in tranquil solitude. It was as if these undisturbed sites were intentionally ignoring the turmoil Germany had recently endured. Passengers on tourist boats would wave, while barge captains and their crews ignored our passage. At the low level I would be flying, I quite often flew below the tops of numerous majestic medieval castles, strategically located on both sides of the river. During medieval times, these castles, manned with cannons, would not allow ships to pass until they paid a toll. I would chuckle as I flew over them at 150 mph and not having to stop to pay. I frequently flew over the city of Mainz, which, as I mentioned earlier, was 85% destroyed by allied bombing during the war. The city was in such a state of destruction that, from the air, it gave the appearance that the bombing raids had ended just weeks before.

One historic sight that I never tired of flying over was a narrow high rocky point of land know as the *Loreley*. This stately rocky overlook rises 630 feet above the Rhine River, and descends almost vertically to a sharp curve in the river, which narrows to a width of only 375 feet. Legend has it that a naked young maiden would distract the attention of passing ship captains, causing them to smash into the rocky shores. I flew over this point of land on numerous occasions, hoping to catch a glimpse of a naked maiden, but the only sight I ever saw were waving German sightseers scrambling about on narrow paths on the top of the rocky cliff.

On Monday, March 27, 1950, I was administered a four-hour first pilot instrument proficiency flight check by Captain C.F. Caskey (another WW II veteran), and was now authorized to fly Combat Readiness Training (CRT) missions outside the local area of Wiesbaden. I felt I was now a real Air Force pilot, ready to take on the Russians.

In May 1950, the Wiesbaden hotel I was staying in was returned to the Germans. I, and my colleagues billeted there, were given the option of a room in another downtown hotel, or a room in the BOQ on Wiesbaden Air Base. Since we would soon be moving to Frankfurt, my good friend Bill (Balls) Bailey and I decided to move into the BOQ. We were assigned adjoining rooms, separated by a door, so we decided to place our steel cots in one room and convert the other one into a living room. However, furnishing it would require some enterprising "midnight requisitioning." We discovered a small padded davenport in the Officers' Club that nobody was sitting on, an end-table and lamp in the service club, and a few chairs, looking for a good home, in the base visitors center. Then to top it off, we discovered a refrigerator, with some major's name on it, sitting in the hall, which somehow made its way into our living room. We were very proud of what a couple second lieutenants could do with a little ingenuity!

One night, soon after going to bed, I was exposed to a bizarre Close Encounter that took me completely by surprise and could have been fatal. Around midnight, I was just drifting off to sleep, when I heard Bill Bailey enter our BOQ room. His shuffling steps told me that he probably had too much to drink, which was not uncommon behavior for any of us. I initially attempted to ignore him, since I was scheduled for an early flight the next morning. But, from past experience, I knew it was difficult to ignore Balls. He turned on the overhead light and started shaking me, stating that he wanted to show me something. I sat up in bed, and through squinting eyes, observed him holding a German 9-mm Luger semiautomatic handgun. He said that he was going to buy it, from the German taxi driver he had waiting outside, for 100 marks ($25), but wanted to make sure it worked before solidifying the deal. I told him, "Its looks authentic to me, so just give the guy 100 marks and let me get some rest." I rolled over, covered my head to shield out the light, and tried to go back to sleep.

Suddenly! I was awakened with a loud "**Bam, Bam.**" I sat up in bed and there was Bill, holding a smoking 9 mm Luger, which he had just fired into a folded blanket. I screamed, "**What the hell are you doing Balls?**" He turned toward me, obviously quite sloshed, while stating that he just wanted to make sure it would fire before buying it. He walked over next to my bed, with the smoking gun pointed in my direction, and apologized for waking me up. (But losing sleep was no longer my main concern!)

The Luger he was holding still had its "breach-block slide" down, and parallel to the barrel. This meant that it still contained one or more live rounds! I told him, "Don't point that gun in my direction, as it is still loaded." Slurring his words, he insisted that it wasn't, as he had only loaded two rounds into the magazine. I tried to convince him that the sliding breach on a Luger will remain open (up) after the last round is fired, but the Luger he was pointing at me, still had the breach down. For a few anxious moments, I was fearful that in his inebriated state, he would pull the trigger to prove that the gun was not loaded.

In a "**Calm**" voice I said, "Balls, point the gun at your bed and pull the trigger." Still not convinced that I was right, he complied with my request. There was a loud explosion, as this round was not muffled by a folded blanket. After the gun went off the "breach-block slide" remained up, confirming that it was now empty! I jumped out of bed, grabbed it out of his hand and threw it out the open window. His response, "Gee, Lou, you didn't have to get so God damn mad." He retrieved the Luger from the grass, paid the taxi driver 100 marks and finally went to bed himself.

Bill was a close friend, in spite of his idiosyncrasy of sometimes pissing people off. He was from Tennessee and one of the first friends I made when an Aviation Cadet. He earned the nickname "Balls" because of an extended scrotum and a "gutsy" streak of independence. Initially he hated the name, but got used to it. When in mixed company, young ladies would ask, "Why do you call him Balls?" We would reply, "He's a champion basketball player!" Bill died in 1996 due to heart failure. (See Photo 23.)

After returning from a three-day trip, I discovered that Bill had set up an electric model train in the middle of our living room. The toy train, running on a ten-foot oval track, occupied a large portion of the room and contained bells, whistles and the standard "click-clack" sound. Bill enjoyed playing with it and said he always wanted one when he was a kid, but his family couldn't afford to buy him one, so I didn't complain.

One night I was again awakened by another one of his antics, but this time it wasn't life-threatening, just harmless buffoonery. I heard Bill and a female German friend enter our living room and recognizing that I was already in bed, he quietly closed the door between the two rooms. I heard him remove a bottle of champagne from our confiscated refrigerator, pop the cork, and the clink of two glasses. They were very discreet when consuming the wine and engaging in adult recreation, but after a few minutes of silence, model train sounds shattered the night solitude. I laid in bed listening to bells, whistles and the standard "click-clack" for some time before thinking that they had played with the train long enough, so I got up to ask them if they could please be a little more quiet.

When I opened the door, my eyes focused on a sight *Playboy Magazine* would have paid big bucks to capture on film. Bill and his female playmate were on their hands and knees, stark naked, and playing with the toy train. Bill's rear end was pointing in my direction, emphasizing why he acquired the ignominious nickname of Balls. I couldn't disturb such innocent behavior, so quietly closed the door and went back to bed.

Bill's true camaraderie was demonstrated one cold winter night in February 1950 when we were still living in the *Bellevue Hotel* in Wiesbaden. I had met a young Spanish girl who was on vacation, took her out for dinner and drinks, and was able to sneak her into my hotel room for some consensual adult joviality. Even though I was a 21-year-old virile Air Force pilot, accustomed to strenuous exercise, she was just more than I could handle. (This was my first encounter with a true nymphomaniac.) I had an early flight the next morning and had to get some sleep, but she was not in a mood for relaxing. I went to Bill's room, woke him up, and said that I had a good looking young female in my room who was eager to entertain him. He headed for my room and I went to sleep in his still warm bed. Around 6 a.m. I was awakened by Bill who said that he could take no more and wanted me to return to my own room. In my early morning stupor it took a minute or so for me to recognize where I was, but when I did I realized it was time for me to get up anyway so I cautiously headed back to my room. I was hoping to quietly get dressed and tell my Spanish female libidinous athlete that it was time for her to leave. Gently opening the door, I was pleased to note that she was sound asleep (hallelujah). I silently put on my flight suit and when ready to depart, woke up the sleeping tigress and told her it was time to say adios (good-bye). Reluctantly, she got dressed, and I slipped her past our German "anti-female-hotel-guard." As she went her own way I said, "Adios, muchas gracias" (good-bye and thanks a lot). I then headed for the airport for an early morning flight to England.

In June 1950 my squadron was transferred to Rhein Main Air Base and I was assigned a BOQ room in the new U.S. Air Force housing complex known as *Gateway Gardens*. I would miss the charm of Wiesbaden, and my downtown hotel room, but Rhein Main had its own unique appeal. The base was extremely active and the home of three squadrons of C-54s, three squadrons of C-82s, a C-47 air evacuation unit, base support aircraft, and F-47s or F-80s, standing "runway alert." I had pilot training classmates in most of these units, which provided for many friendly (sometimes wild) parties in the former Luftwaffe Officers' Club.

I and several of my pilot colleagues were drinking beer in a Frankfurt Gasthaus, in July 1950, when two Army MPs walked in and announced, "All Air Force personnel are required to report to their units immediately." I arrived back at the base around 10 p.m. and entered a madhouse of activity. My first thought was that the Soviet Union had, once again, challenged the West in the control of Berlin. However, I soon learned that the three C-54 squadrons were ordered to McCord AFB, Washington State, to provide transpacific airlift support for the Korean War. The move was to take place ASAP and a few aircraft had already departed. (Almost all aircraft and military personnel would be gone in less than 24 hours.)

The parking lot in front of base operations was illuminated by portable lights and was awash with sobbing wives, crying children, private automobiles and military lawyers. Single men, who were about to board waiting aircraft, were signing "power of attorney" statements, authorizing the military to sell their cars. Wives and children were hugging their husbands and fathers good-bye, before they boarded busses and disappeared into the night mist. Many single men were seeking out friends, who were not part of the exodus, and giving them the names and telephone numbers of German girl friends, with instructions to inform them that they had left Germany and didn't know when and if they would return.

When the dust settled, the Air Force was left with the task of assisting the dependents of the departed units in returning to the U.S. In typical military fashion, it was decided that single male officers would sponsor officer dependent wives, while single noncommissioned male officers would assist enlisted men's wives. I was directed to assist two attractive young wives, not much older than I and kept the association strictly platonic. However, there was scuttlebutt that many men, who were assisting departing wives, provided more than relocation assistance. I'm sure they felt that they were supporting their country and providing needed emotional support to military wives undergoing a very stressful experience. A hidden benefit of the hasty departure of the C-54s and their dependents, was that it left many commandeered furnished German homes and apartments vacant. In addition to fine furniture, they were equipped with silverware, porcelain china and crystal glasses. Being empty, break-ins were occurring at an alarming rate, so to help alleviate the conundrum the base housing officer decided to allow bachelor officers to occupy a scattering of them in areas that had experienced break-ins.

In September 1950, I moved into a fully-furnished, one-bedroom apartment at 167 Garten Strasse in the town of Neu Isenburg (about six miles from the base). Lt. Harry Fielding, a pilot colleague, moved into a second-floor apartment immediately above mine. The apartments came with a full-time maid, a gardener who came around to trim the bushes and an elderly man who came by to stoke the coal-fed furnace. These amenities were not provided to pamper the U.S. Military occupation forces, but were designed to help the German economy recover under the auspices of the "Marshall Plan," and I certainly wanted to do my part! One year after graduating from flight school, I was living like a plutocrat in Germany and only 22-years-old. (I thought, if my recruiting sergeant could see me now, it would provide an excellent recruitment tool.)

I was scheduled to fly a (CRT) Combat Readiness Training mission in a C-82 *Packet*, and to avoid RADAR detection, it was to be flown at tree-top level. The flight would be on a Southern circuitous route from Wiesbaden, to Ludwigshafen, Karlsrule and Stuttgart, then turning east, over high hills toward Augsburg, north to Nurnburg and return to Wiesbaden. This was my first simulated combat military training flight as an Aircraft Commander, so I was determined to fly the mission without being picked up by RADAR, since if spotted, it would indicate that I could not have avoided interception by potential enemy fighters, either F-47s or F-80s.

The flight was proceeding as planned, during the first en route segment, and my new second lieutenant copilot and I were enjoying zooming over the German countryside as we hugged the ground contours. I was flying so low that I would have to climb slightly to avoid hitting fences, and on occasion would hear the swishing of tree limbs scraping the rear of the aircraft as we passed over small patches of woods. I flew over one field so low that when we approached a farmer plowing with a team of horses, I observed him throwing something at the airplane, which was followed by a loud bang underneath the cockpit. (After landing I discovered a small dent on the nose of my C-82.)

As I turned east toward Augsburg and higher terrain, I noted that the cloud base was much lower, but my inexperience, and enthusiasm to complete the mission, convinced me that I still had sufficient clearance between the clouds and the ground to press on. As I continued to climb, to stay above the raising hills, the separation between the aircraft and the clouds was becoming quite narrow, but I was determined to continue.

As I climbed to avoid one particular high hill, I suddenly found myself in the clouds, with no visual contact with the ground. Referring to my flight instruments, I put the aircraft into a tight left climbing spiral, with the intent of climbing above the clouds. As I entered the spiral, I noted brief breaks in the clouds so I directed my attention out the side window, hoping to establish visual contact with the ground. However, the clouds became thicker, and I concluded that my only hope of escaping potential danger was to continue my planned climbing spiral maneuver.

I once again directed my attention to the flight instruments, but to my **Shock,** I realized that vertigo had taken over, and instead of climbing, I was in a descending spiral! To add to the horror, I noticed that our altitude was lower that the surrounding terrain. (What I had mistakenly succeeded in doing was flying a descending corkscrew spiral, into a valley that was lower than the surrounding hills!)

My heart stopped, as I expected to slam into a hill at any second! However, since the aircraft was still flying, I figured that I had blindly corkscrewed into a valley and if I maintained the same angle of bank, and converted it into a climbing maneuver, I may be able to follow the same path to an altitude above the high terrain. If I was successful, it would force the PGR to pursue me during a future screw-up, but not today!

I pulled back sharply on the control wheel, went to full-throttle on both engines, and said a short prayer as the altimeter began indicating a climb. I didn't take a full breath until our altitude was higher than the surrounding terrain, and soon broke out on top of the clouds in bright sunshine!

71

Flying at a higher altitude, we were soon picked up by RADAR, and intercepted by F-47 fighters, who were credited with shooting us down. I flew back to Wiesbaden without successfully completing my first assigned CRT mission, but frankly, I didn't care, as I was still alive and could acquire a mark on the mission accomplishment board later. My copilot and crew chief were not fully aware of the danger they had been exposed to until I briefed them on the risk we had taken later. (Had I flown into high terrain, the wreckage would have been eventually found, but I doubt if anyone would have been able to determine why Second Lieutenant Martin flew his C-82 *Packet* into a German hill south of Stuttgart.)

In early September 1950, the operations officer asked me if I would like to fly as copilot for 1st. Lt. Lee Barrett in ferrying a C-82, with a cracked main wing spar, to the maintenance depot at Warner Robins, AFB, Georgia. Without reservation I said, "Yes." He said the departure date was scheduled for Friday, September 19. Since we would depart 11 days before payday, I thought I would have to visit a bank for a loan but "Lady Luck" saw to my needs and provided sufficient spending money.

The flight operations ready room usually had a poker or black-jack game going whenever there were enough pilots or navigators available to support one. I sat down in a high-stakes, pot-limit, table-stakes poker game, and enjoyed an unbelievable winning streak. When ahead about $500 (equal to $4,000 today), I told my colleagues, "Thanks, guys, I quit!" They were a little pissed off, but when I told them that I needed the money for my flight to the U.S. they reluctantly understood.

Lieutenant Barrett and I, along with a navigator, radio operator and a crew chief, departed Rhein Main Air Base, for a five-hour flight to Preswick, Scotland, the first leg of our trip. After securing the aircraft we obtained rooms in downtown Glasgow and had dinner in a Scottish Pub, but I had difficulty in wading through the thick Scottish accent. (I wondered if they were actually speaking English, but they said they were!)

The next day we flew to Keflavick, Iceland, another five-hour flight. Before landing we made a sight-seeing circle of the island and found the barren rocky landscape, with steam escaping from various crevices, like something from another planet. After landing we took a taxi to downtown Reykjavik for lodging and dinner. Later, recognizing that it was Saturday night, I headed out to explore Icelandic night life, while Lt. Barrett, the navigator, crew chief and radio operator went back to the hotel. It was a pleasant fall night, the town was hopping and with my pockets stuffed with poker winnings, I was eager to lighten the load by supporting the local economy. I wandered into a dance hall, flush with young single blond Icelandic females, looking for a good time. In no time at all I had made friends with four gals who had come to the dance unescorted. They seemed impressed in my willingness to buy drinks for all four, while I concentrated on wooing the prettiest of the lot.

After about an hour of dancing and drinking, I asked if I could take "Miss Pretty" home and without hesitation she said, "Let's go. My apartment is not very far from here." Walking hand-in-hand, down the streets of Reykjavik, I could hear sounds of merriment coming from the bars and dance halls we passed. Enthralled with this lively atmosphere, I wondered if I would be able to score once we reached her apartment. I soon discovered that my fears were unfounded, as she was just as amorous as her Scandinavian cousins in Denmark. About an hour later I walked back to my hotel, feeling sorry for the rest of the crew, since there were extra girls for the taking.

The next day we departed on a six-hour flight to Narsarsuak Air Base, Greenland, code named, "Bluie West One" (BW-1). I considered this the highlight of the trip (not discounting the previous night in Iceland). BW-1 is located near the Southern tip of Greenland and was a secret airport constructed in 1941 to serve as a staging base for ferrying aircraft to Europe and supporting submarine patrols. The base itself is located about 70 miles up a narrow fjord, which in one area is only a half-mile wide as it snakes past a rocky point known as Sugar Loaf Mountain. Both sides of the fjords are rimmed with 5,000 to 6,000 foot mountains and according to reports there are several fjords that are "dead-ends," with the wreckage of aircraft decorating the landscape (a Pilot's Grim Reaper Paradise).

When we arrived over the airport's ocean entrance, we contacted the control tower and advised them that this was our first visit and desired an escort to the runway. They instructed us to hold over a radio beacon, located on a small island called Simiutak, and circle down through the clouds until beneath a reported 2,000 foot overcast. And once in visual contact with the island, continue to circle until they send out a small aircraft to escort us safely through the fjords. What I saw when we broke out underneath the clouds sent shivers up my spine, but at the same time was very exhilarating. The ocean was awash with large "cold-looking" white caps splashing against floating icebergs. The land mass of Greenland to the North looked dark and foreboding with snow filling the narrow gaps in the mountains that faded into low-hanging gray clouds.

After circling for about 30 minutes, a single engine DeHavilland L-20 *Beaver* emerged from one of the fjords, contacted us by radio and said, "Slow-up to about 120 mph, follow me and stay right on my ass. If you take a wrong turn it will probably be your last!" Our guide didn't have to repeat this warning, and when we followed him into what seemed like a black hole fjord, we were right on his ass. We were so close that I'm sure he could hear our two R-2800 engines grinding away, but he didn't complain. It was my impression that he had done this before!

After following our guide for about 20 minutes, he made a radio call stating, "Put your gear down and extend your landing flaps, because as soon as we make the next sharp right turn, the runway will be straight ahead. Let me know when you have it in sight." When we completed the turn, I spotted a short up-hill runway and reported, "Runway in sight," as our escort broke off into a tight circle to the left. The approach end of the runway was next to the water's edge and the far end seemed to disappear into a rising glacier in the clouds.

We spent the night at BW-1 and the next day followed our faithful *Beaver* escort back through the meandering fjords to the open iceberg-dotted ocean. Once over open water we climbed to 10,000 feet and headed out on a six-hour flight to Westover, AFB, Massachusetts. (We all agreed that one visit to BW-1 was enough, and my admiration went out to the young inexperienced WW II pilots, especially fighter pilots, that had to land there on their way to winning the war in Europe.)

Flying across the North Atlantic was my first experience in utilizing the services of the U.S. Coast Guard ocean stations. These stations consisted of Coast Guard Cutters maintaining a relative fixed position, and provided weather data, sea conditions, navigation aids, radar vectors, (baseball scores) and search and rescue (when needed), for surface ships and aircraft passing their position. They were established along well-traveled shipping lanes, and airway routes, in both the Atlantic and Pacific oceans. Their numbers ranged from 13 permanent sites to 46 during WW II. However with the improvement in weather forecasting and 24-hour satellite coverage their services became unnecessary and were discontinued in 1977. However, during their service (1946 to 1977), they provided admirable assistance and saved many lives. More than one aircraft, both civil and military, after encountering serious problems, ditched their aircraft next to an ocean station and survivors were quickly plucked out of the water. Program costs for these stations were shared by nations operating trans-oceanic aircraft. Our crossing of the North Atlantic in 1950 utilized the services of ocean stations India, Allpha and Bravo.

We secured rooms for the night in the BOQ at Westover AFB and went to the Officers' Club for drinks and dinner. When at the bar I met a flying school classmate from T-6 basic training days in Waco, Texas, who went on to William's AFB in Phoenix, Arizona, for advanced training in F-80s. We no more than shook hands, before he wanted to let me know that he was now flying F-86s and assigned to a fighter squadron at Westover. Over a couple of drinks we agreed to meet in base operations the next morning, when he would take me out and show me his *Sabre Jet*. He didn't ask what I was flying, so I didn't bring the subject up.

The next morning we secured a jeep and drove out to a shiny new F-86A with my friend's name painted on its side. He let me sit in the cockpit and while I was admiring it with obvious envy, he handed me a handkerchief, I said, "What's that for?" "To wipe the drool off your face," he said. (I didn't get his handkerchief wet as I used my own!) He drove me back to base operations, where I met the rest of my crew filing a flight plan for Warner Robins AFB, Georgia, a nine-hour flight away.

We landed at Warner Robins around 9 p.m. and an hour later had completed transferring custody of the aircraft to base personnel. I now had five days off before reporting to Westover AFB, for a C-54 MATS flight back to Germany. I was in a "soul-searching" dilemma as to how to spend my time off. Should I visit my girl friend, Carolyn, in Shreveport, Louisiana, or go see my parents in Ladysmith, Wisconsin? I checked the military transient aircraft status board in base operations to see if there were any military aircraft scheduled to fly to Barksdale AFB, Louisiana, but there were none. Without going to bed, I took a bus to the Atlanta International Airport, arriving around 3 a.m.

In Atlanta, I checked on flight schedules for both Shreveport and Chicago, and laid out both plans. I then called my Mother, and told her that I was in Atlanta and thinking of coming home for a few days before heading back overseas. However, I was also thinking of going to Louisiana to see a girl who was very dear to me. She said the decision was mine and she would understand if I didn't come home, but reminded me that my father was 75-years-old! I told her I would call her back. I then made an operator-assisted call to Carolyn in Shreveport. It was 4 a.m. when I made the call and her father, in a very sleepy voice, answered the telephone. The operator said, "I have a person-to-person call for Carolyn

Carroll Is she available?" In a biting tone of voice he said, **"Is this a collect Call?"** When the operator told him that it was prepaid, I could hear him shout, **"Carolyn, it's your Yankee boy friend on the phone. He sure picked a hell of a time to call."** Carolyn and I talked until I ran out of quarters, but in the end I told her that I only had a few days off and decided to go home to see my parents in Wisconsin. She said she understood, although sorry I wouldn't be visiting her in Shreveport.

I took an early morning flight to Chicago, then to Eau Claire, Wisconsin, where my sister Rita picked me up and drove me to Ladysmith. I spent four days sleeping in my own bed, eating delicious home-cooked meals, and letting my father shoot the Italian Beretta semiautomatic pistol I had brought with me. (To reflect on how times have changed, I carried this unloaded handgun in my carry-on luggage while flying on several major airlines, without a hint of trouble.)

When in Ladysmith I made several telephone calls to Carolyn in Shreveport, and we renewed our love for each other and she agreed to wait for me until I finished my three-year overseas tour. The next time I talked to her was in October 1952, when I informed her that I was married. In a halting voice she said, "I hope you find happiness, Lou." Forty-six years later (1998) I was in Shreveport on business and was surprised to see her name still listed in the telephone directory. I called her and asked if she would like to join me for a cup of coffee in the airport cafe. She declined, stating that her fiancé would not approve. (She was getting married for the first time at age 68.)

Five days later I was onboard a MATS C-54 on my way back to Germany. I have often wondered if my life would have been different if I had flown to Louisiana instead of Wisconsin, but I will never know.

One year following my check-out as an Aircraft Commander in the C-82, I still harbored disappointment in not flying an aircraft carrying guns, versus cargo. But at the same time I was thoroughly enjoying flying NATO support missions to many different parts of Europe, while my flying school classmates, flying F-80s, F-84s and F-47s, were generally restricted to their assigned base of operations and accumulating only 15 to 20 hours per month, while I was consistently flying 50 to 60.

Another benefit was that many of my colleagues were WW II combat veterans who had flown B-17 and B-24 bombing missions over Germany.

A few had even been incarcerated in German Stalag Luftwaffe Prisoner of War Camps. (It was heartening to observe this group enjoy the fruits of victory, without showing hostility toward their vanquished former enemy.)

However, not all of my military superiors were role models. The bird colonel commanding Wiesbaden Air Base was a case in point! We referred to him as "Bicycle Joe." He acquired his nickname because he would ride around the base on his bicycle and stop to pick up small bits and pieces of paper or cigarette butts. If during his excursions he spotted a military member, regardless of rank, walk past a small piece of trash he would stop, put him in a military brace, take his name and chew him out mercifully for dereliction of duty for not helping to keep the base neat and clean. Following close behind him on these bicycle junkets was his pet fox terrier, which resembled the RCA Victor Company mascot "Nipper."

"Bicycle Joe" would occasionally hold a mandatory officer's call in the base theater and one of these meetings was more entertaining than informative. (It was the type of event you would expect to see in the movie *Catch 22*, but not in real life.) The theater was about half full when "Bicycle Joe's" adjutant walked in and called the room to **"Attention."** With everyone standing the colonel strutted in, closely followed by his fox terrier. It appeared that they were counting cadence and marching in step, but it was hard to tell since the dog had two more legs than the colonel.

"Bicycle Joe" ordered his dog (I'll call him Nipper) to hop up on a table and assume the recognized "RCA Victor Company pose." The colonel's adjutant ordered the room **"At-ease"** and for everyone to be seated.

Colonel Joe looked around and then launched into a harangue about the stupidity of his officers. His diatribe reached its peak when he pointed to his fox terrier (sitting at attention, with a hard-on) while stating, "Many of you don't have the brains of my dog!" One of my classmates leaned over and whispered into my ear, "At least we don't walk around with our tongues hanging out and our stiff dicks uncovered. That should count for something." I would have liked to have told "Bicycle Joe" about the profound statement coming from my second lieutenant colleague, but I'm sure his military career would have been in jeopardy. Colonel Joe and his dog Nipper were soon transferred, and I hoped not to the Pentagon, but I would not have been surprised if that is where he ended up!

In addition to flying into most military bases in Germany, cities like Manchester, England; Marseille, France; Rome, Italy; Tripoli, Libya; Athens, Greece; Berlin, Germany; and Ankara, Turkey were familiar destinations. I was getting a grand tour of Europe, at taxpayers' expense and only 22-years-old. During a flight to Linz, Austria, I met an Army 2nd Lt. at the Officers' Club and over martinis he asked me if I had ever driven a *Sherman Tank*, which of course I hadn't. The next day he let me drive his 32-ton tin can on their former German training ground, while a 75 mm cannon fired at mock targets. It was quite an experience, and I thanked him for the opportunity, but I was glad I was in the Air Force and not having my insides shaken into mush from bouncing around inside a tank!

Many of my flights to different parts of Europe were eye-opening experiences for a young lieutenant from Northern Wisconsin, but none equaled the surprising outcome of an overnight flight to Burttonwood Air Base in Manchester England, in February 1951. I was flying as copilot for 27-year-old 1st Lt. Ralph Johnson, a WW II combat veteran who, in my inexperienced young mind, was a real hero and a super older pilot.

We landed in Manchester around 4 p.m. and were told that our aircraft would be loaded later that evening, so we were off duty until 9 a.m. the following day. After dinner in the Officers' Club I suggested that we head for the city to see what the English could offer in the form of entertainment. Ralph (who was married) said he was tired, and going to bed early, but wished me a good time and would see me in the morning.

I took a taxi to a pub in downtown Manchester and over a pint of warm beer, asked the bartender if he had any suggestions on what I might do for entertainment. He recommended a large dance hall which featured a "Glenn Miller Style Big Band," adding, "There should be many young single women attending the dance and if I was a 22-year-old American pilot that is where I would go for an exciting night." I downed my beer in a few large gulps and was on my way.

The dance hall was packed with couples of all ages and like the bartender said, there were young single girls sitting around waiting for someone to ask them to dance. With the music from the band encouraging a musical cocky stride, I strolled across the dance floor and asked a pretty young English Lass if she would care to dance. She didn't hesitate for more than a second and we were soon challenging the rest of the revelers for the best-looking couple on the dance floor. I was pleased to learn that she was 21-years-old, a college student and enjoyed dancing. We danced off and on for several hours and during intermissions fought our way to the bar where I learned she favored scotch and water with no ice. We developed a mutual fondness for each other and I asked if I could take her home after the dance. Her answer was an resolute yes!

Before leaving the dance hall, I purchased a bottle of scotch which seemed to please her, since she was quick to state, "I have glasses and water in my apartment, which is just a 30-minute train ride, and a short taxi trip away." The train ride was smooth and quick, followed by a bumpy ride on foggy cobblestone streets in a smoky 1930s-style English taxi. Her apartment was on the second floor and my excitement increased with every step I took. I was hoping that my youthful anticipation of a romp in the sack was not showing and I attempted to hide the obvious signs in the way I carried the bottle of scotch.

Her one room apartment was small, neat and feminine, but extremely cold. As I poured her a stiff scotch and water, she went to the fireplace to start a fire with a couple old newspapers and a few small pieces of coal, which she extracted with fireplace tongs from a full bucket. After several drinks, and fanning the minute pieces of coal into a weak glow with fire place bellows, I could feel a small amount of heat being produced, but not sufficient to warm the room. With teeth chattering I thought my anticipated romp in the sack would be a bit cold!

My excitement grew as my pretty young dance partner turned down the bed, while stating that she was going down the hall to take a hot bath and would be back in about 30 minutes. After she left the room, I put on a Glenn Miller record on her 78 rpm record player, kicked off my shoes, and counseled myself in not looking too eager when she returned. However, there was one important item still lacking, the room was too damn cold! But I figured that with a little bit of good old American ingenuity, I could remedy that.

I went to the fireplace and started laying in additional pieces of coal, while fanning them into a beautiful red glow with rapid squeezing of the fireplace bellows. In the process, I used all the coal contained in the bucket, but was very pleased with what I had accomplished, as the room was starting to warm up and I was anxiously awaiting the return of my partner to show her how an American Air Force pilot could warm-up a room with only one bucket of coal!

The door to her apartment opened and in walked a freshly-bathed young lass, who I was sure would be proud of my accomplishment and eager to make the rest of the night one to remember. However, instead of heading for the bed she went over to the fireplace, looked down at the empty coal bucket, and began to cry. Through tearful sobs, she screamed, **"Bloody Hell, Yank, you used up my entire week's ration of coal. What the bloody hell am I going to for the rest of the week?"**

I tried to console her, but the effects of the scotch, the hot bath and the loss of a week's ration of coal produced more sobs and cussing me out for committing such a stupid gaffe.

I told her to dry her eyes as I would go out and buy her another bucket of coal. She said, "That's impossible, unless your willing to buy one on the black market at an exorbitant price." I told her, "Don't worry. Money is not a problem." I grabbed the empty bucket and headed for an almost empty street to hail a taxi.

It was close to 11 p.m. when I found an elderly taxi driver looking for a fare. I briefly explained my situation to him and solicited his help in finding someplace where I could purchase a bucket of coal. He shook his head in disgust, but said he would do what he could, but added, "It won't be easy, Yank." We made several stops before we found a shop willing to sell me a bucket of coal at five times the going price. With coal in hand, I directed my helpful taxi driver to drive me back to my girl friend's apartment, where I hoped to continue where I had left off. After paying off the driver he drove off in a belch of smoke while stating, "Good luck, Yank, Tally Ho."

With a smile on my face and an eagerness to satisfy my manly lust, I entered her warm one-room apartment proudly displaying a full bucket of coal. I was anticipating a welcome home from my English lass along with a, "Well done, Yank." However, I wasn't prepared for what I found.

The room was nice and warm, no question about that, but my date was sound asleep all curled up in her bed. Next to her, on the night stand, was my nearly empty bottle of scotch. A few gentle pokes to her shoulder told me that she was out for the night and would not be able to engage in any activities other than a deep sleep in her cozy warm bed. I pulled the covers up around her neck, kissed her on the cheek, turned out the lights and quietly left. I never saw her again, but felt some satisfaction in knowing that at least for one night she had a nice warm apartment to sleep in, which was a rarity for a young single lass in England in 1951.

In addition to flying missions throughout Europe, C-82s were directed to provide support for the 36th Fighter Bomber Wing at Furstenfelbruck Air Base, Germany, when they flew their F-80 fighters to Wheelus Air Base in Tripoli, Libya for gunnery and bombing practice. My mission was to fly support equipment and maintenance personnel to Wheelus with an en route refueling stop at Marsellie, France. It was during one of these missions that I experienced another Close Encounter with the PGR.

After landing at Furstenfelbruck, I was informed that my cargo load would be a 5,000-gallon **"empty refueling truck,"** which was so huge that it nearly filled the cargo compartment. When computing my weight and balance, I noted that the stated **empty** weight of the refueling tank resulted in a gross takeoff weight of 2,000 pounds over the maximum allowable design weight of 54,000 pounds for a C-82. But I thought this would not be a problem if I didn't lose an engine during takeoff.

The takeoff roll seemed slower and longer than normal, but I attributed this to the under-powered aircraft with which I had developed a love/hate relationship. When about to run out of available runway, I pulled back on the control column, even though I was a few mph below the normal takeoff speed. As the aircraft became airborne, and out of ground effect, it shuddered slightly as if about to stall and continued shuttering until the landing gear was retracted. However, when I started retracting the wing flaps the shaking returned, so I left the flaps in the takeoff position.

With both engines at full throttle, my rate of climb was only 100 feet per minute and I was precariously skimming over the tops of the trees. Based on such poor performance, I realized I was flying a highly-overloaded aircraft, threatening to stall at any minute. But I thought if I could coax it to remain airborne through gentle manipulation of the controls, I had a chance of flying a low level downwind leg and return to the airport for a safe landing. I declared an emergency with the control tower and was cleared number one for landing.

As I gently banked the aircraft into a 400 foot downwind leg, my crew chief asked, "Should I break out the parachutes?" I told him to forget it, as we were too low to bail out. With precious altitude to spare, and still just clearing the tree tops, it appeared I would be able to keep the aircraft airborne long enough to reach a base leg for a close in final approach. However, my troubles were not over! My alert crew chief called my attention to the cylinder head temperatures gages, which were registering above maximum limits on both engines. The engine cooling cowl flaps were already full open, and not being able to reduce power (for fear of stalling, or diving to increase speed to provide additional cooling), I prayed that the engines would hold together and not start detonating until I could land this cauldron of bolts, rivets and dull sheets of aluminum.

Engine detonation occurs when the fuel-air mixture is ignited by excessively-high temperatures, not by the spark plugs. This pre-ignition results in severe engine vibration which can tear an engine apart.

While struggling to keep the aircraft airborne, and experiencing occasional pre-stall vibrations, I entered a close-in base leg. But before rolling the wings level, both engines started shaking and backfiring so violently I feared they might fail or separate from the aircraft. When I started a gradual descent to a final approach, I was able to reduce a small amount of power which reduced the engine shaking somewhat. When about 200 feet over the approach end of the runway, I directed my copilot to lower the landing gear and obtained three green lights just seconds before the tires made contact with the runway. After coming to a stop, I shut down the smoking engines and ordered the aircraft abandoned as several fire trucks came rushing to our aid.

Post-flight examination disclosed that the so called **"empty refueling truck"** contained 2,000 gallons of jet fuel. This undisclosed weight put me approximately 14,000 pounds over maximum allowable takeoff weight, imposing a severe strain on the aircraft, the engines and my crew. (If an engine had failed on takeoff the PGR would have won.) After the refueling tank was drained and mechanics performed a thorough check of the engines, including replacing the overheated oil, I departed without incident and flew my assigned mission to Libya without further problems.

On a later C-82 flight to Furstenfelbruck, I was instructed to hold over the airport at 5,000 feet until a flight of 44 F-84 jet fighters, approaching the field at 2,000 feet, had landed. Circling above the Bavarian countryside, while watching a long string of smoke trailing F-84s preparing to land, was a beautiful sight. I knew that several of my pilot classmates would undoubtedly be flying several of these sleek fighters and I envied them. From frequent discussions with my jet fighter buddies, I knew that their indicated airspeed, during a 360-degree overhead tactical approach for landing would be 250 mph, with a three-second interval pitchout. I started counting the number of fighters that had already landed, and when I reached a count of 36, I asked the control tower if I would be cleared to land following the last flight of four. The tower controller approved my request, which fit into my plan of showing my fighter-jock classmates what a hot pilot can do in a cumbersome slow twin-engine C-82 *Packet* when he has a fighter pilot audience!

When the last flight of F-84s was approaching the field, I positioned my lumbering transport to parallel their flight path 2,000 feet below. When they were about a half-mile behind and slightly to my left, I went to full-throttle and started a dive. By the time the fighters reached the airport boundary, I was indicating 250 mph and joined their formation as "number five" in an echelon to the right. I held my position in the formation and when the fourth fighter pitched-out, I rolled into a 90 degree bank three seconds later. Looking down at the ground I could see fighter pilots emerging from their parked aircraft and looking up at a C-82 trying to steal their thunder. I maintained my high airspeed and steep bank angle as long as possible, lowered the landing gear on short-final and touched down before the last F-84 had turned off the runway. (See Photo No. 32.)

I spent the night at Furstenfelbruck and it was great to share a few drinks with my classmates. They took great pleasure in shuttling me around the Officers' Club bar and introducing me as the C-82 pilot who joined their formation landing pattern. When introducing me to their friends, they added that I should have gone with them to Williams AFB to fly F-80s, but made the mistake of requesting F-51s and ended up flying B-25s and C-82s. The next day I was back to hauling cargo to Africa, while my fighter pilot classmates were grounded for several days because of inclement weather, which was a piece of cake for us transport pilots.

In the winter of 1951 U.S. Air Force units in Germany were accelerating their Cold War combat readiness capability. The three squadrons of C-82s stationed at Rhein Main were the prime troop carrier transport aircraft available for inter-theater airlift and aerial delivery of men and equipment. The tactical procedure at the time was to deploy paratroopers from large formations so they would be concentrated on the ground after landing. (A concept developed during WW II and still practiced.)

To bolster our combat readiness, pilots were required to be proficient in flying tight, "wing-tip-to-tail" formation in both day and night conditions. As we became skilled in flying 27 aircraft formations in daylight, we progressed to flying them at night ---- first in three-ship flights, then in nine, and finally with 27 aircraft. Night formation, even in clear weather conditions, was very challenging since to simulate combat conditions wing-tip and tail navigation lights were turned off. The only lights visible were a series of dim blue lights on the top of each wing. (Another visual aid, if viewing an aircraft from underneath, was the blue exhaust flames from the engines.) The theory behind this procedure was that by only displaying lights on top of the wings, it would render the aircraft difficult to see by enemy gunners on the ground, but would still allow pilots to remain in formation by flying slightly above the aircraft they were to follow.

To test our combat readiness, higher headquarters inspectors would conduct unannounced Operations Readiness Inspections (ORIs) and in the winter of 1951 our group was selected to undergo such an evaluation.

The first phase of the ORI was a 27-ship daylight formation, on an extended low-level cross country and air-dropping men and equipment on a drop zone designated by the inspectors. With the intent of simulating combat realism, the mission was to be flown without the use of radio communications between the aircraft in the formation or with air traffic control facilities. Signal flares would be used to issue taxi and takeoff clearances and to identify the lead aircraft during the formation join-up. The taxi out from the parking ramp and the takeoff at ten-second intervals went off without a problem. After all 27 aircraft were assembled in formation, we headed out on a designated low level route across Southern Germany. (Our lumbering 27 C-82s in close formation resembled a flock of wild geese heading south for the winter.) Being a newly-qualified second lieutenant Aircraft Commander, my position in the formation was near the tail-end.

After flying the elapsed time that should have found us over the designated drop-zone, we were flying around in circles. The paratroopers and heavy equipment that were scheduled to be deployed by parachute were still on board and the troops were becoming fidgety and some showing signs of airsickness. The circling (over simulated enemy territory) continued as my copilot and I exchanged thoughts of bewilderment, and my crew chief said that he was passing out "barf bags" to the army troops. (If this had been an actual combat mission, our problem would have already been resolved, as the entire formation would have been shot down by enemy ground fire or intercepted by enemy fighters!)

After about 30 minutes of aimless circling, our wing commander broke radio silence and stated that we were returning to Rhein Main. During the postflight debriefing we learned that our formation leader had become lost and we never reached the designated drop zone. (His excuse was outdated maps that confused the navigator.) The first phase of our ORI was a bust and we all felt a sense of disappointment, but no one was more downhearted or embarrassed then our wing commander. He vowed that we would do much better during the next phase of the test, which would consist of a 27-ship night formation flight from Frankfurt, Germany to a French Air Base in Southern France near the city of Toulouse.

Two days later we assembled, at midnight, for a briefing on our critical night formation mission to Toulouse via Strasbourg, Dijon and Lyon. The intelligence officer did an excellent job in providing a realistic combat situation by presenting a WW II style mission briefing, including the opening of a curtain to display our route of flight, a weather forecast, a time hack and a sanctification by an Air Force chaplain. Takeoff was scheduled for 3 a.m. and as before would be flown in "radio-silence" conditions. Colored flares would be fired from the tower to signal start engines, taxi and takeoff times. The last item during the briefing was a statement from the wing commander urging everyone to do their best so we could make up for the fiasco of our recent failed daylight formation flight. He also stated that although the forecasted weather conditions were not the best, he had complete confidence in our being able to successfully complete the mission. He wished us good luck and said he looked forward to seeing us all safely on the ground in Toulouse, where we would be able to enjoy the hospitality of our French NATO colleagues.

My copilot, crew chief and I, lugging parachutes, leather helmets and oxygen masks, were transported to our aircraft by an open-bay truck. As the truck continued moving on down the flight line, discharging other crew members, we walked through a cold night drizzle to our assigned aircraft. I performed a hurried Exterior Preflight Inspection with the aid of a flashlight as I was eager to get out of the cold wet weather. It was difficult to gage the base of the clouds, and I noted that I couldn't see any stars and a thin fog hung over the ground obscuring many airport lights. The rotating airport beacon was visible but each rotation left a lingering ragged hue in the mist. I thought there was a good chance the mission would be canceled but continued with flight preparations regardless.

Approaching the scheduled start-engine time, my crew and I were in position in the cockpit and eagerly looking in the direction of the airport control tower for a start-engine signal flare. The planned start-engine time passed with no flare fired, and based on the deteriorating weather conditions, I was sure that we would soon be informed that the mission was scrubbed. I observed a jeep coming down the flight line and stopping briefly at each aircraft and assumed the driver was delivering mission cancellation notices. However, when he stopped beneath my cockpit window, I was informed that start-engine time had been delayed one hour and we were to standby for a start-engine signal from the tower.

At 4 a.m. a double red (start-engine) flare was observed emanating from the control tower but soon disappeared in the rain and drizzle engulfing the airport. Fifty-four R-2800 engines, spewing smoke and flame, were coming to life up and down the flight line. Fifteen minutes later another double red flare emerged directing the formation to

85

commence taxiing out for takeoff. I taxied out in sequence behind my assigned element leader with the windshield wipers providing visibility.

After allowing time for engine run-ups and completion of Before Takeoff Checklists, the first six aircraft taxied onto the runway in preparation for takeoff. To keep the aircraft directly in front of me in sight through the haze and freezing drizzle, I had to keep the windshield wipers slapping away on high speed. As briefed, all aircraft had their wing tip and tail navigation lights turned off, with only the blue formation lights on top of each wing visible. And for simulated combat secrecy, radio transmissions were still not allowed.

A few minutes after 4:30 a.m., a double green flare sliced through the fog and rain, directing the formation leader to commence his takeoff. All succeeding aircraft would follow at ten-second intervals. When the aircraft in front of me started to roll my copilot initiated a ten-second countdown as I advanced the throttles to 30 inches of manifold pressure. His countdown was oral and in the standard, "4--3--2--1--**Go**," followed by my releasing the brakes and shoving the throttles full forward. (It was standard procedure to initiate the brake release action with a pronounced "jerk", so the aircraft following would have a noticeable start time to initiate their individual takeoff countdown.)

As the aircraft began accelerating, I observed that the C-82 I was to follow was already disappearing in and out of the fog and rain. The only positive visual tracking I had were the bright blue flames shooting out from its engine exhaust stacks. During the climb-out I held a position slightly below, with the intent of using the exhaust flames as a means of forming up on its wing. Once in position, I would be able to use the blue formation lights to remain in position. However, when the pilot placed his fuel mixture control levers into the "fuel-lean-position" (a standard procedure after takeoff) the bright blue hue from the engine exhausts dimmed precipitously and nearly disappeared causing me to momentarily lose sight of his aircraft. (I thought of calling the pilot on the radio to tell him to keep his mixtures in the full rich position, but we were flying a simulated combat operation so this was not an option.)

After losing sight of the aircraft I was to follow, I continued a climb to our assigned "join-up" altitude of 3,000 feet, hoping that the aircraft would once again become visible through the mist, rain and ragged cloud base. When approaching 3,000 feet my copilot stated he had our leader's aircraft in sight and I joined up its left wing, feeling good that I could now remain in position by using the blue formation lights for guidance.

During a brief, but fleeting, improvement in the weather we didn't observe another aircraft flying on his right wing and observed two engine exhaust flames pass overhead and going in the opposite direction. I now began to wonder if I had formed up on my designated element leader or some other aircraft. I instructed my crew chief to momentarily flash our cockpit search light on the tail of the aircraft I was flying formation on to obtain its registration number. When we checked the tail number against our mission briefing setup schedule, we discovered that I had joined up on another inexperienced second lieutenant who was supposed to be flying a wing position in a different section. How I spotted him in the rain and fog, when we should have been flying in different positions in the formation, is still a mystery!

It was now clear that there were 27 C-82s milling around in and out of low-hanging, rain-drenched black clouds, while attempting to join-up in one large formation. With windshield wipers still slapping back and forth in a futile attempt to provide forward visibility, we were constantly alert for other aircraft, while hanging on the wing of an errant low-ranking colleague. There was complete silence in the cockpit as we all thought the night sky may erupt at any moment in a blinding flash of two or more aircraft colliding.

Suddenly the radio came alive with the wing commander breaking radio silence and instructing all aircraft to maintain their present altitude, whatever that may be, and take up a course for Strasbourg, France. He further stated, "By the time we reach Strasbourg the sun will be up and we will join-up in proper position in daylight conditions." I held my position on the left wing of my colleague as he took up a Southern course.

About one hour later our wing commander radioed, "I'm holding over Strasbourg at 9,000 feet, above the clouds in daylight conditions and firing double green flares. All aircraft are to form-up on me according to their assigned positions." After numerous circles 27 aircraft were finally in proper position and flying toward our planned destination of Toulouse. (I think the PGR must have been sleeping that night, because if he had been on the job, he could have inducted several new candidates.)

Approximately six hours after departing Rhein Main the formation was approaching the Toulouse Airport in clear skies above a low-hanging undercast. Our wing commander attempted to contact the Toulouse tower and after many unanswered calls he received a response in very broken, difficult-to-understand English. He responded by stating that he wasn't able to receive the Toulouse radio beacon and inquired if it was on the air.

The tower operator answered in French, which neither our wing commander nor I could understand. A request that the tower operator respond in English was made several times, but only French or unintelligible English came back. The wing commander, with 26 aircraft circling behind him, inquired if anyone in the formation could speak French. A pilot classmate of mine by the name of Scotty responded that he spoke French and said, "The tower operator was stating that the radio beacon was off the air." Scotty was advised to obtain the weather at Toulouse, and when he did, he said that it was 500 foot overcast and 2 miles visibility in light rain. This was obviously too low of a ceiling to sneak in with 27 aircraft in formation, and to complicate the situation, pilots were reporting that they were running low on fuel and didn't think they could divert to another airport. Scotty was instructed to inquire if there was radar available for Ground Controlled Approaches (GCAs). The tower's response, "Negative, the only instrument approach available was a Non-precision RDF, utilizing their Radio Direction Finder."

This type of approach requires the approaching aircraft to transmit a radio signal, by holding down their microphone button for alternating periods of about ten seconds, while the tower determines the position the aircraft is from the airport. This is accomplished by a cone of silence which allows the tower operator to issue course information to steer the aircraft toward the airport. This is a slow, tedious process and requires that both the tower operator and the pilot transmit in a common language. On this day it would have to be French.

The wing commander instructed Lt. Scott to break out of formation, fly a (RDF) approach, and after landing proceed to the tower to act as interpreter to assist the French operator in bringing in the remaining 26 aircraft. I observed Scotty break out of formation and listened to him executing an approach into Toulouse in a chattering of French between he and the French operator. About 15 minutes later, Scotty reported, "I'm on the ground and proceeding to the control tower."

With Scotty interpreting course instructions, the remaining 26 aircraft flew instrument approaches at three-minute intervals. I was pretty much at the end of the stack and was closely monitoring my fuel status when I finally made my approach for landing.

By the time all 27 aircraft were on the ground, it was midmorning and we were hungry and dead tired. Being a typical military operation, no one seemed to know what we were supposed to do next. As we waited for instructions that weren't forthcoming, crew members sought out dry spots on the concrete ramp, stretched out and went to sleep. I joined my exhausted Air Force warrior colleagues and was soon sleeping as soundly on the hard ramp as if I was in a feather bed in some fancy five-star hotel. We spent several days flying and working with the French Air Force, but were not allowed to drink wine with lunch. Later, we flew an uneventful 27-ship daylight formation back to Rhein Main Air Base.

Later that month I was directed to fly a C-82 to Molesworth Air Base, England (a former WW II B-17 base), to pick up cargo and transport it back to Germany. The flight was originally planned for a quick turnaround, but due to heavy rain showers , I decided to remain overnight (RON). The next morning I filed a flight plan for Rhein Main and was preparing to start my engines when a jeep came speeding our way and stopped in front of the aircraft. An Air Force captain jumped out, came to the cockpit and told me to delay our departure as an Air Force colonel wanted a ride to Rhein Main to attend an important meeting. He said the colonel was on his way from London and should be here in about 45 minutes.

Sometime later a blue staff car drove up and a middle-age bird colonel, dressed in a Class A blue uniform and carrying a briefcase, entered the cockpit. He thanked me for waiting and took a seat in the empty navigator's position. After obtaining taxi clearance I advanced power on the right engine and applied hard left brake in order to execute a sharp left turn to avoid striking a nearby hangar with my right wing tip. As soon as the aircraft started its left turn, I heard the sound of gushing water and looked around to see where it was coming from. A torrent of rain water (which had accumulated overnight) was pouring out of the cockpit overhead insulation and drenching the stunned colonel. When I saw what the centrifugal force was doing to the trapped rain water, I slammed on the brakes, but my effort to help only caused another surge of water to hit the colonel in the back of his neck. He was understandably mad as hell and started cussing me out for the ghastly predicament he found himself in. My crew chief, trying to rectify the situation, started wiping him off with an old dirty rag, which pissed him off even more. **"Get Away from me, God damit,"** he snapped at the crew chief.

If the situation had not been so embarrassing, it would have been boisterously entertaining. A full colonel was sitting in the navigator's seat, drenching wet and cussing out the world, while his thin graying (comb-over) hair was running down his face. I asked him if he wanted to get off, but he responded with, **"Hell no, lieutenant. I have an important meeting to attend in Germany. Just get this damn airplane airborne and crank up the heat!"**

During the two-hour flight to Rhein Main I kept the cockpit uncomfortably warm, while the colonel held his shirt and blouse over heat vents. When he deplaned his uniform was nearly dry but it looked more like a pair of blue rumpled pajamas with service ribbons. He never thanked me for the flight, which under the circumstances was understandable. (On page 288 I talk about how I happened to meet this same irate officer "now a general" in Bangkok, Thailand 11 years later.)

In the summer of 1951, I flew several missions to Abington Airport, a RAF base just outside of London, England. My mission was to allow English paratroopers the opportunity of jumping from an American C-82. Abington was the English equivalent of Fort Benning, Georgia and their main base for training paratroopers. To cultivate this training they utilized many simulated devices, such as 35-foot towers with pulleys attached to cables that trainees, suspended in a parachute harness, would ride during their initial phase of qualification. I enjoyed jumping and swinging from these training aids and not only thought that they were great fun but good exposure in the event I ever had to bailout of an airplane myself.

Before English paratrooper recruits would be allowed to jump from an actual aircraft they would be required to make one successful jump from a tethered surplus antiaircraft barrage balloon from an altitude of 800 feet. The Brits would send up five trainees and two burly jump masters per basket who would kick the trainees out one-by-one. There would be another crusty instructor on the ground with a bullhorn barking out instructions as the neophytes floated down. (For some reason, it reminded me of the cat we released from a kite when I was a kid, with one exception, my brother Hank and I didn't have a bullhorn!)

I thought a trip up in the balloon would provide an interesting experience and allow me to take some unique photos, so I asked a couple British Army officers if they could arrange it. Their response, "That shouldn't be a problem, Yank. We'll give it a bit of a go." A few minutes later they returned carrying an English-style paratrooper jump suit, a silly looking round crash helmet and a parachute with a coiled-up lanyard. They told me that it would be necessary for me to wear the jumpsuit, helmet and parachute, because if the balloon broke free from its mooring, it would be necessary for everyone to abandon it by parachute. I naively accepted their explanation and when properly dressed, I looked like any other young English paratrooper trainee.

As the balloon ascended, I was standing in the rear of the wicker basket and snapping pictures with my small German Zeiss Ikon camera. When the balloon bounced to a stop at 800 feet, the two jump masters started pushing the somewhat reluctant trainees out of the basket, one at a time, while barking; "Number one ready, **Go!**" "Number two ready, **Go!**" After the fourth jumper was ejected, I thought we would start descending, but to my surprise the jump masters grabbed me while stating, "Number five ready, **Go!**" Before I had time to object, I was thrown out of the basket!

With my heart in my mouth, I was falling through space, but within seconds the static line opened my parachute and I was floating down toward the English countryside. Before I had a chance to enjoy the experience, I heard the vociferate voice of an instructor on a bullhorn, criticizing my poor descending posture. (When I heard him yelling at me in the same manner that he did his young English novice paratroopers, I realized that this whole episode had been a joke, perpetrated by the English officers I had asked to arrange for me to go up in the balloon and coordinated with the airborne jump masters, but not with the instructor operating the bullhorn. To turn the tables on my capricious English friends, I thought I would have a little fun of my own.)

While dangling from the parachute I started waving my arms and legs in circles, completely disregarding the coaching from the enraged screaming instructor on the bullhorn. The more I waved my arms and legs, the higher the pitch his ranting became. It sounded like he was going to have a heart attack or cause his bullhorn to explode. When I landed on the soft grass the furious "bullhorn instructor" was waiting for me and proceeded to chew me out in a manner typical of a British top sergeant. While he was screaming, I unzipped my English style tunic and displayed my American Air Force officer's blue uniform. He took one look, while shouting, **"Bloody hell, you're a yank. What in the friggen hell were you doing in one of our balloons, dressed like one of our blokes?"** Off in the distance I noted a group of British Army officers pointing in my direction and laughing up a storm. This was my one and only parachute jump, but it provided me with excellent training and a great laugh for my English colleagues. Everyone gained, except the "bullhorn instructor" whose face was orange-red while displaying an inconspicuous half smile.

When we felt lucky, Bill Bailey, Hank O'Neal (another pilot classmate) and I would visit the *Bad Homburg Casino* with the goal of investing some of our black market profits. The casino, about 15 miles north of Frankfurt, emerged from the war intact and was once again popular with German gamblers dressed in outdated dark suits and wrinkled ties.

The Bad Homburg Casino opened in 1841 and was the world's first large gambling establishment. Roulette and blackjack are the popular games played, with slot machines installed just recently. Gambling in the casino is a rather stately affair, requires an entrance fee, passport and proper dress. The proprietors were not too pleased in having a bunch of young Air Force lieutenants invade their aristocratic sanctuary, but there was nothing they could do about it. We met the dress code (military coat and tie), had a lot of geld (money), and Germany was under American military occupation. However, their dissatisfaction in our presence was visibly apparent by the parking lot attendant directing that we park our older-style automobiles, with U.S. Forces license plates, some distance away from their older but polished Mercedes Benz and BMW sedans.

Bill Bailey was the type of gambler who makes you wonder if Lady Luck sometimes sits directly on his shoulder, but at other times didn't recognize his existence. In other words, he was either "hot" or "cold." During one of our visits to the Casino, it was Bill's day, and what a day it was! We started playing roulette by placing modest bets but Hank and I were generally losing. However, almost everything that Bill bet on won! He was betting "odd/even," or "red/black" and was usually right! He was soon placing bets of 100, 500, and even 1,000 marks ($20, $120, and $250) and winning almost every time. Feeling that Lady Luck was his date for the night, he had Hank and I stand between to two adjacent roulette tables, ready to place bets on his command. When he received an "extrasensory message" telling him where the little white ball would drop, he would shout directions, telling us how to place our bets. We would place a 1,000 mark chip on the area dictated by Bill just seconds before the croupier would announce, "Nicht spielen mehr." (No more bets.)

Bill's eccentricity in being able to pick winners caught the attention of German gamblers who would hold their bets until he made a decision and then hurry to place their chips on the same combination that we did. (The whole episode was surreal and something Hollywood would love to portray, but this was real, and I was there!) This unusual winning phenomenon went on for some time and our pockets were soon bulging with high denomination chips. But, all of a sudden, we started losing almost as fast as we had been winning moments earlier. We were not only losing our own bets, but lost the support of our German freeloaders as well. Hank and I persuaded Bill to take a break while we still had chips and to calculate his winnings.

We retreated to the bar and counted the chips still in our pockets. I can't remember the exact amount, but it was somewhere between 30 and 40 thousand marks (approximately $10,000). We attempted to cajole Bill into cashing in and calling it a day, but he was insistent that he felt another lucky streak coming on, and as soon as he made a quick trip to the men's room we would return to the roulette tables.

Hank and I followed Bill back to the gaming room, but he was now just as cold as he had been hot earlier. In a very short period of time we told him that we had no more chips (factually a true statement) and it was time to quit. He accepted our "statement of fact" bravely and we left for downtown Frankfurt for dinner and a show.

When in the restaurant we told "Balls" that we had a confession to make. We told him that when he went to the men's room we cashed in $5,000 worth of chips ($40,400 today) and handed him a bundle of German marks. We weren't sure how he would react to our devious declaration, but he was extremely happy and said, "Thanks guys, tonight the champagne and dinner is on me." He took the rest of his winnings and made a trip to the U.S. and bought a new car, which we all enjoyed.

During my first couple of months in Germany I depended on others for transportation or took a taxi. But in February 1950, I purchased a 1937 Willys sedan from Capt. George Walker, another WW II combat veteran, for $200 ($1,600 today). It was a neat little car but couldn't compete with the high-powered German vehicles on the autobahn as it only had a 48 hp four cylinder engine. It had a heater, but no radio, which was just as well, as even at full volume it wouldn't have been able to drown out the sound of the rattles when driving on cobblestone streets. Nevertheless, I was proud of my car and put it to good use. (See Photo No. 30.)

The German autobahns did not suffer serious damage during the war, and what damage did occur was quickly repaired. The Germans love their autobahn system and in most areas there was no speed limit. I was amazed at how fast prewar and postwar automobiles would race past my 37 Willys, almost sucking it in behind them. U.S. military authorities established a 50 mph speed limit for Americans on the autobahn and MPs would issue citations to speeders. I never received a speeding ticket as my little sedan had all it could do to reach 50, and when I was able to exceed the speed limit on downhill runs, it would start shaking violently. When the military occupation ended on May 5, 1955, and the 50 mph speed limit was lifted, safety experts predicted a large increase in accidents by U.S. military drivers. However, there was no noticeable increase, just satisfaction from drivers in bigger cars to be able to drive without one eye on the rear view mirror looking for overzealous MPs.

Bill Bailey, before his good fortune at roulette, had purchased a surplus military *Jeep* which some previous owner had installed an aluminum enclosure. There were hundreds of such vehicles available and could be purchased for a couple hundred dollars. Several of us were enjoying food and liquor in the *Scala* Officers' Club in Wiesbaden, and challenging each other in chug-a-lugging, in one gulp, "Nicko-lashkas." (A double shot of cognac, topped with a slice of lemon coated with a teaspoon of sugar and fine ground coffee. The object was to chew up the lemon, sugar and coffee into a mush, and wash it down with the cognac. Then, without pausing to take a breath, shout, "I'm a Swamp Stumpier.") With each "Nicko-lashka" consumed the world seem to spin faster and faster until it was just one blur. My friend Balls, who had been drinking more than the rest of us, was having difficulty in standing without leaning against a wall, so I cautioned him not to drive his *Jeep* to our hotel as he could ride with me. He agreed, and I thought the subject was closed. I left him alone for a few moments and went to dance but when I returned he was gone!

I was worried that he may have decided to drive home by himself and went out to the street to see if I could intercept him. I found him sitting in his *Jeep* sound asleep with his foot jammed hard against the starter. The engine hadn't started because the ignition switch was in the off position, but the needless cranking of the engine had completely drained the 6-volt battery. I went back inside the *Scala* and asked one of our buddies to give us a push so I could get his car started.

I pulled Balls into the right seat, climbed in behind the steering wheel and signaled to my friend to "let 'er rip." After making contact he pushed us down the wet slick cobblestone street at a terrific rate of speed and when we crested a small hill he abruptly stopped pushing. I let out the clutch to start the engine, but the sudden drag to the rear wheels caused it to start spinning in rapid 360 degree circles down the rain-swept cobblestone hill. I had absolutely no control over the vehicle's path and unfortunately other drivers didn't have us in sight as we had no lights. After about three spins the *Jeep* smashed into a curb in the opposite direction of the flow of traffic. When it hit the curb it tilted up on two wheels and then settled back down with a thud. The abrupt stop stirred Balls momentarily awake and caused him to state, "Jesus, Lou, take it easy." We left his jeep there for the night and when we retrieved it the next day I was chastised for parking it in such a stupid manner.

On Friday evening, February 23, 1951, my colleague, Lt. Harry Fielding and I decided to visit the Rhein Main Officers' Club for their monthly offer of free booze and food. The club, as expected, was a beehive of activity with drunk and sober patrons fighting their way to the bar for a free drink, while several poker and crap tables were operating at full capacity. After several drinks and eating a big buffet meal, one of my friends shouted, "Hey Lou, there's a seat open at a poker table." I sat down with the hope of winning a few dollars from some of my inebriated colleagues. However, Lady Luck wasn't on my side this particular night, and I not only lost all the cash I had on me, but another $50 that I borrowed from colleagues. I finally realized that this wasn't my night for poker and left for my apartment with empty pockets and missing the company of my American girl friend, Jo Dunham now stationed at an air base near Munich.

After arriving home I decided to call her at the Furstenfelbruck Air Base, with the hope that she could cheer me up. I wasn't able to contact her at her BOQ room so I tried the Officers' Club, where she was enjoying a wild Friday night party with a bunch of F-84 fighter pilots. I told her how much I missed her and asked her to jump on a train and visit me in Frankfurt like she had done several times in the past. But she said that she couldn't this weekend, as she had to work. "To hell with them, jump on a train and come to Frankfurt," I responded. "Well, you know what that means," she said. "I know, so I'll see you tomorrow." After we hung-up I began to wonder what she meant by her comment, "You know what that means," so I called her back and asked her. In a cheerful tone of voice, almost drowned out by background party noise, she said that I had proposed marriage and she was celebrating her engagement with some rowdy fighter pilots, who were joshing her about marrying a multi-engine pilot when there were so many good-looking young bachelor fighter pilots available. Also, she said that she had told her boss that she was quitting and moving to Frankfurt to get married. Realizing that my direct approach in suggesting she come up for a visit could have been interpreted as a proposal, I told her that we would discuss our future plans after she arrived and work something out, but there was an unfortunate misunderstanding regarding a proposal of marriage.

The next day I picked her up at the Frankfurt Haup Bahnhof (main railroad station). I hadn't seen her for two months and was struck with how pretty she looked as she stepped off the train smiling. But I also sensed a confused look in regard to her future.

Jo and I talked about our hopes and aspirations and decided that since we had previously talked, in general terms, about getting married at some future date, there was no need to postpone the inevitable. On April 14, 1951, Elizabeth Josephine Dunham (Jo) and I were married at the Rhein Main Air Base Chapel. Almost my entire squadron attended the ceremony, followed by a lavish wedding party in the Bushlag Officers' Club. After the party we left on a two-week honeymoon trip to Baden Baden, Germany and Switzerland. (See Photos 40 and 41.)

The night before the wedding officers from the 12th TCS decided to throw a bachelor party for me at the home of one of our colleagues. My best man, Balls Bailey, picked me up and drove me to the party so I wouldn't have to drive home drunk and possibly miss, as he put it, my suicide appointment with destiny. My empathetic comrades spared no effort in making the party one to remember. There were catered snacks, beer, wine, champagne, a French 75 punch (a mixture of champagne and cognac) and colorful decorations. To add to the whimsicalness of the event, a young lieutenant came up with a pair of scissors and started snipping off neckties. Initially, several resisted in having their uniform ties circumcised, but as more accepted the seemly harmless ritual everyone was soon sporting a three-inch long blue necktie.

In the midst of the raucous hoopla someone noted a street peddler selling balloons. Several party revelers bought some and brought them inside, thinking that they would add to the party decorum. A few minutes later there was a tremendous explosion. I was standing 15 feet away but felt the concussion of the blast on the side of my face. Col. Kidd, our squadron commander, in a jest of frivolity, pulled out his Zippo cigarette lighter and lit one of the balloons, but he didn't realize that in Germany these decorative balloons were filled with hydrogen. The people standing close to the explosion came away with singed eyebrows, flash-burned faces and ringing ears, but the event did add zest to the party.

Later, several of my colleagues grabbed my arms and legs and threw me to the floor, while others pulled down my trousers. They shaved off my pubic hair and with a red magic marker drew a big arrow, on my lower abdomen pointing to my penis. But they weren't through — they then painted my penis a bright red, and held me down until the ink was good and dry. When they let me up the room erupted in cheer while wishing me good luck on my wedding night. Balls drove me home and was pounding on my front door the next morning to make sure, "I got to the church on time." I tried to wash off my bodily graffiti with soap and water but without success. Fortunately, my bride wasn't aware of my body art during the wedding ceremony as I was fully dressed when I said, "I do."

Jo was a very pretty American girl who I had been dating for over a year. We had met when we were both stationed in Wiesbaden, and after I was transferred to Frankfurt it was only a 20 mile drive to continue our flourishing relationship. Later she was transferred to Furstenfelbruck Air Base, near Munich, but in spite of being separated by 250 miles, I managed to see her quite often and our affection for each other continued to grow. She was a registered nurse and the daughter of a respected pediatrician in Toledo, Ohio. She enjoyed adventure and worked for the United Fruit Company in Costa Rica from 1946 to 1948. She was in Costa Rica when the Communists were active under the "Calderonistas." Her work place was bombed by insurgents throwing cans of dynamite from a C-47 and decided to leave the area while still in one piece. She then sought a more peaceful job as a Service Club director in Germany during the Berlin Airlift in May 1949.

We had fun together for many years, but unfortunately the marriage didn't work out over the long term, which I feel was mostly my fault. Due to long separations and a subconscious subliminal denial of being married, engendered by a feeling that I married too young, I felt I didn't get a chance to "sow-wild-oats" like many of my colleagues who remained single. I believe this feeling haunted me for my third and fourth decade of adult life, but by the time I realized I was succumbing to unwarranted egotistical pride, it was too late to save the marriage which ended in a divorce in 1982. However, a lovely daughter Lynn was born of this marriage on August 5, 1952, and a terrific son Michael on September 15, 1960. They are great kids and turned out well. Lynn, graduated from the University of Guam with a BS degree, and the University of Hawaii with a Masters degree in Pacific Studies. She is presently the Traditional Arts

Coordinator for the state of New Hampshire and lives in Concord with her husband Arnold and son Daithi. Mike graduated from the University of Wisconsin with a BS degree in Mathematics, is a Major in the Air National Guard and a pilot for United Airlines. He flew combat missions during Desert War One in KC-135s, and in Afghanistan and Iraq, flying Special Forces MC-130s. He was recently called back to active duty and is scheduled to return to Iraq in early 2008. (See Photos 16, 60, and 61.)

In the summer of 1951 two flying school classmates cavorted with the PGR, but through good luck escaped his diabolic clutches. The first was Second Lieutenant Hank O'Neal who was part of a large formation of C-82s departing Rhein Main Air Base. Soon after becoming airborne, one of Hank's engines erupted in flames, and as he struggled to gain altitude, he attempted to control the fire, but his efforts were ineffective. Upon reaching an altitude of 1,000 feet, he ordered his crew to bail out. (Fortunately the entire crew were wearing parachutes, which was standard policy when we were flying in formation, and all landed safely.)

After Hank checked to see that his crew had abandoned the aircraft, he bailed out at a dangerously low altitude. During his debriefing he stated, "When my parachute opened, I made one swing and hit the ground." Unfortunately, the aircraft, still burning and trailing thick black smoke, crashed into a German house, killing two civilians. (Hank, continued flying C-82s and I was his best man in South Carolina in 1953, when he married General Strickland's daughter Mary Lee, who he had met in Germany.) The last I heard of Hank he was flying B-57s in South Vietnam.

The other classmate who experienced a Close Encounter was Harvey Trengrove. Harvey was on a flight to Amman, Jordan in 1951 with my flight commander Captain Pete Read. Their mission was to demonstrate the merits of the C-82 (a difficult task) to the Jordanian Air Force. When preparing to return to Germany, Pete told the group gathered for their departure that he would demonstrate a "short-field takeoff."

With both engines roaring at full power, he forced the aircraft into the air at around 90 mph and started a steep impressive climb. However, to everyone's surprise there was a muffled explosion and the right engine burst into flames. Pete reduced power on both engines and put the aircraft into a steep descent, with the intent of executing a forced "straight-ahead" landing. But the flames from the engine had burned off the fabric on the elevator, so when he pulled back on the control column to arrest the descent, it had no effect and the aircraft nose dived into the runway with a thundering crash! Pete and his cockpit crew were able to escape the burning aircraft by removing the navigator's plastic astrodome hatch and jumping off the side of the aircraft to safety.

However Harvey, out of curiosity, had elected to remain in the cargo compartment during the takeoff and when he heard the abrupt reduction of power, unfastened his seat belt and headed for the cockpit. But before he moved more than a couple feet, the aircraft crashed. He was thrown through the cargo compartment and exited the aircraft through the open space of the sheared-off main entrance door. After leaving the aircraft, he tumbled across a patch of high grass like a rag doll. Surprisingly, he only suffered a few scratches, but was minus his shoes! In a stunned state, he picked up a small fire extinguisher that had been ejected from the wreckage and began spraying a piece of burning debris laying out in the middle of the field. He kept spraying this innocuous bit of burning material, until the bottle ran dry, while the main wreckage was going up in flames.

Harvey's miraculous escape is difficult to explain, but obviously cheated the PGR out of a candidate he was probably counting on. With 20-20-hindsight, we concluded that when the aircraft crashed, it was in a yaw to the right while Harvey was making his way toward the cockpit. The yaw, which was the result of the loss of the right engine, provided the required geometric angle needed for him to sail through the main entrance door opening created when it was ripped off by the force of the crash. Miraculously he flew through the opening without coming in contact with sharp ragged edges. (Harvey never appeared comfortable with flying following this incident and left the Air Force in South Carolina when his initial five year service commitment was completed.)

In the fall of 1952, my three-year tour of flying C-82s in Germany was coming to an end and I was hopeful that my next assignment would involve flying jets. I longed for an aircraft equipped with guns, rockets and bombs and since the Korean War was still raging, I requested a combat assignment. I was disappointed when I received orders assigning me to Donaldson AFB, South Carolina and the 18th Troop Carrier Squadron, which had recently converted from Curtis C-46 *Commandos* to C-82s. I had no choice but to accept the assignment but vowed to visit the Pentagon to see if I could get my assignment changed.

Before departing Germany I reflected on additional C-82 events other then my own where crew members experienced a Close Encounter or where the PGR was successful in drafting new recruits. A pilot from my squadron crashed at Neubiberg Air Base when attempting to land in bad weather, after an engine failed when flying over the Alps. He and his crew escaped with minor injuries, but the aircraft was completely destroyed.

A pilot classmate, along with 35 Air Force personnel, was killed when their C-82 slammed into Mount Dorr in Southern France on November 13, 1951. The accident was a calamitous catastrophe and a dreadful loss as the aircraft was transporting 32 skilled aircraft mechanics to a conference in Bordeaux, France. There were many other C-82 incidents, but through skill or good luck none of these resulted in fatalities or serious injury.

In October 1952, accompanied by my wife, ten-week-old daughter Lynn, a new bright red MG TD convertible, and a large pedigree German shepherd (named Varus), I boarded the U.S.N.S. *Henry Gibbons* troop ship (which I was surprised was still transiting the North Atlantic), and ten days later disembarked in New York City and secured a room in the Henry Hudson Hotel. The next day I took a train to Washington, DC to visit my former squadron commander from Germany, Colonel John B. Kidd, who was now stationed in the Pentagon. (Colonel Kidd was a great officer and retired in 1974 with the rank of major general.) He greeted me with a warm handshake, but after reviewing my orders assigning me to a C-82 squadron in Greenville, South Carolina, thought that the assignment was in the best interest of the Air Force. He commented that my three years of experience in flying C-82s in Europe would be put to good use, as the unit I was being assigned to recently converted from C-46s. His final comment, "Sorry Lieutenant Martin, there is nothing I can do to get you a combat assignment in Korea. Anyway, that war is almost over." Figuring that my fate was sealed, I bid Colonel Kidd good-bye and accepted the fact that my days of flying C-82s were not over.

When in New York we were eager to view television (our first opportunity) and had a small ten-inch set sent to our room. We weren't impressed with the programs and in my mind TV programming hasn't improved much in the last 56 years. After shipping our German shepherd to Toledo, Ohio by American Express we wedged ourselves into our small two-passenger MG and headed for Toledo via the Pennsylvania Turnpike. It was early November and since our sports car had no heater and loose fitting side-curtains we thought we were going to freeze. We wrapped our ten-week-old daughter up like an Eskimo and sandwiched her between us over the hand-brake handle. She never complained even when snow flurries started drifting in through the openings from the side-curtains. By the time we reached Toledo I had second thoughts about our decision in buying a small sports car versus a respectable sedan with a heater and roll-up windows, but we were young and carefree and endured the hardship as just another fascinating adventure.

After depositing my wife, daughter and dog in Ohio, I drove to Ladysmith, Wisconsin to visit my family but by the time I arrived I couldn't speak, I had incurred a bad case of laryngitis evidently from the snow and cold air blowing in through the side curtains of my MG. After a short visit I headed for South Carolina and warmer weather. (See Photos 36 & 37.)

I reported to the 18th Troop Carrier Squadron, in Donaldson AFB, South Carolina in late November 1952. The squadron commander, Major Charles R. Vickrey, noting that I had more than 1,300 hours in C-82s, stated that I would be a welcome addition to his squadron. Following a brief local flight check by Captain Tedd L. Bishop, I was designated an instructor pilot. I was a 24-year-old first lieutenant with 1,332 hours in the C-82, 1,657 hours total flight time and eager to start work with a group of pilots recently recalled to active duty and several years my senior.

On December 18, 1952, I was enjoying a martini in the Donaldson AFB Officers' Club when I was surprised by Lt. Bill O'Connell, a pilot classmate, slapping me on the back and offering to buy me a drink. Exchanging warm hand shakes we brought each other up to date on our flying experiences, and when I told him that I was flying C-82s, he emitted a polite chuckle while proudly stating that he was recently checked out as an Aircraft Commander in the Douglas C-124 *Globemaster* and was on a brief en route overnight. He said that he would be departing the next day for Moses Lake, Washington where he would pick up a group of Army soldiers returning from Korea and going home on Christmas leave.

We had more drinks than we should have and while we could still walk, I drove him to the transient officer's quarters and wished him a good flight. As a gesture of friendship he presented me with an expensive-looking silver serving tray. Surprised by the gift, I asked him where he obtained it. "I found it in a show case in the lobby of the Officers' Club and thought it would make a nice farewell gift," he said. (I thanked him for his thoughtfulness but planned on returning it to the club the next day.)

Before I had a chance to return the stolen platter, I learned that Bill O'Connell's aircraft, two minutes after an early morning takeoff from Moses Lake on December 20th, began to lose altitude and crashed and burned in a snow-laden field near the airport. Eighty-two passengers out of 115 and all five crew members were killed. Failure of the pilot to fully unlock a mechanical control handle, which locks the elevators, ailerons and rudder, was stated as the cause of the accident. I prayed that our heavy drinking and limited rest 36 hours before the accident had not caused my friend to overlook such a critical preflight item and assisted the PGR in recruiting 87 new members at such a festive time of the year. (I kept the silver platter in remembrance of my pilot colleague.)

For the next several months I was kept busy administering flight instruction to my fellow C-82 pilots in takeoffs and landings, day and night formation and in air-dropping paratroopers and heavy equipment. Considerable temporary duty (TDY) was spent flying out of Pope AFB, North Carolina in support of Army airborne forces from Fort Bragg.

C-82s also flew support missions for the burgeoning Strategic Air Command (SAC). During one such mission we flew three aircraft to a B-47 SAC base in Kansas where we remained overnight. After checking into the BOQ and changing clothes, we headed for the Officers' Club for drinks and dinner. However, the main dining room on this particular night was reserved for bingo and to be served we would have to buy one or more bingo cards. Although we thought bingo was a boring game we purchased cards and secured a table for six.

Looking around the dining room we were surprised to see that many tables were occupied by unescorted young females. Closer examination revealed that they were all wearing wedding rings, so it appeared they were spending a "lady's night" out while their husbands were on temporary duty defending the country. None of us were winning at bingo, but did enjoy competing (albeit from a distance) in selecting the most beautiful unaccompanied female in the smoke-filled room. We discussed the possibility of hooking up with one, thinking they would be starved for male companionship, but thought the chances were slim. Our spur-of-the-moment beauty contest settled on one undisputed beautiful young wife, who we all agreed was the most gorgeous of the lot. She was a real beauty and even from a distance seemed to possess the personality to match her outward charm.

When intermission was announced a band started playing and couples began dancing. We noticed that the bevy of unescorted females were being asked to dance by male officers on the prowl, but in all cases their offers were rejected. This included rebuffs to my table mates who joined the marauding stags. When they asked our declared pageant winner to dance, she declined with a, "No thank you, but I appreciate your asking." Up to this point I hadn't joined the officers seeking a dance as I didn't wish to expose my male ego to a "cold-turkey-style-rejection."

When my forlorn colleagues were back at the table, I presented a challenge. I told them that they were obviously employing awkward clumsy approaches when asking the ladies to dance and that was the reason they were being rejected. Their response, "You think you could do better, Lou?" "Without a doubt I think I could," I said, "but let's put a wager on my success or failure." I suggested they put up $10 each, against my $50, in betting that I couldn't persuade our selected beauty queen to dance. They thought this was easy money and couldn't wait to put up their ten dollar bills. (The wager today would equal $400.)

With the assurance of a 24-year-old Air Force hot pilot, I strolled across the dance floor, confident of victory. I discreetly folded $25 into the palm of my hand, and when I reached the table of the giggling, chattering young wives, I knelt down next to our selected beauty, introduced myself, and said, "Excuse me, I'm not requesting a dance, but would like to ask you a question." When I had her attention, I told her that I thought I had gone through pilot training with her husband (not true), but this opened the door to some small talk. During the discussion, I told her about my bet of $50 that I couldn't persuade her to dance, but if she would agree to just one dance, I would split my winnings with her. Her lady friends, overhearing my offer, urged her to go for it. She said, "OK, one dance." I slipped her the $25, which she placed in her purse, and we enjoyed a nice long slow dance. When the music stopped, I escorted her back to her table, thanked her like the gentleman I was, and returned to my startled friends, and in a cocky gesture stuffed the five ten-dollar bills into my wallet while stating, "You guys just don't have the right stuff!"

Much to my chagrin, I was beginning to like flying the C-82 *Packet*, which was most likely a result of the many interesting missions I was engaged in, and in the fact that I was developing a reputation as an experienced flight instructor. Another fascinating reality was that I had gone for several months without arousing the attention of the ever-lurking PGR. I doubted that he had given up, but was just biding his time while awaiting a better time to strike.

In January 1953, I was directed to proceed to Barksdale AFB, Louisiana to pickup a load of cargo and fly it to Travis AFB, California. Since the routing after Barksdale was up to me, I thought I would surprise my brother Ben by remaining overnight in Long Beach. When preparing to depart Louisiana, an attractive female Air Force nurse asked if she could ride with us in the jump seat. Naturally I said, "Welcome aboard captain."

En route she said that she had to use the downstairs lavatory and requested that I post it "off limits" to male members of the crew for the next ten minutes! I waited until I thought she would be sitting down and then pushed the aircraft into a shallow dive, creating a period of negative Gs. At the time I thought this was an innocent joke, but in retrospect it was a dirty trick to play on such a pretty young captain. It took her a long time to return to the cockpit and when she did she was (literally) pissed off! She said that she had to change her slacks as she had soiled the others when she found herself floating in space at a very embarrassing moment. She said that she was going to file a violation regarding my disrespectable behavior but I never heard another word. I believe she found it very difficult to put the incident in print, plus I apologized for my thoughtless prank when she deplaned.

After spending a night with my brother, I dressed him in my spare flight suit and allowed him to fly with me to Travis AFB and back to Long Beach. En route I allowed him to set in the pilot's seat, and he thought it was quite a change from flying a 65 hp Piper *Cub.* Whenever we encountered ground crew personnel at either base, I had him hold his hand, or some other object, over the name tag on his flight suit to prevent some inquisitive person from questioning why there were two Lt. Martin's.

In April 1953, I was selected to fly a C-82 to Bolling AFB, Washington, DC to airlift 40 military reserve chaplains to Colorado Springs, Colorado where they would attend a three-day religious conference. The convention was to be held in the famous *Broadmore Hotel* where my crew and myself would also be staying. We were directed to remain with them and fly them back to Washington at the conclusion of their conference. I considered this a plush assignment and my operation's officer, when assigning me the trip said, "I assigned this mission to you, Lou, because of your vast experience in the C-82," adding, "These chaplains range in rank from captain to full colonel, and since they are all from the Washington, DC area, treat them as VIPs." I departed for Bolling AFB a day early and enjoyed a slight diversion by flying up the Potomac River over George Washington's *Mount Vernon Estate* and an aerial panoramic view of Washington (permitted in those days). After a delicious dinner in Georgetown and a night's rest in a Bolling AFB, BOQ room, I was up early and looking forward to my mission to Colorado Springs.

I filed a flight plan of approximately seven hours, preflighted the aircraft and awaited the arrival of my passengers. Around 8 a.m. a blue Air Force bus arrived carrying 40 military chaplains. They wore the uniform of their respective branch of service, which displayed a "Cross" or "Star of David" on their left breast. As briefed, they were of mixed officer ranks. I stood next to the entrance door and as they boarded the aircraft, they extended a blessing consistent with their individual religious beliefs. With just receiving 40 blessings, I figured the PGR would have a difficult time in recruiting me to join his infamous legion during this special mission!

The flight to Colorado Springs, although long, was uneventful. It was in the middle of the afternoon when we landed and a bus was waiting to transport my passengers to the *Broadmore Hotel*. After refueling and securing the aircraft, my copilot, 2nd Lt. Arthur [Cab] Calloway, and my young crew chief followed them by taxi about an hour later. The hotel was far more luxurious than the military billets I had been accustomed to and I looked forward to a pleasurable three-day vacation at taxpayers' expense.

By the third day of our stay, Cab and I had made friends with some local females and planned a farewell party in my hotel room. We had intentionally stayed clear of our chaplain passengers, fearing that they would not approve of our youthful "carefree lifestyle." I even declined to attend their farewell banquet by telling the colonel, who had invited me, "I appreciate the invitation, colonel, but my crew and I will be retiring early so as to be fully rested for our return flight to Washington." He complimented me for my interest in their safety and graciously accepted my justification for not attending.

That night Cab, the crew chief and I were enjoying a farewell party with some young ladies, when there was a loud knock on my door. I put on a bathrobe over my shirt and pants and instructed my guests to remain quiet while I went to see who was interrupting our merry-making.

Standing in the doorway was a chaplain who had been sent to inquire if I would reconsider and honor them by attending a farewell prayer and toast for a safe flight home. With my hair in disarray and my bathrobe loosely covering my body, I politely declined his invitation by stating, "As I told the colonel earlier, I truly appreciate your kind offer, but as you can see, I was already in bed when you knocked and I must respectively decline your invitation. When you and your colleagues say your farewell prayers and drink your farewell toast, please keep me in mind. But I believe God will forgive me for not attending and will agree that, in the interest of safety, it is important that I get a good night's rest." He said, "Bless you my son," and left. I returned to my room, complimented my

105

hidden companions for their silence and continued with our own unpretentious farewell party until around 2 a.m.

The next morning was a beautiful day, with unlimited visibility making the Rocky Mountains appear much closer than they actually were. The 40 chaplains, as they entered the aircraft, blessed me once again. (I figured I had been blessed enough on this trip to keep me safe for several years.) My computed takeoff weight was slightly above the maximum allowable weight of 54,000 pounds, but taking into account that the elevation of the Airport is 6,140 feet above sea level, my maximum allowable takeoff weight would be considerably less. (At the time I didn't realize how serious my taking off in an overweight condition at high altitude would be.)

The acceleration during the takeoff roll was very slow and I was slightly below normal takeoff speed when I reached the end of the runway. I pulled back on the control column and the aircraft reluctantly became airborne, but my climb rate was only a paltry 300 feet per minute. I instructed my copilot to retract the landing gear and wing flaps, knowing that reducing drag would increase the rate of climb. But, when he placed the landing gear handle to the up position, nothing happened. Observing the failure of the landing gear to retract, my crew chief reported, "The landing gear circuit breakers just popped." I instructed him to reset them and again called for the landing gear to be retracted. Once again the gear did not retract and the circuit breakers popped open again. At the same time I began to smell the strong pungent odor of electrical smoke.

Struggling to stay airborne, I kept the engine power at full-throttle and started a gentle turn to a close-in downwind leg for a return to the airport. We declared an emergency and the control tower cleared us for an immediate landing. While flying just above stall speed the crew chief called my attention to the rapidly-rising engine cylinder head and oil temperatures. I ordered the engine cooling cowl flaps and the oil cooling doors fully opened (even though I knew it would increase drag). However, they did not respond to the open command and remained in their semi-closed position. Realizing that almost everything on the C-82 is electrically actuated, and accompanied by the smoke and odor of an electrical fire, I knew I had a serious problem. It was imperative that I get this "Fairchild bucket of bolts" on the ground ASAP, and if I didn't all the blessings I recently received would not keep the PGR from knocking on my door and grabbing 40 unfortunate military chaplains in the process. The C-82 possessed no provisions for dumping fuel to decrease weight, and even if we had parachutes onboard it would have been impossible to get 40 untrained passengers to bail out. I thought of having the passengers throwing out their baggage, but recalled that they traveled light and the order would just create panic and be counter-productive. I coaxed the aircraft up to about 800 feet and by the time I turned onto a close-in final approach, I thought that perhaps the worst of my problems were over, but when I reduced power for landing, a small twin-engine aircraft taxied onto the active runway. I had no choice but to go to full-throttle and commence a go-around. I kept the nose down as long as possible to increase airspeed and enhance engine cooling and passed over the aircraft on the end of the runway by a couple hundred feet. I executed a tight traffic pattern and spiked the aircraft onto the runway at 120 mph. (However, since the airport elevation was more than 6,000 feet, my actual touchdown ground speed was probably close to 150 mph.)

The C-82 was not equipped with anti-skid brakes, nor was it possible to slow down by reversing the propellers. My 54,000 lb. aircraft was screaming down the 5,000 foot-long runway like a drag racer, in spite of my pushing down hard on both brake pedals. I was concerned about applying brake pressure of such force that would cause the tires to skid and possibly explode. However, as the end of the runway was fast approaching, I was still traveling at a pretty good speed, so I had no choice and pushed down hard on both brake pedals. When I did the main tires started skidding as the aircraft came to a rumbling, abrupt stop about ten feet into a sod overrun.

During the landing roll I thought it might not be possible to stop before running off the end of the runway, so I instructed my copilot to give three rings on the cargo compartment alarm bell to alert the passengers that it may be necessary to evacuate the aircraft. (This contingency was covered in my pre-departure passenger briefing, along with informing them that an actual egress would be ordered by one continuous ring.)

When the aircraft came to a stop, I shut off the fuel to both engines, and when the left propeller stopped rotating, I ordered the continuous ringing of the alarm bell. Smoke began billowing up from both sides of the aircraft, creating the sense that it was on fire. My alert crew chief made a mad dash to the front entrance door, opened it and directed our excited passengers to exit the aircraft, and once outside, to move some distance away. After turning off all cockpit switches, except the alarm bell, I descended the ladder to the cargo compartment myself and was gratified to note that all passengers, except one, had left the aircraft. The remaining passenger was struggling to leave his seat, but in his excitement had failed to unfasten his seat belt and was attempting to get moving through rapid stationary shuffling of his feet. I unfastened his seat belt and he was gone in a flash. Taking one last look around to ensure that everyone had evacuated, I placed a handkerchief over my nose and mouth and exited by passing through eye-stinging clouds of arid smoke.

Once outside, I noted that most of the smoke was coming from extremely hot brakes and a ruptured brake line spewing hydraulic fluid onto near red-hot brake pads. The aircraft itself was not on fire, but the clouds of smoke emanating from the landing gear area seemed to indicate that it was. Fire trucks came racing up and began spraying water and foam on the hot brakes, which only served to increase the smoke level and agitate my already excited passengers standing off to the side.

I walked over to join the group of praying passengers, and was greeted with a loud cheer and a big round of applause. I attempted to apologize for the inconvenience and scare I had put them through, but one after another they came forward with embarrassing praises like, "A job well done," "We weren't worried." As one senior chaplain stated, "What could happen with 40 chaplains onboard?" (I guess the PGR was outgunned.)

I contacted my squadron operations officer in South Carolina to inform him of my difficulty, and he said they would send an aircraft to transport my passengers back to Washington, as well as mechanics to repair my aircraft. A bus was arranged to take my cheerful religious friends back to the *Broadmore Hotel* for another night of good food, partying and thoughtful praying. Before boarding their bus they all blessed me one more time. I had now been blessed 120 times since leaving Washington. (I didn't know it at the time, but before returning to South Carolina, I would be calling on all 120 blessings to get me there safely.)

Three days later my aircraft was repaired and I filed a flight plan for Donaldson AFB, South Carolina. I departed Colorado Springs about one hour after sunset for an eight-hour night flight home. The flight would take us over Wichita, Kansas, Tulsa, Oklahoma and Memphis, Tennessee. The Flight Service briefer had warned of a line of thunderstorms forming in Kansas and Oklahoma, but thought I would be able to safely circumvent them. The C-82, like most aircraft in the early fifties, was not equipped with airborne weather avoidance radar, nor were air traffic controllers able to provide accurate guidance in avoiding thunderstorms. It was the responsibility of the pilot to avoid them or, as was often the case, cancel the flight. However, once airborne it was quite possible to find yourself in a situation where you had no choice but to press on and dodge the worst of the storms through visual sightings. This type of avoidance depended on steering around the darkest areas of the menacing clouds and the most frequent lightning flashes. This procedure for avoiding weather was borderline in daylight, but indecisive at best, at night.

The flight was routine until approaching Wichita, where off in the Eastern Kansas sky, I could see frequent flashes of lightning. Initially they appeared widely dispersed and I thought that I wouldn't have a problem in avoiding the worst of the storms, but as I passed over Wichita, the line of thunderstorms intensified and I contemplated returning to Colorado Springs. But the series of storms behind me were now just as intense as the ones in front, so I had no choice but to continue.

By the time I approached Tulsa, I was totally immersed in thunderstorms so intense and frequent that it was impossible to choose a course that would lesson my exposure to continuous heavy rain, lightning and severe turbulence. I instructed my crew and the three aircraft maintenance passengers to tighten their safety belts and hold on. I also turned on the cockpit overhead white lights to lessen the temporary blindness from the frequent lightning flashes. Many lightning strikes were so close that we could hear the loud sharp clap of thunder that followed, while struggling to maintain my assigned altitude of 9,000 feet. I recalled senior pilots recommending that when in extreme turbulence, do not attempt to hold an altitude, just fly attitude to keep from over-stressing the aircraft, which could cause structural damage or the wings to separate.

The severe up-and-down drafts were pushing us up to 11,000 feet and minutes later dropping us down to 8,000. (Racing through my mind was the possibility of flying into an imbedded tornado, a fate which had befallen an aircraft in Texas recently, causing it to break up in flight.) Along with the pounding rain and occasional hail pellets, the cockpit was ablaze with the effects of *Saint Elmos Fire* dancing across the windshield and nose of the aircraft. This erratic discharge of static electricity produced a weird green hue, lighting up the whole cockpit. If it wasn't for the precarious situation I found myself in, the pyrotechnics from the lightning and *St. Elmos Fire,* along with the extreme turbulence, would have made for an exciting ride. I informed the Wichita Air Traffic Control Center that I was unable to maintain my assigned altitude and was unsure of my position on the airways. Through a crackling radio response they acknowledged my advisory call.

I kept on riding our airborne bucking bronco with the hope that we would soon fly through the line of thunderstorms. Minutes later, without warning, the nose of the aircraft was struck by a blinding lightning bolt, accompanied with a loud crash of thunder and an aircraft shudder. Within seconds, we were hit again, this time near the aircraft's tail along with another blinding flash, a loud bang and more aircraft shudder. (Thoughts went through my mind about a C-82 that had recently crashed in Texas after being struck by lightning killing everyone onboard.)

However, I didn't dwell on the possibility of meeting the same fate, as we were still airborne and I had all I could do in just keeping the aircraft upright. A few minutes later, a four-engine aircraft flashed overhead going in the opposite direction, missing our aircraft by no more than a few hundred feet. During my brief visual contact, I saw the exhaust flame from four engines. I reported the sighting to Wichita Center who stated that it must have been an American Airlines DC-4, which had also reported that it was unable to maintain its assigned altitude due to extreme turbulence.

After an hour of fighting the wrath of Mother Nature, we broke out into clear skies. I descended to 9,000 feet and attempted to contact Tulsa Center, but received no response. I made a radio call on the emergency frequency and Kansas City responded. I informed them that I was unsure of my position and through radio direction finding, they determined that I was east of their station, but unable to provide distance. I switched to St. Louis Center, obtained clearance to fly a direct course to their station, and then on my original planned course. We landed in Greenville around 2 a.m., and I complimented my crew for a job well done and promised a round of free drinks. They thanked me for the offer, while stating that although the flight was exciting, it wasn't one they wished to repeat.

I flew the C-82 for two more months, but fortunately experienced no additional Close Encounters. My last flight in the *Packet* was on July 7, 1953, when I delivered one to Kelly AFB, where it was to be used in the training of aircraft mechanics. Many C-82s were transferred to South American Air Forces, who experienced more problems and accidents than we did. Other C-82s were sold on the civilian market, and used as fire bombers or cargo haulers. Most civilian operators installed a jet engine on top of the fuselage to increase takeoff power and provide a comfortable buffer in the event of engine failure. (The nefarious C-82 was made famous in the 1965 movie, *The Flight of the Phoenix, staring Jimmy Stewart.*) I had accumulated 1,600 hours in this ill-famed aircraft and was now ready to move on to another challenge.

Chapter Five --- Baby Grunau Gliders

The attendees at the Yalta Conference on the South Coast of the Crimea in February 1945 agreed that after Germany was defeated, it would be partitioned into four zones of military occupation. They would be controlled by the United States, the Soviet Union, the United Kingdom and France. These zones would be demilitarized, denazified and eventually become part of the new Federal Republic of Germany. In complying with the demilitarized stipulation, all vestiges of the former German Luftwaffe were to be destroyed. Fighters, bombers, transports and gliders were either chopped up for scrap, or stacked into pyramids and burned. However, in England, wiser heads prevailed and many German gliders were stored in hangars in the British Zone for use by the Royal Air Force (RAF) when the fever and passion of the war subsided. Two popular types of gliders saved from destruction, were the Stamer Lippisch Schulgleiter *SG 38 Open* and the Schneider *Baby Grunau.*

The SG 38 (Boat) is a basic trainer with an open fuselage, no instruments, and only the wing, horizontal and vertical stabilizers and control surfaces were covered with fabric. Elevator travel is intentionally limited, making it nearly impossible or very difficult for clumsy student pilots to stall or inadvertently end up in a tailspin. Consequently it's an excellent trainer for novice pilots to learn the basic skills of flying. It has a wingspan of 34 ft., a length of 21 ft. and an empty weight of only 228 lbs.

The Baby Grunau is a light-weight, open cockpit, single place high wing glider constructed of wood and fabric. It has a wingspan of 45 ft. and is stable and easy to fly. It was the most produced sailplane in the world with more than 6,000 manufactured by the Edmund Schneider Company in the town of Grunau, Germany. The first variant was flown in 1931. Today Grunau is known as Jesow and is located in present day Poland.

The German Luftwaffe operated gliders to train pilots without appearing to violate the Post WW I Versailles Treaty that outlawed remilitarization. Fleets of SG 38s and Baby Grunau gliders served as primary flight trainers for thousands of future Luftwaffe fighter, bomber and transport pilots during the 1920s and early 1930s. (See Photos 33, 34, and 35.)

In the spring of 1951 I flew a C-82 to a RAF base in the British Zone of Occupation near Bonn, Germany. The aircraft they were flying was the DeHaviland *Vampire* F3, a neat little single-engine jet fighter which first flew in 1943. It was primarily a ground attack fighter and produced a distinctive high-pitched whistling sound, similar to the Cessna T-37 jet trainer, and not unlike the air-driven "terror" siren on the Junkers JU 87 *Stuka* dive bomber. While waiting for my aircraft to be off-loaded, RAF pilots were eager to show me their glider club, equipped with the *SG 38 Open* and the *Baby Grunau*. I was impressed, and asked if an American pilot could join. Their response, "You're jolly well welcome, Yank, and bring along some of your squadron mates as well."

The following Sunday, accompanied with our operations officer Major Robert B. Hardy, we flew a C-82 to the RAF base with the intent of exploring their friendly offer of allowing American pilots the opportunity of joining their glider club. We were impressed by their spirit of hospitality and their interest in scrutinizing our strange looking Fairchild *Packet.* After completing a simple application form and paying a 10 shilling (about $3) registration fee I and several other pilots were official members. The RAF fighter base was only a two-hour drive so we agreed that future visits would be by automobile which would allow for exploring interesting sites en route and taking our wives along who would pack a picnic lunch. The following weekend, I and several colleagues departed Frankfurt to take the Brits up on their kind offer of allowing us to qualify as glider pilots

To launch their gliders they used a gasoline-powered winch, which during WW II had been used to raise and lower antiaircraft barrage balloons. (Modern glider winches use diesel engines of 250 to 350 hp, but at the time surplus WW II winches were plentiful and free for the taking.) A 3,500 ft. steel cable was stretched the length of a grass strip with communications between the launch pad and the winch operator via a surplus "crank-style" field telephone. With the cable connected to a glider, the launch supervisor would instruct the winch operator to reel in the cable, slowly at first, until it was taut. With a pointed index finger signal from the pilot, indicating that he was ready, the winch operator would be given the signal to reel in the cable at "full-throttle." A head-jerking takeoff acceleration followed which was not unlike being propelled off an aircraft carrier by a steam-generated catapult. The glider would become airborne, almost instantly, and with the elevator control stick held fully aft, the climb-out angle would be close to 45 degrees. It was exciting to watch and I was eager to take part in this exhilarating hobby.

According to the launch supervisor (a *Vampire* jet pilot instructor), before flying the *Baby Grunau* we would have to make one flight in their basic trainer, the *SG 38 Open*, which from all appearances resembled something designed by the Wright Brothers. The pilot sits in a dining-room-style chair in the nose, and can't see any other portion of the airframe without turning around. The glider contained no flight instruments of any kind, not even an airspeed indicator or an altimeter. It was so light that two people could easily lift it off the ground and position it on a three-axis (horizontal, vertical and lateral) stationary gimbal device. Under moderate wind conditions this unique arrangement would allow for a student pilot to sit in its cockpit and literally fly it while an instructor pilot stood next to him providing guidance. (Since the club did not possess dual control gliders this was their method of providing an abinitio trainer for aspiring new glider pilots. See Photo No. 34.)

Once the student mastered flying the stationary *SG 38* by maintaining a straight and level flight attitude and coordinated turns, he was provided slow-speed winch tows that would allow for flights of five to ten feet off the ground and the completion of numerous takeoffs and landings before reaching the end of the field. When the instructor felt that the student could safely fly the glider at higher altitudes he would be provided a full launch of up to a thousand feet, where he would be required to fly a normal traffic pattern and a landing. All this was accomplished without the student ever flying in a dual controlled glider with an instructor. According to our English pilot colleagues this was the same method the German Luftwaffe employed in their pilot training program, which was cost effective and developed a strong sense of individual confidence in the pilots who successfully completed the curriculum.

I and my Air Force pilot colleagues were not required to fly the *SG-38 Open* in the "jury-rigged" stationary simulator so I volunteered to fly first while my companions waited their turn. As the launch supervisor was helping me strap into the simple wooden seat I asked, "How will I know what airspeed to fly without an airspeed indicator?" He replied, "Just fly what feels right, yank." As he hooked up the tow cable, he mentioned that since this was my first flight, I would only be able to reach about 300 meters (1,000 feet) because the launch speed would be somewhat reduced but would still be sufficient to get a feel of the glider. So after releasing the cable make an immediate turn to a downwind leg, perform one or two "deep stalls," and land. With that I was jerked airborne and sailing through the air on what seemed like a "naked chair" in space.

When I felt the tow cable go slack, I pulled the yellow release knob and made a gentle bank to a left downwind. I noted, straight away, how easy it was to fly at the proper airspeed, (just like the instructor said). When lowering the nose to increase speed it felt too fast; when raising it too high, it felt too slow; in between, it felt just right! I pulled the nose up to perform a deep stall, which resulted in the nose dropping so abruptly that if I hadn't been strapped in I would have been thrown out into empty space. My heart was in my throat until I was once again flying with a positive G load. (Now I knew why the instructor wanted me to do a couple deep stalls. It was like topping out on the top of a roller coaster at 800 feet.) I entered a base leg and landed next to the launch site.

My waiting American colleagues, eager to take their turn, asked me for my opinion of the flight. My response, "It's a piece of cake, but I didn't pull the nose up steep enough in the stall, so when you fly, get the nose up real high!" My English instructor held back a smile during my instructional recommendation as we both knew that when the nose dropped you felt like you would be thrown out into open space without a parachute.

Since I was the first to fly the *SG 38*, I was the first American pilot to fly the *Baby Grunau*. My *Vampire* Jet pilot instructor briefed me on the cockpit, pointing out that the only flight instruments were an airspeed indicator, altimeter, rate of climb/descent gage and an unreliable magnetic compass. It also had a round yellow knob, like the *SG 38*, that was to be pulled when disconnecting from the launch cable. However, he cautioned that I should not attempt to disconnect until I fealt the tow line going slack, since the strong tension on the cable during a maximum launch force may not allow the quick disconnect hook in the glider to open. I asked him about the stalling and landing approach speeds. He replied, "Bloody Hell, Yank, you're a pilot! Just fly at whatever speed feels comfortable, just like you did in the *SG 38*."

I strapped myself into the open cockpit, gave a thumbs-up signal to indicate I was ready, and when the cable became taut, signaled with a pointed index finger that I was ready to go. When the launch operator reeled in the cable I knew that the takeoff acceleration would exceed what I had experienced during my first flight, but I wasn't prepared for the thrill of being yanked off the ground, like being shot from a slingshot, and was airborne in about 20 feet of ground roll. I yanked back on the control stick and was heading skyward at a steep 45 degree angle. At around 500 meters (about 1,700 feet) I felt the launch cable go abruptly slack, and as I pushed the control stick forward to avoid stalling, pulled the yellow release handle and observed the cable floating toward the ground attached to a small parachute.

This was my first flight in an aircraft (I didn't consider the *SG 38* a real aircraft) without noisy engines and I felt that I was finally duplicating the flying skills of the eagles and hawks that I had admired soaring in summer thermals in Northern Wisconsin. Back then, as a young boy, I fantasized that someday I would be able to join those magnificent birds in silently waltzing with the clouds and now, here I was---ten years later---living a boyhood dream in a far-off country I only knew from history books.

I loved flying the *Baby Grunau* and understood why it was such a popular design. I also admired the RAF for their foresight in not piling up such beautiful gliders into small stacks and setting them on fire, like the French, the U.S. and the Russian armies did. I performed medium and steep banks, pulled the glider up into a stall, and before I ran out of altitude performed a loop and a descending barrel role. I could easily see why it was an effective tool for training future Luftwafle pilots. I turned onto a 600 foot downwind leg and performed a smooth grass-absorbing landing close to the launch pad. The RAF flight instructor gave me a "thumps-up" while stating, "Well done, Yank, you can stop smiling now!"

During the summer of 1951 I visited the RAF glider club on weekends when I was not flying a C-82 somewhere in Europe and enjoyed the friendly association with the RAF fighter pilots as well as flying the *Baby Grunau.* It was not only a real delight to fly but provided the opportunity of performing loops, barrel rolls or just flying an aircraft solo. The Brits kept about five or six gliders ready for weekend use and by using a winch to launch them, versus towing them aloft with a powered aircraft, resulted in quick turnarounds. It was not uncommon to log five or six flights in any given day. Naturally they called a halt to all glider operations around 3 p.m. for tea, even if the weather was great.

The maximum altitude I could achieve with a good winch operator was around 1,800 feet. And since Northern Germany is not noted for updraft thermals, most flights were a glide back for a landing with a flight duration of around 12 minutes. Another handicap was the German weather! Low clouds and rainy days were common and there were days when we would drag gliders to the far end of the field and sit around and swap flying stories while waiting for a break in the weather. If the weather didn't improve, we would drag them back across the waterlogged airport.

In September 1951, we experienced a typical questionable weather day for gliding, but hoping for the best we positioned two *Baby Grunau*s at the far end of the field to be ready to launch if we got a break in the weather. However instead of it improving it just got worse. It began to rain quite hard and the ragged cloud base appeared to be no higher than 500 feet. After a couple idle hours we were all chilled to the bone and soaking wet so we decided to call it quits. We were preparing to pull the gliders back across the field, with one man driving an open jeep, and another walking a glider wing tip to keep it from dragging on the ground. But since we had only one jeep, it would require two long trips to secure the gliders. To avoid this unpleasant operation, I came up with a brilliant idea on how to get the gliders back across the field without dragging them.

My suggestion was that since the winch was already in position at the far end of the field, we could instruct the operator to perform a short tow. This would allow the glider to reach three or four hundred feet of altitude before releasing, which should be of sufficient height to glide across the field and land next to the storage hangar. This way we wouldn't have to pull them across the field in the rain. The response from my RAF friends was, "Bloody good idea, Yank. Let's do it." I was to fly the first glider and an American pilot colleague was to follow in the second one.

As I was strapping into the cockpit, I amusingly noted rain water running off the nose of the RAF launch supervisor as he bent down to connect the cable. I gave him a "thumps up" ready to launch signal, which he relayed to the winch operator. When he was cranking the telephone, I noted that the weather had deteriorated and it was no longer possible to see the winch at the far end of the field and the cloud base appeared more ragged. But I was still convinced that my idea was sound!

The cable became taunt and with a neck-snapping jerk I was airborne. I expected a launch to about three or four hundred feet, at which time I figured the winch operator would relax the cable, allowing me to disconnect and scoot across the field. However, before I knew it, I was in the clouds and the winch operator was still reeling me in like a fish on a line. I pulled the yellow knob in attempting to release the cable, but like my instructor had warned, it was impossible to disconnect against the force of being towed aloft. At around 700 feet (I'm not really sure) I felt the cable tension go slack and assumed it released when I pulled the yellow knob, but it was impossible to see if it fell free in the rain clouds.

I pushed the stick forward to keep from stalling or going into a tailspin and attempted to keep the aircraft right-side-up by a "seat of the pants" theory of flying. The glider was not equipped for instrument flying and I sensed my brain gearing up to transmit strong false vertigo signals which,

116

with no visual contact with the ground, would make it extremely difficult to maintain a wings-level attitude. I felt completely befuddled and helpless, but tried to keep the yaw string attached to the nose centered but it swung wildly from side to side. I knew I was descending as the altimeter was unwinding quite rapidly, and figured I should break out from the base of the clouds soon and hoped that when I did, I would be right-side-up. I popped out of the clouds at around 400 feet in a 90 degree descending left bank. But thanks to the glider's nimble flight control response, I leveled the wings, pulled the nose up to kill off excess airspeed and scooted across the airport and landed on the wet grass next to the storage hangar. (A piece of cake, exactly according to plan!)

As I climbed out of the cockpit, I looked across the field and peering through the fog and rain I could see that my unsuspecting colleague was getting ready to launch for a similar misguided adventure, but I had no way of warning him that what he was about to do wasn't a good idea!

His glider, being pulled aloft by a wet winch operator eager to close up shop for the day, went racing down the runway, entered a steep climb and disappeared into the rain-drenched clouds. I knew he must be struggling to activate the cable release, but wouldn't be able to until the winch operator relaxed the tension. I just stood there in the rain, with my fingers crossed, hoping that he would also pop out beneath the clouds right-side-up and at an altitude that would allow for a safe recovery.

It seemed like a long time before he came diving out of the rain clouds in a tight descending spiral. He righted the glider and came shooting across the field and landed next to where I was standing. Soaking wet, he climbed out of the small cockpit, shook his head and said, "That was a hell of a lousy idea you had, Lou. It nearly got me killed." Then with a smile he added, "But it was a hell of a lot of fun, but once was enough!"

My buddy and I were quite popular in the RAF Officers' Mess that evening, as our British fighter pilot friends enjoyed telling other chaps about our flying their gliders, equipped only for flying in visual flight conditions, in the rain clouds. We joined them in their friendly joshing, as in the comfort of a warm dry bar and drinking a cool beer it was fun reflecting back on our challenging experience. It was certainly the type of adventure that we couldn't have achieved in our cumbersome C-82s.

Because of busy flight schedules and a series of bad weather weekends, I only flew with my RAF glider club friends a few more times before returning to the U.S. However, I look back on my days of flying the famous *Baby Grunau* German glider with fond affection.

Chapter Six --- Fairchild C-119 Flying Boxcar

My first flight in a Fairchild C-119 *Flying Boxcar* was at Donaldson AFB, South Carolina on May 9, 1953. The C-119 was, in many respects, a redesigned and improved version of the C-82, but in reality it was a totally different aircraft. They were similar in appearance but the similarity ended there. The differences were sufficient to require a separate pilot's type rating (license) when operated in the civilian market. A major cosmetic difference was that the cockpit was relocated near the nose of the aircraft, thereby providing more cargo space and improved pilot visibility.

The C-119 Flying Boxcar was equipped with 3,500 hp engines, either Pratt & Whitneys or Wright Cyclones. It had a maximum takeoff weight of 74,000 lbs, a cruising speed of 200 mph, a maximum speed of 290, a range of 1800 miles, a climb rate of 1,000 feet per minute and cost $623,000, (equal to $4,000,000 today). Like the C-82, it retained removable rear "clamshell doors" and was capable of air dropping paratroopers and heavy equipment. The first C-119 prototype flew in 1947 and deliveries to operational squadrons began in December 1949. During its initial four years of service it developed a reputation of experiencing numerous mechanical problems, was difficult to fly, possessed dangerous stall characteristics and experienced a four-fold increase in accidents when compared to other transport aircraft. There were even reports of engines separating in-flight, which were attributed to one or more of the Hamilton Standard propeller blades separating, resulting in engine vibration so severe that it caused the engine to break away from its mounts. To prevent this catastrophic failure, pilots were required to inspect all four blades before flight by running their fingers over every square inch, to inspect for hidden cracks. Another potential problem was that the steel props, to save weight, were hollow and filled with a sponge-like substance which on occasion would become dislodged and slide towards the propeller tip. This deficiency was evident by a bulging at the blade end, requiring that the entire propeller be replaced. In spite of these problems it was a big improvement over the C-82, one being the aircraft heating system. Instead of the exhaust-heat-exchanger-system, *the C-119 was equipped with eight Janitrol gas combustion heaters on top of the fuselage. They were very dependable and delivered an abundance of heat. (See Photos 38 and 39.)*

In spite of these pessimistic reports, I was excited about flying the Fairchild *Boxcar,* thinking that it couldn't be worse than the under-powered C-82s. I had heard rumors that our squadron was planning on junking our C-82s, but like most military prattle you don't put much faith in it until you see the rumor materialize. However, on May 9, 1953, I was told that our operations officer, Captain Ted Bishop, wanted to see me and the other three flight commanders in his office.

When assembled, he told us that we were finally going to receive our long promised C-119s. We welcomed the news, while asking him, "When?" His answer, "Tomorrow," adding, "We have to send four C-119 qualified Aircraft Commanders to Miami, Florida to pickup the first four of our 18 aircraft." Ted said that higher headquarters had informed him that the troop carrier squadron in Miami was being deactivated and we were to receive their complement of aircraft. When we told him that we didn't see how this was possible since none of us were qualified C-119 drivers, he said not to worry as a C-119 flight instructor was flying in that afternoon to check out his four flight commanders. He acknowledged that this may be a bit hurried, but he didn't want to tell higher headquarters that we weren't able to send pilots to Florida, fearing that they may change their mind and we would be stuck with our antiquated C-82s for a while longer.

After lunch a C-119C taxied into our aircraft parking ramp and shut down its engines. I and the other three C-82 flight commanders met the aircraft and greeted the young instructor pilot as he emerged from the cockpit. He introduced himself as the pilot who was directed to check out four pilots in the C-119 but could only devote four hours to the process. He walked us through an extended two-hour exterior and interior Aircraft Preflight Inspection, which he said would suffice for an abbreviated ground school course. We then assembled in the cockpit to launch a two-hour local flight, which would allow each of us 30 minutes of first pilot time and three takeoffs and landings.

I noted that the cockpit was completely different from the C-82 and a tremendous improvement. Our instructor proudly stated that we would like flying the C-119 as it was equipped with smooth-running Pratt and Whitney R-4360 engines, equipped with automatic power control which would deliver 60 inches of manifold pressure and 2,700 rpm under all atmospheric conditions and was a great aircraft for flying formation.

As he positioned himself in the right pilot's seat he said, "Who wants to fly first?" One of my colleagues, who was standing next to the left seat, volunteered. We watched with intense interest his technique in starting the engines, as he was the only one who would be allowed to perform this phase of our checkout. With both engines running he taxied out for takeoff under the supervision of our instructor. The rest of us remained standing in the cockpit while he performed three takeoffs and landings. In turn, we occupied the left pilot's seat for our own series of takeoffs and landings. I was the fourth pilot to fly so I got to taxi the aircraft back to the parking ramp. Our instructor pilot congratulated us on being checked out in the C-119, disregarding the fact that only one of us had been allowed to start the engines, and had flown it for only 30 minutes. Nevertheless, we thanked him for his time and considered ourselves qualified to proceed to Miami, Florida to pick up our new aircraft.

The next morning four neophyte C-119 Aircraft Commanders, along with four copilots and crew chiefs who had never set foot in a C-119, were flown to Miami Airport in one of our tired, old, creaky C-82s. I was designated the Mission Commander so after landing I proceeded to the unit's operations office to coordinate the delivery of the aircraft.

The Miami operations officer, a young-looking major sporting a deep Florida tan, greeted me with a friendly handshake, but left no doubt that he was disappointed that higher headquarters had directed that his unit be deactivated and directed to give up their coveted C-119s. I sympathized with his dilemma, but pointed out that I had nothing to do with the decision and would like to proceed with the aircraft transfer ASAP, as we were faced with a fairly long flight back to South Carolina. (I thought I saw him wipe away a tear as he agreed to cooperate.)

After a detailed inventory of the equipment assigned to each aircraft, I signed a receipt (in triplicate) taking possession of four C-119 *Boxcars*. (Quite a responsibility for a 25-year-old first lieutenant, four years out of pilot training.) When I presented him a copy of the delivery receipt, I asked if he would direct a flight instructor to visit each aircraft and look over our shoulders while we started the engines. He seemed surprised by my request, but when I told him that I and the other three Aircraft Commanders only had 30 minutes of flight time in a C-119, and this was the first flight for our copilots and crew chiefs, he shook his head in an obvious expression of surprise, but agreed to my request.

I filed a flight plan for a formation flight of four aircraft from Miami to Donaldson AFB, South Carolina and our friendly host had us transported to our respective aircraft by military jeeps. With an instructor pilot standing behind me I started the two P & W 4360 engines, with no back fires, and admired the smooth sound of 56 cylinders and 112 spark plugs, all working together like a well-tuned sewing machine. The instructor pilot slapped me on the back, wished me good luck and departed through a rear door. (Other instructor pilots were providing the same supervised engine start for my colleagues in the other three aircraft.) About ten minutes later all four aircraft had their engines idling smoothly and we checked in with each other on a pre-selected radio frequency. I contacted the control tower which cleared our formation for taxi to the active runway. After receiving a "ready-to-go" from each aircraft, we taxied into position and when cleared for takeoff, departed at ten-second intervals.

We formed up in a "Finger Four" formation and did a sight-seeing circle over Miami Beach before departing on a northern course up the east coast of Florida. We leveled off at 8,500 feet in smooth air and settled back for a four-hour flight to South Carolina. Observing golden sunset rays in the western sky, I felt a real sense of exaltation in finally being able to cast aside our wearied old C-82s and intensify my experience in the C-119. This anxiety was heightened by the realization that after arriving back at Donaldson AFB, I would be required to instruct other pilots in the C-119 starting the next day.

My fellow flight commanders shared in my excitement, and our impending responsibilities were evident by the lively chatter on our discrete radio frequency while winging our way north. As the sun sank below the horizon, I turned on the anti-collision, wing and tail navigation, magnetic compass, pedestal and overhead panel lights, with switches or rheostats clearly visible in the cockpit, but I couldn't locate the controls for turning on the cockpit instrument panel lights. As the sky darkened it became more difficult to monitor the flight and engine instruments, yet I still hadn't located the switches or rheostats to turn them on. My copilot and I continued searching the cockpit for the hidden switches we knew had to exist, but drew a blank. When my young crew chief produced a flashlight to assist in illuminating the instrument panel, I felt utterly stupid! Just as I was basking in the achievement of getting all four aircraft safely airborne, I, as the Mission Commander, couldn't locate the switches to turn on the cockpit instrument lights!

As expected, the other three Aircraft Commanders started calling me on the radio and inquiring as to how to turn on the cockpit instrument lights. I was too embarrassed to tell them that I didn't know, so with the aid of my crew chief's flashlight, I started another hunt for the mysterious switches. I loosened my shoulder harness and lap belt so as to have freedom of movement, and when I leaned forward, I found what I was looking for. Hidden from view behind the throttle quadrant, when sitting in a normal upright position in the pilot's seat, were six rheostats and one on-off switch for controlling the instrument panel lights. Actuation of these controls provided either ultra violet or red light at varying intensity.

With the confidence of an experienced Mission Commander, I informed the rest of the flight of the location of the cockpit instrument light controls. They expressed appreciation for the information, while stating that they would have inquired earlier, but felt foolish in asking such a dumb question. I told them not to worry and that anytime they had a question, just ask, because that's why I'm in-charge! After a night-formation landing at Donaldson AFB, I was up early the next morning sharing my vast C-119 experience with my fellow pilots. One of the first things I made sure of was that they knew the location of the cockpit instrument light switches!

A few days later I was informed that I was to join a small cadre of pilots assigned to ferry C-119s to Ashiya Air Base, Japan. The aircraft were needed to support the Korean War, which showed no signs of ending. I, along with several other pilots, were to proceed to McClellan AFB, Sacramento, California, where we would pickup C-119Cs that had undergone overhaul by a depot maintenance facility and ferry them to Japan. Our operations officer said that this would provide an excellent opportunity of increasing our knowledge of the C-119 along with providing an interesting trip to a war zone in the Far East. I packed a B-4 bag and was en route to California two days later.

When I checked in at McClellan, I discovered that I was one of seven Aircraft Commanders assigned to ferry the C-119s to Japan via Hawaii, Johnston, Kwajalein and Guam Island. To provide sufficient range for the over-water flight to Hawaii, temporary 1,000 gallon extended-range rubber fuel tanks were installed in the cargo compartment. However, even with these additional tanks, we would not be allowed to depart with a wind factor in excess of minus 7 knots. According to weather forecasts it would be several days before we could expect winds that would meet this requirement, so we were free of all duties with the exception of checking in with the operations center duty officer each morning.

While enjoying drinks at the Officers' Club bar, I was surprised to see Captain Larry Thalken, a former C-82 colleague from Germany, sitting a few bar stools down from me. Larry and I exchanged warm greetings and after explaining my reason for being in McClellan, he told me that he was a test pilot assigned to the local depot maintenance facility. He was very enthusiastic about his assignment, stating that it was a pilot's dream, as he was checked out in the C-47, T-33, F-84, B-26, C-119 and B-29 to name a few. He said each day he would fly a different type aircraft so his job was never boring. When I told him that I may be stuck in McClellan for several days he invited me to fly with him on some of his flights.

In the next few days I flew with Larry in a T-33 (my first flight in a jet), a dual control B-26 and a B-29 Superfortress, and was surprised when he allowed me to make the takeoff and landing in each aircraft. I was especially thrilled in being able to fly the B-29, as my brother Hank was a tail gunner in the *Superfortress,* and when returning to Saipan from a combat bombing mission over Japan his aircraft ditched in the Pacific Ocean, but fortunately the entire crew was rescued by a Navy destroyer.

I was having a grand time flying and visiting with my former C-82 colleague, and didn't mind the delay in my flight to Japan. I was equally pleased when he invited me to have dinner with he and his wife, and another former C-82 pilot, Captain MacCallum. Mac was stationed at Travis, AFB (about 40 miles away) and flying B-36s. It was great to relive memories of our scary and exciting days of flying in Europe.

My "vacation" at McClellan came to an end, seven days later when I was advised that wind conditions were favorable for the 2,100 mile flight to Hawaii. Five young airmen (two pilots, a navigator, crew chief, and radio operator, all in their early twenties) boarded a C-119C and headed out over the Pacific Ocean. My navigator, who I had never flown with, possessed a good sense of humor and was fun to fly with. His first instructions, after takeoff were: "Japan is 5,217 nautical miles west, wake me up when we get there!" Thirty minutes later we were cruising above the clouds at 10,000 feet with nothing but open water in all directions. I loosened my shoulder harness and seat belt, to make the wearing of a parachute and life preserver more comfortable, while stating, "Just think, only 12 more hours to go." A bright Pacific sun was bathing the cockpit with warm rays, while the smooth hum of the Pratt & Whitney 4360 engines emitted a hypnotic synchronized lullaby. It was difficult to fight off the tendency of grabbing a quick "snooze," but I knew that if I closed my eyes other crew members would follow, so I stayed awake.

Six hours into the flight we had made radio contact with the U.S. Coast Guard Ocean Station November, which confirmed that we were on course, obtained the latest weather, sea conditions and baseball scores, and thanked them for their assistance. About an hour after overflying November, the navigator stood up in the clear plastic astrodome and took a sun shot with his sextant. After plotting his sighting results on his navigation chart he said, "We have passed the point of no return, and are now committed to proceeding to Hawaii, regardless of any unforeseen problems." My response, "No sweat, hand me another cup of coffee."

As he was handing me the coffee the right engine started backfiring, violently shaking the aircraft and spilling hot coffee on my leg. Forgetting the spilt coffee and my burning leg, I shoved the right fuel mixture control to the "full rich" position! The engine backfiring stopped, but the rich fuel mixture dramatically increased the amount of fuel being consumed. To reduce the additional fuel burn, I slowly moved the right engine fuel mixture control toward the lean position, But I was only able to retard it to a position half-way between "full rich" and "auto lean" to keep the engine from belching loud engine rattling backfires. Taking into account the unexpected increase in fuel burn, we re-computed the fuel remaining upon landing at Hawaii and concluded that it would be sufficient, but less than what we had originally planned.

About one hour later the left engine began backfiring and shaking the aircraft worse than the right engine had. I moved the left engine fuel mixture control to the "full rich" position, which stopped the backfiring, but as with the right engine, the fuel burn increased greatly. I moved the mixture control back and forth in attempting to find a compromised position that would keep the engine from backfiring, and minimize fuel consumption. Unfortunately, the position that would allow the engine to run smoothly was a position close to "full rich," resulting in a fuel burn rate much higher than the flight plan predicted.

An updated calculation of fuel remaining upon reaching Hawaii was not good! Based on our present ground speed, and the increased rate of fuel consumption, we would arrive in Honolulu with close to empty fuel tanks. (Not a happy prospect, since we hadn't planned on swimming the last few miles.) We checked our figures several times, but still came up with the same unpleasant conclusion. We discussed diverting to the big island of Hawaii, but a quartering head wind from the southwest eliminated this alternative. We agreed we were committed to continuing on toward Honolulu, and if the head winds increased, we would be faced with the frightening possibility of having to ditch the aircraft in the Pacific Ocean. (This potentiality caused me to reflect on my brother's B-29 ditching, and I thought if he could do it and survive, I could do the same!)

Confronted with this dire prospect, we transmitted an Emergency call to the Honolulu Center on our long-range high frequency radio. This call initiated an air-sea rescue effort that was truly impressive. I was soon in contact with an operations officer in the Coast Guard Rescue Center on Barbers Point who requested details relating to our emergency. I explained our dilemma regarding the engine backfires and an unanticipated increase in fuel burn, while pointing out that we may be forced to ditch in the ocean if we couldn't reach land before our fuel tanks ran dry. He acknowledged my transmission and reported that they were ordering a PBM Martin Mariner amphibian flying boat be placed on standby for assistance if a ditching appeared likely.

The PBM Mariner was a two-engine search and rescue aircraft, capable of landing on land or water, that was used extensively during WW II. It first flew in 1937 and 1,235 were built.

The air-sea rescue center stated that the sea conditions in our area, were favorable for ditching and an open-water landing by their PBM, if this became necessary. (This was welcome news to my apprehensive crew, but ironically, I felt a freakish sense of excitement regarding the unfolding events that may require a ditching at sea and a rescue by an amphibian flying boat. However, I didn't share this idiosyncrasy with others, as I was sure they wouldn't understand.)

As we droned on toward Honolulu, I discussed with my crew the two options that I felt we had: one, we could ditch the aircraft, before the engines failed due to fuel exhaustion, and after being intercepted by a PBM, since ditching with engine power would be preferred over a "dead-stick" (no power) approach; two, we could remain at 10,000 feet and if we ran out of fuel before reaching Hawaii bail out! I suggested that the second option was the best, by pointing out that even if we didn't have sufficient fuel to reach Hickam AFB, we would certainly be very close. And with a PBM standing by to pick us up, our time in the ocean should be at a minimum. We all agreed that the second option was the best and rechecked our life preservers, parachutes and one-man life rafts.

125

After agreeing on a plan of action we all felt better, as living with indecisiveness---especially when in-flight---is very frustrating. Another bit of heartening news came from the navigator. He reported that the head wind had dropped off to almost zero and in re-computing fuel remaining it appeared that we should have sufficient to reach Hawaii.

Nevertheless, to ensure we effectively used every drop, I instructed my crew chief to tilt the rubber long-range fuel tank, in the cargo compartment in the direction of the outlet opening, thereby providing a few extra precious gallons. I then burned each outboard wing tank dry by switching to an inboard tank only after the engine started sputtering for lack of fuel. After burning the last drop of gas from the long-range auxiliary tank and the outboard wing tanks, the engines were drawing fuel from the two (almost empty) inboard fuel tanks during the last few agonizing miles.

We were still flying at 10,000 feet and when in contact with the Honolulu Airport control tower I informed them that we didn't wish to descend until over the airport. They acknowledged my request and cleared us number one for an emergency landing at pilot's discretion. With runway 04 in sight, we started a descending "power-off spiral" in case both engines quit during the descent. I noted that all four fuel gage indicators were bouncing on empty during our descending roundabout approach.

When on a high final to the runway we extended the landing gear and flaps and even though slightly high and fast, I wasn't concerned as the runway was long and wide. Both throttles were still in idle and as we flared for landing I noted that the engines were still running. After braking hard, to make a high-speed turnoff, I pushed the throttles forward to provide taxi power and was pleased to note that both engines responded. We were able to taxi to the parking ramp and figured the engines must be running on fumes, because the fuel gages registered empty.

After shutting down the engines, a friendly Air Force major came to the cockpit, and said, "Welcome to Hawaii." He identified himself as the chief of aircraft maintenance and inquired about the nature of our emergency. I responded to the good major by stating, "The first thing I have to do is take a long pee, and then I'll tell you about our problem." He smiled and said, "Go ahead. I'll wait." When I told him about the engines backfiring, he asked if the aircraft had just been overhauled by the maintenance depot at McClellan AFB. When I told him that it had, he shook his head while stating, "Let me check on a few things before you leave the area for a well-deserved rest." He left the cockpit and I observed him directing mechanics in positioning a maintenance stand next to the right engine.

A few minutes later he had the engine cowling removed and wearing leather gloves was standing on top of a maintenance stand and inspecting the exposed naked hot engine. As we waited for the results of his cursory inspection, he turned around and said, "Lieutenant, come on up here. I want to show you something." Standing next to him on the maintenance stand he demonstrated that it was possible to remove several spark plugs from the last row of cylinders, with nothing more than his gloved hand as they were only finger tight! He asked, "Have you and your crew been in Hawaii before?" When I told him no, he said, "Plan on spending three or four days here lieutenant, while my mechanics go over your aircraft with a fine-tooth comb," adding, "Enjoy your stay. I'll let you know when your aircraft is ready, and be careful. Don't get sunburned as you and your crew look pretty pale."

After obtaining billets at Hickam AFB, we rented a car and for the next several days visited interesting sights on the island of Oahu. One of the highlights was a visit to Pearl Harbor and the sunken wreckage of the battleship *Arizona* which was still leaking oil. Another interesting remnant from the war was the pockmarked buildings on Hickam AFB. These indentations were made by Japanese *Zero* fighters strafing the base on December 7, 1941. The military decided not to fill then in since they would remind visitors of the price we paid for letting our guard down.

We spent our last day on Waikiki Beach surf boarding. None of us had ridden surfboards before and admired those skilled enough to stand up as they rode their bouncing boards toward shore. My copilot and I swore that we were going to learn to stand on a swiftly moving surfboard before calling it a day. The time seemed to fly by and when we finally gave up our backs and shoulders were a deep red. Before we made it back to the hotel we were suffering from the effects of severe sunburns.

As we were applying a soothing lotion on each others backs, a message arrived stating that our aircraft was now in tiptop condition and we could continue our ferry flight to Japan. The message also stated that in addition to the problems discovered on the right engine, mechanics found several spark plugs on the left engine that were also just finger tight and they were sending a detailed deficiency report to the overhaul facility in McClellan AFB to advise them of their dangerous malfeasance.

The P&W 4360 engines on our C-119C had a combined total of 56 cylinders and 112 spark plugs, so taking into consideration that the mechanics at the overhaul facility were government employees, I guess we were fortunate that only a portion of the spark plugs were not properly installed. Had all of them been loose, we would have been forced to swim to Hawaii or flown there in a Martin PBM Mariner.

When we departed Hickam AFB for Johnston Island, my sunburned back was so tender that I couldn't sit upright in the pilot's seat or wear a parachute. However the engines ran like a freshly overhauled "Singer Sewing Machine." We spent the night on Johnston Island and that evening drank a toast to the Hickam AFB chief of maintenance for taking such good care of a bunch of young Air Force transient crew members.

The next day we flew on to the island of Kwajelien, where we remained overnight and enjoyed a steak dinner at the Navy Officers' Club overlooking the pounding surf. The following day we flew to the Island of Guam and the next morning departed for Ashiya Air Base, Japan, the final leg of our trip. Thanks to the fine tuning by the aircraft mechanics in Hawaii, the engines never missed a beat for the remainder of the flight. When we turned the aircraft over to the Troop Carrier Wing in Japan, we could honestly inform them that they were receiving a good aircraft.

Our orders stated that after delivering the aircraft to Ashiya, we were to proceed to Haneda Air Base, Tokyo for transportation back to the U.S. I asked the base operations officer at Ashiya, how long we could remain in Japan. His answer, "That's up to you, lieutenant. Just let me know when you and your crew would like seats on a courier flight to Tokyo." Since this was our first visit to Japan, we decided to spend four days exploring the Kyushu area and were eager to see what the Japanese had to offer in the form of relaxation and mementos worth taking home.

Ashiya Air Base was an exciting military post in the spring of 1953. The Korean war was still raging and a wartime atmosphere was evident everywhere we looked. The aircraft parking ramp was loaded with C-119s, C-47s, C-54s, C-46s and a few F-84s, F-80s, T-6s and battle-weary looking F-51s. Military personnel of every description were busily coming and going on foot and in various types of vehicles. The Officers' Club dining room and bar, in order to accommodate a 24/7 schedule, never closed, and the industrious ground activity was interspersed with the sound of fighters and transports taking off or landing at all hours. The Officers' Club bar presented a reflective image of WW II military clubs in England, as crew members from several allied countries were elbowing their way to the front for a drink, while swapping combat stories and downing generous amounts of booze. Other crew members were gathered around a slightly inebriated lieutenant, banging out familiar wartime ballads like, *"Throw a nickel on the grass, save a fighter pilot's ass, oh hallelula,"* on a liquor-stained upright piano. Those crowding around him were singing their lungs out, while keeping time with swaying hands clutching drinks. Each rhythmical arm swing would spill a portion of their drink on adjacent revelers or the floor but nobody seemed to care. It was truly exciting to be a part of this carefree Korean War ambiance!

The city of Ashiya was equally exciting and openly displayed the result of thousands of combat servicemen, seeking escape from the burden of war, and possessing the money to delight in this escape like there was no tomorrow. I eagerly threw myself into this jovial lifestyle with the fervor expected of a 25-year-old Air Force pilot 7,000 miles from home.

There were blocks of gaudy cabarets competing for the GI trade by supplying a bevy of young Japanese o-josans (young girls) eager to provide a drink, dance, or in some cases, sexual favors. My impression was that the city was a sensual flea-market, ready to fulfill sexual fantasies at a modest price. There was also a wide variety of restaurants, serving both western and oriental specialties, and countless gift shops selling everything from bamboo fishing poles to unattractive, hastily-drawn oil paintings. All of these pleasures or trinkets were available at a fraction of the cost of what I would have to pay in the U.S. for similar trivialities.

Most of these business establishments were within walking distance of the base, but muscular young Japanese men pulling rickshaws were available for a small fee. One evening my copilot, navigator and I were on our way into town in three separate rickshaws when we noted that the Japanese men pulling them seemed to be competing with each other to be at the head of the line. Observing this, I came up with a brilliant idea! After arriving at our downtown destination, we talked our rickshaw pullers (through sign language) into engaging in a race around the block, with a prize of 1,000 yen to the winner. They eagerly agreed to participate, so we had them line up, three abreast, and standby for my signal to "Go!"

Interest in the race drew a crowd of Japanese civilians and GIs who gathered to observe and cheer on their favorite rickshaw. (Before I gave the order to "Go," I observed them placing bets on who would win.)

I called out, "Ichi, ni, san, Ikimasho," (one, two, three, go) and we were off and running. Three rickshaws, spurred on by the cheers of an enthusiastic audience shouting in both English and Japanese raced down the street. Running neck and neck, we raced around the first corner so fast that I thought my rickshaw was going to tip over. (I think it would have if I hadn't shifted my weight to the inside of the turn.) Coming around the back stretch my puller was running well ahead, and to ensure he maintained his speed around the next corner, I leaned completely out side of the carriage to keep it upright. As we headed into the home stretch, I heard a loud crash behind me and noted that my navigator's rickshaw had tipped over when careening around the last turn. With my trusty Japanese puller running at full speed it was obvious that I would win the race. As we crossed the finish line cheers went up from the crowd and my good-natured Japanese rickshaw puller was smiling from ear to ear, displaying a beautiful set of gold teeth. I was so pleased in his performance that I gave him 2,000 yen (equal to $18.00 today). We gave the other two rickshaw pullers 1,000 yen each for running a good race even though they didn't win. Everyone seemed pleased with the outcome.

I was fascinated by the rickshaws since I had only seen them in movies. In 1953 they were still popular in Southern Japan but had been removed from the streets of Tokyo and other major cities. Rickshaw in Japanese, is spelled "Jinrikisha" which means "Human powered vehicle."

Following our exciting rickshaw race, we visited one of the more elaborate cabarets to enjoy a few beers and dance with some of their young attractive Japanese hostesses. I was impressed with the upscale decorum, a small orchestra (sometimes in tune) was playing Glenn Miller favorites and a bevy of young attractive o-josans were eager to dance or share in a drink. My eye caught an attractive young o-josan apparently not engaged with another customer emerging from a back room. She was dressed in a tight-fitting bright red silk dress, which accentuated her young feminine figure and exposed a tantalizing portion of her long legs through a six-inch open slit on each side of her skirt.

I hurried to intercept her before some other eager American beat me to the punch. (After winning the rickshaw race, I thought I might win in this arena as well.) When I introduced myself, I was pleased to learn that she spoke some English and willingly accepted my offer of buying her a drink. I ordered a beer for myself and a whiskey and Coke for her. As we became more acquainted she told me that her name was Kimiko, that she was 19-years-old, attended a local college and worked in the club part-time to help pay for her education and support her o-tasan (father) who was wounded during the war. As she ordered another drink she advised me that I would be charged 1,000 yen per hour ($20.00 today) for her company, as well as having to buy her an overpriced drink every 30 minutes. However, she added, "Dancing was free and part of the hostess' rental fee." "It would be a good deal at twice the price," was my response!

Dancing close and inhaling the sweet smell of her unfamiliar exotic perfume stimulated my young masculine senses and sent chills up my back. She was an excellent dancer in both slow and jitterbugging which I hadn't enjoyed since high school. Back at the table Kimiko ordered another drink and when I expressed concern about the amount of liquor she was consuming she smiled, while whispering in my ear that what I was paying for was nothing more than straight Coke, with just a couple drops of whiskey on top, to give it the smell of a mixed drink.

We seemed to be enjoying each other's company, so I asked her if I could take her home. She let me know straight out that she was not a call girl, but if I wanted to take her home it would be possible under certain conditions: first, I would have to pay my bar bill, (which I'm sure was several thousand yen); second, I would have to pay the club owner 5,000 yen, to release her from working the remainder of her schedule; third, if I would like her willing cooperation in bodily pleasures, I would have to pay her an additional 5,000 yen, ($100 today). Being a big-spending Air Force pilot, I said, "Let's go!" (Before departing the cabaret, I was required to pony up 9,000 yen, $183 today, but this was no problem for a 25-year-old Air Force pilot under the enchantment of wartime fever.)

We hailed a passing two man rickshaw and following her directions a young muscular puller began a trot toward an unknown destination. I asked Kimiko where we were headed and she said to her house, which she shared with her o-tosan (father). I asked about her mother and she sadly replied that when she was ten-years-old, her o-kasan, while working in a factory, was killed by American bombers. She added that her father was in the Japanese Army at the time and after her mother was killed she lived with an aunt until he returned from the war. I sensed that recalling her war time suffering seemed to intensify the effects of the cool night air, and to offset it, she snuggled up next to me. This closeness started my testosterone juices flowing and making me wish I had a buggy whip to use in getting my rickshaw runner to "motto hayaku" (Go faster).

After about a 30-minute run we were outside of town and traveling on a narrow dirt path with the lights of the city fading off in the distance. Rice paddies glistened in the bright moonlight, which seemed to enhance the mystical sound of chirping crickets, croaking frogs and the flip-flopping of the runner's rubber sandals. The rickshaw came to a stop next to a small cottage and my young Nippon o-josan said, "Here we are." I gave my rickshaw puller 500 yen ($9.00 today), which he accepted with a polite nod and an "arigato gozaimasu" (thank you) and trotted off toward town while singing a Japanese ballad in beat with his flip-flopping sandals.

In a near whisper Kimiko said, "Follow me." We walked across a narrow wooden bridge spanning a section of a rice paddy which led to the entrance of a small bungalow with thin, sliding paper doors and a foot-thick roof made from pads of dried rice stalks. When Kimiko slid the door open, I noted that the interior was illuminated by small peanut-size light bulbs and that I could hear someone snoring in one of the rooms. She said the snoring was coming from her o-tosan sleeping in the next room, but that he was a sound sleeper and would not hear us. Slipping off our shoes we entered a small but neat room with a floor covering of fresh-smelling tatami mats (carpets made from tightly woven rice stalks). In the center of the room was a colorful futon (a padded bed similar to a sleeping bag) spread out on the floor.

I was eager to launch into some form of preliminary foreplay, but before I could make a pass she said, "We will now take an atsui o-furo" (hot bath). She handed me a yukata (bathrobe) and said that while I was getting undressed she would prepare the o-furo and exited the room through a sliding door in the rear of the house. After slipping off my clothes and donning the yukata, I followed her outside where my excitement and curiosity, rose at about the same rapid rate. Soaking in a large wooden steaming tub, with just her head showing, was Kimiko. The tub was heated by a metal firebox, still containing glowing live coals left-over by her o-tosan. She told me that before joining her in the tub I must first wash my body using a small wooden baketsu (bucket) and a washcloth. I turned my back, slipped off the yukata, and sat down on a small wooden stool where I washed my aroused body. After rinsing off, I slid into the tub next to her!

As I settled down into the hot water she began scrubbing my back with a rough sponge. The experience was total ecstasy! Here I was, soaking in a warm outdoor tub, overlooking Japanese rice paddies illuminated by a full moon, and having my back scrubbed by a beautiful 19-year-old female Japanese college student. When we first arrived at her house I was eager to get on with my goal of satisfying my sensuous desires, but I now appreciated her insisting we take a hot bath first and letting the passion build while at the same time relaxing tired muscles.

By the time we left the o-furo, I was an excellent candidate for a Viagra commercial, which was somewhat embarrassing, but the subdued light, and the anticipation of what was soon to follow, didn't allow self-consciousness to deter me from my primary mission. We settled down in her fluffy futon and my youthful desire for sensual gratification was realized with a vivaciousness that I hadn't experienced in the past. Momentarily satisfied I laid down next to her, and with an arm resting gently across her body dozed off into blissful slumber.

I awoke some time later and was able to enjoy the company of my date again before exhaustion and the effects of heavy drinking caused me to snooze a second time. When I awoke it was 4 a.m. and my equally exhausted partner was snuggled up in her warm futon sleeping like a kitten. I was so enthralled by her beauty and peaceful innocent slumber that I didn't wish to disturb her. I quietly got dressed, slid open the sliding door to the street, and departed with a whispered "arigato gozaimasu."

Standing in the dirt road, I hesitated a few minutes to empty my bladder and absorb the beauty of the countryside, while giving thanks to the world for being a healthy contented, 25-year-old American Air Force pilot. The sky was bristling with blinking and shooting stars, a setting full moon had turned the flooded rice paddies into flickering silver streaks, the crickets were still singing their nighttime song of life, and the lights from the city of Ashiya were casting a faint glow in the distant horizon. I knew there wouldn't be a rickshaw available to transport me back to town, but figured if a Japanese, pulling two people in a buggy, could make the trip on foot, I could certainly do the same. I knew the approximate direction to town and scanning the skyline spotted the rotating "Green, Double White," flashing beacon from the Air Base. With a buoyant bounce in my step, I allowed the beacon to set my course and 30 minutes later was displaying my military ID to an Air Force MP guarding the main gate. As I settled down in an uncomfortable cold steel BOQ cot, I was already missing my Japanese college student, and wondered if the whole evening had been just one beautiful alcohol-induced fantasy, but when I checked my almost empty wallet I knew with a smile that it really happened.

The next night my navigator, copilot and I visited the same cabaret for an Ashiya farewell party, since we were leaving the next morning on a military charter flight for Tokyo. I scanned the club for my pretty Japanese college student, hoping I may have another opportunity of contributing to her college fund, but didn't see her. I bought a drink for one of the other hostesses and inquired if Kimiko was working this night. She said that she wasn't as this was her day off. I asked her if she knew where she lived but she didn't, and of course there was no way that I could direct a rickshaw runner to take me to her house. I thought of helping out another attractive young Japanese o-josan, but I was afraid it would destroy the wonderful image Kimiko had created, so we just had a few drinks, bought a few for some pretty young hostesses, and headed back to the air base to get ready for our flight to Tokyo.

The next morning we boarded a C-46 military charter flight for Haneda Airport with an en route stop in Osaka. When I checked in with the Military Air Transport duty officer in Tokyo to arrange for a flight back to the U.S., he said, "When would you and your crew like to depart, lieutenant?" I asked him if we had a choice. "The departure date is up to you," he responded. Since this was our first visit to Tokyo, I said, "How about in four days?" "No problem. I'll make flight reservations accordingly. See you in four days," he said. With that we rode a military bus to downtown Tokyo and secured billets. My copilot, navigator and I obtained rooms in the *Sanno Hotel* (a senior officer's facility). I was surprised that we were able to obtain rooms in the *Sanno*, but since we were on official travel orders in support of the war, we were given priority over officers on a three-day pass or leave from Korea. My crew chief and radio operator obtained rooms in a nearby enlisted men's hotel.

The Sanno Hotel was a former Japanese senior officer's facility built by the Imperial Army during the 1930s and Japanese officers considered it a prestigious honor to be able to stay there. When Japan surrendered, in August 1945, several despondent senior Japanese generals committed "Hara-Kiri" in the hotel's lobby. Fortunately they installed new carpets since those dark days. The hotel operated a five-star restaurant and a fabulous piano bar, both of which were available at reasonable prices. A popular feature of the Sanno was the continuation of a policy initiated by former Japanese officers. A room could be rented for only two or three hours (day or night) for the entertaining of female guests with no questions asked. The hotel was closed in October 1983 and replaced by a New Sanno Hotel that provides modern facilities for military personnel but lacks the charm of the original and doesn't rent rooms by the hour.

(Hara-Kiri is suicide committed in accordance with the "Bushido Code," which dictates the cutting open of the stomach with a sharp knife, followed by an assistant severing the victim's head with a Samurai sword. Consequently the need to change the carpets.)

For the next four days we toured Tokyo by taxi and on foot and noted that much of the city still reflected the scars of war but was making huge strides toward recovery. The large infusion of capital in support of the Korean War was very beneficial to Japan's economic recovery.

When our short Tokyo vacation ended, we boarded a PAA DC-7 for a return flight to the U.S. We made en route stops at Wake Island, Honolulu, San Francisco and Dallas Ft. Worth, Texas before arriving back at Greenville, South Carolina 30 hours later. Our C-119 ferry flight to Japan, which took 30 days to complete, was history. I was naturally happy to be home, but found myself enthralled with Japan and its people, and hoped my military adventures would take me back there in the future.

At the time I didn't realize the extent Japan would play in my future life, but eight years later I would spend three years at Misawa Air Base, fly as a captain for Japan Domestic Airlines for five years, and meet and later marry Chieko Hara, who was a Japanese senior JDA flight attendant. The cross-roads of life certainly have a strange way of affecting the future!

After returning to South Carolina I was saddened to learn of the PGR's success in recruiting five new candidates from my former organization in Germany on May 15, 1953. Subsequent to my returning to the U.S., the 60th TCW retired their C-82s and were now flying C-119s. Eighteen of them were circling south of Rhein Main Air Base, Germany at 5,000 feet in preparation for a flyby honoring the retirement of an Army general. Twelve F-84 jet fighters from the 36th Fighter-Bomber Wing at Bitburg Air Base, also participating in the flyby, were directed to orbit at 9,000 feet (four thousand feet above the C-119s). However, the F-84 formation leader, apparently unaware of the C-119s and confronted with low clouds, informed his flight that they would also orbit the area at 5,000 feet.

Flying on a head-on flight path, the fighters flew directly into the formation of C-119s. When the F-84 formation leader spotted the C-119s, he called for an immediate break, but one F-84 smashed head-on into the C-119 formation leader, clipping off his right wing. It then caromed off and smashed into a second C-119! The first C-119, minus a wing, spun to the ground and crashed in flames. Miraculously, two enlisted crew members were able to escape by parachute, but both pilots, including Lt.Col. John W. Osborn, my former group operations officer, were killed!

When the F-84 smashed into the second C-119, the resulting explosion ignited the jet pilot's ejection seat and he escaped with minor injuries.

However both pilots of the second C-119 were also killed. Two enlisted crew members, finding themselves floating in space, deployed their parachutes, but one of them had lost both legs above the knee and died from injuries in a German hospital! I had personally flown with Lt.Col. Osborn and was acquainted with the other crew members. A pilot friend, who had been flying further back in the formation, stated that he observed two fiery explosions, followed by bits and pieces of aircraft debris flying past his and other aircraft! One large chunk of a UHF radio smashed into the front of his aircraft making it very difficult for him to land!

After a few days off, I was once again instructing new pilots in flying the C-119 at Fort Bragg, North Carolina, in both single and formation flights while dropping paratroopers and heavy equipment, and flying airlift support missions for jet fighter units. One such mission was supporting an F-86F unit in deploying from George AFB, California to McCord AFB, Washington State. The F-86s were conducting a joint Army/Air Force combat exercise, culminating in a realistic "Firepower Demonstration," involving both ground and air units. I was told that after arriving at McCord, I was free from all duties until a return flight to George AFB, three days later, and I and my crew would be provided VIP seats for the thrilling military exercise. Expecting to be off duty for several days, my copilot and I joined several fighter pilots in visiting local clubs for drinks and a few laughs, returning to our BOQ rooms around midnight.

However, to my disappointment there was a note attached to my door advising me that we were to fly to George AFB the following morning to pickup a spare J-47 jet engine, which would result in our missing the "Firepower Demonstration." Not wishing to miss this joint Army/Air Force exercise, we woke up our crew chief, drank several cups of strong coffee, chewed several sticks of Dentyne gum (to mask the smell of alcohol) and departed for George AFB around 1 a.m. Two hours later we were shutting down our engines on a very dark ramp at Geroge Air Base, and told the base operations duty officer to wake up a loading crew to load a J-47 engine in our aircraft. After pissing off a few sleepy aerial port personnel, we were back in the air two hours later and landed back at McCord AFB at 7 a.m. After a shower and a big breakfast we were in our VIP seats enjoying the airshow at 9 a.m. while fighting to stay awake.

My cargo load for the return flight to George AFB was a J-47 jet engine, a liquid oxygen cart and about ten aircraft mechanics, culminating in a computed takeoff weight of 74,000 lbs. The taxi and takeoff, with the exception of a long ground roll, was normal. After retracting the landing gear and flaps, I allowed the aircraft to accelerate to 145 knots and initiated an en route climb. I was adjusting the throttles and propeller RPMs when my crew chief called my attention to the rapidly-rising oil temperatures. I positioned the engine oil cooler exit flap switches from auto to open, but the oil temperatures continued to rise precipitously. I declared an emergency and was cleared for an immediate landing. Before I completed a 180 degree turn the oil temperature gages, for both engines, were registering dangerously high and a few minutes later exceeded allowable limits. Reducing power and opening the engine cowl flaps did nothing to lower the ominously high oil temperatures. I was concerned that the extreme temperatures may cause the oil to boil, which would deprive the engines of proper lubrication and cooling, and inflict internal damage.

I set up a high altitude, minimum power traffic pattern, and when stopped on the runway, shutdown both engines. There was no smoke or fire so I dismissed the fire trucks that had followed us down the runway during the landing roll out. I then called for a tug to tow us to the maintenance ramp.

During the slow tow to the ramp, I conducted a crew "skull session" in attempting to determine why the oil temperatures rose so rapidly on both engines and did not respond when the controlling switches were placed in the open position. In the midst of our discussion, I scanned the overhead circuit breaker panel and was shocked when I discovered the circuit breaker for the engine oil cooler doors "popped" (open). The discovery surprised us all, as it seemed remote that both oil cooling doors would simultaneously fail and cause an overload condition.

I pushed the circuit breaker in, turned on the ships battery, and it remained in. I then positioned the oil cooler door switches back and forth from closed, open, and auto and the circuit breaker remained in. I concluded that, for some unknown reason, the circuit breaker was open when we departed and I had missed recognizing this potential problem during the Before Start Engines Check.

When parked the base maintenance officer came to the cockpit and requested the reason we had returned and what type of maintenance support I required. I told him that apparently I had screwed up and departed with the oil cooler temperature control circuit breaker open. With a shake of his head he said, "What do we do now, lieutenant?" I told him that the oil temperatures had been so high that I was sure the oil was no longer useable and we would need an oil change on both engines! Still shaking his head he said, "How much oil does each engine require lieutenant?" His head shook for the third time when I told him, "60 gallons each." About one hour later we departed with 120 gallons of new oil, the oil cooling door circuit breaker double checked in, and flew a normal flight (albeit behind schedule) to George AFB.

In July 1953, Captain Ted Bishop, the operations officer, requested that I select a copilot for a C-119 ferry flight to Rhein Main AB, Germany. This was considered a plush assignment, and in keeping with my goal of distributing desirable assignments, I selected Lt. Sam Eppley.

The next day, Lt. Bill Hanson(N), also a member of my flight, requested that he be assigned the trip in lieu of Sam. Bill told me that he was to be released from active duty in two months and would be returning to civilian life to work with his widowed mother. He said that his mother never approved of his being an Air Force pilot and after the untimely death of his father, pressured him to give up flying and return home. Reluctantly, he acquiesced in her wishes and would soon be discharged. However, since he had never been to Europe, he requested that he be assigned the ferry flight to Germany. I told Bill, that if it was OK with Sam, it was OK with me. There was no objection from Lt. Eppley, so Bill left on the flight to Germany a week later.

According to the accident report, the C-119 flight from Dover AFB, Delaware to Bermuda and the Azores Islands was routine, However, when it was passing over Paris, France, ground witnesses observed the aircraft going into uncontrolled erratic maneuvers, followed by an in-flight breakup. The resulting crash killed all five crew members! Post-crash investigation disclosed that as the aircraft passed over Paris at 9,000 feet in clear skies, the navigator went to the rear of the cargo compartment, opened a paratrooper door, and began taking pictures. Sometime later he attempted to close the door and when he did it separated from the aircraft and wrapped around the horizontal stabilizer. This caused the aircraft to go into uncontrolled maneuvers and exposed it to such high stress loads that it experienced an in-flight breakup!

Accident investigators, inspecting the wreckage, discovered the rear paratrooper door still wrapped around the separated horizontal stabilizer. And when the film from the navigator's camera was developed it clearly showed aerial pictures of Paris along with fringes of the open paratrooper door. It was determined that when the navigator attempted to close it at an indicated airspeed of around 175 knots, it was sucked out and struck the horizontal stabilizer. The paratrooper door was not normally opened in-flight at speeds greater than 130 knots. The navigator should have known this, but apparently ignored the danger, and the PGR recruited five more candidates. The irony of this accident was not only the untimely loss of Lt. Bill Hanson, who was to be discharged in a few weeks, but the Aircraft Commander was recently married to a girl who had lost two other Air Force pilot husbands killed in aircraft accidents. She was a beautiful gal, but I believe she would have a hard time in convincing a fourth pilot to join her in exchanging wedding vows!

One Friday afternoon in August 1953, I and several other pilots were preparing to head for the Officers' Club for the customary Friday night beer call. As I was about to head out the door, the operations officer told me to grab a copilot and perform a functional test flight on one of our C-119s. He said that the aircraft had just completed some minor maintenance and all that was needed was a short trip around the pattern to declare it in commission, so just a 15-minute flight would satisfy the test flight requirements and still allow us time to attend Friday's beer call.

Since it was to be a short flight my copilot and I didn't go to the trouble of checking out parachutes and oxygen masks, which we normally carried on test flights. But when we arrived at the aircraft, I noted that my young crew chief had a parachute and oxygen mask slung over his shoulder. I jokingly chided him by stating, "If we have to bailout sergeant it will be a little crowded with all three of us using the same parachute!"

The start-engine and taxi out for takeoff were routine, with the exception of the outside temperatures being in the high 90s, so we kept the sliding cockpit windows open until starting the takeoff roll. Soon after becoming airborne, I thought I smelled unfamiliar odors and before reaching 500 feet, clouds of smoke began flowing from the cargo compartment into the cockpit. The crew chief, with a fire extinguisher in hand and wearing his oxygen mask, plugged into a portable oxygen bottle, headed for the cargo compartment. He soon returned, stating that the area was so thick with smoke that it was hard for him to see and he couldn't pinpoint the source of the fire. Consequently he hadn't been able to use the fire extinguisher. (In our haste to perform a quick test flight, and not miss Friday night's beer call, my copilot and I not only didn't have parachutes, but more importantly we didn't have oxygen masks, which were essential in preventing smoke inhalation.)

I declared an emergency and started a full power climbing turn at 140 knots to a downwind leg. At the same time I ordered the raising of the landing gear and flaps and the opening of the cockpit windows and rear paratrooper doors. (I was hoping this action would help dissipate some of the smoke entering the cockpit.) However, when the landing gear lever was positioned to the up position the gear remained down. When the flap handle was placed in the up position, the flaps---like the gear---did not move. I checked the gear and flap circuit breakers, but found them both in. With the temperatures in the 90s and unable to raise the landing gear and flaps, the cylinder head temperature on both engines began to rapidly rise to dangerous levels. Realizing that the engine cooling cowl flaps, like the landing gear and flaps, require electrical power for operation, I didn't think attempts to open them would be successful, which was exactly the case, as they remained in a half-closed position.

Flying a 500 feet downwind leg, with smoke burning my eyes and without an oxygen mask, normal breathing was becoming difficult. The landing gear and flaps --- being extended --- were producing considerable drag and with the engine cooling cowl flaps inoperative, the engines were starting to overheat, with no way of cooling them off. As I prepared to turn onto a low altitude, close-in base leg, both cylinder head temperature gages were off scale high and the engines began to vibrate from internal detonation. Turning onto a low final approach at just above the tree tops the engines were shaking like a belly dancer. (Thoughts went through my mind of reports of C-119 engines separating in-flight, but I knew this couldn't happen to me, especially on a Friday night. However, I did say a quick prayer that the aircraft would reach the runway in one piece.)

On short final, I voiced a weak joke to my crew stating, "At least we don't have to worry about lowering the gear and flaps." The touchdown was smooth and I applied full reverse thrust and hard anti-skid braking. When the aircraft stopped rolling, I shut down the engines and ordered an immediate evacuation of the aircraft to a welcoming committee of fire fighting and rescue personnel. Fire fighters, wearing protective face masks, entered the aircraft and since there was no visible flames opened the rear "clam-shell" doors allowing the smoke to dissipate at a faster rate.

About 15 minutes later, the cargo compartment was free of smoke so I entered it to see if I could determine the source of the electrical fire. I noted that the aluminum cover on the main electrical power junction box was smudged from apparent smoke. When the cover was removed, the burnt remnants of a large metal flashlight tumbled out. Apparently, an errant mechanic had failed to remove his flashlight after working on electrical problems and the acceleration forces, during the takeoff, caused it to short out the power source to critical systems.

By the time I reached the Officers' Club most of the free snacks were gone and most of my squadron mates had left for home. However, I did have time to drink a defiant toast to the PGR, stating that he had lost another round and I was beginning to learn his devious ways of acquiring new recruits, so he shouldn't count on me joining him anytime soon.

In August 1953, Captain Harry Luke, a former colleague from Germany and now a headquarters staff member at Donaldson AFB, called to give me a heads-up on a request he had just received from the Pentagon. Washington was requesting C-119 pilots be sent to Germany to replace rotating pilots from the 317th Troop Carrier Wing.

The 317th was a former Ohio Air Reserve unit that had been activated during the Korean War, supplied with new C-119s, and relocated to Rhein Main Air Base, Germany in the summer of 1951. The unit was later transferred to Neubiberg Air Base near Munich and would be needing pilots to replace those completing an overseas tour. I was excited with the prospect of returning to Germany, but especially ecstatic at the possibility of spending three years in Munich, close to the famous Alp Mountain ski resorts, and a relatively short drive --- through the Brenner pass --- to Italy. I told Harry to put my name on top of the volunteer list.

A couple weeks later, I and about 20 other pilots received orders transferring us to Germany. The orders did not specify a base of assignment, but I assumed it would be Neubiberg since they would be losing pilots to stateside rotation. The only other base in Germany operating C-119s was Rhein Main, but it didn't appear that they were faced with a pilot shortage and I had already served a three-year tour there, so I was anxiously looking forward to a tour in Southern Germany.

In mid October 1953, I presented my military travel orders to the Air Force representative at Camp Kilmer New Jersey. He, in turn, would coordinate my movement to Germany by troop ship, or more likely, since I was traveling unaccompanied, by Military Air Transport Command C-54s from Westover AFB, Massachusetts. I pointed out to him that my orders didn't specify a base of assignment in Germany, but assumed it would be Munich. He agreed, since that is where the need for C-119 pilots was most critical. Also, since I had already served three years in Rhein Main, it would be contrary to Air Force policy to send me there again, as it would result in six years out of seven at one base. However, to guarantee my choice of assignment was clear to headquarters personnel in Germany, he recommended that I write a letter outlining my desires and situation, which he would attach to my military record's file that would be air mailed to Germany in the next couple of days. I followed his recommendation and my hand-written letter was attached to my personnel file. I felt very confident that my next assignment would be Munich, not Frankfurt.

About one week later, I and about 20 other C-119 pilots were onboard a MATS C-54 heading for Rhein Main, Air Base Germany with a refueling stop in the Azores. When we arrived in Germany we were assigned rooms in a military hotel in downtown Frankfurt and instructed to check the bulletin board in the Army/Air Force personnel office for information relating to our base of assignment orders, which should be available in two or three days.

It was great to be back in Germany and since I had spent three years in the Frankfurt area, I became the unofficial guide in showing my new colleagues how to have a good time in Deutschland. A couple days later one of the pilots came into the hotel dining room, where a group of us were eating breakfast, stating, "Our base of assignment has been made and is posted on the bulletin board." I quickly finished my breakfast and joined the procession hurrying to learn of where I would be assigned, which I was sure would be Neubiberg Air Base in Munich.

To my surprise, every pilot --- except one --- was being assigned to Neubiberg. The one exception was a first lieutenant by the name of Martin who was being assigned to Rhein Main! I was not only shocked, but highly pissed-off, since I was the only one who had indicated an assignment preference, and was the only one who had served a previous three-year tour in Germany. The note following the list of names stated that travel orders were ready for pickup from our Air Force representative.

Several of my colleagues noted my disappointment and inquired as to what I was going to do in regards to my posted assignment. I responded by stating, "The first thing I'm going to do is not pick up my orders. The second thing I'm going to do is take a train to Wiesbaden to visit the Air Force Headquarters at Camp Lindsey to get my orders changed!" My former copilot, Arthur Calloway, asked if he could accompany me, even though his orders were for Neubiberg. I asked him why and he replied that he thought he might learn something!

Following a 30-minute train ride and a 10-minute trip by taxi, we were standing at the front entrance to a large former German Luftwaffe building, which housed the Headquarters of the U.S. Air Forces in Europe (USAFE). I told the sergeant at the front desk that I wished to see the chief of personnel on a matter of extreme importance. When he asked me what it was about, I said that it was personal, but very important. A few minutes later we were escorted into a plush office, where a full colonel, with a chest full of ribbons, was sitting behind a large oak desk. We saluted smartly and he said, "At ease, lieutenant. Have a seat and tell me about your problem." After telling him the full story, including my session with the Air Force officer in New Jersey, including my letter that was attached to my military records and forwarded to Germany, he expressed sympathy and said, "Just make yourself comfortable, lieutenant, while I make a phone call."

I could only hear one side of his phone conversation, but after discussing golf scores with an apparent colleague, he said, "I have a young C-119 pilot by the name of Lieutenant Louis Martin in my office who has just arrived from the U.S. and there is a mistake in his base of assignment. His orders have him assigned to Rhein Main, but they should read Neubiberg, along with a large group of C-119 pilots he shipped with." He closed out his telephone conversion with, "Thanks, Hank. I'll see you on the links this weekend." The colonel told me to return to Frankfurt, where I would be able to pickup revised orders assigning me to Neubiberg, as the orders assigning me to Rhein Main were being canceled. He asked about my friend Calloway, who up to this point had said nothing. I told him he was OK, as his orders were for Neubiberg and now, thanks to his help, we would be able to continue the friendship we had enjoyed when flying together in the states. We saluted and were out of his office in about 15 minutes. After a 30-minute train ride and a short walk, I was back in the hotel in time for happy hour.

The next morning, bright and early, I went to the military personnel office to pick up my orders. When the sergeant handed me orders assigning me to Rhein Main, I handed them back stating, "These orders are in error, sergeant. My next base of assignment is Neubiberg, not Rhein Main." He seemed surprised in my comment and inquired as to why I considered them in error. When I told him of my visit to USAFE Headquarters, and that the chief of personnel had directed that I receive new orders, he displayed a surprised look and disappeared into a side office. A few minutes later a non-rated (no aircrew wings on his chest) captain appeared and commenced to reprimand me for going to Wiesbaden to complain about my assignment. After he had his condescending say, I politely requested that he check with USAFE Headquarters to confirm that my orders had been revised. Still maintaining his sharp tone he said, "I already have, lieutenant and new orders are being prepared as we speak, but you were way "out-of-line" in going to higher headquarters to complain about your assignment without talking to me first." I apologized for any embarrassment I may have caused him, followed by, "When will I be able to pick up my new orders?" He said, "Come back in 30 minutes."

When reporting for duty with the 317th TCW at Neubiberg AB, I was informed that I would be assigned to the 40th Troop Carrier Squadron, and was warmly welcomed by the operations officer, Major William E. Barnett. The squadron commander, Lt.Col. Evan R. Bruner, was on annual leave. When Major Barnett learned that I had served three years as a C-82 pilot at Rhein Main and had flown C-119s in the U.S., his welcome was very enthusiastic and stated that he would have me flying the line as an Aircraft Commander in no time at all. (See Photo No. 25.)

I was pleased that I had fought hard to be stationed at Neubiberg, as it was readily apparent why it was a choice assignment for Luftwaffe fighter pilots and had suffered little damage during the war. After the war it was occupied by the 86th Fighter Bomber Wing flying F-47s, and later F-84s, but in 1952 it had been reallocated to Landstuhl Air Base, west of the Rhine River. After the fighters left, the 317th Troop Carrier Wing, with 54 C-119s, was relocated from Rhein Main to Neubiberg in March 1953. They shared the base with the 5th Tow Target Squadron flying B-26s. It was a great area to be assigned and lived up to my expectations.

In less than 30 days I was checked out as an Aircraft Commander, and it was great to once again be flying to destinations throughout Europe. In 1953 NATO had been in operation for four years and the 317th TCW was charged with the primary mission of supporting their airlift needs, another reason to be pleased with the assignment.

A typical NATO support flight was a night courier mission to Bordeaux, France and Burtonwood Air Base in Manchester, England. Departure time from Neubiberg was around 9 p.m., Bordeaux, around 1 a.m., with an arrival in Manchester around 3 a.m. The flight from Bordeaux would overfly the cities of Paris and London and under good weather conditions, provided thrilling nighttime scenes. After a 12-hour crew rest, the flight back to Neubiberg would be a reverse of the inbound route.

The flight from Neubiberg to Bordeaux was routine, and I decided to let my copilot fly the leg to Manchestor from the left seat. We were overflying the city of Paris at 9,000 feet when I commented on how interesting it was, that even though we were in the clouds and heavy rain, the lights of Paris caused the clouds to glow, almost white, and turned the rain droplets into sparkling diamonds. The light show phenomenon was even more spectacular when I turned on the bright landing lights. We were enjoying this innocent diversion when suddenly, without warning, the propeller on the right engine raced into an over speed condition with a screaming rise to around 3,000 rpm! If the problem was not immediately corrected the propeller may spin off from the engine shaft and slice through the fuselage, like a freshly honed spinning scythe.

I quickly disengaged the autopilot, went to full power on the left engine, retarded the right engine throttle to idle, positioned the right propeller switch to its low rpm stop and placed the right engine fuel mixture control to cutoff. I then attempted to position the propeller blades into a featherd (minimum drag), streamlined position. However, repeated attempts in feathering the propeller were unsuccessful, and we were faced with four large propeller blades stuck in a "flat-pitch-high-drag-position." To offset the sharp yaw and tremendous drag from the defective propeller, I pushed hard on the left rudder pedal, while realizing that we would not be able to maintain our assigned altitude of 9,000 feet.

I instructed the copilot to take over the controls, initiate a 180 degree turn to the right (a left turn would have been more difficult) and maintain 9,000 feet until the airspeed decreased to 140 knots (minimum safe single engine speed), and then allow the aircraft to descend, at whatever sink rate it takes, to maintain 140. I declared an emergency with Paris Air Traffic control and requested a lower altitude and radar vectors to Orly Airport (a joint French/U.S. Military base that I was familiar with and had flown into in the past). However, my call was not answered! After several more attempts, a sleepy-voiced French controller, who spoke very little English, answered. When he finally understood my request he cleared us to descend to 5,000 feet, but was unable to provide radar vectors, as their radar was not operating! But he did clear us to fly a direct course to the Orly Airport's low frequency radio beacon. When I asked him for the latest weather at Orly, he said it wasn't available, but thought it should be suitable for landing.

I attempted to tune in the Orly radio beacon, but due to heavy precipitation static, the radio homing needle just swung in aimless circles. My copilot was doing a good job of holding the bucking aircraft at 140 knots, but when we approached 5,000 feet, we were still descending at about 300 feet per minute. It was obvious that we would have to continue our descent to a lower altitude before we would be able to maintain level flight. My crew chief asked if he should start throwing smaller pieces of cargo out the rear of the aircraft to lighten the load, but I told him that this was not an option, pointing out the bright glow from the clouds indicating we were flying over the city of Paris. I informed the "half-French, half-English" speaking air traffic controller that I could not maintain 5,000 feet and requested a lower altitude. In an excited, difficult-to-understand voice he cleared us to 4,000 feet, but no lower. But by the time he had cleared us to 4,000 feet we had already passed through it, and were still descending at 100 feet per minute while maintaining 140 knots.

Approaching 3,000 feet, we were still flying in heavy rain, unable to receive the Orly radio beacon and still in a slight descent. To add to the problem, our left legs were beginning to ache from the strain we were putting on them in correcting the severe yaw to the right. I was also concerned about the possibility of crashing into the Eiffel Tower, since I knew that it was more than 1,000 feet high, and Paris was a little over 400 feet above sea level. (The thought ran through my mind that smashing into the Eiffel tower would certainly cause an international incident, and wouldn't make me very happy either.) With these facts spinning through my mind the crew chief wanted to know if he should bring three parachutes to the cockpit. I told him this wasn't an option for the same reason that we couldn't throw out cargo to lighten the load. (I knew that the crew chief was just trying to help, as it must have been hell for him to just sit there unable to do anything but watch his two pilots fighting to keep the aircraft airborne.)

Upon reaching 2,500 feet we were able to level off while maintaining a bucking airspeed of 140 knots. However, the radio beacon needle was still doing circles so I wasn't sure of our exact position. However, from the bright glow of the clouds, I knew we were still somewhere over Paris. It was still raining, but I was starting to observe breaks in the clouds and at times, could even see lights on the ground.

Suddenly, we were flying in a clear area between clouds and off to my right I spotted a lighted airport runway, which I assumed to be Orly

146

Airport. I told the copilot that I had control of the aircraft and put it into a tight diving spiral to the right. I ordered the landing gear and flaps extended (even though a little too fast) and started to reduce power on the left engine. Without forewarning, the differential drag we had been fighting suddenly disappeared, and I noticed that the right propeller had gone into a (low drag) feathered position. (I thought, well, it was about time things started working out in our favor.)

My landing on the wet runway was smooth, but a little fast, and as I turned onto a blue-lighted high-speed taxiway, I told the copilot to switch the radio to Orly Tower. Repeated attempts to contact Orly were unsuccessful, so I just followed the blue taxiway lights to the airport terminal. Approaching the terminal, the reason we couldn't contact Orly Tower became surprisingly and embarrassingly clear! We had landed at **Le Bourget Airport,** not Orly, which was about 20 miles further south.

It was around 3 a.m. when we parked the aircraft, unassisted, and walked to the airport terminal and surprised a night watchman. Through a combination of sign language and broken English, we were finally able to persuade him to call a taxi which took us to a nearby hotel.

However, my crew rest was very short, as around 8 a.m. there was a loud knock on my door and an English-speaking hotel clerk said that I was to report to the manager of Le Bourget Airport ASAP. When I arrived at his office, he was quite upset and said that I had really screwed up when I landed at his airport the night before without contacting the control tower. According to him, I caused an Air France DC-4 to execute a missed approach. I apologized for screwing up Air France, but pointed to my aircraft sitting on the ramp with its right propeller in a feathered position. He responded that he was also a pilot, and since the propeller was feathered, I should have been able to land at Orly. I thanked him for his concern, but said that the reason for landing at his airport would be covered in the written report he requested me to write. With that he left me alone, while stating, "I'll look forward to reading your report and will withhold any further comments until I do." When he read my report, everything was forgiven, and he couldn't have been more helpful. He even expressed a little humor by stating, "I don't think the Air France captain has a complaint, because as far as I'm concerned they need practice in executing go-arounds." Three days later a new propeller was installed, and as I departed Le Bourget Airport I thought of Charles

Lindbergh's night landing there 27 years earlier. (I am sure he experienced a more amicable welcoming than I did!)

My flying throughout Europe during my second tour in Germany was more expansive and interesting than during my first three years. This was due partly to the fact that the C-119 was a more versatile aircraft than the C-82, and the overall airlift support for NATO was more demanding. One NATO support mission I really enjoyed was dropping English paratroopers from Royal Air Force bases in England.

A typical mission was one in which I led three C-119s to an air base in Northern England near New Castle. We arrived on a Monday and were scheduled to drop British paratroopers from a reserve Army unit on Tuesday, Wednesday and Thursday, returning to Germany on Friday. However, on Tuesday, the air base and nearby drop zone were fogged in, making flying impossible. The same weather conditions existed on Wednesday and the forecast for Thursday was no better. We hadn't turned a prop since arriving but did drink a fair amount of scotch at the Officers' Mess and improved our 301 dart throwing skills.

On Wednesday evening the British Army colonel in charge of the reserve paratroopers, bought me a drink and inquired about the chances of flying the next day. When I told him that it didn't look good he was very disappointed, stating, "I have 120 reserve paratroopers who must make at least one jump or they won't be paid, is there anything you can do?" I told him, "All we can do, colonel, is to hope for better weather, but you can rest assured that if there is anyway I can fly your troops I'll do it, as we don't enjoy sitting on the ground." He thanked me for my concern, so we dropped the subject and played a game of darts for a drink, which I naturally lost. (It was almost impossible to beat the Brits at darts.)

The weather conditions the next morning were 500 foot overcast, 2 miles visibility in fog and forecasted to remain so for the remainder of the day. As expected, the British Army colonel, with a group of junior officers backing him up, was soon breathing down my neck wanting to know if we could fly. I reluctantly told him no, because with a 500 foot overcast we would be in the clouds when I climbed up to the minimum drop altitude of 1,000 feet. The colonel responded with, "Captain, my men and I are willing to try anything. We just need one jump." I mentioned that I had operated out of his base several times in the past and was very familiar with the large flat area just a few miles south of the airport that was used as their drop zone. (Confident that there were no hidden radio towers or obstacles in the vicinity, and that a light wind was blowing toward the shore, I concluded that I could probably drop all 120 English paratroopers safely if they would agree to jump from my aircraft when I was in the clouds.)

I told the British Army colonel of my plan. His response, "Jolly good show, Yank. Let's give-it-a-bit-of-a-go." I loaded the colonel and 40 paratroopers in my aircraft and went skimming down the coast at about 400 feet. When I located the drop zone I slowed to 130 knots (standard speed for dropping paratroopers). I then flew inland for three minutes to ensure I was over the center of the drop zone, reversed course and flew back toward the coast. Upon reaching the coast I flew out to sea for three minutes and executed a climbing 180 degree turn, leveling off at 1,000 feet and 130 knots. After flying this reverse course for six minutes, I instructed my copilot to turn on the green jump light which was the signal for the colonel (only) to exit the aircraft.

In accordance with a prearranged plan the colonel was to jump by himself first, and if he landed successfully on the drop zone, he would advise me by radio. Based on his satisfactory report, I would then drop the remainder of his troops.

About three minutes after the colonel had jumped through the clouds, he called me on the radio, stating; "Bloody good show, yank. I landed smack-dab in the middle of the drop zone," adding, "This was my first jump in the clouds and it was a smashing good experience. You can start kicking my chaps out in the same manner." Before the day was over, I flew three flights and dropped all 120 English paratroopers. They all landed in the middle of the drop zone, in spite of the fact that they exited the aircraft when in the clouds. By the time I finished my last flight, the first group was already back at the base and waiting for my return. When I emerged from my C-119 *Boxcar* they carried me on their shoulders like a "conquering hero" to the Officers' Mess where I was celebrated with rousing cheers and free drinks. If I had the stomach for it, I could have drowned myself in free drinks.

The next day we flew back to Germany and I forgot all about my challenging experience with the British paratroopers. About three weeks later I was told that our Wing Commander, Colonel Joseph Cunningham, wanted to see me in his office. After reporting Col. Cunningham handed me a letter from the British Army and wanted to know if it was true.

The letter was a commendation from a British Army general complimenting me for exemplary service above and beyond the call of duty. The letter continued by explaining how I had air dropped 120 English paratroopers, through the clouds, thereby increasing their combat readiness, and ensuring they received their reserve jump pay.

I sensed that Colonel Cunningham was somewhat confused and upset over the letter, so before he could launch into an "ass-chewing session," I thought I would beat him to the punch. Returning the letter to his desk, I said, "That's a nice letter, colonel, but I don't think a commendation was warranted. I didn't do anything that you wouldn't have done, faced with the same set of circumstances. My concern was to assist our British NATO allies in accomplishing their war-time mission, and do it safely. My intent was to carry out the goal of the 317th TCW by overcoming all obstacles in getting the job done." Colonel Cunningham dismissed me, with a weak compliment, while stating that he didn't wish to make the commendation public, as it might give other pilots the wrong idea. He added that if I promised not to pull such a stunt in the future, the subject was closed. (I agreed to his request and as I presented a smart departure salute, I thought I saw him wink, but I couldn't be sure. Perhaps it was just something in his eye.)

On a cold clear morning in February 1954, I departed Burtonwood Air Base, Manchester, England on a flight to Neubiberg Air Base. The flight path would take me over London, the White Cliffs of Dover, Brussels and Frankfurt. After leveling at 9,000 feet, I engaged the auto pilot and sat back to enjoy the rarity of viewing London, void of fog, rain or clouds. However, upon reaching the southern section of the city the aircraft, without warning, began shaking violently and began oscillating up and down. The elevator flutter was so intense that I had difficulty in keeping my hands on the control column or reading the engine instruments.

Thoughts ran through my mind, regarding the C-119 from my squadron, in Greenville, South Carolina that experienced an in-flight breakup over Paris less than a year ago, and I wondered if I would end up in a similar situation, but I didn't think I had time to dwell on this possibility.

Instinctively realizing that reducing airspeed should decrease the violent flutter, I pulled back on the shaking control column and reduced power on both engines. As the airspeed decreased, the vibrations abated at a corresponding rate. When the airspeed reached 120 knots, the shaking disappeared completely. I instructed my crew chief to bring up three parachutes from the cargo compartment which we quickly donned. I declared an emergency with London Center and informed them that I was diverting to the RAF fighter base at Manston.

With the security provided by a relatively high altitude of 9,000 feet, and parachutes tightly strapped on, I decided to engage in some experimentation to test the flight capabilities of my wounded aircraft. When I allowed the airspeed to rise above 120 knots, the vibrations reoccurred, but when I slowed back to 120 knots, they stopped. As I set up a slow descent toward Manston Air Base, I directed my crew chief to perform a visual inspection of the aircraft to see if he could observe any irregularities, but when he returned to the cockpit he reported that everything appeared normal. I leveled off at 5,000 feet, with the intent of extending the landing gear and flaps to see if the aircraft was flyable in a landing configuration while we were still over open country and high enough to bail out, if things didn't work out.

With the landing gear and flaps extended and maintaining 120 knots, the aircraft remained stable, so I was confident I could safely land, in spite of the unknown mechanical problem. The landing was uneventful and I dismissed the fire trucks that followed us down the runway. After a normal engine shutdown, I performed an external inspection to see if I could determine the reason for the in-flight vibrations. To my surprise, the cause was quickly discovered!

The elevator trim tab is permanently connected to a moveable push-rod by a bolt and self-locking nut. The bolt and nut were missing, which allowed the trim tab to flutter "uninhibited" up and down. This pulsating movement caused the entire elevator to flutter, which in turn, caused the aircraft to "tap dance" through the sky. The higher the airspeed the greater the dance, but stopped when I slowed to 120 knots!

The bolt had either sheared, or the nut had not been properly torqued, allowing it to come loose. We obtained a new bolt and a maintenance stand from the RAF and had the aircraft back in commission about 30 minutes later. After returning to Neubiberg I wrote a detailed report about my in-flight flutter incident, with a recommendation that the bolt used in connecting the push rod to the trim tab be inspected for proper strength, and that all C-119 pilots be briefed on my in-flight incident. I stressed that if they encountered a similar problem, slowing the aircraft to 120 knots would most likely stop the severe vibrations.

Ironically, a C-119 crew from Rhein Main, Air Base experienced a similar failure a month later, but the pilot did not slow the aircraft and as the severe vibrations continued, he ordered his crew to bail out. The four crew members all survived, but examination of the accident disclosed a missing bolt from the elevator trim tab and a copy of my incident report, and recommended corrective action, were not provided to the pilot. (I think the PGR had a hand in this oversight.) Final corrective action to eliminate this problem was the istallation of a modified bolt on all aircraft.

After living in the Munich area for a year it was easy to see why this Southern Bavarian City was so popular with the Germans and also a favorite with American military personnel. Wiesbaden could rightfully boast of the finest Rod and Gun Club in occupied Germany, but no military installation could match Munich's downtown Officers' Club. In 1933 Hitler ordered that a large Neoclassical style building be built to display modern and abstract art, enclose a theater, a concert hall and room for holding political and industrial conventions. The building occupied an entire city block on Prinregentenstrasse and was faced with a long row of tall white columns, similar to buildings in the old Roman Forum. The *Hau der Kunst* (House of Art) was opened with much fanfare in 1937 by Adolph Hitler. When General Patton's Army marched into Munich in 1945, they requisitioned it and converted it into an Officers' Club. It was the place to be on Saturday nights and reservations were a must, as the food was exceptional along with a first-rate floor show.

A popular live vaudeville act playing the military club circuits at the time was the Great Anthony Marlo, a very entertaining hypnotist. He would hypnotize volunteers from the audience and direct that they perform like kindergarten kids, bark like dogs, crow like roosters, etc. Since the volunteers were friends and colleagues we knew that their bizarre behavior was not faked. Hypnotism, as a stage act, was made popular by the interest in a young Irish girl, who under hypnosis, reportedly regressed to a past life 200 years earlier. The story was made famous by the book, *The Search for Bridey Murphy.* I became a casual friend of Anthony Marlo and took up hypnotism as a hobby. I read many books on the subject and began hypnotizing friends at house parties. I was having great fun in this seemingly harmless whimsicalness hobby until one night when I hypnotized my C-119 colleague, Captain Billy Prim. When under hypnosis I had his arms outstretched like steel rods and was sticking pins into his fingers until his wife Doris became uneasy and told me to bring him out of his hypnotized state. I went through the standard procedure, that hadn't failed me in the past, but I couldn't bring Billy out of his state of hypnosis. I became very concerned and was almost ready to call for professional help when he suddenly snapped out of it, although a little groggy. I gave up my ill-advised hobby about the same time it disappeared as a stage act out of fear of law suits (When Billy was told later that he experienced difficulty in recovering he wasn't concerned.)

In the summer of 1954 I was selected to perform the duties of a C-119 pilot examiner under the direction of Capt. Joseph Bessler, the 317th TCW Standardization Director. Each of the three squadrons were required to designate four experienced instructor pilots to administer annual proficiency and upgrade checks to pilots other than their own squadron. At first I thought that this procedure inferred that we would not be objective if we administered flight checks to fellow squadron pilots. But I soon realized that this was the right approach, as it was much easier to fail a pilot, or send him back for more training, if I didn't fly with him on a regular basis. The duties of a flight examiner included administering formation qualification checks, both day and night, and air dropping of paratroopers and heavy equipment. With these extra duties I was flying about 60 to 70 hours a month and, as they say, "having a ball."

A good example of this good life was demonstrated in August 1954, when I was the mission commander for three C-119s on an airlift support mission to an RAF base in Northern England. We were to spend several days with our English colleagues in introducing them to the marvels of the Fairchild *Boxcar*. As in the past, crew members assigned to this trip carried cans of Spam, slabs of salami, boxes of crackers, soft drinks and dozens of small candles. The snacks would be used to ward off hunger pains in between meals at the RAF Officers' Mess, as the English cooked the hell out of everything, and the candles would be burned in our BOQ rooms to raise the temperature a few degrees and help dry the cold damp air. (It was amazing what a few burning candles could do.)

The base visited on this trip, in addition to accommodating a reserve paratrooper unit, also accommodated a RAF *Gloster Meteor* jet fighter squadron, which I enjoyed watching fly and became friendly with several of the pilots operating them.

The Gloster Meteor was the RAF's first operational jet fighter and became operational in 1944. It flew combat missions during WW II, but never in aerial combat against German ME-262 jet fighters. However, it did see combat during the Korean War and proved to be a very effective ground attack aircraft, but with limited range. It had a wing span of 34 ft., a length of 40 ft., max. weight of 15,666 lbs., max. speed of 600 mph and powered by two Rolls Royce Derwenti engines of 3,894 pounds thrust.

During one of my non-flying periods, I visited the Gloster *Meteor* squadron and asked the operations officer if it would be possible for me to take a flight in one of their two-place fighters. He was very obliging and thought it would be no problem. He called over a young flight officer who was about to fly a tow-target mission for a flight of *Vampires* and said I was welcome to go with him. He then accompanied me to their personal equipment room, where I was fitted for a parachute, hard hat and oxygen mask. During our short walk to the aircraft he briefed me on our flight, pointing out that the *Meteor* was not pressurized, nor did it have ejection seats, so if we had to bail out he would roll the aircraft inverted, jettison the canopy and we should push away from the aircraft with our legs. He also said that once we lined up on the runway he would let me make the takeoff and talk me through the landing at the end of the mission. He estimated we would be airborne about two hours.

I found the back seat quite roomy, but with limited forward visibility. The two large engines imbedded in each wing gave the impression of speed just sitting on the ground. Starting the engines was smooth and simple and we were soon lined up on the runway. My friendly Brit fighter jock said, "You have it, Yank. Push the power levers to the hilt and let her fly off." The acceleration was exhilarating and after becoming airborne we made a pass over the airfield to snatch the colored tow target. With the target in tow he instructed me to climb to 20,000 feet and level off. He then cleared the *Vampire* fighters to commence their live firing passes. It was exciting to watch them attack our towed target, while observing the muzzle flashes from their 20-mm cannons. If I placed my helmet against the canopy I could hear the "rat-a-tat-tat" from their guns. After about 45 minutes we felt the aircraft "lurch" and one of the *Vampire* fighter pilots reported that a cannon round had severed the cable to the target.

My RAF colleague said that we still had about one hour of fuel remaining so we might as well have some fun. He talked me through aileron rolls, loops, Cuban eights, high speed dives and high G pull outs. He seemed pleased with my flying which made me feel good when he said. "You should be a fighter pilot, Yank." I did note that at high speeds the flight controls became very stiff and brute force was needed to yank and bank at these speeds. When our fuel state was such that it was time to head back to base we were at 40,000 feet. My pilot said, "Watch your ears," and rolled the aircraft inverted into a high speed dive. With my ears popping we made a pass down the runway doing 500 mph. We pulled up into a chandelle topping out at 10,000 feet. He then talked me through a touch-and-go landing followed by a full stop. I was on cloud nine when we walked back to the operations building. His response, when I thanked him for the flight was, "Jolly good show, Yank. I enjoyed flying with you."

When turning in my parachute and helmet my RAF friend asked, "What else can we do to make your visit with us more enjoyable?" I pointed to two DeHavilland 82 *Tiger Moths* sitting outside and said that I would sure enjoy getting a flight in one of them. He didn't think that would be a problem and said, "Come with me." He stuck his head into the doorway of the pilot's ready room and called out, "Any of you chaps planning on flying the *Tiger Moths*?" Hearing nothing, he turned to me and said, "No problem, Yank. Help yourself." I asked him if he or another RAF pilot was going to fly with me. "Bloody hell" he said, "You're a pilot. Just go fly it." Surprised by his answer, but not wishing to pass up a chance of flying a different type of aircraft, I strolled over to the nearest *Tiger Moth* sitting idle on the ramp and obviously waiting for someone to fly it.

The De Havilland Tiger Moth was developed in the early 1930s as the basic pilot trainer for the RAF. It was not an easy airplane to master and therefore enabled instructors to identify and correct novice pilot weaknesses early, or eliminate them from the program before expending a lot of time on students who would not be able to complete the program. (This characteristic was shared with the American PT-17 which served the same purpose.) This open-cockpit biplane was used by many countries prior to the outbreak of WW II and 8,700 various models were built. The later versions had a 145 hp engine, a max. takeoff weight of 1,825 lbs., a wing span of 29 ft., a max. speed of 160 mph., a cruising speed of 90 mph., a ceiling of 14,600 ft. and a range of 275 miles. (See Photo No. 77.)

I found a RAF mechanic lounging near one of the *Tiger Moths* and told him that I was given permission to fly it. His response, "Yes sir, how can I help?" I told him that I understand that it has no brakes and no starter, is that correct? "Right you are sir, anything else?" "Yes," I replied. "Just give me a few minutes to look over the airplane, and when I'm ready I would appreciate you cranking the prop for me." The walk-around inspection was nothing more than seeing that the wings were attached and there was a prop connected to the engine crankshaft. I sat down in the cockpit and the nose high attitude and old airplane smell brought back fond memories of flying Piper *Cubs* and Taylorcrafts.

I was soon ready and called, "Switch on, contact," to the RAF mechanic. The engine caught on the first pull and I taxied out to the active runway, made an engine run-up and wiggled my ailerons toward the control tower (the aircraft had no radio). The tower gave me a green light and I was soon airborne. Other than having to use left rudder on takeoff to offset the torque in the opposite direction from American aircraft, it flew like any other light plane. I enjoyed the open cockpit sensation and flew around boring holes in the sky for about an hour. I returned to the airport, received a green light for a landing and made several "touch-and-goes" before returning the aircraft, intact, to the ramp. I poked my head into the pilot's ready room, and told the group of RAF pilots, shooting darts, thanks. They responded with, "Tally hoe, Yank. Thanks for helping out with our paratroopers."

There had been rumors that our C-119Cs would be transferred to the Italian Air Force and reserve units back in the U.S., and in October 1954, this rumor became a reality when we were directed to send a group of flight crew members to Frankfurt for airlift back to the states to pick up new C-119Gs from the Fairchild Factory in Hagerstown, Maryland.

Before departing Germany we were briefed on the differences between the C-119s we had been flying and the new G. Model. The most conspicuous change was that they were equipped with Wright R-3350 Cyclone, turbo-compound 18 cylinder engines, instead of the smooth running, 28 cylinder, P & W 4360s. The reason for the engine conversion was that Pratt & Whitney engines were in high demand since they were being used on C-124s, B-36s, KB-50s and KC-97s, to name a few. And there were not enough being produced to hang on new C-119s, which had a lower military priority.

The Wright R-3350 Cyclone engines were unique in that they were equipped with three power recovery turbines (PRTs), driven by engine exhaust gas and connected by fluid couplings to the main engine crankshaft. This innovative arrangement increased the power output by 600 hp. The engine was also equipped with a Water-Methanol Anti-Detonant Injection System to boost takeoff power. These modifications were on an engine that produced less than 2,000 hp when used on B-29s, but would now develop 3,500 hp, quite an improvement.

The G. Model was also equipped with an Aeroproducts four-bladed propeller, instead of the Hamilton Standard model used on previous C-119s. (This eliminated the problem of cracks, bulging tips and blade separation, but presented another potential catastrophic problem which will be discussed later.) Two other prominent modifications were an updated high-frequency, long-range radio, which eliminated the need for carrying a radio operator for sending position reports by a telegraph key in Morse Code, and a cockpit emergency escape hatch for use in bailout.

The last modification noted was the installation of two vertical stabilizer extensions, mounted underneath the ends of each tail boom. They were added to enhance directional control in the event of an engine failure, especially during takeoff, however they presented some unanticipated problems. (See Photos 38 and 39.)

We discovered that these hollow stabilizer extensions would sometimes fill with water and if the bottom drain holes were clogged, the trapped water could freeze. If this occurred, it could seriously affect weight and balance by shifting the center of Gravity (CG), toward the rear of the aircraft. This shifting of the CG could increase the danger of a stall, especially when slowing to 130 knots when dropping paratroopers, who, when preparing to jump, also shifted the CG aft by bunching-up in the rear of the cargo compartment. The ice problem was eliminated when ensuring that the drain holes were open became an item on the mechanic's and pilot's exterior preflight inspection. However, the weight shifting by bunching-up paratroopers was something we had to live with.

Unfortunately, these stabilizer extensions did not markedly improve the inherent instability of the C-119 in the event of an engine failure shortly after takeoff. The normal rotation (liftoff) speed of the C-119 was 125 knots. However the "safe-single-engine-airspeed" (SSES) was 140 knots. The standard pilot technique, after becoming airborne, was to accelerate *to above SSES as quickly as possible, because if an engine failed below this speed, at heavy weights, it was necessary to reduce power on the operating engine to avoid an uncontrollable roll and an unmanageable crash. This is exactly what happened to two good friends of mine, Dutch Kemerling and Bob McNeal, in separate accidents, who experienced an engine failure soon after becoming airborne and crashed with everyone onboard killed. The elapsed time between liftoff and accelerating to 140 knots was brief, but always a period of anxiety. If an engine was approximating internal failure, it would most likely occur during takeoff, as the engine would be operating at maximum power.*

Following our differences briefing, I was looking forward to picking up a new aircraft right from the factory, an experience I had not enjoyed in the past. On Monday, November 8, 1954, I arrived at the Fairchild Factory in Hagerstown, Maryland to pickup my new $650,000 aircraft (equal to $4,731,928 today), and after signing a receipt the factory Air Force representative said the aircraft was all mine. Brushing off our shoes, my crew and I entered our new C-119G, which had strips of paper spread out on the cargo and cockpit floors and smelled like a new car! I went through a little different, but similar Start Engine Check List, and had the Wright Cyclone 3350 engines up and running with no back fires. The engines produced a "sports car" like sound, which I attributed to the exhaust being muffled when passing though the three power recovery turbines. We flew a one-hour local acceptance test hop and landed without any maintenance squawks to report. I was now ready to depart for Germany in my taxpayers-provided new airplane!

On Tuesday, November 9, 1954, I made a one-hour flight to Dover AFB, Delaware, where I received my overseas briefing. Several C-119 crews were assembled for this Military Air Transport Service (MATS) orientation and Aircraft Commanders were given the option of crossing the Atlantic with refueling stops in Bermuda, or the U.S. Navy station in Argentia, Newfoundland, before proceeding on to Lajes Airport, in the Azores. Lt. Arthur (Cab) Callaway (flying a separate aircraft) and I chose Newfoundland, while the remainder of the crews elected to go through Bermuda. On November 10th, we departed Dover AFB for Argentia, landing seven hours later. My aircraft ran beautifully the entire flight and was just what you would expect from a new five million dollar aircraft.

The next morning, November 11th, we visited the U.S. Navy base operations center to file a flight plan for the Azores. However the operations officer told us that we were not allowed to depart until released by MATS headquarters. He showed us a message which stated that our aircraft were not equipped with high frequency (HF) radios that would allow for voice transmissions, and since we were not carrying radio operators we wouldn't be able to transmit position reports by Morse Code when flying the North Atlantic. I tried to explain to him that both aircraft were new C-119G models, equipped with updated HF radios that could dial in any and all frequencies listed in the radio spectrum, transmit by voice, and therefore we didn't need radio operators. However, my comments fell on deaf ears as he remained adamant that his orders were clear, and he wouldn't allow us to takeoff until released by MATS Headquarters. He suggested we return to the BOQ and he would advise us as soon as he received further guidance.

Five days later we had propositioned most of the U.S. Navy nurses, drank up a good share of the liquor in the Officers' Club bar and still hadn't received permission to depart Argentia, a bastion of ice, snow and bitter cold winds. Not wishing to make a career out of sitting idle in Newfoundland, I figured it would be necessary to resort to some Air Force ingenuity to secure a release from our screwed-up, higher headquarters directed imprisonment. So I visited the local Military Affiliate Radio System Station (MARS) and made friends with the Navy volunteer manning it.

MARS is a department of defense sponsored program which consists of licensed amateur radio operators interested in assisting weak or out-of-service official military communications. They provide World-Wide auxiliary communications and are still used to some extent today.

I asked the MARS operator, "What's your favorite drink? "Johnnie Walker Black Label Scotch," was his response. Fifteen minutes later I returned with two bottles of Black Label and presented them to him as a gift from two Air Force C-119 Aircraft Commanders, in recognition for all the assistance their stations have provided in the past. He acknowledged the gift of booze by stating, "Thanks for the scotch, lieutenant. Is there some way I can repay you and your colleague for your generosity?" "I'm glad you asked," I said. I showed him a copy of the message from MATS, restricting us from proceeding on to the Azores. I stressed that it was a typical military snafu (situation normal all f - - d up), since our aircraft were equipped with radios fully capable of maintaining voice communications when crossing the Atlantic Ocean, plus that we had heard that the C-119s that had gone through Bermuda were not delayed and were already in Germany. (Being a radio expert, he quickly grasped our predicament.) He repeated his previous statement by asking how he could help. I said, "I would like to ask you a hypothetical question." "Go ahead," was his reply. "If you received a phone message from MATS Headquarters stating that the C-119s being held at Argentia possessed proper HF radios and should be allowed to proceed to the Azores, would you type the message up on official military stationary and deliver it to the base operations officer?" "Of course, that's my job," he said. I thanked him for his candid response and said he could expect a phone call from MATS Headquarters in the U.S. shortly.

I proceeded to the Officers' Club, called my scotch-drinking friend at the local MARS Radio Station, and told him, "I was a staff officer from MATS Headquarters in the U.S., and requested he inform the base operations officer that the two C-119s he was holding were authorized to depart for the Azores, as they were equipped with HF radios that were capable of providing proper communications when crossing the Atlantic Ocean." He acknowledged receipt, while stating that the message would be typed and delivered right away. One hour later the Navy operations officer called, stating that he had some good news! He said that he had just received a message from MATS Headquarters, authorizing us to depart his station!

The next day, still nurturing a hangover, we departed Argentia and seven hours later landed at Lages Airport. If I hadn't made friends with the MARS radio operator, I think we could have spent our entire military careers in Newfoundland. But in retrospect, I think the Navy nurses would have had our small Air Force contingent kicked out long before we reached 20 years of service.

On November 17th, we departed the Azores for the longest leg of our ferry flight to Neubiberg, Germany (11 hours). The flight over the Eastern Atlantic Ocean was above the clouds and in smooth air, and by the time we reached the Coast of France the sun was setting and it was great to see lights on the ground versus the emptiness of the ocean. When overland we removed our life preservers and settled down for an airways flight to Neubiberg which we hadn't seen for almost a month. When approaching the French/German border I heard the telltale audible sound of a propeller failing to stay in synchronization. Checking the engine tachometers, I noted that the right propeller was about 100 rpm higher than the left prop, so I retarded the right prop control lever slightly, bringing the propellers back into synchronization. But a couple minutes later the right propeller rpm started increasing again. I retarded the prop control a bit more and repeated this procedure several times until I had the right prop control lever all the way back against its low stop. However, this had no effect in reducing the orratic rpm, which was now indicating a worrisome, and nauseating 3,000, (500 higher than the left propeller). I considered placing the prop control lever into the feathered "low drag" position, but this would result in shutting down the engine and require that we land at the nearest suitable airport. I discussed the problem with my crew and we all agreed that we wished to get home, so I retarded the right engine throttle some, which seemed to stabilize the uncontrolled rise in the rpm to around 2,900 (about 200 above allowable limits). We maintained our altitude of 9,000 feet for more than two hours, while enduring the nerve racking sound of propellers wildly out of synchronization, and the right prop control lever <u>back against its low stop position,</u> a full four times the width of the control shaft.

The significance, and danger, of continuing flight with such a large displacement of the ineffective propeller control shaft will be revealed later. But at the time, I was ignorant of the danger I was exposing myself and my crew to, especially since we were not wearing parachutes. I didn't realize that the PGR was breathing down my neck for the entire two and one half hours it took us to reach our destination.

After landing at Neubiberg the only squawk (discrepancy) I entered in the aircraft maintenance log book was the right propeller problem. I added that the aircraft had been flown only 24 hours since new, and the problem should be corrected without taxpayers incurring additional expense. The aircraft maintenance officer, who debriefed me after landing, stated that this was not the first reported deficiency with the Aeroproducts propellers, and the Air Force was looking into the problem.

Following a few days off, I was instructing other pilots in the C-119G while the majority of our old C models were being transferred to the Italian Air Force. I enjoyed flying the G model, but quickly noted that we had to use caution when operating the Turbo-Compound Wright Cyclone engines in formation. Low altitude and low airspeed formation flying requires frequent fore and aft throttle movements to offset the effects of air turbulence, wing tip vortices and prop wash from other aircraft. When flying in formation with the P & W 4360 engines we didn't have to worry about over boosting, as they were equipped with automatic power control

(APC), which limited engine power by automatically adjusting for temperature and pressure altitude. (A pilot caught in turbulence could push the throttles of the 4360 engine full forward without fear of over-stressing the engine.) However, the Wright 3350 engine was not equipped with APC and on cold days it was possible to reach maximum designed power limits with several inches of forward throttle movement remaining. Pushing the throttles full forward under these conditions would easily "over-boost" the engine! (There were actual cases of cylinders being blown off the 3350 engine when the pilot rammed the throttles full forward like he was accustomed to with the P & W 4360.) Our procedure to prevent exceeding power limits on the Wright engines was for the pilot not flying to closely monitor the engine torque instruments and physically prevent the pilot flying from moving the throttles beyond allowable limits.

In addition to closely monitoring the engine limits, another risky component of flying C-119s in formations of three, six or nine aircraft, was during the dropping of paratroopers or heavy equipment at 1,000 feet and 130 knots with the flaps extended. This slow speed, while holding a "wing-tip-to-tail" position, resulted in a high angle of attack which increased "wing-tip vortices" and "prop-wash," making it very difficult to remain in formation. Maintaining this slow speed was essential, as speeds in excess of 130 knots could cause panels in the paratroopers parachutes to rip, resulting in a higher rate of descent and possible injury when they made contact with the ground. It was easy to determine an Aircraft Commander from a copilot, as he had calluses on his left hand while the copilot had them on his right hand. When flying tight formation, at low altitude and low airspeed, the pilot workload was so intense that it was quite common to swap control of the aircraft every 15 minutes. Since the C-119 was not air-conditioned we generally flew with the cockpit side windows open during the summer.

An example of the danger involved in formation flying was exhibited when two C-119s from a sister squadron collided in midair when flying in formation over Edelweiler, Germany on August 10, 1955. All 20 persons onboard both aircraft were killed.

We had been operating the C-119Gs for about six months when we started hearing reports of serious problems with the Aeroproducts propellers. The information received stated that if rpm control is lost, the failure could propagate to the extent that the propeller could go into a negative angle of attack, or reverse thrust position in-flight. If this

162

*catastrophic failure occurred, the severe differential drag would cause the aircraft to go into an uncontrolled "pinwheel" maneuver from which recovery may not be possible. There were two reports of such failures resulting in both aircraft crashing and causing numerous fatalities. The Air Force issued a **Red Bordered** emergency revision to the pilot's flight manual which, as I recall, stated, "If a propeller rpm control problem occurs, which will be recognized by a notable out-of-synchronization aural sound and a rise in rpm, and you are incapable of reducing rpm by retarding the propeller control lever, the Emergency Procedure is as follows: If a rising propeller rpm cannot be corrected by retarding the propeller control lever, equal to one width of the control shaft (about one inch) the recommended procedure is, **Bail out!** This procedure will remain in effect until a modification is made to prevent propellers from going into a reverse thrust position in-flight."*

When I read this emergency notice I thought of my propeller malfunction during my recent flight from the Azores to Germany, where I flew for several hours with the prop control lever all the way back against its low stop position, (A full four inches.) I didn't realize that the propeller could have gone into reverse thrust at any time, which would have resulted in an out-of-control condition and a night-time crash somewhere in Germany. (The PGR missed another opportunity of drafting me and my crew into his infamous legion of departed aircrew members.)

Not long after this emergency flight manual revision was issued, I was on a flight from Neubiberg, Germany to Athens, Greece. After crossing the Alp Mountains at 18,000 feet, I descended to 9,000 over the East Coast of Italy, and upon reaching the Italian Boot turned east toward the Ionian Sea. I was occupying the pilot's left seat while our group commander, wishing to pick up some flight time, was in the right seat. My displaced copilot and crew chief were sitting in the unused navigator's and radio operator's seats. Since we were flying in a clear blue sky, and on an easterly heading, the right side of the aircraft was bathed in warm sunshine. This unruffled solitude prompted our exhausted, and overworked bird colonel, to tilt his seat to the full reclined position and close his eyes, giving me the impression that he was engaged in a higher headquarters form of problem solving through deep meditation!

When I first detected the telltale audio signs of a propeller going out of synchronization, I thought no, not again! But, in spite of my ineffective wishing, the left propeller started a slow insidious rpm rise. Moving the prop control lever toward a low rpm position had no effect, and in a matter of minutes the propeller was growling away at 3,000 rpm, even though the prop control lever was <u>back against its low stop position</u>. It was positioned about four times the width of its shaft, way past the one shaft width the emergency order allowed before a bailout was directed. My crew chief and copilot recognized the seriousness of the problem and, without any urging from me, headed for the cargo compartment to bring up parachutes, one-man inflatable rafts and individual life preservers.

I reached over and shook the colonel and his first words upon waking up were, "Lieutenant, do you know that the propellers are out of sync?" I said, "Yes sir, I certainly do," as I pointed to the split position of the prop control levers. This got his attention as he asked, "What does that mean?" I had already pulled out a copy of the Emergency Order to the pilot's flight manual which I handed to him at about the same time that my crew chief and copilot arrived on the flight deck carrying parachutes, one-man rafts and life preservers. After a quick review of the emergency order, the colonel stated, "According to this Order we should bail out! Is that what we are going to do?" I told him that it may come to that, but we are not going to do so when over open water as long as the airplane is still flying.

With the left throttle retarded to help control the "runaway propeller," I put the aircraft on autopilot and briefed my crew on our plan of action: I pointed to a small island about ten miles ahead and stated that once over it, I will move the left prop control lever into the feathered (low drag) position. When I do this the prop may either feather, or go into a negative thrust (reverse) position. If it feathers, we're home free, but if it goes into a reverse position, I'll immediately position the right prop into reverse to help equalize the differential drag. However, if I'm forced to do this, the aircraft will begin to drop like a rock, hopefully straight ahead and we will immediately bail out, with me being the last one to go. So if I give the order to jump, don't screw around! I then instructed the crew chief to take up a position next to the cockpit emergency bailout hatch with his hand on the jettison handle, ready to pull it if I give the order. I added that if we bail out and land in water, do not inflate your life preservers and one-man-raft until you have released your parachute canopy. When everyone nodded their head in agreement, I switched the radio to the emergency frequency and called "Mayday, Mayday." To my surprise, and delight, I received a quick response from a Greek operator but I didn't note his location. I told him to stand by and I would get back to him.

When over the small Island, I placed the left fuel mixture control lever to off, and with eight crossed fingers in support, snapped the left prop control lever into the "Feathered Position" (minimum drag). The propeller rpm fluctuated for a few seconds, decreased slightly, and then in a flash feathered. I sensed that my crew was still very tense and with the intent of easing the anxiety, I told my crew chief, "I would like a cup of coffee with a little cream and no sugar." This broke the ice, and with the aircraft operating smoothly on one engine, they asked if we were going to proceed on to Athens or land at a closer airport. I told them that I didn't wish to top the mountains en route to Athens on one engine so we would land at the nearest suitable airport.

I remembered flying over the Greek Air Force base of Araxos on the Western Coast of the Peleponnessos Peninsula, which couldn't be more than 80 miles away, and said that we would land there. I made another call on the emergency radio frequency and requested the source of the station that had responded to my previous call. To my surprise the caller stated that his location was Araxos Tower, exactly where we were headed. I told him of our intention of an emergency landing at his base and he cleared us for a straight-in approach and said that fire trucks would be standing by in case we needed them.

The descent, approach and landing were routine and when on the ground I noted that the airport was a Greek F-84E jet fighter base. After shutting down the right engine a small detachment of smartly-clad fighter pilots came out to greet us and seemed especially interested in the fact that we were able to land with one engine shut down. In addition to a very warm welcome, they wanted to know if they could look inside our aircraft. My answer, "Be my guest."

Most of the Greek pilots spoke English and were eager to let us know that they had attended pilot training in the U.S. and when doing so were treated exceptionally well and now wanted to reciprocate in any way possible. I told them that I would greatly appreciate their help and that the first thing I had to do was to make a telephone call to our detachment Air Force Commander in Athens. A few minutes later I was talking to a major at Hellikon Airport, briefed him on our emergency and said that I would need mechanics to repair the propeller. He said he would send what I needed the next day.

Our Greek colleagues helped us secure the aircraft and then drove us to a hotel in downtown Araxos, where they helped us secure rooms overlooking the town square. Before they left, they said they would be back later to take us out for dinner in an elegant restaurant overlooking the Ionian Sea. The food was delicious, along with a never-ending supply of Ouzo (an 80% proof anisette-flavored liquor). Our hosts wouldn't let us pay for anything, stating that we were their guests!

My group commander copilot and I staggered into a taxi that was to take us back to our hotel, and sitting between us was one of the young Greek female dancers our fighter pilot friends had invited to entertain us during dinner. It was obvious that she, like ourselves, had consumed far too much Ouzo, which seemed to arose her sensually. In a frolicking gesture she grabbed my hand and placed it on her well developed chest! I assumed this amiable act gave me the liberty of exploring more delicate parts of her anatomy and my fingers crept further "south." However, to my shock, as I did so, my fingers came in contact with the colonel's probing hand! Adhering to the long established tradition of RHIP (rank has its privileges), I quickly withdrew my hand and kept it on my lap.

The next morning a C-119 from Athens arrived carrying needed parts and four mechanics, who assisted by my crew chief went to work in repairing the aircraft. After off loading, the aircraft would return to Athens and my colonel colleague, after thanking me for a very interesting flight, decided to go with it. Several Greek mechanics volunteered to help out in the repairs and since there was nothing else I could do, and nursing an Ouzo hangover, my copilot and I headed to town for a guided tour of this historical interesting city. This was followed by another elaborate dinner with some of our friendly Greek friends, but this time I insisted that the dinner was on me, which they reluctantly accepted. After dinner they took us to a Greek night club where we enjoyed some strange sounding music, engaged in *Zorba the Greek* style dancing with young ladies dressed in authentic Greek attire, who promised to make the remainder of the evening enjoyable, memorable and satisfying. (Which it was!)

When I visited the airport the following day, the mechanics were just finishing up on repairing the propeller and said the aircraft should be ready for a functional test hop in a couple of hours. The fighter pilot group commander invited us for lunch at their Officers' Club and as a receptacle gesture of good will, I asked him if he would like to accompany me on the test hop to check out the propeller. He jumped at the chance, stating that he had hoped for a flight in our C-119 but was hesitant to ask.

With the Greek F-84 group commander in the right seat I climbed to 5,000 feet, where I feathered and unfeathered the left propeller and proclaimed the aircraft operational. We then flew around the area on a sightseeing tour with our guest pointing out historical and significant sites. Heading back to the airport I told the group commander that he could make the landing after I made a low level flyby over the airport!

After obtaining permission from the tower, I went to maximum continuous power, put the aircraft into a steep dive and roared over the runway at around 50 feet doing 275 knots (over 300 mph.) I then pulled the aircraft up into a steep left climbing turn to a downwind leg, and with wings level, I told the smiling Greek commander that he had the controls and could make the landing.

With just a little coaxing he flew a very nice traffic pattern and made an acceptable landing. When we taxied in he was grinning from ear to ear and obviously pleased in being able to fly and land, what was to him, a giant two-engine aircraft. After parking he inquired as to when we planned on departing. I told him that since we hadn't checked out of our hotel we would spend one more night and depart in the morning. With that he said that my crew and I would be his guests for a farewell dinner that night in his favorite restaurant overlooking the Ionian Sea Coast. He added that he and several of his pilots would pick us up at around 6 p.m.

At exactly six o'clock a crew bus arrived containing our friendly group commander and four of his F-84 fighter pilots (which I assumed were his flight commanders). The dinner was great, the Ouzo glasses were never empty and the entertainment consisted of several young Greek male and female dancers. Before departing for our hotel I raised my glass and said I would like to propose a toast. Everyone rose and my toast went something like, "I would like to propose a toast to thank our Greek pilot colleagues for their excellent hospitality during our short stay. I would also like to thank the Aeroproducts engineers, because if they had not screwed-up when designing their propeller, none of this would have been possible." There was a uniform, "here-here" as we clinked glasses and drank to my toast. (The next day we departed for Athens, as I supraliminally thought that the PGR lost another round.)

Araxos Air Base remained an active Greek Base until 2001, and until 1996 was used as an auxiliary location for storing nuclear weapons for the U.S. Air Force. The former military base is now a civilian airport to support an ever-increasing tourist interest in this fascinating area of ancient Greece. Not long after my vacation in Araxos, the Air Force issued a field modification order for all Aeroproducts propellers installed on C-119Gs. The order required the installation of a mechanical low pitch stop which is retracted electrically when the throttles are moved into the reverse thrust position after landing. This eliminated the danger of a propeller going into reverse thrust during flight and solved a serious design defect. However, this propeller modification did not address another serious problem, the potential failure of one or more of an engine exhaust driven power recovery turbine (PRT).

The PRTs installed on the Wright R-3350 Cyclone engines, rotate at terrific speeds and a slight imperfection, or metal fatigue would cause them to literally explode, with the force of a small bomb! This explosion would result in considerable peripheral damage to the surrounding area and spew out hot pieces of turbine blades at bullet-like speeds in all directions. The potential danger to passengers from flying shrapnel, was so serious that sections of the cargo compartment adjacent to inboard PRTs were reinforced with steel bulletproof plates.

I experienced a PRT failure on a flight from Athens, Greece to Germany in the summer of 1955, and can personally attest to the magnitude of the problem. I had climbed to 18,000 feet, in preparation for crossing the Alp Mountains, and when I moved the throttles to a cruise power setting, the aircraft shook violently and a muffled explosion rattled the right engine. Engine instruments confirmed that I had a serious problem as the torque meter (which reflects engine performance) indicated a significant loss of power and the propeller rpm, manifold pressure and fuel flow gages were all fluctuating wildly. Visual observation of the engine confirmed the instrument readings, as it was vibrating so erratically that I feared it might separate from the aircraft. It was obvious that the engine should be shut down immediately or a more serious problem was sure to follow.

I positioned the right engine throttle to idle, placed the fuel control lever to off and attempted to move the prop control lever to the feathered (low drag) position. However, it would not move beyond an intermediate position, something was binding or restricting the linkage between the control lever and the engine, which I'm sure was related to the engine explosion. I continued pulling on the control lever, trying to dislodge it, but it would not move. With fuel to the engine shutoff, the propeller was in a "flat-pitch" wind-milling position and causing considerable drag, making it imperative that we start an immediate descent!

168

I was faced with the possibility of applying so much force to the prop control lever that it might break off, or live with the tremendous drag of a wind-milling propeller, which would render the aircraft difficult to fly, even at low altitudes. Deciding on the former as the best course of action, I placed both hands on the prop control lever and pulled back on it with all my might! Suddenly, it broke free and slammed into the feathered position, but for a couple seconds I wasn't sure if it broke off or performed its designed function. However, my concern was short-lived when I looked at the right engine and saw four propeller blades in a feathered position.

With this segment of the emergency solved, I instructed my copilot (who had been flying the aircraft) to execute a 180-degree turn to the right and initiate a descent at an airspeed no lower than 140 knots. In a shaky, and obviously excited voice, he said, "What are we going to do now?" I told him we would declare an emergency and divert to the joint U.S. Italian Air Base at Aviano, Italy. Glancing at my young crew chief, I noted that he was strapping on a parachute and appeared as nervous as my copilot. I realized I would have to find a way to eliminate their anxiety if I was to benefit from their assistance in safely landing my crippled aircraft, but what to do? I reached into the top pocket of my flight suit and pulled out an unopened package of Double Mint chewing gum. This seemingly incongruous action captured their attention, so I slowly, and nonchalantly, opened the package and took a long sniff. I then turned to my two nervous crew members and said, "Have you ever noticed how a fresh pack of gum smells when you first open it? It not only smells great, but has a lot better flavor." With that I handed each of them a stick as I slowly unwrapped one for myself. This simple gesture of confidence snapped them out of their temporary onslaught of "Cockpit Buck Fever" and were once again productive members of my crew.

I contacted Aviano Air Base on the emergency radio frequency and advised them of our problem and requested a Ground Controlled Radar Approach (GCA). Shortly thereafter, they had us on radar and directed us in for an uneventful landing. When I parked the aircraft in front of the Base Operations building, a small group of American and Italian military personnel came out to meet the aircraft. Before the left engine shutdown was complete, I noted a group of onlookers gathered around the right engine, pointing up at it and shaking their heads. (Not a good sign!)

When I joined the group gathered around the engine, the reason for their head shaking became clear. The right lower portion of the engine cowling looked like we had received a direct "flack hit." Pieces of the cowling were missing and small and large shrapnel holes were everywhere. Fortunately, the holes in the underside of the wing did not penetrate the self-sealing fuel cells and cause a fire. (Which would have been uncontrollable.) With the help of local Air Force personnel, I made a phone call to our base in Germany and told them that we would need a new engine, new cowling and a sheet metal mechanic. Later when we removed the engine cowling, I discovered the reason for the jammed propeller control lever. A piece of the exploding PRT had impacted the prop control push rod, bending it upwards about 30 degrees, and nearly cutting it in half. It was a miracle that it didn't break when I used both hands in forcing it to move! We spent the next five days in Italy, enjoying good food, fine wine and even managed to get in a trip to Venice before the aircraft was repaired and we could continue on to Germany.

In concert with the expansion of NATO, I was flying more and more trips to military bases and cities throughout Europe, but none were more enjoyable than Ciampino Airport, Rome, Italy. Rome, because of its geographic location was a perfect refueling and layover stop for aircraft flying to Africa and Greece. The U.S. Air Force maintained a small contingency of active duty personnel to service both fighters and transports, but possessed no military quarters, so all overnights required procuring a hotel room downtown. I made so many flights to Rome that I became very familiar with its many historical sites and fine restaurants. One of my favorite bistros was *Alfredo di Roma*.

Mr. Alfredo di Lelio opened his restaurant in 1914 and in addition to other fine culinary achievements, was the originator of Fettuccine Alfredo. He concocted this egg-noodle dish, heavy with fresh cream, butter and parmesan cheese, to tempt the palate of his pregnant wife, who had lost her appetite. Alfredo di Roma was the restaurant silent movie stars, prominent business executives, German, Italian and American Generals, and celebrities from all walks of life felt obligated to visit, and have their picture added to the restaurant wall. Alfredo was a great showman and a very colorful man with a bubbling personality. He was especially proud of a large solid gold fork and spoon set, presented to him by silent movie stars Douglas Fairbanks, Sr. and his wife Mary Pickford, when they visited his restaurant during their honeymoon in 1927. He proudly displayed them in a glass case on the wall of his restaurant. However, for special customers he would remove them from their protective case and use them in a flamboyant table-side mixing ceremony of his famous Fettuccine noodles. After the mixing was complete, which was accomplished with flowing arm movements and off-key singing, he would dish out equal amounts of Fettuccine to dinner guests seated around the table, except one! He would then set the large plate he used in the mixing ritual in front of the person he choose as the table leader. This would be accompanied by a cheer and applause from customers seated at adjacent tables, who had been observing this entertaining performance.

I'm proud to say that I visited the *Alfredo di Roma Restaurant* so often, and brought in so many new customers, that Mr. Alfredo often honored me with the gold fork and spoon table-side mixing and set the large platter in front of me. This would be accompanied by a beaming smile from underneath his flowing mustache and a "bon appetite." (I'm sure Mr. Alfredo is now mixing Fettuccine for St. Peter, but without his gold fork and spoon, I don't think St. Peter is enjoying it as much as I did.)

When visiting Rome, be sure to visit Old Alfredo di Roma, not one of the newer reataurants, which lack the charm of the original and do not have a gold fork and spoon displayed on the wall. To ensure you visit the original Alfredo's have your hotel write a note for your taxi driver, but be sure you agree on the fare or you may be faced with an argument over it later.

Of the many flights I made into Rome's Ciampino Airport, one stands out as a potential Close Encounter. I was cleared for an instrument approach when the airport and the surrounding area was being buffeted by thunderstorms. Air Traffic Control in those days did not provide weather advisories and the C-119 was not equipped with weather avoidance radar. I was flying in heavy rain and moderate turbulence while observing frequent lightning flashes from nearby black rain clouds. After turning inbound, I switched on the windshield wipers, ordered the copilot to lower the landing gear and flaps and called for the Before Landing Check List. One of the items on the check list required the copilot to start the auxiliary power unit (APU and check it for proper operation. The APU start switch and voltmeter are located on the lower instrument panel in front of the copilot, but due to the turbulence I noted that he was having difficulty in steadying his bouncing arm when actuating the start switch.

Ironically, when he finally steadied his bouncing hand, sufficiently to activate the switch, we experienced a thundering lightning strike on his side of the aircraft. It was so bright that we were momentarily blinded. (Lightning strikes can and have on occasion knocked aircraft out of the sky, but if after a strike you are still airborne, the next big concern is --- did it damage the aircraft's electrical system?) To evaluate if any electrical impairment had occurred, I flipped on the radio receiver switch and found it still receiving a signal. I then made a radio check with the Ciampino Tower which was also OK and instructed my copilot, who was sitting motionless and staring into space, to check the APU for proper operation. His response was somewhat humorous, but considering his relative inexperience was understandable. He said, "No sir, I'm not touching the start switch to the APU again. The last time I did there was a big explosion and a flash of light." I was too busy to laugh, or savor the unintended humor in his remark, so just repeated my order by stating, "You had nothing to do with the explosion or flash, as we had been struck by lightning, and there is nothing to worry about as we are still in one piece." He seemed somewhat relieved, but still displayed a certain amount of hesitance when conducting the APU electrical check, which was satisfactory. Before we broke out of the clouds we were struck by lightning once more, but this time somewhere near the tail of the aircraft. After the second strike, our check of the electrical system went much smoother, as I now had the copilot working with me. Fortunately, the aircraft suffered no apparent damage from the second strike either.

After landing, I decided we would spend the night in Rome and were driven to a hotel by taxi in heavy rain. The next day, in clear weather, we checked over the aircraft for any signs of damage. Just below the copilot's floor level side window were charred burn marks that formed two complete circles which looked like "ring worm." We couldn't find any burn marks from the second strike, so following a thorough preflight, I filed a flight plan and we continued on our mission to Wheelus Air Base, Libya.

When in Rome I never tired of walking the ancient streets, visiting St. Peter's Basilica and exploring Roman ruins like the Forum and the Coliseum. In the 1950s these ruins were open day and night and I was able to wander in and around them freely. I was walking the cobblestone streets one evening when I met a young Italian girl from Naples who was also out for a stroll. I asked her if I could buy her dinner and wine, which she accepted. After exploring each other's backgrounds (she spoke English with a pleasing Italian accent) over a two-hour dinner, we decided to go for a late night walk to enjoy the full moon and a cool evening breeze. Our stroll brought us to the gates of the famous Roman Coliseum (known as the Amphitheatrum Caesareum to ancient Romans).

We walked through isolated passages, illuminated by broken shafts of moonlight, and sat down in the area close to the Roman Emperor's private box, and after a session of heavy breathing we thought it was time to engage in some adult consensual pastime. At the climax of our merrymaking, I fantasized that I could hear the approving cheers of 60,000 Roman spectators and a "thumbs-up-signal" from the Emperor. When our passion withered, and I no longer heard the imaginary cheering, we left the Coliseum and I walked her back to her hotel. With a joyful, youthful skip, I then walked to my own hotel. Another wonderful night in Rome was history.

February 1955 was a memorable month in Germany. I was notified that I was promoted to the rank of captain, which in addition to an increase in salary, provided what I thought was a respectable title. (I guess the epithet, Captain Martin, reminded me of legendary aviation heroes like, "Captain Midnight" and "Captain Jimmy Allen" who entertained kids with their adventurous aviation radio programs in the 1930s and 40s.) There were about 15 other first lieutenants promoted at the same time, so we decided to throw an open-house, open-bar party at the Neubiberg Officers' Club. I was elected chairman of the party committee and told our club officer, Captain Kirby Quinn, to spare no expense. It was a grand night with balloons, a German polka band, free food and all the trappings of the type of party Air Force officers in those days considered standard events. Unfortunately, parties like this are no longer a component of the military; they would not be considered politically correct.

The Officers' Club chief bartender, a German by the name of Gunther, kept his staff on their toes and made sure our glasses were never empty. Gunther was a chubby, beer-bellied, fun-loving guy who spoke English with a thick, pleasing German accent. He had tended bar when the club was occupied by rowdy young Luftwaffe fighter pilots, flying FW-190s and ME-109s, by American pilots flying F-47s, F-84s, and now C-119s. Gunther and I became friends and I asked him, "Gunther, what is the difference in tending bar for German Luftwaffe pilots and American pilots?" His answer, "Except for the uniforms and language, there isn't much, as all pilots are klein verruckt (a little bit crazy). (I thought his answer was quite profound and right on the mark.)

One Friday night at the club I asked my operations officer, Major Hurst, if I could dance with his attractive wife. They were sitting on swivel bar stools when I posed the question and in accepting my request, his wife playfully spun rapidly around, slipped off the stool and lost her footing. I grabbed her arm, which prevented her from falling, but she thought she may have twisted her ankle but didn't think it was very serious. Before the dance was over she started complaining about pain in her ankle so I escorted her, limping, back to her husband.

The following Monday Major Hurst told me that the next day his wife was complaining about pain in her ankle, so he took her to the hospital. After x-rays it was determined that her ankle was broken and they put her in a "walker-cast" which she would have to wear for six weeks. Major Hurst's wife (who enjoyed a good joke) never tired of telling people who would ask, "Did you break your leg skiing?" "No," she would reply, "I broke it when I agreed to dance with Lou Martin." (For some reason I had a difficult time in getting other attractive wives to dance with me following this unfortunate incident.)

There were occasions when the PGR seemed to extend his recruitment campaign to crew members other than pilots and not necessarily when they were flying. An example of this occurred on one warm summer day, when our squadron was having a picnic and a softball match between the officers and enlisted men at a nearby German beer garden. Everyone was having a good time in cheering on their favorite team (the enlisted men won), enjoying good food, consuming large amounts of strong German beer and dancing to a small *Lawrence Welk* style polka band. Events like this were great for morale and solidifying esprit de corps.

When the event was winding down my wife and I, and Major Phil Currier and his wife Anne (who we were riding with), were preparing to leave. A group of six, well-mannered, handsome young airmen were standing near the front door. As we approached, a young crew chief, dressed in a bright yellow sweater, who I had flown with on many occasions, asked if he could dance with my wife. She accepted his polite request and while waiting for her, I enjoyed a friendly conversation with his buddies. When the music stopped, he escorted her back to where I was waiting, politely thanked her for the dance and joined his comrades. They were obviously eager to "hit-the-road" and when their apparent leader said, "Let's go," all six headed for the parking lot in a youthful rush.

As we were walking toward Phil's car we observed the six airmen we had just been talking to race out of the gravel parking lot at a high rate of speed, with the rear tires of their late model Hudson sedan spinning and spewing out gravel! We shook our heads in disgust, while commenting, "We hope they reach Neubiberg Air Base safely."

About three miles from the beer garden we were rounding a curve in the narrow two-lane road when we observed German farmers running across a field. As we came closer, the reason for their running became clear. The Hudson sedan we had observed racing out of the parking lot a few minutes earlier was laying on its side between two large trees. Spread out in the middle of the road were three lifeless bodies and one young crew chief, obviously dazed, leaning against a tree. Phil stopped the car and I ran over to the first unconscious victim. As I looked down at a shoeless, lifeless body, I was struck with the fact that he was wearing a bright yellow sweater, now torn and dirty. (Just a few minutes earlier he was dancing with my wife, and politely thanking me for the privilege.) I knelt down beside him, felt a weak pulse which stopped beating shortly thereafter. The other two young men, laying in the middle of the road, were also dead and beyond help. Including the young man leaning against a tree, we counted four victims, leaving two unaccounted for.

A German farmer shouted that he found a dead body, laying in tall grass off to the side of the road, but this still left one airman missing. Phil, Anne, my wife and I, along with about ten Germans, fanned out to look for the sixth victim. Our search of the immediate area turned up nothing, so I decided to exam the wrecked Hudson, which had its roof peeled back like an open "Sardine" can and still smoking. Standing next to the smashed sedan I thought I heard a faint groan, and upon investigation, I discovered the sixth airmen pinned underneath, but still alive!

I shouted for the group of onlookers to join me, next to the hulking wreckage, and in an "all-together-effort" to lift it up while I crawled underneath to drag the injured young man to safety. With adrenaline infused strength, the car was raised enough for me to crawl under it and rescue the young crew chief. As I was sliding him out, I could hear stressed grunts coming from the people holding up the wreck, but felt confident they wouldn't let it drop until both I and my injured colleague were clear. When we were clearly safe, the heavy automobile was dropped with a loud thud! The injured airmen was rushed to a hospital and although seriously injured survived, as did the young man who was leaning against the tree (who turned out to be the driver).

The primary cause of the accident was obviously due to excessive speed and alcohol, but a contributing factor was the dangerous German narrow asphalt rural road, with high built-up edge lips of several inches. In addition there were no shoulders, just rows of large trees lining both sides. Apparently, the driver allowed his automobile to swerve off the hard surface and when he attempted to steer back onto the paved road, the high lip caused it to overturn. Sliding along on its side, the windshield slammed into a tree, ripping open its steel top and ejecting its passengers. (There were no seat belts, or shoulder harnesses in those days, and ironically rural German roads present the same potential danger today.) I felt demoralized over the loss of four young comrades, and compassion for our squadron commander who would be faced with the responsibility of explaining this tragic loss to their loved ones.

One dark night in September 1955, I was leading a three-ship cross country C-119 formation flight, designed to fulfill one of our combat readiness requirements. We departed Neubiberg Air Base at 8 p.m. with a scheduled return time of midnight. When approaching our home base, I was advised that the weather conditions had deteriorated, and the airport was below landing weather minimums and expected to remain so for the rest of the night. We were directed to divert to Rhein Main Air Base and remain there overnight (RON).

We landed around 2 a.m. and just ahead of an approaching fog bank. The visibility was so bad that it was difficult to taxi to the parking ramp. Based on my five years of experience of flying in Europe, I thought we might be stuck in Rhein Main for two or three days while waiting for the weather to improve. We bought toothbrushes, a couple cases of beer, two decks of cards and secured rooms in the base transient aircrew building. We figured we could buy fresh underwear and anything else we needed in the BX the next day. In the meantime, we would gather in my room for our favorite pastime of playing poker and drinking beer. We played cards until 7 a.m. since with the field socked in we were not concerned about having to "rise-and-shine" anytime soon.

I drifted off into a beer-induced sleep around 7:30, but three hours later I was awakened by a loud knock on my door. A bright-eyed airmen, performing the unpleasant knocking, told me I was wanted on the telephone. Major Hurst, our operations officer in Neubiberg, said, "Get dressed, wake up your crew and return ASAP." I reminded him that Rhein Main was below takeoff and landing weather minimums and I wasn't sure about the weather in the Munich area. He said that the weather in Munich was improving slightly and I should be able to sneak in, and since I had a Green Instrument Card, if I could see well enough to taxi to the end of the runway at Rhein Main, I could legally takeoff. He emphasized that he needed the aircraft and crew back at Neubiberg for a special mission, which he would brief me on when I returned.

The Air Force at the time had two levels of pilot instrument ratings, White Card and Green Card. Pilots holding white cards were restricted to published weather minimums. However, for pilots holding Green Cards there were no takeoff or landing minimums; if you could see to taxi you could takeoff. Likewise, if you could see the runway during the approach, you could legally land. This dual instrument qualification practice was discontinued in later years due to a series of weather-related accidents.

I woke up my copilot and crew chief and told them to get dressed as we were departing for Neubiberg, and if they needed toothpicks to keep their eyes open, I had plenty. The visibility at Rhein Main was almost zero, so I requested a "Follow-Me" vehicle driver, who was familiar with the airport, to lead me out to the end of the runway. (I thought the visibility was too bad to attempt to taxi out on my own.) When positioned directly over the runway marker 25 Left, I turned on the landing lights, set the directional gyro on a heading of 250 degrees, locked the brakes, shoved the throttles to full takeoff power, turned on the water injection and released the brakes! The aircraft, being empty, accelerated to takeoff speed of 125 knots in about 15 seconds. (Apparently I stayed somewhere near the middle of the runway during the takeoff roll as we became airborne without hitting any runway lights.)

En route to Neubiberg all I could think of was heading for my apartment for a good rest immediately after landing. We landed around 2 p.m., and when taxiing to the ramp, I observed an unusual amount of activity in and around our squadron area. Aircraft were being refueled, crews were preflighting aircraft and vehicles were scurrying about everywhere. Something was up, but I didn't know what. As the engines were spinning down, Major Hurst came to the cockpit and told us to go home, pack a bag and return ASAP. He added, "By the time you return, long range auxiliary fuel tanks will be installed in the cargo compartment, the aircraft will be refueled and in-flight lunches will be onboard." When I asked where we were going, he said, "Lages Airport in the Azores, to join in the search for a military C-118 *Liftmaster* which disappeared on a flight to Manchester, England with a full load of military personnel and their dependents. The Air Force is launching a maximum effort to find survivors, and we are sending several aircraft to help." (The civilian version of the C-118 was the 74 passenger Douglas DC-6.)

Two hours later I was back at Neubiberg and departed around 4 p.m., for a ten-hour flight to the Azores. Fighting off sleep, I landed at Lages around one o'clock in the morning (local time), and parked on a ramp loaded with C-54s, C-47s, C-118s and C-119s. As the engines were spinning down, I mentioned to my crew that perhaps now we would be able to hit the sack for eight hours of well-deserved rest. However, this was not to be! We were met by a major who identified himself as the search-and-rescue coordinator. He asked if our aircraft was operational. When I told him that it was he said, "Fine, report to billeting to obtain a bunk, get something to eat, and be back in three hours for an aircrew search briefing." With less than two hours sleep, we were roused out of bed by a sergeant going through the barracks banging on a steel triangle.

The briefing area was standing room only and was called to attention when a full colonel entered. He walked to a large wall map and pointed to a section of open water which reflected the flight track the missing C-118 would have flown en route to England. He said that its last reported position was about 300 miles northeast and nothing was heard from it since. He then pointed to sectional squares, on either sides of the track, that were identified with letters and numbers. Navigation folders were then issued to each Aircraft Commander, identifying the specific area he would search. The colonel stated that our search altitudes would be flown at 500 feet and continue until sunset (about 9 to 10 hours). He briefed on discrete radio frequencies for reporting sightings or in communicating with the search and rescue command post. The colonel concluded his briefing with a time hack and a statement that since the present weather favored visual flight, we were free to taxi out and takeoff when ready, but wanted all aircraft airborne one hour before sunrise.

I flew a nine-hour search mission at 500 feet while crisscrossing the same area over and over. I was so tired that I often thought I saw life rafts or survivors bobbing in the water, but after close scrutiny they proved to be nothing but hallucinations created by water spouts or large whitecaps. When returning to Lages, I was faced with another barrier that was preventing me and my crew from getting some sleep. A 1,000 foot overcast shrouded the field, with cloud tops of around 3,000. About 25 aircraft, all on visual flight plans and some low on fuel, were returning to land at about the same time. Lages Approach Control, overwhelmed with the sudden arrival of so many aircraft, made a radio call "in-the-blind" stating that aircraft were to maintain their own separation above the clouds and their own individual sequence for an instrument landing.

The first aircraft to arrive over the station advised that he was initiating a non-directional radio beacon approach and succeeding aircraft should follow at three-minute intervals. In a very short period of time there were numerous aircraft arriving overhead and calling out that they were setting up holding patterns at 500 foot intervals. On our own initiative, the stack of aircraft holding allowed those who were short of fuel to jump to the head of the line. The rest kept descending down the stack, at 500-foot increments, as the aircraft at the bottom of the heap broke off for its individual approach and landing. It took about an hour for all aircraft to land safely! After landing I was advised that a hot meal was waiting for us in the mess hall, but I was too tired to think about eating since I had only slept six hours in the last three days. I passed out on my bunk, fully clothed, and slept for seven straight hours before my bladder demanded attention. I then undressed and slept through the rest of the night.

I was expecting to be directed to fly another search mission the next morning, but when I awoke I was advised that pieces of burnt wreckage, broken seats and a few floating bodies had been found. The nature of the discovery indicated that the aircraft, for unknown reasons, had apparently experienced an in-flight fire or explosion and crashed, killing all onboard. Therefore, there would be no further search for survivors. After a hearty breakfast of steak and eggs, we departed the Azores for a long flight back to Neubiberg Air Base, Germany.

After Turkey and Greece joined NATO in 1952, and Italy in 1955, air transport support to the Southern Mediterranean area grew in importance. To support this increased airlift requirement, C-119 squadrons from Neubiberg were directed to station 12 aircraft in Athens Greece on a 30-day rotational basis. The 41st Squadron was the first unit to send aircraft to Athens, and the 40th Squadron (my unit) was to follow. In preparing for my 30-day stint in Greece, I thought it would be great to have some means of touring the Greek countryside when not flying missions to Turkey, Libya and Morocco. I visited a BMW Motorcycle shop in downtown Munich and purchased a used 500 cc. motorcycle. It was a marvelous machine with large cylinders poking out from each side and a raised buddy seat with a large handhold. When It became my turn to fly to Athens, I put the motorcycle in my aircraft and took it with me.

Some pilots from the squadron that had preceded our unit to Athens, had rented a large house capable of accommodating about ten crew members, and I arranged to take it over when they rotated back to Germany. I thought living in a private home would be more desirable than staying in a noisy downtown hotel. There were a number of colleagues who agreed with me and decided to move in and share the expenses. With a mixed flight schedule, pilots and navigators were coming and going at all hours. This chaotic schedule, combined with a youthful exuberance to enjoy life at its fullest, caused the house to take on the atmosphere of a lively fraternity house, similar to the 1978 movie *Animal House*. To accommodate crew members about to fly, or those just finishing a long mission, there were parties either starting or just ending. I was fortunate to have a private room and would quite often have to lock my door to get some rest, or to keep out a wandering young Greek female from dropping in for a drink or some consensual adult entertainment.

When scheduled to fly, a military bus would pick up crew members to take them to the airport. However, owning a motorcycle my copilot, 1st Lt. Ed Collins, and I didn't have to ride the slow, uncomfortable bus. We could make it to the airport on our own. One morning around sunrise we departed our rented "nut house" by stepping over sleeping bodies in the living room, and climbed on my BMW motorcycle and headed for the airport for an early morning flight to Morocco. Because of the early hour, traffic was light, and I was allowing the motorcycle to demonstrate what it could do in the arena of speed. We were zooming along the Kavos Bay coastal highway, at about 70 to 80 miles per hour, as daylight was beginning to brighten the Eastern sky. Without slowing down, I drove into the left lane in preparation for passing a slow moving bus. However, what I didn't see before passing the bus was that the left lane was blocked by an unmarked two-foot high mound of loose gravel and sand. I was going too fast to stop, so I just shouted to my copilot, "Hold on, Ed," and gunned the engine as we hit the mound of dirt. With the unloaded engine roaring in defiance, we flew past several windows of the bus in mid air. From a peripheral view, I noted startled passengers aghast at seeing a motorcycle soaring past like a Greek Evil Kanevil. When we came back down to Mother Earth, the motorcycle wobbled back and forth, but stayed upright, and I avoided what could have been a fatal crash. (I believe our high speed, although reckless, produced sufficient gyroscopic force to keep the motorcycle from going into a spin.)

With another burst of power, we passed the bus and continued on our way. When we arrived at the airport, Ed told me that he hoped I wouldn't take it personal, but in the future he would take the crew bus, adding, "I joined the Air Force to fly, not ride on the back of an overpowered BMW motorcycle with a crazy Aircraft Commander." I told him that he had no guts, as I had gotten him to the airport safely. His response, "We made it this time, but I'm concerned about the future, which would seem bleak if I continue to ride on a motorcycle with you!"

I enjoyed the freedom my motorcycle provided and when not flying I would head for the hills surrounding Athens and visited parts of Greece that my landlocked colleagues never saw. When my 30 days in Athens were up, I put a For Sale sign on my motorcycle, parked it in front of the main terminal and sold it for twice what I paid for it on the first day.

It was a beautiful warm summer night in Athens when my copilot, navigator and I finished a leisure dinner in a beach-side restaurant, near the Hellinikon International Airport. When having after-dinner drinks we met a good-natured retired English medical doctor and his wife vacationing in Greece. They were a delightful couple, who seemed to take pleasure in our youthful approach to life and our funny American accents. They invited us to join them for a night cap in their bungalow, just a short walk from the restaurant. Sitting on their verandah we marveled at the full moon, the landing lights of aircraft approaching and departing the airport and the distant glow of the lights of Athens. After about an hour of enjoying their charming company and rare scotch, they decided it was time for them to retire and bid us good night. Succumbing to our youthful zest for life, we thought it was too early to head for the sack and were looking for some other form of entertainment. I suggested that we go for a late-night swim in the warm waters of Kavos Bay.

We stripped down to our shorts and swam out several hundred feet into the bay and started treading water to take in the sights. The lights of the city cast a blinking panoramic view to the north and looking to the west we could see the shining lights of the harbor of Piraeus, with boats departing and entering. To the south a full moon was casting its reflective light upon the entire scene. With our eyes now adjusted to the darkness, the entire horseshoe harbor of Athens was bathed in a silver hue. We lingered in the warm water for a considerable length of time while reflecting on how fortunate we were in being provided the opportunity of enjoying such pleasures in a far off land, at taxpayers' expense.

After fulfilling our thirst for adventure, we started to swim toward shore. After swimming a few feet, I felt like I had swum into a mess of weeds, or perhaps garbage. However, It was soon apparent that it was something more sinister, as my upper body and arms developed a sharp painful sting. I thrashed wildly to escape whatever it was I had encountered and was soon free of the entrapment, but my troubles were not over. My arms and chest were in terrific pain and partially paralyzed! In addition, I was having difficulty in breathing. I called to my colleagues for help and they responded by grabbing a hold of my arms and pulled me to shore.

After leaving the water, I was able to walk, but my upper body was still in intense pain. My buddies half carried me to the English doctor's bungalow, and knocked on his door. Apparently he was not yet asleep as he responded quickly and after taking one look at me directed my buddies to bring me inside and place me on his bed. When the lights were turned up, the nature of my pain was obvious. My chest and arms were streaked with red lines and small white lesions, and I was still having difficulty in breathing. The doctor said that it was apparent that I had come in contact with a colony of *Portuguese man-of-wars,* whose tentacles had secreted a poison into my body through sharp barbs. He put a soothing salve on the lesions and injected a blood thinner into my veins. He said that I was fortunate that I was not alone when I encountered the poisonous jelly fish or I wouldn't be here. He and his wife nursed me for about an hour before I was able to walk and display full upper body mobility. We headed for our own quarters and the next morning I was in good shape except for a few faint red marks and a slight stiffness in my shoulders. (Another Close Encounter with the PGR that did not involve flying.)

Many of my C-119 flights were to Wheelus Air Base, Libya in providing logistical support for jet fighter units performing gunnery and bombing practice. The shortest route to Libya was crossing over the Austrian Alps, flying down the Italian Peninsula and over the Mediterranean Sea. However, when our cargo load included transporting military support personnel, it was usually necessary to fly a much longer route, by way of the French Rhone Valley with a landing at Marseille, France for refueling. This long way around was necessary because flying over the Alps required a climb to 18,000 feet and the C-119 was not pressurized, nor did it have supplemental passenger oxygen outlets in the cargo compartment. However, there were occasions, when carrying only one or two passengers, I would allow them to sit in the unused navigator's or radio operator's position, which were equipped with demand-type oxygen systems. An alternate method, which would accommodate up to three passengers, would be to allow them to suck on one of our three portable oxygen bottles for the short 30-minute flight over the mountains.

However, starting in May 1955, all flights to Libya, Italy, Greece and Turkey were forced to fly via the Rhone Valley and Marseille. The four occupying powers (The U.S., Great Britain, France and the Soviet Union) granted full sovereignty to Austria, ending the military occupation they had been in force since the end of WW II.

The Austrian Government elected not to become members of NATO, and therefore prohibited the overflying of their territory by military aircraft of NATO members. I think it was a big mistake for the allied powers to allow Austria to enact this costly and burdensome restriction against overflying the Austrian Alps. Certainly with a bit more diplomatic pressure the U.S. could have forced the Austrian Government to allow over-flights by way of a narrow corridor. It should be noted that Austria is still not a member of NATO but enjoys the protection it provides at no cost to them.

Flying around Austria and Switzerland not only increased crew duty times, but increased wear and tear on the aircraft, increased operating costs, and at times, caused the cancellation of flights due to labor strikes by French Air Traffic Controllers or severe weather in the Rhone Valley. One such bad weather encounter occurred in January 1956. Passing over Dijon at 9,000 feet, I was flying in a solid overcast and picking up moderate amounts of "rime ice." (Rime ice is a white granular type of crystallized water, similar to what you find inside a refrigerator.) However, as I approached Lyon, the icing problem became more serious. We began picking up the more dangerous type of aircraft icing, known as "clear ice." (Clear ice can accumulate at extremely rapid rates and is more difficult to get rid off.)

The C-119 was equipped with eight Janitol gas fed heaters on the top of the fuselage designed to provide heat for anti-icing the leading edges of the wings and tail surfaces, as well as heat for the interior of the aircraft. Under most icing conditions these heaters provided excellent protection against in-flight icing. But in severe icing conditions, there was the possibility of ice forming behind the heated sections from melted ice runoff. Also the nose of the aircraft did not have ice protection and ice built-up in this area not only caused a disruption of air flow but increased aircraft weight. The engine carburetors were protected from ice by the ducting of hot engine exhaust and the propellers were protected by electrical heated strips on the leading edge of each blade.

When about 50 miles north of Lyon, I was employing all the aircraft anti-icing, and deicing, equipment available but in spite of my efforts the ice buildup was increasing at an alarming rate. Airspeed was dropping off precipitously, even with the engine power advanced to maximum continuous. I could hear chunks of ice banging against the side of the fuselage, in sequence with the electric cycling of the propeller blade deicing, the windshield wiper blades had large chunks of ice adhering to them and the small outside air temperature gage probe had accumulated an ice cone resembling a foot-long megaphone. I knew I was also picking up unseen ice on the nose section, as the "angle-of-attack" was approaching dangerous levels as the autopilot was attempting to maintain a constant altitude. I knew I had to do something, and do it quickly, or the aircraft might go into a stall, or tailspin, making recovery questionable.

I declared an emergency with the Lyon control tower and even though the operator spoke little English, he understood my request for an immediate descent. Pushing the nose over I requested the airport's weather and temperature. He reported a 2,000-foot overcast, heavy rain and a temperature of 38 degrees. I continued a high speed descent in the published airport holding pattern and broke out of the clouds at around 2,000 feet. Large chunks of ice began breaking off the aircraft, along with sheets of it flying past the windshield from the nose section. I leveled off at 1,000 feet and when I was assured that I had shucked all accumulated ice, filed a VFR (Visual Flight Rule) flight plan to Marseille. After landing, I drank a couple cups of strong cappuccino coffee, refueled the aircraft and continued on to Libya, where I enjoyed a warm swim on a sandy beach next to the Mediterranean Sea before heading back to Germany.

During my second tour in Germany, there was a growing fear that the Cold War may become hot, so there was more emphasis on ensuring that all combat crew members were properly trained. One such training activity was "Escape and Evasion." This realistic program required navigating on foot through simulated enemy lines consisting of U.S. Army soldiers on maneuvers, who were promised a three-day-pass for every Air Force pilot they captured. Apprehended pilots were searched, trussed, stripped of their boots and turned over to U.S. Special Forces personnel who were dressed in authentic Soviet Union Army uniforms. Since I was able to avoid capture, I was allowed to observe the interrogation of a colleague through a one-way mirror. He was led into a cold, bare room stark-naked, except for a hood over his head, and ordered to sit down on a cold steel stool under a bright overhead light. The hood was removed and his naked body shivered from the cold and obvious effects of sleep depravation.

His interrogators began to orally berate him with screaming accusative questions that made fun of the position he found himself in, the small size of his penis, while stating that his comrades were screwing his wife back at his home station. This training was so realistic that some men broke down into uncontrolled sobbing and begged to end the session. This type of indoctrination, although unpleasant, involved no physical torture but was extremely valuable as evidenced by U.S. pilots being able to resist extreme harsh conditions, for up to seven years, as POWs in North Vietnam. (Today our "tepid" leaders would consider this "Cruel, Inhuman and Degrading Treatment," but to us it was realistic valuable training.)

In the spring of 1957, I was preparing to return to the U.S. and still hoping to be assigned to a jet squadron. With this in mind I requested reassignment to a B-57 light bomber squadron, but even though my request was "Recommended Approved" by my squadron commander, and USAFE Headquarters in Wiesbaden it was disapproved at higher headquarters in Washington. My next base of assignment was to the 2256th Air Reserve Flying Center, Niagara Falls, New York. I would be instructing Air Reserve pilots in their recent transition from F-84 jet fighters to C-119Gs. Even though it was not what I had requested, I thought the assignment would be challenging and looked forward to it. However, before concluding my recollections of my life at Neubiberg Air Base, Germany I will comment on a few colleagues, who for different reasons, left a lasting impression.

Colonel Joseph A. Cunningham, the 317th TCW Commanding Officer, received his pilot wings in 1939, and during WW II flew B-26 light bombers in Africa and Europe. He was one of the finest officers I had the pleasure of serving. I often flew with him in the C-119 and recognized his exceptional pilot expertise. Being too young for WW II, I enjoyed sharing the cockpit with him whenever the circumstances allowed. Major General Cunningham, USAF (ret.) died on November 23, 1991 at the age of 76.

Colonel Luther Howell(N) was a headquarters senior staff officer who I also remember, but for different reasons. He was a WW II veteran, but seemed to derive perverted pleasure in inspiring officers, and enlisted men, to do anything to avoid him. He led a 12-ship C-119 formation on a good-will flight to Athens, Greece with a refueling stop in Italy. When preparing to depart Italy, one of our aircraft experienced a minor mechanical problem and couldn't make the scheduled takeoff time, so the crew planned on joining us later in Athens. After landing in Greece, Colonel Howell gathered us together and stated with a tone of hostility, "I don't want anyone to be seen in a downtown hotel in flight suits." Based on his unusual edict, we were required to change into civilian attire, over hot sweaty bodies, before leaving the airport.

Sometime after dinner, several of us were sitting in the hotel lobby when the crew that had been delayed in Italy walked in to register, still wearing their flight suits (which was common practice when on cross-country flights). Col. Howell, grim-faced, and extremely angry that his orders had been disobeyed (the crew that had landed late were not present when he issued the flight suit edict), walked over and put them in a military brace, and started screaming obscenities at them for disobeying his orders. When he finished berating them, he snarled, "This is not the end of this issue. You will hear more when we return to Germany."

The next morning we were gathered in the hotel dining room eating breakfast, and as directed dressed in civilian slacks and sport shirts. Colonel Howell entered, dressed in a flight suit and a gaudy baseball cap with "thunder and lightning" on its visor, and took a seat at a separate table. (A perfect example of the negative type of leadership he instilled.)

Most Friday nights at the Officers' Club there would be a poker table operating, along with a crap game so crowded that it was difficult to find a spot to place bets. Colonel Howell would show-up, half-drunk, and in a few minutes lose the few dollars he would have on him at the crap table. He would then reach over and borrow money from adjacent dice throwers, by just pulling bills out of their hands. His brusque unsolicited borrowing tactics resulted in players pocketing their exposed cash and leaving the game, which would not resume until he left the club.

On another occasion my wife and I were entering the club and observed Col. Howell and his wife arguing loudly in the narrow entrance hallway. As we were about to excuse ourselves past them, he hauled off and smacked his wife so hard she bounced off the wall. He then strolled into the club while his wife began crying. Colonel Howell was transferred to Wiesbaden and I had the dubious honor of flying him there in a C-119.

Major William A. Jones III was a West Point graduate, and a member of the headquarters staff, but assigned to my squadron for flying. Bill and I became great friends and were both members of an Air Force downhill ski team in 1956. He was a great pilot, loved the military, and his enthusiasm for flying helped in establishing excellent squadron "esprit de corps." In the summer of 1956, he was preparing to rotate back to the U.S. and requested reassignment to a B-47 jet bomber squadron. However, when his orders arrived they stated that his next assignment was to a C-124 *Globemaster* cargo unit. Bill was very unhappy with the prospect of flying lumbering cargo aircraft and stated, "I'm not going to accept that assignment, and will not leave Germany until I'm assigned to B-47s." I told Bill that he couldn't go on strike when in the military, but this didn't deter him from his planned objective. "Just watch me," was his response. He wrote to his senator and congressman and allowed his scheduled rotation date to lapse, without making any effort to depart. We were all eager to see what would come of his "one-officer insurrection," but we didn't have long to wait. Bill won the fight and was assigned to a B-47 squadron in Lake Charles, Louisiana.

During the Vietnam War, he volunteered to fly Douglas A-I *Skyraiders* and was awarded the Medal of Honor for meritorious service over North Vietnam on Sept. 1, 1968. After returning to the U.S. he called to let me know that President Nixon was going to present the medal to him in the Oval Office and after the ceremony, he and his wife Lois were going to visit us in Dover AFB. However on November 15, 1969, he was killed in a Piper *Tri-pacer* soon after takeoff from Woodbridge, Virginia. The cause of the accident was <u>Undetermed</u>, but it was thought that he may have experienced a heart attack due to combat injuries he incurred over North Vietnam. His wife Lois accepted the medal in his behalf from President Nixon in a White House ceremony in 1970. (Lois never remarried, we still exchange holiday greetings and she has a copy of this book.)

There were other officers and enlisted men that were worthy of mention, but too numerous to comment on. My assignment to the 317th TCW and the 40th TCS at Neubiberg Air Base, Germany was the best assignment in my Air Force career --- not only because of the people I had the pleasure of serving with, but also having the opportunity of being part of the flourishing freedom engendered by the expanding formation of NATO. My last flight in a C-119 in Germany was on May 3, 1957. A few days later, my wife, five-year-old daughter Lynn and I were on a train for Bremerhaven Germany, where we would board a troopship for the U.S.

In 1957 most Air Force personnel transferring between the U.S. and Germany was by military aircraft. Movement of personnel by air was cheaper and shortened the time spent in the travel pipeline. However, since I was rotating back to the U.S. in late May, I thought a leisurely ten-day trip on a ship would be an enjoyable way to end a very pleasant overseas tour. I was especially eager to return by ship, since being promoted to captain, my family and I would be authorized a private cabin.

Our chief flight surgeon, Captain C.H. Dudley, was a personal friend and I asked him if he would write a letter stating that my wife was fearful of flying (not true), so we would be authorized to return to the U.S. by troop ship. His response, "No problem, Lou. You can pick up the letter tomorrow." I presented Dr. Dudley's letter to our transportation officer and was promptly issued orders authorizing surface transportation to New York. Our train from Munich to the seaport of Bremerhaven stopped within walking distance of the gangplank of the U.S.N.S. troop ship *General Patch.* (The long cumbersome, "hurry-up-and-wait" process, that was evident years earlier, was no longer in existence.)

The General Patch was an improvement over the older ships the Navy was nursing toward retirement. It was launched in 1944, was 608 feet long, could accommodate 5,200 troops, a crew complement of 618, cruised at 19 knots and continued in service until 2001.

Once onboard, a crew member directed us to a bulletin board, listing cabin assignments, and other pertinent information relating to the voyage. I was pleased to learn that we were assigned a private cabin on A Deck. However, there was an asterisk next to my name which indicated I should check a second bulletin board for determining my military duties once the ship was underway. Much to my disappointment I was designated as a Compartment Commander for a group of enlisted men (crammed in like sardines) in the bowels of the ship. An Army 2nd Lt. was assigned as my assistant. The order, signed by an Army major general, stated that compartment commanders, and assistants, were to report to the ship's main lounge at 1400 hours (2 p.m.) In Class A uniform for a briefing.

About 40 field grade officers (second lieutenant through captain) were assembled when the general's aide called the room to attention. Instruction booklets (containing about 20 pages) were distributed, followed by a monotonous "pep talk" on how important it was that we ensure strict military discipline be maintained during the crossing, while stressing that compartment commanders, or their assistants, would inspect their assigned areas twice daily for cleanliness, no lounging on neatly-made bunks during the daytime, floors swept, clean latrines, etc. When making these inspections, we were to be in Class A uniform. (Listening to this boring briefing, I thought, well there goes my plan of a leisurely relaxed ocean crossing, but I wasn't ready to give up.)

At the conclusion of the briefing, I met with my young 2nd Lt. assistant and asked him how long he had been an officer. He said, "One year, sir. I graduated from West Point last year and was assigned to a unit in Germany, but it was recently deactivated and I'm now on my way back to the U.S. for reassignment." I asked him about his accommodations on the ship, to which he replied, "I'm assigned a bunk with seven other junior officer in a cabin below decks." (I remembered the experience well.)

I asked my young "Shave-tail" if during his military career he had received a letter of commendation, to which he replied, "No sir, not yet." Hearing that, I told him that I was going to do him a big favor, which would help his military career. He seemed interested, as I explained that since I had recently made captain I didn't need any recognition for "exemplary service," so I would like to see him reap all the benefits of a well-managed compartment. I told him that I would allow him to assume full responsibility for ensuring our assigned compartment meets all military requirements, as set forth in the general's briefing. In return for his diligence, at the completion of the cruise, I would present him with a letter of commendation, adding that such a letter, endorsed by an Air Force captain, would look great in his military personnel file. He seemed pleased by the proposal and responded, "That sounds great, captain. Don't worry about a thing. I'll do a good job and make you proud of me!"

For the next nine days I lounged on the warm open decks, dressed in shorts and a short-sleeve shirt, enjoyed an occasionally martini from my hidden bottle of gin and took long naps after lunch. My capable assistant would hunt me down to report on his findings from his twice daily inspections of our assigned compartment, which I listened to, with intense interest, and told him to keep up the good work!

Lounging on a deck chair, with just one day remaining in our enjoyable ocean cruise, I reflected back on a few highlights of the voyage --- I had acquired a good tan, put on a few pounds, and had time to read several good books. But my reflective meditation was interrupted by my faithful assistant, who located me lounging in the sun with a newspaper covering my face. He handed me a memorandum from the Army general stating that the following morning, the last day of our voyage, there would be an open-bay inspection of all compartments. It directed that all compartment commanders, and their assistants, be present for this important inspection. The memo went on to state that following the inspection, the results would be posted, along with a ranking of how each compartment was rated. A letter of commendation, signed by the general, would be presented to the first, second and third place winners.

My assistant and I, with shined shoes, fresh haircuts and pressed uniforms, were standing at attention in our respective compartment the following morning. The general and his aide, wearing white gloves, walked in and went about inspecting our area for dust, beds made with eleven-inch white collars, shoes aligned, clean latrines, etc. The general's aide, walking behind him like a trained poodle, recorded their findings. When they left, I told my assistant I was going to change into more comfortable clothes, and if he needed me for anything else, I would be lounging on an open deck.

A couple hours later my assistant, with his head bowed, came walking slowly in my direction. I could see that he was depressed and asked him why he was so forlorn. He said, "I have some bad news to report captain, but I don't know exactly where to begin." I told him, "Just spit it out!" With almost a tear in his eye, he said, "Captain, I'm sorry to report that our compartment was considered the worst compartment on the entire ship, and as far as the inspection rating was concerned, we came in last!" I could see that he really felt bad after all his hard work, so I didn't make fun of his "West Point Style" sincerity. I handed him the promised glowing typed letter of commendation, while stating, "Lieutenant, you were the best compartment assistant on the entire ship, regardless of what some tired old general says." After reading the letter, his composure brightened somewhat and he thanked me for taking the time in writing such a complimentary letter. He said that the first thing he was going to do when he reported to his new post was to present it to his new commanding officer. I congratulated him for a job well done and said that I was very fortunate to have an assistant as trustworthy and conscientious as he had been. We shook hands and went our separate ways.

After a 30-day home leave, I reported for duty with the Air Force Reserve Organization at the Niagara Falls, New York Airport. I would be part of an active duty force of approximately 20 Air Force specialists (both officer and enlisted) with the primary responsibility of training members of an Air Force Reserve Squadron. The airport was shared by the Bell Aircraft Company (which produced the P-39 and P-63 during WW II), a Navy Reserve Squadron flying Grumman F-9F Panthers, an Air National Guard Squadron flying F-86Fs and an active duty Air Force Interceptor Squadron flying F-86Ds. The Air Force maintained a small military base, including a BX, mess hall, and NCO and Officers' Clubs, which were frequented by both reserve and active duty personnel.

I presented a copy of my orders to my new commander, Lt.Col. Donald Pricer, who I took a liking to straight away. He told me that he had already reviewed my military background and was looking forward to my assuming the duties of chief instructor in checking out former Air Force Reserve fighter pilots in the C-119. Col. Pricer added that our unit was also responsible for training and maintaining the currency of a group of reserve navigators, utilizing two TC-47 aircraft, but I would not, at least initially, be involved with this mission. He said that I would have my hands full with the C-119 program. He also mentioned that we had two Beechcraft C-45 *Expeditors* assigned for administrative support missions but weren't flown very much and I could fly them whenever I wished. I was then introduced to our operations officer, Major Lawrence H. Tate. (Major Tate had recently checked out in the C-119, but had thousands of hours in the C-47.) Like Col. Pricer, he extended a very warm welcome.

The other active duty officers consisted of C-119 pilots, Major Clarence G. Weslar(n), Captains Charles W. Sperling, Charles Hoggat and Joe Loucks. Captain Loucks had the additional duty as commander of the TC-47 Navigator Training Detachment with Captain Charlie Carpenter as his chief pilot. Captain Carl Sheldon was the aircraft maintenance officer.

Major Tate stated that since our primary mission was working with the reserve units, my normal work days would be Wednesday through Sunday, with my two days off being Monday and Tuesday. He added that once I became accustomed to working weekends, I would enjoy it, since no matter what I wanted to do on my days off, I could avoid weekend crowds. (I soon discovered that he was correct, and since my daughter was only five-years-old, and just starting kindergarten, I would be able to spend Monday and Tuesday afternoons with her.) My first flight in a C-119G at Niagara Falls was on Wednesday, July 17, 1957, during a local flight check with a reserve pilot already qualified in the aircraft.

I found the majority of the reserve pilots eager to check out in the C-119, even though they missed the excitement of flying jet fighters. However, they were realistic in recognizing that with the Korean War over, many reserve fighter units were being deactivated, and if it wasn't for the C-119s they would have been transferred to the inactive reserves with no aircraft to fly. They also felt fortunate that their unit was equipped with the C-119G, the latest model of the *Flying Boxcar*. The reserve pilots came from all conceivable cross sections of the surrounding Western New York State area, so if I wanted to buy a television, washing machine, rent a house or fix a traffic ticket, there was a member of the reserve squadron who could help out. The fact that I was their chief instructor certainly increased their willingness to provide assistance wherever possible.

As more and more reserve pilots became qualified in the C-119, my cockpit duties consisted mostly of conducting annual proficiency checks, formation qualification, and higher headquarters directed support missions. Typical of these was the flying of a group of college Air Force ROTC cadets to a basic pilot training base in Bartow, Florida and staying with them for five days. When in Florida each cadet was given an orientation flight in the T-34 Beechcraft *Mentor* while I enjoyed visiting local sites including *Cypress Gardens.* Most parents came to the Niagara Falls Airport to see their sons off and I'm sure prayed that when they climbed onboard my C-119 they would return safely. (All of them did!)

Another interesting support flight was flying several low level trips up and down the Saint Lawrence Canal during its construction phase. These flights were made with the rear clamshell doors removed so engineers and cameramen would have an open view to take pictures. (When flying these missions I insisted that the cameramen wear parachutes and be anchored to the interior of the aircraft by long nylon straps.)

In the summer of 1958 I accompanied my reserve squadron on their annual two weeks of active duty to Grenier Field, Manchester, New Hampshire. The summer camp session evaluated all aspects of simulated combat flying and I was very proud when our unit was rated number one of the reserve squadrons participating. So as to have local transportation I drove my 1953 Nash *Ambassador* versus flying there with one of the flight crews. The Nash was a neat car and equipped with a split bench-style front seat that folded back flat to form a bed. (I was hoping this unique feature would become useful during my stay in Manchester.)

Most of the reserve pilots were now fully qualified in the C-119 so it was not necessary to fly with them on every mission, leaving me with a fair amount of free time to enjoy the excitement of the "simulated wartime" atmosphere and the surrounding New England area. I had become friendly with an attractive secretary, and recent divorcee, working at the airport who gave me the impression of a gal who would be interested in showing a visiting pilot the local sights. I asked her if she would care to go out for dinner. She readily said, "Yes."

After dinner she suggested I purchase a bottle of booze at one of the state operated liquor stores, followed by visiting her apartment for a nightcap. This captured my interest and I was soon mixing drinks in her one-bedroom, second-floor dwelling in downtown Manchester, when I noticed her making frequent trips to a window overlooking the parking lot. When I inquired as to what she was looking for, her answer not only surprised me, but put a damper on any amorous plans I had for the night! She said that she was concerned about her former husband who was extremely jealous and had recently visited her apartment and threatened a male visitor with a gun and wouldn't leave until the police arrived. **(Gulp!)** I finished my drink, said it was quite late and that I had to get back to the base. As I was leaving, I said, "Perhaps we can go out for dinner tomorrow night, to some 'out-of-the-way' restaurant that your ex-husband is not familiar with?" "I know just the place," she said.

I picked her up as she left work in my shiny blue "*Nash Bedmobile*" and drove about 30 miles outside of Manchester to a quaint country restaurant nestled amongst a thick grove of tall pine trees, where we enjoyed a couple martinis and a leisurely dinner complemented with a fine bottle of wine. After dinner we took a drive through some back woods and found a delightful secluded parking spot, about 20 feet off the main road.

I tuned the radio to a station playing romantic music and started making advances that were warmly received. In my exuberance in testing out the "*Nash Bedmobile*" feature, I reached across her, firmly grabbed the seat back release handle and broke it off. When the release handle snapped, the seat slammed back into a prone position with a bang. (I wondered how I would be able to raise it later, with the release handle broke, but that was not a problem that required immediate attention.) The folding seat lived up to its reputation and being tired of swatting mosquitoes, I thought it was time we headed for town. But leaving, as I soon discovered, was not going to be easy!

Operating the old vacuum tube radio on the six-volt battery had discharged it to the point that it didn't have enough power left to turn over the starter, and we were parked some distance off a deserted country road. What to do? Searching through the woods, I found a long pole which I used as a prying implement against the rear bumper. With my good-spirited companion steering, I was able to move the heavy sedan "inch-by-inch" back onto the highway and to the top of a small hill. I then got behind the wheel and with my date half sitting and half laying on the collapsed passenger seat, released the brake and allowed the car to gain speed down the hill. When I released the clutch, the engine started and I drove to a nearby gas station, where under the guise of a smiling attendant, I borrowed a pair of pliers to reposition the passenger seat into an upright position. When I thanked him for the use of the pliers, he said with a wink, and a glance at my pretty date, "If you like, you can keep them as you may wish to lower the seat again before the night is over." "Thanks, but no thanks," I said, "I'm all tuckered out and need some rest!"

I devoted the rest of my time in Manchester flying with pilots that still required a bit more massaging before they were qualified C-119 Aircraft Commanders. There was one likable captain, who was a promising twin-engine pilot, if I could cure him of one chronic problem. When I would simulate an engine failure he would become confused as to which engine had failed and waste critical minutes in trying to figure out which one he should shutdown. I recommended that he adopt the tried and true method of "dead-foot-dead-engine," but he still paused before making a decision.

The "dead-foot-dead-engine" technique refers to the fact that if the left engine failed the aircraft would naturally yaw to the left, because of the increased drag on that side of the aircraft. To correct for this the pilot would be required to push hard on the right rudder, to keep the aircraft going straight. Once he accomplished this he could "snap" his left unused (dead-foot) back against his seat, which would indicate that the left engine had failed and should be shut down. (A tried and true procedure.)

In spite of my stressing this proven simplistic technique, which seemed to confuse him, I thought a more radical approach was required. When simulating the loss of an engine it was standard procedure to retard one throttle to the idle position and state, "engine failure!" For most pilots this procedure worked fine and they would identify which engine supposedly failed and perform the proper corrective action in a timely manner. However, I thought that perhaps this former single-engine jet fighter pilot, when looking down at misaligned throttles, with his instructor calling out "engine failure," may have caused unnecessary confusion.

When flying in clear skies at 7,000 feet east of Manchester I instructed him to make a turn to the left, and as expected, he turned his head to check for the presence of other aircraft. When his head was turned, I reached up and switched the left engine fuel selector to the off position. About three seconds later, the left engine gave out with a "big grunt" and quit, causing a sharp yaw to the left. My surprised student gave me a startled look, as the throttles, prop and fuel mixture controls were all in a normal cruise "engine running" aligned position. In an excited voice he said, **"What do you want me to do?"** My answer, **"It appears we lost an engine, so take the proper action!"** He pushed on the right rudder pedal (to arrest the yaw to the left), snapped his left foot back against his seat, and called out "dead foot." Following this correct call, I expected him to retard the left throttle, left fuel mixture control and feather the left propeller. However, to my surprise, and before I could stop him, he reached up, shutdown the right engine and feathered the right propeller!

With both engines shutdown, the aircraft became very quiet as we had just become a 44,000 lb. Fairchild glider! I think my student was just as surprised, in the sudden silence, as I was and said, **"What do you want me to do now?"** My answer, **"You got us into this mess, now get us out of it, and don't let the airspeed fall below 140 knots in the glide."** He was a good "stick and rudder" pilot and kept the airspeed at 140 kts, and I thought at first he would be able to get an engine restarted before we were dangerously close to the farm fields of New Hampshire. However, indecision was still his systemic problem and as we were approaching 2,000 feet and still sinking, he hadn't been able to restart an engine. I couldn't wait any longer so shouted, **"I've got it!"** and took over control of the aircraft. I switched the left fuel selector to the on position, and retarded the left throttle to idle. Since the left fuel mixture control was still in the fuel-on position, and the left propeller had not been feathered, the engine roared back into life. I then unfeathered the right propeller, started the right engine and directed that he return to Grenier Airport. After landing my affable, but unpredictable former single-engine jet fighter pilot admitted that he may never master twin-engine aircraft and withdrew from the program. I trust he is alive today, as I'm sure the PGR had marked him as a potential candidate had he continued flying the C-119.

A former C-119 pilot colleague, Captain Donald E. Born, who I had served with in Germany, was not as fortunate and was involved in a rare fatal Encounter with the PGR in the winter of 1958. Don, like myself, was a C-119 instructor pilot, but working with an Air Force Reserve Squadron at Hill AFB, Utah. He had departed Randolph AFB, Texas for Utah after a ten-day TDY trip. Onboard his aircraft were two pilots, one navigator, two crew chiefs and three passengers. The flight was routine until about 50 miles east of Ogden. They were flying in the clouds at 12,000 feet, and picking up ice, when the carburetor heat control for the right engine failed. Following this failure the engine began backfiring and finally quit. Don was forced to feather the propeller and with only one engine operating could not maintain altitude, even when going to full power on the left engine. As he began to lose altitude he was concerned about crashing into high mountainous terrain, so he ordered the three passengers and the two crew chiefs to bail out. He was still losing altitude, and with the aircraft's speed dropping, he put the aircraft on autopilot and ordered his student pilot and navigator to bail out. He soon followed them after ensuring everyone onboard had abandoned the aircraft.

All eight crew members landed safely, but unfortunately they were dressed in summer flight suits and came down in high desolate snow-covered mountainous terrain, with temperatures below freezing, and less than one hour of daylight remaining. Captain Born had managed to make a "Mayday" (emergency) radio call before bailing out, but with the bad weather and failing daylight, rescue could not be expected before the next morning. Don and three other crew members could not last through the night and were found the next day frozen to death. Ironically, the aircraft continued flying, missed the mountains, and crash landed on relatively open prairie after it ran out of gas. (I often thought that Don may have been able to restore partial power to the right engine by use of the engine primer, but we will never know.)

The operations officer of the F-86D Fighter Interceptor Squadron at Niagara Falls was a fine officer and an excellent pilot. He loved to fly and checked me out in the Aero Club's T-34. He was a fighter pilot's pilot and respected by all who had the pleasure of knowing him. One foggy Sunday afternoon a local county sheriff called the air base and requested a helicopter to help search for some reportedly lost hunters. A helicopter could not be launched without his permission so the duty officer called him at his on-base military quarters. His wife said later, that when he received the call he was watching a football game on television, but since the team he was cheering for was losing, he told her he would join the helicopter pilots to help look for the lost hunters. During the low altitude search the helicopter struck high tension wires hidden in the fog and all onboard were killed. As often happens, the hunters were not lost, but had stopped to have a few beers on their way home, but failed to call their wives who were naturally worried and called the Air Force for help.

During the same time frame Major Tate and myself observed fire trucks racing toward the west end of the airport. We jumped into a jeep and followed. About 1/4 mile short of the runway a T-33 had crash-landed in a frozen swamp on its extended landing gear. The pilot in the front seat appeared dazed, but was conscious. The pilot in the rear seat was slumped forward and appeared unconscious. The area reeked with the smell of jet fuel so crash rescue personnel smashed the canopy with an ax versus attempts to raise it electrically. The pilot in the front seat recovered quickly, but the pilot in the rear seat was killed when his forehead slammed into the trim switch on the top of the control stick. His forehead contained a small deep indentation not unlike a bullet hole.

Investigation of the accident disclosed that the pilots were making an instrument approach in freezing rain and had failed to turn on the pitot heat, which resulted in inaccurate airspeed indications, allowing the aircraft to stall just short of the runway. The pilot in the front seat had his shoulder harness locked, which prevented him from slamming forward, but the pilot in the rear seat had failed to lock his shoulder harness and therefore his upper body slammed forward with such force that his head struck the trim button on top of the control stick. If they had not forgotten to turn on the pitot heat, or if the rear seat pilot had locked his shoulder harness, he would have survived the crash. (The PGR never sleeps.)

In the summer of 1958 I was administering an annual proficiency check to one of our reserve pilots a few miles east of Buffalo at 7,000 feet. It was a brilliant sunny day with a cloudless blue sky and unlimited visibility. Suddenly, a large fiery explosion, a few miles south and about 5,000 feet above my altitude, erupted in the clear sky. It grew in intensity for a few seconds, then split into two distinct fireballs and crashed into desolate farm land. I made an emergency radio call to the Niagara Falls tower, reporting that two fighters had collided, that I didn't observe any parachutes, was proceeding to the crash sites and would provide their exact locations. Following my call an aircraft stated, "Aircraft reporting that two fighters had collided, what is your call sign?" When I responded, I was informed that the crash did not involve two fighters, but a B-47 jet bomber. This information was coming from a KC-97 pilot, who sounded like he was under a lot of stress. I circled over the flaming craters, noted their location and returned to Niagara Falls.

The next day an Air Force major from Columbus AFB, Ohio arrived to lead a team of inspectors in investigating the accident. To my surprise the team leader was Major (Pappy) Hurst my former boss from Germany. Pappy told me that the aircraft that crashed was a B-47 from his base in Ohio and that it was preparing to take on fuel from a KC-97 tanker at 15,000 feet when its right wing sheared and folded back over on top of its fuselage. The four crew members onboard were unable to eject and were killed in the crash. He added that when the bomber exploded it was so close to the tanker that it nearly blew it out of the sky as well.

On Saturday, October 12, 1957, I was administering an annual proficiency check to a reserve captain when I received a radio call instructing me to land and contact my operations officer. Major Tate told me that my father had died and he and Colonel Pricer expressed their condolences. This was naturally sad news, but not unexpected, as he had been battling prostate cancer for some time. I went home to pack a bag and check on flight schedules to the nearest city to my hometown with a commercial airport. While I was packing, Colonel Pricer called and said that he had arranged for a reserve crew to fly me home in a C-119. I called my brothers, Hank and Ben, and told them that I would be arriving at the Eau Claire Airport around noon the next day. I didn't tell them what type of aircraft I would be arriving in, assuming they would think it would be a twin-engine Beechcraft, similar to what I had flown home in before.

When a large Air Force C-119 landed at the Eau Claire Airport, it created quite a sensation. It was a warm day and there were a number of sightseers watching small airplanes takeoff and land, so the appearance of a 74,000 pound Fairchild *Boxcar*, with huge rumbling 3,500 hp engines, was a star performer. We parked in front of the small terminal and I spied my two brothers waving along with a group of curious bystanders. I waved to them from an open cockpit window and then proceeded to the rear of the aircraft where I exited from a paratrooper door. I picked up my B-4 bag, walked to the front of the aircraft and gave a thank you salute to the crew. They acknowledged my wave off, taxied out to the runway and departed with the roar of two 3500 hp Wright Cyclone engines reverberating across the field. The sound of the C-119 racing down the airport runway was accompanied by "Ohs and Ahs" from the crowd gathered to watch it blast-off. I felt real proud as I shook hands with my admiring brothers, while subliminally giving thanks to a fine commanding officer that made this flight possible.

My years in the Air Force not only provided an interesting range of flying experiences but also the meeting of likable and interesting characters that injected humor into a sometimes dangerous profession. One such individual at Niagara Falls was Major Clarence Weslar. He was a bachelor officer, about 35-years-old, and always seemed to have an easy-going smile. He lived in the BOQ, which was adjacent to the Officers' Club, and because of his rank was authorized two adjoining rooms. His hobby was wood working so he converted one room into a work shop and installed all the tools he deemed appropriate to support his noisy pastime. His array of equipment included a table saw, sander, drill press and a wood lathe. Needless to say his hobby generated considerable noise and complaints from other BOQ residents, which rose and fell, in concert with his off-duty hours. Since our scheduled off days were Monday and Tuesday, he could create wood-working noises to his heart content, during the day, but quite often he was eager to finish a project and continued working into the evening. (His BOQ colleagues didn't think the expression "sawing wood" when trying to sleep, needed any help from Clarence and would bang on his door to get him to turn off his machines.)

Clarence, like myself, loved martinis, but where I had learned to taper off after two or three, he was just getting started. He also loved playing pinball machines, and would set his martini on the glass top of a pinball machine, while kicking its supporting legs and banging its sides in attempting to coerce the steel balls into the high numbered holes. When things didn't work out the way he thought they should, he would accuse the machine of cheating him. His "earthquake type" shaking and kicking would cause his martini to spill and create a slippery puddle on the floor where he was standing. The spilling of his drink didn't deter him from his goal of defeating the "stealthy devious machine," as when his glass was empty, he would just order another, set it on the glass top and continue his kicking, cussing and hand slapping the machine.

One evening several of us were enjoying a drink at the Officers' Club bar, when our attention was directed to watching Clarence courageously battle a dishonest and conniving pinball machine. The machine seemed to be particularly ornery and was not responding to his usual abusive, coercive tactics. (It obviously took advantage of his inebriated state and beat him royally!) Clarence became more agitated than usual, took a step back from the diabolical machine, curled his upper lip into a snarl, cocked his right leg back like a "NFL field-goal kicker" and prepared to teach the errant pinball machine a lesson it wouldn't soon forget. With all the force his small frame could muster, he started to swing his cocked leg forward, but before he could deliver the kick, he slipped on the puddle of spilled gin and landed "slam-bam" on his ass! The machine had won round one, but Major Weslar didn't accept defeat lightly! He got up off the floor, shouted, "You son-of-a-bitch," at the machine, and in two strong kicks broke off it's two front legs! As the pinball machine came crashing down on the floor he smashed his foot through the glass top! Internal electronic relays were still clicking away wildly, which we interpreted as a coded message of surrender! Clarence proudly staggered away in a cocky, victory-style gait. (He was naturally charged for the damage to the club's property, but we were not charged for a free floor show.)

On another night, we were playing a Roll-A-Score machine for drinks and a dollar per game. The machine had a "bowling-style-alley" for the rolling, by hand, of fairly large hard balls. The object of the game was to sink the balls into numbered holes, on an elevated surface, behind a protective glass containing a tabulated electronic score graph. The smaller the hole, the higher the score. Clarence was having a bad night and losing dollars and drinks and the more martinis he consumed the more convinced he was that the bowling-ball machine was built by the same company as the pinball machine and conniving against him.

During one of his underarm softball pitcher style throws he struck the knuckles of his right hand on the metal edge of the machine. This obviously caused considerable pain and his ball to go shooting across the bar room floor. We could see that he was angry and wondered what type of revenge he was going to take out on the machine. We didn't have to wait long, he picked up a ball, muttered, "You S.O.B." and threw it through the protective glass score chart. As the glass came crashing down I said, "Well, the game is over as we can no longer identify the players with the scores, without the glass covering." Clarence's answer, "Yes we can. I'll run over to my BOQ room and get some duck tape. This is the first time that I'm ahead and I don't want to quit now." The duct tape didn't work and he had the cost of repairing another machine added to his bill.

Major Weslar, when not entertaining his fellow tenants by the whirring sounds from his wood working shop or engaging in mortal combat with amusement machines, would be speeding around the countryside in his 1958 Chrysler Imperial sedan, while listening to sporting events on the radio. It was a beautiful car with a four-barrel, 345 hp Hemi engine, capable of creating clouds of smoke from spinning rear tires.

One night I had invited him to our house in North Tonawanda for dinner. His arrival was announced by the sound of his Chrysler swerving into our driveway, accompanied with screeching tires as it came to a stop. I mixed him a double Beefeater gin martini, and without the spillage he normally experienced when playing pinball machines, the entire drink went down his throat. He thrust out his empty glass for a refill, but I said, "This one will be a single." "Bullshit," he answered, and went to the bar and mixed himself another double. I momentarily left him alone to assist in preparing the dinner and when I returned he was on his third martini.

Dinner was served with wine and after the meal Clarence went to the bar and helped himself to a double shot of Cognac, which he poured into his coffee. I was worried about him being able to drive home and made an earnest effort to get him to spend the night in our guest room. However he had a better idea! "I would like to take you and your wife for a ride in my Hemi-powered Chrysler Imperial. You won't believe the acceleration," he said. I emphatically, but with respect to my good friend, declined his offer and again insisted that he spend the night with us and drive back to the base the next morning. I think our declining his offer of accompanying him in a "death-defying" ride in his Chrysler, and insisting that he spend the night with us, insulted his macho bachelor image. He stormed out of the house, while muttering a half-hearted, "Thanks for a great evening, Lou."

He climbed into his Chrysler, backed out of our gravel driveway with the rear wheels spewing rocks against the house, and in a cloud of smoke from spinning tires, disappeared around the nearby corner. Even when he was out of sight, I could still hear the sound of screeching tires. I went back into the house, and told my wife that I hope he makes it back to his BOQ room safe and sound, but there was nothing more I could do!

When reporting for work the next morning, Major Tate told me that Colonel Pricer wanted to see me in his office. The first question he asked was, "Did Major Weslar have dinner at your house last night?" When I said that he did, he lit into me for allowing him to drive home by himself. After explaining that I had tried to get him to spend the night in our house, he calmed down and proceeded to tell me about Clarence's wild escapade after he left our house. Apparently he had become lost and was driving aimlessly around the countryside trying to find Niagara Falls Air Base. But in his wandering he came across the main gate of a *Nike Ajax* surface-to-air missile base, off limits to all personnel, both civilian and military, unless you possessed a special security pass.

During the 1950s there were approximately 145 Nike Ajax, surface-to-air missile sites in the U.S. They were designed to shoot down Soviet Union bombers that escaped our fighters. Most of them were small highly restricted military bases, complete with mess halls, barracks, recreational facilities, a small PX and highly motivated security police.

Clarence, thinking he had arrived back at his own base and eager to get some rest, attempted to drive through the front gate with just a wave of his hand, but was stopped by a military guard. He lost patience in being questioned on his authority to enter and, with rear wheels spinning, drove onto the base. The guard called the MPs who chased him down narrow streets before cornering him in a dead end. They escorted him to their infrequently used "cooler," and after identifying who he was, the site commander called Colonel Pricer to come and pick up his rowdy major. However, before Col. Pricer was allowed to take custody, he had to sign a release form and promise to take proper disciplinary action.

I told Colonel Pricer that I was sorry he was called out in the middle of the night and that I felt a certain amount of responsibility for Major Weslar's troubles since he was allowed to drink too many martinis when having dinner in my house. Adding that we all liked and respected him and hoped he would go easy when administering discipline, as many of us, under similar conditions, could have found ourselves in a similar predicament. I'm not sure he bought my (weak) argument, but he thanked me for my concern. Clarence was restricted to the base for a period of time, which seemed to temper his wild off-base escapades, but I'm sure it didn't please his fellow tenets in the BOQ, who were now subjected to an increase in the operating hours of his wood working shop. (Major Weslar died on September 3, 2003, and we lost a good Air Force officer, in spite of his infrequent eccentricities.)

Sometime later I was having a drink in the Officers' Club at Pope AFB, North Carolina. An officer sitting next to me asked where I was stationed. When I told him Niagara Falls, he asked if I knew a Major Weslar. When I told him that I did, he said what a great guy he was, and then added, "Is he still trashing pinball machines?" When I said on occasion, he told me of an incident that topped my observations. He said Clarence was playing a pinball machine in the Officers' Club one night and when the machine was getting the best of him, he got so mad that he pushed it out an open window and It crashed into a million pieces two floors below. Naturally, he had to buy a new one for the club. I said, "That's our Clarence!"

In November 1958 I was informed that my job would be taken over by an Air Reserve Technician and that I would be transferred to the 14th Air Force Inspector General's Staff at Mitchell AFB, New York. In a letter from Colonel Wildes, he congratulated me on being assigned to his unit, along with a notation that must have been dictated by my "Guardian Angel." It read, "Your new assignment will require that you be jet-qualified. If you are not presently qualified, please let me know and I will obtain a priority quota for you to attend a jet qualification course." So after all my failed attempts in becoming a jet pilot, the opportunity was dished out on an unexpected "silver platter." My last flight in a C-119 *Flying Boxcar* was on December 7, 1958. I had flown it for five years and 2,500 hours, and escaped the clutches of the PGR many times over. I had fond memories of flying the various models of this perfidious Fairchild aircraft and would miss the excitement it provided, but thought there must be other aircraft that would embolden my desire for excitement. I was now ready to move on to other assignments. I knew that whatever fate awaited me, it would be interesting and the PGR would be close at hand.

As I prepared to leave Niagara Falls, I reflected back on the wonderful experience it provided, including seeing the falls frozen to a complete "standstill" in the winter of 1958. Also the experience of flying and associating with a great bunch of pilots who had flown F-51s and F-47s during WW II and F-84s during the early fifties, followed by my introducing them to the C-119 and watching them master and accepting it in a very short period of time. I left with fond memories, but as in the past, eager to see if "the grass was greener on the proverbial other side of the airport!"

Chapter Seven --- Douglas C-47 Skytrain

In the spring of 1958 most of the Niagara Falls Air Force Reserve pilots were qualified in the C-119, allowing me time to checkout in the TC-47.

The C-47 is the military version of the famous Douglas DC-3, which was one of the four weapons singled out by General Eisenhower as the most instrumental in helping win WW II. (The others were the bazooka, the jeep and the atomic bomb.) The C-47, affectionately known as the Gooney Bird, was a product of the Douglas DC series dating back to 1936. However, in 1937 the Army ordered a new model based on its own specifications. It was an improved version of an earlier aircraft and represented the Army's goal of providing critical airlift capability. In 1941 the U.S. Army revised its requirements and directed that the new aircraft have a reinforced fuselage floor, a large side cargo door, external cargo hooks, and a tail mount for towing gliders. After these modifications were made, the aircraft was designated the C-47 Skytrain.

As a cargo aircraft it could carry up to 6,000 pounds, a jeep or a 37-mm cannon. As a troop transport it carried 28 paratroopers, (in full combat gear) or 14 stretcher patients and support nurses. It saw action in all theaters of the war and during the 1943 Sicily campaign it towed gliders and dropped 4,381 paratroopers. In the 1944 invasion of Normandy it towed thousands of gliders and dropped 60,000 paratroopers.

By the end of WW II, 9,348 C-47s had been produced. After the war C-47s remained in service for many years and flew missions during the Berlin Airlift and the Korean and Vietnam wars. The C-47 has a wing span of 95 ft., a length of 64 ft., a maximum weight of 33,000 lbs., two Pratt & Whitney R-1830 engines of 1,200 hp. each, a cruise speed of 160 kts, a maximum speed of 224, and cost $138,000. (Equal to $1,600,000 today.) The models I flew were the basic C-47, the VC-47 (VIP version) and the TC-47. The latter was used for navigator training and equipped with three additional plastic astrodomes for taking celestial observations and six additional navigator plotting tables. (See Photo No. 42.)

On March 2, 1958, I was assigned to fly as copilot in a TC-47, commanded by Captain Charles (Charlie) Carpenter, on a reserve navigator training mission to Miami, Florida, with an en route stop at Mitchell AFB, New York. From Mitchell wo flow oast until 500 miles over the Atlantic Ocean before turning south toward Florida. This circuitous route allowed the navigators the opportunity of acquiring long-range over-water navigation proficiency. We would then spend several days in Miami flying extended navagation flights over the Gulf of Mexico. Charlie was a delightful pilot to fly with, possessed a wonderful sense of humor and a "homespun" Will Rogers-style philosophy on almost every aspect of life. When I complained about the slow cruise speed of the C-47 Charlie said, "We get paid by the month, not the speed we fly, so what difference does it make in how long it takes?" He was right!

After landing in Miami, we rented a car and obtained billets in an airport motel. The next night we filed a flight plan which would have us flying on a western course of approximately 500 miles over the Gulf of Mexico, followed by a northern course of 100 miles and a direct course back to Miami. The purpose of the mission was to provide night celestial navigation training for 20 reserve navigators.

After reaching our 500 mile turning point, we headed north and stood-by for our navigator's command to head east. However, no such course change came forth from the cabin and I couldn't raise an instructor navigator on the interphone. Charlie, noting that we had been flying on a heading of north much too long, directed that I go to the cabin to check on why we hadn't been instructed to take up a heading of east.

What I observed would have been humorous if it was being portrayed in a movie, but this was real life. Several of the navigators were in a heated argument as to our present position and obviously couldn't come to an agreement. Three of them had their heads in the astrodomes, taking star fixes with their sextants, while others were leaning over charts arguing and pounding index fingers on different geographical locations. Others were just sitting around, either too confused to participate in the position dispute or just didn't care. I returned to the cockpit and reported my observations to Charlie, who decided that we couldn't wait any longer for instructions from the navigators and took up an easterly heading.

There was no question that we would eventually reach Florida, but in 1958 the U.S. was surrounded by "Air Defense Identification Zones" (ADIZs) that were designed to provide radar protection against a surprise attack by Soviet Union bombers. Authority for penetrating an ADIZ was by prior permission, at specified locations, and at a time and altitude as indicated on an approved flight plan. Deviations would trigger an intercept by Air Defense fighters and a possible violation against the Aircraft Commander. Since we were now approaching the Florida coast from an unknown position, the possibility of being intercepted and incurring a violation was very real. To offset this possibility we contacted Miami Radio and reported that we were approaching Florida from the West, but due to a failure of navigation equipment (mostly true), we were unsure of our position. At the time we were beyond radar coverage, but Miami Radio attempted to "pinpoint" our position through triangulation from our HF radio transmissions, but this method was unreliable. However, when they determined our approximate position, they said they would relay it and the failure of our navigation equipment to the Air Defense Command. At least the problem of a possible violation seemed to have been resolved.

After flying on a heading of east for some time the chief navigator came to the cockpit and told us we should take up a heading of 090, but he wasn't sure of our exact position! Charlie told him, "Thanks, how about getting me a cup of coffee?" When in radar contact we took up a direct course for Miami and landed in time for breakfast. We were scheduled to fly a similar mission the following night, hopefully with better results.

Our rental automobile was a 1958 Plymouth sedan with a stick shift (manual transmission) and a key ignition switch on the dashboard. (The ignition switch in those days did not lock or unlock the steering wheel.) We were heading out for dinner when Charlie attempted to change radio stations, but he unintentionally turned the ignition switch into the off position. I reached over, turned it back on, which brought the engine back to life, but also ignited the accumulated fuel/air mixture in the exhaust pipe with a loud "backfire." We felt that we had just discovered a novel way of announcing our presence in Florida and began experimenting in ways of producing louder and more spectacular backfires!

We discovered that if we accelerated to a high rate of speed in second gear, turned off the ignition switch and pushed the accelerator all the way to the floor, we would pump raw gas not only into the cylinders, but the exhaust pipe, muffler and tail pipe as well. Then, when the ignition switch was turned back on, there would be an awe-inspiring explosion, accompanied by a ten-foot long flame shooting out from the tail pipe. (We called our discovery "Our Plymouth afterburner" and would repeat this frivolity whenever we felt a need for a "jocular fix.") It wasn't long before our improvised afterburner blew out the insides of the muffler and with a hollow tube from the engine to the tail pipe, the backfires and tongues of flame were more spectacular. (We also discovered that the pyrotechnics were slightly more thrilling when burning high-test gasoline.) When we returned the automobile to the rental agency, I told the young lady that the car ran fine, but needed a new muffler. Her response, "Thank you for letting us know, sir. We will have it repaired right away. Have a nice day!"

After returning to Niagara Falls, Major Lawrence Tate, our operations officer, decided to administer a checkout in the famed "Gooney Bird" to Charlie Hoggat, another C-119 flight instructor, and myself. On Wednesday, March 26, 1958, we departed on a local three-hour training flight, with Charlie in the left seat and Major Tate in the right seat as instructor pilot. While awaiting my turn to fly, I would observe by standing in the aisle between the two pilots.

We climbed to 5,000 feet where Larry demonstrated approaches to stalls, followed by Charlie performing the same maneuver. Larry then shutdown the right engine, feathered the propeller and had Charlie unfeather it and restart the engine. He then retarded the left throttle to idle and declared, "Simulated engine failure." Charlie shut down the left engine and feathered the propeller in a proficient manner that evidently pleased our flight instructor, who stated that he had control of the aircraft and would demonstrate a situation that could get us in a lot of trouble if we allowed the airspeed to decrease below "minimum-control-speed" when flying on one engine.

His first demonstration was simulating a landing with the left propeller feathered and executing a go-around from an imaginary low altitude, final approach. He went to full power on the right engine, pushed hard on the right rudder pedal, retracted the landing gear and while the aircraft was struggling to maintain altitude, stressed that he didn't allow the airspeed to fall below 85 kts. (The minimum safe single engine airspeed required for flight on one engine.) The aircraft settled several hundred feet before accelerating sufficiently to climb at around 300 feet per minute.

Larry then, while talking, said he would demonstrate the danger of allowing the aircraft speed to fall below the single engine minimum control speed of around 75 knots. With the left engine still shutdown, he reduced power on the right engine, pulled the nose up slightly, and at the first indication of a stall advanced the right throttle to full power of around 48 inches of manifold pressure and 2,700 RPM. As the power on the right engine approached maximum, the aircraft, without warning, "snap-rolled" inverted to the left. Standing between the seats I observed the horizon spin around 180 degrees and had to grab onto the sides of the cockpit to keep my head from hitting the ceiling.

Major Tate, who had thousands of hours in C-47s, and was a good "stick-and-rudder" pilot, reduced power on the right engine, allowed the inverted *Gooney Bird* to fall through the horizon with a positive G load, and when the nose was pointing toward Mother Earth, applied full left aileron and rolled the aircraft upright. With the airspeed approaching the "red line" (maximum) he pulled back on the control column to pull the aircraft out of a screaming dive. The positive G load recovery pulled me off the ceiling, but forced me onto the floor with a thump. Before the recovery maneuver was complete, we had lost about 3,000 feet of altitude and I picked up several strands of gray hair. (Larry said later that it was fortunate that we had climbed to 5,000 feet, as he initially planned on leveling off at 4,000. Had he decided on the lower altitude, it's quite possible that the PGR would have recruited three new candidates.)

The lesson learned from this incident was twofold: first, never allow the airspeed to fall below 85 knots, when flying on one engine; second, when administering flight instruction, never allow your attention to be diverted from flying the aircraft. Major Tate had considerable experience in C-47s, but allowed complacency and inattention to interfere with good sound judgment. (A contributing factor, which caused the aircraft to "snap-roll" to the left, was that the most critical (left) engine was shut down. This resulted in a yaw to the left which was exacerbated by the natural tendency of the aircraft to roll left, known as the "P Factor.")

After both Charlie Hoggat and I completed a more unruffled exposure to airwork, we returned to the airport to perform a series of landings and takeoffs. We flew the traffic pattern at a comfortable 110 kts with 90 knots on final approach. Larry suggested wheel landings (touching down on the main gear only) and not attempting "three-point" landings, as a high angle of attack flare would block airflow to the all important rudder. After one hour and 30 minutes in the left seat, I was checked out as an Aircraft Commander in the TC-47.

I flew a couple more navigator training missions to Miami, Florida and fortunately on these missions the navigators were able to accurately plot our position over the Gulf of Mexico. (However, during these trips, our rental automobiles still had a habit of backfiring and blowing out mufflers. We felt that there must have been something in the salt air that caused this systemic problem.) When preparing to return from Miami the chief navigator told me that one of his reserve navigators had refused to get out of bed and was still asleep in the BOQ and in a cantankerous mood. He added that he was a good navigator, but his heavy drinking and hot temper had caused problems in the past.

I visited the BOQ and discovered our missing navigator curled up in a fetal position in his bunk and sound asleep. I pulled back the bed covers, shook him awake and told him in a firm voice to "rise and shine!" My attempt to rouse him was met with flaying arms and cussing to leave him alone. I grabbed a pitcher of ice water, held it over him, and told him that if he didn't get up by the time I counted to five, I would pour it on top of him. When I reached a count of five, he hadn't stirred so "splash" went the ice-water. More arm flaying and profanity erupted, but he remained in bed. I didn't want to leave him in Florida, but knew that more drastic measures were required if I was going to get him onboard the aircraft!

I took the crew bus back to the flight line and procured about ten feet of nylon rope from a maintenance hangar. Returning to the BOQ, the chief navigator and I "hog-tied" our errant and protesting rebellious navigator, dressed only in his wet underwear, and carried him to the crew bus. We then placed him, still bound head to toe, in the aircraft cabin and covered him up with some blankets. In spite of his protesting and obvious discomfort, he was soon sound asleep on the cold floor. (I suspect that the high alcohol content in his blood stream was keeping him warm.)

En route to Niagara Falls, one of the navigators came to the cockpit and said that our rowdy navigator was awake and wanted to be untied. I went to the cabin and encountered a very cold, but apologetic Air Force captain who expressed remorse in causing so much trouble and thanked me for not leaving him in Miami. He said that if he failed to return home his wife would probably divorce him and he would lose his civilian job. I untied him, handed him some dry underwear from his suitcase and after he got dressed gave him a flight lunch and a hot cup of coffee. I returned to the cockpit and the remainder of the flight was routine. As our wayward navigator left for home, he thanked me once again for not abandoning him and promised to do something about his drinking.

I was beginning to enjoy flying the TC-47 in spite of its slow speed, but like Charlie said, "We get paid by the month, not by the mile or airspeed." Keeping that in mind I found it an interesting aircraft to fly, especially in icing conditions. The wings and tail surfaces were deiced by expanding rubber boots, which worked fairly well. The engine carburetors were anti-iced by heat from engine exhaust and the propellers and windshield were deiced by spray nozzles dispensing ethylene glycol. When the intermittent spraying of the propellers occurred you could hear ice chunks breaking off and hitting the sides of the fuselage. When this happened you knew the propeller deicing systems were working. To deice the windshield I would turn on a valve directing deicing fluid to flow over its outside surface. However, a portion of the pungent-smelling liquid would leak into the cockpit and drip onto my legs. To keep dry I would spread out old maps across my lap. An alternative for deicing the windshield was to let the ice build up and then open the pilot's side window and reach out and scrape it off with an automobile plastic ice scraper.

I flew a couple navigator-training missions to St. Johns, Newfoundland, which were considered fun flights by both pilots and navigators. When in Newfoundland we could purchase fresh lobster and cheap liquor, plus the navigators relished being able to navigate over Northern Atlantic waters. I instructed the navigators that they could purchase as much booze as they wished, but anything over the allowable duty-free limit would have to be reported to customs. (Customs inspectors were starting to clamp down on unreported alcohol, and the Aircraft Commander would be held accountable for any violations.) They acknowledged my verbal warning while stating that I had nothing to worry about.

When en route to the U.S. I requested to review the customs declaration forms to be submitted so I would have prior knowledge of what customs inspectors would be interested in when we landed at Mitchell AFB. Since our first point of entry in the U.S. would be a military station, we could expect to be met by military police, who normally substituted for government customs inspectors. The military tended to be more lenient in overlooking small amounts of excess liquor; however, there was always the possibility that U.S. customs inspectors would meet the aircraft themselves. But the Aircraft Commander always had the option of requesting U.S. Government customs personnel from the New York Idelwild Airport meet the aircraft.

The customs declaration forms for this flight reflected "nothing to declare," other than the allowable duty-free amount, so I felt that our ground time before proceeding to Niagara Falls would be at a minimum. When still several hours out, I went to the cabin to return the customs forms to the navigators, stretch my legs and have a cup of coffee. I sat down on a stack of cargo, covered with a piece of canvas, and languished over coffee and a couple navigator-supplied cookies. I sensed that the navigators were overly friendly and appeared anxious for me to return to the cockpit, but I shrugged it off as nothing more than their concern that I not spend so much time in the cabin and return to flying the aircraft. When I finished my coffee, I stood up to leave, but for some reason wondered about the canvas covered boxes I had been sitting on. I didn't recall any opportune military cargo being loaded and I didn't think we were bringing back cases of duty-free frozen lobsters.

I uncovered a section of the canvas and discovered numerous cases of liquor of every description. Disregarding the stares from the navigators, I didn't say a word and returned to the cockpit. I contacted New York Control and requested a "phone patch" (a connection with a telephone land line) with the Mitchell AFB operations center. When in contact, I requested that a U.S. customs inspector from Idelwild Airport, meet our aircraft, as we had considerable amounts of liquor onboard to declare.

When taxiing into the Mitchell AFB parking ramp, I noted a gray government customs vehicle waiting for the propellers to stop rotating and the main entrance door to open. When a uniformed customs agent came onboard, my copilot and I handed him our customs forms, which listed only an authorized amount of duty-free liquor. When he was finished with us, which took less than a minute, I told him that the navigators were waiting for him in the cabin, as they had quite a lot of liquor to declare.

About an hour later, after checking weather and filing a flight plan for Niagara Falls, I returned to the aircraft and the customs agent was just finishing up with collecting cash and checks from my "rum-running" navigators. They didn't ask me why a U.S. customs agent decided to inspect our aircraft, but if they had I would have told them the truth. What I did tell them was that we may not be able to land at Niagara Falls due to high winds, but we would give it a good old "college try!"

When in radio contact with the Niagara Falls tower I was advised that the airport was experiencing gusty winds of 50 mph from 280 degrees (the runway heading), so I decided to shoot an approach to see if it was safe to land, and if not, I had sufficient fuel to divert to a suitable alternate.

I flew a long straight-in final at around 110 knots, with gear down and partial flaps. Surprisingly there was only light turbulence, but with a 50 mph head wind my ground speed was slower than a 65 hp Piper *Cub*. I made a powered wheel landing and after touchdown gradually retarded the throttles. When the aircraft stopped rolling, the tail was still in the air and it felt like we were still flying. I decided not to force the tail down with elevator control or turn off the runway in fear of ground looping when I turned crosswise to the wind, so I called for a truck to tow us in. When it arrived I shut down the engines and slowly lowered the tail. A tow bar was connected, external control gust locks installed and we were towed to the parking ramp. With the aircraft secured we braved the wind and made our way to a waiting crew bus. Another interesting flight was entered in my expanding pilot's log book.

I continued flying the *Gooney Bird* even after transferring to Mitchell, AFB in December 1958, but not the TC Model. When at Mitchell I flew the standard C-47 and a plush VIP model with the designation VC-47. My C-47 flights from Mitchell AFB were sometimes just proficiency flights, where we would see who could make the best three-point landing, a real challenge. I would also occasionally fly one to an Air Force Reserve or Air National Guard base on inspection trips. And in the summer of 1960 I called my former C-119 buddy from Germany, Captain John (Spider) Webb who was working toward a masters degree with Columbia University and asked him if he would like to join me in flying our retiring Inspector General, Colonel Wildes to Love Field, Texas for a job interview with Texas Instruments. It was great to fly with Spider again and Colonel Wildes picked up the tab for the hotel, meals and drinks.

Later that year, when I was preparing to transfer to Chanute Air Force Base, Illinois, to attend the Aircraft Maintenance Officer's Course I asked the transportation officer if they would ship my Vespa motor scooter as part of my household goods. His answer, "Not authorized." So I requested a personal C-47 cross-country flight, called Spider to see if he could break away for a day and after loading my motor scooter in the back of the aircraft we flew it to Chanute and left it with a friend. It certainly would have been cheaper for the Air Force to ship my Vespa as part of my household goods, but it wouldn't have been as much fun. With that flight my days of flying the famous C-47 *Gooney Bird* were over. Checking my personal flight log book I noted that I flew it for around 250 hours and in retrospect admit that it was one of my favorite aircraft.

Every time I started the engines on a C-47 and prepared for a flight it was like turning back the pages of history, an experience few pilots can enjoy, especially today!

Chapter Eight --- Beechcraft C-45 Expeditor

In September 1957, I checked myself out in the twin-engine Beechcraft *C-45 Expeditor*, of which we had two. After studying the flight manual, I made a two-hour (solo) local flight and considered myself qualified. It was an easy aircraft to fly, but due to a narrow gear it could be very tricky on crosswind landings. They were assigned to our reserve training unit for the purpose of supporting administrative missions, but sat idle most of the time. Consequently I could fly them solo, or with a fellow pilot, whenever time and desire were in synch. The Air Force had thousands of these neat little twin-engine aircraft left over from the war and Air Force bases throughout the country had one or more sitting on their parking ramps. Our C-45s were H models configured for carrying passengers, but the seats could easily be removed to accommodate small amounts of cargo.

The C-45 was the military's version of the Beechcraft Model 18 commercial light transport. Between 1939 and 1945, 4,526 were built for use in training multi-engine pilots, navigators, bombardiers, aerial gunners, photographers and as utility transports. It has a wingspan of 47 ft. 8 in., a length of 34 ft. 2 in., a height of 9 ft. 2 in., a maximum weight of 9,300 lbs., a cruising speed of 150 mph, a maximum speed of 225, powered by two Pratt & Whitney 450 hp R-985 engines, and cost $57,838. (Equal to $641,000 today.) It has an internal heater for cabin comfort, inflatable deicing rubber boots on the wings and empennage, on some models, ethylene glycol spray for deicing the propellers and windshield, and hot engine exhaust for carburetor anti-icing. The cockpit was small but once seated it was fairly comfortable. (See Photo No. 43.)

Most of my flights in the *Expeditor* were for personal pleasure and provided a diversion from flying the C-119. I flew one to Northern Wisconsin to visit my parents, made low level flights to seek out favorable duck-hunting sites and, just for kicks, flew one to 21,000 feet without oxygen, but when I became "light-headed," I made a rapid descent.

My most serious Close Encounter in a C-45, was in January 1959. I and a fellow pilot, Captain Jim North, were flying our Inspector General,

Colonel Wildes, to Griffis AFB, New York. We were flying in the clouds and picking up light "rime ice," but the aircraft and engines were confronting the problem quite well. However, as the flight progressed the icing conditions became severe and there was a steady staccato of ice chunks flying off the propellers and striking the sides of the fuselage. Peering out the side windows (the front windshield was covered with ice) I noted that ice was building up on the leading edge of the wings faster than the deicing boots could remove. (I assumed the same conditions existed on the tail surfaces, which I couldn't see.) The carburetor heat temperature gages indicated a steady drop of intake temperatures, even though I had both carburetor heat controls in the full hot position. I requested a higher altitude with the hope of climbing above the clouds, but ATC said, "standby," as there was other IFR traffic above us.

While awaiting a higher altitude both engines began backfiring, small jolts at first, but soon became more severe while rocking the engines from side to side. I realized that the carburetor air intakes were starting to ice-up and if something wasn't done soon both engines would most likely fail. I told Jim to declare an emergency with ATC and start a rapid descent, while I actuated the engine fuel prime switches. (The fuel prime system is used when starting the engines by injecting raw fuel into the top cylinders. By using it in-flight, the engines continued to operate at reduced power, but at least the propellers kept turning!)

We broke out underneath the clouds at around 4,000 feet, and after I opened a side window and scrapped off a portion of ice from the windshield, I spotted Griffis AFB about five miles west of our position. This was accompanied by ATC clearing us for a straight-in approach. With Jim flying, I kept the engines running with the fuel prime switches, but when on short final, I took over the controls since he hadn't had time to open his side window and scrape off the ice from his windshield. I made a smooth landing on a snow-covered runway and had sufficient engine power, without using the primers, for a slow taxi to the parking ramp.

My second exciting C-45 experience, although not a PGR Encounter, is nevertheless worthy of note. In the summer of 1960, I flew my boss, Major Carl Doughman, to Boston, Massachusetts to conduct a one-day staff visit. We left Mitchell Field in the morning and planned on returning that night. While waiting for Carl to complete his task, I spent the afternoon visiting historical sites in downtown Boston. We met back at the airport later that afternoon for dinner and departed for Mitchell Field as the sun was setting in a clear western sky. After takeoff I climbed to 8,000 feet, engaged the autopilot and set a course that would take us over Providence, Rhode Island across Block Island Sound and along the South Coast of Long Island. Visibility was unlimited and the air was smooth as silk. It was a beautiful night to fly! Major Doughman was not a pilot, but a great guy to fly with and since I flew this trip without a copilot, he settled down in the copilot's seat. During the hour and a half flight, we marveled at the intricacy of millions of sparkling city lights competing with a sky full of stars for prominence. The hum of the 450 hp engines added to the majestic setting and I secretly gave thanks to the taxpayers for allowing me to indulge in such pleasure while receiving a decent salary.

Approaching Mitchell Field, I canceled my instrument flight plan and made a few circles around the area known as Levitown, where Major Doughman lived, but we couldn't locate his house. He jokingly said, "I forgot to tell my wife to turn on the porch light." I turned onto a downwind leg for runway 04 and as I was turning base leg Carl asked, "Can you make a three-point landing in the C-45?" My answer, "Sure, if you're a hot pilot. I'll show you how it's done." When I turned final I noted a slight crosswind from the right, but didn't think it was strong enough to ruin my guaranteed demonstration of superior airmanship. I executed a normal flare-out for landing, but kept the nose of the aircraft high, while holding a bit of left rudder and right aileron to correct for the crosswind.

The aircraft was very light and tended to float in a nose-high attitude, which resulted in the landing lights pointing skyward and not down the runway. This created a black hole beneath the aircraft which affected my depth perception, but I rejected it as a potential problem. Suddenly, the aircraft stalled, and we fell flat for maybe three or four feet. This sudden drop caused the aircraft to do a "Charleston-style-dance" down the runway, while trying to decide if it was going to ground-loop, spin-off the runway, or come to rest all in one piece. During this brief, but uncomfortable excursion, I was just a passenger as the aircraft was doing its own gymnastic maneuver, without any assistance from me. I had no more control over it than my stunned non-pilot passenger in the right seat! The bouncing was so erratic that, even though it was at night, the tower operator called to inquire if I needed assistance from the crash vehicles. (How embarrassing!) When we stopped bouncing, Major Doughman turned to me and said, "Lou, that was the worst landing I have ever been through. I thought you were going to show me a three-pointer." My comment, "Carl, you're right. That was a bad landing and the worst one I ever made, but I think you must admit that it was exciting!"

Chapter Nine --- Lockheed T-33 Shooting Star

In late December 1958 my wife and six-year-old daughter Lynn crammed into my 1957 Volkswagen *Karmann Ghia* and departed Niagara Falls for Mitchel AFB, New York. The *Karmann Ghia* is a 36 hp, two-seat sport model of the standard VW *Beetle* with a tiny rear jump seat. The small interior space was "jammed-packed" with suitcases, clothes and boxes leaving barely enough room for my daughter and her big doll. As we headed south from Niagara Falls, I looked back at my little princess, squeezed in between boxes and her doll, and although obviously uncomfortable, she didn't whimper or complain. My fatherly love took over and I decided I couldn't expose her to this torture for a two-day drive to New York City, so I pulled into the parking lot of the first Chevrolet garage we came to and told my wife, "We're going to buy a bigger car!"

A salesman met us and said, "May I help you?" I told him we wanted to trade in our *Karmann Ghia* for a new or late model American car, and wanted to be back on the road in a couple hours. (I noted a big smile of satisfaction appear on his face as he escorted us into a warm waiting room and poured a cup of coffee for my wife and I, and opened a can of Coke for my daughter.) While his mechanics inspected our almost-new Volkswagen sports car, he showed us his collection of new cars but nothing struck our fancy. However, all of them were much bigger than our little VW. I noted a couple of men washing a tan 1958 Chevrolet *Impala* convertible and asked him if it was available. He told me that he had just taken it in on a trade as the previous owner didn't like driving a convertible in the snowy streets of Buffalo, that it only had 12,000 miles on the odometer, was equipped with a 280 hp V8 engine, an air suspension system and was still under warranty. I said, "I'll take it. Now all we have to do is discuss how much you will allow me for my VW." We finally agreed on the VW and $1,800 ($12,000 in 2008 dollars).

However, he said we would not be able to pick it up until the next morning as it had to go through their pre-sell inspection program. He provided us with a loaner for our unplanned night in Buffalo.

Where to stay? My friend Captain Bruce Owen, a jet fighter pilot, who was assigned duties with the joint Army/Air Force recruiting office in downtown Buffalo but had been attached to our unit for flight proficiency. I called his wife Peg, and asked her if we could spend the night with them in their comfortable house in the suburbs of Buffalo. As expected, she said we were welcome and could stay as long as we wished and hoped it would be more than just one night. (Captain Owen and his wife, in opening their house to unexpected Air Force friends, epitomized the camaraderie practiced throughout the Air Force in those days and was one of the reasons I enjoyed serving in the military.)

The Owens not only put us up for the night, but turned it into a farewell party and tried to get us to stay longer. We declined their kind offer and were back at the Chevrolet garage at 9 a.m. the next morning to pick up our shiny, (nearly-new) *Impala* convertible. After storing all our baggage in the large trunk, I was pleased to see my daughter, and her dolls, enjoying the entire back seat all by herself as we headed for New York. I was looking forward to my assignment at Mitchel AFB because, as a student of history, I knew the importance it played in military aviation antiquity.

Mitchel Field was named after the former Mayor of New York City, John Purroy Mitchel, who was killed while undergoing pilot training in Louisiana prior to WW I. It was developed from a large potato field in 1917 and hundreds of pilots were trained at Mitchel flying the famous open-cockpit Jenny. The field saw considerable expansion during this period and remained an active military station after the First World War ended.

In 1929 a major construction program was initiated which included permanent brick barracks, clubs, housing, warehouses, operations buildings, a modern hospital and eight large steel and concrete aircraft hangars. During the 1930s it was the prestige base of assignment for Army Air Corps personnel. It had excellent housing, swimming pools, polo fields and tree-lined streets, which created a Country Club appearance. Several early observation, fighter, and bomber squadrons were stationed at Mitchel and it hosted the U.S. National Air Races in 1920 and 1925. Major C.S. Mosely established a new speed record of 156 mph in 1920, while Cyrus Bettis topped that with 249 mph, in a Curtis Racer, in 1925. In 1922 the Army Air Corps established the country's first airway and in 1938 the Army launched the first nonstop transcontinental flight with B-18 bombers. In 1939, three B-17s, led by Lt. Curtis Lemay, flew 750 miles out to sea to intercept the Italian ocean liner Rex. During WW II, it was utilized as an air defense field for New York City, flying P-40s. After the war it was the home base of the Air Defense and Continental Air

Commands, but when jet aircraft entered the Air Force inventory its relatively short runways (5,000 feet) became a problem. In 1954 several airplane crashes, including an F-47 into Hofstra University, along with a constant growth of housing and businesses, resulted in considerable pressure to close the base. This onslaught was led by the newspaper, Newsday. When I was assigned to Mitchel Field in December 1958, the last remaining aircraft operating were C-119s of the 514th Troop Carrier Wing, seven T-33s and a few C-47s and C-45s. Mitchel Field was closed in 1961, with the land turned over to the county of Nassau. However, many of the original buildings still remain and are being used by Hofstra University. Several of the original hangars have become the Cradle of Aviation Air Museum and contain not only a history of Mitchel Field, but many historical pictures, restored aircraft and aviation memorabilia.

A few days before Christmas I placed my wife and daughter in a WW II barracks, used as transient family quarters, acquired a discarded evergreen tree branch and decorated it with cotton balls and strips of toilet paper as an improvised Christmas tree for my six-year-old daughter.

The next day I reported to my new assignment as an operations inspector with the 14th Air Force Inspector Generals' Staff, and met my boss, Major Carl Doughman and Colonel Wildes, the IG. It was vividly apparent that I was to become a member of a select group of experienced officers charged with the oversight responsibility of Air Force Reserve and Air National Guard units in the Eastern third of the U.S. Col. Wildes, during his orientation briefing, informed me that I would be responsible for ensuring units operating F-86s, F-84Fs, F-89s, TC-47s, C-119s, C-123s, C-124s, B-26s, SA-16s and T-33s were capable of performing their war-time assigned missions. After reviewing my military personnel file, he said that I would be able to evaluate, without additional training, squadrons operating propeller driven aircraft, but reiterated that it would be necessary that I attend a jet qualification course as soon as possible. He asked me when I would be able to depart for Randolph AFB, Texas. I told him, "You name the date, colonel, and I'll be on my way."

I obtained a three-bedroom apartment in the military family housing area know as "Mitchel Manor," enrolled my daughter in a local public school, and while awaiting jet qualification training, participated in Operational Readiness Inspections (ORIs) of Air National Guard and Air Force Reserve units. However, not being jet qualified, my expertise was limited to checking training records when visiting jet fighter squadrons.

In March 1959 I departed New York, in my *Impala* convertible, for Randolph AFB, Texas to attend a two-month jet qualification course (Class 59-E), in the Lockheed T-33. En route I visited my former Neubiberg operations officer Major Burnott, working in the Pentagon, and my friend Major William Jones, who was flying B-47 jet bombers at Lake Charles, Louisiana. When I drove through the main gate at Randolph, I experienced a "flashback" relating to my fascination with the 1935 movie, *West Point of the Air*. It was difficult to acknowledge that I was actually reporting for flight training at the same base made famous in the movie. However, when I realized that I wouldn't have Wallace Beery as my mentor, I knew it was 1959, not 1935. But still, I was fulfilling a childhood fantasy in becoming a student at the "Showplace of The Air Force!" With the convertible top down, I circled the base, including several turns around the famous *Taj Mahal Tower*, before obtaining housing.

Randolph Air Force Base, like Mitchel Filed, is steeped in military history. The base was dedicated on June 20, 1930 and was used for the training of pilots during the 1930s, WW II, the Korean and Vietnam wars and continues to this day. The base was named for Captain William Randolph, who was killed in an aircraft crash in Texas on February 17, 1928. The most notable, and famous, building on the base is the 147 foot high water tower, referred to as the Taj Mahal. The nickname was derived from a famous building which it resembles in India. The tower is capped by a blue and gold mosaic tiled dome, and ornamental pre-cut concrete grill work. It was declared a Texas historical site on March 2, 1976. When I arrived at Randolph it was being used for training pilots in the T-33 and the KC-97 Boeing Stratacrusier.

I was assigned a two-bedroom apartment which I would share with a jet qualification pilot classmate. I was unpacking my B-4 bag when I heard the front door opening. Assuming it would be my roommate I went to the living room to meet him. When the door opened I couldn't believe my eyes! My roommate for the next two months would be my Waco AFB, Texas basic flight instructor, Captain Ray Meador (now a major). We hadn't seen each other for ten years, but neither had changed, except for our military ranks --- he a Major and I a Captain. He fancied in addressing me in the familiar greeting used for Aviation Cadets, as "Mr. Martin," and I, in referring to him as "Captain Meador." As he shook my hand he said his name was "Ray" and I said my name was "Lou." It took us several minutes before we could refer to each other by our first names. (The military training, and discipline, imbibed in both flight instructor and cadet was difficult to breach, even after ten years.)

After becoming comfortable in addressing each other on a first name basis, we couldn't get over the coincidence, and mutually agreed in our good fortune in being assigned as roommates for our two-month stay. As Major (excuse me, "**Ray**") was unpacking his suitcase, I said, "Ray, do you remember who was the first student pilot to solo the T-6, when you were my flight instructor at Waco Air Force Base in the fall of 1948?" He dropped what he was doing, turned in my direction, and with a big smile said, "I sure do, Mr. Martin (excuse me "**Lou**") and tonight the drinks and dinner are on me!"

I was introduced to my T-6 basic flight instructor, Captain Meador, on October 28, 1948. Each instructor was assigned four Aviation Cadets and our first flight was a 30-minute orientation ride in the back seat of the North American Texan. I was the third student to fly, and as far as Captain Meador knew this could have been my first flight in an aircraft, but most certainly my first in a T-6. After level-off he told me to take a hold of the stick and place my feet on the rudder pedals. He then went through a very basic explanation of what causes the aircraft to fly straight and level and what makes it turn, climb and descend. Following this explanation he asked me to try to keep it level and make a few turns. (Since I had a Private Pilot's Certificate, and 120 flight hours, I had no problem in holding the aircraft on the horizon and made several coordinated right and left 90-degree turns.) Captain Meador asked, "How much flying time do you have, Mr. Martin?" When I told him, he talked me through a landing and took his fourth student up for his 30-minute orientation flight. After all four students had flown their back-seat ride, we were lined up abreast while Captain Meador briefed us on what to expect in future flights. He stressed that from this day on we would be flying from the front seat and to study the flight manual until we could locate all the cockpit switches and controls blindfolded and could recite all limitations and normal and emergency procedures from memory. He then called us to attention and said, "Dismissed." We tossed him a smart salute, did an "about-face" and prepared to leave. But as I turned to depart, he said, "Mr. Martin, hold up a minute. I would like to talk to you." I thought at first that I had done something wrong, but I soon learned that there was a personal devious reason for him wanting to talk to me.

His opening comment stressed that he was not inferring that I violate the Aviation Cadet honor code which states, "I will not lie, steal, cheat, nor tolerate those that do," and asked if I understood. I nodded my head in agreement but wasn't sure what I was agreeing to. He then went on to explain that each flight instructor puts five dollars into a "kitty" and the instructor who has the first student to solo wins the pot! With that said, he stressed that it wasn't necessary for me to broadcast that I had 120 flight hours and a Private Pilot's Certificate. "Do I make myself clear?" he asked. "Yes sir, I understand completely. Good luck," I responded. With that I was dismissed, and less than a month later I was the first Aviation Cadet in my squadron to solo and Captain Meador won the pot.

After unpacking Ray and I headed for the Officers' Club and, good to his word, we enjoyed martinis, a big steak and a bottle of excellent wine and he picked up the tab. I wondered what I had done to be so lucky. Since leaving Niagara Falls, I was hand-picked for a coveted position with the 14th Air Force Inspector Generals' Staff, bequeathed priority to attend a jet qualification course at Randolph AFB (fulfilling a childhood dream), and now sharing an apartment with my flight instructor from Aviation Cadet days. "What a deal!"

The next day I was issued a helmet (hard hat), oxygen mask, parachute, T-33 flight manual with checklist, and a Jet Qualification Training Manual. Following this I and my 49 classmates met our flight instructors and started half-day ground school and half-day flight training sessions. My first instructional flight in the T-33 was on Friday, April 3, 1959. I loved flying the Lockheed Shooting Star and looked forward to each flight with the same anticipation a kid would experience if given unlimited access to a candy store.

The Lockheed T-33 Shooting Star is a two-place jet that was used to train pilots to fly jet fighters, transports or bombers. It was also used to administer annual proficiency checks to jet pilots for many years. It was developed from the single-seat F-80 fighter by extending the length of the fuselage to accommodate a rear cockpit. The T-33 made its first flight in 1948 and was in production until August 1959 with nearly 6,000 built. The T-33 was not limited to the training of pilots, but used in the towing of aerial targets and in some countries as a combat aircraft. It has served with the Air Forces of more than 20 countries for close to 55 years. The T-33 has a wing span and length of nearly 38 ft. and a fully loaded weight *of 15,000 lbs. As a combat aircraft it was equipped with two .50-cal. machine guns. It has an Allison J-33 engine of 5,400 lbs. of thrust, a crew of two, a maximum speed of 525 mph, a cruising speed of 455 mph, a range of 1,000 miles and a service ceiling of 45,000 ft. (Although I was able to climb to 50,000 ft. during a flight over Japan in 1962.) When produced it cost $123,000 ($891,000 today). (See Photo No. 44.)*

I found the T-33 unique in its simplicity, although it did require some adjustment after flying nothing but big round-engine airplanes. It was a nice change to be able to perform a Preflight Walk-Around Inspection at eye-level, but loosening and checking seven separate fuel tanks, without getting splashed with jet fuel, took some getting used to. Another important area of inspection was to ensure that the nose gun bay doors were tightly secured. (If these doors came open during takeoff it could cause the aircraft to crash.) After climbing the entrance ladder and settling down into the snug cockpit, I would experience a raptured sense of excitement of finally being a single-engine jet pilot. The engine start procedure was much simpler than starting a reciprocal engine, as I didn't have to be concerned with backfires, but did have to focus on the possibility of a "hot start," which could occur from low electrical output from an external power unit or a tail wind up the tail pipe.

Taxing the T-Bird requires moving at a fairly good clip so as to provide steering through the use of differential main gear braking, which is very effective. Takeoff was smooth and fast without any torque or yaw experienced in propeller powered aircraft. I had no problem in adapting to the high speeds and control sensitivity (the ailerons are hydraulically boosted), and was signed off for solo flight in seven hours. It's difficult to put in words the exhilaration I felt when I flew my first solo flight over Southern Texas. I climbed to 35,000 feet, and although instructions in aerobatics were to come later, I performed wing-overs, aileron rolls, loops, immelmanns, Cuban eights and streaked through clouds at 500 mph. I was as giddy as an 18-year-old experiencing his first sexual encounter, with one important difference. I was old enough to realize that what I was experiencing was meaningful and would change my life!

The ground school portion of the course was a "piece of cake" as my roommate had spent the last 12 years in the Air Training Command and possessed an uncanny sense of what material would appear as questions on pop quizzes and weekly exams. He would tell me, "Study this, disregard that, memorize this. Let's go have a drink." We would head for the Officers' Club, while our classmates burnt the midnight oil studying. They never understood how Ray and I scored nearly 100% in all the tests while spending so much time in the bar. (I never shared my secret weapon with any of them.) On weekends Ray and I would jump into my *Impala* convertible and head for downtown San Antonio for Mexican food, or drive the short distance to the city of New Braunfels.

This unique European style German town was founded by Prince Carl of Solms in 1845. After landing at Galveston, he traveled north by horseback, where he purchased the tract of land now encompassing the city of New Braunfels. The area is inhabited by German-speaking people and presents the impression of being in Germany itself.

Ray was acquainted with a secretary, who lived in this German enclave, who said she had a girl friend for me. We made several trips to this German community and I was delighted to note that my blind date adhered to the same relaxed attitude toward consensual adult recreation as her cousins in Europe and was eager to demonstrate this proclivity during my occasional visits. She was especially fond of entertaining her adult companion in the art of fellatio and was not bashful in practicing it.

I thought that she was well ahead of her time, as this was 38 years before it was, reportedly, a form of entertainment between a 22-year-old White House intern and an American President in the Oval Office.

I completed jet qualification on May 19, 1959 with 42 hours of flight time and an overall grade average of 94% (a grade of 93 to 100 was considered superior). The remarks section of my Training Record stated:

"Captain Martin received an excess of formation and navigation flight time at the expense of instrument time because his proficiency in instruments was attained with less than the prescribed flight hours."

After returning to Mitchel AFB, I completed a local field check (with emphasis on short field takeoffs and landings on Mitchel's short runways), with Captain Warren F. Aderholt on May 26, 1959. I was now qualified to provide a greater expertise in evaluating Air Force Reserve and Air National Guard units flying single-engine jets, assisted by current jet fighter pilots from Tactical Air Command Squadrons or Air Defense

Command units. These pilots would fly the fighters while I administered instrument checks or conducted chase flights in a T-33. I was having so much fun I was almost ashamed to accept my monthly pay check, but I acquiesced as I didn't want to set a bad precedent and needed the money to support my family.

I was flying a T-33 from Mitchel AFB to Niagara Falls New York in the summer of 1959, with full 230 gallon tip tanks, so I planned my takeoff in the early morning to take advantage of the cooler temperatures. I filed an instrument flight plan with a request for a VFR en route climb. When airborne I contacted New York Air Traffic Control (ATC) who cleared me as filed. As I was passing through 12,000 feet the cockpit fire warning light illuminated, which is about the size of a quarter coin, but to me it appeared the size of a "grapefruit." I rolled into a sharp left bank to see if I was trailing smoke but saw none. When in the bank I looked down and noted that I was directly over the heart of New York City and came to the realization that if my aircraft was actually on fire, an ejection and bailout would not be advisable. I retarded the throttle and rolled into a right bank to check again for smoke trails. I was still not trailing any and retarding the throttle had no effect on the fire warning light, which seemed to be competing with the morning sun in brightness!

A scan of the engine instruments showed the engine still developing power, so I restored the throttle to an intermediate setting, declared an emergency with ATC and diverted to Stewart AFB. When over Stewart I flew a simulated flameout (SFO) pattern and landed without difficulty. Maintenance personnel checked the aircraft over and found no discrepancy with either the engine or fire warning system, which went out during their troubleshooting process. They cleared the discrepancy by signing the 781 aircraft maintenance log book as, "Ground checked OK." The aircraft was refueled, I filed a new flight plan and proceeded to Niagara Falls and later back to Mitchel AFB with no further difficulty. To this day, I don't know why the fire warning light decided to come on when it did, but in retrospect I'm glad it did as it increased my confidence in handling an emergency in a single-engine jet in an unruffled manner.

After qualifying in the T-33, I spent another year and a half at Mitchell and could fly one of our seven T-Birds just about any time I wished. Not only was an aircraft almost always available, but my position with the Inspector General's Staff provided me with a certain amount of priority. I would often fly a T-33 to an Air Force Reserve or Air National Guard fighter unit we were inspecting and along with administering "no notice" instrument proficiency checks to pilots selected at random, use the T-Bird to chase F-86s on low level navigation flights and F-89Js on practice intercepts. When my mother was visiting my brother in Detroit I flew one to visit her and to a colleague's wedding in South Carolina.

One type of T-33 solo flight I really enjoyed was to wait for a night with no moon and cloud tops of around 30,000 feet. I would file a "round-robin," (out & back) VFR on-top cross-country flight of about two hours. After breaking out on top of the clouds, I would dim the cockpit instrument lights and after my eyes became adjusted to the dark cockpit the stars would brighten with such intensity that they appeared to touch the top of the canopy. Being on top of the clouds there were no ground lights visible and since the aircraft was not equipped with the type of radio used by civilian aircraft the radio was almost silent. I would settle down in my snug warm cockpit, strapped in tightly by parachute, lap belt and shoulder harness, my head encapsulated in a helmet and oxygen mask, and the hum of a well-tuned jet engine providing a soothing background ballad. I would feel like I was separated from the rest of the world and floating in space. I was always sad when these infrequent night fantasy flights came to an end and looked forward to recapturing this experience.

I was flying in the back seat of a T-33 mission that had us towing a "Delmar" target for F-86Ds, on practice rocket attacks, over Lake Erie, which provided an interesting Close Encounter with the PGR.

The Delmar target is a Styrofoam structure, in the shape of a large dart and covered with aluminum foil so as to provide an excellent radar return for the fighters. It is slung underneath the wing of the T-33 and reeled out about 1,000 feet which is then fired on by the fighter interceptors.

After we leveled off at 35,000 feet I reeled out the Delmar target and we cleared the F-86Ds to commence their practice rocket-firing passes. The fighters would be vectored in for a 90-degree deflection intercept by Ground Controlled Intercept Radar (GCI), and when the pilot's onboard radar locks on to the target, he literally buries his head in his radar scope and requests permission from the tow pilot to continue with his live fire intercept. If the fighter pilot's radar is tracking the Delmar, and not the T-33, he appears to be heading directly at us, since he has to compensate for the 90-degree deflection offset. When this occurs the fighter pilot is given permission to fire his rockets.

However, if the fighter pilot's radar is tracking the T-33, instead of the Delmar target, he will appear coming in pointing well ahead of the tow plane. If this occurs the pilot is not cleared to fire his rockets and instructed to break off his attack. The first couple of firing passes by the fighters went off without a hitch, but their salvo of rockets failed to strike the Delmar target. However, the third firing pass by a fighter was a different story. During his 90-degree deflection run he was flying on a course well ahead of us, so it was apparent that his airborne radar was tracking our aircraft, not the towed Delmar target. We told him to break off his pass, but he kept on boring in like we were the enemy. We were aware that when the fighter reached a predetermined position his rockets would fire automatically, so he was told several times to break off his attack, but he didn't respond and just kept boring on in toward us!

With a closure rate of over 500 knots, he was coming at us with his rocket pod extended, and in the next instance we observed a salvo of rockets heading in our direction. We popped the stick forward and the cluster of rockets went zooming over the top of the canopy. The pilot's aim was good, but we weren't too happy with being his intended target.

Reviewing the incident later we discovered that the screw-up was the result of a second lieutenant on his first live firing intercept, and he became so excited that he held his radio microphone button down, thereby blocking out the calls for him to break off his attack. He apologized for the screw-up and bought us drinks at the Officers' Club.

My responsibility, as an operations officer for the Inspector General's Staff, involved participating in readiness inspections of Air National Guard and Air Force Reserve units in many different locations. It was amazing the differences in combat readiness, between one unit versus another, even with similar missions and flying the same type of aircraft. I attributed this variance to the effect certain squadron commanders had on their respective organizations. A 30-year burly master sergeant, who was a member of our team and inspected mess halls, told me that he could visit a military dining facility, order a cup of coffee, and sit down and write his report without inspecting the facility itself. He based his hypothesis on the quality of the coffee, how long it had been sitting in the pot, the cleanliness of the cup, etc. I wasn't this perceptive in evaluating the readiness of combat flight operations, but I did learn that first impressions are important and says a lot about what I would find when turning over the "proverbial rocks."

When visiting an F-86 Air National Guard unit in the New England area, I was randomly inspecting pilot training records to confirm the number and date of completed required flight sorties. After making note of the dates these flights had taken place, I then started checking the aircraft maintenance flight records to see if a flight had actually taken place on the dates indicated in the pilot's training records. To my surprise, I discovered several instances where pilots had taken credit for sorties on days when there were no aircraft flying. (I noted that the operations officer was observing my spot checking of these records from a distance, and was apparently concerned about my note taking.) Before I had completed my inspection, our team leader poked his head in where I was working and invited me to accompany him and the rest of the IG team for lunch. When at lunch, I briefed my boss on my findings while promising that I would check further to see if the problem was isolated or systemic.

When we returned to the Air National Guard unit, the squadron commander was waiting for us and told my boss that he had a telephone call from Washington. Sitting next to my boss as he took the call, I could only hear one side of the conversation, but noted many "Yes sirs." When he hung up he told me to discontinue my checking of the pilot's training records and go onto something else. He wouldn't tell me who he had been talking to in Washington, just stating that it was better that I didn't ask. We rated the unit fully operationally ready!

At another F-86 guard unit, my assistant, Master Sergeant Robert Battleson, came to me and asked if I could do something to get the operations officer off his back. He said that he was making his inspection chores extremely difficult and expressed a very negative attitude toward being bothered by the Inspector General. I told Sergeant Battleson I would see what I could do, but couldn't promise any relief due to the strong politics permeating Air National Guard units. However, I sought out the troublesome major and told him I would like to administer a "no-notice" instrument proficiency check to him in one of their T-33s. His response, "Sure, let's go. I'll show you how to fly a T-Bird on instruments, Captain."

I climbed into the front seat while the "hotshot" major climbed into the rear cockpit. When lined up on the runway I had him position the instrument hood (which enclosed his canopy), and instructed him to make an Instrument Takeoff (ITO) and climb to 25,000 feet. Still under the hood I had him perform steep turns, intercept VOR headings and recover from almost inverted unusual attitudes. He was an excellent pilot and performed everything I threw at him in an outstanding manner. It didn't appear that I could find fault in his flying and use it as a wedge in getting him to lay off my sergeant, but I thought I would try one more high speed, high G load, unusual attitude maneuver.

I dove the T-Bird to around Mach .80, and while pulling about 4Gs rolled it inverted and said, "You've got it, major, recover." He reduced power, kicked out the speed brakes, rolled the aircraft upright and seconds later we were flying straight and level. He then, in a sarcastic tone of voice, said, "What's next, Captain?"

We were in clear skies at around 18,000 feet and with him still under the instrument hood, I told him to contact approach control, obtain a clearance to climb to 20,000 feet and set up a holding pattern over the VOR station, followed by a jet penetration and non-precision low approach. With a cocky smirk in his voice he obtained ATC clearance, made a turn toward the station, set climb power and started climbing. However, to my surprise he flew right through 20,000 feet without leveling off! To make sure he didn't misunderstand my instructions I told him to report level at twenty thousand. His response, "Roger-dodger-captain." I now knew that he had allowed himself to commit the cardinal sin of misreading the altimeter by 10,000 feet. (Not uncommon with the old style altimeter.) With a gloating smile hidden underneath my oxygen mask, I reached down and turned off the altitude reporting feature of the transponder, so as to prevent ATC from ruining my devious plan of upsetting the ego of my smart-ass F-86H jet fighter pilot.

He continued the climb, leveled off at 30,000 feet, but reported level at 20,000, made two practice turns in a holding pattern and reported to ATC that he was initiated a jet penetration to a VOR low approach. (I sat chuckling in the front seat, but had to keep my teeth clenched so that my giddy excitement would not show through the hot microphone between the cockpits.) He flew a beautiful teardrop penetration turn, and at what he thought was 10,000 feet, but was actually 20,000, turned inbound toward the airport. The minimums for this approach were 500 feet above the ground, so I instructed him to shake the stick when we were over the field. Another, "Roger dodger" came from the rear cockpit.

It was a beautiful clear day and as we approached overhead, I could see the field 10,500 feet below. But my confused "hot-shot" major firmly believed we were only 500 feet above the ground. When he shook the stick, I said, "I've got it," and rolled the jet inverted and started a split-s (half loop) maneuver. My fighter jock, thinking he was a dead man because the stupid-ass inspector in the front seat rolled the aircraft inverted when only 500 feet above the ground, threw back the instrument hood covering his cockpit. With the hood rolled back he noted that the airport was 10,000 feet below, not 500, and with a changed tone of voice said, "Holly shit, I thought we were only 500 feet above the airport and you were going to kill us both when you rolled the jet inverted."

I didn't say another word and flew the jet down into a beautiful overhead approach and a full-stop landing. I let the major stew in the back seat for a while over what he thought would be a busted check ride and an embarrassment to him and his squadron. After I shut down the engine, installed the seat and canopy pins and climbed down the ladder, I asked him what he thought about the ride. In a strained voice he said he thought it should be a bust. I responded with, "You allowed yourself to fall into the trap of misreading the altimeter through complacency which can happen to anyone, so I'll make a deal with you. You lay off my assistant, Sergeant Battleson, and I'll rate the check ride satisfactory and keep the screw-up just between you and me." "You've got a deal," he said, as he shook my hand. Later that day Sgt. Battleson wanted to know what I did to the major as he was nice as pie and even bought him a cup of coffee.

In August 1960 the Mitchel AFB operations officer called me to inquire if I would be interested in accompanying another T-33 pilot on a flight to Volk Field, Wisconsin, to recover a T-33 that had been left in Wisconsin for maintenance. As usual, I jumped at the chance telling him, "You bet." He said the takeoff time was scheduled for 7 a.m. the following morning to take advantage of cool temperatures.

I met the pilot that I was to share the flight with in base operations at 6 a.m. We flipped a coin to see who would fly the front seat, on the outbound flight, thereby being able to fly both legs as PIC. (I won the toss, and if I hadn't, it's quite possible my aviation career would have come to an early end and you wouldn't be reading this book!) After filing a flight plan we proceeded to the aircraft, conducted a joint preflight and by the time I had strapped into the front cockpit, I was wet with perspiration as it was to be another hot humid August day in New York. The engine started with the customary rush of air, but seemed to accelerate slower than usual which I attributed to the high ambient temperature and density altitude ---- or perhaps a weak ground power unit ---- but the engine came up to idle speed of 35% without exceeding temperature limits. While going through the Before Taxiing Checklist, the crew chief gave me a cut-engine signal. After I shut down the engine he came to the cockpit and said that we had a hydraulic leak in the speed brake area which would have to be corrected before we could continue. I told the tower to cancel our clearance, but keep the flight plan open and we proceeded to a nearby air-conditioned maintenance shack to wait out the aircraft repairs and bum a cold soft drink from the line crew.

It took some time for maintenance to secure a "hydraulic-mule" (portable hydraulic cart) and a hydraulic specialist to make the necessary repairs. About two hours later the aircraft was reported ready to go and we secured ourselves back into the hot, steamy cockpits. I knew the air temperature had increased considerably since our first engine start, but didn't think it would be a problem if we could takeoff on one of Mitchel's 5,000 foot runways.

Because of the relatively short runways at Mitchel AFB, the base operations officer had established an "80/80/80" rule for T-33s. This rule required a maximum of 80% RPM power when lining up for takeoff at the end of the runway, and if the air temperature was more than 80 degrees Fahrenheit the wing tip fuel tanks (which have a capacity of 230 gallons each) would be limited to 80 gallons (160 gallons total).

When taxiing out for takeoff I requested the 5,000 foot runway to the southeast, but was told by the tower that it was closed for temporary repairs. I was instructed to taxi to runway 18 which was only 4,700 feet long, if every inch was used. This particular runway had no runway distance markers, nor did it have an overrun. The runway end was marked by a 12-foot high chain-link wire fence with the Hempstead Expressway on the other side. I figured the takeoff run might be a bit tricky, but with the canopy down and enjoying air conditioned air, I didn't wish to taxi back and abort the mission, so I pressed on!

When lined up on the runway thoughts ran through my mind that I was already in violation of the "80/80/80" rule, so I may as well violate one more restriction and make it a clean sweep. Holding the brakes, I advanced the throttle to 100% RPM (disregarding the noise complaints I knew would come from nearby home owners), allowed the engine thrust to stabilize and released the brakes. The jet rattled down the rough runway, but didn't seem to accelerate in a manner I normally expected. By the time we reached the halfway point we were well below normal takeoff speed and I knew we had passed the point where I would be able to abort the takeoff and stop the fully-loaded jet in the runway remaining. I kept pushing on the throttle, but it was already full forward so it had no effect on increasing power. (The normal takeoff speed of a T-33 is around 120 knots, but I normally used 125.) When green grass appeared below the jet's nose (indicating the end of the runway) my airspeed was around 112 knots. I eased back on the control stick, cleared the chain-link fence by mere inches and zoomed across the busy Hempstead Expressway and the tops of cars by a few feet. I'm sure we scared the living hell out of numerous motorists on their way to work! Fortunately, there were no trucks crossing in front of us, or we never would have made it!

After passing over the highway, I reached down and raised the landing gear, and as the gear doors opened I thought I felt a slight stick nibble when the open gear doors caused an increase in drag. On the opposite side of the expressway was a series of civilian homes, but fortunately there was a narrow clear-way, which we raced through. Once the gear was retracted the jet started to accelerate at a normal pace and as we raced past civilian houses, at eye-level, I retracted the flaps at 140 knots and zoomed up to a safe altitude and 240 knots. Up to this point my colleague in the rear seat had been quiet and I heard nothing over the "hot mic interphone," except heavy breathing. When the gear and flaps were up and we were zooming up to a higher altitude, my friend in the back of the bus said, "Well, we made it!" I believe this was one of the Closest Encounters I had with the PGR and it all could have been avoided if I had exercised good judgment and not allowed my self to become complacent. (In reviewing this near-fatal mistake later, I discovered that when we took-off, the temperature was + 95 degrees Fahrenheit, the density altitude was 2,500 feet and we had a slight tail wind. Under these conditions the required takeoff ground roll distance was close to 5,100 feet on a runway length of 4,700. If I had not advanced the power to 100%, before releasing the brakes, we never would have made it!)

The above incident could have resulted in the same fate as the Comair Flight that crashed at Lexington Kentucky, on August 27, 2006, killing 49 people, after the pilots attempted a takeoff on the wrong runway. The runway length they used was too short not unlike my T-33 episode.

After leveling off at 39,000 feet we proceeded to Volk Field, Wisconsin without incident and after I made a couple touch-and-go landings we taxied in and had lunch while our aircraft were being prepared for the return flight to New York. At first we had planned on flying back to Mitchel AFB in formation, but a crew chief, who had worked on the stranded aircraft, had to fly back in one of the T-birds. Since he had not been certified for high-altitude flight the aircraft carrying him would be restricted to 18,000 feet. My colleague agreed to fly the crew chief and making a refueling stop at Wright Patterson AFB, thereby giving us both two flights in the front seat. I would fly the jet that had undergone repairs back to New York nonstop. The jet I was to fly had been grounded for a crack in the speed-brake area and therefore the return flight would have to be made without its use. I didn't think this would be a problem and departed Volk Field right after lunch.

I leveled off at 37,000 feet and encountered a strong, intermittent, tail wind during my uneventful flight east. Approaching New York, ATC cleared me for an expedited descent to 20,000 feet, but what I had not counted on was that not being able to extend the speed brake, I was not able to descend at a rate requested by ATC. Even with the throttle fully retarded the engine fuel regulator would not allow the RPM to decrease much below 70% and with this high power setting my airspeed, during the descent, was quickly approaching the aircraft Mach limit of .82. I therefore raised the nose, allowed the speed to decrease to 195 knots, and lowered the landing gear, which increased my descent rate, but I had to be careful not to exceed the gear-down speed limit. When I finally leveled off at 20,000 feet I was able to retract the landing gear and assume a near normal flight profile. I was instructed to hold over the Hemstead low frequency beacon with an expected approach clearance in ten minutes.

I flew east for one minute, executed a 180 degree turn and flew toward the radio station with the intent of entering a standard holding pattern. When inbound, ATC stated that when overhead the beacon, I would be cleared for a jet penetration approach to Mitchel AFB, and to report leaving 20,000 feet. I was flying at the standard holding airspeed of 200 knots, but failed to get a swing on my radio compass needle (which would indicate passage of the station). After several minutes on this course, without getting a needle swing, I wondered if my radio had failed, but a check showed normal operation. I then increased my airspeed to 275 knots and after a seemingly long period of time I finally obtained a needle swing and flew a modified jet penetration approach, using the extended landing gear (instead of the speed brake), to control my speed and made a normal landing. I was concerned about my not being able to reach the beacon on my inbound course at an indicated airspeed of 200 knots, so I visited the weather office to inquire about winds at 20,000 feet. The meteorologist said that he had reported winds from the west as high as 225 knots. (This explained the problem. When I was flying at an airspeed of 200 knots, inbound to the Hempstead radio beacon, I was actually being pushed further east at 25 knots per hour. If I hadn't increased my airspeed to 275 knots, I never would have reached the beacon.) Another interesting day of flying complete and another exciting day of being an Air Force jet pilot in the fun days of 1960.

In the summer of 1960 Mitchel AFB received its last T-33, a brand new 1959 model. It had an improved fuel system, a civilian style VHF radio (in addition to the UHF), a smooth running engine that seemed to have slightly more thrust and an improved cockpit pressurization system. This aircraft was a pleasure to fly and was popular with my jet pilot colleagues.

One beautiful Thursday afternoon in July 1960, I felt fortunate when I was able to schedule it for a solo local flight. I had requested that the aircraft be serviced with only 150 gallons in each 230 gallon tip tank, which would require less time to run dry, as I was planning on performing aerobatics. (We were not allowed to do aerobatics with fuel in the tip tanks, so with only 150 gallons they would be close to empty by the time I reached our area set aside for aerobatics.) However, when I reported to base operations to file a local flight plan, I noted from the setup schedule that the aircraft was serviced with full fuel of 813 gallons. A fellow T-33 pilot, who was the Officer in Charge (OIC) of the base altitude chamber, approached me and said, "I hope you don't mind, Lou, but I noticed that you were flying solo this afternoon, so I scheduled myself to fly in the back seat and requested they put on full fuel." I told him, "Not at all, as the airplane belongs to the taxpayers and you're certainly welcome." I suggested he fly the jet until the tips ran dry (about one half the period) and asked what he would like to do.

He told me that he was coming due for an annual instrument proficiency check and had put in for a cross-country flight to Warner Robins AFB, Georgia over the weekend and would like to get some instrument practice under the hood. With that as our plan, he put up the instrument hood and we headed for Suffolk County AFB, Long Island for practice instrument approaches. His instrument proficiency had deteriorated to the point that we were forced to abandon several approaches, because he was unable to maintain proper course and altitude. To provide him with additional practice, I reluctantly allowed him to fly a portion of my allocated time. After about 30 minutes of aerobatics we returned to Mitchel AFB for a

233

routine landing. We discussed his need for additional instrument proficiency training, before he took his annual proficiency check, and I agreed to fly with him again the following week.

I asked him if another pilot was flying with him on his approved cross-country flight to Georgia, the next day. He said, "As far as I know nobody has volunteered to go with me." I surreptitiously didn't like the thought of him flying on his own, but didn't attempt to dissuade him from going. I did, however, offer a suggestion. I recommended that if he was flying by himself to restrict himself to a ceiling of at least 1,000 feet and 3 miles visibility, as an added measure of safety, at both Mitchel and his destination in Georgia. He accepted my recommendation and said he would contact me the following week for additional instrument practice!

On Monday morning my boss asked me if I had heard about our T-33 accident in Georgia. He said that the OIC of the altitude chamber crashed right after takeoff from Warner Robins AFB. According to preliminary reports he was on a solo return flight to Mitchel and apparently became disorientated when departing in a 200 foot ceiling and restricted visibility due to light rain. (Not only did we lose a pilot, but he crashed in our newest T-33.) I felt a certain amount of responsibility for this tragic accident as I should have insisted that another pilot fly with him on his planned cross-country or the flight be canceled. I should have expressed my concerns to the base operations officer, but I said nothing! I vowed never to repeat this mistake and have never failed to speak up when I think a pilot is not capable of meeting accepted standards.

The cause of the accident was listed as "pilot error," which I'm sure was the correct call. A solo takeoff and initial climb in the T-33, like any single-engine jet, is a critical phase. And when performed with a 200 foot ceiling, and restricted visibility, can easily result in the pilot losing situation awareness, if he doesn't plan ahead. After becoming airborne at 125 knots, the pilot must concentrate on keeping the jet upright, by reference to cockpit instruments, reach down and retract the landing gear, accelerate rapidly to 140 knots, raise the flaps, continue a climbing acceleration to 240 knots, switch his radio to a departure control frequency, turn to a heading specified in his departure clearance (sometimes as much as 90 degrees different than the takeoff heading), while being cognizant of the increasing sensitivity of the flight controls due to the increase in airspeed. To keep ahead of the jet under these conditions, I would instruct my students to take control of the situation by incorporating a few basic safety procedures before takeoff: first, when departing under adverse weather conditions do not attempt to switch radio frequencies until the aircraft is all cleaned up (gear and flaps retracted) and above 1,000 feet; second, before takeoff determine how many clicks of the radio tuning dial is required to go to the new frequency (by following this procedure it's not necessary to look down at the radio control panel, which is especially important at night); third, refuse a departure clearance which requires large heading changes immediately after takeoff by requesting to climb on runway heading, even if only up to four or five thousand feet before turning; fourth, when flying proficiency flights throughout the year perform frequent instrument takeoffs under the hood. (Many pilots only practice instrument flying just before their annual proficiency check.) Flying a high speed jet on instruments requires frequent practice, not unlike a piano player who, if he doesn't practice, will never be ready for a command performance. A jet pilot, whose lack of instrument flying doesn't qualify him for a "command-style performance," will gratify nobody except possibly the PGR.

On September 15, 1960, my son Michael was born at the Mitchel AFB hospital, and I thought that he would be pleased to learn that he was born on an Air Force base with such historical significance. I fantasized that this may influence him to become a pilot himself when he grew up. He fulfilled my wish as he is presently a pilot with United Airlines and a major in the Air National Guard. He has served his country in both peace and war and when he completes his 2008 combat tour in Iraq he will have over 20 years of creditable service as a pilot with the United States Air Force. Mike and I were flying together in my Cessna 150 on September 10, 2001, when he was on a short vacation from UAL and was scheduled to return on **9/11/01,** but was delayed from returning for duty by several days. We sat together before a television set watching Islamic terrorists fly airplanes into the WTC buildings and the Pentagon. (A sight neither of us will ever forget, but I fear many Americans have already forgotten the significance of this vicious attack by crazed Islamic Fundamentalists whose goal was to kill as many Americans as possible.)

In the fall of 1960 it was announced that Mitchel AFB would close. Protesters, championed by the *Long Island Newsday Newspaper,* had won! My planned four-year tour with the 14th Air Force Inspector General's Staff would only last two years, along with it my ability to fly the T-33 at just about any time I desired. There was a mad scramble by Air Force personnel stationed at Mitchel in finding assignments somewhere else in the world. The Air Force at the time had a surplus of pilots, so finding a flying job seemed remote. I tried obtaining an assignment with a B-57 jet bomber squadron or F-94s, but was unsuccessful. The chief of personnel presented me with a choice of three assignments: one, as an Intercontinental Ballistic Missile (ICBM) launch officer with the Strategic Air Command, which would deposit me in a hole in the ground, like a ground hog, for up to three days at a time. I told him I wasn't interested; two, attend a training program as a supply officer, a pencil pushing job behind a desk. I told him, "No thanks;" third, attend a nine-month training program at Chanute AFB Illinois, as an Aircraft Maintenance Officer (AMO). The latter assignment would allow me to continue flying the T-33 and after completing the program, I would be assigned to a jet flying unit somewhere in the exciting world of aviation. I told him, "Sign me up for the AMOC." As I was preparing to depart Mitchel AFB, the 14th Air Force IG presented me with a Commendation Award, which read in part:

"As Chief Tactical Inspector, Captain Martin was responsible for conducting operational readiness tests for Troop Carrier, Fighter Interceptor, Tactical Fighter (both conventional and special weapons), Photo Reconnaissance and Aeromedical Evacuation units. His outstanding operational and evaluation ability enabled him to singularly supervise a section formally requiring two officers. He frequently participated in aerial flights, both jet and conventional, with Air National Guard and Air Force Reserve Units, and frequently worked 16-hour days without complaint. Signed: Burton K Voorhees, Colonel, USAF, Detachment Commander, 14th Air Force Inspector General."

On November 16, 1960, my wife, eight-year-old daughter Lynn and two-month-old son Michael, loaded up my Chevrolet *Impala* convertible and headed for Chanute AFB in Rantoul, Illinois. Returning to Chanute was a nostalgic event, as it was where, after my 20th birthday in June 1948, I spent three days undergoing testing for an appointment as an Aviation Cadet. Now 12 years later I was returning as a captain, senior jet pilot, and married with a wife and two small kids.

Chanute Air Force Base, like Mitchel and Randolph, was a historic military installation. It was named after Octave Alexander Chanute (1832-1910) whose early aviation research inspired the Wright brothers' success. The base was opened in July 1917 and played an important role in WW I, WW II, and the Korean and Vietnam Wars. When it was closed on September 30, 1993, it was the third oldest active military flying field. It now houses an aviation museum and civilian establishments.

I obtained a three-bedroom apartment in base housing and enrolled as a student in a nine-month AMOC. I would attend six-hour daily class sessions, five days a week, commencing at 6 a.m. one week, and alternate with a starting time of 12 noon the following week. My 12 Air Force classmates were all pilots, and like myself, hoping to remain in a career field closely relating to flying. Also attending, the same class were an Iranian captain, a Turkish major and a captain from Venezuela.

Rated Air Force officers were to maintain flight proficiency in the T-33, T-28, or the C-47. I was pleased that I was to continue flying the T-33, and received my local day flight check on December 9, 1960, with instructor pilot Captain M.J. Adams, and my night check on December 21, with Captain C.L. Wheeler. The T-33 instructor pilots were assigned to the Air Training Command and treated us like inexperienced cadets. Gone were the days of flying the T-Bird any time I wished, like I was accustomed to at Mitchel AFB. I was only allowed to fly when scheduled by our "distinguished instructors," which alternated between front and rear cockpit. We were never allowed to fly the aircraft solo and would only fly about ten hours per month (the minimum number of hours required to remain current). Our flight instructors would perform unannounced ramp checks on aircraft taxiing out for takeoff and if both pilots were not wearing boots, gloves, and the proper flight suit they would cancel the flight and send us back to the ramp.

The nine-month AMOC was designed for young college ROTC graduates with no previous knowledge of flight operations; therefore, many parts of the training curriculum were routine, but there was no way to change the military bureaucratic wheels of inefficiency to accommodate more experienced officers like ourselves. We decided that the best course of action was to enjoy our nine-month vacation, which would occasionally bring to light areas useful in our new career field of aircraft maintenance. The course consisted of aircraft maintenance fundamentals, shops and systems, electrical components, power plants, weight and balance, inspection systems, management techniques and a myriad number of other related subjects designed to make us competent supervisors. I graduated on August 8, 1961, with a final course grade of 87%.

I enjoyed the carefree attitude of my classmates and at times, our cavalier attitude of engaging in silly, but humorous "frat-boy-style-tricks," drove our young instructors up the wall. When studying hydraulics a young second lieutenant instructor was explaining the functions of a hydraulic system by utilizing a wooden pointer on an overhead schematic projection. His pointer was following heavy **red** lines, representing high pressure outflow, and heavy **green** lines, representing low pressure return flow. In the middle of his presentation it was time for a pee and coffee break and during the instructors absence one of my enterprising classmates drew a detailed and realistic false **red** line on the instructor's projector transparency that ended in a blind alley.

When the instructor continued his lecture, he picked up his pointer and attempted to follow the false **red** pressure line to explain a typical aircraft hydraulic system. However, when his pointer came to a dead-end his face turned red and his presentation stumbled as he tried in vain to explain a hydraulic system that had no logical explanation. Naturally we peppered him with questions about the pressure line that had no **outlet**.

When studying engines, installed in a test cell, we would compete in seeing who could generate the most number of backfires when starting a Pratt & Whitney 4360 engine, and engage in similar contests in seeing who could create the longest flame shooting out of a J-47 engine tailpipe. These engine cell contests were not popular with the instructors who would give us hell and threaten to wash us out if they continued! The time passed quickly and we became a very harmonious group and participated in many weekend parties. We were able to provide the happy juice for these parties at discount prices as our three foreign students could order booze from Canada duty free.

During my stay at Chanute I only experienced one incident in a T-33 that was somewhat exciting. A fellow classmate, Captain Jack Lowrey, and I put in for a night cross-country flight to Andrews AFB, Maryland, which to our surprise was approved. I was to fly from the front seat to Andrews and Jack would fly it on the return leg. When we filed our flight plan the weather forecaster stated that we might encounter some thunderstorm activity over Ohio, but thought we could pick our way through the area with no problem. (We didn't want to cancel the flight as obtaining approval for a T-33 cross-country from our "training command nursemaids" was extremely difficult.) After takeoff we climbed to 37,000 feet and when approaching Ohio we observed lightning flashes so numerous that it appeared we would have difficulty in avoiding the worst of the storms, so we climbed to 41,000 feet. We still couldn't top all of them, but were able to circumnavigate the ones that looked the most menacing. The ride was bumpy, but exhilarating as we dashed from right to left in attempting to evade the lightning strikes. We picked our way through the area unscathed, but decided to spend the night at Andrews AFB and fly back to Chanute the next morning.

As graduation day grew closer there was much speculation as to where we would be assigned, once we were certified as Aircraft Maintenance Officers. The possible assignments were as varied as the Air Force itself, but we felt confident that they would relate to some type of jet aircraft support. About a month before graduation our next base of assignment was posted, with mine being the 39th Air Division at Misawa Air Base, Japan. In checking the type of aircraft operating at Misawa, I discovered that there were two squadrons of F-100s, one squadron of RF-101s, and F-102s, plus support T-33s and C-47s. It was a fighter base in every respect and my heart jumped with joy. I had no idea which type aircraft I would be required to maintain, but I would consider any one of them, except the C-47, acceptable and an answer to a 13-year-old Ferry-Godmother wish.

I didn't think my Chevrolet *Impala* convertible would be the type of car to take to Northern Japan so I traded it in for a 1960 bright red Plymouth *Valiant* sedan. It was a new design, had a manual transmission, a slant-six cylinder engine of 101 hp and very roomy --- a perfect car for the back roads of Japan. I purchased a second car for my wife, who would remain behind until I secured housing in Misawa and left for Travis AFB, California for further transportation to Japan in September 1961.

After arranging shipment of my Plymouth *Valiant*, I was on a PAA B-707 for Yokota Air Base, Japan, with refueling stops in Hawaii and Wake Island. En route to Hawaii I engaged in a lengthy discussion with a group of staff officers from Pacific Air Force Headquarters (PACAF), who, when they learned that I was a recent AMOC graduate and heading for Misawa, were eager to brief me on the many problems the F-100s were experiencing at Misawa and Itazuke Air Base and wanted to know if I was being assigned to an F-100 squadron. I told them that my final assignment had not been determined, but this didn't discourage them from telling me horror stories about F-100 problems and accidents. They deplaned when we landed in Hawaii and I was glad to be rid of their pessimistic reports about an aircraft that I knew nothing about.

1. Author, in June 1929, celebrating his first birthday. Six months later the stock market crashed, sending the country into an economic depression.

2. Author at age eleven, 1939. Note the necktie and full head of hair. Schools at the time required boys to wear neckties and hair neatly cut.

3. Author and high school girl friend, Erna Lou Jones in 1946. She later married a returning local WW II navy veteran.

4. Author's 1947 high school graduation photo. After graduation his first job was in a Ladysmith photo studio.

5. Author in the summer of 1941 (age 13) holding a model airplane he built. It was made with balsam wood and powered by a "wind-up" rubber band. They didn't last long, but after it crashed a replacement was soon available.

6. Author and seven high school classmates assembled in Duluth Minnesota, seeking employment in early June 1944. Initially we had hoped to work on Great Lake steamers, but ended up as "Gandy Dancers" on the Soo Line railroad. L. to R: Author, Jim Wilkinson, Rusty Anderson, Bob Morris, Richard Siefert, Bob Biller, and Jim Blanchett.

7. Author as 16 year old "Gandy Dancer" on the Soo Line Railroad in Northern Minnesota in the summer of 1944. He worked 10 hour days, six days a week, at 60 cents per hour. His weekly salary was $36, equal to $384 today.

8. The Martin family in 1968: L. to R. Back row, Dan (Air Corps WW II), Joe (Army WW II), Jerry (U.S. Marines during Korean war), insert photo of father who died eleven years earlier, (Army National Guard WW I), George (WW II instructor pilot CAP), Hank (Air corps WW II), Author (U.S. Air Force 1948 to 1970. Front row, Betty, Rita, Mother, Ben (Navy WW II), Dolores.

9. Author, at age 17, standing next to Aeronca Chief at Triangle Airport, Michigan. This is one of the aircraft he flew after his first solo on July 21, 1945. He had spent the summer working for his brother George, a CAP flight instructor, who provided him with the means of obtaining a Private License.

10. Author standing next to Taylorcraft BC-12 during EAA Air Venture Oshkosh 2005. This is the type aircraft he flew on his first solo sixty years earlier. Note that he has put on a few pounds since that memorable day!

11. A 1945 Department of Commerce Civil Aeronautics Administration Identification Certificate, designating my brother George as a certified airman. This type of identification was required during WW II.

12. Author's 1945 Department of Commerce Civil Aeronautics Administration Identification Certificate. Private flying during WW II was very restrictive, especially when flying near either coast. Another factor, which made private flying difficult, was "gas rationing." However, my brother being an instructor pilot with the Civilian Air Patrol I was able to fly almost any time I wished.

13. An Aeronca 7AC Champ, the type aircraft I flew when creating snow clouds by skimming over the frozen Flambeau River in the winter of 1946. The Champ was a fun airplane to fly as it had a 65 hp engine, a maximum speed of 129 mph and a takeoff ground roll of only 224 feet.

14. A Piper J-3 Cub, the type aircraft I was flying on a cold January day in Northern Wisconsin in 1946, when the top entrance door blew off and struck the right horizontal stabilizer. My high school classmate, in the rear seat, almost froze before we were able to make it back to the Rusk County Airport. The aircraft had a 65 hp engine and cruised at around 80 mph.

15. Author on wing of North American T-6 Texan in April 1949. He flew this aircraft during basic training at Waco AFB, Texas. The T-6 was a two-place advanced trainer in WW II, but the Air Force had thousands left over after the war so they used it as a basic trainer. It has a 550 hp engine and cruised at 205 mph. More than 21,000 T-6s were built.

16. My son, Michael, next to a T-38 he flew in pilot training in 1989. The T-38 is a twin-engine supersonic jet trainer built by Northrop. It has two engines of 2,900 pounds thrust, with afterburner, cruises at 812 mph and has a maximum ceiling of above 55,000 feet and can climb at 30,000 feet per min. When I took Mike for a ride in the T-6, he was amazed in how far we had come in forty years.

17. Author next to T-6 Texan at Waco, AFB Texas in April 1949. Note new style flight jacket and WW II type leather helmet. By this time I had about 160 hours in the T-6, and most of my fellow students who were to be washed out had already been discharged.

18. Results of fatal accident that killed a classmate in the rear cockpit of a T-6. He was under an instrument canvas hood and preparing to make an instrument takeoff (ITO), from the rear cockpit, when another aircraft climbed up his tail. He was shredded into a thousand pieces by a spinning propeller.

19. Formation of T-6s owned by civilian pilots. The T-6s the author flew as an Aviation Cadet in 1949 were not as shiny, but he didn't have to pay for the gas. Perfecting formation flying was an integral part of pilot training and flights of up to twelve aircraft were not uncommon.

20. The B-25 Mitchell bomber, the type aircraft I flew in advanced pilot training at Barksdale AFB, LA. General Jimmy Doolittle flew the B-25 when he and 15 other Mitchells bombed Tokyo on April 1942. More than 9,800 were built and used as multi-engine trainers and military executive transports after the war.

21. Second Lieutenant Lou Martin in October 1949, after graduating from Air Force pilot training. Shortly after this photo was taken he was en route to Germany.

22. Lieutenant Colonel Lou Martin, in September 1966 at Dover AFB, DL. At age 38 he was the youngest Lt. Col. on the base, however promotions came fast during the Vietnam war.

23. William (Balls) Bailey and author celebrating Christmas 1949, in their Bellevue Hotel in Wiesbaden. Balls was from Knoxville, TN. and an Aviation Cadet colleague. After pilot training they were both sent to Germany.

24. Col. Red Forman, on Nov. 15, 1949, welcoming the ten 2ndLts. selected to fly C-82s in Wiesbaden Germany. L to R: Col. Forman, Hank O'Neal, Edward Scott, Don Iannia, Willard Wicklund, Lou Martin (author), name missing, Balls Bailey, James Cooley, Jack Rossell, & Harvey Trengove. (Note the variety of uniforms; Air Corps Pinks & Greens and Air Force blues).

25. Author giving a "thumbs up" in cockpit of C-119 over Germany in 1954. The wearing of a parachute indicates that the flight was in formation with other Packets, as we always wore them when flying in formation.

26. A C-82 Flying Boxcar in Wiesbaden AB, Germany., which I flew when assigned to the 12th TCS. It was the first aircraft designed to be loaded from trucks at ground level. It was originally designed to support the planned 1945 invasion of Japan, but was later assigned to troop carrier units worldwide.

27. Four C-82s in formation over Germany. The photo was taken by the author from the right seat of another Packet. The aircraft was powered by two P & W R-2800 engines of 2,100 hp each and cruised at 162 mph, could carry 42 troops or 34 stretchers. When production ceased in 1948, 223 had been built.

28. A view of the C-82 Packet showing the opened rear clam-shell doors which allows for direct loading from trucks. The rear doors could be easily removed for the air drooping of heavy equipment. There was no notable difference in the flight characteristics with the doors removed.

29. A C-54 at Rhein Main AB in 1950. It was the first four-engine transport to enter military service and 1,164 were built. It could carry 28,000 pounds of cargo or 49 passengers, was powered by four P & W R-2800 engines, cruised at 239 mph, and saw extensive service during the Berlin blockade in 1948/49.

30. Author's 1937 Willys sedan in Mainz, Germany in early 1950. The Willys was a neat little car, but couldn't compete with high-powered German cars on the autobahn. It was equipped with a four cylinder 48 hp engine and cost me $200 (equal to $1,470 today).

31. A view of the ruins of Mainz, Germany, which was 85% destroyed by bombing raids during the war. This photo was taken in 1950 and reflects on how difficult it was to rebuilt German cities. If it hadn't been for the "Marshal Plan" reconstruction would have taken many more years.

32. Author returning from a high altitude formation flight in a C-82 in 1951. It can be recognized as a high altitude mission by the wearing of a "quick release" parachute harness and a leather helmet with attached oxygen mask. Also note the A-2 leather jacket which was still standard issue.

33. Author standing next to German glider SG 38 boat, which he flew as a member of an RAF Glider Club in the British occupied zone of Germany. It was one of the gliders the Brits confiscated from the German Luftwaffee.

34. An SG-38 open glider. It was the type of aircraft German Luftwaffee pilots first flew during their training and was also the type I first flew with the RAF Glider Club. It was like sitting in a dining room chair in flight and possessed no instruments of any kind. (Note the swastika on the rudder).

35. Author sitting in cockpit of German "Baby Grunau" glider and waiting to be towed aloft by a surplus barrage balloon winch. The Baby Grunau was the most produced sailplane in the world with more than 6,000 produced. It was an excellent primary trainer for thousands of future Luftwaffe fighter pilots.

36. A bright red 1952 MG-TD I purchased new in Germany for $1,500 and shipped to the U.S. It was a wonderful little sports car, but had no heater. After picking it up at Staten Island, NY. we drove it to Toledo Ohio, with our two month old daughter wrapped up like an Eskimo over the brake handle.

37. Author's 1950 Buick Roadmaster in Greenville, SC., in 1953. It had belonged to a local rich boy who fell in love with the MG and wanted to trade cars. He wanted my MG and $500, but I held out until we made an even trade. The Buick was a neat car for a young pilot. (Note police dog in rear seat).

38. Paratroopers preparing to board a C-119G at Neubiberg AB, Germany in 1955. By the time they strap on all their equipment they are usually carrying so much weight that they have to be helped into the aircraft. When they move to the rear of the aircraft, to jump out, they will shift the aircraft CG aft.

39. Paratroopers jumping from a C-119G over Germany in the mid 1950s. They will exit the aircraft from a door on either side of the aircraft while the pilot maintains a maximum airspeed of 130 KTS. in close formation with other aircraft. Their parachutes are opened by a "static line" in the aircraft.

40. Author and wife leaving the Rhine Main AB chapel following their marriage on April 14, 1951. Officers no longer carried sabers so in lieu of a canopy of raised swords colleagues lined the sidewalk and presented a salute. The chapel, along with the rest of the base, has since been destroyed by the Germans after the base was returned on Dec. 30, 2005.

41. Flying school classmates and their wives get together for dinner in the Donaldson AFB, Officers' Club in the summer of 1953. L to R: Author, and his wife Jo, Bill Wicklund and his wife Joan, Mary Lee and her husband Hank O'Neal. (I was best man for Hank and Mary Lee's wedding).

42. The C-47 Skytrain which I flew when stationed at Niagara Falls, NY., and Mitchel Field. Gen. Eisenhower stated it was instrumental in winning WW II.

43. The C-45 Expeditor. A twin-engine Beechcraft used extensively during WW II as a trainer and light transport, 4,526 of them were built.

44. The Lockheed T-33 Shooting Star. It was a two-place jet developed from the F-80 fighter, and used worldwide. I flew this aircraft for four years and loved every minute of it. It was one of my favorite airplanes.

45. North American F-100 Super Sabres in formation over Japan. . It first flew in 1956 and was the first fighter to exceed the speed of sound in level flight. I flew this aircraft when stationed at Misawa AB, Japan.

46. The North American T-39 Sabreliner was the Air Force version of a popular jet executive aircraft. I flew this aircraft at Misawa, Japan.

47. The Fairchild C-123 Provider was a short range assault transport originally designed as a glider. I flew in the C-123 during my TDY in Thailand.

48. Author in front of his tent at Don Muang Airport, Bangkok, Thailand in October 1962. Lou and a major colleague from Tachikawa, Japan, spent three months on temporary assignment in Southeast Asia establishing logistic support utilizing a fleet of Fairchild C-123 Providers.

49. General Wallace, Commander of Dover AFB, presenting a C-133 Aircraft Commander designation certificate to me in July 1965. The general was also qualified in the C-133 and when he wished to fly a mission he would request that I accompany him. He was instrumental in my promotion to Lt.Col.

50. A C-133A Cargomaster on the ramp of Dover AFB. (Note the mechanic standing on top of the fuselage.) I flew the C-133 for six years (1964 to 1970) and 4,700 hours. Fifty C-133s were built with seven crashing for mysterious reasons before the problem was solved.

51. Author in front of C-133 he flew to a base in South Vietnam in 1966. The rear ramp is lowered for the unloading and loading of cargo. Ground time in Vietnam was kept to a minimum as the large Cargomaster was a tempting target for North Vietnam insurgents manning mortars

52. On April 30, 1967 A C-133 , en route to Midway Island, ditched in the Pacific Ocean after it experienced unprecedented problems in all four propellers. I was the pilot investigator for this accident .

53. A proud Laysan Albatross (Gooney Bird) found on the Pacific Island of Midway. About 400,000 of these magnificent birds make Midway their nesting location for about five months of the year. They were an amusing nuisance, but at the same time provided a welcome diversion.

54. Japan Domestic Airline Gaijin pilots training with Piedmont Airlines in Winston Salem, NC (Dec. 1970) L to R: Bob Frazier, Chris Weitzel, Frank Plonowski, Jack Spence, Dick Emery, Bob Ammon, Mike Michelis, Dusty Rhodes, Randy Hayes, Penrod Rideout, Lou Martin, Bucky Blair, & two instructors. Insert photo, L to R: Bob McLin, Bob MacClelland and Jim Treacy.

55. A Japan Domestic Airlines YS-11 on takeoff. I flew this twin-engine Japanese turbo-prop for nearly five years. One hundred and eight-three were built by the Nihon company and served not only Japanese airlines, but Piedmont and other airlines worldwide.

56. Author in the cockpit of a YS-11 in 1974. Photo was taken by a Japanese Sport Aviation magazine photographer who wrote an article relating to my smooth landings. This article, in its English translation, appears on page 443.

57. Author with Japan Domestic Airlines crew in summer of 1972. L to R: Capt. Lou Martin, senior flight attendant Chieko Hara (his future wife), second flight attendant and two trainees (under the supervision of Chieko), and Japanese copilot. (Note the mini skirts and proud appearance of the group).

58. Author on 750 CC Honda Motorcycle in Yokohama (1972). My landlord, an American JAL B-727 captain, owned two motorcycles and I could ride them anytime the desire and time were in sync. He also owned the house I was renting and had a Japanese wife. They were great friends.

59. A chance meeting, in 1974, with my landlord Captain Joe Burke, who parked his B-727 next to my YS-11 in Fukuoka Airport. L to R: Joe Burke, two JAL flight attendants, and author.

60. Author and daughter Lynn, after her graduation from the University of Hawaii , in 1981, with a Master's degree in Pacific Studies. Lynn remained in Hawaii for a number of years, but now lives in Concord, New Hampshire, with her husband Arnold and son Daithi.

61. Author, Lt.Col. Martin, USAF (ret), swearing in his son Mitchel, as an Air Force officer, after his graduation from the University of Wisconsin in 1987. Mike is also a pilot and flew combat tours in Gulf War I, Afghanistan and Iraq. He is presently a pilot with the Air National Guard and United Airlines.

62. Author and Chieko in Tehran, Iran in 1978. They are standing in front of the Volkswagen that was abandoned during the revolution that overthrew the Shah. Their story is covered in the author's book "Wings Over Persia." This photo was taken near the swimming pool at the U.S. Army base.

63. Author enjoying a martini in his apartment in Tehran, in 1978. This was obviously before the worst of the revolution because Chieko was still in Iran. What the picture doesn't show is the strong odor of onions coming from my landlords downstairs apartment.

64. Chieko enjoying a Beefeater Martini while toasting to a future of happiness, which I feel was realized when we were married on November 13, 1982. Chieko and her Japanese colleagues left Tehran soon after this picture was taken as their Japanese boss felt they were in danger.

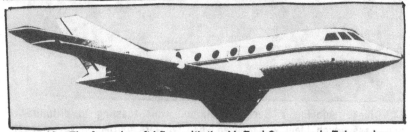

65 to 68.   The four aircraft I flew with the Air Taxi Company in Tehran, Iran.
From the top: Fairchild F-27, & FH-227, Rockwell 690A, & French Falcon jet.

69. Author in cockpit of F-27 somewhere over Iran in 1977. When Chieko obtained a job in Tehran, in January 1978, she had me shave off my mustache.

70. Author enjoying a ski trip with friends in Austria in 1995, when assigned to the U.S. Consulate office in Frankfurt Germany from 1992 to 96. From L -R : Lee Brooks, Eric Elmgren, Chieko and author. (Unfortunately, Lee Brooks was killed in an auto accident after returning to the U.S.

71. Author and wife celebrating their twenty-second wedding anniversary in a Minneapolis restaurant on November 13, 2004. This was a very happy occasion for both and we toasted to many, many more to follow.

72. Chieko and author overlooking a coffee plantation in Costa Rico in December 2005. We spent two weeks touring this friendly country and can recommend it as a place to escape the winter snow.

73. Kermit Laquey, chief pilot for the Planes of Fame Air Museum at Flying Cloud Airport in Eden Prairie, MN. Kermit was instrumental in my checking out in several WW II restored aircraft operated by the museum. Kermit was tragically killed in a F-51 accident on July 19, 1990.

74. Author (left) and a retired Air Force pilot towing aerial targets for Luftwaffle Tornado jet fighters in a F-100F. I was able to make one more flight in this famous fighter in 1993. Once airborne I flew it from the rear cockpit for the two hour mission. It was amazing how quickly the feel for it returned.

75. Author taxiing out on a passenger flight in a PT-17 Stearman primary trainer when flying for the Planes of Fame Air Museum. in 1992.

76. Author taxiing out, on April 20, 1991, for a test flight in the Air Museum's restored T-34. It had been 33 years since I had flown a Mentor.

77. Photo of a restored De Havilland Tiger Moth in Oshkosh in July 2005. It was the same type aircraft I had the pleasure of flying in England the 1950s.

78. The *Bob Pond Racer,* a light weight composite aircraft designed by Burt Rutan and initially test flown by his brother Dick. Jim Duffy, Al Pike and I witnessed the "roll-out" of this unique aircraft at Mojave, Ca. , in April 1991. Veteran race pilot Rick Brichert, was killed when flying it in 1993.

79. Author caressing the FM-2 after his last flight in a Wildcat on August 14, 1995. He had just returned from flying it to Sioux Falls, SD for the dedication of the "Joe Foss Airport." Gen. Foss welcomed him and introduced him to his admires as the pilot who flew his favorite aircraft in for the celebration.

80. Author proudly displaying his book, "Wings Over Persia" in 2004 after he was informed that his book had been selected as The Best Aviation Writing by a Minnesotan for 2004, by the Minnesota Aviation Hall of Fame. He is standing next to his C-150 which he flies to Midwest fly-ins and air shows.

81. The author signing books, in the Author's Corner of the warehouse building, during the EAA's Air Venture Oshkosh 2005. He shared space with many other authors and had the opportunity of meeting many of them . (Note the plaque from the Minnesota Aviation Hall of Fame sitting on the table).

Chapter Ten --- North American F-100 Super Sabre

When I arrived at Yokota Air Base, Japan I still had four days before I would have to report for duty in Misawa, so I decided to spend a couple days exploring Tokyo. It had been eight years since I had last visited this bustling city and I was eager to see the changes, which I assumed would be many. I rode a train downtown and a taxi to the former Imperial Japanese Army *Sanno Hotel.* I spent several days walking the streets and couldn't believe the progress the Japanese had made in rebuilding a city that was nearly destroyed by B-29 bombing raids 16 years earlier. Many sections no longer bore any evidence of the tremendous destruction this aerial bombing caused, while other areas were undergoing extensive rebuilding. Construction cranes sprouted up everywhere!

Three days later I rode an overnight train to Misawa (400 miles north), arriving early on the morning of September 25, 1961. I called the base duty officer and ten minutes later an Air Force staff car arrived to transport me to the headquarters of the 39th Air Division. I presented a copy of my travel orders to a staff officer who informed me that General Ernest Beverly, the Division Commander, would welcome me personally.

I was ushered into his office and after presenting a smart salute, the general said, "At ease, Captain Martin, welcome to Misawa. Have a seat." I was impressed that the general had a copy of my personnel file on his desk and was reviewing it. He asked me if I would like to check out in the F-100. (I couldn't believe what I was hearing as I had been trying for years to qualify in fighters and now I was being asked if I would like to check out in the North American *Super Sabre.*) I told the general that I certainly would and inquired if it could be accomplished in Japan or if I would be required to attend a qualifying course at Luke AFB. He told me that it could be achieved in Japan since they had four two-place F-100Fs and Itazuke Air Base had a simulator, but it would be a slow process and require a lot of hard work on my part. He repeated his question regarding my desire to fly the F-100. When I told him again, that I would. He said, "That's great, as Major Craig Nolan, the squadron commander of the 416th Tactical Fighter Squadron, has reviewed your personnel file and would like to have you assigned to his squadron, providing you were willing to checkout in the F-100." We shook hands and as I snapped him a farewell salute, he said that he would have a staff car drive me to Major Nolan's office, as he was looking forward to meeting me.

Nolan's office was located adjacent to the flight line and when I stepped out from the staff car my heart was racing from the scene unfolding before me. The ramp was awash with shiny new F-100s, while others were taxiing in and out of the area. Adding to the thrill was the thundering sound of F-100s, RF-101s and F-102s taking off with long shafts of flame shooting out from their afterburners. As I walked into Major Nolan's office I had to rub my eyes to make sure I wasn't dreaming. My reporting salute was returned along with a handshake and a request to take a seat. I was immediately impressed by Major Nolan who fit the image of the type of officer you would like to see on a recruiting poster. He was handsome, intelligent looking, dressed in an immaculate tailor-made blue uniform adorned with an impressive array of ribbons and senior pilot wings.

He welcomed me to his squadron while stating that he was eager to match his sister squadron, the 531st, commanded by Lt.Col. Sollars, who had a maintenance officer qualified in the F-100, and an assistant who had flown F-104s. Therefore he would like to have me checked out in the F-100 ASAP. He added that my assistant, 2ndLt. Bob Anderson, was not a pilot, but an extremely sharp young officer who I would enjoy working with in maintaining his fleet of 24 aircraft. And, he added, as soon as I was comfortable in my new job, he would arrange for me to attend a two-week F-100 ground school and flight simulator course, with the 8th Tactical Fighter Wing at Itazuke Air Base. After completing training at Itazuke, he and his highly qualified flight instructors would check me out in the Super Sabre, utilizing their "two-place" F-100-Fs. With that he escorted me around the squadron to meet his operations officer, Major Les Levoy, and fighter pilots milling about the operations center. Following this he accompanied me next door to the aircraft maintenance hangar where he introduced me to my assistant, Lt. Bob Anderson, and my line chief, Senior Master Sgt. Longacre. He then said he was returning to his own office, allowing me time to get acquainted with my staff. But as he left, he welcomed me once again and said that if there was anything I needed I shouldn't hesitate in letting him know.

Misawa Air Base was established by the Imperial Japanese Army in 1935, and in 1942 the Japanese Navy assumed control to study the feasibility of using it for long-range bombing raids on the U.S. mainland, however this objective was never achieved. Near the end of the war the base was used for training kamikaze pilots. In July 1945, B-29 bombers destroyed 90% of the base infrastructure, rendering it inactive. After the war the U.S. took control and it became the home base for the 49th Fighter Group flying F-51s, F-80s, F-84s and F-86s. It was an active support base during the Korean War with F-100s arriving in 1959. When I arrived in the fall of 1961, it housed two squadrons of F-100s, a squadron of F-102s, a squadron of RF-101s, a Japanese Air Self Defense (JASDF) squadron flying F-86Fs and support aircraft flying T-33s and C-47s.

I secured a room on the second floor of the BOQ, unpacked my bags and looked forward to starting work in my new exciting job the next morning. Sometime during the night my cot began shaking and in my half-asleep condition I thought someone was attempting to rouse me out of bed. However, when I woke up my room was still dark, but from the dim light shining in from the window, I observed the entire room and my bed shaking sideways and up and down. I popped out of bed and almost fell flat on my ass because of the violent shaking. Dressed in my underwear, I steadied myself by grabbing a hold of the wall and staggered out into the hallway. When I entered the hall I noted several colleagues making their way toward the nearest exit, while steadying themselves by holding onto the walls. I joined this "drunken-like-march," but had only taken a few wobbly steps when the shaking abruptly stopped. I stood in silence for a couple minutes while other residents started moving back to their rooms. As one of my colleagues made his way past me he said, "Welcome to Japan. I assume this was your first experience with an earthquake? But I can assure you it won't be your last." I went back to bed, but it took me a long time to go back to sleep!

Early the next morning I went to my office and found my assistant already on the job. Bob was a young ROTC college graduate who loved aviation but wasn't able to qualify for pilot training because of a minor medical problem, so he choose to attend the AMOC to be close to airplanes. He was a tireless worker who had an uncanny ability of getting along with noncommissioned officers many years his senior. He lived off base in a small Japanese built "shack" with an equally impressive young wife. In discussing our mission with Lt. Anderson and Sergeant Longacre, it was apparent that it was going to be a real pleasure to work with such intelligent and dedicated individuals. The F-100 was our front-line tactical fighter bomber and the Air Force was doing its best to assign well qualified officers and enlisted men to maintain this important strike force. I was proud to be a part of it!

Bob introduced me to a Japanese man named "Willie" who owned a tailor shop in downtown Misawa and was also a contractor for constructing small "off-base" houses for newly-arrived military personnel who would live in them while awaiting sufficient seniority to move into government housing on base. (The waiting period was generally a year.)

Willie drove me to a farm field east of the city, where he was building two and three-bedroom homes. He asked me how many bedrooms I needed and when I told him three, he showed me a couple different floor plans. After making a selection, I asked him how much it would cost. He said, "$2,500." ($16,439 in today's dollars). Surprised at the low cost, my next question was how long would it take to build. His response was also a surprise, "Once my crew can commence construction it will be finished in less than two weeks!" I went to the base credit union, took out a loan and put $1,000 down with the remainder to be paid when the house was completed. Willie told me that there was a long waiting list but he hoped to have it finished in three months, which would be just before Christmas 1961. This was great news since, if true, it would allow me to have my family in Japan for the Christmas and New Year's holidays.

I returned to my office and while awaiting F-100 familiarization training I decided to learn as much as I could about the North American *Super Sabre* jet fighter and what was expected of me in my new assignment of maintaining 24 of them in combat-ready status.

The F-100 first flew on January 24, 1956 and delivered to operational squadrons later that same year. The last F-100D was produced in August 1959 after a production run of 1,274. (However there were 1,020 other models produced for a total of 2,294.) The initial cost for each aircraft was $664,000, ($4,471,685 in today's dollars). The aircraft experienced several major deficiencies when first introduced that were not easily corrected. There were problems with the electrical system, autopilot integration with the Low Altitude Bombing System (LABS), afterburner fuel system, occasional inadvertent bomb releases and in-flight refueling probes, to name a few. There were so many field modifications that maintaining them in combat-ready status was initially a real problem. It was equipped with a Pratt and Whitney J-57 turbojet engine of 16,000 pounds thrust (with afterburner), had a wingspan of 38 feet 9 inches, a maximum speed of 770 mph at sea level and 864 mph (Mach 1.3) at

36,000 feet. Its initial climb rate (clean) was 19,000 feet per minute, a service ceiling of 36,100 feet and absolute ceiling of 50,000. It had a normal range of 534 miles, but up to 2,000 miles with external fuel tanks installed. Its empty weight was 21,000 pounds, with a maximum takeoff weight of 35,000 or higher. Our F-100Ds were equipped with four internal 20-mm cannons and wing mounts for the Sidewinder air-to-air infrared missile and tactical nuclear weapons. (See Photo No. 45.)

As I became more familiar with the F-100 I was fascinated by the marvels of its construction and diligently studied the pilot and maintenance manuals. The pilots assigned to fly this prestigious fighting machine knew they were on the cutting edge of our defense posture and were a proud lot, and It was an honor to be assigned to their unit. They openly accepted me as one of their own which fulfilled my dream of becoming a member of a front-line jet fighter squadron.

Soon after arriving at Misawa I looked up my Niagara Falls, New York buddy Charlie Carpenter. (Charlie and I had shared many laughs together in Miami, Florida when flying reserve navigators over the Gulf of Mexico in TC-47s and in blowing out mufflers on rental cars.) After leaving Niagara Falls, Charlie had attended Radar Approach Control (RAPCON) training and was now assigned as a RAPCON supervisor at Misawa Air Base.

RAPON worked in concert with Japanese Air Traffic Controllers and assumed radar control of military aircraft arriving and departing Misawa.

Charlie maintained flight proficiency in the C-47 and thought I was playing with fire, and somewhat daft, for planning on flying the F-100. However, except for blowing out auto mufflers, he was never very adventurous so I disregarded his concerns. Charlie, his wife Pat and their two kids were living in an extremely small Japanese constructed shack in an area referred to as "B Battery." The area presented the image of a slum community with dirt roads producing either clouds of dust or seas of mud. However, Charlie, like many military personnel awaiting on base housing, accepted it as a way of saving money knowing that it was only a temporary hardship and a part of military life that others also endured.

In early December 1961 Major Nolan told me that he had arranged for me to go to Itazuke Air Base for F-100 ground school and when there obtain as much time in the simulator as I could talk them into. The ground school course was designed primarily for mechanics and presented more detail than normally offered to pilots. However since I was an Aircraft Maintenance Officer, I had no problem in absorbing the material presented and thought it would advance my capability of ensuring the aircraft in my charge were properly maintained. The simulator was fantastic and approached the utility of a full flight simulator, even though it didn't provide a visual scene or motion. However, all the instruments were operative and it had a built-in sound effect system that, when the canopy was closed created the feeling that you were flying a real aircraft. Another benefit that I hadn't anticipated was that F-100 pilots from the 8th TFW weren't too fond of flying it so I had it almost to myself. I was able to secure a F-100 flight instructor to look over my shoulder during my first few simulator periods, but he soon lost interest and left stating, "Hell, Lou, you're doing great and won't have any problem in flying the airplane, so I'll just leave you alone to enjoy yourself." I would spend two to three hours each day, after ground school, flying the simulator and was welcomed by the civilian technician hired to maintain it. I think he enjoyed my interest in his excellent training device and it gave him a break from reading magazines. I not only flew all the maneuvers that I would be exposed to when flying the actual aircraft many times over, but went through the abnormal and emergency procedures so often that I could go through them without reference to the checklist. When my two weeks in Itazuke were over, I was eager to put my F-100 knowledge to the test.

When I returned to Misawa (around the middle of December 1961) I was hoping to find my off-base house completed, as my wife and kids were scheduled to arrive just before Christmas. But when I visited the construction site there was nothing in place except a cement block outline, and a loose pile of lumber, kitchen sink, toilet and bathtub sitting in the field next to where the house was to be built. I went to Willie's tailor shop and gave him hell for not completing my house as promised, but he said that bad weather had prevented construction. However, he would send a crew out the next day to start building. I wasn't sure if I believed him, but his slanted half-open eyes appeared to be telling me the truth.

After work the next day I visited my building site, known as W-19, and was aghast at the activity in place. It gave me the impression of an "ant hill" by the number of Japanese workers bustling about. There were so many workers shifting lumber, hammering and just hustling about that I wondered how they kept from running into each other. They had only been working one day, but were already installing the roof, plumbers were hooking up water pipes and electricians were stringing wires. I quickly got out of their way and left, eager to see what I would find the following day. The next day the house was structurally complete and workers were inside installing flooring and thin plywood walls. When I visited it on the third day workers were plastering the outside walls of the house and painting the tin roof a bright red. I couldn't get out to inspect it on the fourth day, but when I visited it on the following day workers were testing the water and electrical system. On the way back to the base I stooped by to see Willie who said that as soon as I paid him the remaining $1,500 he would give me a stamped three-page deed to my house. I made another visit to the base credit union, withdrew $1,500, presented it to Willie and was now the proud owner of a house in Northern Japan --- one week before my family was scheduled to arrive.

A few days before Christmas my wife, nine-year-old daughter Lynn and 14-month-old son Michael arrived and we moved into our new "varnish-smelling" Japanese shanty. The heat source was a kerosene space heater in the front room, but since the house was not insulated the only warm area was right next to a "red hot" stove or under tons of blankets. Pilots and wives from the 416th Tactical Fighter Squadron descended on us the day after my family arrived bringing with them food, liquor and Christmas presents for the kids. It was great to be part of such a harmonious Air Force unit!

Following the Christmas holidays my "Pilot Flight Record" was transferred from the base flight T-33 Section to the 416th TFS. I was now an official member of a fighter squadron, after a 12-year struggle since graduating from pilot training. (A little late, but the road leading to this juncture was interesting and bountiful in regard to total flight time, which totaled 4,800 hours with nearly 500 hours being single-engine jet. This was twice as much as many of my new squadron colleagues had.)

My first flight in the F-100 was with my squadron commander, Major Nolan, which included a detailed flight briefing and procedures for ejecting from the aircraft. (As PIC he would announce, "Eject," and after he blew the canopy I was to eject immediately and not hesitate as he would follow seconds later.) He also requested I recite, from memory, the "Bold Face" emergency procedures. We then proceeded to the aircraft on a cold winter day in January 1962. Major Nolan said that he was impressed with my knowledge of the aircraft and could see that I didn't waste time in Itazuke. I performed an Aircraft Preflight Inspection under the watchful eye of my instructor and climbed the ladder to the front cockpit. The cockpit was more spacious than the T-33 and considerably higher up off the ground. My heart was racing with euphoric excitement as I looked down at the maintenance men gathered around on the ramp with the sole purpose of assisting me during my first flight in an F-100. The engine start was straight forward and the J-57 engine was soon emitting a tuned hum as it stabilized at 55 percent RPM. After the crew chief performed his check of the hydraulic system, I closed the canopy and called for taxi and takeoff instructions from the control tower. I advanced the throttle to get the aircraft moving and engaged the nose wheel steering by depressing a small button on the control stick. As we began to roll I felt a series of bumps, which I called to Major Noland's attention, but he said not to worry that they were the result of temporary flat spots on the tires from sitting in one place and would soon disappear while taxiing, which they did!

Sitting in the number one position for takeoff, I went through the Before Takeoff Check including the canopy locked and freedom of movement of the controls. When cleared for takeoff I taxied into position on runway 28, held the brakes, ran the power up to 100% RPM, checked the engine instruments for proper readings, all annunciation warning lights out, and with the nose wheel steering button depressed, released the brakes. As soon as the aircraft started rolling, I moved the throttle lever into the afterburner position and within a second or two felt and heard a "kick-in-the-ass" as we accelerated rapidly down the runway. (Up to this point everything was similar to my 30 hours of flying the fixed-base simulator in Itazuke, but nothing could duplicate the thrill and excitement I felt in shooting down the runway at breakneck speed.) I knew I was supposed to monitor the instruments during the takeoff roll, but in what seemed like seconds the airspeed was approaching 140 knots. I pulled back on the control stick, to raise the nose to about ten degrees pitch and let the beast fly off the runway. With my mind racing to equal the speed of the aircraft I heard a voice coming from the rear cockpit cautioning me to raise the landing gear before exceeding 220 knots, which we were fast approaching. When the gear and flaps retracted, I discontinued the use of the afterburner, and the jet quickly accelerated to the climb airspeed of 350 kts. With the vertical speed indicator pegged at the top of the gage, we busted through some snow showers, broke out on top at around 10,000 feet, and were heading for clear blue sky in about a 45 degree climb angle. **(What a machine! There is no way a pilot could have more fun than this with his clothes on!)**

I leveled off at 25,000 feet and was just beginning to feel out the aircraft, in gentle turns, when we received a call from the supervisor of flying to return to Misawa due to snow showers approaching from the west. I kicked out the speed brakes, reported over the airport at 10,000 feet and flew a simulated engine out approach (SFO). I held around 300 knots airspeed during the descending 360 degree circle and since we were still quite heavy I slowed to about 220 knots on the base leg and 190 knots on final approach. My touchdown was a little long, but with the drag chute deployed and a 10,000 foot runway, stopping was not a problem. Major Nolan was pleased with my performance, but I didn't want to tell him that my mind was still on the takeoff roll and just mentally into the climb phase when I shutdown the engine at the end of the flight. I could see that I required more mental fine tuning before my next flight.

Major Dave Gosser, the aircraft maintenance quality control supervisor and a high-time F-100 pilot, called and invited me to accompany him in the back seat of a F-100F functional check flight. He said Major Nolan thought I would benefit from a flight in the back seat, where all I had to do was observe. I told him that I agreed with Nolan and after picking up my parachute and helmet, I met Dave on the flight line about one hour later.

This was the first time I had met Major Gosser but had heard good things about him and now that I met him in person, I could attest first-hand to his personable character. He was a few years my senior, conveyed a very pleasing disposition and gave me the impression of the type of individual I would like to have as a big brother. After checking the aircraft records, we settled down in our respective cockpits and after a normal engine start taxied out for takeoff on runway 28. During the taxi Dave asked me if I would like to make the takeoff from the rear seat, but I told him I would prefer to sit back and watch an expert "Hun Driver" (F-100 pilot) make the takeoff without the pressure of trying to mentally stay ahead of the aircraft. With a chuckle, he said he understood.

Observing the rapid unfolding events from the rear cockpit was extremely helpful and I was confident that my next flight from the front seat would be less stressful and my brain would be able to match the rapid acceleration from an unleashed *Super Sabre* in afterburner. Once airborne, Dave turned over control of the jet to me and a couple minutes later we leveled off at 35,000 feet. We checked the operation of the afterburner, which took a lot longer to ignite than at sea level. He then lowered the nose and we went supersonic. I was amazed that when exceeding the speed of sound there was no noticeable indication other than a higher indicated airspeed on the Mach meter. The purpose of the flight test was a functional check of all components after the completion of a 100 hour inspection. The aircraft flew great and we didn't note any squawks, but Dave said that there was one more system he wanted to check before heading back to Misawa --- the autopilot performing a Low Altitude Bombing System (LABS) maneuver.

The LABS is a computerized system designed for delivering a nuclear bomb, from low altitude and performing a maneuver that allows the pilot to escape the area before the explosion. Prior to takeoff the pilot inserts settings in an onboard computer and when approaching the target descends to 500 feet while zooming in at 500 knots. When crossing a predetermined Initial Point (IP), he starts a stop watch count down while flying a precise heading to the target. When the inserted run-in time expires he engages the afterburner and starts a 4 G pull-up into an Immelmann. (A cockpit instrument should then be utilized to guide him through the maneuver.) Keeping the horizontal needle centered would indicate a constant 4 G pull; keeping the vertical needle centered would indicate he was maintaining the proper course. With the aircraft going straight up, the bomb will release automatically and continue zooming upwards before falling back to earth and detonating. (A bomb release light will illuminate informing the pilot that the bomb has left his aircraft.) The pilot completes the 180-degree Immelmann by rolling wings level at 10,000 feet and, when still in afterburner, dives toward the ground, accelerates to supersonic speed and races along the ground at tree top-level to escape the blast of the nuclear bomb. The F-100 autopilot was integrated to perform this maneuver automatically.

To test the system we descended to 5,500 feet, engaged the autopilot, accelerated to 500 knots and punched the timer to start the maneuver. (Dave said he was simulating a field elevation of 5,000 feet.) When the time ran out the aircraft went into an abrupt 4 G pull-up and as it did he moved the throttle into afterburner. The LABS needles never varied from the vertical and horizontal positions and the aircraft (still on autopilot) rolled wings level at 15,500 feet. I commented to Dave that this was very impressive and asked if he, and other Hun Drivers, used the autopilot when flying practice LABS drops on Rip Saw range at 500 knots and 500 feet above the ground. "Not on your life," he said, "we don't put that much confidence in the autopilot, especially at such a low altitude."

We returned to Misawa and Dave let me make a couple low approaches (we never made touch and go landings in the F-100 because the high landing speeds would result in heavy tire wear and increase the chance of a blowout). The low approaches were followed by a full-stop landing utilizing the drag chute to slow us down. I truly enjoyed this flight and felt I would be able to fly my next transition mission with considerable more confidence and the ability to mentally stay ahead of the fast-moving jet.

On Friday, January 26, 1962, I flew in the front seat of an F-100F with instructor pilot Eugene C. Buttyan in the rear cockpit. After a thorough pre-mission briefing, in which he also complimented me on my knowledge of the aircraft and emergency procedures, we headed for our assigned aircraft. Approaching the jet I noted red streamers hanging from the gun ports and practice bombs on the wing-mounted pylon rack. I mentioned to Gene that there must have been a mistake in the configuration of the aircraft, since initial training flights are not to be loaded with bombs or ammunition, and we didn't have a time slot for bombing and strafing runs on the Rip Saw Range! Gene's response, "Hell, Lou, who wants to fly a fighter without loaded guns and bombs hanging from the wings?" When I told Gene that I hadn't flown a LABS maneuver or made strafing runs, he said, "Don't worry, Lou. I'll talk you through it from the back seat!"

With a call sign of "Hardy Five" I completed a supervised Preflight Inspection, followed by a normal engine start and a taxi to runway 28. My takeoff airspeed was 5 knots too high and pitch angle a couple degrees high, but according to Gene I made corrections without a comment from him. We climbed to 25,000 feet where I performed standard rate banks to predetermined headings, steep turns, pitch and roll maneuvers, airspeed changes, speed brake exercises and throttle changes. When the 270 gallon drop tanks indicated empty, Gene had me perform maximum rate turns so I could experience the tendency of the aircraft to "tuck under" (tendency to dive in banks). I then flew a series of lazy eights, chandelles, a clean stall and slow flight at 160 knots. The only thing remaining, according to Gene, before heading for the Rip Saw Bombing Range, was to experience the F-100s "Adverse Yaw" characteristic (the tendency of the aircraft to turn in the opposite direction during steep banks, especially at low airspeeds, sometimes called a "Dutch Roll").

Gene had me deactivate the yaw damper by pulling the circuit breaker, slowing the aircraft, and gently moving the control stick from left to right. Apparently I was to observe the aircraft's nose swinging in the opposite direction of bank which would get worse as the airspeed decreased.

But seemingly, I didn't get the nose high enough, and hadn't deflected the control stick far enough to produce the effect he wanted. He said, "I have control." He pulled the nose up and moved the stick back and forth almost full travel. The aircraft snapped-rolled upside-down and went into an inverted tailspin. While inverted, we were plunging like a rock with the world spinning around like a kids "toy top." The altimeter needle was unwinding so rapidly that it was difficult to read and I was bouncing from side to side in the cockpit. Gene said he was flying the jet while stating, "If it's not under control at 10,000 feet we will eject, agree!" (For some strange reason I had a flashback of laying on my back on a playground merry-go-around while other kids spun it wildly.) Around 12,000 feet the spinning stopped and Gene rolled the wings level, as we bottomed out of a screaming supersonic dive at around 4,000 feet. In a 5 G pull-up we zoomed up to around 10,000 feet, where, in a calm voice Gene said, "I'll sign you off for adverse yaw exposure, Lou. Now let's head for Rip Saw Range and have some fun in dropping bombs and shooting the guns!"

Gene talked me through two LABS maneuvers, but I tossed the bombs so far off the target that the range officer said he didn't see the small explosive charge that they would produce, and inquired if our bombs had actually released (which they had). Since Gene was the PIC, his reputation was at stake, so he made the last two bomb drops from the rear cockpit and was able to obtain good circular error scores. Next I fired our 20-mm cannons on strafing runs, and I didn't do much better than I did on my bomb drops. Approaching fuel minimums we returned to Misawa ten miles to the south, flew one low approach and a full-stop landing. Gene's written comments on my training mission report stated:

"This training mission was considered to be a very satisfactory flight. Captain Martin corrected all in-flight errors quickly and even recognized errors and corrected them before being instructed to do so. Captain Martin is eager to learn and I consider him to have had no outstanding difficulties throughout the transition phase."

Major Nolan told me that Captain Buttyan was pleased with my performance and didn't think I would have any problem in checking out in the F-100. He asked for my comments. I related that my exposure to the "Adverse Yaw" characteristics was very impressive and left me with the wariness of avoiding high rate roll maneuvers at low airspeeds and low altitudes. He nodded his head in agreement. I then told him that I would prefer to delay dropping bombs and flying strafing runs until I obtained a little more time in the aircraft. He agreed and said that my next training flight would not include Rip Saw Bombing Range activity.

The next day I was leaving the Officers' Club and encountered Captains Tom Stinson and Joe Greco standing outside. (Tom and Joe were recent AMOC graduates and attached to the 531st TFS for flying. They were both jet pilots, but not qualified in the F-100, and were awaiting the opportunity to attend the same ground school course in Itazuke that I did.) Being members of the 531st *Ramrods* they were both wearing their squadron's bright red blazers with their squadron patch over the left breast pocket. I, in turn, being a member of the 416th *Silver Knights*, was wearing a dark blue blazer with a squadron patch depicting a medieval knight, in full body armor, sitting on a large white horse.

I asked them why they were standing out in the cold, and they said that their squadron was having a party at the golf course club house and one of the pilots had promised to pick them up, but apparently forgot. They asked me if I would give them a ride. I said I would be glad to if they didn't object to riding with a pilot wearing a blue blazer. They chuckled when responding, "No problem. A ride is a ride." Countering in reciprocal humor, I told them that at least my Plymouth *Valiant* was a bright red so that should provide some comfort!

I pulled up in front of the club house with the intent of just dropping them off, but they insisted that they be allowed to buy me a drink in repayment for the transportation. I told them that I hated to pass up a free drink, but didn't think my blue jacket would go over very well in a room full of red coats. They insisted that I have just one drink!

When I entered the club I was greeted by Lt.Col. Sollars, the 531st Squadron Commander, and Major Dave Gosser (who was my pilot during my second flight in the F-100) both were wearing their standard *Ramrod* red blazers. They found harmless fun in joshing me about my blue sports jacket and Silver Knight emblem, while I, in turn, shot back with, "I always wanted to stand out as a fighter pilot and being the only one wearing a blue jacket, I finally achieved my goal." Dave, with a smile, told his boss that he had flown with me recently and thought I would be a welcome addition to Misawa and wished I was assigned to their squadron, but Major Noland got to him first. I thanked Dave for his kind words, finished my drink and left with a handshake from both he and Colonel Sollars.

In less than ten days, both of these fine officers, and seasoned jet fighter pilots, would become victims of the PGR in separate F-100 accidents, which will be covered in detail on pages 254 and 256.

On February 1, 1962, I was scheduled to fly a F-100F mission with instructor pilot Captain John D. Parker. After a thorough preflight briefing and a "skull session" on the blackboard, we picked up our parachutes, donned G-suits, grabbed our helmets and headed for our assigned aircraft. Approaching it I was pleased to note that their were no red streamers hanging from the gun ports or bombs on the wing pylons. I commented to John that I was pleased that I could just concentrate on flying the jet and not be concerned with dropping bombs and shooting the guns. His comment, "I wanted the aircraft armed, but Major Nolan told me to just let you fly the aircraft and worry about fighting the Russians later."

The Aircraft Preflight Inspection, start engine and taxi out for takeoff was accomplished with no comments from Captain Parker. I felt comfortable in the takeoff, along with an increased rush of excitement, since I was mentally able to keep pace with the rapid acceleration, the bang of the afterburner and the high rate of climb. (It was a great feeling to be the pilot and not a passenger!) We leveled off at 25,000 feet and performed chandelles, lazy eights, slow flight and steep turns. I knew, from my many hours in the air, that on this flight I was in control, not the other way around. John asked me if Captain Buttyan had demonstrated "Adverse Yaw" maneuvers when I flew with him. Before, he got any crazy ideas, I replied. "Gene and I went through adverse yaw very thoroughly and there is no reason to waste fuel to do it again." He said, "OK. Then let's shoot a Simulated Flame Out Approach (SFO) and use up the rest of our fuel in making approaches to landings."

After a couple low approaches we heard a "May Day" call from an F-100 which had just departed, so I broke out of the landing pattern to the south, climbed to 5,000 feet, reduced power and set up a holding pattern. The pilot who had declared "May Day" reported that he was south of the field and had experienced an engine flameout and in a calm voice stated that he was flying east to jettison his bombs over the ocean and was attempting an engine relight. A few seconds later he reported a relight utilizing the normal fuel system failed and he was going to try a relight on the emergency system. As calmly as if he was in a simulator, he stated, "No luck. I'm ejecting about five miles east of the base." That was the last call from the pilot, but our rescue H-43 helicopter (which was always on standby alert when we had fighters flying) reported that he was airborne and proceeding to pick up the pilot. I reported to the tower that I was low on fuel and was cleared to land.

After engine shutdown my instructor pilot and I proceeded to our flight operations center to monitor the recovery of the pilot, and to find out who it was. We soon learned that Major Dave Gosser, after ejecting, had come down in the ocean about five miles from shore. The rescue helicopter pilot reported that the F-100 pilot's parachute had not collapsed and was being dragged further out to sea by a strong wind from the west. He added that the pilot was making feeble attempts to release his parachute harness, but wasn't haven't any success, and that he was going to attempt to deflate the parachute with downward wash from his rotating blades. A few seconds later he reported that they had been successful in collapsing the parachute, but the pilot was too weak to climb into a deployed rescue sling, so a crew member was jumping into the water and would roll him into a rescue basket.

I and several other pilots rushed over to the helicopter pad to observe the return of our downed pilot. After the helicopter landed medics carried Dave into the rescue building and as he passed our position I noted that his skin was a dark blue and he appeared unconscious. About 30 minutes later it was announced that the flight surgeons were unable to revive him and he was declared dead.

We learned later that when the helicopter hovered over Dave's parachute in attempting to collapse it, portions of the canopy became entangled in the landing skids of the helicopter, endangering its ability to stay in the air. It was close to crashing on top of the downed pilot, until entangled portions of the parachute were cut loose by crew members. It was estimated that Major Gosser was in the water only 15 minutes, but since he was not wearing an anti-exposure water survival suit he suffered from severe hypothermia from a water temperature of around 45 degrees Fahrenheit. He was also close to drowning from being dragged across the water like a surfboard behind a speedboat. The cause of the accident was listed as Undetermined. Following this loss we were required to wear the balky "poopy suits" anytime the water temperature dropped below 50 degrees, which was the norm from early November to late March.

Major Gosser was an ardent golfer and in memorializing his service, the golf course at Misawa AB was named the Gosser Memorial Golf Course.

Captain Parker seemed pleased with my last F-100F flight and his mission critique sheet contained statements like:

"Nose wheel liftoff was at the proper airspeed and rotation to takeoff attitude was good. Captain Martin seems to have no trouble with aircraft control. His turns were aggressive and he was able to hold the aircraft on the buffet during turns with no over-controlling. The base leg and final turn attitudes were good. Glide slope on the final was just right. Captain Martin did very well especially considering his limited fighter experience."

Following the flight Captain Parker told me that he was going to recommend to Major Nolan that I be allowed to fly the single seat F-100 with an instructor pilot flying as my wingman for two or three flights. Major Nolan said that he was pleased with my performance and would allow me to fly the single seat jet, with himself or one of his instructors acting as "chase pilot." But several days of bad weather prevented this and while awaiting for the weather to improve, I was sent to Kunsan, Korea, for ten days temporary duty (TDY). My assignment in Korea was to oversee F-100s on combat alert. Nolan recommended that I read up on the weapons systems carried on the F-100 so that when I returned I could resume flying the Super Sabre. I boarded a C-130 for Korea the following Monday, February 5th, 1962.

Several F-100s from Misawa were kept on combat alert status at Kunsan Air Base, Korea. Normally four aircraft, armed with nuclear weapons, were kept mission-ready, 24 hours a day, seven days a week. Pilots would be scheduled for this important but tedious, assignment for seven days on a rotational basis. They were required to remain in a double-barbed-wire enclosure and be ready to launch at a moments notice. Each pilot was committed to perform a Target Study on pre-selected sites until he was as familiar with it as he was to the back of his hand. Targets were generally in the Southern section of the Soviet Union, North Korea or China. Most pilots considered them one-way missions, since if we ever went to war, they felt that being able to rendezvous with a KB-50 aerial tanker after dropping their bomb and en route back to South Korea or Northern Japan was unlikely. They accepted this risk without question knowing that they were defending their country. My job was to ensure that the aircraft were ready for launch and capable of performing this important cold-war mission.

When I was on TDY in Korea, Lt.Col. Sollars (the 531st TFS Commander) and his wingman departed Misawa in two F-100Ds for Sendai, Japan. Colonel Sollars was to deliver a Commendation Award to a JASDF F-86 squadron and after completing his mission return to Misawa. Sollars was flying a Ground Controlled Radar Approach (GCA) into Sendai, in clear skies and light winds, when on final approach with gear and flaps down, his aircraft crashed into a shallow bay several miles short of the runway. His wingman, noting his unexplained dive toward the water, called for him to pull-up or eject, but received no response. Col. Sollars was killed instantly and his aircraft and remains were recovered from shallow water. Several local fishermen observed his aircraft crash and reported seeing no fire or smoke before it impacted the water in a nose down attitude. A thorough examination of the wreckage did not indicate any abnormal aircraft discrepancies and the cause of the accident was listed as Undetermined. The elementary dependent school at Misawa was renamed the Sollars Elementary School in his honor.

My ten days TDY at Kunsan Air Base, Korea were interesting, but not an experience I would care to adopt as a routine. Our F-100s were parked in a double barbed-wire fence enclosure, which encompassed a dormitory, dining room and recreation hall, and its perimeter was patrolled by armed guards 24 hours a day. The fighter bombers were kept fully armed with nuclear weapons and ammunition, full fuel loads and rested on quick release jacks, which could be removed by a pull on a chain. Since the aircraft were loaded with atomic bombs no one individual was permitted on or near the aircraft by himself. A "two-man-concept" was employed with the intent of preventing one deranged individual from exploding a nuclear bomb and starting WW III. In my ten days at Kunsan, I left the enclosure only once to visit the Officers' Club and BX, since to leave the enclosure involved cumbersome security checks in both departing and returning. I was glad when I was able to return to Misawa and looked forward to flying the single-seat F-100D.

After returning to Japan there was a note on my desk that Major Nolan wanted to see me. When I entered his office, he told me that he had some bad news. The 39th Air Division Commander had directed that all aircraft maintenance facilities be reorganized into a consolidated unit. The new organization would be known as the Organizational Maintenance Squadron (OMS). The goal of the reorganization was to eliminate the duplication each squadron employed in retaining maintenance specialists that would be far more cost effective if they were consolidated and dispatched through a radio controlled Maintenance Control Center.

Major Nolan continued --- an integral part of this change was that the four fighter squadrons would not be authorized individual Aircraft Maintenance Officers, as they would be assigned to the OMS. And since they were no longer members of a fighter squadron, they would not be allowed to fly their aircraft. Consequently, my flight records were being returned to the T-33 section. He said that he was sorry that this came about after all my effort in checking out in the F-100 but did promise me occasional flights in the F-100F. He sensed my disappointment and with the intent of easing the pain, added that this not only affected me but my maintenance officer colleagues in the other squadrons. He mentioned that Captains Joe Greco and Tom Stinson were also looking forward to flying the F-100 but were --- like myself --- being reassigned to the T-33 unit for flight proficiency. I asked Major Nolan if it was possible for me to be transferred to his squadron as a line fighter pilot. He said that he had already checked on this possibility, but since I had attended the AMOC, I was restricted from serving in any other Air Force Specialty Code (AFSC) other than 4344 (Aircraft Maintenance Officer) for three years.

I thanked him for his concern, saluted and returned to my office. I was naturally disappointed, but at least I would still be flying the T-33 and like he said, I would be able to occasionally fly the F-100F which I did for my remaining time at Misawa. (See Photo 74 for my last flight in an F-100.)

My line chief, Sergeant Longacre, briefed me on additional concepts of the reorganization as it affected my job. The new OMS Squadron Commander was a Lt.Col. Ken Rasmussen, a recent arrival to Misawa but not rated in jets. His assistant was Major John Shippey, the former Aircraft Maintenance Officer for the F-102 fighter Interceptor Squadron, also not jet rated. My assistant, Lt. Bob Anderson, was reassigned duties overseeing the maintenance of the F-102s (a good choice). According to the plan, I would continue to serve as the maintenance supervisor for the 416th TFS's F-100s but report directly to the OMS commander.

About two weeks after the reorganization I was informed that I would proceed to Itazuke Air Base for ten days temporary duty (TDY) as the maintenance officer in support of ten F-100s participating in a PACAF directed operational readiness exercise between the 8th TFW and the 39th Air Division. The mission commander would be Col. Dean

Davenport, while I would be supported by 30 aircraft mechanics. I had heard many interesting stories about Colonel Davenport and was looking forward to meeting and working with him.

Second Lieutenant Davenport was Lt. Ted Lawson's B-25 copilot on April 18, 1942, when a group of 16 Army Air Corps bombers took off from the aircraft carrier Hornet for a low-level daylight bombing raid on Japan. His aircraft was the seventh aircraft to takeoff and flew 700 miles to bomb a steel plant in Tokyo, and then flew on to China, but ran out of gas before reaching a planned airstrip. Lt. Davenport's B-25 crashed in the East China Sea at night, about a quarter-mile from a wide beach. Both pilots were severely injured, resulting in Lt. Lawson loosing his left leg. The Doolittle raid was recounted in Lt. Lawson's 1943 book, Thirty Seconds Over Tokyo and in the 1944 movie in which Lt. Davenport was employed as a technical advisor. He flew 86 fighter combat missions during the Korean War and continued flying fighters when the war ended. After being promoted to full colonel, he was assigned as the Wing Commander of the 39th Air Division and attached to the 416th TFS for flying, but during my short stint with the squadron I had not had the opportunity of working with him. He retired from the Air Force in 1967 and died in Panama City, Florida on February 14, 2000 at the age of 81.

My mechanics and I, along with spare parts, were transported to Itazuke in a C-130, and the following day ten F-100Ds, led by Col. Davenport, arrived. We parked them in an impressive straight line on the concrete ramp. The weather was beautiful and forecasted to remain so for several days, so it appeared we would have the opportunity of demonstrating what a good fighter unit can do, and everyone from the pilots to the mechanics were intent on fulfilling this goal. I started down the line of aircraft to see if the pilots had any "maintenance squawks" that needed attention, with Col. Davenport's aircraft first on my list. I climbed the ladder to his cockpit and stated, "Any squawks during your flight, Colonel?" Colonel Davenport snapped back, "Captain Martin, I don't want you to screw around with my airplane and break something that ain't broke. All I want you and your mechanics to do is make sure it's serviced with gas and oil and don't touch anything else. Is that clear?" "Yes sir," I said, "gas and oil only. How about the bugs on the windshield? Should we remove them or just leave them alone?" "Don't be a smart-ass Captain. Clean the windshield too," he quipped. "Yes Sir, we'll remove the bugs!"

Close to Itazuke is the fun city of Fukoka which in 1962 had not changed from what I experienced in 1953. It contained long lines of bars, cafes and establishments, with pretty young Japanese o-josans prepared to provide all forms of entertainment at reasonable prices. Naturally my mechanics were eager to head for town at the end of each day's exercise, but my mission was to have ten operationally-ready aircraft ready for Col. Davenport and his pilots each morning. To accomplish this, and still allow ample time for my men to enjoy the pleasures of the city, I gathered them together and put out the following edict: "No one will be allowed to leave the flight line at the end of the day until all ten aircraft are in commission, serviced, armed and ready for the next day's mission. I don't care what your specialties are in regard to the new OMS job codes. You're all mechanics and an avionics specialist can assist in changing tires, as well as an electrician helping to pump gas. No one heads for town until all ten aircraft are ready to fly." They all nodded in agreement.

It was a wonderful sight to see the mechanics working together with a single goal in mind: "Have ten aircraft ready to fly, followed by 30 horny and thirsty American GIs heading for town at the end of each day." When we got back to Misawa, Colonel Davenport called me off to the side and said, "Captain Martin, I don't know how you did it, but that was one hell of a show we put on in Itazuke. We not only beat the shit out of the 8th TFW, but we had ten aircraft, ready to fly each day, which allowed us to rub their nose in it. Good show, Captain!"

I was talking to a group of pilots in our operations center when we heard a "Mayday" call over the radio speaker. Everyone quieted down so we could hear the unfolding event. A pilot, with a 416th TFS call sign, transmitted a "Mayday" stating his fire warning light came on soon after takeoff. Another pilot (identified as Col. Catt, a headquarters staff officer) reported that his wingman's aircraft was trailing smoke and he was dropping back to see if he could determine the source of the fire. The following radio transmission soon followed, "Jim, you're on fire, bail out!" Response, "I'm ejecting now!" After a few seconds of silence, Col. Catt came back with, "Canopy gone, pilots out." More silence, then the cut-short radio call, "Good Chu------," and silence. The next radio call heard was from our rescue helicopter, "Rescue One airborne and we have two burning crash sites in view --- one south and one east. We are proceeding to the crash south of the airport, since it is emitting the most smoke." The next call from the helicopter was that they had picked up a pilot south of the airport who appeared to be in good condition. (This pilot we learned later was Jim, the pilot who transmitted the Mayday call.)

Investigation revealed that Col. Catt was leading a two-ship F-100 flight with Captain Jim (I don't remember his last name) as his wingman. After takeoff Jim's fire warning light came on along with a "thumping" in his control stick. Col. Catt dropped back to scan Jim's aircraft and reported that he was on fire and recommended he eject. Jim bailed out at around 5,000 feet, but his "man-seat-separator" (an automatic device which forces the pilot out of his seat after ejection) failed and he was tumbling through space still strapped to his seat. Jim stated later that when he realized he was still attached to his seat he manually unfastened his lap belt, kicked free of the seat and pulled his parachute ripcord. The chute opened, and after one or two swings, he hit the ground.

Jim's unmanned aircraft circled the air base and crash landed in a frozen marsh (wings level) a couple miles east of the airport. After coming to rest over an open ditch a fire developed which consumed a large portion of the center section of the aircraft. However, the aft section, including the engine afterburner area, sustained no post-crash fire damage. Ground witnesses stated that the aircraft, in its unmanned glide, barely missed striking a large JP-4 fuel storage tank before bouncing along the frozen ground.

Investigation disclosed that Col. Catt was flying next to Jim's aircraft when he ejected, and when he started tumbling earthward still attached to his seat, he put his aircraft into a diving spiral to observe Jim's dilemma. Unfortunately, he became so engrossed in his problem that he allowed his aircraft to assume such a negative nose down, low altitude angle, that it was impossible for him to pull out. His last radio report confirmed this as it was cutoff short at "good chu------." (It was determined that he observed Jim's chute opening at about the same time he realized his own problem and meant to report, "good chute.")

Col. Catt's aircraft crashed at high speed, in a wings level attitude, and burst into flames. The aircraft broke-up into a thousand pieces, but investigation disclosed that the horizontal stab actuator was fully deflected to a nose-up position. Apparently, when he realized the dangerous diving attitude he was in at such a low altitude, he pulled his control stick full aft, but didn't have sufficient altitude to recover. Col. Catt was killed instantly and left a wife and nine children.

Post-crash investigation of Jim's F-100 disclosed that a fire of high temperature had existed in the rear of the aircraft near the landing drag-chute compartment. The fire was sufficient to burn into the drag-chute enclosure leaving large deposits of molten nylon. It was determined that the smoke trailing behind his aircraft was coming from a smoldering, partially burnt, drag-chute still stored in its closed compartment. Further investigation discovered that one of the 24 fuel lines (pigtails) which supply fuel to the afterburner suffered a fatigue break. The remaining 23 pigtails were pressure checked at 150 PSI, revealing fuel leaks on two additional fuel nozzle lines. Sometime during the takeoff, these fuel lines began leaking raw fuel into the airframe area between the afterburner and aluminum aircraft skin in the vicinity of the horizontal stabilizer and the drag-chute. The leaking fuel allowed a fire to erupt, which caused the actuation of an overheat warning detector, and due to extreme heat fused its contacts together. The leaking fuel allowed a fire to continue burning until the afterburner was shut down. However, a series of explosions of fuel vapors continued due to trapped fuel fumes vaporizing, igniting, blowing out and continuing this process through continuous explosions. The primary fire extinguished when the pilot shut down the afterburner, but the fire warning light remained illuminated because the contact points were fused together. The pilot not only had a fire detector warning light that wouldn't go out, but he was trailing smoke from a burning drag-chute. This was not the first time we had experienced problems with the F-100 afterburner fuel system and wouldn't be the last. But ironically, it's possible this tragic accident could have been avoided. If Jim had discontinued the use of the afterburner earlier, and jettisoned his drag chute, or the big if ----- had his "man-seat-separator" not malfunctioned, which resulted in him tumbling toward the ground still attached to his ejection seat ---- Colonel Catt would not have allowed himself to fly a critical low altitude (fatal) diving spiral. However, like most accidents, this is hindsight thinking and does not cast doubt on the actions the pilots took when faced with the stress of a serious in-flight emergency, in a high speed jet fighter, of dubious reliability.

As an AMO I intended to do what I could to detect potential afterburner fuel nozzle failures, and engaged in what I admit was a stupid and dangerous preventative procedure. F-100 engines were tested by anchoring the aircraft, with heavy chains, in an area know as "the-engine-trim-pad." Because of the noise created from engines operating at full 100% power in afterburner, it was located in an isolated area of the base. I noted that when we removed the inspection panels bordering the afterburner fuel nozzles, leaking fuel lines that caught fire would give off a small blue flame (similar to a blow torch). We could then tighten the faulty "B-nut" and hopefully correct the problem. However, we couldn't eyeball the fuel nozzles located directly above the afterburner, so this is where my well-intended --- but dangerous --- procedure came into play.

I would stand on top the aircraft fuselage, straddle the dorsal fin above the afterburner area, hold on to the vertical stabilizer with both hands and with a nod of my head signal a mechanic to shove the throttle into afterburner. The aircraft would buck and jerk along with a ten-foot flame shooting out the rear, while I peered down into the engine area looking for the telltale signs of a leaking fuel nozzle. A second nod of my head would signal the mechanic to come out of afterburner and shut down the engine. I detected several leaking fuel nozzles following this risky action and fortunately never fell off (If I had of I would have been burnt to a cinder).

One day Colonel Lou Cole (our deputy commander for material) wandered out to the engine trim pad area when I was standing on top of an aircraft operating in afterburner and nearly had a heart attack. He started waving his arms in a frantic gesture directing that the aircraft engine be shut down. He gave me holy hell for performing such a stupid act and directed that I never do it again. (I didn't disagree with his concerns and was surreptitiously happy he came along and forced me to discontinue my improvised preventative maintenance procedure.)

The afterburner fuel leak problem was soon corrected when it was discovered that the afterburner fuel lines and "B-nuts" were made of different metal composition. Therefore when they were tightened to a proper cold torque setting they expanded at different rates when heated and loosened sufficiently to allow for mist-type fuel leaks. The fix was to use the same type metal for both fittings. The RF-101s and F-102s did not experience a similar afterburner fuel system problem, even though they were equipped with Pratt an Whitney J-57 jet engines, since their engines were encased in thick aluminum-type shrouds.

My line chief and I were touring the ramp to observe and direct the turnaround of F-100s, returning from dropping bombs and strafing on the Rip Saw Bombing Range. With the ramp activity humming along, like the erecting of a circus tent, I asked my line chief to drop me off at the squadron operation's center where I could enjoy a cup of coffee. The room was full of noisy pilots, boasting and arguing about their bombing and strafing scores, and while sipping my coffee I enjoyed listening to their "hot pilot" anecdotes. I was standing "back-to-back" to Colonel Davenport, who hadn't noted my presence, and when I heard him call out to the dispatcher requesting the name of the pilot who was going to fly the aircraft that he had just flown, my audio senses went on full alert.

The dispatcher shouted back, "Lt. Smith, Sir." Spotting Lt. Smith, Col. Davenport motioned for him to come over as he wanted to talk to him. "Smitty," he said, "when you select afterburner in the aircraft you're about to fly you will note that the nose tends to yaw to the right, but it's easily corrected by kicking in a little left rudder. This occurred during my last two LABS maneuvers, but I just held a little left rudder, to keep the ball centered, and my bomb drops were good. I just wanted you to know this before you fly." Lt. Smith, with a puzzled look on his face, said, "Thanks for the tip, colonel, I'll keep your recommendation in mind."

I left the building and signaled my line chief to pick me up. While driving to Col. D's aircraft I told Sergeant Longacre about the conversation I had just overheard. The first thing we checked when reaching the aircraft was the aircraft maintenance log and, as I expected it was signed off as, "OK flight." (A typical Col. Davenport log entry and shades of what I experienced during my ten days with him in Itazuke.) We then removed several panels surrounding the "airframe-engine-mount area." The engine was still too hot to inspect with bare hands so I secured a burlap bag, from the back of our jeep, wrapped it around my arm and reached down into the area surrounding the engine. When I did I discovered the top right engine mount loose! I then checked the other mounts and found a lower mount also loose. (Obviously what Col. Davenport was experiencing, when he selected afterburner, was a shift of the engine exhaust to the right which he offset with left rudder.)

I took out my red pencil, grounded the aircraft and headed back to the squadron operations office. Being as pissed off as a captain can be with a full colonel, I sought out Col. D., and told him that I had discovered why it was necessary for him to use left rudder when in afterburner. I then requested he come with me as their was something I wanted to show him. He wanted to know what I had in mind, but I think the stern look on my face compelled him to accompany me without further questions. By the time we reached the aircraft my mechanics had more panels removed and the broken engine mounts were clearly visible. I pointed out the loose mounts to the colonel, whose only response was, "Well, that explains it.

Thanks Captain. How about running me back to the squadron?" (If I had not discovered this unreported serious aircraft discrepancy and grounded the aircraft, it's quite possible that Lt. Smith, when flying an aircraft with broken engine mounts, would have joined the PGR's infamous fraternity very early in his flying career.)

The warm sun rays in June 1962 made living in our small Japanese-built hubbell much more enjoyable, as we were able to strip off the insulating sheets of plastic covering the windows and enjoy the close association of our Air Force neighbors without wading through deep snow drifts or thick mud. Directly behind our house was a thoroughbred horse ranch and it was great to watch these magnificent animals sprinting across open fields. The Japanese caretaker was a friendly elderly gentleman who would greet us with a smile when we wandered next to the fence to admire his horses. One foggy Saturday afternoon our two-year-old son Mike was playing outside and the next minute he was missing. The visibility was less than 20 feet and in a few minutes the whole neighborhood was searching the area for our lost boy. Our frantic calls went unanswered and no one shouted through the fog that they had found him. I stopped my own search when I thought I heard approaching footsteps and out of a thick fog bank came our friendly Japanese rancher holding Mike's hand. My wife was so grateful that she presented him with a prized vase she had purchased when working as a nurse for the United Fruit Company in Costa Rica years earlier.

Directly in front of our house was the home of Major Bob and Fran McDonald, the base Public Relations Officer and a classmate from jet qualification training at Randolph AFB in 1959. Next to their house was the home of Captain Mitchel, General Beverly's aide. We didn't have a washer/dryer and when I checked with the base housing officer, he told me that they were not authorized in off-base Japanese-built homes. I accepted this until I saw a washer/dryer being off loaded at Captain Mitchel's house. I paid another visit to the housing officer and told him that if I was not supplied with a washer/dryer I would send a complaint letter to the Division Commander with an information copy to the Inspector General in Hawaii. We had a washer/dryer the next day.

We had hired a full-time Japanese maid for around $40 per month, who assumed a secondary role as nanny for our young son. After living in our house for four months, we noted a foul odor coming from the bathroom. Following my Air Force-trained sensitive nose I discovered that it was coming from the bathtub drain. The Japanese plumbers had installed a straight pipe (absent a 180 degree water trap) directly from the bathtub drain to the cesspool. We could prevent this offensive odor from entering the house by keeping the drain plug installed, but our maid kept leaving it out since the odor didn't seem to bother her.

Off base hutches were not equipped with telephones so when it was determined that I was needed, during off-duty hours, a vehicle would be sent to pick me up or to deliver a message. During military alerts, when all military personnel were required to report to the base, trucks were sent throughout the area blowing their large trumpet-like air horns, which could be heard for miles. (This sleep-shattering exercise was referred to as a "Misawa Recall.") Another sleep disrupter was the frequent blast of J-57 afterburners as engines were being tested on the engine trim pad. I often wondered what the Japanese thought about our frequent Misawa Recalls and afterburner blasts at 3 or 4 a.m., but they never complained.

On April 11, 1962 I was cruising the flight line while overseeing the launch of F-100s on combat practice sorties. I stopped next to two pilots preflighting an F-100F and recognized one of them as Lt. Bob Wunderlich, with whom I had spent ten days with in Itazuke. Bob told me he was being administered a tactical evaluation flight check in special weapons bombing, by Captain Richard Hale from the 531st Squadron. During our brief discussion I commented that I thought they would be flying a good aircraft as I had just flown it the day before with Ed Henely.

I continued working the flight line and noted that they taxied out for takeoff around 11:50 a.m. About 15 minutes later I observed signs of excitement near our squadron operations center and drove over to see what the commotion was all about. I was told that an F-100F had just crashed east of Rip Saw Range, but there was no immediate report on the status of the two pilots. I knew that accident investigators would soon be requesting the maintenance records from the aircraft involved, so I headed for my hangar to direct that they be secured. When I reached my office my line chief informed me that the deputy commander for material, Col. Cole, had just called stating that I was to be a member of the accident investigation team, and a Lt.Col. from division headquarters was on his way in a four-wheel drive weapons carrier to pick me up.

Following directions by radio from our airborne rescue helicopter we drove through narrow dirt roads and trails toward the crash site. When we ran out of roads we put the vehicle in four-wheel drive and drove across open country toward a rising black cloud of smoke. Reaching the crash site it was apparent that the aircraft impacted the soft volcanic black soil in a near vertical attitude and at a terrific rate of speed. The only portions of the aircraft still recognizable were the seemingly intact empennage sticking up from a 20-foot wide, ten-foot deep crater. Calm winds were allowing streams of black smoke and steam from the heated moist soil to rise straight up into a clear blue sky.

Both pilots had ejected, but apparently at a very low altitude and were fatally injured. Lt. Wunderlich's body was found 110 feet from the aircraft wreckage and still in his parachute harness. His pilot chute had deployed, but the shroud lines were still intact in the parachute bag. His seat was located 20 feet from where he impacted the ground. Captain Hale's body was found 44 feet from where the aircraft impacted, along with his parachute which had partially deployed but not opened. His ejection seat was found 25 feet away. Both pilots had impacted the soft ground with such force that when their remains were removed, a three-dimensional ghostly outline of their bodies, including out-stretched arms, remained. After pictures were taken we covered the indentations with shovels of dirt.

Investigation disclosed that nine minutes after takeoff the aircraft was granted permission to enter the bombing range and space themselves behind other F-100s. There was no further radio transmissions heard. Japanese farmers reported the crash to Japanese police, who advised Misawa Air Base and a helicopter was dispatched to the scene.

The aircraft, except for the empennage, was broken into small pieces when it impacted the ground at an estimated speed of 350 knots. Its weight was estimated at 31,000 pounds (which included 6,000 pounds of fuel). The post-crash fire was soon smothered out by the wet soil that flowed into the crash crater, so we were able to retrieve all major components for detailed laboratory analysis. I experienced a Close Encounter when working in the crater when I disturbed a condenser, still containing an electrical charge, which sparked and ignited pools of jet fuel. I quickly scrambled out of the crater, ahead of the expanding flames, which were quickly extinguished by a fire truck standing by.

Following a detailed inspection of the engine, fuel, egress, hydraulic, oxygen, heat and vent and electric systems; plus the instruments, radios, flight controls, autopilot, yaw damper, and the pilots' physical condition, we could not determine if the loss of control was pilot-induced, maintenance malpractice, or material failure, so the cause of the accident was listed as <u>Undetermined</u>. However, it is my personal opinion that the crash was due to a loss of aircraft control by inadvertent autopilot actuation of the flight controls. Captain Hale had 1,000 hours in the F-100 and 2,000 total hours. Lt. Wunderlich had 524 hours in the F-100. It is not likely that such experienced pilots would intentionally place themselves in such a precarious flight condition when performing a maneuver they had performed many times over, on a clear VFR weather day.

The Misawa Officers' Club was the center of most social events and featured a large dining room, huge upstairs barroom, and a stag bar in the basement, which was "off-limits" to females, with no exceptions. The club employed a full time dance band known as *Tiny and His Skyliners* that had been an integral part of the facility since the U.S. took over the base in late 1945. Friday evening was "beer call night" and was attended by one and all. It was the one night that you didn't want to miss. In June 1962, the 531st Squadron was buying drinks for everyone in the stag bar as a welcome gesture for their new commander, Lt.Col. Roland J. DuFresne, who was replacing Col. Sollars lost in a F-100 accident five months earlier during a landing attempt at Sendai. (See page 256.)

Colonel DuFresne was a respected fighter pilot, who received his pilot wings during WW II, and flew combat missions in P-40s and P-47s. His last assignment was as squadron commander of a F-106 unit at Minot Air Force Base, North Dakota. He had 4,000 hours total flight time, of which 2,200 hours were in jet fighters, and recently completed F-100 transition training at Luke AFB. He was a likable officer and fit right in with his younger rowdy fighter pilots. I had talked to him briefly in the stag bar and admired his obvious zest for life and his delight in flying jet fighters. Unfortunately, Col. DuFresne, like his predecessor, was caught up in the PGR's wide net while flying an F-100 on Rip Saw Range. (See page 299.)

One rainy Friday afternoon, my mechanics and I were in the process of moving 18 F-100s into a hangar for the weekend, and I was eager to complete the task so I wouldn't miss the traditional Friday evening "blow out" at the Officers' Club. Cramming all 18 aircraft inside, without crunching wing tips, was like assembling a "jig-saw-puzzle." While moving the last aircraft inside, we were preparing to close the hangar doors when a muffled explosion erupted from the center of the tightly packed fighters. An avionics mechanic, working on a F-100 parked in the center of the hangar, mistakenly jettisoned two 450 gallon external drop tanks unto the concrete hangar floor. The wing pylons were still armed with explosive cartridges, which slammed the tanks against the floor with such force that they ruptured. Within seconds, 900 gallons of JP-4 jet fuel covered the entire hangar floor, leaving 18 F-100s resting in a pool of highly volatile gasoline. One spark, and 18 front-line fighters, mechanics working amongst them, and an aircraft hangar would go up in flames. I ordered an immediate halt to actuating light switches, the starting of power units or tugs and told my line chief to call the fire department and request an aircraft refueling truck to start sucking up the spilt fuel. I then secured two tugs equipped with "spark-arrestor" exhaust systems and directed that they start moving the aircraft outside into the rain.

When the refueling truck arrived, I ordered the second lieutenant commanding it to move his truck close to an open door and start vacuuming up the fuel from the hangar floor. He took one look at the potential disaster and refused to move his truck close enough to do any good. He finally relented when I gave him a signed statement assuming full responsibility for his actions. With the aircraft slowly moving out, I directed aircraft mechanics to man mops and buckets to soak up as much fuel as they could and deliver it to the refueling truck, while others, using squeegees, were pushing fuel toward sewer drains. When there was room to move about the hangar we carried the ruptured wing tanks outside and had them hosed down with water and fire retardant foam. My feet, and those of my mechanics, were soaked with JP-4 and beginning to smart, and the noxious fumes were starting to make us dizzy. (If the hangar had caught fire we would have all gone up in flames faster than a Buddhist Monk in downtown Saigon.)

About one hour later we had all 18 aircraft safely outside and were able to hose down the hangar floor with water and foam. With the doors open on both ends of the hangar, we were finally able to start moving the aircraft back inside. Around 9 p.m., all 18 aircraft were put to bed and I headed for the Officers' Club for a beer and sandwich. When I took a stool in the stag bar my colleagues moved off to one side, complaining that I smelled like an open bucket of JP-4 jet fuel, but I figured it was better than smelling like a barbecued Buddhist Monk.

This incident, like all accidents or incidents, was the result of more than one failure: first, the wing pylons on the aircraft involved did not have safety pins installed which would have prevented the fuel tanks from being inadvertently jettisoned by an errant mechanic; second, the explosive devices (large shotgun-like cartridges) were not removed from the wing pylons before moving the aircraft inside the hangar. (These combustible cartridges are installed to ensure that when external fuel tanks are jettisoned, in-flight, they will be propelled out a safe distance from the aircraft.) Had either of these safety procedures not been overlooked, the potentially dangerous incident would not have occurred. We discovered one more aircraft in the same unsafe condition and took the proper safety precautions before moving it back inside. I didn't press court-martial charges against the airman, who mistakenly caused a potentially catastrophic accident, since my mechanics were equally responsible and I was hoping that senior officers were so busy drinking beer that they wouldn't hear how close we came to making international news. (Fortunately, I was never questioned about the incident by any of the many irritating bird colonels, prowling the base looking for problems.)

Later in the month we experienced an F-100 accident at our alert base in Kunsan, Korea. Two pilots were on a local flight and started chasing each other around the sky in mock combat. The problem was that their aircraft were prohibited from aerobatic maneuvers, since they were equipped with two 450-gallon drop tanks still containing fuel. One young lieutenant lost control of his aircraft, when inverted, and ended up in a tailspin (a situation similar to what I had also experienced). He didn't think he could recover from this uncomfortable, self-induced maneuver and ejected, leaving the aircraft to crash into a Korean rice paddy. The aircraft impacted with such force that it disappeared in the centuries-old soft soil and could not be reached, even with 20 foot probing poles. Since JP-4 fuel kept seeping into the farmer's field he was provided with a life-time payment for his loss, and the aircraft wreckage was not recovered. The pilot, who landed unharmed, was temporarily grounded, and after meeting a Flight Evaluation Board was no longer allowed to fly the F-100.

In May 1962 I was notified that I had been promoted to the rank of major, with an effective date of July 15th. Several other captains were also promoted along with a number of first lieutenants to captain. We all went together and threw a big party at the Officers' Club that was long remembered as one big drunken celebration. I was naturally thrilled with the promotion, but wondered how it would affect my position as an Aircraft Maintenance Officer for maintaining F-100s, as the position only authorized a captain. However, my curiosity was short lived.

On Friday, June 29, 1962, Colonel Cole (deputy commander for material), walked into my office unannounced. I started to rise, but in a friendly tone of voice (unusual for him), he said, "At ease, Lou. There are a couple questions I would like to ask you." He then inquired if I was aware of the problems the Periodic Maintenance Branch (PMB) was experiencing in completing sequential inspections on RF-101s, F-102s, and F-100s on schedule. I told him that I was, since many of my own aircraft were not returned in a timely manner. He went on to state that he felt it was time to replace Major George Little, the present Officer in Charge (OIC). Pointing out that the position authorized a major, and since I was recently promoted, he wanted to know if I was interested in replacing him. My response, "If you are asking, colonel, my answer is no!" "That's too bad," he said, "because starting Monday you will be the new OIC of the PMB. Major Little will be transferred to the engine overhaul facility, which is being run by a sharp chief master sergeant, and since he only has six months left on his overseas tour, he won't be able to screw things up before its time for him to leave." I asked the colonel why, if he had already decided that I would be reassigned, did he ask me if I wanted the job? He smiled while stating, "Well hell, Lou, I had a 50/50 chance you would give me the answer I wanted to hear, but even though you didn't, it doesn't change my decision. Starting at 0800 hours Monday you will replace Major Little as I don't want to drag this assignment change out! When I leave your office I'll go over and tell George to have his mechanics assembled for an "all-hands meeting" Monday morning for a formal change of command ceremony. I want you there, ready to take charge, at that time." "Yes sir," I replied, "I'll be there." I went over to tell Major Nolan that I was being transferred to the Periodic Maintenance Branch, but he said that Colonel Cole had already told him of the change and he thought it was a good move. He wished me well in my new job while stating that I would still be able to fly the F-100F from time to time.

Although my new assignment as the OIC of the PMB came as a surprise, it wasn't totally unexpected, since with every promotion an officer is expected to take on more responsibilities. Otherwise the promotion is meaningless. As OIC I would supervise about 70 aircraft mechanics assigned to ten maintenance docks (units), comprised of two for RF-101s, two for F-102s and six for F-100s. Each dock had from seven to eight mechanics assigned, along with a NCO in charge. I knew Major Little and although pleasant to talk to, he was not the type of officer that fit-in well in a jet fighter base. He was not a pilot and his off-base hobby was that of a Christian preacher (a tough job in a country where only one percent of the population are Christians). In keeping with his religious calling, he would often preach to his men on the evils of drinking and fornicating with young cooperative Japanese o-josans and had a policy of no swearing in his hangar. (I guess his mechanics, when they smashed their finger with a hammer, were supposed to say "bless me Lord" instead of "oh shit" or some other appropriate expletive.) Unfortunately, Major Little's management style did not promote a sense of esprit de corps and this low morale was reflected in poor productivity, which resulted in aircraft not completing scheduled inspections on time. Some were as much as a week behind schedule!

I had two days to plan for a "change-of-command" presentation to the PMB mechanics and wanted to let them know, straightaway, that they had a new OIC who operated under a different philosophy. I felt that it was quintessential that I lay the ground work for improving morale, increase productivity and getting everyone to work as a well-oiled machine. The next day I visited the base library and checked out a couple books on General Patton, an officer who had no problem in expressing himself in plain language. From these books, I memorized a few colorful phrases he used when addressing his troops and didn't think he would object to me plagiarizing some of his choice words for a good cause.

At 0800 hours on Monday morning, July 2, 1962, Major Little and I were standing before 70 assembled enlisted mechanics in the PMB hangar. Major Little addressed the assembly by stating that Colonel Cole had decided that effective that day, he would be reassigned as OIC of the Propulsion Branch and Major Martin would replace him as OIC of the Periodic Maintenance Branch. He thanked everyone for their past support and wished them well. He then turned to me, asking if I would like to say a few words. I said, "Yes, I sure as hell would, major. First I would like to wish you success in your new assignment and don't let the wrench twisters over there f - - k you up." Turning to the assembled mechanics, I continued, "Last Friday Colonel Cole asked me if I would be interested in taking over as OIC of the PMB. I told him, you bet your ass I would, colonel. It would tickle the shit out of me to lead such a fine bunch of hard working men like yourselves. I'm sure you all share with me the need to move aircraft through this hangar like shit through a goose, as the defense of Misawa depends on it. If we don't provide the squadrons with operational aircraft in a timely manner, our chance of pounding the crap out of those God Damn Soviet Union shit-heads won't amount to nothing more than a good pile of horse dung. From this day on, I want to see nothing but assholes and elbows when your working, and boozing, whoring or spending time with your family when you're off duty. As a start, I want to announce that this Sunday the hangar will be closed as everyone will be off! Now let's get our asses in gear and go back to work." Major Little left with a red face, while the mechanics were fighting back smiles. I thought I had opened the door for raising the morale. At least I hoped so, without embarrassing Major Little too much!

My next move was to get together with my NCOIC, Chief Master Sergeant Hank Moon. Hank was a WW II vet, about ten years my senior, and obviously possessed a lot of experience. Over coffee I asked him to level with me in stating what our unit needed to make it one of the best sections on the base. Hank told me that indeed the morale had hit rock bottom, but it wasn't all Major Little's fault. But he seemed more concerned with saving souls than getting aircraft out on schedule. I told Sergeant Moon that this would change! "Our first goal is to move aircraft out on schedule and let the men worry about their souls, because if we don't win the Cold War there won't be souls to save!" He agreed.

The next problem to solve was the long hours the mechanics were working, which was a product of low morale and a lack of replacement aircraft parts. He said that many aircraft could not be moved through the pipeline in a timely basis, because they went NORS (not operational ready for lack of supply). I told him we would work on reducing the long working hours first and the supply problem second. He thought that my declaring the coming Sunday off was a step in the right direction.

I knew that the PMB consisted of ten inspection docks, but beyond that I wasn't exactly sure of how the system worked, so I asked Sergeant Moon to fill me in. He told me that aircraft inspections took on three distinct phases. All fighters underwent a thorough inspection every 100 hours of flight time and were scheduled in our hangar for three days. At 50-hour cycles they were in our docks for two days and after 25 hours underwent an inspection which took only one day. There were a specific set of "work cards" outlining what must be inspected at each interval and the cards listed the recommended time to accomplish each task. However Hank reminded me, once again, that the biggest obstacle in meeting these time constraints was the lack of spare parts.

Being located in Northern Japan, we were on the tail-end of the supply chain and critical parts were often "back-ordered," resulting in aircraft sitting idle until the parts arrived. I suggested that the dock chiefs prepare a list of the most essential parts that had been "back-ordered" and we would then pre-order them and store them in a secluded location in our hangar. Sergeant Moon said that this wouldn't work, as when we ordered a new part we were required to turn in a "non-serviceable" like item to supply. Regardless, I told him to prepare the list and I would figure out some unconventional surreptitious way to beat the system.

With the critical parts list in hand, Hank and I visited the base salvage yard and secured everything we needed from the wreckage of aircraft involved in accidents. We then started a "land-office" business of ordering parts, along with submitting "non-serviceable" parts we obtained in the salvage yard, to supply. As boxes of parts started accumulating, we built a false wall in a secluded corner of our hangar and within a couple weeks we had our own supply of parts. Except in rare cases, this surreptitious operation prevented aircraft from going NORS. The inefficiency of our supply system was vividly brought to my attention one day when a dock chief ordered a F-100 hydraulic actuator, which the supply warehouse stated was in stock. However, when the so called actuator was delivered, it turned out to be a pencil sharpener. I took the pencil sharper to the supply warehouse, went to the bin listed for pencil sharpeners, and found our needed F-100 actuator. (We kept the pencil sharpener and installed it in my office, since I figured I would need sharp pencils to do my job.)

When aircraft started meeting established inspection schedules, we were able to eliminate working on both Saturdays and Sundays, which had a very positive affect on raising morale and improving unit esprit de corps. In attempting to keep the spirit alive, Hank and I designed an individual unit patch, which (at my expense) we had Willie's tailor shop in downtown Misawa produce. We issued them to our mechanics who, with great pride, had their wives, girl friends, or a tailor shop sew them on their fatigues and jackets.

Friday night beer calls were just as popular with the enlisted ranks as they were with the officers, so I devised another method of increasing morale. I told my dock chiefs that I would allow them to knock off from work 30 minutes early each Friday afternoon if they met certain conditions: one, that their aircraft were on schedule; two, that their docks were properly cleaned, drip pans installed, aircraft grounded, fire extinguishers in-place and all rubbish discarded. To ensure these requirements were met Sergeant Moon and I inspected five docks each, and if everything was in order those assigned to that dock would be free to leave and get a head start at beer call. This practice worked like a charm and it was heartening to see the enthusiasm it generated for just an extra 30 minutes of free time, which in reality, was not lost productivity because to meet this objective dock chiefs had to ensure that their individual aircraft were either on schedule, or slightly ahead.

Sergeant Moon briefed me on a unique situation we had with one of our F-102 docks and what he had been doing to protect the NCO in charge. He confessed that he had not told my predecessor, Major Little, about the problem and how he was handling it as he was sure he would not have approved. The dock chief was an African American staff sergeant by the name of Thomas, who was a slow-talking, Southern black, who presented the impression of being somewhat uneducated and not the type of individual you would want in charge of seven men performing maintenance on one of America's top-line fighter interceptors. But, according to Sgt. Moon, he was an excellent supervisor and the aircraft his mechanics inspected experienced fewer quality control (QC) squawks than aircraft coming out of almost every other inspection dock.

Because of Sgt. Thomas' extrinsic character, Sgt. Moon had assigned like-minded personnel to his dock, knowing that he would ensure that they work hard and not screw up. He did not assign sharp young airmen with high school diplomas or some college to his dock because it would create a conflict. Hank added that whenever we had higher headquarters inspectors visiting he would give Sgt. Thomas and his dock the day off, because he feared their slow-talking, methodical ways would give the wrong impression to inspectors looking for weak spots and eager to find problems to justify their existence. I complimented Sgt. Moon for his past actions and told him not to change a thing. I added that I had personally talked to Sgt. Thomas and found him to be a real asset to our unit.

Not long after my discussion with Sgt. Moon regarding Sgt. Thomas, I was returning from a T-33 flight and observed two C-130s parked in front of base operations. I recognized them as aircraft from PACAF Headquarters in Hawaii and feared inspectors had sneaked in to conduct a no-notice Operational Readiness Inspection (ORI). My thoughts immediately turned to Sgt. Thomas and his dock, knowing that Sgt. Moon was on leave and not available to send them home.

When I entered my hangar my clerk told me that Colonel Cole wanted to see me in his office ASAP. I snapped a salute to Colonel Cole, while a "snarling-bird-colonel" sitting next to him looked on. Col. Cole stated that the {snarling} colonel was the OIC of the Inspector General's Staff that was conducting an ORI of our maintenance facility. Having said this, he handed me seven multiple choice test answer sheets, while stating, "Major Martin, look at these pitifully written test results that your F-102 dock chief, Sgt. Thomas and his men, submitted to ORI inspectors. They range from 35 to 50 percent. How in the hell can you have a group of men in charge of a F-102 dock with such limited knowledge?" (I had dealt with Col. Cole before and considered him a man who would listen to reason, but I wasn't sure about the growling I "gotcha" type colonel from Hawaii.)

I explained that indeed Sgt. Thomas gave every appearance of being slow, and perhaps even somewhat lacking in basic smarts, but that he turned out the best airplanes of any of my dock chiefs and was a real asset to the unit. I went on to explain that he and his men were not the type who would excel in written tests, but knew the F-102 inside and out. I suggested that the ORI team have a couple sharp NCOs take Sergeant Thomas and his men over to the BX snack bar, buy them a cup of coffee, and administer oral exams on the F-102 and their assigned duties. The ORI colonel finally spoke up and said, "Well major, what do we do with those failing test score results you're holding?" I looked him in the eye, and said, "This is what we will do with these spurious test results!" I then tore them up and threw them in the nearest waste paper basket. Both bird colonels were stunned into silence by my action and stared at the waste paper basket as if they expected the torn-up answer sheets to reappear in their original form. Before they could gather their thoughts, I told them I would have Sgt. Thomas and his men in the BX snack bar in ten minutes and trust there would be a couple ORI experts there to administer oral exams. The ORI chief thought that this was highly unusual, but said he would go along with it if Col. Cole approved, which he did, with a nod of his head. I snapped them a salute, did an "about face" and left the room. As I was leaving I noted that they were still glancing over at the waste paper basket, and Col. Cole's enlisted clerk, sitting in an outer office with the door open, was giving me a "thumbs up" signal. (Apparently he had overheard the entire exchange regarding the written tests fiasco.)

The oral exam results were outstanding and I was no longer questioned about Sgt. Thomas' qualifications by members of the ORI team and they left to harass some other base. The next day Sgt. Thomas and his crew, dressed in clean pressed fatigues, visited my office and told my clerk that they would like to see me. They formed up in a straight line, popped me a smart salute, while Sgt. Thomas said, "Sah, we-all shoo wanna thank ya, foo saving our ass. What can we-all do foo you sah?" I responded, "Sergeant Thomas, what you and your men can do for me, and for the country, is to continue the excellent work that you have been doing. I'm proud to have you and your men as part of our team." They saluted and went back to work. (I assumed they heard about my exchange with the two colonels, and what I did with their written test results, from Col. Cole's enlisted clerk, the one who gave me a thumbs-up.) When Sgt. Moon returned from leave, I told him about the episode and he also talked to Sgt. Thomas to lend his support as well.

On another occasion I wasn't as successful in protecting one of my hard-working mechanics, this time a young 19-year-old Caucasian. He and several of his young colleagues were enjoying beer and laughs (expected of young men in a far-off foreign land) in a local unsavory bar in downtown Misawa, while a young Japanese stripteaser was entertaining them with seductive gyrations. They encouraged her to strip beyond her normal scanty g-string, and ribbon-size-brassiere, by throwing rolled up 1,000 yen notes at her feet. This innocent frivolity grew in excitement and she was soon dancing on their table stark naked!

Spur-of-the-moment excitement took over and several giddy (slightly inebriated) teenage airmen began daring one of their more aggressive merrymakers to kiss it (meaning the naked dancer's "black forest"). He made a fleeting gesture of acquiescing to their demands and with a red face quickly sat down accompanied by a round of cheers from his friends! Immediately following this innocent expression of youthful exuberance two plain-clothes OSI agents, who had been sitting in the back of the club, placed him under arrest, put him in handcuffs and locked him up in a jail cell on Misawa Air Base.

He was charged with committing "lewd and lascivious acts" in a public place and court-martialed. The prosecuting attorney was a gruff old major who appeared to be a product of the type of military lawyer in the movie, From Here to Eternity. The appointed defense attorney was a young lieutenant, not much older than the accused airman. I and several of my mechanics appeared as character witnesses at his trail and I despised the arrogance of the prosecuting attorney in his attempts to cast doubt on my own veracity. However, I shot back with equal fervor and in the end I think

I made him look bad by attacking a respectable Air Force major. I had hoped that my young colleague would suffer no fate greater than a reprimand but apparently the legal zealots were looking to set an example. He was sentenced to a bad conduct discharge and one year of hard labor in prison. (What a terrible miscarriage of justice.)

Just before he was shipped back to the U.S. I visited him in his jail cell. He was in tears, but thanked me for supporting him. His main concern was that he was worried about what his parents and siblings would say, as he hadn't told them about his court-martial. I assured him that they would still love him and that the first thing he should do is demand a transcript of the trial and allow his parents to read how I and others that knew him supported him. He said that he would request one immediately. He left for the U.S. the next day and I pray he was able to overcome the hostility shown him by an overzealous military system. He would now be 65 years old and most likely has kids and grandkids of his own. (I feel that had he been an African American, political correctness at the time would have dictated that he receive a much lessor sentence.)

In a little less than three months, after assuming the position as OIC of the PMB, we had eliminated working on Sundays and except for occasional catch-up periods most Saturdays. The mechanics were putting in 40-hour work weeks and 75 percent of the aircraft were being returned to operational squadrons on time. However, Sergeant Moon and I were still working long hours, and would continue to do so until we eliminated all working on weekends and our On-Time inspection cycles were close to 100 percent. My goal for achieving this was October 1962.

But I did have Sundays off and I would load my wife and kids into my Plymouth *Valiant* and take day trips around Northern Honshu. One of our favorite excursions was to drive to the Emperor's horse farm, about 50 miles north of Misawa, where we would enjoy a picnic. To reach the farm required driving on narrow rough gravel roads and I was glad I didn't ship my Chevrolet *Impala* convertible to Japan. Returning to Misawa, a big rock flew up and bounced off the underside of the car. It hit so hard that I feared that it must have caused damage, so I stopped to investigate. The rock had bounced off the gas tank so hard that it punctured it and fuel was running out at a pretty good rate. Unless I did something fast, the tank would soon be empty and we would be stuck in the hinterlands with no way to call for help. (We didn't have cell phones in those days.)

I had my ten-year-old daughter Lynn, place a finger over the leak while I figured out a way to stop the flow. I broke off a branch from a nearby tree and, using a jackknife, whittled it down to a point and shoved it up into the hole in the gas tank. It did the trick and we were able to make it back to the base before we ran out of gas. The next day I took my car to the BX automotive garage and had the Japanese mechanics remove the tank and weld a patch over the hole. I assumed they drained the tank of gasoline before using a welding torch, because I didn't hear an explosion coming from the area of the garage.

In August 1962 we lost another F-100 and an experienced pilot, but there was no way we could investigate the cause of the accident. A highly experienced *Super Sabre* pilot had departed Misawa on a solo night round-robin (out and back) cross-country flight. It was a beautiful clear night, but he never returned. There was no distress radio call, so we didn't know if he went down in the ocean or land. We flew search missions along his intended route of flight in T-33s and helicopters but never located any sign of his aircraft. I flew several T-33 search missions, at 500 feet, but after a couple days of finding nothing we had to give up the search. Since we thoroughly covered his overland route we assumed he went down in the ocean. The cause of the accident was listed as Undetermined with the most probable cause as pilot incapacitation due to oxygen starvation, or aircraft malfunction, but we will never know.

In 1962 Misawa had been charged with sending pilots to South Vietnam for 120 days temporary duty. I had talked to a couple pilots who recently returned and although they were not allowed to engage in any combat flying they said that their tour of duty, in a developing combat zone, was interesting, so I put my name on the list of volunteers! On Saturday morning, September 29, 1962, a staff car pulled up in front of our off-base house and a personnel officer informed me that I was being sent to South Vietnam for 120 days. "When do I leave?" I asked, and as he handed me my orders he said, "On Monday's courier flight to Tokyo, where you will spend the night, and then proceed to Clark Air Base, for further transportation to Tan Son Nhut Airport, Saigon. After arriving in Saigon you will be advised on your specific assignment." He then told me that I should visit base supply to pickup a steel helmet and a side arm.

I had been expecting a TDY assignment to Southeast Asia, so my family had been prepared and I knew that my wife could take care of things until I got back. But I did feel guilty, in feeling a rush of excitement over the assignment, since it would mean leaving my ten-year-old daughter and two-year-old son for up to four months. I stopped by Sgt. Moon's house to let him know I was leaving and that he would be in charge and had my full support in any decisions he made. He wished me well and said he looked forward to my return, and not to do anything stupid when in South Vietnam. I assured him I wouldn't! Hank also told me to tell my wife that if she needed anything while I was gone not to hesitate to request it. (A typical Air Force colleague's response.)

The following Monday morning my family drove me to the passenger terminal, where I boarded a C-47 for Tachikawa AB, Tokyo. My orders stated that I was one of four operations officers being assigned to South Vietnam and would be joined by a major from Tokyo and two from Clark Air Base. When I arrived in Tachikawa, I secured a room in the BOQ where a message was waiting informing me that I was scheduled to depart the next morning at 10 a.m. on a C-130 for Clark Air Base.

Boarding the C-130, I met the second member of our group, Major Avon Ernst. Avon told me he was assigned to a C-54 squadron and was a native Hawaiian. (We became good friends during our tour of duty and shared many mutual interests.) I spent a second night in Clark Air Base and the next day Avon and I, and two additional majors, departed on a flight for Saigon. When we landed at Ton Son Nhut, it was pouring rain and we were transported, soaking wet, to a nearby tent where we presented copies of our orders to an Air Force master sergeant reading the *Stars and Stripes*. I asked him if he knew where my colleagues and I would be assigned during our TDY tour. "I have no idea, major," he said, "What you and your friends should do is secure rooms in the Majestic Hotel in downtown Saigon, which is reserved for field grade officers, and make a daily check of the bulletin board for assignment instructions." We threw our wet B-4 bags into the trunk of a staff car which drove us downtown. We walked into the Majestic Hotel lobby around 4 p.m. on Wednesday, October 3, 1962, and was immediately impressed by the old world charm of this classic French Colonial style hotel.

The Majestic Hotel was opened in 1925 during the golden age of the French Colonial period. It had 122 rooms and 30 executive suites, provided an excellent view of the Saigon River and was within walking distance of many shops and tourist attractions. It had a large swimming pool and an open-air skyline bar on the top floor which offered a panoramic view of the city and surrounding area.

Avon and I were fortunate to be assigned adjoining rooms with small balconies overlooking the Saigon River and the bustling activity of the street below, which produced never-ending strange noises. The river was awash with small sampan boats to large ocean-going vessels sounding their loud horns. Men, dressed in black pajama-style loose-fitting garments, were busily shuffling up and down the street, while women in flowing silk dresses and wearing large "pizza-size" straw hats followed close behind. The streets were jam packed with small taxicabs belching smoke, motorized and pedal-powered pedicabs, plus a few standard rickshaws. It was my impression that the taxicab drivers thought their engines would stop dead if their horns were not blowing continuously. Fortunately, the hotel was air-conditioned and had thick double-glass windows that blocked out most of the street noise when closed.

After a shower and a change into casual dress, Avon and I went to the open-air skyline lounge for a drink and had to elbow our way to the bar, past men in civilian and military dress, to obtain a 25 cent drink. Officers ranged in rank from major to general, with a drink in one hand and a snack in the other. The few American females present seemed to be enjoying themselves as they were surrounded by horny-looking men competing with each other for their attention. Trays of free snacks were everywhere and the temperature (since it was early October) was near perfect. (I wondered if my 120 days in Vietnam would be spent in such luxury or perhaps billeted in some tent in the boonies of South Vietnam.)

We had dinner that night in a wonderful large dining room, adorned with crystal chandeliers, round white-clothed tables, exquisite silverware and white-gloved waiters. It was obvious that the European style living, established by the French, was still being followed. What seemed completely incongruous to the four-star atmosphere were little lizards running up and down the walls and across the ceiling. A colonel sitting at an adjacent table noted our concern regarding these little creatures, and asked if we were new to Saigon. I told him that we had just arrived that afternoon! He chuckled and said, "Those little lizards you see running across the walls and ceiling are called geckos, and have little microscopic suction cups on their feet which allows them to hang from the ceiling." Obviously, he was a gecko expert and continued, "Their chief diet is grabbing mosquitoes with their long lightning-fast tongues. We consider them our little friends as they are innocuous, not venomous and help control the spread of malaria-carrying flying insects. You will see them everywhere and the only caution required is to hold a hand over your soup when they are on the ceiling above your table." (I noted that they were almost transparent and when next to a light you could see mosquitoes sliding down their throats and into their stomachs.) Our meal was delicious and I rushed through my soup before the geckos had a chance of adding their own brand of indigenous flavoring.

The next morning I checked the bulletin board and finding nothing regarding an assignment, headed for the dining room for breakfast. After eating, Avon and I hired a 19-year-old Vietnamese female guide, who spoke Vietnamese, French and English to show us the sights of Saigon. In the fall of 1962, the emerging war between the South Vietnamese and the Vietcong had not yet reached Saigon and it was still referred to as the "Paris of the Orient" and lived up to its reputation. Sidewalk cafes were everywhere, along with excellent French and European culinary style restaurants. Temples, museums and cathedrals were open and free to visitors. In addition to our intelligent attractive guide, we hired an air-conditioned limousine to chauffeur us around the city.

The following day the bulletin board was still void of any instructions so we again contracted with our guide and limousine driver to continue with sightseeing. We finished the day by treating them to dinner in a top-scale French restaurant, and continued with our "tourist-like" activity for a full week, branching out further each day with our guide exposing us to additional exceptional restaurants and interesting sights. So after a week of acting like tourists, with no assignment, I told Avon that the following morning I was going to put on my uniform and take the 7 a.m. work bus to Tan Son Nhut Airport to see if I could find out what I was going to do for the next 110 days. Avon said, "I'll go with you."

Arriving in clear weather at the same tent we reported to a week earlier, we found a different sergeant manning the desk. I asked him if he knew what my duty assignment would be during my TDY tour in Vietnam. "Who are you, major, and where did you come from?" was his response. After answering his question, he asked for a copy of my orders. He then suggested I obtain a room in the Majestic Hotel and make a daily check of the bulletin board for further instructions. (I had gone through this run-around a week earlier and was starting to get a little pissed off.) I told the uninformed sergeant, in a stern voice, "I arrived in Vietnam seven days ago during a driving rain storm, and a sergeant sitting in your chair told me and my three colleagues to get a room in the Majestic Hotel and check the bulletin board for further instructions. We have been doing this for the past week and still don't have an assignment. While waiting for someone to tell me what I'm supposed to do, I have visited all the tourist spots, eaten in all the five-star restaurants, and don't want to stand around waiting for the latest copy of the *Stars and Stripes* and a cup of coffee for the next four months. If you have nothing for me to do, get somebody of authority to release me and let me return to Japan, where I have an important job at Misawa in maintaining 24 F-100 jet fighters."

As I was concluding my uncompromising comment, an Air Force bird colonel, dressed in starched fatigues, walked around from behind a partition and gave me a stern look! While continuing his stare, he said, "Major, I've been listening to your bitching, and frankly I'm getting a little tired of listening to it, so knock it off!" "OK. I'll stop bitching, but can you tell me what my job in Vietnam is?" I snapped back. His response, which I'll never forget, was, "Major, just like the rest of us you're doing your job by just being here. You're one of President Kennedy's 17,000 advisors. We're like firemen without a fire to fight, but with one big difference, we don't have fire engines to polish while waiting for something to happen." Softening his approach, he said, "Do you know what a TMC is?" I said that it's usually used in reference to "Transport Movement Control." Noting that, he seemed impressed. I added that I had flown C-119s for several years and this was a common term used in troop carrier operations. Hearing this he said, "Well, I may have a job for you if your interested. How about your quiet friend standing there (referring to Avon) --- does he have any transport experience?" Avon spoke up and said that he was an operations officer for a C-54 squadron in Japan. "Well," the colonel said, "I think I may have something that you two officers may be interested in."

The colonel asked me if I was familiar with the Fairchild C-123 *Provider*. I told him that I was, but had never flown it. He continued, "That doesn't matter, as you and your buddy will not be required to fly them, just oversee them." He said that a squadron of C-123s were being based at Don Muang Airport, Bangkok, with the mission of providing logistical support during the constructional phase of military bases throughout Thailand. To support the mission, the general in charge of Joint Task Force 116 has requested that two Field Grade officers, experienced in troop carrier operations, be assigned to his staff to help organize an airlift support operation. He asked if we would be interested in taking on the assignment. When we said that we were, since we have seen all the tourist sights in Saigon, he smiled and said that orders would be prepared and we would leave for Bangkok the next day. We returned to the Majestic Hotel, enjoyed an excellent dinner, while quickly eating our soup as geckos were racing up and down the walls and across the ceiling.

The next morning Avon and I were on an Air America DC-4 for Bangkok, arriving a couple hours later. We were met by our immediate boss, a pleasant non-rated Air Force major, who said he had reserved rooms for us in a hotel in downtown Bangkok and that a staff car would pick us up for work each morning and drive us back to the hotel in the evening. He added that our unit was under the command of Brigadier General Stephen D. McElroy (Mac), who was an old fashion officer, commissioned in 1933 and although a pilot thought it was a mistake when the military eliminated horses and open-cockpit airplanes. "Can we assume, from your description, that the general is a little strange?" I asked. "Don't quote me, but you nailed it exactly," he replied. As we headed for our hotel, I noted several C-123s parked on the Royal Thai Air Force ramp (more would arrive in the next few days), plus several 45th Tactical Reconnaissance RF-101s from Misawa Air Base, Japan and F-84s bearing Royal Thai Air Force markings.

The Fairchild C-123 Provider is a short-range twin-engine assault transport designed for airlifting troops and cargo in and out of unprepared airstrips. It evolved from earlier designs for a large assault glider, but was equipped with engines at the end of WW II. The first of 300 Providers produced entered service in July 1955, and by 1969, 184 were modified with two J-85 jet engines for increased performance, when flying low-level defoliant spray missions in South Vietnam. The C-123s that I would be associated with were not equipped with jet engines, but the standard Pratt & Whitney R-2800 engine of 2,300 hp each. It had a wing span of 110 ft., a maximum gross weight of 60,000 lbs., a cruising speed of 170 mph, and cost $602,000 (equal to $3,370,000 today). (See Photo No. 47.)

Reporting for work the next morning we were shown a tent which would be our TMC. It was one of many, aligned in a perfect row, which we were told was General Mac's requirement. According to our boss the general would make frequent inspection visits and would raise hell if even one tent stake was out of alignment! Our tent was located next to a much larger one used by the headquarters staff, and was the only one with air conditioning. C-123s were already flying support missions, but on a "you-call-we-haul" basis. Our mission was to set up a mini-airline type operation with published departure and arrival times, for overlapping airports, which would be used as "hub stations." In addition to publishing flight schedules, we would establish basic parts supplies at each airport and develop Standard Operating Procedures (SOPs), advising crews on messing facilities, refueling procedures, telephone numbers and if the need arose, overnight lodging. To accomplish this Herculean task it would be necessary for Avon and I to visit each airport many times before our task was complete. The first thing we did was procure a large wall map of Thailand and identify the airports under construction or alteration that our aircraft would support. They included: Don Muang (Bangkok), Chiang Mai, Korat, Nakhon Phanom, Takhli, Ubon, Udorn, and U Tapao. Since many of these bases were under construction our C-123s were required to land and take off on partially completed runways, taxiways or ramps.

Within a few days more C-123s began arriving, after flying from the U.S. via South America, Morocco, Turkey and India. It appeared that most of the young crew members had seen too many John Wayne movies as they stepped off their aircraft wearing leather hip holsters containing Smith & Wesson .357 magnums or .45 caliber pistols with glistening ivory hand grips and wide decorative leather belts ringed with polished rounds of ammunition. (I'm sure their protective weapons must have weighed about ten pounds, and without a doubt, General Patton would have been proud of them.) Avon and I didn't want to disappoint their desire for an "OK Corral-style shoot-out" by telling them that the only dangers they faced when flying in Thailand were mosquito bites, poisonous snakes, VD and diarrhea, and that their expensive sidearms would not be effective in protecting them against any of these combat hazards. We knew that within a few days they would figure this out for themselves and leave their weapons in their footlockers before somebody got hurt. (This is exactly what happened and our fear of being shot by some C-123 crew member accidentally discharging his weapon was no longer a problem.)

Avon and I took turns in visiting each airport and formulated appropriate support procedures. We transferred them into published SOPs, along with flight routes and departure and arrival times for each location, but left the scheduling of flight crews up to the C-123 operations officer. We then plotted the entire operation onto a large map of Thailand and covered it with plastic, which allowed for erasable grease-pencil notations. We placed this map in General Mac's command tent, which was used for flight following during a daily 3 p.m. briefing. Within 30 to 45 days our C-123 *Provider* Airline was a reality and everyone was pleased with its dependable On Time operation. The *Provider* was an extremely reliable aircraft and the crew members were great to work with. They were housed in open-bay barracks on the Royal Thai Air Force side of the base and were off duty about two days per week. When not scheduled they would head for downtown Bangkok which provided all forms of entertainment for young American warriors 7,000 miles from home.

Avon and I, for the first two weeks, maintained rooms in a Bangkok hotel, which was convenient for enjoying the fruits of Thai night life and young Siam girls eager to provide various forms of recreation. We discovered that the Thai people had a passion for apples, as they loved fruit, but apples were not indigenous to their country. I would purchase a sack of them at the U.S. Embassy Commissary and place them in a bowl in my hotel room, which were a hit with visiting guests.

However, I think General McElroy thought we were having too much fun and directed that we move out of our air-conditioned hotel rooms and into a BOQ building on the Royal Thai Air Base at Don Muang Airport. I was assigned a steel cot in an open-air bay with a community latrine and shower room down the hall. Each cot was equipped with a mosquito net which was kept rolled up off the floor during the day, and when retiring for the night, I would tuck it in around the base of the mattress and spray the inside area with a "bug bomb."

A short walk from the BOQ was the Royal Thai Officers' Club which was referred to as the "Air House." It had an American-style bar, a lounge, served a delicious (tree-ripened) fruit lunch and a family-style dinner, which was usually quite good. There was an upstairs theater, equipped with overstuffed furniture, that provided free nightly Hollywood movies from a 16-mm movie projector. The movies were generally current productions and I had to get there early to get a good seat.

I was surprised to see several pilots wearing "polka-dot" silk scarves drinking at the Air House bar, which I recognized as members of the 45th Tactical Reconnaissance Squadron from Misawa, Japan. I was aware that the squadron was operating RF-101s on a secret mission called "Able Mable," but until I saw their aircraft in Thailand, I wasn't aware of the location of their operational base. The pilots wouldn't discuss their mission, but it was common knowledge that they weren't in Thailand to take aerial photos of elephants! They were flying dangerous low level photo reconnaissance missions over North Vietnam at a time when

President Kennedy was telling the country that we had no American combat aircraft flying in Vietnam. (I guess they were just advisors, like myself. They lost several pilots in this dangerous clandestine style combat mission and their spouses, back in Japan, or family members in the U.S., were told that their husbands or sons were killed in a training accident!)

I continued visiting Bangkok on my days off and would ride an open-air smoky bus for the 30-minute trip. The fare would be one Thai baht (five cents). I enjoyed visiting Buddhist temples, open-air cafes and even made friends with a young "yellow-robed monk" who invited me to visit his humble room. At first I was suspicious of his intent, but soon learned that his only interest was to practice his English, and I would often visit him when I was in town. His payment for my English lessons was escorting me through sections of temples not open to tourists.

Because of the serious danger of VD, I usually limited my adult entertainment junkets to occasional visits to one of the many massage parlors located in a back room of most barber shops. The charge for a massage was 100 baht (five dollars), with an extra cost for any special request. After a busy and interesting day in Bangkok I would ride the bus, by hanging on to the sides, back to the Royal Thai Air Base.

There were many nights that I did what I could to help the Thai Air House bar by spending several hours enjoying a wide variety of cheap liquor. Following these marathon drinking sessions, I would head back to the BOQ by walking along a narrow concrete sidewalk illuminated by a couple low wattage bare light bulbs. One night, I was skipping back to my room, while struggling to stay on the narrow path, since on either side were high weeds populated by a variety of snakes, which I didn't wish to disturb! In the dim light I noted a long black object spread across the sidewalk and for some odd reason (influenced, I'm sure, by my inebriated state of mind), I thought it was a garden hose and stepped on top of it! However, it wasn't a garden hose, but a large Black King Cobra snake, enjoying the relative warmth of the concrete. The King didn't appreciate being disturbed and quickly coiled, spread its hood and in a very aggressive manner lunged out at me with a menacing hiss while spitting a spray of venom. Since I was now three feet in the air, he missed my leg by a wide margin and before he could recoil for another attack, I was several feet down the path and running like hell. The incident had an immediate sobering effect and would be an excellent method of shucking the effects of alcohol, but I don't think it will become a popular ascetic remedy. (I never expected the PGR to go after me with the assistance of a King Cobra snake, but I guess they must be colleagues and work together in inducting unsuspecting inebriated pilots.)

Sometime later, after contributing to the coffers of the Air House bar, I was returning to my room and cautiously calculating each step, when navigating the narrow path. I entered the BOQ quietly as most of my bunk mates were already asleep and engaging in a lively snoring contest. Approaching my cot I noted that the mosquito netting was untied and touching the floor. Apparently the Thai maid, after making the bed, forgot to tie it up into a knot. However, I didn't give it much thought and stripped down to my shorts, and bare feet. After a visit to the latrine, I walked back to my dimly lit cot, grabbed a hold of the mosquito net and gave it a good shaking. When I did, my heart almost stopped! From the bunched up mosquito net a three-foot long Banded Krait snake scooted out, crawled across my bare toes and disappeared under an opening in a screen door. During the brief moment it took to slither over my toes, its black body and yellow bands were clearly visible, just like the pictures shown in survival school. I immediately sobered up and it took me a long time to go to sleep. (See Photo No. 48 for author next to his working tent in Thailand.)

The Krait snake is 15 times more deadly than a cobra, as its venom is a powerful neurotoxin that affects the central nervous system, causing respiratory failure. They seek shelter in sleeping bags, boots and tents.

However, I was not the only one that had to deal with King Cobras! Aircraft crew chiefs, performing sunrise preflights, carried long sticks and flashlights. Cobras would wrap themselves around warm tires and brakes for protection against the relative nighttime cold. The crew chiefs would spot them with a flashlight and sling them out onto the concrete ramp with their long sticks. The snakes, pissed off from being disturbed, would slither off into the tall grass, while announcing their displeasure with continuous loud spitting sounds and spreading their threatening looking wing-like hoods. It was not unusual to count 20 or more heading for the weeds after being dispatched by crew chiefs with long sticks.

On October 15, 1962, my concern over poisonous snakes was trivial in comparison to the news affecting military units worldwide. Reconnaissance aircraft had detected missiles capable of launching nuclear warheads against the U.S. from Cuba. And even though the crisis was on the other side of the world we were put on "DEFCON 2," an alert status one step short of going to war. For 12 days we were on edge while trying to figure out what we would do in Thailand if the U.S. went to war with the Soviet Union, and worried about our families in Japan. Fortunately by October 27th the crisis was over and we were allowed to resume our day-by-day routine of providing inter-theater airlift.

One morning in early November my boss asked me to join him and two other officers in a round of golf. The other two making up the foursome were a visiting general and his aide. The 18-hole course we would play on was maintained by the Royal Thai Air Force and located between runways 21R and 21L. It was a well-maintained course, but presented a couple distinct differences compared to golf courses in other parts of the world. The first notable contrast was that participants were not restricted to a maximum of four players per group. Thai golfers played in large numbers and it was not uncommon to see up to 12 golfers, along with a like number of female caddies, moving down the fairways. When approaching the green, they didn't wait for the golfer whose ball was the furthest out to swing first, but would hit their own ball when they reached it and didn't shout "Four." The fun really began when they reached the green and totaled up their scores! The few times I played the course we limited our group to the standard foursome and were somewhat frustrated when these large groups would not let us play through, but even if they did, it would have been almost impossible to coordinate playing through such a large group without being hit by a golf ball. The second notable contrast was that the "out-of-bounds" areas, on both sides of lush green fairways, were covered with knee-high thick grass and weeds. We were advised that if your ball landed off the fairway, not to attempt to find it, but take the one-stroke penalty and make your next swing along the edge. The reason for this caution was twofold: first, it would be almost impossible to find your lost ball in the tall grass; second, in searching for it you would stand a good chance of disturbing an aggressive King Cobra snake, who has no patience with two-legged adversaries hitting little white balls into its private domain and disturbing his afternoon siesta.

When we picked up the general and his aide, my jaw dropped! I recognized him as the colonel that I drenched with dirty rain water when I flew him from England to Rhein Main, Germany in a C-82 eleven years earlier (see page 89). However, it didn't appear that he recognized me as

288

the second lieutenant who nearly drowned him in 1951 and I certainly wasn't going to refresh his memory. We briefed our two guests on the hazards of hitting a ball out-of-bounds and were able to play the first nine holes without following a small army of Thai golfers, an unusual treat.

Before playing the back nine we were resting over cold drinks in the club house when I noted that the general was giving me an inquisitive once-over. After a few minutes he said, "Major Martin, you look familiar. Have we played golf together before or met someplace?" "Yes," I said. "We did meet before. It was when I flew you from Molesworth, England to Rhein Main Air Base, Germany in a C-82 in 1951." He burst out laughing, while telling my boss and his aide about the event. (I often wondered how he explained his rumpled, wrinkled uniform when he showed up for his staff meeting and now, after all these years, I was about to find out.) The general said that when he got off the airplane at Rhein Main he was really pissed off, but didn't blame the young second lieutenant (me) who flew him there, since he was obviously not aware that the cockpit overhead was full of rain water. He said that when he showed up for his meeting the other members, noting his disheveled appearance, asked him what in the hell had happened to his uniform. When he told them about his being drenched during his flight from England, the room erupted in laughter and he became a celebrity, not rejected because of his appearance. The general shook my hand while stating, "Major, I knew it wasn't your fault and I'm happy to be able to tell you this in person. Now let's play the back nine, while avoiding the snakes."

The warning about the snakes when playing golf was not issued without justification. A couple days after playing with the general, an Air Force major from our task force hit a ball into the weeds and decided to find it rather than take a penalty stroke. He was searching through the high grass when he disturbed a King Cobra that struck him in the chest close to his heart. His golfing partners helped him to the club house (the course did not have carts) and called for medical assistance. However, from the time he had been bitten to the time he reached medical attention was too long to save him and he died from respiratory paralysis, a terrible loss in exchange for not wishing to take a one-stroke penalty. (Another example of how the PGR never relaxes in his search for additional victims.)

One of our transportation department NCOs kept a small squirrel monkey named "Mickey" as a pet. He was a well-mannered little guy who reminded me of the type of monkey organ grinders use to solicit money while he entertains passer-bys with music. I would stop by to see Mickey on my way back from lunch at the Air House and bring him bits of fresh fruit, which he dearly loved. Mickey and I became friends and when the sergeant left for the U.S. he brought Mickey over to my tent and asked if I would like to have him. I welcomed the gift and Mickey now had a new home and human friend. (I was sorry I didn't have an organ to grind.)

He was tent-broken and when he wanted to go outside, he would chirp loudly. I would put him on a long nylon cord and when he wanted to come back inside he would scratch on the screen door. He would often sit on my shoulder while I was working at my desk, or curl up inside my pith helmet to take a nap. He loved to play tricks and would often grab my pencil and dash around the tent while I chased him to retrieve it. He was a great little companion and admired by everyone, even our hard-nosed General McElroy liked him!

One day I tied Mickey outside while I went to lunch, but when I returned with some fresh fruit snacks, he was gone. The nylon leash was cut, or chewed through, and there were fresh blood spots nearby. I and many of my colleagues searched the area (except the tall grass) looking and calling for him, but we never found him. I believe a large King Cobra, which can reach a length of 16 feet, found him and dragged him off. I hope he is in monkey heaven, because he provided me and my friends with many smiles while faithfully serving as one of President Kennedy's 17,000 advisors in Southeast Asia.

As previously mentioned, I was a frequent patron of the Thai Air House bar and would usually have one or more Beefeater gin martinis before dinner. Colonel Hongsakul, the Royal Thai Air Force F-84 Squadron Commander, was also a Beefeater gin aficionado and in sharing this mutual fondness for martinis we became good friends. He spoke excellent English, had trained with the U.S. Air Force in the United States, and was familiar with the use of a dice cup in determining who pays for the drinks. It didn't matter to him if he won or lost, he just enjoyed the game. He was great fun and one day he took me on a personal tour through the Royal Thai Air Force Air Museum that contained many unique aircraft.

In early November Col. Hongsakul and I were enjoying drinks in the Air House when he asked if I was familiar with the Festival of Lights (Bang Sai Loi Krathong). When I said no, he ordered another round of drinks and began telling me about one of the most popular festivals in Thailand.

According to the colonel, it is celebrated annually on days when there is a full moon, the rainy season has ended, the weather is pleasant and the rivers are at their highest level. In 1962, the dates for the festival were the second week of November. He continued, "Loi means to float, and a Krathong is a lotus-shaped boat made of banana leaves. Thousands of these boats are filled with candles, flowers and modest coins and after making a wish, are floated down canals as an offering to the *Goddess of Water*. Some people believe that when the Krathongs float away they carry with them the sins and bad luck of the people who launched them." However, the colonel thought he was too much of a reprobate to benefit from a floating banana leaf, but considered the festival a wonderful event. He invited Avon and I to be his guests for drinks at his house, followed by VIP seats for viewing the nighttime festivities.

A chauffeur-driven, pre-WW II, Yellow Rolls Royce sedan arrived in front of our BOQ to transport us to Col. Hongsakul's house. His home was positioned above ground level on long sturdy supporting poles, and with the exception of window and door screens, was mostly open. However, there were wooden shutters available for blocking out wind, rain, or providing privacy. The colonel met us at the door and invited us inside to meet his wife and two beautiful daughters, ages 15 and 17. The women were dressed in colorful long flowing silk dresses and wearing expensive looking gold necklaces, earrings and bracelets. The colonel was wearing white trousers and an Aloha-style short-sleeved shirt. Our introduction to his family was limited to handshakes and slight bows, as the women did not speak English, but friendly smiles and the musical Thai language salutations made us feel welcome. The house was sparsely furnished with rich-looking rattan furniture capped with silk cushions. The floors were varnished wood and brightly polished to the point that in stocking feet they were quite slippery. I presented the colonel with a bottle of Beefeater gin, which he accepted with a gracious thank you. Inviting us to sit down he asked if we would like a drink before leaving for the festival. We responded that we thought this was a grand idea.

The colonel clapped his hands and a Thai Air Force enlisted man instantly appeared, slid across the polished floor on his knees and bowed down in front of the colonel. (The image was like a scene from the musical, *The King and I*, except the colonel didn't have a shaved head like Yul Brynner.) The colonel spoke to his servant in Thai, who rose to his feet, bowed again and disappeared into a back room. Within a couple minutes he was sliding back across the floor on his knees, but this time coming to a stop in front of Avon and I and holding a silver tray containing a bottle of Johnnie Walker Black Label Scotch, a bucket of ice cubes, a seltzer bottle and a dish of mixed nuts. After we helped ourselves he set the tray on a nearby coffee table, bowed and left the room. With the colonel acting as a translator his wife and daughters peppered us with questions about life in the U.S. and our thoughts about Thailand. During the conversation I mentioned that we were impressed by his chauffeur-driven Rolls Royce and wondered how he acquired it. He chuckled at the question, while stating that it had belonged to a Japanese general, who abandoned it when the Japanese Army surrendered, and he grabbed it before a Thai general could commandeer it. After a couple drinks he suggested we head for the celebration, where we would enjoy a buffet-style dinner before the Festival of Lights commences.

The limousine was equipped with folding jump seats so there was plenty of room for our party of six. We were driven right up to the entrance of a grand gazebo situated on the shores of a large klong (canal). The colonel led us to a table overlooking the festival grounds marked "reserved." Several other guests had already arrived and according to our host they were colonels, generals and their families. In the middle of the pavilion was a long table covered with a colorful array of food.

With plates in hand we helped ourselves to appetizers of deep-fried chicken in pandan leaves and a spicy minced pork salad. The main course consisted of fried prawns, yellow crab curry, sautéed bean sprouts, mixed vegetables and steamed fish in rolled banana leaves. The desert was assorted tree-ripened fresh fruit and coconut pudding. For beverage the colonel opened a couple bottles of French champagne and later offered cups of strong black coffee. The food was scrumptiously delicious, and the weather was in the high 70s with light winds. The golden rays of a setting sun added a nice touch to the sounds of a strange, but pleasant, distant Thai band. (I couldn't help but feel sorry for my family and colleagues back in Japan, because in November they were probably shoveling snow.)

By the time we finished dinner the sun had disappeared in the Western sky and a full moon, in compliance with the colonel's schedule, began rising at 6:22 p.m. Thousands of people had gathered on both banks of the klong and were launching Krathongs containing burning candles. Each boat christening was accompanied with musical vocal prayers and happy cheers from both children and adults alike. The sight of thousands of small flickering banana leaf boats, slowly floating down the klong, mixed with the sounds of merriment from thousands of happy people, was an experience I'll never forget. The gala event terminated with a gigantic 30-minute fireworks display. I reached across the table, patted my Thai colonel friend on his shoulder and said, "Thanks, colonel, for a great experience." His response, "No problem, major, I was always treated extremely well in the U.S. and this was my chance to reciprocate."

During the entire evening I found it difficult to keep my eyes off the colonel's exceedingly beautiful 17-year-old daughter, whose name was Apasra. My attraction was not in any way associated with lustful thoughts, as it was not in keeping with my character, and would have been an insult to my gracious host. The fascination was similar to viewing a beautiful portrait that is difficult to ignore. She not only possessed attractive feminine features, but even without being able to speak to her in her native language it was apparent that she possessed inherent charm, remarkable poise and a regal bearing. (In a later chapter, I will disclose how her beauty did not go unnoticed by feminine beauty connoisseurs associated with the Miss Universe contest and my chance meeting with her father in the Travis Officers' Club three years later, on page 344.)

I had mentioned that our commanding general was a carry-over from the early military days of the 1930s and was a little bizarre. (He reminded me of Col. Sherman Potter in the popular TV show *M*A*S*H.**) But nothing demonstrated his bizarre behavior more then what he requested one day when I was preparing to brief him and his staff on our daily airlift accomplishments. I had just taken my position before the podium when the general said, "Major Martin, before you brief us on the airlift achievements of your C-123s, I want to know why there's a God Damn large noisy refrigerator van parked outside of my office. The noise of the constantly-running engine is driving me nuts, and I want it moved!" I had no idea what he was talking about and whatever it was it shouldn't be my concern. I looked over at a Lt.Col. sitting next to him who was obviously just as confused as I was, and shrugging his shoulders while nodding his head in an obvious signal for me to acknowledge the general's order and proceed with my briefing, which, like a good solider I did.

When the briefing was over the room was called to attention and the general and his aide left. I went over to the Lt.Col., who had been sitting next to the general, and said, "What in the hell was the general talking about in regard to a noisy van sitting next to his office?" "I don't know," the colonel said, "but let's go find out." Indeed, there was a large refrigerated trailer parked next to the general's office, and like he said a noisy auxiliary power unit was running continuously. We drove over to our motor pool and ordered the officer in charge (OIC) to take a tractor and move it somewhere on the outskirts of the base. We waited around until we saw it being towed away, thinking the problem was solved, we retreated to the Thai Air House for drinks, dinner and our nightly movie.

The next day we were gathered in the air-conditioned command tent, awaiting the general to begin our daily briefing. When he and his aide arrived, the room was called to attention and as the general took his seat he bellowed out, "Where in the hell is Major Martin?" "Right here," I responded. "Major, yesterday I ordered you to move that God Damn noisy van parked next to my office but it's still there. Are you deaf or deliberately ignoring my orders?" I looked over at the shoulder-shrugging lieutenant colonel, who was obviously just as perplexed as I was. I told the general that we had it moved yesterday, but would go see why it was moved back, right after today's briefing. "Make damn sure you do major," he said. "Present your daily briefing and make it short!"

Just like the general had said, the van was back in its original site and just as noisy as before. We drove over to the motor pool to discuss the van problem with the OIC, who said that after he had his men move it the day before, an Army major general "two-star" gave him hell and demanded it be moved back to where it was. He added that he had told the Army "two-star" that an Air Force "one-star" didn't want it where it was and wanted it moved. However, the Army "two-star", obviously pissed-off, said, "I don't give a good God Damn what General McElroy wants captain, move that friggin trailer back where it was, right now!"

When General Mac arrived for the next day's briefing, he blurted out, "When are you going to move that God Damn van, Major Martin, or am I going to have to march you over there personally to get it moved?" I told him that we had moved it when he first complained about it, but an Army major general said he wanted it exactly where it was and ordered it moved back! He wrinkled up his nose, paused a minute, and then said, "Forget about that God Damn van, major, and brief me on your friggin C-123s." The subject of the van never came up again and within a few days it had fulfilled its mission and was gone!

I was sitting in my office tent one day when General Mac's aide came in and said that the general wanted to see me. I checked that I had on a clean uniform, that my shoes were shined, my mustache neatly trimmed and jumped into a jeep and drove over to his office. I popped him a smart salute which was returned with, "At ease, major, have a seat." After I sat down he stated, in a fatherly like manner, "Major Martin you impress me as an officer who doesn't hesitate to speak his mind, and with your permission, I would like to ask you a question." "Yes sir." I said, "Go ahead." His question related to his perception that the troops didn't like him and he wanted to know why. (This was a delicate subject to explain, but I thought I would do my best to provide him with some constructive information, without pissing him off and putting my own career in jeopardy.) I suggested to the general that it wasn't that his men didn't like him, but that there was a generation gap between the time he joined the military and the time almost all his subordinates did. I referred to the fact that he was probably the only member of our Task Force that had served prior to WW II, and, using myself as an example, I pointed out that I graduated from flight school in 1949 and my immediate superiors joined during WW II. Noting that he was listening, I continued. I said that he was not much younger than my father and earlier in life I had many disagreements with him, but later I realized that his experience and foresight was far more valuable than my youthful "care-free" irreverence. And I thought the same situation was occurring here, and that he shouldn't worry about what some of his subordinates think, as he knows what's best for the unit and those that bitch the loudest are least prepared to become leaders. I told him, "Personally, general, I respect your leadership and enjoy being a part of Task Force 116." His comment, "Thanks, major, you're excused." (Not long after my informal conversation with the general he returned to the U.S. and retired. Even though his behavior was somewhat bazaar, I enjoyed serving under him and felt that he had served our country well during three wars and was a credit to his uniform. (Brig. Gen. Stephen D. McElroy died in May 1991 at aqge 79.)

By mid December our "mini-airline" was operating on its own like a finely-tuned watch, and there wasn't any need for both Avon and myself to sit around in our tent reading the *Stars and Stripes*. To provide for sufficient time to enjoy our success we took turns working three days on, and three days off. During my days off I would frequently take the five-cent bus ride to downtown Bangkok to visit my Buddhist friend, gift shops and Johnny Gems Jewelry store. (I had given up on the massage parlors as they no longer appealed to me.) I also spent time walking the streets and taking boat trips through the Floating Market to observe the many different and sometimes weird items people would buy as food, such as deep fried giant water bugs, worms and grasshoppers. Priding myself on having an adventurous pallet, I tried a couple fried water bugs (which tasted like burnt breakfast cereal), but passed on the worms and grasshoppers. I was told that Thai food is often flavored with ground up water bugs which provides a spicy flavor, similar to red peppers.

During one of my trips to town, I visited a King Cobra snake farm where they harvest venom for medicinal purposes. The farm contained thousands of snakes crawling over each other in high walled enclosures, while one of the workers demonstrated how he milked them for their venom and gave an interesting lecture on the snakes' habits. When he finished his presentation he asked if there were any questions. I asked him what would happen if you stepped on a King Cobra while he was stretched out resting. His answer, "Well, I can assure you that he wouldn't be too happy and would most likely bury his fangs into your leg with the speed of lightning." (I was glad to hear him say "most likely.")

I was a frequent visitor to Johnny Gems Jewelry Shop in downtown Bangkok and became quite friendly with the owner. Even if I didn't make a purchase Johnny would invite me to join him in a cup of tea and a chat about life in America. His shop was popular for princess rings, blue-star sapphires, and various gold adornments for both men and women. One day I was haggling with Johnny over the price of two princess rings I was planning on purchasing for my wife and daughter. He insisted that the lowest price he would accept was $100 each, while my top offer was 50. We had gone back and forth in friendly bickering, when Johnny finally agreed to come down to $75, but I insisted that 50 dollars was my limit.

Unexpectedly, a taxi came to a screeching stop in front of his store and two American women jumped out and entered. They said they were on their way to the airport, but before departing they wanted to pick up some princess rings. Johnny showed them rings from the same tray that I had been looking at, and without any fanfare the women said they wanted to buy five and asked Johnny for the price. He said, "$100 each." The lady who seemed to be in charge said, "Fine, put them in a box" and signed five $100 travelers checks. I said nothing, but Johnny and I knew that they were the same rings that he had agreed to sell to me for $75. The women picked up their rings, dashed out the door and jumped into their waiting taxi. After they left, I looked Johnny in the eye and said, "My offer to buy two at $50 each still stands." "Sold," Johnny said. I later purchased a set of Thai bronze-ware and hand-carved wooden elephants, at a discount, which I took back to Japan as Christmas presents.

On another three-day vacation, I signed up for a tour of the Thai countryside, while riding on the back of an elephant. The experience certainly provided an excellent elevated view of klongs and ancient ruins, but even though I was a seasoned pilot I nearly got seasick from the constant back and forth swaying. However, I did become adept in getting on and off the big beast by stepping on his bent knee and long trunk. (Until you've heard an elephant fart, you don't know what a good fart is!)

Around mid December Chiang Mai Airport was experiencing refueling and turnaround problems, so I decided to fly there in one of our C-123s and remain overnight. (Chiang Mai was our most Northern base and close to the border with Burma. I had visited the base once before, but never stayed overnight so I was looking forward to the experience.) The refueling and related problems were easily solved and the Air Force NCO in charge offered to take me out for dinner in a unique Thai restaurant in downtown Chiang Mai. I noted that the people living in this Northern area were quite dark in skin color and the women wore brightly colored clothes with strands of beads and layers of gold necklaces.

We ate in a true ethnic style restaurant which prepared a sort of "Mongolian Beef Barbecue" dinner which was very spicy and to my taste the beef was much too rare (almost raw), but I washed it down with a couple bottles of Thai beer. (More on the results of this rare beef dinner on page 304.) I spent the night in an open dormitory, sleeping on a standard military steel cot covered with a mosquito net, and the next afternoon I flew back to Don Muang Airport. Soon after returning, my boss told me that he was very pleased with my performance, during the past three months and with our mini-airline running smoothly there was no need for both Major Ernst and myself to remain in Thailand. He added that he was aware that I had a family in Japan and it was only five days before Christmas. So, if I wished he would cut orders and I could leave the next day. I told him that this sounded great, but didn't think it would be fair to Avon. He said that he had already talked to Major Ernst, and since he didn't have any children in Tachikawa Air Base, he was in full agreement that I should be the one to be released early.

I packed a footlocker with my Thai purchased presents, stuffed everything else in my B-4 bag and on the morning of December 22, 1962, I was on an Air America DC-4 for Tachikawa with en route stops in Saigon and Clark Air Base. I arrived in Tachikawa late that same day and called my wife telling her I would take a train for Misawa the next day. I also talked to my ten-year-old daughter Lynn, who was overjoyed that I would be home for Christmas. After an all-day train ride my family met me at the Misawa train station in the evening of December 23rd. My deep tan, slim body and full mustache surprised them, but in spite of the snow it was good to be home. The next day I called my boss, Lieutenant Colonel Ken Rasmussen, who welcomed me back and authorized ten days leave. When talking to him I was pleased to learn that during my tour in Southeast Asia we hadn't lost any more F-100s.

When I returned to work my NCO, Chief Master Sergeant Hank Moon, told me that during my absence the performance of our inspection branch had steadily improved, and for the 90 days that I was TDY, approximately 95% of the aircraft we inspected were returned to the squadrons on schedule. I was also heartened by the many "welcome back" comments expressed by my ten dock chiefs, and felt very fortunate in having such an outstanding NCO as Sergeant Moon. (This would allow me more time to fly the T-33 and occasionally bum a flight in the F-100.)

One method I employed to obtain extra flight time was to volunteer for simulating attacks by Soviet Union bombers, especially during the winter months. With the assistance of Master Sergeant Hart, our personal equipment specialist, a fellow pilot and I would wiggle into rubberized anti-exposure (poopy) suits and wearing a hard seat-pack parachute and one-man life raft, slither into the cockpit of a T-33. We would climb to 34,000 feet, fly approximately 300 miles out over the Northeast Pacific Ocean, turn off our radar responding transponder, descend to 500 feet and head back toward Misawa Air Base.

The object of the exercise was to test the capability of our air defense radar network in detecting an unidentified aircraft approaching Misawa. If spotted by radar, F-102 jet fighter interceptors would be launched to identify the fast-approaching aircraft as "friend-or-foe." The reason these flights were not very popular was due to the fact that we would have to wear the uncomfortable tight-fitting poopy suit and sit on a hard one-man life raft for three hours or more. And, after descending to 500 feet over an iceberg-infested ocean, we would be out of radio contact for almost an hour. The thought of flying a single-engine jet at low altitude over cold water dotted with icebergs made some pilots apprehensive. (I flew this type mission often and on more than one occasion I was able to reach Misawa and drop an imaginary atomic bomb without being detected.)

The anti-exposure (poopy) suit was one size fits all and required the help of an assistant to put on. It had tight-fitting rubber openings for the ankles, wrists and neck and to allow for blood circulation stainless steel rings were inserted around each wrist and neck opening. (In the event of a bailout, these rings were to be removed when descending by parachute.) Experts estimated that without the poopy suit our expected useful consciousness in the cold ocean would be approximately 15 minutes. However, wearing a poopy suit this time would be extended to around 45 minutes. (I guess the additional 30 minutes would provide sufficient time to re-enlist.) The suit was also provided with a rollout opening for urinating, but it was so long and difficult to use that you would have to be equipped like a stud horse to use it! F-102 pilots standing runway alert would plug in air conditioning hoses to keep from roasting.

An interesting phenomenon associated with these low altitude over-water flights was the feeling that the engine, quite often, would appear to be running rough. I would lean my helmet against the canopy, to act as an improvised stethoscope, and ask my colleague if he thought it sounded a little strange. However, by the time we reached landfall, or were within radio range, the engine sound would be normal!

My high spirits on being back home, and once again flying single-engine jets, were dashed when on January 14, 1963, the PGR struck again. Lieutenant Colonel Roland J. DuFresne, the new commander of the 531st TFS, was killed in a violent F-100 crash a few miles north of the base. Colonel DuFresne, whose radio call sign was **Mint 3**, was part of a three-ship flight scheduled for LABS training at the Rip Saw Range, 10 miles north of Misawa. After takeoff the flight climbed to 15,000 feet, moved into a spread formation, checked out their LABS equipment and gun sights and proceeded to the bombing range. After contacting the range officer the flight was advised of snow showers on the downwind leg for the standard left-hand pattern, so the flight leader advised that they would fly right-hand patterns. He received an acknowledgment from both aircraft regarding this transmission. After making three right-hand pattern bombing runs, the snow showers dissipated, so the flight leader advised that their next bombing run would be flown in a standard left-hand pattern. Both wingmen acknowledged this call.

During their first left-hand circuit, **Mint 3** called the flight leader and advised that he was aborting his bombing run because his LABS gyro had tumbled (failed). During his next pass, he again reported that his LABS gyro had tumbled, but a few seconds later he reported that it was working and completed a normal bomb run, but shortly after that he reported that his slave gyro was inoperative. The flight was to make one more bombing run before returning to Misawa and the flight leader reported that when he was about four miles out he heard **Mint 3** reporting that he was turning inbound toward the bombing range. He also heard him acknowledge a radio call from Mint 2, who was a few miles ahead of him. (This was the last radio call from **Mint 3**.)

After the number two aircraft completed its bombing run the range officer was expecting **Mint 3** to soon follow. When he didn't, he made a radio call requesting his position, but received no reply! The flight leader also made several radio calls which also went unanswered. A rescue helicopter was launched and a smoking crash site was located five miles east of the village of Noheji. The aircraft struck the ground at high speed in an approximate 53 degree right bank and a 30 degree dive angle. Investigation revealed that the pilot had made no attempt to jettison the canopy or eject from the aircraft. Inspection of the wreckage disclosed that when the aircraft crashed the ailerons were positioned to provide a left roll, the rudder was deflected to the right, the horizontal stabilizer was positioned for a climb and the engine was operating at full military power without afterburner. There was no evidence of a mid-air collision, in-flight fire or structural break-up, and all aircraft components inspected disclosed normal operation. We couldn't determine why the rudder was deflected 20 degrees to the right, while the aileron servos were commanding a left roll, but we all agreed that the pilot was attempting to roll the aircraft into a left climbing maneuver when it crashed.

Why a highly experienced jet fighter pilot crashed, when performing a low altitude bombing run, in good weather, could not be determined. The Aircraft Accident Investigation Board stated that the primary cause was Undetermined with a most probable cause as "flight control malfunction."

I was a member of the Aircraft Accident Investigation Board, and it was my welcome-home assignment after returning from Southeast Asia.

In February 1963 I received notice that we could move into military "on-base" housing on March 1st. This was certainly good news and it even got better when I learned that we were authorized a single unit versus an apartment. The military helped us relocate and our freshly painted house was within walking distance of my office, the Officers' Club and my daughter's school (renamed in honor of Colonel Sollars). Before I had a chance to list our off-base house for sale a young second lieutenant, who had recently joined the 416 TFS, contacted me stating that he was interested in purchasing it and wanted to know my asking price. I told him I would sell it for exactly what it cost me, $2,500. He considered it a very fair price, stating he would arrange for a loan from the credit union and present me with a check within a week, adding that he was expecting his wife to join him sometime in April. In the meantime, he would spend the time getting the house ready for her arrival, while completing his local check out in the F-100.

When several of my former off-base neighbors heard that I had sold my house for what it had cost me, they were very upset. Several contacted me and requested I reconsider the asking price, stating that there was very little land left for building additional off-base houses, which made existing homes more valuable. They thought that I should have set the asking price at $5,000 as a minimum. I told these miserly selfish greedy S.O.B.s to go to hell and that they should be ashamed of themselves for trying to make a buck off the backs of their fellow Air Force colleagues! (I was pleased to note that none of these greedy bastards were pilots or members of any of the four fighter squadrons.)

The young lieutenant's wife (they had no children) arrived in late April, and while she was unpacking, a chaplain and the lieutenant's squadron commander paid her a visit to inform her that her husband was killed in an F-100 crash! I and several others consoled her the best we could and helped her sell the house for $2,500, to a recently arrived sergeant.

The lieutenant's accident was similar to Col. DuFresne's crash, and following an extensive investigation, the primary cause was listed as Undetermined, with a possible cause of flight control malfunction. Everyone was naturally concerned about our F-100 fatal accidents, especially when a flight control malfunction was listed as a possible culprit. The 8th TFW at Itazuke Air Base, which operated three F-100 squadrons, had removed the autopilots from their aircraft, right down to the wiring and hydraulic servos. However, the 39th Air Division insisted that we retain them, which in my estimation was a mistake as none of our pilots felt confident enough to engage them at low altitudes. Our North American technical representative expressed an opinion that with the autopilot turned off, there was no way that an autopilot servo could become inadvertently engaged. However, the wing commander at Itazuke didn't adhere to this thinking, and after he had the autopilots removed from their aircraft, their undetermined crashes were history. Based on this, PACAF Headquarters in Hawaii ordered our base to remove the autopilots and our <u>Undetermined</u> accidents also ended.

Downhill skiers at Misawa formed a ski club and on several occasions traveled to the famous Japanese ski area known as Zao Onsan. It is located about halfway between Tokyo and Misawa and provided excellent snow conditions until late spring. The village adjacent to the area was built with a European Alpine atmosphere in mind and featured a western style hotel with a huge community hot bath (o-furo) facing a large heated plate-glass window. We could sit in this steamy hot tub while drinking a cold beer and look out at the snow-covered mountains. (However, even when skiing there was the off chance that the PGR was looking for an opportunity of recruiting another victim.)

Our base meteorologist took a bad spill while skiing and thought he may have twisted his ankle. He said that he was returning to the hotel to soak it in hot water and would meet us in the bar later. We stopped skiing around 4:30 p.m. and headed for the hotel bar, but our injured weather man never showed. We became concerned, so one of our members said he would go to his room to see if he was all right, but he came back a few minutes later stating that he wasn't there. We thought that he may be in the community men's bath house but he wasn't there either.

With a heightened concern several of us spread out to see if we could find him. I and a couple other club members went back to his room but he still wasn't there. We looked down the hall and noted steam coming out from underneath a door leading to a small private o-furo. Thinking he might be inside we tried to open the door, but it was locked and our knocking drew no response. A Japanese house maid, hearing our pounding, opened the door with a pass key and we discovered our missing skier laying in the hot tub unconscious, with his head just inches above the water level. We thought he might be dead as he didn't respond to slaps on his cheek or shaking, but we dragged him (naked) out into the cold hallway, threw a towel over his midsection, and started resuscitating his chest. After a minute or so he was breathing on his own and started shivering from the cold (a good sign). A little later he was sitting up and asking us what happened. He told us later that after he went back to his room, he had a couple stiff drinks and went to the private hot bath to soak his ankle. The last he remembered was that he was getting sleepy and

302

thought he would close his eyes for just a couple minutes. (His couple minutes of planned relaxation almost ended up in eternal repose, if we hadn't become concerned about him!)

On Friday afternoon, March 22, 1963, I experienced my last Close Encounter with the PGR in a T-33. I could have discussed this incident in the previous chapter, but since it occurred in Japan, I thought it appropriate to include it when discussing my life in Misawa. I was preparing to leave my office for the standard Friday evening beer call at the Officers' Club when my telephone rang. The Base Flight NCO called to inquire if I would perform a functional test flight on one of his T-33s. He said that all his assigned pilots had already left and he would like to list the aircraft as operationally ready before he left for home himself. He added that they had replaced the engine fuel control unit and all the aircraft needed was a functional check of the normal and emergency fuel system at ten and twenty thousand feet. Recognizing that it was Friday evening, he said if I was willing to fly the test hop he would have the rear seat secured, and the jet ready to go by the time I arrived. I told him, "No sweat, sarge, I'll be there in a few minutes."

I grabbed my helmet and parachute, jumped into a jeep, and headed for the T-Bird area. Mechanics assisted me in a quickie preflight and ten minutes later were helping me strap into the cockpit. The start engine and taxi for takeoff were routine and since there were no other aircraft flying, the tower cleared me for takeoff before reaching the end of the runway. I completed the Before Takeoff and Lineup Check by memory and made a rolling takeoff without stopping at the end of the runway.

The acceleration was normal and at 120 knots I rotated the nose and after becoming airborne, raised the gear at 140 knots and retracted the flaps while allowing the jet to accelerate to 240 knots. However, at around 190 knots the aircraft started vibrating and the canopy began shaking up and down. I looked at the canopy latch lever and was shocked to note that it was still in the "unlocked position." (In my rush to get airborne I neglected to lock the canopy, a stupid and potentially fatal mistake.)

I was concerned about the canopy separating from the aircraft and striking the empennage, which would render the aircraft uncontrollable. (I remembered reading about T-33 fatal accidents when their canopies separated and certainly didn't want to add my name to the list.) I pulled back on the throttle, banked into a wide downwind leg and reduced the air speed, but the canopy just kept bouncing up and down. I placed the control stick between my legs to steady the aircraft and pulled down hard on the rearview mirror with both hands, hoping to lower the canopy enough to engage the lock, but my effort was futile. I thought of climbing to a higher altitude and jettisoning the canopy, but rejected this outright! I called the control tower operator and requested an immediate landing and he wanted to know if I was declaring an emergency. I said, "**No**." (If I had declared an emergency it would have alerted the wing commander, who I'm sure was tossing down drinks at the Officers' Club and I didn't want to let him know about my dim-witted mistake.) When turning base leg I lowered the landing gear and flaps and when I slowed to around 140 knots the canopy stopped vibrating. The landing was routine and upon reaching the end of the runway, I locked the canopy, requested a downwind takeoff and was airborne minutes later.

I climbed to 10,000 feet, checked out the fuel system and repeated the check at 20,000. With the required checks completed I flew a series of aerobatic maneuvers and just enjoyed flying the T-33 solo. I entered the traffic pattern, made a normal "Martin" smooth landing and taxied back to the waiting Base Flight NCO. After shutting down the engine the sergeant asked me why I had returned after my first takeoff. I thought I could bullshit my way out of admitting an error and told him that the remote magnetic indicator (RMI) was 180 degrees out of phase and I thought I had an electrical problem, but after landing everything was normal, so I made another takeoff. "Don't bullshit me, major" the sergeant said, "You forgot to lock the canopy, but I have to assume part of the blame by rushing you to get airborne. But don't worry I won't say a word! Thanks for flying the test hop. I hope you're still in time for beer call." "Anytime sergeant," I said, and headed for the Officers' Club with an unpretentious feeling of not being such a "hot pilot," but still a live and thirsty one!

Of all the schemes the PGR employed in his efforts in inducting me into his domain, I believe the following was his most imaginative. In late March 1963, my appetite was waning and I felt bloated and was experiencing difficult bowel movements. I was sitting on a toilet in the men's room in my hangar when I felt a tickling sensation in the area of my anus. I dropped my head down between my legs to investigate, and to my shock and disbelief discovered the reason for the titillating sensation. There was a six-inch white worm, about the diameter of a shoe string, wiggling back and forth in its struggle to escape the confines of my colon. (**My first thought was that this can't be real, but indeed it was!**)

I grabbed the little bugger, still wiggling, wrapped it in a piece of toilet paper and rushed over to our base hospital. I told the administrative assistant that I needed to see a flight surgeon right away! When he asked why, I told him that it was personal, but very important! (I believe he thought I wanted to report a case of VD, so he didn't ask any further questions.) I reported my unusual rear-end tickling experience to a young doctor and showed him the specimen wrapped-up in toilet paper. His comment, "What is it major?" "You tell me, doc. You're the expert," I responded. He called in his colleague, another young "two-year-type" and they began probing the worm which had stopped moving.

The expression "two-year-type" was used to identify young doctors who had accepted government education assistance. In repayment they were committed to serving two years active duty upon graduation. This was true for physicians and dentists alike, We generally joked that they were using military personnel as guinea pigs before obtaining enough practical experience to go out into the civilian world to get rich.

Still mystified in the specimen, they started leafing through the pages of a medical journal and transferred the worm to a slide under a microscope. (I felt like a bystander watching two medical students preparing for a final exam, as they seemed more interested in the parasite than their patient.) Finally, after several minutes, one of the doctors said to his colleague, "By golly, I believe it's a beef tapeworm. What do you think?" The other doctor said, "You know, I believe your right. Very interesting!"

I hated to interrupt their euphoria in discovering something new, but was getting a little anxious, so in an inquisitive tone of voice I said, "Will one of you highly learned doctors tell me what in the hell is going on?" With that they became very considerate, and started asking me questions in relation to where I may have eaten improperly cooked or tainted beef in the last several months. I told them about my TDY in Southeast Asia and my "Mongolian Beef Barbecue" dinner in Chiang Mai, Thailand. They both agreed that this was most likely where I had picked up my tape worm.

The beef tapeworm (Taenia Saginate) is the most common of the big tapeworms that parasitically attacks humans and is contracted from infected raw or rare beef. The worm can grow up to 12 to 25 feet long in the intestine, which it latches onto and feeds from. It is made up of small white segments which can grow at the rate of six inches per day. It tends to block bowel movements, produce abdominal pain and nausea. (All the symptoms I experienced.) About ten or more segments are passed each day in feces or in just seeking escape by crawling out the anus. If not killed, it will eventually take over and kill its host. According to the doctors it is difficult to get rid of and the procedure is quite painful.

After their diagnosis I was weighed and briefed on what I must do to rid my body of my "Thai hitchhiker." The doctors prescribed a strong liquid toxin, in a dosage amount based on my body weight. They said that when I drank it, I would become very sick, but hopefully it would be strong enough to kill the parasite but not me. Thirty minutes after swallowing the poison, I was to take a strong laxative which would force a bowel movement, and if the tape worm was dead it would be discharged from my body. They issued me a bedpan and requested I bring the liberated worm back to them for inspection. They emphasized that it was important that we obtain the head of the worm, or it may reappear. Their last bit of instruction was that before taking the medication I was not to eat or drink for 24 hours and not allow myself to go to sleep after taking the poison. When I left with my medicine and bedpan the two young doctors were still reviewing a medical textbook and talking about their most interesting day since graduating from medical school.

Following a 24-hour fast, I drank the bottle of toxin and within a few minutes I felt like I was going to die. I experienced severe stomach cramps along with spasms of shooting pain throughout my entire body. If my beef tapeworm was feeling half as bad as I was, I thought it would surely call it quits and just give up and accept a dignified death. I endured the agony induced by the toxin for the required 30 minutes and then headed for the bathroom with the bedpan. I swallowed the two large laxative capsules and in a matter of minutes felt the need for a bowel movement. Sitting on the bedpan I ejected whatever was in my bowels and colon with a wind breaking explosive force. I looked back into the bedpan and there, coiled up, was a white segmented tape worm at least 20 feet long. It was hard to believe that this organism had been living and growing inside my body for the last three months, but there it was in all its gruesome detestable form. I felt so good in getting rid of it that I mentally formulated a headline for the Misawa base newspaper. I thought it should read: **"Air Force major conquers a 20-foot-long beef tapeworm, with the assistance of two local Misawa flight surgeons."**

I covered the bedpan with a piece of Saran Wrap and rushed it over to the "two-year-type" doctors. Looking down into the bedpan the lead doctor said, "Amazing, simply amazing! We will rinse the specimen off, and examine it. Hopefully we got its head. Go home and have a well cooked meal major, you've had a hard day." However, after seeing what I discharged from my body, I wasn't very hungry. (Forty-five years later, I still quiver with repulsion when I think about my Thailand freeloader.)

In April 1963 Misawa Air Base received two T-39 *Sabreliners* to augment our fleet of T-33s. They were to be utilized for pilot proficiency training, annual instrument checks, administrative support and flying high and low level tracking missions for our F-102 fighter interceptors. I was one of several Misawa pilots selected to check out in this unique aircraft.

The T-39 was the Air Force version of the North American Rockwell's twin-engine jet executive aircraft. It's first flight was on September 16, 1958 and shortly thereafter the Air Force ordered 149. It had a wing span of 44 feet, a maximum takeoff weight of 17,760 pounds, a cruise speed of 500 mph, a range of nearly 2,000 miles, an altitude ceiling of more than 40,000 feet and a remarkable single engine cruise altitude of 20,000 feet. It would accommodate four passengers and two pilots, and was powered by two Pratt & Whitney 3,000 pound thrust engines. Production costs were $810,000, or approximately $5,602,200 today. (See Photo No. 46.)

The T-39 was a pleasure to fly, but during my first few flights it felt very strange not to be wearing a helmet (hard hat) and having an oxygen mask strapped to my face. (In fact I felt somewhat undressed.) The cockpit was very quiet and there was no problem in conversing with the other pilot in a normal tone of voice. Soon after checking out in the *Sabreliner* I would be flying proficiency flights, transporting F-100 pilots to and from Kunsan Air Base, Korea, and faker missions simulating encroaching Soviet Union bombers. Being a twin-engine aircraft there was no requirement to wear the uncomfortable poopy suit, a welcome change.

On high altitude faker missions I would fly about 300 miles north of Misawa, turn off the transponder (a device that transmits a response to ground radar), climb to 35,000 feet and fly back toward Misawa. I would be on the same radio frequency that ground based radar controllers were using in directing F-102 jet fighters, and would hear them state, "Buster climb to angles 35, heading 350, bogey 150 miles," (meaning use afterburner to 35,000 feet, fly a heading of 350 degrees, unidentified aircraft 150 miles). We knew that the F-102s would struggle to climb above 40,000 feet when fully loaded, and the T-39, with more thrust than an F-86L, and with just two pilots onboard could easily climb to 45,000 feet or higher. When the F-102s were about 50 miles out, we would start climbing and by the time they were within range to fire their simulated missiles, we would be well above 40,000 feet, forcing them to struggle to get within firing range. We thought we were providing realistic evasive training for the fighters while at the same time enjoying a game of "cat-and-mouse," but the F-102 pilots, not being able to simulate the firing of their missiles, were not able to log a successful combat mission. The wing commander, hearing about our out climbing the F-102s, issued an order stating that we would no longer climb when being intercepted by the fighters. (We wondered if he was issuing the same instructions to Soviet Union bomber pilots. However, to be fair, it should be noted that if the F-102s were intercepting real hostile aircraft, they would jettison their external drop tanks and the Soviet bombers would be toast.)

I also flew a T-39 to Saigon with stops in Kadena, Okinawa and Clark Field in the Philippines. On the return leg to Clark we lost all radios and made a descent through the clouds at our Estimated Time of Arrival (ETA). But in spite of following the rules, the base operations officer gave us hell for not contacting the control tower before landing. On the en route leg back to Misawa there was a line of thunderstorms around the Tokyo area and we climbed to 51,000 feet, but still couldn't top some of the granddaddy thunderstorms. However, the performance of the *Sabreliner* was really impressive. This was the highest I had ever been in an aircraft and noted that the sky was starting to darken. We stayed at this altitude for some time to be able to enjoy the experience.

I also flew the T-39 to Kadena Air Base, Okinawa to engage in competition skeet shoots. A colleague pilot, my NCOIC Sgt. Moon, Sgt. Hart (the personal equipment NCO) and his colleague and I would load our shotguns into the aircraft and three hours later would be in Okinawa. On one such flight we were preparing to depart when we observed a lot of excitement around the base operations area. We soon learned that we had lost another F-100 and pilot, from Undetermined causes just north of Misawa. We stood by while the rescue helicopter took off and didn't have to wait long before it returned with medics carrying a body bag into the flight line dispensary area. We naturally felt bad and weren't sure if we should cancel our flight, but knew that if we did, it wouldn't help the unfortunate young lieutenant who had just died. We discussed it for a while when I noted our wing commander, Col. Davenport, standing off to the side. I told my waiting skeet shooting partners that I would go talk to the colonel and ask him what he thought we should do. I told him that we were about to depart on a flight to Okinawa, when we heard about the accident, and wanted to know if we should cancel our flight. In answering he said, "There is no need to cancel your plans, major. We don't need the T-39, and the best thing we can do to honor the lieutenant is to carry on. That is exactly what he would want us to do. Have a nice flight!"

On Saturday, June 8, 1963, we were celebrating my 35th birthday with cake, ice cream and too many candles. My wife and 11-year-old daughter had baked a large cake and with the help of my three-year-old son Mike, had decorated the house to commemorate the occasion, but unfortunately I had lost my appetite and was feeling abdominal pains. I was worried that my beef tapeworm had returned, but didn't want to embrace the thought or ruin the party. However, the next day my worst fears were realized when I felt another worm wiggling its way to freedom from the confines of my colon. (Apparently it didn't care for the birthday cake and ice cream I had consumed the day before.)

I pulled out a five-inch squirming specimen, wrapped it in toilet paper, and headed back to the base hospital. When I showed it to the two young doctors, now beef tapeworm experts, they expressed disappointment in the fact that the parasite had returned, but I sensed that secretly they actually enjoyed the challenge of treating something more complicated than common colds on relatively young healthy Air Force personnel. They examined the section of worm I brought and agreed that it was a sibling of what I had encountered three months earlier. They said that they had pickled the other worm in a bottle of formaldehyde and asked if I wanted to see it. I declined, stating that I had already seen it, in its natural repulsive state.

The diagnosis was that during the first eradication treatment I had failed in killing the worm's head, which contains the tiny suction cups which latch onto the intestinal tract, thereby allowing it to grow back. The plan of attack this time was to repeat the previous treatment, but with modifications: first, the amount of orally-administered toxin would be increased and I was requested to allow it to stay in my system a minimum of 45 minutes; secondly, I was requested to fast for 30 hours instead of 24; third, I was issued a mild laxative to take right away, with the goal of ensuring my colon was empty before taking the poison. I left the hospital with the familiar bedpan and went home to do battle, once again, with my Thai repugnant foe with the hope of killing it this time.

Thirty hours later I drank the liquid toxin and battling severe stomach pains and a feeling of vomiting, watched the clock run down to 45 minutes. I then retreated to the bathroom, took the strong laxative and in a few minutes ejected another 15 to 20 foot long white segmented worm. Once again I wrapped the pan in plastic and made tracks for the hospital. My doctors were waiting for me, and as I presented them the bedpan I said, "Hi Doc, I have another candidate for your formaldehyde specimen jars. Now you'll each have one of your very own."

They congratulated me for going through the painful treatment for the second time and said that after the worm was cleaned off and examined they would give me a call. The next day the doctor called and said he was positive that the head was ejected and hopefully my "beef tapeworm battle" was history. Stool samples confirmed that the parasite was in worm heaven, and I have never eaten rare or raw beef since. (During this entire painful experience a thought raced through my mind relating to a popular commercial which states, "I should have used preparation H." However, I don't think it would have discouraged the tapeworm from setting up housekeeping in my colon!)

By the time the snow and cold winds of January 1964 started buffeting, the base the Periodic Maintenance Branch was becoming a desirable place to work. Not only did it allow mechanics to work in a warm inside environment, but because our On Time reliability rate was close to 95 percent they were off duty most weekends. Based on this, I maintained a long list of outside flight line mechanics, who wished to escape the rigors of the harsh Northern Japan winter weather, and volunteered to join their colleagues in working inside our PMB heated hangar.

My NCO, Sergeant Moon, and I had worked very hard in improving the esprit de corps and satisfying the real and imagined needs of our aircraft mechanics. But it appeared that our enthusiasm in creating a contented working environment was, in some sense, coming back to bite us. Working conditions had become so relaxed that a few of my dock chiefs were taking advantage of their newly found independence and forming an autonomy that was not conducive to overall cohesiveness, so essential in the event we had to go to war. I figured I had to do something to reverse this trend, reinstate good military discipline, but without destroying the good will and esprit de corps we worked so hard to achieve. (The solution to our problem came about unexpectedly one cold windy day in January.)

My RF-101 dock chief and his six mechanics were off duty since their maintenance dock was empty. It had been my policy that if a crew did not have an aircraft to work on, they were allowed to stay home or attend some form of military training. This policy was well received by the men and met my goal of not having mechanics standing around with nothing to do. The deputy commander for material, Colonel Lou Cole, came by my office and noting that one of my RF-101 docks was empty inquired if they could perform a 100-hour inspection on an F-100. I told the colonel no problem, but since they were not thoroughly familiar with the *Super Sabre*, I would like to allow them four days to complete the inspection versus the normal three. He agreed, shook my hand and returned to his own office. I told my clerk to tell Sgt. Moon that I would like to see him.

I told Hank about my agreement with Col. Cole, and he thought it made good sense and would contact the dock chief and have him and his crew report for work the following morning. A few minutes later he came back and said that when he informed the dock chief that he was to perform an inspection on an F-100, he said that they only work on RF-101s.

I picked up the telephone and called my boss, Lt.Col. Ken Rassmusen. I briefly told him about my RF-101 dock mechanics' refusal to work on an F-100 and requested he immediately transfer seven qualified line mechanics I had on my volunteer list to the Periodic Maintenance Branch. In return, I would transfer the seven recalcitrant RF-101 mechanics to the flight line. I stressed that this was necessary to maintain good military discipline without resorting to a messy court-martial of a group of men, who in spite of their momentary lapse of good judgment, were excellent workers. He agreed and a couple hours later I had seven new mechanics chucking their winter parkas and reporting for work in our warm hangar.

I then had Sgt. Moon issue a direct order to the militant RF-101 dock chief directing that he and his men report to my office the following morning. When they arrived they were surprised to see their tool boxes and personal items in a pile next to my office and seven new mechanics working on a F-100 in their former dock. When they asked me for an explanation, my answer was simple and direct, "Sergeant, you and your men do not decide when and where you work. That decision is mine and Sergeant Moon's. As of today you and your men are being reassigned to the flight line. I would suggest that before reporting for work you go by supply and check out winter parkas, warm gloves, boots and long underwear. You're dismissed!" Following this unpleasant but necessary episode, the individual independence that was starting to creep into our unit disappeared and a spirit of cooperation was once more prevalent. (Sgt. Moon and I could now spend more time shooting skeet!)

On Friday, January 27, 1964, at around 3:30 p.m., the PGR discovered a very bizarre method of drafting two more aviation support personnel into his formidable domain. I was sitting at my desk when I heard a muffled explosion which rattled the windows and shook my desk. My first thought was that some young fighter jock had exceeded the speed of sound over the base and if the wing commander found out who it was his ass would be toast. A couple minutes later I received a telephone call from the deputy commander for material, who asked me if I had heard and felt the recent explosion. When I said that I did, he responded with, "There was a big external fuel tank explosion in the Fuel System Tank Repair Shop. Get right over there and see what happened, as you have been selected as the officer in charge of the investigation. Keep me posted."

The Tank Repair Shop was located in the southeast corner of a large hangar shared with the Engine Propulsion Branch and about 300 feet from my office. By the time I reached the scene fire trucks and ambulances had already arrived and air policemen were roping off the area to keep back curious spectators. The windows surrounding the Fuel Tank Repair Shop were all blown out and smoke was drifting out through the openings. An air policeman attempted to stop me from entering the building, but when I identified myself he allowed me to proceed as he had been informed that I was charged with investigating the accident.

When I entered the interior of the disaster area I wasn't prepared for the amount of destruction that had occurred. Work benches were scattered about, sheet rock for about 50 feet was in small pieces, bare wires were hanging down where ceiling lights had been, steel personnel lockers were caved in, and there were two bodies covered with white sheets laying off to one side. Several other workers were burned, but were able to escape the area unaided and were being treated by medics. Workers who escaped injury were blackened from smoke and shaking their heads in attempting to restore lost hearing. I stood there, in the middle of the destruction for a few seconds, while asking myself where do I start in investigating the accident? However I quickly realized that the only person who could answer that question was me and standing around thinking about it wouldn't get the job done!

The fuel System Tank Repair Shop was responsible for cleaning and repairing external fuel (drop tanks) for F-100s, RF-101s and F-102s. Fuel tanks of various capacity were transported to the shop for routine cleaning and repair of fuel shutoff valves and quantity indicating systems. Fuel tanks awaiting cleaning or repair were stored both outside and inside the shop depending on storage space available.

Three days before the explosion a 450-gallon drop tank was removed from an F-100 and transported to the shop to repair a quantity indicating system. However, the tank still contained small amounts of residual fuel. The standard procedure, before moving a fuel tank inside, was to partially disassemble it, purge it with steam, and perform a fuel vapor concentration check with an Explosimeter. But, for unknown reasons, none of these precautionary safety measures were performed. The tank was moved directly into the heated shop where dangerous fuel vapors were allowed to mature.

Three days later, a fuel system mechanic, Mr. Aoki, started working on it and decided to test a "jury-rigged" electrical tester he was designing for the checking of fuel shutoff valves. The makeshift tool consisted of eight 1.5 Volt D flashlight batteries taped together in series and was a prototype suggestion he was planning on submitting for evaluation. When he connected the wires from his "home-made-tester" to the fuel tank electrical leads, it ignited the accumulated fuel vapors and a terrific explosion followed, killing him, his assistant Mr. Higoshi, and severely burned Mr. Takahashi. I interviewed Takahashi, bandaged from head to toe, in the hospital who told me, through an interpreter, that Mr. Aoki had tested his invention on other tanks in the past, but obviously all of them had been purged of residual fuel. This was a sad accident that resulted in the PGR gaining two more recruits, injured many others and destroyed a lot of valuable property. The accident could have easily been avoided if simple safety procedures had been followed.

In February 1964, I was 90 days from my rotation date back to the U.S. and had mixed emotions regarding a continued assignment with Tactical Air Command. My impression of several high ranking officers whom I had served with during the last three years was that they were more interested in saving their own ass then in fulfilling the Air Force mission. I already discussed their attempt to fire my F-102 dock chief, Sgt. Thomas, the court-martial of one of my young mechanics and instructing us not to climb our T-39s during practice intercepts by F-102s, but there were other examples worth noting. The 39th Air Division Commander held a daily 3 p.m. "stand-up briefing" in the command bunker we called the "Mole-Hole." The briefing included an update on the operational status of our aircraft and as a casual observer, I had witnessed the fudging of status reports intended to please the general and allowing the reporting officials to "save face." One day I was sent to represent the maintenance organization at the briefing and presented a true aircraft status report. The general quizzed me extensively on the information I presented and I answered all his questions truthfully. When the deputy commander of material and the chief of maintenance heard about my briefing performance, word went out that I was never again to be allowed to represent our organization at the general's daily briefing.

One Saturday afternoon I was conducting a safety walk-through of my hangar when I observed Major Jack Jolly, the OIC of the Field Maintenance Shop, standing next to my office. Jack was an old ski buddy from Germany and had been a major for many years. We exchanged greetings and were engaging in small talk when Major Edwin Henely, a pilot classmate who worked in the chief pilot's Office, walked over and joined us. My German colleague, in a friendly tone of voice, said, "Hey, Lou, how about calling in some of your off-duty troops to give me a hand in field maintenance?" "Like hell," I said, "if you can't run your shop efficiently don't expect me to save your ass." With that I walked into my office to check on a few things before heading home. My phone rang and my boss, Lt.Col. Rassmussen, said that he had to see me right away! His office was a short walk from my hangar and when I entered he said, "Lou, you're in a lot of trouble. Major Ed Henley is going to recommend you be court-martialed for insubordination to a senior officer, namely the comments you made to Major Jolly, the OIC of the Field Maintenance Shop when he asked you for assistance."

I couldn't believe what I was hearing, but was not totally surprised. I told my boss that before he makes a fool of himself he should call the Major I supposedly showed disrespect to and ask him if he wishes to press charges. He called my old German ski buddy who said he thought the whole idea of a court-martial was ridiculous. He told my boss that Lou Martin and he were old friends from Germany, had belonged to the same ski club and often snapped back and forth at each other in jest. When he asked to have some of my men come in to help him in his shop, my answer was exactly what he expected and had I asked him for help he would have responded in the same offhand manner. (Case closed.)

I had also been critical of the base security system and reported that it was in many respects just a charade, designed to make people feel good, and wouldn't stop intruders striving to penetrate the system, but my comments went unheeded! When it was my turn to perform the duty as the monthly base security inspector, I figured it was my chance to prove what I was saying was true. However, I didn't want to be handcuffed and hauled off to jail by over zealous security guards, so when I made my inspections I had my NCO follow me around carrying a copy of my special orders and my security badge. Excerpts of some of the comments that appeared in my report to the Inspector General were:

Aircraft line maintenance personnel displayed a complete lack of security awareness. They allowed an unfamiliar airman (directed by me) to freely roam the restricted ramp area, ask questions and exit without being challenged or apprehended. During his time on the ramp he did not wear or display a security badge.

Security at the Air Division Command Center "Mole-Hole" is a farce, as I was allowed to enter without displaying proper identification. I waited outside and walked in with a group of officers, while carrying a briefcase and giving the appearance that I knew what I was doing.

I was allowed to enter three different alert pads by displaying a security badge issued to my NCOIC, who is a chief master sergeant, and whose physical appearance and rank did not match mine in any form.

After my report was submitted, I heard by the grapevine that I would no longer be assigned the duty of security inspector!

During an Operational Readiness Inspection (ORI), when we were supposed to be simulating actual combat conditions, I was assigned line duties to expedite the quick turnaround of F-100s. I noted that a flight of four fighters that had recently landed were sitting idle on the ramp with no mechanics working on them. I located the master sergeant in charge and asked him what in the hell was going on. He told me that it was lunch time and he had sent his people to chow! I told him, "Sergeant, get on your bicycle, or jeep, and get those men back here right now to turnaround these aircraft. We are supposedly at war and the mess hall is open 24 hours, so your men can eat when the aircraft are flying. Now get your ass in gear!" He got his men back, and the aircraft were refueled, rearmed and ready to go by the time the next group of pilots showed up. But about 30 minutes later I was told to report to Colonel Rassmussen. He began chastising me for mistreating enlisted men by not allowing them to eat. He said that he was considering court-martial charges! My response to this stupid statement was, "Colonel, your insinuation is a bunch of bull shit and I don't have time to stand around and discuss it, as I have jet fighters to attend to!" I walked out of his office, returned to the flight line, and never heard another word about mistreating enlisted men.

During another ORI we lacked one additional operationally-ready F-100 to meet our war time goal of 80% in commission. There was a *Super Sabre* in my hangar that was close to being returned to the flight line and if we could move it out within the next hour we would meet our objective, and all eyes were focused on my mechanics in their anxiety to complete the last few remaining inspection items. Everything was humming along smoothly and it appeared we would roll the aircraft out with time to spare. However, just before I was about to inform maintenance control that the aircraft could be considered in-commission a mechanic came to my office and informed me that they had discovered a "popped rivet" adjacent to an internal fuel cell. Before they could declare the aircraft safe for flight, the rivet head would have to be retrieved. Otherwise vibration might puncture the fuel cell. I relayed this information to maintenance control, telling them to hold off on declaring the aircraft "operationally ready."

A few minutes later, Colonel Cole, the deputy commander for material, stormed into my house, slammed his hat down on my desk and snorted, "God Damnit, Martin, if we fail to meet our ORI goal it will be the result of you being a piss-poor supervisor of inept mechanics!" (He gave no thought to the fact that the popped rivet was due to a manufacture defect, not my mechanics.) He continued to rant and rave while blabbering irrelevant bull shit like, "For the want of a nail a horseshoe was lost, for the want of a horseshoe a horse was lost, for the want of a horse a battle was lost," and so-on. While he was going through this outburst, which was going in one ear and out the other, I was observing my mechanics through my second floor office window, working on retrieving the popped rivet. A tall thin mechanic, who had stripped down to his waist, was reaching his long bare arm into the fuselage of the F-100. With a big smile he retracted his scratched arm and proudly displayed the rivet head to a cheering group of colleagues. While he was holding up the rivet head, like an "Academy Award Oscar," the aircraft crew chief was giving me a thumbs-up signal. I turned to the colonel, who was still babbling about my inefficiency and horseshoe nails, and told him to turnaround so he could see the critical operationally-ready F-100 being towed out to the flight line. He shrugged his shoulders in a condescending manner, plopped his hat back on his head and stormed out of my office. As he left, he turned around and snarled, "You're damn lucky, Martin. That's all I got to say!"

Another area of concern was the approach my superiors observed when submitting Officer Effectiveness Reports (OERS). The report contained five specific rating columns (one through five) plus a comment section. It was an accepted practice, within most Air Force commands, that if the officer's performance was above average his ratings would be in columns four or five. It was recognized that this philosophy resulted in inflated ratings, but if not followed the officer stood little chance of being promoted. However, my rating officials in Misawa decided to fight the system, by asserting that all officers are expected to perform in an exceptional manner, so therefore a rating in the middle column is a good rating. The problem with this stupid philosophical approach was that the officers selected for promotion were made by a board of senior officers in Washington, and all they had to work with were the OERs submitted by the various commands. (I was concerned that my effectiveness reports, from Misawa, although submitted with the best of intentions, would result in me being passed-over for LT. Col. This is exactly what happened and I'll discuss how I overcame this obstacle in the next chapter.)

In the spring of 1964 it was common knowledge that the F-100 squadrons at Misawa would be transferred to England Air Force Base, Alexandria, Louisiana. It was also well-known that I, and my F-100 Aircraft Maintenance Officer colleagues, would be sent there as well. After some soul searching, I decided that I was ready for a new assignment and wished to return to the cockpit. I had four years before being eligible for retirement and was hoping for a civilian flying job after leaving the Air Force. I therefore felt a return to transports would be in my best interest.

The Lockheed C-141, a four-engine jet transport, was about to enter the Air Force inventory and would replace the C-130s based at McGuire AFB, New Jersey and Travis AFB, California so I sent a letter to my former wing commander, Joseph Cunningham, now a major general, requesting he use his influence in securing me an assignment flying turboprop transports on the East Coast. (I figured if he was able to help me in obtaining this position, I would soon be flying a four-engine jet transport and would have several thousand hours in it by the time I retired and would be in a good position for a civilian flying job.)

Almost by return mail I received a letter from General Cunningham, informing me that he had spoken to a colleague in the Pentagon and my next assignment would be as a Douglas C-133 *Cargomaster* pilot with the 39th Military Airlift Squadron at Dover Air Force Base, Delaware. This well-intended support was not what I had in mind. I was hoping to be assigned to C-130s, plus the C-133 had a ignomious reputation as a number of them had disappeared, with no trace, when flying over the Atlantic and Pacific Oceans.

I sent another letter to General Cunningham, thanking him for his help, but explained that I was seeking an assignment to C-130s not C-133s and wanted to know if he could help in making this change. His quick response stated, "Lou, you asked me to help you in obtaining an assignment flying turboprop transports on the East Coast and I did exactly what you asked. The C-133 is a four-engine turboprop and Dover AFB is on the East Coast! I don't feel it would be prudent for me to go back to my friends and request another change. The C-133s are in need of experienced pilots and I'm sure your expertise will be put to good use. Good luck and stay in touch." The general was right and it was my fault by not specifying C-130s instead of just stating "turboprops."

As I prepared to depart Misawa, I reflected back on my very interesting tour of duty. Many of the problems first beset the F-100 were now corrected, but it cost far too many pilots and aircraft in achieving this goal. We lost around 13 F-100s during my tour in Misawa, while experiencing zero pilot error losses in the F-102 or RF-101 fleets, which were equipped with nearly identical engines. Fleet-wise, over 500 F-100s were lost in accidents between 1956 and 1970. Many of them were due to pilot error as the aircraft was somewhat unforgiving when compared to earlier jet fighters. Pilots had to take note of the fighters' inherent odious personality during low altitude, high G maneuvers and during landing to avoid its dangerous adverse-yaw tendency. It was unfortunate that large numbers of F-100s were allowed to enter operational squadrons before many potential critical deficiencies were corrected. However, by the late 1960s the F-100 was becoming a reliable close air support fighter, and by 1967 only five squadrons remained in the U.S., with most of the rest transferred to Vietnam where it proved itself in actual combat.

Bases operating F-100s in South Vietnam were: Bien Hoa, Phan Rang, Phu Cat and Tuy Hoa. During its use in Vietnam, there were a total of 243 aircraft lost. (198 charged to combat and 45 to accidents.) From July 1964 to November 1968 the Air Force Thunderbird flight demonstration team operated the F-100D. However, during an air show at Laughlin AFB in Texas on October 21, 1967, Captain Merrill McPeak's F-100 disintegrated in midair during a solo high speed pass. Fortunately he was able to eject safely. The accident was the result of wing cracks due to metal fatigue. Some Vietnam combat losses were thought to be the result of similar failures and all F-100s were temporarily restricted to 4-G maneuvers until a modification of the wing structural box was completed. Following their withdrawal from Vietnam in 1970, many F-100s were transferred to Air National Guard squadrons and remained in service until 1979.

Air Systems Inc., located in Mojave Airport, California, operated a combination of remote-controlled and pilot-controlled F Models as target drones. Under contract they operated seven pilot-controlled F-100Fs in Germany, towing Delmar targets for German Luftwaffe pilots flying Tornadoes. When working in Germany I had an opportunity for one more flight in the back seat of an F-100 in 1993. I was allowed to make the takeoff but didn't think the jet demonstrated the engine thrust that I was accustomed to. To explain this difference in power the pilot told me that to preserve engine life the engines were de-rated since they were flying the aircraft at a reduced weight.

Unfortunately, the following year a retired F-100 pilot in his early sixties and thousands of hours in the aircraft was killed when returning to their Luftwafle base after completing a tow-target mission. I believe he was the last pilot who met the PGR in a *Super Sabre*.

On Thursday, May 21, 1964, my family and I departed Misawa on a C-47 courier flight to Tachikawa Air Base, followed by a chartered Canadian CL-44 four-engine Turbo-prop transport flight to Travis AFB, California, with an en route refueling stop in Anchorage, Alaska. When in Alaska, the devastation caused by the 1964 earthquake was still visible.

Chapter Eleven --- Douglas C-133 Cargomaster

After arriving at Travis AFB, I picked up my Plymouth *Valiant* (which had been shipped earlier) and started our long drive east to visit my family and friends in Ladysmith, Wisconsin and my in-laws in Toledo, Ohio. When in Ladysmith I stepped on a broken glass bottle when assisting my brother Hank launch his small speed boat and nearly severed the big toe on my right foot. Hank drove me to the emergency room of the local hospital where Doctor Pagel, a WW II vet, stitched it up without the use of anesthetics. He said that he had to stop the bleeding right away and couldn't wait for a sedative to numb my foot. (My personal opinion was that he wanted to return home before his dinner got cold.) The injury limited my vacation activity and I had to modify a canvas shoe with a wooden sole to be able to drive. After a brief stay in Ohio, we continued on to Dover Air Force Base, Delaware, arriving on Friday June 26, 1964.

There were two C-133 Military Airlift Squadrons assigned to Dover, the 1st and 39th. I was assigned to the 39th, commanded by Lt.Col. Hank Wurster, a jolly likable father-like figure. Within a few days after reporting for duty I was enrolled in a eight week C-133 *Cargomaster* pilot transition course. I still had mixed feelings about flying an aircraft with such an ignominious reputation. However I figured it would provide its own unique form of excitement, but I didn't know to what extent until some time later.

Following the end of the Korean War Intercontinental Ballistic Missiles (ICBMs) were beginning to supplement long-range bombers as our Cold War deterrent weapon. To support this new weapons system, and related balky military cargo, a large-capacity transport aircraft was essential. Lockheed and Boeing aircraft companies had nothing to offer, as they were engrossed in developing jet transports, but Douglas was working on a large four-engine turboprop transport with the designation C-133 Cargomaster. The DOD decided that this was exactly what they needed and ordered 50 on a fast-track production program. The order called for 32 A models and 18 modified B models capable of airlifting large ICBMs. The C-133 had a 180 ft. wingspan, carried 18,000 gallons of fuel, cruised at more than 300 mph, was powered by four turbo-jet engines of 7,500 hp each, equipped with 18-foot diameter Curtis-Electric propellers, had a maximum weight of 275,000 lbs, a 90 ft. long cargo bay and cost $10,000.000 ($72,727,630 today). (See Photos 50 and 51.)

The C-133 made its initial flight on April 23, 1956 and was flying with operational squadrons 16 months later. It was the largest transport flying at the time and was a featured aircraft at a Paris Airshow. In 1958, a C-133 set a nonstop transatlantic record by flying 80,000 lbs. of cargo to France, and in the same year, another record was established by lifting 118,000 lbs. to 10,000 feet. The first round-the-world flight of three Cargomasters took place in 1959, and aircrews selected to fly this new Giant of the Sky walked tall and proud. During the Vietnam War the C-133 was an integral part of heavy combat airlift support, carrying cargo loads that would not fit in the C-141 or C-124. A standard load was airlifting five UH-1 Huey helicopters directly into combat zones and returning battle-damaged ones to overhaul depots in the U.S. Other missions included transporting armored equipment and ammunition into combat areas in support of key battle campaigns. However, before the aircraft became a reliable transport it experienced many Unexplained fatal accidents, which resulted in the Air Force questioning its future role. (Note: Readers interested in learning more about this unique aircraft should read Cal Taylor's, Remembering an Unsung Giant, available at: Firstfleet Publishers, 2154 Beverly Beach Dr. NW, Olympia, WA 98502 .)

On April 13, 1958, a C-133, commanded by Captain Raymond R. Bern, crashed and burned in an inverted attitude 17 minutes after departing Dover AFB, Delaware. All four crew members were killed. The cause of the accident was Undetermined, but it was thought that the aircraft entered a stall and rolled inverted at an altitude too low to recover.

On June 9, 1961, a C-133, commanded by Major Lawrence J. Ceretti, disappeared over the Pacific Ocean 30 minutes after takeoff from Tachikawa, Air Base Japan. Only floating debris was recovered. Eight crew members were killed and their remains were never found. The cause of the accident was Undetermined.

On May 27, 1962, a C-133, commanded by Lt. James A. Higgins, disappeared over the Atlantic Ocean 32 minutes after departing Dover AFB, Delaware, en route to Lajes Air Base, Azores. The aircraft was cleared to 17,000 feet by New York Center but 50 seconds later disappeared from radar. A life raft and nose gear assembly were the only *pieces of the aircraft recovered, but the remains of the six crew members were not found. The cause of the accident was <u>Undetermined</u>.*

On April 10, 1963, a C-133, commanded by Major Roy M. Johnston, crashed near Travis AFB, California. The aircraft went down while executing a low altitude circling instrument approach. Nine crew members were lost and their bodies burned beyond recognition. The cause of the accident was <u>Undetermined</u>. (Ironically, killed in this accident were two young second lieutenant navigators, who volunteered for the flight to qualify for their monthly four hours hazardous duty flight pay.)

On September 22, 1963, a C-133, commanded by Captain Dudley J. Connolly, disappeared from radar over the Atlantic Ocean 28 minutes after takeoff from Dover AFB. No trace of the aircraft or the ten crew members were found. The cause of the accident was <u>Undetermined</u>.

On November 12, 1963, a C-133, commanded by Major Burnett, experienced an in-flight stall following a night takeoff from Etain Air Base, France. After leveling off at 10,000 feet at an airspeed of 160 knots, the aircraft shuddered and went into a 45 degree right bank. The alert pilot pushed forward on the control column and went to full power, but the uncontrolled rolling movement continued. When the bank angle approached a dangerous 90 degrees, he extended the flaps to 15 degrees and after one more shudder, aircraft control was regained. Major Burnett, faced with an unprecedented emergency, canceled his flight to Lages Field, Azores and diverted to Chatereaux Air Base, France. He left the flaps at 15 degrees and performed controllability checks at 10,000 feet and 140 knots, before making an uneventful landing. The cause of the in-flight problem was <u>Undetermined</u>, Burnett's incident and his preventative stall actions, were included in the emergency section of the pilot's flight manual. His cool head and quick action saved him and his crew from becoming a C-133 statistic and new recruits for the PGR.

Armed with these alarming statistics, I wondered if I had made a potential calamitous mistake in petitioning General Cunningham to assist me in obtaining a turboprop assignment on the East Coast of the U.S. but it was too late to dwell on the past! So I accepted my assignment as just another interesting chapter in my expanding aviation career, while hoping that I would be able to broaden it while at the same time manage to avoid the PGR's clutches in spite of the fact that it appeared he may have found fertile ground in the C-133 Cargomaster.

The first four weeks of the transition course consisted of ground school, with the final four weeks a combination of simulator and aircraft transition flights. When I first met my flight instructor, he asked me what type of aircraft I had been flying in Japan. When I told him the T-33, F-100 and T-39, he said, "You may have a problem flying the C-133 Lou, as it has a 180 foot wingspan." I responded, "I promise never to taxi through an area less than 181 feet." The subject was dropped! My first flight in the giant Douglas *Cargomaster* was on July 14, 1964, which introduced me to one of the many surprises I would encounter when flying this four-engine behemoth. The first one was that the crew entrance door was located on the right side of the aircraft!

When the U.S. Army first considered adding aircraft to their military units in 1908, commanders had to decide if the pilots would enter the cockpit from the right or left side. However, since the majority of the early pilots were cavalry officers, who mounted their horses on the left, it was axiomatic that they enter the aircraft cockpit on the left side as well. This tradition has been followed throughout the years and 99% of aircraft, both military and civilian, have their entrance doors on the left side.

When I asked my flight instructor why the C-133 crew entrance door was on the right side, since we mount horses on the left, he said, "Douglas Aircraft engineers don't ride horses, but more importantly, there is a large hydraulically-operated cargo door on the aircraft's left side, which left no room for a crew entrance door. So, at the risk of offending horse lovers, they put the crew entrance door on the right side." Since, I was no longer riding horses, nor wearing spurs, I ignored this break from tradition and entered the aircraft on the right side with my instructor.

After flying small jet aircraft I felt like I was flying an ocean liner or hotel with wings, but surprisingly it was quite maneuverable when you exerted the right amount of movement and force on the flight controls. Because of its long wings, abrupt movement of the ailerons (wing controls) would set up a ripple effect that would travel, like ripples in a pond, toward the cockpit about two seconds later. The secret was to ease into aileron control movement, until the aircraft started to bank, and then increase the amount of bank desired by a smooth increase of aileron pressure.

I discovered years later that this inherent characteristic of large aircraft was also prevalent in the B-747 Jumbo Jet.

Another characteristic of the aircraft was its tremendous vibration and noise. It was equipped with four three-bladed 18-foot diameter propellers with its tips spinning at supersonic speeds. This supersonic disruption of air flow set up horrendous vibrations and noise throughout the entire aircraft. However, the cockpit, with both ears covered with a headset, was tolerable. But the cabin would loosen tooth fillings if you spent much time standing in the prop line. An amusing demonstration was to have new pilots position themselves in the cargo compartment and stand on a piece of Bond typing paper, while the instructor would slide it out from underneath their feet. After about 15 hours in the aircraft and an equal amount of time in the simulator, I was administered a four-hour Proficiency Evaluation flight check by Lt.Col. John Dyer on September 9, 1964, and was designated a *Cargomaster* Second Pilot (the lowest ranking of the five pilot qualifications in the Military Air Transport Service).

The five pilot rankings were:

Second Pilot: Authorized to fly from the right seat only, and not allowed to make takeoffs and landings unless accompanied by an instructor pilot or flight examiner in the left seat. The primary job of a second pilot was to read the checklists, raise and lower the landing gear and flaps, make radio calls and keep his mouth shut!

First Pilot: Authorized to fly from the right seat only, but could make takeoffs and landings with a benevolent Aircraft Commander in the left seat. The primary job of a first pilot was much the same as a second pilot, but could occasionally offer suggestions, if they were complimentary to the Aircraft Commander.

Aircraft Commander: Authorized to fly as Pilot in Command (PIC) on airlift missions while flying from the left seat. He could allow first pilots to make takeoffs and landings, but only if they carried his B-4 bag and bought the first round of drinks in the Officers' Club bar on layovers.

Instructor Pilot: Authorized to act as PIC on airlift missions when flying from either pilot's seat. He was also required to continually remind other crew members that he was an instructor, knew everything, was not to be questioned and was never wrong.

Flight Examiner: Authorized to administer oral exams, proficiency flight checks, fly as PIC from either pilot's seat and sit in the cockpit jump seat during airlift missions, while passing judgment on the flying proficiency of pilots of all categories. He considered himself the God of the cockpit and his decisions should never be questioned. One of the primary responsibilities of a flight examiner was to assume a superior attitude and never allow himself to become friends with fellow crew members of lesser rank unless they bought the drinks and carried his bags..

In mid September 1964, I started flying airlift missions with various Aircraft Commanders within the lower contiguous 48 states. One of the first things that I observed was that many ACs appeared skittish and somewhat apprehensive regarding the reliability of the C-133 and wouldn't hesitate to abort a mission for any unexplained strange sound or minor propeller fluctuation. However, taking into consideration the unsavory reputation of the aircraft, I didn't think them over-cautious. I was told that there were even a few pilots that had refused to fly the *Cargomaster,* stating a "fear of flying" and were grounded and transferred to non-flying assignments. However, I found flying this mystery aircraft somewhat exciting! (I suspect that this "cavalier" attitude was the product of flying several different types of aircraft with questionable safety records in the past.) We didn't carry parachutes, which would have been of questionable value even if we did, because of the difficulty of reaching a suitable exit. (This lack of parachutes didn't bother me since reflecting back on the many pilots we lost in F-100s, who were provided with ejection seats and automatic opening parachutes, but still experienced an early end to their flying careers.)

One of my earliest overseas flights as a new second pilot was to Thule Air Base, Greenland. The Aircraft Commander was Captain Rolland Schoonover and the first pilot Major Pat Fiore. Thule is located in Northern Greenland and served as a support base for Strategic Air Command bombers and Ballistic Missile Early Warning System (BMEWS) radar towers. These radar installations were designed to detect the launching of Soviet Union ICBMs, thereby providing a minimum 30-minute warning of an attack on the U.S. This would be sufficient time to determine if the attack was real, and if it was, to launch ICBMs that would destroy both countries and kill tens of millions of people. This Cold War concept was known as Mutual Assured Destruction (MAD) and prevented both countries from launching preemptive strikes. Also based at Thule was a squadron of single-engine jet F-102 fighter interceptors. I admired the courage of these pilots to launch in total darkness over the frozen ice fields of Greenland, since if they were required to eject from their aircraft, chances of survival were almost zero.

Our mission in Thule was to fly resupply trips to *Station Nord,* located about 500 miles northeast of Thule and 500 miles from the North Pole. Due to its extreme northern location, resupply by surface ships was not possible, so it could only be supplied by air during the daylight periods of summer. The runway was rolled snow, which resulted in extremely soft landings. We made three shuttle flights to Nord, airlifting food, gasoline, cooking oil, heavy equipment for maintaining the runway, mail and miscellaneous cargo. The base was operated by approximately 30 Danish civilian workers, on one-year isolated tours. We were told that in two one-year tours they could save enough money to return to Denmark and purchase a small farm. The terrain we flew over was the most inhospitable area I had ever seen and resembled what you would expect the backside of the moon to look like, as there were no visible signs of habitation, just sheer mountains and frozen ice fields in all directions. I was glad when we completed these missions and were flying back toward civilization along the West Coast of Greenland.

Station Nord was built by the U.S. in 1952. Its purpose was to fill the gap for weather stations and serve as an emergency landing strip for military and civilian aircraft flying over the North Pole. In July 1972 the U.S. terminated its support of Nord, since the weather information it provided could now be obtained by satellites. Faced with the cancellation of U.S. support the Danish Government closed the base, but in 1975 it was reopened as a remote military base in support of scientific expeditions. The number of personnel stationed at Nord has been reduced to about five men on one-year tours.

In October and November 1964, I began flying missions to Hawaii and Europe and was beginning to enjoy the versatility and variety of the trips. In early November I was on a flight to Rhein Main Air Base, Germany, which provided me with the opportunity of, once again, eating German food and drinking strong German beer. Our return flight to the U.S. would be via Chateauroux, France and Lajes, Azores. When preparing to depart the Azores on November 7, 1964, we heard that we lost another C-133.

A *Cargomaster,* commanded by Lt. Guy L Vassalotti, crashed soon after takeoff from runway 09 at Goose Bay, Labrador. The aircraft appeared to stall soon after takeoff, then dropped sharply and impacted the ground in a left wing down, nose high attitude. All seven crew members were killed and their bodies burned beyond recognition. A stall due to ice was suspected, but the factual cause was Undetermined. The news of this accident put a damper on our holiday spirits and the cockpit chatter during our return to Dover was quite subdued. However, the Aircraft Commander managed the crew anxiety in a professional manner. In December I made more flights to Europe and was able to do my Christmas shopping in the military BXs in Germany and France. In early January I started flight training for first pilot when tragedy struck again.

On January 10, 1965, a C-133 commanded by Captain Arthur F. Wiegand, crashed soon after a night takeoff from Wake Island. The aircraft attained an altitude of about 500 feet before crashing into the 10,000 foot deep Pacific Ocean. Some floating debris was recovered, but the bodies of the six flight crew members were never found. The cause of the accident was listed as Undetermined.

The Wake Island crash was the seventh unexplained accident of a C-133. Compounding the mystery was that in each accident there were no radio reports from the pilots indicating an impending emergency. Obviously what the pilots encountered was sudden and so catastrophic that they were unable to inform ground personnel of the nature of their emergency. Faced with such unprecedented accident statistics the Department of Defense (DOD) grounded all C-133s and ordered a thorough investigation to determine the cause of these perplexing tragic accidents. The order stated; **"C-133 Cargomasters will not be allowed to resume flying until a cause factor is found, and corrective actions are taken to prevent similar loss of aircraft and crew!"**

This grounding came at a very bad time for the Air Force, as the war in Vietnam was expanding rapidly and the need for heavy combat airlift was growing at the same pace. The C-133 was the largest aircraft in service and could carry loads that couldn't be accommodated in smaller aircraft like the C-124 and C-130. In addition, the C-141 was not yet in service and the C-5A (which would eventually replace the C-133) was delayed due to production problems. It was imperative that the C-133 be returned to service ASAP, but only if it could be operated safely. Flight crew morale was at an all time low, but we were as eager as the Air Force in discovering why our aircraft, and fellow airmen, were disappearing with no report of an emergency from the pilots. A figurative "blank check" was issued by the DOD with instructions to: **"Find and fix the problem and get the C-133s back in the air ASAP!"**

Post grounding actions ordered by the DOD were:

1. Two C-133s were loaned to the Air Force Flight Test Center at Edwards AFB, California for operational testing by experienced test pilots.
2. A scale model was built and sent to Langley AFB, Virginia, for profile flight testing (including power-on stalls) in their giant wind tunnel.
3. To determine if the aircraft involved in the accidents were overloaded, Air Freight Centers worldwide were ordered to recalculate cargo loads carried in C-133s during the last several years.
4. Since severe vibration was a known inherit problem in the C-133, a fleet-wide study was ordered to determine if air sensing lines, that provide altitude and air speed data, had loosened. If not properly connected they could produce incorrect critical cockpit instrument readings.
5. A study was ordered to determine why it had become an acceptable practice of releasing aircraft for flight with inoperative stall warning systems. (An assemblage designed to alert pilots of an impending stall.)
6. A study was ordered to determine why it had become an acceptable practice of releasing aircraft for flight with autopilots that have a history of producing sporadic, unprogrammed, pitch-up (climb) signals.

While actions were being taken on the above listed directives there was a problem of what to do with C-133 crew members temporarily out of a job. One project I engaged in was restoring an old speed boat powered by an antiquated 65 hp outboard motor. Once the renovation was complete, I planned on using it for pulling my 13-year-old daughter on water skis. An integral part of this project was to install a trailer hitch on the rear bumper of my 1961 Cadillac, so I took it to the base auto hobby shop, raised it up on a hydraulic hoist, and began drilling holes into the heavy gage steel bumper. In the process I felt something flick into my right (unprotected) eye, but thought it was just a piece of dust and didn't give it much thought. I finished the project and to ease the discomfort I administered Visine eye drops, which seemed to ease the annoyance.

The next morning I was scheduled for a four-hour simulator training period but before one hour had elapsed my right eye began bothering me so I told the instructor I was going to visit our flight surgeon. After one quick look at my eye he sent me to see our resident optometrist, who examined it with a magnifying glass, and said that he thought he could see a small speck of metal imbedded in the thin transparent film covering the cornea. He asked me if I had any idea how this could have occurred. When I told him about my drilling into my automoblle bumper the previous day, without the use of protective plastic goggles, he shook his head while stating, "Major, you may lose that eye, but I want an ophthalmologist to examine it. I'll call the Naval Hospital in Philadelphia and send you there in an ambulance, as time is critical in trying to save that eye." He administered some drops to anesthetize it and had a nurse cover it with a large white bandage while he went to call Philadelphia. He came back a few minutes later, stating that he had talked to an ophthalmologist who wanted to examine me ASAP.

I sat in the passenger seat of a blue Air Force ambulance, while a young NASCAR-aspiring driver raced through the main gate and headed up Highway 13 toward Philadelphia, about 50 miles away. He turned on the siren and rotating red light and even with the use of only one eye, I could see that he was using me as an excuse to fine tune his stock car racing technique. At the pace he was driving, I worried more about finishing the trip in one piece than I did in saving my eye. I told him, "Airman, dead men don't need two eyes. Slow down, turn off the siren and flashing light, or I'll drive the ambulance myself." I'm sure I ruined his day, but we finished the trip in one piece, and only a few minutes later than we would have at the pace he had been driving, if we arrived at all!

Two ophthalmologists were waiting for me and rushed me into their examination room. They removed the bandage and had me rest my chin in a metal frame designed to prevent unwanted head movements. After a detailed examination, they agreed that it didn't appear the speck of metal, now coated with rust, had penetrated deep enough to allow critical fluids to escape. They thought they could remove it with a "pencil pointed magnet." With the aid of a strong light, and a steady hand, the doctor lightly touched the surface of my eye and removed a small piece of a Cadillac bumper. After further examination, the doctors stated that I was very lucky and within a couple days I would be as good as new. Indeed I was lucky, but at the same time I felt very stupid in not wearing protective goggles, as my career in aviation almost came to an abrupt end and this book would never have been written. Two days later the patch over my right eye was removed and my vision was still 20/20 in both eyes.

While grounded we were encouraged to take annual leave, perform housekeeping chores around the squadron, or perform the duty of mortuary escort officer for servicemen killed on active duty. In this capacity we would accompany their remains home to their families. I assumed this sad task several times but one such trip to Wyoming stands out in my mind and is worth recalling.

Captain Gary L. Gaffner, whose hometown was Buffalo, Wyoming, was killed in a KC-97 crash in Newfoundland. I was directed to escort his body to Buffalo, where his young widow and parents resided. In order to preclude any screw-ups, I was required to personally observe the loading and unloading of his coffin, be it on a commercial aircraft, train, or mortuary hearse. During the trip we traveled by air to Denver, train to Cheyenne and hearse to Buffalo. My driver, during the six-hour 290-mile trek across the plains of Wyoming, was a young apprentice mortician from Cheyenne, who was directed to transport Captain Gaffner's body to Buffalo and assist the local undertaker during the funeral.

I found him to be an interesting person to spend a few hours with and he seemed equally intrigued in my life as an Air Force pilot. I mentioned to him that my instructions stated that the body was not suitable for viewing, as it had been badly burned during the post crash fire, and had to be identified through dental records. He acknowledged this and said he would discourage the family accordingly, but if they demanded that their local undertaker view the remains, there was nothing we could do to stop them. He said that when he was going through mortician training in Texas, an Army soldier's remains were returned to his parents for burial, and it was also stated that the remains were not suitable for viewing. However, the soldier's mother insisted that the local funeral home open the casket to determine the state of the body, and that he was present when it was to be examined, but all they found inside was a metal plaque that stated, "This represents the remains of (the soldier's name). May he rest in peace." He said that the soldier's mother was suing the military, but he had left Texas before the case was settled.

We arrived in Buffalo on a Thursday afternoon and after delivering the casket to the local undertaker, I was informed that the funeral was not scheduled until the following Monday and that Captain Gaffner's widow requested that I remain in Buffalo to present her with the U.S. flag that would cover the coffin of her deceased husband. I naturally agreed to honor her request and obtained a room in a local motel.

330

The Gaffner family was well know in Wyoming and ranchers from far and wide began gathering for the funeral. Family members and friends congregated at the Gaffner ranch for a typical Western style barbecue on Friday and Saturday evening. I was invited to attend, but thought It proper protocol to decline. However, when Capt. Gaffner's father came to my motel room and said that his son loved the Air Force and he would consider it a fitting tribute to have a pilot colleague, in uniform, present for his son's "send-off-parties," I agreed to attend both gatherings.

When performing the duty as mortuary escort officer, I was required to be in a Class A uniform at all times, not to consume alcoholic beverages and present the best image of the Air Force.

After driving my rental car to the Gaffner ranch, about 15 miles outside of Buffalo, I had a difficult time in finding a place to park. The area surrounding the ranch house was packed with late-model pickup trucks (most with rifles in gun-racks across their rear windows) and Cadillacs covered with prairie dust and strands of sage brush. Approaching the Western style, open-porch ranch house, I could hear the sound of cattle grazing in a nearby field and the whinny of horses in an adjacent barn.

I was greeted at the door by Captain Gaffner's father and with his hand on my shoulder, he escorted me inside to meet his rancher friends. The house was packed with six-foot-tall men, with most wearing ten-gallon Stetson hats with sweat stains around the brims and shiny silver belt buckles the size of small dinner plates. The women were dressed in skin-tight blue jeans, but with smaller belt buckles. A Western style band was banging out cowboy ballads in a far corner. I was treated like one of the family and shuffled around to shake hands with everyone in attendance. Every handshake was accompanied with an expression of appreciation for bringing their native son home to his final resting place and were impressed that the Air Force would send a major as his escort. This was always followed with, "What would you like to drink, major?" They seemed surprised, and perhaps a little disappointed, when I declined an alcoholic beverage. They insisted in enticing me into having just one or two belts of bourbon whiskey, as a toast to Captain Gaffner, but I stuck to the rules and respectively said "No thanks."

The following Monday was a crisp February day with bright sunshine and calm winds. A local American Legion chapter provided a military rifle salute and a former high school colleague blew taps that echoed mystically across the desolate Western plains. After the flag was folded, I presented it to Mrs. Gaffner with these words: "Mrs. Gaffner, I present this flag on behalf of the United States of America, in honor of your husband, Captain Gary L. Gaffner, who gave his life in the defense of our country. We are forever grateful and share with you in the sorrow of his death." While presenting the flag I gave her a prolonged salute. She responded with a weak, "Thank you, major." As she pressed the flag to her chest streams of tears were running down her young pale cheeks.

After the funeral there was a gigantic lunch at a local church meeting hall and after the meal, I left with a prominent funeral home director and his wife from Cheyenne who had driven to Buffalo for the funeral. He had invited me to ride back with him, providing I didn't object to his stopping en route to visit his brother who ran a funeral home in Casper.

Two hours later we parked in front of an up-scale funeral home with adjacent living quarters. A professional looking middle-age man came out to greet his brother and sister in-law and invited us into his home. I was impressed by the opulence of the living quarters, which had large rooms, high ceilings, overstuffed leather furniture and a Western style motif throughout. The host's wife, when welcoming me to her home, said, "What would you like to drink, major?" Before I could reply, my Cheyenne undertaker friend said, "Major Martin doesn't drink!" I quickly corrected him by stating that Air Force rules precluded me from drinking when performing mortuary escort duty for an Air Force colleague, but that task was fulfilled and I could sure use a double Beefeater martini. My hostesses' comment, "Coming right up, partner. Would you like your martini with a twist or olive?" "Olive please, and light on the Vermouth."

While I was sipping my long overdue drink, my host and his brother started talking about their chosen profession of making dead people appear happy they died, and how competitive their business was becoming. During the conversation the subject turned to two young girls our host was working on in his basement. He said that they were recently killed in a head-on collision and were both thrown through the windshield of their pickup truck. He went on to state that their facial features were almost destroyed and he was rebuilding them from pictures provided by their families. He told his brother that he was nearly complete in rebuilding their facial traits, suitable for viewing, and was quite proud of his work. He invited him downstairs to view his project, and as they rose to leave he said, "Major Martin, would you like to see my reconstruction work also?" "No thanks" I said, "I'll just sit here and enjoy another martini."

A couple hours later, we drove the remaining 160 miles to Cheyenne, where I boarded a commercial flight to Philadelphia, with an en route stop in Denver. In Philadelphia an Air Force staff car picked me up and drove me back to Dover AFB Delaware.

The commander of Francis E. Warren AFB, Wyoming, Colonel William Brier, sent a favorable letter of communications to my Wing Commander, General Wallace, which stated in part: "I wish to commend the performance of Major Martin in his duties as escort for the remains of Captain Gary L. Gaffner. His cooperation with my Mortuary Officer and thoughtful consideration of the family was outstanding. No one could have done more to facilitate matters. His unerring attention to detail resulted in exact plans and a smooth, beautiful service. I have received several letters from the funeral home and members of the family complimenting Major Martin. His actions were in keeping with the highest traditions in performing escort duty reflecting respect and credit to the U.S. Air Force."

By mid March, 1965, results of the DOD mandated C-133 special investigation were beginning to emerge. Test pilots reported that considerable altitude was lost when recovering from power-off stalls by stating that the aircraft, after stalling, would waddle back and forth while falling flat for several thousand feet, before the nose would drop sufficiently to allow for a resumption of normal flight. Wind-tunnel tests, of the scale model concurred with actual test pilot findings. However, a disturbing characteristic was the predictable behavior of the aircraft in a high angle of attack, full power-on stall. According to the test results, there was a tendency of the aircraft to "snap-roll inverted," which would result in an in-flight breakup due to high stress loads. Test pilots discussed performing power-on stalls in an actual aircraft, but after reviewing the wind-tunnel test results would only do so if ejection seats were temporarily installed in their C-133 used for testing. This was deemed impractical so the wind-tunnel test results were accepted as valid data.

However, before concluding the flight test program it was decided to perform one additional power-off stall analysis in a line aircraft selected at random. A professional test pilot and flight engineer visited our squadron and asked for a volunteer to fly as copilot when performing these collateral stalls. For some unknown reason, I eagerly stepped forward. We loaded a C-133 with cement blocks to its maximum weight of 275,000 lbs. and climbed to 16,000 feet over the Chesapeake Bay. As a false

333

sense of escape we wore parachutes, but I doubt if we would have been able to reach a usable exit in the rear of the 90 foot long cargo compartment if we had to abandon the aircraft.

We performed a series of power-off stalls with the landing gear and flaps extended and with them retracted. I was amazed in how such a large aircraft could be flying normally one minute and, without warning, go into a violent shaking mode, roll into a sharp bank, and fall, like a dry leaf, for a thousand feet or more before the nose would drop and a return to normal flight could be resumed. We would climb back to 16,000 feet, and perform stall after stall. I lost count in how many we made, but was glad when the flight test was over. I chastised myself for volunteering, but like many interesting aerial excursions it was fun to talk about later at the bar.

About three months after the C-133s were grounded we were hearing rumors that they would soon be back flying. In April 1965, flight crews and maintenance personnel were assembled in the Dover Air Force Base theater for a briefing on the findings of the special investigation. Representatives of the Air Force Material Command and Flight Test Center would conduct the briefing, which we assumed would explain why C-133s had, from Undetermined causes, mysteriously disappeared or crashed and what actions would be taken to prevent similar accidents.

The Air Force colonel conducting the briefing stood next to a large round board that had strips of paper covering individual sections, like the spokes of a wheel. The enlarged center section was covered with red paper resembling a target. As the colonel started his briefing, he removed the first strip of paper which revealed the words, **Cargo Loads.** He stated that their investigation revealed overload weight discrepancies as much as 20,000 lbs. on many C-133 load manifests. In the future accurate load accounting would be a special emphasis item.

The next strip of paper removed disclosed the words, **Pitot Static System.** The colonel stated that a fleet-wide inspection disclosed a systemic air leak problem in the sensing lines that provide airspeed, rate of climb and altitude information to the pilots. These leaks were serious enough to produce noticeable false readings and were the result of the tremendous vibration inherit in the aircraft. In the future, pitot static lines would be inspected for potential air leaks every 100 hours of flight.

The next message uncovered contained the words, **Stall Warning System.** The colonel acknowledged that It had become common practice to defer corrective action on inoperative stall warning systems, that were designed to alert pilots of an impending stall, by first shaking the pilot's control column, followed by a mechanical movement of the entire column forward. Considering the importance of this safety device, an inoperative stall warning system would be cause for grounding the aircraft.

The next message displayed was, **Autopilot.** The colonel acknowledged that C-133 auotpilots would occasionally produce sporadic pitch-up signals, and when this occurred quick action by the pilot was required to prevent the aircraft from reaching a dangerous nose-up attitude, and possible stall. Autopilot maintenance would be a special emphasis item for early correction of this idiosyncrasy and, in the interim, the autopilot would be restricted for use in cruise and descent flight only. It would not be used during climb.

The next message bared the words, **Flight Test Results.** He stated that test pilots had completed their extensive flight evaluations with special emphasis on stall characteristics. However, only low angle of attack, power-off stalls were performed in an actual aircraft. Under these conditions the aircraft gave almost no warning of a pending stall and after stalling considerable altitude was lost before a recovery could be made. High angle of attack, power-on stalls were not performed in a real aircraft due to the likelihood of unpredictable controllability problems, which may result in the aircraft snap-rolling inverted.

The last subject, on the spokes of the briefing wheel, revealed the words, **Wind Tunnel Tests.** According to the colonel, these tests predicted that a fully loaded C-133, flown into a full power-on, high angle of attack stall, may snap-roll inverted without warning. If the stall was entered at above maximum certified weights, or above maximum service ceiling, the maneuver would be more severe. Recovery from this condition was deemed unlikely as high stress loads would most likely cause the aircraft to break-up in flight.

At this point in the briefing, only the large center section of the display board was still covered. A sense of anticipation engulfed the room as the colonel prepared to slowly uncover the remaining message! When he did, it revealed the word, **Stall.** This certainly got everyone's attention, as stall is recognized as an enemy of flight safety, and a tool of the PGR, from the days of the Wright Brothers to the Comair accident in Lexington, Kentucky, on August 27, 2006, which killed 49 passengers and crew.

The briefing was concluded by the colonel stating that incorporating the recommendations presented, C-133s would be allowed to resume flying. In addition, the investigative team recommended early installation of "angle-of-attack" indicators in all aircraft. Based on what we heard, pilots and maintenance personnel alike left the theater with a positive attitude toward resuming flight operations. (However, there was nothing that could be done to eliminate the tremendous vibration that would result in the loss of two more aircraft before they were retired from active service, more on this problem later in this chapter.)

All the safety recommendations were adopted and I started flying C-133s again on May 3, 1965. We never lost another *Cargomaster* for Undetermined causes and it was obvious that the majority of the previous accidents were the result of inadvertent flight into a catastrophic full power-on stall, resulting in the aircraft snap-rolling inverted and breaking-up. This type of failure would explain why the pilots never had time to make an emergency radio report. Within a year all aircraft were equipped with "angle-of-attack" indicators, thereby providing visual guidance to the pilots in avoiding attitudes that may result in a stall.

Following four months of inactivity, C-133 pilots were required to undergo refresher flight training and complete a proficiency flight check before being allowed to resume flying. To expedite returning the aircraft to full airlift support status, it was directed that pilots be re-certified in their former crew position only. This would dictate that I be returned to line flying as a second pilot, with the opportunity of upgrading, to a higher crew position, sometime in the undetermined future. The flight examiner scheduled to administer my recertification check was Lt.Col. John C. Dyer from Eastern Air Force Headquarters at McGuire AFB, New Jersey.

The flight check consisted of instrument flying, engine failures during takeoff and three and two-engine circling approaches to a full stop landing. I knew that the flight went well, but Colonel Dyer's comment during the post-flight debriefing caught me by surprise. He stated that my performance was exceptional and that he was going to recommend that I be upgraded directly to Aircraft Commander, bypassing returning to line flying as a second or first pilot. He said that he wasn't sure if my operations officer would agree, but he felt that it would be a waste of time not to allow me to upgrade immediately. I thanked him for the unexpected promotion and his confidence in my flying capabilities. He said, "No problem, major. Let's go talk to your squadron operations officer."

We walked into Major Roy L. Meyer's office and Colonel Dyer informed him that he was recommending me for immediate upgrade to Aircraft Commander. Meyers was not receptive to the idea stating that pilots were to be returned to flight status in their original crew position only. Colonel Dyer stated that this concept was OK for most pilots, but it would be a waste of time in my case, as my performance was better than most of the rechecks he administered to previously qualified Aircraft Commanders. Major Myers finally agreed to upgrading me to first pilot, but Colonel Dyer wouldn't back-down. The colonel finally convinced the major that he was right and he accepted his recommendation. I was congratulated by both with a handshake and a smile. Things were certainly looking up!

In 1965, new C-133 Aircraft Commanders (ACs) were required to complete an Initial Operating Experience (IOE) training flight, under the supervision of an instructor pilot. This would be followed by flying a regular line check administered by a pilot flight examiner (PFE). The IOE flight would be flown without cargo or passengers and the itinerary was at the option of the new AC and instructor, providing at least one flight segment included a 500-mile over-water route. I suggested that the flight be flown from Dover, Delaware to Argentia, Newfoundland, Sondre Stromfjord, Greenland, and an extended over-water leg back to Dover. The flight was completed without a hitch and except for a very interesting circling approach up a fjord to Sondre Strom, the instructor had little to comment on. I was now ready for an operational line check by a PFE.

These Initial Operating Experience (non-productive) 709 training flights for new ACs were later eliminated as they were an expensive waste of valuable pilot and aircraft flight time.

The Air Force was eager to return the C-133 Cargomasters to line flying as the war in South Vietnam was rapidly expanding. In January 1965, Vietcong forces seized control of a village 40 miles from Saigon and killed 200 South Vietnam troops and five Americans. On February 7th, a U.S. advisory compound in the central highlands was attacked killing nine Americans. This was followed by an explosion in a hotel in the coastal city of Qui Nhon, killing 23 Americans. There was no doubt that the U.S. was now engaged in a serious shooting war against a determined enemy whose goal was to defeat the South Vietnamese Government! On March 8th, 3,500 marines were sent to Danag, followed by a rapid increase in additional U.S. military troops in the coming months. In March 1965, President Johnson authorized Operation Rolling Thunder, a massive bombing offensive utilizing Air Force and Navy aircraft. Like in all past wars, an increase in combat activity requires a four-fold increase in logistic support --- in this case, a maximum effort by C-133 Cargomasters.

337

In early June, I was scheduled for an initial operational line check to Clark AFB, Philippines, with en route stops in Corpus Christie, Texas, Travis AFB, California, Hickam AFB, Hawaii and Wake and Guam Island. My pilot flight examiner (PFE) was Captain Gordon S. Pink. Gordon and I flew C-119s together in Germany eight years earlier and it was great to share a cockpit with him once again. In 1965 C-133 missions were flown under a crew stage concept, which meant that when you landed at an en route base, another crew would be scheduled to takeover the aircraft and fly it to the next down-line station. We would be assigned billets and "take-a-number" for taking over an inbound aircraft that was heading in the same direction after completing the required 15 hours of crew rest.

Paper pushing generals in MATS Headquarters at Scott AFB, Illinois, felt that this would expedite the movement of aircraft, since a rested crew would be available to move the aircraft toward its next intended destination as soon as it was refueled. Conceptually, this made sense, but the generals who directed this stupid policy knew nothing about C-133s. The *Cargomaster* was a rogue aircraft and did not share a commonality with other four-engine transports. Also, its uniqueness required C-133 mechanics, specifically trained, to keep it moving in any semblance of a regular schedule. Compounding the problem was that since there was a limited number of C-133s in service, there was a finite number of spare parts available. In addition, the tremendous vibration inherent in the aircraft, resulted in reportable in-flight discrepancies on almost every leg segment. However, flight crews would be willing to carry them forward if they were allowed to stay with the same aircraft, but would be forced to record them in the aircraft maintenance log if they were going to turn it over to a new crew. Once these deficiencies were recorded, the aircraft would sit for days awaiting repair. It was not uncommon to see the same aircraft you flew 15 hours earlier still sitting on the ramp when you came out of crew rest and there were several crews ahead of you waiting for an in-commission aircraft to fly.

Under this ill-conceived concept I spent a week's vacation in Hawaii, five days sun-bathing and fishing on Wake Island, and several days of drinking and chasing Air Force nurses on Guam Island before finally arriving at Clark Air Base. At the time C-133s were not allowed to land in South Vietnam, as it was felt that there was a good chance they would be stuck in a combat zone and become a target for the Viet Cong. Our cargo was transferred to the smaller C-130s for delivery to Saigon.

I arrived in Clark Air Base on June 18, 1965, the same day B-52s were returning from a bombing mission in North Vietnam. The raid was not well organized and several of the bombers, for various reasons, were not able to return to their home base on Guam Island. One of the bombers made an emergency landing at Clark and that night its five officer crew members had joined a mixed group of pilots, navigators, flight nurses and flight attendants in the "Ratskeller" of the Officers' Club. The smoke-filled room was exploding with raucous laughter, backslapping, heavy drinking, men propositioning giggling females and just loud typical war-inspired frivolity. In a far corner a jukebox was blaring out sixties ballads, surrounded by couples engaging in upright foreplay (dancing).

In the midst of this bedlam the B-52 crew members rose to their feet, let out loud cheers, while their Aircraft Commander (a major) stood on a chair and started punching holes in the ceiling with a clenched fist. Each time he punched a new hole his drunk crew members would give out with a loud "hurrah." I thought this destruction of club property was unnecessary and walked over to see if I could put a stop to such foolishness. My attempt to interfere with the bomber crew's exuberance was met with "evil-eye" stares and a threatening clenched fist from the intoxicated AC.

I was soon joined, in my standoff with the B-52 crew, by crew members wearing MATS and TAC patches. A silence fell over the previous rowdy bar, as it appeared a riot could break out with the slightest provocation. The "hole-puncher" stepped down from the chair, twisted his upper lip into a snarl and stared into my eyes, like an owl eyeballing a field mouse! His facial expression was so contorted that it excited my funny-bone and I started to laugh. He responded to my martini-induced joviality with, "What in the hell is so God-damn funny, major?" Still smiling I responded with, "You and I standing here stone-drunk and ruining a perfectly good party. Let's split the cost of buying a round of drinks for the house and shake hands." He nodded in agreement, while breaking out in unconstrained laughter. A cheer went up from the room, while someone began ringing a brass bell hanging over the bar, which signified a free drink for one and all. As I recall it cost us about 20 dollars each, which was repaid several times over by the many slaps on the back the B-52 major and I received from the raucous crowd. (War can be a lot of fun, if you don't get killed!)

Five days later I started a frustrating trek back east, transiting Wake Island, Hawaii and Travis AFB, while following the same cumbersome aircraft swapping at each station. Thirty days after leaving Dover my initial line check, as a C-133 Aircraft Commander, was history. I was now authorized to fly Pacific Ocean odysseys on my own! (See Photo No. 49.)

Once again, I began to mull over the circumstances that found me flying the C-133, but it was too late to worry about that now. With the U.S. involvement in a war in South Vietnam, which was growing day-by-day, I was frozen in my assignment and it appeared that I would spend considerable time away from home. But, at least I knew my family was being properly cared for, by a trustworthy wife, living in base housing. If they needed any help, all they had to do was call, and our Air Force friends would respond immediately.

A couple days later I was flying my first trip as a C-133 Aircraft Commander, delivering a load of miscellaneous cargo to Kadena Air Base, Okinawa. However, on this mission I would fly the same aircraft during the entire trip. Air Force generals in charge of airlift had finally taken a good dose of "Get-Smart Pills" and decided that C-133s crews would remain with the same aircraft for the entire mission. Crew members and maintenance personnel alike welcomed this decision. Flight crews would now be able to form a personal covenant to an aircraft they would fly for up to 75 hours and ten days during a mission to South Vietnam.

The first leg of my initial trip was a nine-hour flight to Travis, AFB, California. The next day I departed on an eight-hour flight to Hawaii. About three hours out from Honolulu, the flight engineer called my attention to the illumination of the number three engine "start button."

The pilot's overhead panel contains four start buttons, one for each engine, and when pushed directs high pressure air to a pneumatic valve that rotates the engine during the startup sequence. When the engine reaches approximately 40% RPM, the start valve will close and the light bulb in the starter button will extinguish. Illumination of this bulb during flight could indicate that high pressure air, at extremely high temperature, may be entering the engine accessory section and could result in a serious engine fire that would be difficult to extinguish.

When the flight engineer called my attention to the illumination of the start button, I had no idea how long it had been on. We were flying into the setting sun and it was very possible that the bright sun rays, shining directly into the cockpit, could have prevented early detection of the light.

I directed a crew member to inspect the number three engine from a window in the cargo compartment. He reported no visual indications of a fire or abnormal condition so my flight engineer thought that it was probably a false indication that required no corrective action. However, I was uncomfortable with just doing nothing! Having consumed enough fuel to provide a comfortable three-engine cruise ceiling, I shutdown the number three engine and feathered the propeller. We descended to 16,000 feet, computed a new estimated time of arrival for Hickam and pressed on to an uneventful landing.

When parked mechanics moved a maintenance stand next to the number three engine and when they opened the cowling several pieces of burnt metal came tumbling out and smashed onto the concrete ramp. In addition, high temperature air lines, in the vicinity of the engine start valve, were twisted from excessive heat. From all appearances the area had been exposed to extreme high temperatures and an uncontrolled fire could have occurred at any time. We spent five days on the beaches of Waikiki before our aircraft was repaired and ready for the eight-hour flight to Wake Island. The maintenance repairs made in Honolulu seemed adequate, but I was concerned about a high fuel flow and a slightly higher Turbine Inlet Temperature (TIT) when starting the number three engine.

We spent two days on Wake Island, while a few minor discrepancies were taken care of before proceeding on to Okinawa with a refueling stop in Guam. After landing in Okinawa, I expected my cargo to be off-loaded for transport to South Vietnam by C-130s, but was told that C-133s were now allowed to fly into the combat area, providing we land at Tan Son Nhut Airport, Saigon. After a 15-hour crew rest I departed on a six-hour flight to South Vietnam. It had been two years since I had been in Saigon (the last time in 1963 in a T-39) and I was stunned in how much the military activity in and around the airport had increased. Everywhere I looked there were B-26s, C-47s, C-123s, C-124s, T-28s, B-57s and numerous civilian airliners. There was no question that the U.S. was ramping up its war effort in Southeast Asia. After my aircraft was off-loaded and refueled, I was taxiing out for takeoff three hours later. After a long wait for permission to takeoff, I flew back to Okinawa, arriving there about 3 a.m. in heavy rain and strong cross winds.

Before returning to the U.S. we were authorized 24 hours crew rest in Okinawa, but due to several maintenance discrepancies, I thought we would be there for two or three days. After a couple beers and a hot

341

breakfast my crew and I hit the sack for a well-deserved rest. Falling asleep, however, was difficult because of the noise of heavy rain and strong winds beating against the thin walls and metal roof of our barracks.

Around 9 a.m. an orderly was pounding on my door informing me that I was to contact the area command post. Donning my flight suit, I hurried to the nearest telephone and called the operations officer, who told me that the base was under a typhoon evacuation and all flyable aircraft were to be flown to a safe harbor. He instructed me to round up my crew and report to base operations ASAP. Less than an hour later my crew and I, rubbing sleep from our eyes and dripping wet from the rain, were assembled in operations and fighting our way through crowds of crew members attempting to find out where they would take their aircraft.

When I finally reached the head of the line I was issued orders to depart for Tachikawa Air Base, Japan. We felt good about our evacuation destination as Tachikawa was famous for shopping, cheap booze and tons of night clubs featuring cute young Japanese o-josans. About one hour later we were taxiing out for takeoff, behind a long line of aircraft, with the windshield wipers slapping and the aircraft rocking from side to side from strong gusts of wind. When It was our turn for takeoff, I rolled the ailerons into the cross wind, turned the windshield wipers on high position, turned on the jet air blast to the windshield, flipped the engine water injection switches on, and advanced the power levers to full throttle and when the engine power stabilized released the brakes.

In harmony with the copilot shouting "Go" (takeoff decision speed or V_1), the aircraft began to vibrate like a belly dancer. I instinctively knew that the gyrations were not related to the typhoon and to confirm my suspicion the flight engineer and copilot were shouting, "We are losing the number three engine!" (the same engine that I had problems with in Hawaii). While fighting the strong wind gusts, turbulence, and heavy rain, I eyeballed the engine instruments and noted that the torque oil pressure, RPM, turbine in-let temperature, fuel flow, and other engine readings, for the number three engine, were all dancing up and down. This was accompanied by a scanner, in the cargo compartment, reporting that the engine nose case was shaking badly. I ordered the engine shutdown and the propeller feathered, and 30 seconds later we were climbing through heavy rain clouds on three engines. My copilot asked if he should declare an emergency for a return to Kadena. My response, "No way, Jose. We're not going to return under these weather conditions and have the aircraft destroyed by a typhoon. We will continue on to Tachikawa on three engines and have the aircraft repaired there. After all, it's only about a three-hour flight, and since our cargo compartment is empty, we can still make landfall for an emergency landing if we lose another engine!"

After landing at Tachikawa, we had to hold on a taxiway for an hour, while they repositioned other aircraft on the parking ramp to make room for our mammoth C-133. When a parking spot was finally available, and the engines were shut down, a grumpy Aircraft Maintenance Officer came to the cockpit and demanded to know why I had landed at his base with an aircraft in need of an engine change. "I was just following orders, captain, and as soon as you fix our aircraft, we will be on our way," was my response. He left in a huff and my crew and I secured quarters in the transient crew area. I knew that we would be in Tachikawa for at least five days, as a new engine and propeller would have to be flown in by a C-124 and installing it would go slowly as the transient maintenance mechanics were extremely busy and unfamiliar with the C-133.

After five days of shopping, drinking, visiting the many local off-base clubs and bartering with the bar girls, I received a call that our aircraft was repaired and released for flight. The next morning my crew and I were in base operations where I filed a flight plan for Yokota AB (twenty miles to the west) where we would refuel before flying on to Wake Island.

The reason for not refueling at Tachikawa was because man-made obstacles, on both ends of the runway, required a steep climb after takeoff to avoid hitting them. It was therefore necessary to keep the aircraft as light as possible. The obstacles were the handiwork of radical Japanese demonstrators opposing the existence of the base, and to make flight operations difficult they erected high steel towers, along with the constant flying of large kites and balloons. Every so often Japanese police would storm the shacks, where the demonstrators were living, tear down the obstructions, throw a few in jail, but a couple days later the towers, kites and balloons would be back. (The demonstrators finally won the battle and the base was closed and turned into a park in 1977.)

After referring to performance charts to ensure a safe climb gradient, we proceeded to the aircraft for our short five-minute flight to Yokoto. But just prior to taxiing unto the runway, the master cockpit fire warning bell sounded, along with the number three engine fire warning light illuminating. I quickly shutdown all four engines, had a flight engineer scan the number three engine (who reported no indications of a fire) and declared an emergency. In a matter of minutes fire trucks had assembled around the aircraft, but were soon released as there was no indication of an actual fire. However, the fire warning light problem had to be addressed, so a tug was sent to tow us back to the parking ramp. The same disgruntled maintenance officer came to the cockpit, and before he could say a word, I said, "Guess what, captain? We're back. We love your base so much we hate to leave." He didn't appreciate my humor, but understood the seriousness of a fire warning light and said they would look into the problem right away. We spent another night in Tachikawa while maintenance personnel repaired a bad electrical connection in the engine fire warning system. The next day we departed for Yokota, and after refueling, made an uneventful eight-hour flight to Wake Island.

Following a 15-hour crew rest we flew on to Honolulu. My copilot and I were walking into the Officers' Club when I was approached by Captain Robert L. Carpenter, a PFE from my squadron. He began to orally reprimand me for flying a C-133 on three engines from Okinawa to Japan. He accused me of compromising safety, violating MATS directives and committing an overall stupid act! I responded to his criticism in an equally stern voice, by stating, "Captain, you're way off-base and even though your a supposedly "know-it-all" flight examiner, you don't know what in the hell your talking about. Also, keep in mind that your addressing a superior officer and I would suggest that you show proper respect. The reason I didn't return to Kadena, after losing an engine on takeoff, was that the base was undergoing a typhoon evacuation and if I had returned it would have placed the aircraft in severe danger. Before you start accusing a fellow pilot of screwing-up, you better get all the facts. Otherwise keep your mouth shut." Bob calmed down, while confessing that he didn't realize the base was being evacuated because of an approaching typhoon and apologized for jumping on me before gathering all the facts. Bob and I had a drink together at the bar and remained good friends.

The next day we flew to Travis AFB, where we would spend the night. After a shower and a change of clothes I was elbowing my way to the Officers' Club bar for a Beefeater's gin martini. While sipping my drink, I was surprised to see Colonel Hongsakul, my Thai Air Force friend from Bangkok, nursing a martini a few stools down from me. Colonel Hongsakul (reference chapter 10, page 290), was the Thai officer who invited me to be his guest during the *Festival of Lights* in Bangkok in 1962. I walked over to him, said hello, and to my surprise he shook my hand while stating, "Hello, Major Martin. What a nice surprise. Let's shake dice for a drink." (He hadn't forgotten that we had frequently engaged in this game of chance in the Thai Air House three years earlier.) As he rattled the dice box, I asked him what he was doing in the U.S. He told me that his daughter Apasra, now 20-years-old, was selected as the 1965 Miss Universe Queen, and he was returning from the Miami, Florida pageant. He proudly showed me a picture of her being crowned, as the winner of the event. I told him that I wasn't surprised, as I was very impressed with her beauty and charm when I met her in Bangkok. We enjoyed a few more martinis and then adjourned to the dining room for dinner. I insisted that he be my guest and after some "arm-twisting" persuasion he agreed. Following a steak dinner and a bottle of fine wine, we enjoyed a farewell drink at the bar and went our separate ways. (I never saw Col. Hongsakul again, but through a Google Search you can see a picture of his daughter Apasra as the 1965 Miss Universe Queen.)

It's interesting to note that Colonel Hongsakul's daughter, after returning to Thailand, became a very popular social figure. She later married a cousin of Queen Sirikit, and when the 2005 Miss Universe pageant was held in Bangkok, she was one of the VIP guests attending. She would now be 65-years-old, but I'm sure still a beauty!

The next morning, I left on a nine-hour flight to Dover, Delaware and my first flight as a C-133 Aircraft Commander was history. It required 21 days and 75 flight hours to complete. Based on the results of my first solo mission, it was obvious that I was going to spend a lot of time away from home, while enjoying the exciting life of a C-133 *Cargomaster* pilot.

In mid August 1965, the first major battle of the Vietnam War occurred near the city of Chu Lai when the U.S. Army, supported by Naval air support, killed 700 Vietcong soldiers while suffering 45 dead and more than 200 wounded. During this same time frame General Westmoreland was put in command of the approximately 60,000 American troops in Vietnam. My part in this expanding military buildup was to fly frequent combat cargo support missions, carrying the tools of war to our troops.

In less than a week, after returning from my first solo flight to Southeast Asia I was heading west on another mission to Saigon and would keep the same aircraft for the entire flight, so barring any unusual maintenance delays the trip would take about ten days and 75 hours of flight time.

The normal flight crew assigned was two pilots, one navigator, two flight engineers and one loadmaster. However, due to constant training, upgrades, and flight checks it was not unusual to have three or more additional crew members sharing the cockpit. It was great to keep the same aircraft and same crew for the entire flight and the mission was flown without any major problems and I was back in Dover ten days later.

I discovered that I was becoming quite fond of the C-133, in spite of its frequent "jack-in-the-box" surprises. The cockpit was spacious, the pilot seats were like overstuffed chairs and would tilt back almost 45 degrees. The navigator sat directly behind the Aircraft Commander and the engineers panel faced the right side of the cockpit, behind the copilot's seat. I could coordinate with the navigator without using the interphone and by turning my head I could view the entire flight engineer's panel. Directly behind the flight deck was a bulkhead, separated by a curtained doorway, which contained two airline-type seats, equipped with reading lamps, a full galley (with an oven and hot cups), a sofa that folded into a bed and a pull-down bunk that was reserved for the Aircraft Commander. (Air Force rules, on long over-water flights, allowed one pilot at a time to be absent from his assigned crew position, but falling asleep in the bunks, due to high noise and vibration levels, was difficult.)

The lavatory was located in the cargo compartment, but visits there were short. The cargo area contained two additional bunks but were rarely used. The cargo compartment was always freezing cold, extremely noisy, and vibrated so much you were in danger of losing tooth fillings inserted by young "two-year-type" inept dentists. During the rare occasions when we carried military passengers acting as couriers or escorts for military equipment, we strapped down a row of seats in the rear of the cargo compartment (where the noise and vibration was tolerable) and issue these unfortunate souls blankets and ear plugs, and briefed them that once airborne they were free to visit the cockpit, in shifts, to keep from freezing. If we didn't see or hear from them for awhile one of the flight engineers would walk the 90 feet to the rear of the cargo compartment to see if they were still breathing. Usually he would find them still conscious, but wrapped up in blankets, like Eskimos, and sound asleep. It's amazing what our G.I.s can endure and still sleep.

In November 1965, I was upgraded to instructor pilot and felt that this was quite an accomplishment. In less than a year (when considering the four months the C-133s were grounded) I had gone from flying F-100s,

T-33s and T-39s to being an instructor pilot in America's largest transport, bypassing many colleagues who had flown the aircraft for several years.

Flying from the right seat, with my copilot in the pilot's seat, we departed Wake Island for Hickam AFB, Hawaii. About 50 miles west of Honolulu at 23,000 feet we were cleared to descend in preparation for radar vectors to a straight-in instrument approach to runway 08. We reduced power and programmed the autopilot to commence a descent, but the aircraft did not respond. I disconnected the autopilot and pushed forward on the control column, but it would not move toward a "nose-down" position. I requested that my copilot join me in pushing forward on the control wheel, but no matter how much pressure we applied, it would not move! Surprisingly, we discovered that we could move it aft, toward a "nose-up" position, but not forward beyond a neutral position. I didn't know what caused the problem, but ruled out the elevator being frozen in position due to ice. (I jokingly said to my copilot, that unless we can find an airport with an elevation of 23,000 feet, we may have a problem in landing. However he didn't seem to appreciate my unusual humor.)

I declared an emergency with Honolulu Approach Control, and requested a long straight-in descent on the Instrument Landing System (ILS). Experimenting with the other aircraft controls, I discovered that the ailerons and rudder were fully operational and as previously stated, up elevator. When we intercepted the 2.5 degree glide-slope of the ILS, I reduced power and with my copilot and I pushing forward on the control column, I rolled in a climb command on the elevator trim tab. When the airspeed decreased to about 150 knots, I lowered the landing gear and flaps and by adjusting engine power and the elevator trim tab we were able to keep the aircraft on the instrument glide path. And, since we still had aileron and rudder control we were able to remain on the course center line. I figured that we would be able to fly this unorthodox approach right down to the runway threshold, at which time I would reduce the engine power to idle and with up elevator control available, execute a standard "Martin-style" smooth landing. And while the aircraft was being repaired we would enjoy several days of paid vacation in Hawaii.

The reason the copilot and I pushed forward on the control column, when I rolled in a nose-up command on the elevator trim tab, was to prevent the elevator from moving up and forcing the aircraft into a climb. Normally, when the relatively small trim tab is used to command an aircraft nose-up or nose-down, it will move in the opposite direction of the elevator. But, with an elevator that would not allow for a nose-down command, I used the trim tab as a mini elevator by not allowing the elevator to move. This may sound complicated, but it worked great and prevented the PGR of another opportunity of recruiting new members.

Working in close harmony, my copilot and I were flying a beautiful instrument approach and had the Honolulu runway in sight when passing through 10,000 feet. Suddenly, the elevator broke free and we had unobstructed forward and aft movement. A normal landing followed and after engine shutdown I made a detailed write-up in the aircraft maintenance logbook, and orally briefed an Aircraft Maintenance Officer on our in-flight emergency. He assured me that he would find and fix the problem and advise us when the aircraft was back in commission. My crew and I secured quarters in the transient crew area and looked forward to several days of frolicking on Waikiki Beach.

But to my surprise, 12 hours later, we were alerted by the command post duty officer, who stated that our aircraft was in commission and we could proceed to Travis Air Force Base. I was anxious to review the aircraft log book, to see what our maintenance friends discovered, but was aghast when I read the stated corrective action, "Could not duplicate the problem, flight controls ground checked OK, aircraft released for flight." I radioed the command post and told them that I wanted the director of aircraft maintenance to come to my aircraft ASAP, and that no one of lesser rank need show-up. About ten minutes later a Lt.Col. (who was not a pilot) came to the cockpit and wanted to know why I wanted to see him. I showed him the corrective action his mechanics had taken to clear our serious in-flight control problem, stating that it amounted to "no corrective action at all." He attempted to defend their action, by stating that they couldn't find anything wrong with the controls, as they moved freely in all directions. I responded by telling him that of course they couldn't, because after we descended to 10,000 feet the elevators operated normally, but at higher altitudes the control column could not be moved forward. He said, "Maybe the problem was ice?" I told him that this assumption was stupid as they were only jammed in one direction. I demanded that the floor panels around the base of the control columns be removed to inspect the hidden linkage underneath. His response, "That's a hell of a lot of screws to remove, major!" "And I want every damn one of them replaced, after you complete your inspection colonel," I

348

said. "Now if you will hand me a 'speed wrench' I'll work on the copilot's side, while one of your mechanics works on the pilot's side."

After removing a zillion screws, I discovered the problem beneath the copilot's control column. A series of rivets had popped loose from a section of aluminum support (probably from vibration) which allowed it to lodge against the hidden base of the control column, as there were visible scar marks, indicating rubbing. Apparently, the aircraft pressurization differential, at higher altitudes, was sufficient to force the loose metal section against the base of the control column, thereby forming a wedge. But, when the differential pressure decreased during descent, the natural spring tension of the bent metal was sufficient for it to become dislodged. The fix was nothing more than having a sheet metal mechanic install new and stronger rivets on the panel that had broken loose and on the panel that was still in place on the pilot's side. After replacing both floor panels, and a zillion screws, the flight back to Delaware was uneventful.

In late December 1966, the callous disregard by higher headquarters toward maintaining high morale within the flight crew ranks was demonstrated when we were directed to schedule three C-133s on a flight to Saigon with a departure from Dover AFB on Christmas morning, December 25th. I was to be the mission commander, and when I complained that this would not allow 25 flight crew members, and an equal number of support personnel needed to launch the aircraft, to spend Christmas Day with their families, my objection met with little empathy, even when I pointed out that under normal conditions our crews were away from home about 50 percent of the time. I was told that General Westmoreland had complained to President Johnson that he was lacking some critical supplies and in response the president promised him that they would be delivered by New Year's Day. Therefore by allowing one or two days for possible en route problems, it was necessary that our aircraft depart Dover, AFB on Christmas Day.

I proposed that we augment our crews with one additional pilot, which would allow us to fly all the way to Honolulu, before stopping for crew rest. This plan would honor President Johnson's promise to Westmoreland and allow our crews to depart on December 26th. Higher headquarters approved my recommendation providing I contact all the crew members involved and confirm that they agreed to the change, and if they did, we could depart on December 26th. I thought this was a dumb requirement, knowing that everyone would be in favor of my proposal, so without bothering to make 25 phone calls, I called higher headquarters and told them that everyone agreed to the change. The departure date was changed to the day after Christmas and about 50 military men were able to spend Christmas Day with their families.

In early 1966, the majority of our C-133 missions were in support of the ever-increasing U.S. military commitment to South Vietnam. There were constant clashes between American and Vietcong forces and more Americans were dying. Flights across the Pacific Ocean were becoming routine and surprisingly the reliability of the C-133 was markedly improved. However, there were still surprises yet to be discovered, which will be revealed later. However, before doing so, I will attempt to provide a "snap-shot" of the routine C-133 combat cargo crew members experienced during a typical mission to and from the war zone.

The majority of the people in Dover, Delaware, with the exception of flight crews and their families, went about their daily life as if the war news, 9,000 miles away, did not affect them. (I think President Johnson's program of "guns-and-butter" created this false sense of euphoria.) They seemed to be more interested in a new Mexican restaurant opening than they were in the war in South Vietnam. (Surprisingly, our war in Iraq and Afghanistan seems to be creating this same false sense of "well-being" on the home front today. If the military troops lose the support of the country, they are defending, they tend to say, "What in the hell am I fighting for if nobody cares?" We must preserve the will to win, or we will lose.)

However, getting back to the Vietnam War: Upon reaching Travis Air Force Base, California, we would note a gradual change in attitude. Travis was a staging base for troops coming and going to South Vietnam and both groups, for different reasons, were in high spirits. To enhance this feeling of well-being they shared one common pastime, heavy drinking, back slapping, propositioning female officers and swapping war stories. The bar at the Officers' Club was always crowded and it was necessary to elbow your way to the front of the crowd to obtain an inexpensive drink.

Honolulu took you 2,100 miles closer to the war and was the primary location for troops spending two weeks on Rest and Recuperation (R&R), after serving six months of a 12-month tour. Single men found females eager to share in having a good time and every night was "party-night." The Fort DeRussey Army Officers' Club was awash with men, sporting beautiful tanned bodies, drinking too many Mai-Tais, and obviously living it up like there was no tomorrow. Married troops had their wives join them and were not as visible and when in public would be walking hand-in-hand. The husbands would be dressed in loud Aloha shirts, their wives in flowing (obviously new) flowered muumuus and both would be wearing fresh flower leas around their necks. A common watering hole, in addition to the Officers' Club, was Duke Kahanamoku's Night Club in the Honolulu International Center. Playing nightly was Don Ho and his band singing "Tiny Bubbles." Don was a former Air Force pilot and knew how to relate to a military audience, but his remarks sometimes surprised married couples in the audience when he asked them how much of their R&R was spent in their hotel room, but it was all in good fun. Don was an Hawaiian Living Legend and was on R&R himself in 2006 after recovering from a heart operation in Thailand in December 2005. After recovering he continued entertaining Hawaiian vistors at the Waikiki Beachcomber Hotel with dinner shows on Thursday and Sunday evenings, even though he was wearing a pacemaker. However, he died suddenly on April 14, 2007 of heart failure. His final show was on April 12th with a standing ovation.

Moving 2,000 miles further west, to Wake Island, disclosed a totally different atmosphere. There were no military dependents on this small desolate island and it was absent of military men going to or returning from Vietnam (except aircrews). The aircraft parking ramp was usually loaded with C-124s, C-130s and C-133s, while their crews were on 15-hour crew rest, or longer if their aircraft required maintenance. The housing, for both officer and enlisted men, was stacked steel cots, next to an open-air theater and a crowded bar serving 25-cent drinks. Nightly high-stake poker and crap games were always available and if you were required to spend several days on Wake Island, it was interesting to explore old Japanese military bunkers and machine gun nests overlooking the beach area. My personal enjoyment, when visiting the island, was to walk to the edge of the coral barrier reef at night during low tide, and listen to the ocean waves crashing into the rocks. With my back to the lights of the compound, the stars would blend in with the distant horizon and when a shooting star would streak across the sky it seemed to smash into the distant ocean. I don't think an artist could adequately capture this magnificent scene on canvas!

The island was operated by civilians who did an excellent job of supporting the continuous flow of aircraft and even provided an unofficial "mail box" for transient crew members. Those who wished to maintain correspondence with female friends could give their address as "Name, MATS Flight Crew Member, Wake Island." The civilian staff would place incoming letters in a stand-up alphabetical file located in flight operations. It was not uncommon to hear crew members, flying across the Pacific, radioing friends to check their mail when visiting Wake Island. In front of the operations building was a memorial to the Marine fighter pilots that defended the Island against the Japanese attack in December 1941. The memorial was the cowling, engine and propeller of the last F-4U *Wildcat* fighter that fought off the Japanese invaders. It was dredged up from shallow water in the bay.

Guam Island was normally just a refueling stop and unless we required maintenance we would not remain there overnight. However, flying the troublesome C-133 into Guam often required a one or two-night stay. Anderson Air Force Base was a main B-52 bomber base and on many occasions I had to hold for an hour or more before landing because of large numbers of B-52s departing for, or returning from, a bombing mission over Vietnam. The atmosphere of the base and Officers' Club was not what you would expect of a front-line combat base, compared to what we recall of WW II "devil-may-care" bomber bases in England. I believe this was the result of the strict military discipline demanded by the Commander, General Curtis LeMay. (I believe his philosophy was, "It's OK to die for your country, but don't have any fun in the process!")

After refueling in Guam, there were three bases that were used by C-133s before flying into South Vietnam or Thailand: the first, and one of the busiest was Clark Air Base, which I have already described during my first C-133 flight there in June 1965, but was now more raucous than before; the second was the Philippine base of Mactan, across the bay from Cebu City in central Visayas Province. Overnights in Mactan were very enjoyable as there were a limited number of military barracks available on base and we were normally required to stay in hotels in Cebu City. To reach it we traveled by crew bus which had to be ferried across the Cebu River on an old U.S. Navy Landing Ship Tank Boat (LST). When in Cebu City we would have dinner in a large Chinese restaurant, that in addition to serving excellent food at a reasonable price would present a floor show featuring cute young Philippine dancing girls. I personally enjoyed visiting Mactan, as my former colleague from Niagara Falls, New York and Misawa Air Base, Japan, Major Charles Carpenter, was the operations officer of the local command post. Charlie would meet me in the hotel bar and we would enjoy reliving our fun days stationed at the same base. I was even able to get in a round of golf with Charlie on one of my visits, but once was enough in the heat and humidity of the

Philippine Islands; the third possible stop, was Kadena AB, Okinawa. Kadena, without a doubt, was the liveliest combat base in the Pacific. The airfield was home for a mixed bag of aircraft, including fighters, transports, helicopters, rescue aircraft and civilian airliners (with cute flight attendants). Adjacent to the base were dozens of bars, cafes, restaurants and brothels operating 24/7. The Officers' Club bar was always crowded and high-stakes gambling was active day and night. The transient crew quarters were within walking distance of the club and PX, which were awash with military men of all branches of service coming and going. By the time you reached Kadena you knew you were near a combat zone!

The routing when returning to the U.S. was usually a nonstop flight from Okinawa to Midway Island, a distance of 3082 nautical miles and 11 hours, followed by a 2752 mile, 10-hour nonstop flight to Travis Air Force Base. If possible I would adjust my departure time from Kadena for early evening, which would have us arriving at Midway in mid-morning and a night departure. (Departing Midway at night would decrease the chance of striking large Albatrosses "gooney birds" during the takeoff and provide for an arrival time at Travis in time for happy hour at the Officers' Club.)

We could generally count on spending several days at Travis because the base contained a squadron of C-133s and experienced *Cargomaster* mechanics who could correct a variety of discrepancies we had been accumulating and carrying forward. Travis not only provided a good place to unwind after a long hectic mission to Vietnam, but insured we would return our aircraft to Dover, Delaware, in good shape.

I always enjoyed visiting Midway Island and looked forward to crew resting there. The island was operated by the U.S. Navy which took possession in 1867, and in the early days was used as a coal refueling stop for ocean steamers and later as a refueling stop for Pan American Transpacific Clippers. It was also famous for The Battle of Midway in June 1942, which turned the tide of WW II in the Pacific. The Navy moved out in 1993 and the island is now a bird sanctuary and is difficult to reach without prior permission from the U.S. Fish and Wildlife Service.

The small U.S. Navy staff stationed on Midway was extremely friendly and we could always count on a breakfast of steak and eggs no matter what time of the day we arrived. The transient crew quarters were exceptionally clean and there was a white sandy beach available for swimming or taking a snooze while listening to the pounding surf.

Midway Island is also the mating and nesting location for the Laysan Albatrosses "gooney birds" and about 500,000 adult mating pairs spend eight months of the year spread out across the entire landscape in hatching and raising a single chick. When not taking over the island they wander great distances over the North Pacific, never touch land, and sleep while floating on the ocean surface. Their annual arrival back at Midway Island, in late October, is accompanied by considerable amusement, because after spending four months in mastering water landings, they forgot how to land on a hard surface. They glide in with their feet stuck out in front of their 24 pound, 11-foot-wingspan, expecting to skim over a smooth water surface. However, when their webbed feet make contact with the hard surface their legs buckle and they tumble "head-over-heals" in a ball of ruffled feathers. When they stop tumbling, they stand up, shake their heads in bewilderment, as if to say, "What in the hell happened? I thought I was setup for a smooth water landing!"

A harmless activity enjoyed by some Navy sailors would be to gorge several of them with scraps of food from the mess hall until their stomachs were bloated. They would then flush them into attempting a takeoff by waving white T-shirts. The gooney birds would turn into the wind, start running as fast as they could to obtain takeoff speed, but due to their overweight condition would only be able to gain a height of a few inches before stalling, crashing back to earth and tumbling "ass-over-tea-kettle." They would attempt several more takeoffs before giving up, completely exhausted, and wouldn't be able to fly until they digested their U.S. Navy supplied banquet, and discharged a couple pounds of gooney-bird- poop.

Gooney birds mate for life, up to 60 years, and return to the exact spot every year where the female lays an egg and both the male and female take turns in sitting on it until it hatches. Infertile females become depressed in not having an egg to sit on, so enterprising sailors would provide them with a pool or tennis ball, which they would adopt and sit on for months, waiting for it to hatch. However, I never saw a chick emerge from these simulated eggs. But, I guess it was better than administering Prozac to these frustrated dejected females. (See Photo No. 53.)

Another reason I enjoyed visiting Midway was that one of the Air Force officers assigned there was a colleague by the name of Dick Bonds. Dick and I were in the same C-119 squadron in Neubiberg, Germany nine years earlier and he was a great and entertaining friend. He and his wife

Jackie would invite me for drinks and a steak dinner in their beach-style home during many of my Midway stops. One of these enjoyable dinners was during the gooney bird nesting season and a large female was sitting on an egg next to their front screen door. The gooney bird is very territorial and had settled down so close to the door, that it could only be opened a few feet without knocking her off her nest. Entering and leaving required positioning your body sidewise and shuffling in and out through a narrow opening. Jackie had assumed a female fondness for this struggling future 24-pound feathered mother and named her Matilda.

Dick was in the process of mixing me another Beefeater gin martini, when he noted that the bottle was empty. He shouted to Jackie, who was in the kitchen fixing dinner, that he and I were going over to the liquor store to get some more gin and a bottle of wine. As we prepared to leave, Jackie shouted out in a loud voice, **"You guys be careful when you leave, and don't disturb Matilda!"** Dick, who didn't share Jackie's concern for Matilda's maternal proceedings, swung the screen door wide open, knocking her off her nest. Matilda, shaken and obviously pissed off, expressed her displeasure through loud clucking sounds, in concert with rapid up and down head movements. Dick didn't take kindly to being reprimanded by an irate gooney bird and, to express his anger, pointed his index finger close to her head while snarling, "Screw you, Matilda. I have had just about enough of your shit." Matilda, also pissed off, snapped back with lightning speed and struck Dick's hand with her razor sharp beak, creating a one inch long cut. I wrapped a handkerchief around Dick's bleeding hand and we headed for the hospital emergency room, dripping blood on the way. As we left, I noted that Matilda was settling back on her egg, while emitting loud clucking sounds of victory.

The Navy doctor, after stitching up Dick's hand and giving him a tetanus shot, wrapped it in a bulging white bandage. When we returned to the house, carrying a couple bottles of booze and Dick's hand wrapped up in a bandage, Jackie asked what took us so long and what happened to Dick's hand. Dick's response, "That damn Matilda bit me when we left the house." "Dick, I told you to be careful and not to disturb her. If you had knocked me off my nest I would have bitten you as well, but in a place that would have been a lot more difficult to bandage than your hand," was her answer. We enjoyed a great dinner but I had to help Dick cut his steak! The next day I left for the 2752 mile, 10-hour flight to Travis AFB.

In the summer of 1966, the U.S. involvement in the Vietnam War was rapidly expanding and our C-133 missions to the war zone were becoming more frequent. We were carrying a wide variety of military equipment and delivering it directly into combat zones, which included Da Nang, Chu Lai, Phu Cat, Pleiku, Qui Nhon, Cam Ranh Bay, Phan Rang, Bien Hoa, Tan Son Nhut and Nakhon Phanom in South Vietnam and Udorn, Ubon, Korat, Takhii, Don Muang and U Tapao in Thailand. Many of these flights were in direct support of Army and Marine Corps forces engaged in mortal combat. Because of this, I would be advised to keep the ground time to a minimum as the Viet Cong would attempt to get close enough to destroy my aircraft with mortar rounds.

One such mission will illustrate the importance of this warning. I was delivering about 40,000 pounds of small arms ammunition and artillery shells to a forward airstrip being defended by a group of U.S. Marines. Active fighting was taking place in close proximity to the airport, and to avoid enemy ground fire, I flew a steep four degree final approach. In addition, *Huey* helicopters flew alongside each wing tip and kept spraying the surrounding jungle with automatic machine gun fire. The runway was less than 5,000 feet long and after touchdown I went to full reverse, on all four engines, and maximum anti-skid braking. The small narrow runway didn't provide sufficient space for a standard 180 degree turnaround, so I had to reverse course by moving the aircraft back and forth by alternating the use of forward and reverse thrust from the propellers. When turned around, I kept the engines running, while my loadmaster opened the rear cargo ramp, and a long string of Marines began unloading our precious cargo by passing the boxes from man-to-man in a conga line.

Before the off-loading was complete one of my flight engineers came to the cockpit and informed me that we had a badly cut tire. (It had apparently been pierced by bits of debris on the runway.) I left the cockpit to exam the damage and noted a rear external truck tire completely flat and hanging in shreds. I didn't wish to attempt a takeoff with a tire in this condition, as it would most likely tear itself completely apart, damage the aircraft and possibly affect the operation of the landing gear. What to do? While I was deliberating in how to solve the problem, a Marine Corps major arrived on the scene and said, "It will be dark in about one hour, major, and if you don't get your aircraft off the ground before sunset, it won't be here in the morning." (The runway wasn't equipped with lights.)

I asked my flight engineer if he had a hack saw in his tool box. When he said he did, I said, "Get it!" We took turns in cutting through the damaged tire, which required the replacement of several hack saw blades before we could cut through the strong steel bands. We removed the tire, section by section, and threw them off to the side of the runway About 30 minutes later, with blistered hands and bodies soaked in sweat, the tire was removed leaving just a bare rim.

I held the aircraft in place with brakes, advanced all four throttles to full power, turned on the engine water injection system and released the brakes. With an empty cargo compartment and a light fuel load the aircraft was airborne, in a cloud of dust, in less than 3,000 feet. I departed the area in a steep climb while banking from left to right, with the intent of minimizing the chance of being hit by VC gunners striving to improve their small arms skill. After reaching an altitude of 3,000 feet I took up a heading for Clark Air Force Base, 948 miles and four hours to the east.

An uneventful night landing was made at Clark and after the engines were shutdown a Lt.Col. Aircraft Maintenance Officer came to the cockpit and announced, "Major, do you know that you had a right rear tire blowout upon landing?" I told him that it didn't blowout during our landing at Clark, but failed during a landing in Vietnam and we cut it off and flew here with just three tires on the right side. He seemed surprised, and snapped, "Who gave you permission to fly an aircraft in this condition? A missing tire is a grounding item, and I have to make a report." Rising up from my seat and heading for the cockpit door, I told this nincompoop, "You do what you want, colonel, but my crew and I are heading for a shower, a cold beer and a big steak." With that we climbed into a waiting crew bus.

A new tire was installed and I flew an uneventful trip back to Dover, Delaware. About a week later our Wing Commander, General John B. Wallace, called me and asked about a report he had on his desk relating to me flying an aircraft with a missing tire. When I told him about the circumstances surrounding the incident he said that he was throwing the report in the waste paper basket and congratulated me for doing the right thing and probably saving a valuable aircraft in the process.

General Wallace was born in Florence, South Carolina in 1918, graduated from pilot training in 1940 and flew combat missions in B-17s. He was an excellent commander and we became friends. While many general officers avoided flying the C-133 (because of its reputation), he qualified as an Aircraft Commander and when he wished to fly, he would request that I fly with him. He was instrumental in my promotion to Lt.Col., which I will discuss in a subsequent section. He died on Dec. 21, 2004.

In May 1966 I was upgraded to pilot flight examiner (PFE), the highest crew position. I would now, in addition to flying missions as an Aircraft Commander and instructor pilot, administer local annual proficiency checks and perform operational line checks. I was pleased with the promotion, but promised myself that I would not adopt a pretentious attitude toward my pilot colleagues like some other flight examiners did.

One of my first flights in this new status was administering an initial line check to Captain Richard Alexander who at a relatively young age had whipped through the pilot upgrade program. He was a quick study, possessed a remarkable ability for recalling complex aircraft statistics and reflected a likable sense of humor that was not appreciated by some of my "hard-nosed" colleagues. An integral part of the upgrade program to Aircraft Commander was an oral exam administered by a board of senior flight examiners. The exam was designed to evaluate the candidates knowledge of the aircraft, and related subjects, but in my opinion it often digressed into asking ridiculous mundane unimportant questions. I felt that it should last no more than one hour and only encompass important subjects. But some of my colleagues seemed more intent in displaying their own personal knowledge than evaluating the candidate.

This was the case when Captain Alexander went before the board. He had answered everything that we could throw at him correctly, but after sitting before us for nearly two hours some of my colleagues were still asking stupid questions, i.e. "How many knots in the cockpit escape rope?" I could see that Dick was becoming frustrated with the direction the oral exam was taking and his answers were becoming short and somewhat curt. Our operations officer, Major Roy Meyers, asked him to define excessive TIT (a metaphor for Turbine Inlet Temperature). In a firm strong voice Dick said, "Excessive tit is that what you can't get in your mouth." I thought his comment was funny, but Major Meyers considered his answer vulgar and disrespectful. Dick was excused from the room while we deliberated on rating his oral exam satisfactory or unsatisfactory. I argued that it be considered satisfactory since he answered all the important questions properly and to disregard his comment about excessive TIT, which I thought was right on the mark. When the vote was taken it was three for and two against.

After passing his oral exam, I would now have the opportunity of seeing if he could transfer his excellent technical knowledge of the aircraft to practical use. His initial Aircraft Commander line check was to transport a load of war-essential miscellaneous cargo from Dover AFB, Delaware to Tan Son Nhut Airport, Saigon.

Initial line checks required the satisfactory completion of a minimum of two over-water route segments. But the PFE could extend the evaluation to include additional segments at his discretion. According to our route of flight, the two required over-water legs could be fulfilled between Travis AFB and Wake Island, which would include a 15-hour crew rest and refueling stop in Honolulu.

The nine-hour leg from Dover to Travis AFB, California was flown without a problem as well as the eight-hour flight to Honolulu. The aircraft ran like a well-tuned sewing machine and Captain Alexander's crew performed extremely well so there was very little that I could comment on. I thought that the next day's flight to Wake Island, would provide more material for me to form an opinion on Dick's ability to command a sometimes cantankerous C-133. However, once again the weather was great and the aircraft was trouble free, so I had little to use in rendering a final judgment on his performance. I wasn't looking for problems, but I felt like there was something missing. I told him that I would extend the line check to the turnaround point of Tan Son Nhut Airport, Saigon. He had no choice but to accept my decision, so after a refueling stop in Guam and an overnight crew rest in Okinawa, we departed for Saigon.

When over Tan Son Nhut we were instructed to hold at 16,000 feet and subsequently cleared to descend to 9,000, while awaiting our turn to execute an instrument approach. Upon reaching 9,000 feet we detected the strong odor of hydraulic fumes and a flight engineer hurried to the cargo compartment to investigate. A few seconds later he was making a frantic call on the interphone informing the Aircraft Commander (Dick) that there was a high pressure hydraulic leak in the cargo compartment, and it was rapidly filling up with fumes. He requested that the hydraulic pumps be turned off and the aircraft pressurization system be placed in "Ram Air." (This was the correct call for the emergency situation we were facing, as hydraulic fluid, in vapor form, is highly volatile, and the slightest spark could result in one big fiery explosion.) The flight engineer placed his fingers on the appropriate switches, while awaiting the Aircraft Commander's authority to act. However, Captain Alexander appeared to be in a state of immobility and was just staring straight ahead. He appeared to be in a frame of mind that I call, "Cockpit Buck Fever." I said,

"Dick, issue the proper commands to your crew," but he took no action! I couldn't wait any longer for him to act, so I instructed the flight engineer to turn off the hydraulic pumps, depressurize the aircraft, open the outflow valves, go to ram air, and for the crew to don oxygen masks. I then told Dick to get out of the left seat and I took over command of the aircraft. We declared an emergency, lowered the landing gear by an alternate procedure and made an uneventful landing.

After engine shutdown a section of hydraulic line was quickly replaced, and the aircraft was back in commission. I informed Dick that he had failed his initial line check and sent him back to Dover in the jump seat of a C-141. He naturally felt bad but I told him to cheer-up and I would outline additional training requirements I felt he needed before his next line check when I returned to Dover. I then sent a message to our squadron operations officer, informing him of my actions, stating that I would provide additional details after my return.

Back at Dover, with my office door closed, I sat down with Dick and discussed his succumbing to a mental state of paralysis when faced with an actual in-flight emergency. His explanation was honest and not far from what I expected. Before commencing pilot training, he had never piloted an airplane, and during his year as a student pilot he never experienced an actual aircraft emergency. I also discovered that he was not as adventurous as many Aviation Cadets in seeking out audacious exploits and had no desire to fly fighters. He also told me that he had lived a very sheltered youth, was not allowed to drive a car until he was 18, never experienced an auto accident, and most surprisingly, had never been a crew member on a C-133 that experienced a serious incident. The bottom line was that he didn't mentally accept the fact that he was faced with a real live emergency when holding over Saigon and succumbed to a temporary mental block. (A perfect example of "Cockpit Buck Fever.")

I liked Dick and thought he possessed a lot of potential, so I exposed him to a series of every type of emergency I could think of in the C-133 simulator, while not allowing his copilot or flight engineer to assist him in taking proper and immediate corrective action. I then flew with him for four hours in the aircraft and exposed him to simulated emergencies that required both pilot skill and a clear mind to solve. Confident he was ready, I recommended him for another initial line check and gave him the option of having myself or a different PFE administer it. He choose me to administer his repeat flight check.

A few days later we departed for another flight to South Vietnam, with the first segment a 2203-mile, 9-hour night flight to Travis AFB, California. We were approaching Denver, Colorado at 22,000 feet in smooth air, when the flight engineer informed the pilot that he was experiencing a rapid loss of oil on the number three engine. Captain Alexander, without hesitation, ordered his copilot to shutdown the affected engine and feather the propeller, instructed the standby flight engineer to scan the engine from the cargo compartment, called for the Engine Shutdown Check List, directed the copilot to set the transponder code to 7700, declared an emergency, and advised the flight engineer to compute a three-engine cruise ceiling. He then picked up the microphone and told Denver Center that he was diverting to Buckley AFB and requested radar vectors and the latest weather. I didn't have to do a thing but sit in the jump seat and witness a classic example of an Aircraft Commander taking control of a crew and directing proper and quick action when faced with an actual emergency. There was no sign of "Cockpit Buck Fever" and I was proud of the fact that I may have had a hand in bringing his hidden talent to fruition. Dick made an uneventful night landing at Buckley AFB and after the aircraft problem was corrected we flew unto Travis two days later. After transiting Honolulu and landing at Wake Island (which fulfilled the two required over-water route segments), I congratulated Dick on becoming our newest C-133 Aircraft Commander.

Approximately 70 percent of my officer colleagues during the Vietnam War were married and generally in their late twenties or early thirties. (There were no female flight crew members.) Supplying the tools of war resulted in them being absent from their families about 50 percent of the time, and in some cases more. These long separations, in combination with the historical lowering of individual inhibition during times of war, resulted in some interesting behavior.

The unmarried officers, as expected, were more adventurous than married men in pursuing lively off-duty entertainment, including excessive drinking, scrimping on sleep and female companionship. In contrast, married officers would usually fall in one of three categories:

The first group were "Straight Arrows" and their off-duty activity was limited to a few beers, a good meal, a movie and retreating to their room to read or enjoy a good night's rest. If a strange female smiled at them, or said hello, they would quickly recoil into their manly shell and head for the BOQ, not to be seen again until the next morning. This uncorrupted group were constantly displaying pictures of their wives and children and boasting about how lucky they were to have such a great family.

The second group would occasionally take advantage of their temporary status as displaced married bachelors and have several drinks with the boys, say hello to good-looking females and occasionally ask one to dance. They would also visit a topless bar, if accompanied by other men, and may even visit a massage parlor in Okinawa, Saigon or Thailand, but would never visit a bordello. If propositioned by a horny female they may allow the wartime euphoria to influence their behavior, but would be back in the BOQ a short time later taking a long hot shower, to cleanse their bodies and erase any feelings of guilt.

The third group, which included myself, took full advantage of their temporary bachelor status and enjoyed the relaxed atmosphere prevalent during times of war. We drank too much, stayed up too late and could always be found asking good-looking female officers for a dance in the Officers' Club. If conditions were favorable for a one-night romp in the sack, we would almost never turn it down and probably spend the whole night savoring the moment. This "carefree, devil-may-care-group" felt that resisting the healthy temptation of being a virile man, and suppressing the natural flow of testosterone working overtime, could cause frustrations of such magnitude that it could jeopardize flight safety. Most, for unexplained reasons, felt a greater animalistic need to enjoy the natural release of their seeds of life, than their "Straight-Arrow" colleagues. The general consensus of this group was that there was a war on and "their behavior was not unlike their father's or grandfather's in previous wars."

No matter which group you happened to be in, there was a mutual respect for colleagues anonymity, knowing that everyone loved and missed their wives and children and would give up their philandering in a heartbeat, in exchange for being home with their families. There was also a "Band-of-Brothers Code-of-Silence," in that what happened on layovers would not be discussed back home. From what I observed, a certain amount of "sowing-wild-oats" resulted in most men loving their wives even more. This was due to a feeling of guilt, accompanied by the realization that "one-night stands" could never compete with what they had waiting for them at home! Wives usually benefited from this feeling of remorse by being recipients of frequent and expensive welcome home gifts!

On Friday afternoon, June 24, 1966, I landed at Travis AFB, following a 10-hour flight from Midway Island. After a shower and a change of clothes my navigator and I headed for the Officers' Club for the Friday night "happy hour." As usual, the club was crowded with servicemen and women from all branches of the military and we had to fight our way to the bar to obtain a drink. I looked across the bustling room and spotted two young women entering and looking for a place to sit. To their good fortune, four patrons were vacating a table and they quickly grabbed it before anyone else could lay claim to it, but this left two empty seats.

My navigator (who was also from group three) and I walked over and asked if we could join them. They readily accepted and in our "get acquainted" discussions we learned that they were Air Force captains and registered nurses who worked at the base hospital. One of them, who I took a special shining to, was named Helen, who had recently returned from a three-year tour in Torrejon Air Station, Spain. I asked her to dance and when holding her close experienced a rush of excitement that I hadn't experienced in 17 years. This was the fourth time in my life that I had felt such an instant attraction toward a female: the first time when I was a junior in high school, the second time when I was an Aviation Cadet in Shreveport, Louisiana, and the third time when I met my wife, Jo Dunham, in Wiesbaden, Germany, (Ironically she was also a nurse).

I'm sure Doctor Kinsey could explain the reason why some women have an instant effect on certain men. But all I knew was, that at age 38, I felt like a teenager with a heart-throbbing crush on my newl friend. Their was a definite interchange of body chemistry that I sensed was mutually felt. I believe this inexplicable sensation can best be described in a refrain from a song from Rodgers & Hammerstein's, South Pacific, which states: "Who can explain it who can tell you why? Fools give you reasons, wise men never try!"

As the night drew on we talked, drank Beefeater gin martinis and danced to the music from a jukebox. The atmosphere in the club was one of war-time merriment, filling the room with laughter, clinking glasses, Barbara Streisand singing "People," or Jerry Vale's "Strangers in the Night" and male and female officers just having fun. Little thought was given to the fact that there was a war raging 7,800 miles on the other side of the ocean and military colleagues were fighting and dying in greater numbers every day. But for the moment, thoughts of the war were drowned out by the extravagant consumption of liquor, the enjoyment of good company and being part of a family of military officers, all sharing the same goal. At least for the moment everyone was having a good time and not worrying about tomorrow, as tomorrow would take care of itself.

This jovial atmosphere helped me forget that during my last departure from Saigon, I flew 15 aluminum coffins, containing the remains of young men killed in combat, to Okinawa, where they would be flown to the U.S. in C-141s. Around 1 a.m. our drinking partners dropped us off in front of the BOQ, but before departing Helen invited me for a home-cooked meal in her apartment in Fairfield the following night.

I took a taxi to her apartment, located in a housing complex known as Phoenix Court, and upon entering was welcomed with a chilled Beefeater martini and the pleasant aroma of a beef roast simmering in her small kitchen. Several martinis later I was treated to a delicious meal, accompanied with a bottle of excellent French red wine, a fattening dessert and after-dinner drinks of Cointreau on the rocks. Following dinner we made ourselves comfortable on the living room floor, engaged in subdued conversation about our military experiences (I learned she was 28-years old), while listening to her excellent collection of stereo records. Feeling the effects of the alcohol (we drank nearly a full bottle of gin, a bottle of wine and after-dinner drinks), we allowed ourselves to occupy the same floor space. When I suggested that it would be more comfortable if we relocated to her soft bed upstairs, she readily agreed. I found the bed more commodious than the hard floor and when I awoke around 4 a.m. I took a taxi back to Travis Air Force Base.

The following evening my navigator and I were invited to her apartment to enjoy a bottle of Chivas Regal Blended Scotch Whisky with her nurse colleague, who we had met the previous Friday night. In a quiet corner, I apologized for taking advantage of her the night before, but she responded with, "It takes two to tangle, Lou, so it was my fault as much as yours, but what happened was not my normal behavior and it won't happen again!" After finishing the bottle of scotch my navigator and I took a taxi back to the base and departed the next day on a 9-hour nonstop flight to Dover, AFB, Delaware.

Three days later, our wing commander, General John B. Wallace, contacted me and said that he wished to fly one of our nightly nonstop flights to Chateauroux Air Station, France and wanted me to accompany him as instructor pilot. Naturally the general, as in past flights, would fly from the left seat while I occupied the copilot's seat.

Our night flights to the U.S. Air Station in Chateauroux, France (about 125 miles south of Paris) were very popular with staff pilots and for administering annual line checks to Aircraft Commanders. The distance to Chateauroux was 3289 nautical miles, but due to prevailing Westerly winds, the east-bound flight could be flown nonstop in 12 hours. After a 24-hour crew rest the return west-bound flight would make a refueling stop at Lages Airport, in the Azores. In a period of three days it would generate a flight time of close to 27 hours. The departure time from Dover was 7 p.m., providing an arrival time in France of around noon (local time). After an afternoon crew rest we would normally enjoy a seven-course dinner in a fabulous French restaurant. The next morning we would visit the BX for shopping before returning home.

However, on this particular Chateauroux flight, an Air Force friend of General Wallace, also a general, would accompany us and we would be authorized 48 hours crew rest before returning. General Wallace said that the additional ground time would allow us time to attend the 24-hour auto race at LeMans, but only under certain conditions. After arriving in France he asked me to see if I could arrange transportation to LeMans but not to seek any special favors that would invoke impropriety on his part. I told him that I fully understood and would see what I could do.

After the long overnight flight from Dover, the two generals and the rest of the crew went to bed, while I headed for the Special Service Office. I talked to the OIC and asked him if he was planning on sending a military bus to LeMans, so base personnel could attend the famous LeMan's Auto Race. He said that he hadn't thought about it, but it sounded like a good idea and he would make an announcement over their local Armed Forces Radio Network (AFN), stating that anyone interested should contact him for a free bus ride. I suggested that the bus should depart around 10 a.m. the following morning so as to be in place for the start of the race at 4 p.m. He agreed. Before leaving his office I requested that he reserve seven seats for my crew. (I didn't tell him that two of the crew members were general officers.) When I told the generals of how we were to travel to LeMans they were pleased and the prospect of a long uncomfortable military bus ride didn't dampen their spirits.

The next morning we boarded an Air Force bus for the 100-mile drive to LeMans arriving around 2 p.m. In addition to our group of seven, there were about 20 airmen riding with us, so there was no way the generals could be accused of misuse of government transportation. When purchasing race tickets we were told that there were no more bleacher seats available, but they did have "standing-room-only" space in the mid-field. We purchased what they had, while our two generals, who had made previous arrangements, were afforded seats in a VIP section.

The LeMan's Race Track is 8 1/2 miles long and soon after watching the drivers sprint to their cars to start the race, the cars became widely spaced. After about two hours of standing in a dusty field and watching one car at a time zoom by, I became very bored and said to my navigator, "Just think, only 22 hours more to go." I retreated to the carnival grounds adjacent to the race track, had something to eat and wrote post cards.

That evening there were occasional scattered light showers, but the shrill whine of the cars racing around the track never stopped. When darkness fell the cars kept zooming around the course, while hundreds of vendors and carnival rides were operating at full force. Later that night I returned to our bus to try to get some sleep, but it was too hot inside so I, and other standing-room-only race fans, crawled under the bus. (We didn't want to lay on the grass outside, in fear of being run over by automobiles coming and going.) In an attempt to drown out the ear-splitting sound of the race cars, I stuffed cotton, obtained from a first-aid kit, into my ears. I had only been asleep a short time when it started to rain quite hard and water began flowing under the bus. I retreated to the inside, which was still very warm, but managed to get a few hours of uncomfortable sleep, while sitting upright in a hard seat.

I awoke as it was getting light, removed the cotton from my ears, and went looking for a place to take a pee and brush the dust out of my teeth. The night before the rest rooms were separated by signs stating "Hommes" and "Dames" (men and women), but by the following morning the differentiation was meaningless. The rest rooms were jammed packed with both sexes and nobody seemed to mind. After finishing my morning hygienic chores, I stood in line for crepes suzette and strong coffee, and after finding a secluded spot addressed a few more post cards, glancing at my watch I noted, "Only eight more hours to go!"

Around 2 p.m., I elbowed my way toward the race track and watched a Ford GT40 Mark II win the race. "Whoopee, it was over!" After a long wait to escape the confines of the parking lot we were back on the road to

Chateauroux. Four hours later I was standing in a hot shower and washing the sand and dust out of my nostrils, ears and other body crevices. I stood in the shower for 30 minutes before I felt clean enough to emerge. The next time someone asks me If I would like to attend the 24-hour auto race at LeMans, I'll pass. The next day we departed France and after a refueling stop in the Azores, were back home in Dover.

By late July 1966 there was no question that we were fully engaged in a seemingly never-ending war in Vietnam. Thousands of U.S. troops were battling the Vietcong and 1,300 were killed near the town of Con Thien. Much of the brunt of this new fighting initiative was the incorporation of large numbers of Bell UH-1 *Huey* Helicopters. More than 16,000 of these versatile mobile fighting machines were built and the Army and Marines went through them in rapid order. To maintain a steady supply, C-133 *Cargomasters* were assigned the task of airlifting them directly into combat areas. I was directed to proceed to the Naval Air Station in Corpus Christi, Texas (a distance of 1290 miles and 5 hours flight time from Dover, Delaware), load five UH-1s and deliver them to Qui Nhon, Vietnam. Corpus Christi was the prime overhaul facility for the *Hueys* and was to become a regular stop. By folding the rotor blades, and retracting the stairway to our flight deck, five helicopters could be loaded in the cargo compartment. The empty weight of each helicopter was 4,750 lbs, so with five onboard the total cargo load was only 23,750 lbs. This would allow for departing with full fuel loads and initial climbs to 20,000 feet. When the aircraft was loaded and refueled, I flew on to Travis AFB, (a distance of 1430 miles and 6 hours) arriving there around 5 p.m. Before departing Texas, I called Helen and invited her out for dinner. She was glad to hear that I would be remaining overnight and said she would pick me up in her new car, which she was eager to show me.

She drove up in front of the BOQ in a new 1966 light green, two-door, Pontiac *Grand Prix* with white leather interior. It was a beautiful car and she was rightly very proud of it. She jumped out and asked me if I would like to drive. We drove to what would become our favorite restaurant in Fairfield called *Dick's Seafood Grotto* which was operated by an Air Force friendly Italian by the name of Dick Stellina. The ambiance was Hawaiian and the quality of the food was worth the long wait for a table. While waiting to be seated we enjoyed Beefeater martinis at the bar. After dinner we drove to her apartment for after-dinner drinks and to listen to some music, but before we became too entangled in affectionate body language, she let me know, in a very gentle but sincere manner, that her bedroom was off-limits and what happened when we first met was not to become a regular event. Even though this created a certain amount of frustration on my part, I understood and respected her for "just saying no!" Later that night she dropped me off in front of the BOQ and I told her that if I was on schedule, I would be back in about eight to ten days.

The next morning I departed for South Vietnam, with stops in Hawaii, Wake Island and Okinawa. This was to be my first landing at Qui Nhon and I was looking forward to the challenge. The runway was only 100 feet wide, 5,000 feet long and constructed of perforated steel planking (PSP). (A rough temporary runway made famous during WW II.) One end of the runway was a few feet from the South China Sea, while the opposite end embraced Vietnamese peasant shacks. A fairly large aircraft parking ramp was located on the West side of the airport. After a full reverse, anti-skid landing, I taxied to the parking ramp and before we completed the Engine Shutdown Check, the rear aircraft loading ramp was open and eager Army troops were off loading the first of five helicopters. They would position an "over-center" wheeled dolly underneath a helicopter, raise it up off the cargo compartment floor and slowly remove it from the aircraft.

Once the helicopter was positioned on the parking ramp, mechanics would start unfolding the propeller blades, while a refueling truck filled it with gas and ground crewmen plugged in an auxiliary power unit. Before the third helicopter was off-loaded the first one was already airborne. The entire ramp area was bustling with activity, with jeeps pulling artillery cannons and trucks loaded with young troops racing toward the sound of battle. I could hear the intermittent chatter of machine gun fire, along with the deep bark of outgoing artillery and muffled mortar rounds. The concussion blasts from the 105 howitzers could be felt on my cheeks.

Four of the helicopters had been off-loaded when it became apparent that there was a problem in removing the fifth one. An Army lieutenant told me that the axle on the dolly broke and they were trying to figure out how to remove the remaining helicopter sitting in the far end of the 90-foot long cargo compartment. A variety of ideas were put forth but none seemed to solve the problem. An Army major approached and said that it was imperative that I get my aircraft off his ramp ASAP as the VC had already spotted it and would soon be lobbing in mortar rounds in attempts to destroy it. I looked at the group of men attempting to off-load the last chopper and felt that if I left the scene they would find a way to remove it, without damaging the aircraft floor, my only requirement. In other words, I

368

felt that they could solve the problem without me looking over their shoulder, and walked across the ramp to see if I could find a cold drink.

I entered a small building, that had an air conditioner poking out through a window, hoping I could find a cold Coke in a cool environment. Inside were two young airmen watching the TV program Gunsmoke, on a small 17-inch screen sitting on top of a steel filing cabinet. As I entered, one of them looked up and I asked him if they had any cold drinks. "Sure, major, over there in the ice chest. Help yourself." he quipped, and went back to viewing the TV. I opened a cold can of Coke and joined my two battle-hardened airmen in watching the program. The reception was surprisingly good, but every time a 105 Howitzer artillery round went off, the steel cabinet would shake and the TV picture would momentarily disappear, but come back on when the shaking stopped. (I wondered if Matt Dillon, Katie and Chester ever thought that they would be entertaining troops in a battle zone in South Vietnam.) I thought the scene was quite bizarre, but in spite of this I soon became immersed in wondering how Matt Dillon was going to solve his latest problem in Dodge City, Kansas. However, before I finished my Coke, and before the TV episode was over, a soldier stuck his head through the door and announced, "Major, they got the last helicopter off your aircraft and the CO wants it off the ground ASAP." I left not knowing how Matt Dillon solved his problem with the "black hats", but I had a dilemma of my own and couldn't hang around to find out. Thirty minutes later I was racing down the runway for takeoff and with an empty aircraft, I flew a steep climb-out to minimize the chance of being hit by ground fire. I then headed for Kadena, Okinawa, five hours to the east.

I arrived back at Travis AFB around 5 p.m. three days later and called Helen, but discovered that she was on duty in the Intensive Care Ward of the base hospital, so after a shower and a change of clothes I walked over to see her. She said that she was on-duty until midnight, but had the next couple days off. This would work out well with my schedule, since the maintenance discrepancies on my aircraft would take two or three days to repair. She handed me the keys to her Grand Prix, suggesting I use it to take my crew out for dinner, with the understanding that I pick her up at midnight. (My copilot and navigator were impressed when I offered to drive them to Dick's Seafood Grotto restaurant in a shiny new Pontiac.) After dinner and a couple drinks at the Officers' Club, I was parked in the entrance to the base hospital waiting for Helen. When she walked through

369

the front door and headed toward me waiting in her car, I couldn't help but note how pretty and distinguished she looked in her white nurse's uniform. As she approached she smiled, and while offering one in exchange, I mentally asked myself, "Where is this mutual affection heading?" We drove to her apartment, enjoyed a late-night martini, listened to a few records, exchanged a few warm hugs and went to bed. She in her upstairs bedroom by herself, and me on the downstairs sofa.

The next day we drove to San Francisco to see the movie *Sound of Music,* and later had a late-night dinner in a restaurant on Fisherman's Wharf. (Another movie we saw during this visit was *Doctor Zhivago* and I thought the love triangle between Dr. Zhivago and Lara, in an obligatory way, echoed my relationship with Helen. I, like Zhivago loved my wife and kids but at the same time had unwittingly fallen in love with another woman who was also a nurse.) After returning to Travis AFB, we enjoyed night caps and dancing in the Officers' Club bar, followed by her dropping me off in front of the BOQ. The next morning I flew back to Dover, AFB.

Back in Delaware I learned, to my disappointment, that I had been passed over for lieutenant colonel. This was a real blow to my self-esteem and was also a surprise to my mentor, General Wallace. He called me at home to express surprise and to inquire if there was any hidden reason that he was not aware of as to why I was not promoted. I told him that my last assignment was Misawa Air Base, Japan, and my rating and endorsing officials possessed a warped opinion that Air Force Officer Effectiveness Reports (OERs) were inflated documents. And that they felt that all officers were expected to perform in an outstanding manner and OERs should reflect an average performance rating. I told General Wallace that before being assigned to Misawa, I served a tour with the 14th AF Inspector General's Staff and my OERs were rated in the highest column (outstanding). Yet my Misawa friends, in spite of my objections, insisted on rating me and other outstanding officers as average. They felt that they were being the vanguard in bringing down inflated reports. (This may have been a noble goal, but when my performance reports were reviewed by the promotion board in Washington, they didn't consider me worthy of promotion.) Gen. Wallace thanked me for filling him in and said, "Don't worry, Major Martin, there is another Lt.Col. promotion board in a few months, and I guarantee that you will be promoted when they meet."

General Wallace directed, that during the next several months, my reporting official would be changed every 60 days. This would require that each previous reporting official submit an OER, and in compliance with his desires, these additional OERs would reflect outstanding ratings. In addition, he voluntarily added personal endorsements to each report. His first endorsement read: "I have observed the absolutely superior performance of Major Martin and concur with this report, which documents his achievements. He is a definite asset to this command and the United States Air Force. *Promote him now.*"

Another endorsement, from General Wallace read: "I concur with this absolutely superior report. I know Major Martin well and have flown with him on a number of occasions. He is one of the finest pilots in the business. His vast experience in the C-133 has been put to good use in his duties as a Pilot Flight Examiner and he is now being assigned as Squadron Chief of Aircrew Standardization. He sets a fine example for others, is neat in appearance, thorough in his paperwork, pleasant in personal contacts and articulate in discussions. *This is an all-round superior officer who should be retained on active duty and promoted as soon as possible!* He has great potential."

In November 1966, I was promoted to Lt.Col. with a back-dated rank of September. (At the time I was 38 years old and the youngest Lt.Col. on the base). Subsequent to being promoted, General Wallace added additional voluntarily endorsements, which read in part: "I concur except for the overall evaluation which I have raised from Outstanding, Almost Never Equaled, to Absolutely Superior. I have worked closely with this officer and consider him to be one of the finest pilots I have known. He is doing a superior job as the Squadron Standardization Officer. He sets an example and people like and respect him. He is quick, thorough, and dedicated. His recent promotion was well deserved. *This officer should be retained on active duty.* We need more like him." (See Photo No. 22.)

Another Wallace endorsement read: "Lt. Colonel Martin is 'Absolutely Superior' in all respects. I have worked closely with him (being attached to his squadron for flying) and consider him one of our top experts in the C-133. He is now ready for bigger jobs with more responsibilities and I intend to move him for career broadening at the first opportunity."

A later endorsement read: "Truly one of the finest officers I know, Lt. Colonel Martin has demonstrated superior abilities in all his endeavors. He sets an example and has the respect of his superiors and subordinates alike. He has shown great potential and should be moved to various duties for career broadening. *Award him a regular commission and promote to Colonel.*"

371

(Thanks to General Wallace, I lost very little in date of rank as a Lt.Col. by not being promoted on the first go-around.)

General Wallace retired in 1969 and was replaced, as Wing Commander, by Brigadier General Fred W. Vetter, who added the following endorsement to my first OER under his command: "Lt.Col. Martin is an officer of numerous outstanding qualities, has contributed substantially to the 200,000 accident-free flying hours by the 39th Military Airlift Squadron. His knowledge and proficiency in the C-133, as well as his dedication to the mission, are unsurpassed and well recognized throughout the Military Airlift Command. As the back bone of the standardization program, his dynamic efforts have indeed enhanced overall C-133 aircrew proficiency. I have personally observed his superior managerial skills in directing a squadron sponsored off-duty activity in the Officers' Club which was an overwhelming success. Promote to Colonel at the earliest opportunity."

These endorsements by two general officers recommending that I be promoted to Colonel, be afforded a regular commission and be retained on active duty, were ignored when Richard Nixon was elected President in 1968. His campaign promise was to end the war in Vietnam "by surrendering" and reducing our military strength. Part of this draw-down was forcing career reserve officers eligible to retire to do so with an effective date of March 30, 1970. Officers who were affected by this decision were lumped into one category --- the good, the bad and the ugly. (A typical government bureaucratic knee-jerk decision.)

The stupidity of a March 30 separation date would mean that Air Force officers would have to pull their children out of military schools and find someplace for them to finish their last 60 days of the school year. (So much for good human relations and taking care of Vietnam War veterans.) In my case, it would result in my daughter Lynn, who was a senior and honor student in the Dover AFB High School, not being allowed to graduate with classmates with whom she had spent the last six years. I was outraged, and submitted a request for a 90-day extension to my forced retirement date. I pointed out that extending it to June 30 would result in me retiring within the same fiscal year, and therefore would not have a serious effect on the budget but would mean a great deal to my children attending a military school, especially my 17-year-old daughter.

General Vetter recommended that my request be approved, but other staff officers held out little hope that it would be looked upon favorably in Washington. However my request was approved in a message dated

November 1969, which read: "The Secretary of the Air Force approves the request submitted by Lt.Col. Louis J. Martin for extending his Date of Separation (DOS) from 31 March 70 to 30 June 70." I was pleased to learn that we still had a few conscientious leaders in Higher Headquarters. Based on the approval of my extension request, the forced retirement order for officers with dependent children in military schools was revised to allow them to remain on active duty until June 30, 1970. I received many phone calls of thanks from officers throughout the Air Force who were helped by this retirement extension approval. (Once again it proves that one person can make a difference.)

In late August 1966 I took five days annual leave to visit my brother Ben, in Los Altos Hill, California, but also to accompany Helen to Reno, Nevada to register her new car. (Registering automobiles in Nevada, was a common practice by military personnel to avoid the high taxes in California.) After registering her car we drove to Lake Tahoe, for a short overnight holiday. I had hopes of repeating the stimulating success I enjoyed when we first met, but Helen held true to her program of self-denial and insisted on separate motel rooms. In spite of this "lockout" we had a wonderful time and I could sense that our fondness for each other was growing stronger each time we met. I didn't know how to handle this new unplanned affection and felt a strong sense of guilt regarding my wife and kids living in Delaware without a husband and father about half the time. I'm sure other men, especially military ones during times of war, have experienced this same troubling situation, but this was new to me and I was confused in how to confront it. But for the moment, I decided to just enjoy the company of my newly found soul mate and worry about tomorrow, tomorrow. We enjoyed a wonderful dinner, played the slot machines, slow danced until the wee hours and retired to our respective individual motel rooms.

The next day we drove back to Travis, where Helen prepared another delicious home-cooked meal. She was an excellent cook and a real joy to be with. After another night on the sofa, I left the next morning for Dover, Delaware and home. After arriving home I gave my two kids an unusually long hug, which to me made sense, but to them was a little surprising!

As the war effort expanded, I continued to fly frequent combat support trips to South Vietnam and Thailand. Flying back and forth across the Pacific Ocean became very routine and it seemed to grow smaller with each crossing. The C-133 was performing surprisingly well, and by allowing crews to remain with the same aircraft was keeping them pretty much on schedule. Our primary mission was still airlifting *Huey* helicopters and general cargo, but at times critical material was flown directly to our front-line troops fighting the Vietcong. Under these conditions I would execute a steep approach in the landing pattern, while being escorted by helicopters spraying the surrounding jungle with automatic machine gun fire. I'm not sure how much enemy ground fire this action suppressed, but it no doubt killed a lot of monkeys! The U.S. Government, as an incentive to improve morale, allowed a $500 tax exemption per month for officers serving in Vietnam and a total tax exemption for enlisted men. (It only required one combat flight per month in or over South Vietnam to qualify for this exemption.)

By the end of 1966 American forces serving in South Vietnam reached a total of 365,000, in addition to the 60,000 Navy personnel stationed offshore. More than 6,000 American servicemen had been killed in the past year, along with 30,000 wounded. It was estimated that 61,000 North Vietnamese had been killed, out of an indeterminate force of 280,000.

During my frequent stops in Travis AFB (which usually lasted two or three days while my aircraft was being repaired), I was still seeing Helen and borrowing her car when she was on duty. We enjoyed leisurely dinners in local restaurants and even attended a Catholic mass together one Sunday morning. (Helen was a devout Catholic, which most likely provided her with the willpower to engage in abstinence from libidinous encounters.) I was born and raised a Catholic and probably should have shared in her adherence to coitus self-denial, but I figured that if God wished me to abstain from male behavioral peculiarities, he wouldn't have made me so damn horny! Nevertheless, I respected her dedication, and it didn't diminish my respect for her. I was becoming a frequent member of her social group and was recognized as a frequent visitor by her many friends. Where this relationship would take us was an unsolved question, and I felt that I would have to make a decision soon, regarding our future life, if there was to be a future, but not today!

In December 1966, General Wallace called and invited me to accompany him and a two-star general from McGuire Air Force Base, New Jersey and General Robert D. Forman, the former commander of Chateautoux Air Station, France, on a ski holiday to Switzerland. We would take ten days annual leave, fly to Chateauroux in one of our C-133s, and meet General Forman, who had arranged to charter a civilian bus to drive us to Switzerland. He said that Major Gordon S. Pink (my former C-119 pilot colleague from Germany) would be going with us.

I had met General Forman when I first arrived in Germany in 1949, when as a colonel he welcomed our group of 20 new second lieutenants to Europe. I liked him then and as a general he was still pleasant to be around. The bus he chartered had the last four rows of seats removed and in their place was a fully-stocked bar and cooler with a variety of snacks. General Forman invited eight of his former staff members to join us, so with a party of 12 "happy-go-lucky" Air Force men and women of mixed rank and dressed in ski clothes, we headed for Switzerland.

It took us a full day of drinking to reach Switzerland, followed by a staggering stroll to our cozy hotel rooms. After five days of skiing, we restocked our bar and headed back to Chateauroux. The trip back was not as raucous as the outbound trip, as skiing had sapped a goodly portion of our party luster, but we still managed to empty numerous bottles of champagne. We drove through the main gate of Chateauroux Air Base around 9 p.m. on a Saturday night, and I thought the bus would take us directly to our BOQ rooms. However, this was not to be!

General Forman announced that everyone was to be his guest for a nightcap at the Officers' Club and he directed the bus driver to take us there. As the bus pulled up to the front of the club, we noted that the parking lot was full of cars and officers milling about in their mess dress uniforms (military tuxedos) and women were dressed in full-length evening gowns. Apparently, the officers were holding their formal annual Christmas party and this fact had been overlooked by General Forman. Since we were all dressed in rumpled ski sweaters and the men in need of a shave, we figured the general would cancel his invitation of buying us a drink, but with a wave of his hand he said, "Follow me, fellow skiers, and don't let the Air Force monkey suits bother you."

When 12 unkempt ski bums, dressed in their disheveled attire, entered this formal dress setting, all eyes were focused in our direction. Gordon Pink and I stayed close to our general officer friends, least some colonel decided to make our presence an issue. General Forman made room for us at the bar, by asking several formally-attired officers and their wives to move, and asked us what we wanted to drink. I ordered a double Beefeater martini. As I was sipping my drink, a drunk colonel came up to me and said, "You're out of uniform, sir. What is your name and rank?"

Before I could answer his wife started tugging on his sleeve, and said, "Leave them alone, honey. They're with the generals." He showed good sense and followed his wife's advice and staggered away.

I thought that after our one drink at the bar we would leave the club and head for our rooms, but General Forman was not through entertaining us. He discovered that they were about to start a floor show and he was having club employees bring in two large tables and chairs from a back room. He and several club employees had patrons, already seated, move their tables off to the side so ours could be placed directly in front of the stage, providing an excellent view of a professional entertainment group from Paris, while silver champagne buckets were setup and waiters started filling our glasses. I still have visions of this strange sight --- here we were, dressed in ski clothes, and attending an officer's formal mess dress party, while sitting at tables in front of the stage and drinking French champagne. What a night! The next day we left for Dover, and I'm sure the local inhabitants were happy to see us leave.

General Forman retired in 1966, and became the manager of the Dover Delaware Downs horse and auto race track. He was killed in a tragic auto accident in 1971 while riding with General Wallace and his wife, who escaped injury. He was a WW II Combat veteran and served his country well. They don't make men like General Forman anymore!

Our longest nonstop Pacific Ocean flight was from Okinawa to Midway Island, a distance of 3082 miles, and depending on the prevailing winds the trip segment would take 11 to 12 hours. We would usually depart Okinawa in the evening, climb to an initial altitude of 15 to 17 thousand feet and request higher altitudes as we burned off fuel. By the time we approached Midway we would normally be at an altitude of 23,000 feet. Even though these flights were long, they were very enjoyable. We could normally expect smooth air, and for about two hours enjoy the Eastern horizon grow from a pale blue, to a light pink and finally a bright red, as the sun came into view. On one of these flights we were experiencing an unusually-strong tail wind, giving us a ground speed of 380 knots, which shortened the estimated en route time to about nine and a half hours. My navigator, when announcing this phenomenon, said, "Colonel, I bet we can fly all the way to Honolulu tonight and set a new nonstop distance record for C-133 Pacific flights!"

His comment interested me, as this would result in a nonstop flight of 4,223 nautical miles in less than 15 hours! I got up from my pilot's seat, reviewed the navigator's "crunch numbers" and agreed that it was possible to overfly Midway, and continue on to Honolulu, but I wanted to build in a safety caveat before making a decision! Addressing the navigator I said, "Taking into consideration a worst case scenario of zero winds between Midway Island and Honolulu, will we still have sufficient fuel, including an adequate reserve, to overfly Midway?" His answer, "Yes, sir, colonel, no sweat."

I contacted Honolulu Radio and obtained a clearance to overfly Midway, and took up a heading for Hawaii, 1141 miles and four and a half hours away. Looking down at the crescent-shaped island, 23,000 feet below, was a sight I hadn't seen before and I surreptitiously wondered if I had made the right decision. Initially my navigator informed me that the strong tail winds we had experienced earlier had dropped off to about 20 knots, but this was still well above my worst case scenario of zero winds, so I wasn't too concerned. By the time we were approaching our halfway point, or point of no return, the navigator reported that our tail wind had dropped off to zero. And shortly thereafter he reported that we were now experiencing a 20-knot head wind, but was rechecking his figures to confirm this unexpected result. Once again, I got up from my seat and joined the navigator at his station. I checked and double checked his figures and came up with a head wind even stronger than he reported. I then checked with my flight engineer for a report on fuel remaining. Combining the fuel onboard, with the reduced ground speed, we would arrive in Honolulu with fuel remaining at a dangerously low level. However, this was based on the fuel gages providing accurate information, but I questioned the reliability of gages exposed to the tremendous vibration of the C-133, and was concerned that there was an indisputable possibility of running out of gas before reaching Honolulu.

We departed Okinawa with a full service of 18,000 gallons, but based on our latest estimates, we would arrive in Honolulu with a mere one thousand, or one hour endurance at reduced power. The C-133 had eight separate fuel tanks and I instructed the flight engineer to either burn or transfer the fuel from tanks 1,2,7 and 8, and go "tank-to-engine" on the four inboard tanks. When about 500 miles from Honolulu, and two hours out, everyone in the cockpit was wide awake with one eye on the fuel gages and the other eye ready to shout "Land Ho" when we sighted the island of Oahu. We felt somewhat relieved when our Distance Measuring Equipment (DME) locked on at around 200 miles, and I was in radio contact with Honolulu Approach Control.

We were cleared to descend to 10,000 feet, but I requested to remain at 23,000 until intercepting the Instrument Landing System (ILS) "glide slope," and then execute a gradual 2.5 degree descent to a landing. My request was approved without comment. (I planned on maintaining the higher altitude as long as possible to conserve fuel, and would delay extending the landing gear and flaps for the same reason.)

During the descent, I could hear approach control working other aircraft, but hoped that our "straight-in" approach to runway 08 would not be interrupted. However, as we were passing through 7,000 feet, approach control directed that we take up a heading of south, to allow a Pan American B-707 to land. I continued inbound and informed ATC that I wanted to continue my approach as I was short of fuel! He came back with, "Are you declaring a fuel emergency?" Before I could answer, the PAA pilot told ATC to go ahead and let the Air Force transport land ahead of them. My comment, "Thanks, Pan Am." "No problem" was the response. "This will give my passengers a better view of Hawaii." (I was very grateful to the PAA captain, because if I was forced to declare a fuel emergency, I would have had to submit a report that would go all the way to the top. I'm sure higher headquarters personnel, when reviewing it, would have asked why I was so stupid as to overfly Midway Island and take a chance of running out of gas and having to ditch in the ocean, which would have been a legitimate question.)

After a 16-hour flight, I made an uneventful landing and taxied to the ramp with 500 lbs. of fuel showing on the four inboard tanks, not a good sight on an aircraft that carries 117,000 pounds. Needless to say, I didn't submit the flight for consideration of an award. If I had, I'm sure I would have received a picture of a fat turkey, with an inscription reading: "Awarded to Lt.Col. Lou Martin for the dumbest act of the year." After a 24-hour crew rest in downtown Honolulu, we departed the next morning on a 2060-mile and eight-hour flight to Travis Air Force Base, California.

I contacted Helen, and after a couple Beefeater gin martinis and dinner at the Officers' Club, she left for her apartment as she had to report for duty at 7 a.m. the next morning and I was expecting an early alert for my flight back to Dover. However, when I reported to the operations center I was advised that I, and another C-133, commanded by Major Tom Honeywell, would be returning to Saigon on a presidential directed flight.

Apparently General Westmoreland told President Johnson that the Army was not receiving camouflaged colored fatigue uniforms, similar to what U.S. Marines were issued, and this deficiency was costing American lives. Hearing this the president promised Westmoreland that he would have several thousand new fatigue uniforms sent to him within a few days and more would soon follow. Our mission was to fly to Hill Air Force Base, Utah, pick up two loads of uniforms and fly them to Saigon.

Aerial Port personnel were waiting for us in Utah, but we were told it would be several hours before enough boxes of uniforms could be assembled to fill our two aircraft, but they had a team of people working on it. In the meantime we were allowed to stretch out on bunks in a nearby barracks for a short nap.

Within a few hours truck loads of fatigues arrived and our aircraft were loaded, from the floor to the ceiling, with hundreds of cardboard boxes. My aircraft was soon balked out, but lightly-loaded in regard to weight. I filed a flight plan for Travis and departed Utah as the sun was setting in an orange-filled Western sky. My level-off altitude would be 24,000 feet.

Passing through 18,000 my flight engineer reported that he was having difficulty in pressurizing the aircraft and that our cabin altitude was slowly raising above 10,000. He said that we were experiencing an air leak somewhere in the cargo compartment and our second flight engineer was investigating to see if he could find the source of the problem. Based on this, I stopped my climb at 20,000 feet. A couple minutes later there was a loud explosive rushing of air and the cockpit filled with a cold fog. (We had experienced a rapid decompression and our cabin altitude quickly rose to 20,000 feet.) I instructed my crew to don oxygen masks, disconnected the autopilot, pushed the nose over to commence an emergency descent and instructed my copilot to declare an emergency with Air Traffic Control. We were immediately cleared to descend to 12,000 feet (the minimum en route altitude for our route of flight).

With an emergency rate of descent of around 6,000 feet per minute, we soon leveled off at 12,000 feet and removed our oxygen masks. I turned to my flight engineer and asked if he had received any report from his colleague, who had gone to the cargo compartment to check on our pressurization problem. He said that he hadn't heard from him nor had he returned to the cockpit. I began to worry as it wouldn't be the first time that an explosive decompression was accompanied with a crew member being blown out of the aircraft. As I was mulling over in my mind what I would do if I lost a crew member overboard, the missing flight engineer

379

entered the cockpit. He was as white as a ghost, wearing no hat and his hair sticking almost straight up. It took him a minute or so to catch his breath before he could unwind and tell us what had happened.

He said that when he went to the cargo compartment to check for an air leak, his task was made difficult because of the boxes stacked all the way to the ceiling. He checked all the doors, which seemed to be OK, but thought he heard air leaking from an emergency escape hatch on the cargo compartment ceiling. He climbed on top of the boxes and was crawling on his belly toward the hatch, when it blew off. The explosive rush of air, moving with hurricane-force in the direction of the open hatch, carried him along with it like a rag doll. As he was about to be ejected through the opening, he grabbed a hold of a cargo tie-down strap and was able to keep from tumbling into the Rocky Mountains, 20,000 feet below. With his upper body outside the aircraft, and bouncing up and down like a "Bobblehead Doll," he maintained a firm death grip on the strap. When the rush of air escaping from the aircraft subsided, he pulled himself back inside. (We figured that when the boxes of fatigues were being loaded, an errant member of the loading crew inadvertently used the emergency escape hatch release handle as a handhold and loosened it.) We continued on to Travis, secured a new hatch, bought our flight engineer a new hat, and 12 hours later were en route to Saigon.

My return flight to the U.S. was routine except on the route segment from Midway Island to California. When at Midway, a Navy sailor reported seeing a rat run across the cargo compartment. This always raised considerable concern, as rats not only carried many diseases, but could chew on aircraft wiring. Whenever a rat (the four-legged kind) was observed on an aircraft, it was automatically grounded. Pest control personnel would don gas masks, set off canisters of poison gas inside the aircraft, close and seal all openings and place it off limits for 24 hours. When my aircraft was released for flight, I wondered if they had killed all the little hitchhikers as we didn't see pest control personnel leave the aircraft carrying small "rat-size" body bags. I was concerned that if before being sent to rat heaven they might have crawled into hidden areas to die in peace, and their decomposing bodies would cause a terrible stink. However, I thought that by the time they started putrefying, some other unlucky crew would be flying the aircraft, so why should I worry!

We were flying at 23,000 feet and four hours into a ten-hour flight, when my load master came to the cockpit and reported that he saw a rat run across the cargo compartment floor. I ordered everyone to don oxygen masks and directed the flight engineer to depressurize the aircraft. With a cabin altitude of 23,000 feet, I thought that any rat that survived the poison gas treatment would surely succumb to a lack of oxygen and soon join his colleagues already in "rat Valhalla." My flight engineer wanted to know how long we should maintain a cabin altitude of 23,000, I said, "30 minutes, sarge, if we find any rats still alive after that I'll take them home as pets." Thirty minutes later we were starting to feel the cold, so I told the flight engineer he could repressurize the aircraft.

To test my theory on how to rid an aircraft of rats, I told my load master to spread out some bread crumbs on the cargo compartment floor. I figured that if any of the rats had survived the poison, and lack of oxygen, they would be hungry as hell and need a snack. About an hour later my load master told me that he saw a rat nibbling on the bread crumbs and tried to catch him, as he knew I would want to take him home as a pet, but he was too fast and escaped. (I don't know how rats can endure 24 hours of poison gas and 30 minutes at 23,000 feet without oxygen! But obviously they had rat-size oxygen masks and small oxygen bottles hidden somewhere in one of the many concealed crevices in the aircraft.)

Later in the flight my copilot had gone back to the crew lounge for a short rest. I had my seat titled back like a lounge chair, my flight engineer was fighting to stay awake as he starred at 101 heat emitting gages, and my navigator's head occasionally dropped, from an upright position, into a "Japanese-style bow" before he would catch himself and jerk it upright. I was singularly enjoying the solitude as all four engines were purring like kittens and I could confirm, at a glance, that we were on course by seeing the Big Dipper and North Star (Polaris) off the left wing tip, exactly where they should be when flying east. Everything seemed to be humming along, so I tuned in the KBAL radio station in San Francisco and enjoyed listening to the latest hits being played by my favorite disc jockey.

Sometime later a shooting star, off to the left side of the aircraft, caught my eye and I watched it disappear in the distant horizon. But in watching it something else caught my attention! When I looked out over my left wing tip I couldn't see the Big Dipper or North Star! Something was wrong with this picture! I woke up my navigator and called his attention to this unexplained sighting. I then turned up the cockpit overhead lights, noted that the Remote Magnetic Indicator (RMI) was indicating 090, but the Standby Compass was indicating 180 degrees. I disconnected the autopilot, started a turn to the left, but the RMI didn't move. Apparently the Flux Gate Compass had failed and the aircraft, being on autopilot, had slowly drifted to a southern heading. The question was, how long had we been flying 90 degrees from our planned course? The navigator took some star shots and he discovered that we were 200 miles south of course. I contacted the San Francisco radio center, told them of our problem and requested to proceed from our present position direct to SFO, which they approved. I don't think the pissed-off rats had anything to do with the compass failure, but it was certainly coincidental!

After landing at Travis, I reported live rats observed on the aircraft and the failure of our RMI, which would allow a minimum of 24 hours, or more, to repair. Helen picked me up at the BOQ and I invited her to have dinner in *Dick's Seafood Grotto* in Fairfield. While waiting for a table we took a seat in a booth and ordered Beefeater martinis. When the drinks arrived, I told her that there was something I wanted to tell her. Gazing into her eyes, I prefaced my statement by stating that what I was about to say I should have said a long time ago. But I procrastinated because I didn't want to fracture what was becoming a close bound of affection between us. I believe she sensed what I was about to say and probably considered the possibility earlier, but like myself, was ducking reality. I told her that I was married, had two loving kids, and after much soul searching, decided that I would not abandon them and seek a divorce. I added that it would be unfair to my 14-year-old daughter, my six-year-old son and my wife, who was raising them almost by herself, since the demands of the Vietnam War resulted in me being gone most of the time.
   Helen's eyes moistened, she fought back tears, and with a weak smile kissed me on the cheek and said, "I understand, Lou, and I respect your decision. Now let's have another martini and a bottle of wine with dinner." My eyes also moistened, as I slowly nodded my head in agreement. As a nurse she was adept in healing broken bodies and I prayed she would be equally successful in mending a broken heart. To hurt someone you love is a painful experience and I felt a deep sense of guilt, as it was I who allowed this to happen. It saddened me more than I can describe, to throw cold water on a relationship that, at times, I hoped would have a happy ending. In a different time and a different place, I'm sure this would have been the outcome. But I was wrong in allowing this subterfuge to continue. I had told Helen that my address and telephone number, in Delaware, was that of my bachelor ski buddy, Dan Ruskaweitz. Dan had promised to save any mail he received for me and if called by telephone, to state that I was not in, but would take a message. (I'm quite sure my

wife sensed that I was seeing someone else, as women have a way of knowing such things, but she never embarrassed me by asking.)

Our dinner that night was quite subdued and we ate quietly. We were both in a state of mind, similar to hearing that a good friend had just died! Helen and I remained friends, but the sparkle in her eyes when we would meet was gone. When in Travis, I would occasionally invite her out for dinner, but not surprisingly there were times when I called that she would say that she had other plans and couldn't see me.

In 1968 she became a flight nurse and made frequent trips on C-141 Air Evacuation flights to Vietnam, caring for wounded American soldiers. I was very proud of her and her flight nurse colleagues. They put in extremely long hours and not only cared for our combat-injured servicemen physically, but comforted them emotionally. Their service to our country has not received the recognition it deserves.

In the summer of 1968, I was on a flight with General Wallace that had us remaining overnight in Hickam AFB, Hawaii. We walked into the Officers' Club dining room, and to my surprise Helen and three other flight nurses were having dinner at a nearby table. I walked over, said hello, and invited to buy her an after-dinner drink in the bar. But after only one drink, she said she had to get some rest. I walked her to her BOQ, and said goodnight with a handshake and a kiss on the cheek.

The last time I saw Helen was in December 1968. She was stationed in Tachikawa Air Base, Japan, and I was on a flight that remained there overnight. I visited the base hospital, found out the ward she was working in, and invited her to have dinner in the Officers' Club. It was good to see her again and after a couple Beefeater martins, we enjoyed a steak dinner, a bottle of wine and after-dinner drinks. Later she drove me to my BOQ in her small, not-so-new, little Japanese car. I never saw her again, but heard from friends that she married an Air Force officer in 1977, retired as a Lt.Col. and she and her husband live in Florida.

I regret that my succumbing to a natural human weakness may have caused pain to others, but I can't apologize for grabbing a few months of happiness during a time when flying in and out of Vietnam was mentally depressing. However, I felt a special sense of failure toward my 14-year-old daughter, my six-year-old son and my wife, who was forced to be both a mother and father to our children. I consoled my daughter when her puppy, Curly, was run over before her eyes at age six, I watched her smile at me during her First Communion, ran beside her when she learned to ride a bike, talked to her about boys when she became a young lady and looked forward to her hugs when I returned home from my overseas flights. When she saw me walking up the front steps, she would run to greet me, wrap her arms tightly around my neck and say, "Welcome home, daddy. I love you. Can we go water-skiing on Silver Lake?" I recall my son showing me his broken arm after he fell out of a tree at age eight and holding back tears asked, "Are they going to have to cut it off, daddy?" He was also happy to see me when I returned home and couldn't wait for a ride on my motorcycle, throwing him balls to bat or flying in my Ercoupe. This was an interesting chapter in my life, mixed with both happiness and sorrow, but I'm glad it occurred. I think if Helen and I had met in another place or time, it might have affected our lives differently but it was not to be. However, some friendships last forever and I hope if she ever thinks of me it will be with a smile. I hope Helen has found happiness commensurate to what I encountered when I met Chieko Hara in Japan six years later and she agreed to become my wife!

On April 30, 1967 I received a telephone call from General Wallace. He told me that a C-133 had just ditched in the Pacific Ocean but didn't have many details, however from the information received so far, the aircraft was from Travis AFB and went down north of Okinawa. He told me that I was assigned as the accident pilot investigator, to pack a bag and be on a C-141 leaving for Okinawa in two hours. He added that he didn't know how long I would be gone, but estimated about two months. He said travel orders would be waiting for me in base operations.

Two hours later I was sitting in the jump seat of a C-141 heading for Fairbanks, Alaska. In Fairbanks, the aircraft was refueled, a new crew came onboard and two hours later I was en route to Okinawa. When I stepped off the aircraft eight hours later, I was met by Colonel W.A. Williams from Travis AFB, who had been designated as the President of the Accident Board. After securing a room in the BOQ, Colonel Williams filled me in on the latest information regarding the accident.

He said that a C-133B, commanded by Capt. James C. Regan, departed Kadena Air Base at 6:48 a.m. local time with a destination of Midway Island. The aircraft at takeoff weighed 262,000 pounds, which included 103,000 lbs. of fuel and 25,190 lbs. of general cargo. The Okinawa weather was light drizzle, 900 foot broken clouds with higher layers and tops approximately 6,000 feet. The departure was normal and the aircraft was given radar vectors for an on-course climb to 15,000 feet.

Passing through 12,000, the pilot experienced torque oil pressure fluctuations on the number one engine, followed by similar oscillations on engines 2, 3, and 4. The pilot declared an emergency and requested a return to Kadena. He was cleared to reverse course and to descend to 6,000 feet at pilot's discretion. Shortly after reversing course the number four engine developed serious problems and the pilot shut it down and feathered the propeller. To reduce weight, the flight engineer began dumping fuel and when approximately 30 miles from Kadena, the pilot discovered that he had no control over the propellers on engines 1, 2, and 3. (They were stuck in approximately a 40 degree angle of attack, which was determined during the post accident investigation, and was not information known to the pilot at the time.) The crew made a thorough check of cockpit instruments and circuit breakers, but couldn't locate the source of their unprecedented propeller malfunction. The pilot directed that the second flight engineer check the master electrical junction box in the cargo compartment to see if he could determine the problem.

Shortly thereafter their two auxiliary gas turbine units flamed out and the flight engineer extended the emergency ram air driven electrical generator. The pilot had descended to 6,000 feet and was on radar vectors above the clouds for a straight-in approach to runway 23. Approaching the Northern Coast of Okinawa the pilot noted breaks in the clouds and made a left turn to descend visually down through a large open area. As the aircraft descended the engine electrical generators began operating intermittently and when he leveled off at 2,500 feet, all hell broke loose! The engine-driven generators and compass power failed, and even with the throttles fully advanced he was losing power on the three remaining engines. Shortly thereafter, they "flamed out."

The pilot was now flying a 250,000 pound glider at 2,500 feet over the Pacific Ocean. He ordered his crew to don life jackets, lowered the nose to maintain 150-160 kts. airspeed and extended the landing flaps to 25 degrees. Approaching the ocean surface he reduced the airspeed to 135 knots and then to about 110 knots as the aircraft slammed into the water. Touchdown impact was reported as normal to severe, depending on the individual crew member's remembrance and his location in the aircraft.

Everyone on the flight deck escaped without injury through the overhead cockpit crew escape hatch or the pilot's clear view sliding window. After leaving the aircraft they attempted to inflate a large life raft, but it was badly torn and was of no use. So they inflated their individual life vests and assembled around a floating nose gear, where the pilot noted that they were missing the flight engineer, Sergeant Wetsel, who had gone to the cargo compartment to investigate their propeller problem.

Two rescue helicopters quickly arrived and began hoisting the cold, wet men out of the water. The pilot insisted that he be the last one rescued, and when onboard reported that a crew member was missing and insisted that they search the area in attempting to locate him. The helicopter pilot thought they should head for Kadena, as they were already overloaded and the wreckage appeared to be sinking. But Capt. Regan was adamant in his demand for a search so the helicopter hovered over the tangled remains of the *Cargomaster.* (See Photo No. 52.)

The aircraft, after impacting the water, had rolled inverted and the bottom of the fuselage had peeled back like an opened sardine can. From the hovering helicopter they were peering into the interior of a cargo compartment which was a snarled mess of aircraft debris and loose cargo. Sergeant Leonard Fullerton, a pararescueman thought he saw a body amongst the semi floating wreckage and requested to be lowered, by sling, into the interior of the sinking aircraft to investigate.

Upon reaching the debris, he discovered the unconscious missing flight engineer and ordered the lowering of a rescue basket. He rolled Sgt. Wetsel into the basket and signaled for it to be raised. He remained in the rapidly sinking wreckage until the injured flight engineer was safely onboard the helicopter and a sling could be lowered for him. After all ten crew members were rescued the helicopters headed for Kadena.

I interviewed nine of the crew members in a round-table discussion, and Sgt. Wetsel in the base hospital. It was obvious that they had experienced an unprecedented catastrophic failure that was not addressed in the Pilot's Flight Manual or included in training programs. The injured flight engineer stated that when he went to the cargo compartment to see if he could find a reason for their conundrum, he observed sparks coming from the main electrical junction box and in the process of climbing over sections of cargo to reach the area, the engines flamed out. The abrupt lack of engine noise was followed by the loud ringing of the alarm bell, but since he was not in contact with the flight deck, he didn't hear the pilot's preparatory warning to prepare for a ditching. However, with the loss of all engines he knew that they were in real trouble and rather than attempting to climb over cargo and return to the cockpit, he strapped himself into a passenger seat just forward of the rear cargo ramp. He was wearing a life preserver, but didn't remember the aircraft hitting the ocean. The next thing he recalls is waking up in the hospital.

I spent two weeks in Kadena gathering data, and even had a helicopter fly me over the accident site at 2,500 feet (the altitude the C-133 was at when its engines flamed out). By now there was nothing to see but open water, but it gave me a better sense of what the pilot faced. Soon after the aircraft ditched, rescue personnel reached the site by boat and attempted to retrieve the flight data recorder, but the wreckage sank before it could be removed. The Accident Investigation Board President decided that we had accomplished all we could in Okinawa and that we should reconvene in Travis Air Force Base to evaluate the data collected.

The accident board was made up of ten members representing experts from the aircraft manufacturer, propellers, engines and various aircraft components. Additional members were a flight surgeon, military lawyer, recorder, and myself, representing the flight crew members affected. It didn't take us very long to agree that the reason electrical power to the propellers was lost was due to a rupture of the electrical power coming from the main junction box in the cargo compartment. We were also in agreement that this fracture was most likely due to the inherent tremendous vibrations of the aircraft. What was not immediately clear was why the engines continued to operate at 12,000 and 6,000 feet, but abruptly flamed-out at 2,500. However, our propeller and engine experts soon solved this problem. (The C-133, like all modern propeller-driven aircraft, was equipped with constant speed propellers, which results in the blade angle automatically, and constantly, adjusting to power, altitude, speed, and atmospheric conditions.)

At lower altitudes, where the air density is high, the propeller blade angle must be relatively low to maintain a desired RPM. However, at higher altitudes, where the air is less dense, the propeller blade angle must be greater to prevent the propeller from over-speeding.

From examination of photos of the wreckage, and expert testimony, it was determined that the propellers were locked in a 40 degree blade angle, when electrical power was lost at 12,000 feet. And when the aircraft descended to 2,500 feet, this high blade angle resulted in such a large drag factor that the engines stalled, or flamed out. All accident board members were in agreement in the findings, up to this point. What was remaining, was to determine the primary cause of the accident and submitting recommendations.

Similar to the voting process employed by juries, board members submitted sealed votes as to the primary cause of the accident. I was shocked when the votes were counted by the Board President. Nine members had stated "Pilot Error" as the primary cause, with just one vote, (mine), stating "Material Failure!" I couldn't believe the thinking of my learned colleagues and one by one I engaged them in arguing against their onerous perceived position.

The most stupid contention taken by most board members was that if the pilot had not descended to 2,500 feet the engines would not have flamed out. I shot this argument down very quickly by pointing out that unless Kadena could have raised the altitude of their airport to 6,000 feet, the pilot was going to have to descend if he was going to successfully land the aircraft. It didn't matter whether it was 40 miles north or over the airport itself. After a second vote the count was five/five and seemed to be stuck at that number. However, I was not going to cave in and told the Board President that if we couldn't arrive at an unanimous vote of "Material Failure," I was going to submit a dissenting unacceptable "Minority Report." He didn't relish this prospect so we continued to deliberate on the primary cause of the accident.

I felt like Henry Fonda arguing his case against Lee J. Cobb, and ten other holdouts in the 1957 movie, Twelve Angry Men. I thought that If Hank Fonda could prevail in a movie, I should be able to do as well in real life and we continued to deliberate without taking a break.

Finally, after a few more secret votes we were unanimous in listing the primary cause as "Material Failure." It was now time to vote on the primary "Contributing Cause." Colonel Williams turned to me and said, "Colonel Martin, as the pilot member of the board, what do you think it should be?" Without hesitation I told him, "Supervisory Failure." I amplified my position by stating that there were procedures in the Pilot's Flight Manual in how to deal with a single propeller failure, but nothing addressing a failure of all four. The pilot in this accident was faced with an unprecedented catastrophic failure and in spite of a lack of procedural guidance, he successfully ditched his C-133 (the first time this had been done) with such skill that all ten crew members survived. After only one vote, all board members agreed. (This was further proof that one person can make a difference, when convinced his position is correct.)

The accident board was now required to come up with recommendations to prevent similar accidents. The first one was a "no-brainior," as it was obvious that the main electrical lines, coming from the main junction box, would have to be replaced with heavier material and inspected frequently for excessive wear due to vibration. However, we knew that this would require time for an engineering study, and once the proper fix was accepted, it would take time to incorporate it into all C-133s. So, in the interim, what course of action should flight crews take, if faced with a similar failure? We knew that if a deficiency of this magnitude occurred at higher altitudes (which was the most likely scenario), the high fixed blade angles of the propellers would result in the engines flaming out when the pilot descended in preparation for landing.

Taking into account my past experience of flying single-engine jets, I suggested we study the feasibility of establishing an Estimated Engine Flameout Procedure (EEFA) for C-133s, which would remain in effect until all aircraft were modified. My suggestion was initially met with laughter and sarcasm from my fellow board members, as they thought it would sound ridiculous to suggest such a maneuver for a four-engine transport. However, my suggestion was taken more seriously when I pointed out that if the pilot in the ditching accident we were investigating had access to such a procedure the accident may have been avoided.

My suggestion was fully coordinated with Headquarters 22nd Air Force Staff, and sent to the Flight Test Center at Edwards Air Force Base for procedural development by test pilots. When developed, the procedure required the aircraft to circle down to a "high-key-position," 5,000 feet over the end of the runway, place all four engines in idle power (to simulate all engines flamed out), lower the landing gear and flaps and circle down to a power-off landing. All C-133 Aircraft Commanders were required to satisfactorily demonstrate three of these approaches. After all aircraft were modified, the requirement for this procedure was discontinued. This recommendation, which was initially scoffed at, was recognized as a significant recommendation by the president of the Accident Board, and Major General D.W. Graham, Commander 21st Air Force, who in a letter of Appreciation stated, "Please convey my appreciation to Colonel Martin for his outstanding performance during this investigation. His idea of establishing an EEFA was accepted, and when developed through Flight Test may be significant in averting another accident of this type."

After returning to Dover AFB, I delivered a briefing on the accident in the base theater and in McGuire AFB, for the 21st Air Force Headquarters Staff. Following my trip to New Jersey, I drove to New York, and treated myself to a couple Beefeater martinis, an expensive dinner and the new Broadway show, "*I Do! I Do!*" featuring Mary Martin and Preston Foster. I then returned to Dover to resume flying C-133 combat cargo missions.

My next flight to Saigon was by the standard routing of Honolulu, Wake and Guam Island and Okinawa. When I arrived in Kadena I hurried over to the base barbershop for my customary haircut, shave, shampoo, manicure and boot shine. The barber and manicurist would be attractive young Japanese females while the shoe shine boy would be a young Japanese male. This entire routine would cost one dollar and tipping was not recommended. The next day I delivered my cargo to the Tan Son Nhut Airport in Saigon and was instructed to stand by for my return load, a battle-damaged F-4 *Phantom* jet fighter.

We lowered the rear cargo ramp, allowing aerial port personnel to load the jet, which was packed in three dollies. I asked the Air Force sergeant, in charge, if the jet was purged of all JP-4 fuel. His response, "Absolutely, colonel," pointing to bright yellow tags hanging from the F-4 stating, "**Purged of all Fuel**." I departed Saigon just as it was getting dark and took up a heading for Clark Air Base, four hours to the east.

The empty F-4 constituted a load of only 30,000 lbs., so my initial level-off altitude was to be 21,000 feet. As I approached the East Coast of South Vietnam I could see numerous flashes of lightning over the China Sea, but they seemed widely dispersed so by employing my weather avoidance radar I thought I would have no problem in steering around the worst of them. By the time I was climbing through 19,000 feet, the night sky was embedded with violent thunderstorms and I was picking my way through towering cumulus clouds and continues flashes of lightning, when suddenly, my radar screen gave off with a bright flash and went blank. I was now forced to attempt to avoid the worst of the storms by steering away from the brightest lightning flashes. I told my crew, "Tighten your safety belts and hang-on" as I leveled off at 21,000 feet.

About this time we detected the strong odor of jet fuel and my reserve flight engineer, holding on to the sides of the bulkheads, to steady himself from the turbulence, headed for the cargo compartment to investigate. A few seconds later I received the following call on the inter phone, "Colonel, we have a real problem. Fuel is spewing out from that F-4 like a fire hydrant, and there is already about a half inch of JP-4 fuel covering the cargo compartment floor and sloshing back and forth from the turbulence." This was not good news! We were picking our way through numerous thunderstorms and lightning, our airborne radar was out and the cargo compartment was awash with jet fuel. One spark and we would disappear in one big bright flash over the China Sea and the Air Force would be faced with another C-133 mysteriously disappearing.

A subliminal thought ran through my mind that if we blew-up, it would send everyone back to "square one" in regard to investigating the cause of mysterious C-133 crashes, and I wouldn't be around to tell them what really happened and participate in the investigation!

I told my copilot to take control, do the best he could in avoiding the thunderstorms and start a descent to 10,000 feet. I then instructed the flight engineer to adjust the cabin altitude, which was now around three thousand feet, to as low an altitude as possible, because the higher cabin altitude was obviously forcing the residue fuel in the F-4 to spew out from open fuel lines. (It was readily apparent that I was lied to, in regard to the jet fighter being purged of all fuel, but that was not my immediate concern.) It was imperative that we descend to a lower altitude ASAP, get rid of the fuel sloshing around in the cargo compartment, avoid the use of electrical components (which might generate a spark) and pray we don't get hit by lightning! (I was sure the PGR was behind this entire mess and eagerly monitoring its outcome!) My copilot asked if he should obtain clearance before descending. I told him absolutely not, don't key the HF radio or actuate anything which may cause a spark. With that, my navigator and I grabbed our oxygen masks, plugged them into walk-around bottles and headed for the cargo compartment.

After descending the cockpit stairs, I was shocked, and somewhat frightened, by the scene that unfolded before me. Raw fuel was spewing out from several open orifices of the folded wings and cradled fuselage of the jet, and the cargo compartment floor, like the flight engineer had reported, was saturated with about a quarter to a half inch of highly volatile JP-4 fuel, swishing back and forth in tune with the rocking aircraft. To add more drama to the potential explosive scene, continuous lightning flashes could be seen through the small round windows lining both sides of the cargo compartment. My loadmaster, and extra flight engineer, were both wearing oxygen masks, plugged into yellow portable oxygen bottles (hooked to their flight suits by alligator clamps) and busily at work in soaking up the spilt fuel.

The loadmaster was sweeping puddles of it into pools so the flight engineer could soak it up with the use of a large deck mop. When the mop could hold no more, he squeezed its contents into a bucket with a foot activated wringer. I admired their sterling effort, but they appeared to be just keeping pace with the amount of fuel pouring out from the F-4. It appeared that the situation was so critical that just the smallest spark would ignite the whole mess.

I returned to the cockpit, while my navigator remained in the cargo compartment to assist in sweeping the fuel into pools. I told my copilot to slowly reduce engine power to idle, assume a nose high attitude and increase the rate of descent. (I wanted the aircraft's nose to assume a high angle of attack to force the fuel to run toward the rear of the aircraft.) I grabbed another portable oxygen bottle and returned to the cargo compartment. I was pleased to note that our descent, to a lower altitude, had slowed the amount of fuel spewing out from the jet to just a trickle. Also the nose high attitude had forced the spilled fuel to pool in the rear of the cargo compartment. (I now thought we had a chance of licking the problem before the PGR had an opportunity of blowing us up.)

The flight engineer busily mopped and squeezed, while the loadmaster and navigator swept fuel in his direction. When the bucket was nearly full, I carried it to the top of cargo ramp and dumped its contents out the open pressurization outflow valves. With eyes and feet burning from the effects of the raw fuel, we continued with the cleanup process until all the fuel that was able to be soaked up with a mop, was dumped overboard. We congratulated each other for still being alive and headed for the cockpit where we would be able to breathe without the use of an oxygen mask.

When back in the cockpit I noted that we were flying at 10,000 feet in smooth air, our cabin alitude was zero, and the line of thunderstorms was many miles to the rear. However, my boots were soaked with jet fuel, so I took them off to let my fuel-saturated feet dry out. My loyal crew members who assisted in the cargo compartment clean-up did the same. My copilot asked if we should inform anyone, by use of the radio, that we were flying at such a low altitude, but were OK I said, "No, the cargo compartment still reeked of fuel fumes and I don't want to take a chance on the HF radio creating a spark, as fuel vapors are more dangerous than raw fuel." He agreed, so we just kept flying toward Clark AFB and would contact them when we were within VHF radio range.

Fortunately, we had departed Saigon with excess fuel so remaining at 10,000 feet was not a problem as far as fuel-burn was concerned. When about 75 miles from Clark, I called them on the VHF radio and they were delighted to hear from us, since they had not received any radio calls, since shortly after we had departed Saigon, and had already reported us missing and presumed lost. They were also surprised to learn that we were flying at only 10,000 feet, but I told them I would explain everything after landing. We made an uneventful landing and after shutting down the engines a maintenance officer came to the cockpit and said, "Colonel, I think you have a fuel leak. I can smell fuel fumes in the cargo compartment!" My answer, "No shit, I guess we will have to check it out!"

I demanded that the F-4 *Phantom* be off loaded and emphatically stated that I was carrying it no further. I then submitted a detailed report of the incident, outlining how close we came to becoming another C-133 statistic, but I never received a reply. (I accepted the incident as the perils of war, and let it go at that.) We opened the large side cargo door, and the rear cargo ramp and left them open overnight. The next day, with our radar problem corrected and the fuel fumes gone, we departed for home and three days later were back in Dover, Delaware.

On Wednesday, September 27, 1967, five crew members from my squadron died in a bizarre aircraft accident that did not relate directly to the *Cargomaster*, but was nevertheless just as tragic. The Air Force had contracted with a civilian maintenance facility in Greenville, Texas to perform overhaul maintenance on C-133s. We would assign crews to ferry them there as a bonus for good service, since it was a welcome break from the drudgery of flying long cargo missions to South Vietnam. After delivering the aircraft, the Electro Systems Facility would fly the crew to Love Field, Dallas in one of their corporate aircraft, put them up in a first class hotel, and provide airline tickets for their return trip home. Major Jack H. Culp, a C-133 Aircraft Commander, had never flown one of these trips and asked me if he could fly the one scheduled for September 27th. I was happy to approve his request, as Jack was not only a friend, but a pilot I admired. He was a former WW II P-47 fighter pilot, had flown 33 combat missions and shot down two German fighters, before being shot down himself and taken prisoner. Accompanying Jack on this ill-fated flight was Capt. Donald Cook as copilot, Capt. Anthony Lucci as navigator and Sergeants Kenneth Kennedy and Julius Lee as flight engineers.

Our five crew members were on board a North American Rockwell *Aero Commander,* en route to Love Field Dallas, when the right wing, without warning, separated. The aircraft went into an uncontrolled spiral, bounced off a passing car (whose driver escaped injury), careened through rows of school bike racks, slammed against a brick building adjacent to a school yard, and finally came to rest within 50 feet of a group of assembled teachers. All five C-133 crew members, and two Electro Systems civilian employees on board the aircraft, were killed instantly. (On any other day, the school yard would have been full of children lingering to visit and pick up their bicycles.)

Post-crash investigation disclosed that a mandatory Federal Aviation Administration Airworthiness Directive, that required that the main wing spar be reinforced, had apparently not been complied with. Lawsuits were filed and dependents of our crew members received an undisclosed settlement, but money did not ease their pain. It appeared that the PGR had been after Jack Culp for a long time and finally because of a weak wing spar was able to grab him along with six other unfortunate airmen.

On January 31, 1968, approximately 37,000 Vietcong troops began attacking more than 100 cities throughout the breadth of South Vietnam. The attack was supported by tanks and heavy artillery and resembled a classic style WW II military campaign. Most of the Vietcong soldiers involved were killed, including their best fighters and political officers, and by any measure this attack was a disaster for the Vietcong, but faced with a loss of 2,500 U.S. troops, and CBS journalist Walter Cronkite telling the American public that the war was unwinnable, public support was waning. After Cronkite's defeatist statement, President Johnson stated, "If I've lost Cronkite, I've lost Middle America." However, this VC attack, commonly referred to as the "Tet Offensive" generated several months of hard fighting. In April and May of 1968 I flew a total of 231 hours.

Ironically, Cronkite, who is now 91-years-old reportedly told the Television Critics Association on Jan. 15, 2006, "If I were on the air today, I would say the same thing about the Iraq War. We should get out now!"

To support an earlier war commitment, in December 1965 and January 1966, C-133s were directed to move the 25th Infantry Division from Hawaii to Pleiku. The Air Force positioned a number of aircraft in Hickam AFB to begin a round-the-clock airlift. Maintenance personnel and C-133 spare parts were positioned at all en route stations and the practice of crews remaining with the same aircraft was temporarily suspended for the duration of the exercise, called *Operation Blue Light*.

After departing Hickam and landing at Wake Island, we were authorized 12 hours crew rest, before picking up a different aircraft and flying it to Kadena for another 12-hour break. We would then fly a different aircraft to Pleiku and return to Okinawa. After a short crew rest in Okinawa we would fly back to Hawaii, where it would start all over again. This 24/7 routine lasted one month and I personally flew 203 hours in 30 days.

Fierce battles were raging in and around Pleiku and to minimize ground fire, we were advised to fly four degree steep approaches when landing (especially during daylight hours) and equally steep climb-outs after takeoff. In addition, during the final phase of our daylight landings, we would frequently be escorted by *Huey* Helicopter gun ships on each wing spraying the surrounding countryside with machine gun fire. When landing at Pleiku during the hours of darkness, we were instructed to turn off our navigation lights and rotating beacons when below 10,000 feet. I thought this procedure was stupid as the sky was always crowded with aircraft of every description, both day and night. I was more concerned about the possibility of a mid-air collision than I was about ground fire.

My fears were brought to fruition one night when holding over Pleiku at 9,000 feet, awaiting my turn to land. Riding in the jump seat was my friend and colleague, Major Gordon S. Pink, who was now assigned as a staff officer in Wing Headquarters. While circling, a large black object passed over my aircraft, by no more than a couple hundred feet and appeared and disappeared so fast that no one else saw it. I reached up and turned on my navigation and rotating beacon lights, which resulted in Gordon expressing opposition. He told me that I was violating military directives and should turn them off! I refused, and in spite of our close friendship, he remained adamant that I turn off the lights. I reminded him, that I was the Aircraft Commander and the lights were going to remain on, and that he could put anything in his report that he wished, and if he didn't have a pen he could use mine. After landing Gordon was so upset that he didn't join me and my crew in drinking a cold Coke. Less than a week later this stupid directive was rescinded by MAC Headquarters, stating, "There is a greater danger of midair collisions, than there is in ground fire, and we don't want aircraft flying around in crowded skies at night without lights." Gordon, and I never spoke of this incident again and remain close friends, renewing this friendship during a recent reunion in Las Vegas, Nevada.

Ironically, disciples of some of these dull-witted generals, who thought we should fly around the crowded night skies of South Vietnam with our navigation lights off, were in positions of authority 24 years later. My son Major Mike Martin flew KC-135s during Desert Storm One in 1991 and initially they were directed to refuel fighters over Iraq at night with their external lights off. However, after several close-calls the procedure was discontinued and the lights went back on. (Deja vu.)

In late 1968 I was conducting "no-notice" line evaluation checks on C-133 crews flying throughout the Pacific Ocean. When performing this function I would not be assigned to any particular crew, but would check in with Area Command Posts at each base and advise the duty officer of my presence and on which aircraft and crew I would fly with next. The purpose of these checks was to ensure that good safety procedures were being followed by crews thousands of miles from their home base, to provide expert guidance where needed and be able to fill in for a pilot that may not be able to continue the mission due to sickness or incapacitation. It was due to the latter situation that I was requested to assume the duty as Aircraft Commander on a C-133 returning to the U.S. from Okinawa. The assigned pilot, my young friend Captain Dick Alexander, had come down with a very bad cold and was in the base hospital.

The flight to Midway Island and Travis AFB was routine and I was enjoying a beer with my copilot and navigator in the Travis BOQ lounge, when two burly air policemen walked in and asked if I was Colonel Martin. When I said that I was they said, "You will have to come with us, colonel. Put down your beer!" I inquired as to the reason, but they said that they weren't told why, just instructed to find and escort me to the Office of Special Investigations (OSI). I asked them if I could shower and change clothes first, but they said no, that their instructions were to escort me to the OSI peaceably if possible, but forcibly if needed. I put down my beer and followed them to their squad car. A few minutes later I was escorted into an interrogation room and surrounded by grouchy obnoxious looking OSI agents who started peppering me with questions.

The inquiry was routine at first and related to name, rank, serial number, age, home town, etc., but then centered on my flying a C-133 from Southeast Asia to Travis. When I asked the reason for all the questions, they responded with, "We will ask the questions, colonel, you just provide the answers." During the question/answer session, it became clear that they, at first, weren't aware that I had only flown the aircraft from Okinawa and had not been in South Vietnam with this particular C-133. When this fact was disclosed they started asking me questions about Captain Alexander and why he didn't fly the aircraft to the U.S. himself. I told them that he was sick and that they could check this out with the hospital in Kadena! They said they already had. After about one hour of grilling, they finally told me the reason I was being rigidly interrogated.

The Cargomaster I had flown to the U.S. had about a dozen Russian made AK-47 automatic rifles hidden behind a bulkhead. They had been investigating a group of Vietnamese civilians who were smuggling weapons into the U.S. by hiding them in large aircraft. They were quite sure that flight crews were not involved in this activity and the smugglers were informing accomplices at Travis, through code, as to which aircraft they would find the weapons. They had broken the code, which indicated that there were weapons onboard my aircraft. The aircraft was now under surveillance and I would not be allowed to fly it to Dover, Delaware until further notice. They said that the weapons were still onboard and were not being removed, as they were hoping to grab gang members on this end when they attempted to remove them. After two days of surveillance the guns were not picked up by accomplices, who apparently smelled a rat (the two-legged kind). So OSI agents removed them and released the aircraft and the next day I flew it back to Dover AFB.

By 1969 there was an ever-increasing number of C-141s providing combat cargo support for the Vietnam War. This allowed C-133s to fly oversized cargo loads to other parts of the world that could not be accommodated in smaller aircraft. I flew a large radar van to Addis Ababa, Ethiopia, with en route stops at Torejon, Spain, Tehran, Iran and Dhahran, Saudi Arabia. Except for Torejon, these were all new locations and made the trip very interesting. The flight across the Arabian Desert was impressive by its thousands of miles of nothing but sand. The airport elevation at Addis Ababa is 7,625 ft. above sea level and in spite of the fact that we departed with a light fuel load it felt like we were taking off with partial power (which in reality, after compensating for the high altitude, we were). Even with a light load I still used almost 9,000 feet of runway during the takeoff.

Another interesting mission was flying an electronics van to Christchurch, New Zealand by way of Pago Pago, American Samoa, 2258 nautical miles, and 9 hours south of Honolulu. My cargo load was quite heavy, so I was not allowed to carry enough fuel to fly to a distant alternate airport, if we could not land in Samoa. Our alternate plan was to hold overhead for three hours and await favorable weather conditions.

Seven hours after departing Hawaii we were flying at 25,000 feet, in smooth air, about 500 miles north of Pago Pago, as a tropical red sun was setting in the western sky. I had not flown this far south before, nor had I been to the Samoa Islands, so I was excited about what may lie ahead. I attempted to obtain the latest weather on our HF radio, but the reception this close to the equator was very bad. I would have to wait until I could contact the airport on our VHF radio, when about 100 miles out.

About 120 miles from Pago Pago we were flying in solid clouds and picking up numerous rain showers on our radar but didn't observe any lightning flashes. The weather appeared to be a typical series of tropical showers that move back and forth across the equator producing changeable weather conditions. So if the airport was below landing weather minimums when we arrived overhead, we could expect to hold for a relatively short period of time before commencing an approach. It was about this time that our VOR radio receiver came alive, so I figured I would be able to contact the airport by radio.

My first call was quickly answered, by a native Samoan with a peculiar accent, but easy to understand. I asked him, **"What is your latest weather?"** He came back with, **"Three hundred foot overcast and one mile visibility in heavy rain. You are cleared to descend to 20,000 feet and cleared for a VOR approach at pilot's discretion. There is no other reported traffic in the area."** The reported latest weather was below landing minimums, so I planned on holding overhead at 20,000 feet, awaiting an expected improvement. After descending to 20,000 we were still in solid overcast and had no visual contact with the surface.

I reduced power, entered a holding pattern and about every ten minutes repeated my request for the latest weather. However, each time I did the radio operator came back with the same gloomy report. After holding for one hour and the reported latest weather didn't show any signs of improving, I started to become concerned. I told my copilot to continue holding while I got up from my seat for a confab with my navigator. We poured over his charts to see if there were any airports we could divert to, with the remaining fuel onboard, and determined that Tahiti was the only one. However, according to our aeronautical publications it would be closed by the time we arrived and in addition I had no idea of its weather conditions. I had to figure out another option!

The non-precision VOR approach to Pago Pago is quite demanding, as there is a high hill about a mile from the end of the runway and several aircraft, during bad weather and at night, had crashed into it including a recent PAA B-707. Because of this hazard, the landing minimums were higher than most non-precision approaches. Since I had never landed at Pago Pago, I figured that it may require two or three approaches before I could safely descend below the published landing minimums for a successful landing. With this in mind, I computed how much fuel it would require for three approaches, plus a 30-minute reserve for setting up a ditching pattern if I couldn't find the runway. I then added this amount to our remaining fuel onboard and figured we could hold for another 30 minutes, before we would have to start down.

With my copilot flying the holding pattern, I studied the Approach Chart, until I had every aspect of it committed to memory. Approaching the 30-minute bewitching hour, I directed that we all don life vests, reduced the power on all four engines, took a deep breath and started down. During the initial phase of the descent we flew through scattered rain showers, but no lightning or heavy turbulence. As we descended through 12,000 feet the rain abated and suddenly, at 9,000 feet, runway lights on the airport were clearly visible. I put the aircraft into a tight descending spiral, while keeping the runway in sight. I wasn't sure how large the break in the clouds was as all surrounding quadrants contained black rain clouds. I had no problem in keeping the runway in sight and by the time we reached 4,000 feet, lights from the nearby city and surrounding hills were clearly visible. I flew a normal VFR downwind leg, lowered the landing gear and flaps and turned onto a base leg. As I did a red rotating beacon on the top of the hill short of the runway, was clearly visible. I made an uneventful wet runway landing and taxied to the parking ramp, void of anyone to assist us. After completing the Engine Shutdown Check, my copilot and I walked over to a small building which appeared to be the operations office.

We walked into a windowless room, occupied by a man sitting before a radio console and reading a comic book. I asked him for the latest weather. He grabbed a clip board off the wall and said, "**Three hundred foot overcast and one mile visibility in heavy rain**," and went back to reading his comic book. Shocked, I told him that the weather outside was Visual Meteorological Conditions (VMC), with good visibility and no rain. He shrugged his shoulders while stating. "Captain, you asked for the latest weather and that is what the weather office reported three hours ago, before they closed for the day! If you had requested the present weather I would have gone outside and taken a look, even though I'm not a weather observer." He then went back to reading his comic book!

Ever since this incident I instruct my students never to request just the latest weather, but to specify the weather for a specific time period. If questionable weather is reported, request the time sequence this observation was made. Had I done this for Pago Pago, I would have more hair and saved the taxpayers two hours worth of fuel.

There was no military office in Samoa, so I decided (on my own) that we would take 48 hours crew rest to allow for a little sight-seeing. We rented a couple straw-covered beach bungalows and explored the area in the company of a tour guide. Two days later we departed for Christchurch, New Zealand, 2,000 miles further south. As we flew over the equator, we noted that we were all "Pollywogs" (those who have never crossed the equator) and held a low-key initiation ceremony in the cockpit. We didn't have any garbage to crawl through, fresh eggs to crack over each other's heads or a "Shellback" (someone who had crossed the equator before) to officiate over the ceremony, so we just shook hands and hoped *King Neptune* would accept our subdued ceremony at 24,000 feet above his domain. After landing at Christchurch, an Air Force representative said that the electronic van we had onboard would be off loaded and shipped to McMurdo Sound, Antarctica, on a Navy ship. He added that we were authorized 24 hours crew rest before heading back to the U.S. This was our first visit to New Zealand and my crew was looking to me to come up with a plan that would allow us to spend two or three days without fabricating a lie about a mechanical problem with our aircraft, which we all agreed was not an option. I needed to come up with more evenhanded plan.

I suggested to our Air Force representative that instead of shipping our cargo to Antarctica by surface ship, why not allow us to fly it directly to William's Field in McMurdo Station 2,000 miles away. He said that he thought it was a good idea, but didn't have the authority to authorize it on his own, but would send a message to MAC Headquarters, in Scott AFB, Illinois, seeking permission. He would let me know when he received their response and while awaiting their reply we could remain in Christchurch. After three days of sight-seeing and enjoying the warm hospitality of New Zealand, we flew back to Dover, Delaware.

My devious plan to spend a few extra days in Christchurch worked like a charm. The message to MAC Headquarters, would not arrive until Saturday morning (U.S. Time). Consequently, it would not be reviewed until Monday. I was confident that my request to fly to Antarctica would be disapproved, but awaiting a reply would provide us with three days free time to explore New Zealand. (There is more than one way to skin a cat, while being complimented by your crew for exercising self initiative.)

On February 6, 1970 we experienced our last fatal C-133 accident. A *Cargomaster* en route from Travis AFB, California to Harrisburg, Pennsylvania crashed in Nebraska, killing all five crew members. The cause of the accident was relatively easy to determine as the nose section, just forward of the wing, separated in flight. It floated to earth and came to rest miles from the rear section, with all five crew members still strapped in their seats. Metallurgists discovered a fatigue crack in the fuselage metal skin adjacent to the propeller line. Seemingly, the metal had weakened through thousands of hours of vibration from the sonic boom pulsations from propeller tips that rotate at super sonic speeds.

As the aircraft was climbing to 25,000 feet, the undetected fracture could not support the pressure differential of high altitude and suddenly, like a crack in an eggshell, propagated around the entire fuselage. Experts estimated that the front severed section, which contained the cockpit and crew, took several minutes to float to the ground.

This accident was especially painful for me as the Aircraft Commander, Bill Tabor, was a personal friend. We had flown C-119 *Boxcars* in Germany 14 years earlier and had escaped the clutches of the PGR many times in the past. A few weeks before he died, Bill was on an overnight in Dover AFB and over several drinks in the Officers' Club bar we discussed what we were going to do when we retired. Unfortunately Bill's retirement plans were determined by the PGR.

Following this accident C-133s were inspected for fatigue cracks, and to prevent a similar catastrophic failure, the fuselage forward of the wing was wrapped with 16 steel straps. All but one were three-inches wide and spaced 22 to 28 inches apart. The spacing was predicated on aligning them with inside fuselage ribs. The second to the last strap, near the leading edge of the wing, which failed during the accident, was in two sections --- the top half being five-inches wide and the lower half three inches. The purpose of the straps was to prevent any future fatigue crack from spreading and causing another accident. C-133 Cargomasters on static display at various air museums all have these steel straps installed. (From a distance, they resemble strips of Duct Tape and crew members, in a jocular manner, would state, "Now the generals are having us fly airplanes held together with duct tape!")

In March 1970 I was directed to fly to Howard AFB, Panama in a C-54 to conduct a survey of airports throughout the Caribbean that would be suitable for C-133s, in case a need arose requiring rapid movement of men and material to that part of the world. I considered the highlights of the mission sitting in the bar at the Hilton Hotel in Panama City, drinking martinis and listening to the Giant Wurlitzer organ. A fellow officer stationed at Howard AFB asked me if I had ever visited a bordello. I told him no, that I had never felt the need or the desire. But after a few more martinis he convinced me that I owned it to my masculine legacy to try it, at least once. He told me that there was a first class brothel in Panama City that was highly rated, inspected weekly by health authorities and maintained a beautiful "pride" of young Panamanian girls. He was a convincing salesman so we jumped into a taxi and headed out.

As we entered an opulent plush waiting room, equipped with overstuffed furniture, expensive-looking purple silk lamps and soft music, a well-dressed madam asked if we would like a drink, while we selected a companion. We both ordered a Beefeater martini! So far, what my new friend had said was true as across the room sat 12 young ladies, well-dressed, well-groomed and flush with youthful beauty. By the time the madam returned with our drinks, I had made my selection and pointed her out to our hostess. She called her over, introduced us, and asked if I wanted a half-hour or one-hour session. I told her I thought 30 minutes would be enough and with that I was escorted to a cashier's window, where I forked over $20 (equal to $106 today). I was issued a receipt, while my female entertainer was handed a basket containing a towel, a small bar of soap, a condom and a room key. Gripping the basket she said, "Follow me please," and led me to a clean room containing a single bed (with clean sheets), a chair and a night stand with a 25-watt bulb. The whole event was so mechanical and commercialized that it took me awhile to live up to my self image of a virile horny Air Force pilot on the prowl. After accomplishing what I had paid $20 for, I walked out with the feeling not unlike that of leaving a drug store. I'm glad I had the experience, but once was enough. I never visited a bordello again but my friend told me he was a regular customer. (I wondered if he was accumulating frequent screw miles.) A couple days later I was back in Dover and flying another trip to South Vietnam.

During my return flight to the states, I was filing a flight plan in the Kadena Air Base operations center next to a Continental Airlines captain. I struck up a conversation and inquired if Continental was hiring pilots. He said that he didn't know, but suggested that when I get back to Travis AFB, I call the International Air Service Company (IASCO) in Burlingame and request a copy of their employment application, as they hire pilots for foreign airlines in many different parts of the world. He asked if I had an Air Transport Pilot Certificate (ATP). When I said no, he recommended that I obtain one before looking for a job flying for a civilian airline, as they most likely wouldn't hire me without it. I thanked him for the good advice and flew back to the U.S. When in Travis I contacted IASCO and requested they send me a job application.

After returning to Dover I sent for an ATP written study guide from Acme, spent an entire weekend reviewing it and drove to the FAA Office in Baltimore, Maryland, to take the written test, which I passed with a grade of 77% (seven more than needed). To complete the process I now had to pass a flight check in a multi-engine aircraft. I knew that the Air Force frowned on FAA inspectors flying on C-133s, but I figured if I didn't ask for permission, they wouldn't have the opportunity of saying "no."
I called inspector Altman in the Valley Stream, New York office, and asked him if he would be willing to administer an ATP flight check in a C-133 in Dover AFB. In our discussion I discovered that he was a retired Air Force pilot and expressed a desire to fly in a *Cargomaster*. I told him I would call him back as soon as I could coordinate a flight schedule.
When conducting annual proficiency checks we were authorized to schedule an aircraft for four hours, but with a sharp pilot, it was possible to accomplish all the required maneuvers in half that time. I arranged to administer a flight check to a young Aircraft Commander, who I knew would be willing and able to complete his check in two hours, and then fly copilot for me while I received my ATP evaluation from a FAA inspector. I called Mr. Altman, who said he would meet me in base operations.
I made sure that the FAA inspector's name was on the local flight plan I filed with base operations and listed as Lt.Col. Altman, USAF, retired. (I thought by listing him on the crew manifest as a retired officer, and not a

FAA Inspector, it might prevent some eager "whistle blower" from questioning a civilian's presence on the aircraft.) We flew to Wilmington, Delaware, where I devoted the first two hours in completing the flight check on my sharp young captain, and then switched seats while I was administered my flight check. When we landed four hours later, I was handed my ATP Certificate, with a Douglas C-133 type rating. I thanked Mr. Altman for his cooperation and called it a day.

The following morning I received a call from the bird colonel in charge of Wing Standardization who said that he heard that I had allowed a FAA Inspector to give me an ATP flight check in a C-133 and wanted to know if this was true. I said, "Yes sir, what you heard is true." He then, in a long-winded fashion, proceeded to reprimand me for allowing a civilian to fly in one of our aircraft. I allowed him to have his say, which I'm sure he felt was necessary to justify his position, but when he finished chewing me out, I said, "Colonel, you're absolutely right. I agree with everything you said and promise never to do it again." There was momentary silence, while he was trying to figure out whether I was being a "smart ass" or just being respectful. He finally said, "OK. I accept that colonel" and hung up.

The next day there was a notice sent to all squadrons that FAA inspectors were not authorized to fly in our aircraft to administer ATP flight checks. (I thought this was a good policy and certainly intended to follow it. I didn't want to be accused of violating Air Force directives.)

My next goal was to obtain a Flight Instructor Certificate. I completed another Acme study guide and after passing the written test, enrolled in a flight instructor's training course with Summit Aviation in Wilmington, Delaware using benefits from my GI Bill. On May 5, 1970 Inspector James Graham, from the North Philadelphia FAA Office, administered a flight evaluation in a Cessna 150 and issued me a CFI certificate. I now figured that I was ready for the world of civilian aviation. I held an ATP and CFI certificate, had 10,031 flight hours (800 in jets) and was only 42-years-old. With this in mind I sent job applications to the IASCO and FAA offices in Burlingame, California and the FAA office in Washington, DC.

My last C-133 flight to South Vietnam was in June 1970. After eight years of fighting a irresolute war with a no-win policy, I didn't see an end in sight. President Nixon agreed and the U.S. decided to cut-and-run by ending the war in 1972, and removing all American troops on March 29, 1973. This futile war resulted in 58,000 U.S. military dead, 1,000 missing and 150,000 wounded. (From 1965 to the end of the war the average number of U.S. military killed was 7,250 per year or 604 per month.)

I reflected back on my five years of flying combat cargo missions to South Vietnam with mixed emotions. I was naturally pleased that the war was coming to an end, but at the same time my flights to and from the Far East were exciting and professionally fulfilling. My final route segment on return flights was usually a nonstop night flight from Travis AFB, California to Dover AFB, Delaware. By the time I crossed south of Chicago I would be at 25,000 feet and marvel at being able to see the glistening lights of Chicago, Milwaukee and the outline of Lake Michigan. I would wonder if the five million people living in this area had any concept of the number of Americans that were dying 8,000 miles away or did they just carry on with their daily lives as if the war didn't affect them. I suspect it was the latter.

As I would head southeast toward Delaware I would experience feelings of nostalgia in that another mission was about to end. I would naturally be eager to see my family but at the same time miss the excitement of the last ten to twelve days of flying halfway around the world and back with the same aircraft and crew. Flying the C-133, an aircraft that had a enigmatic reputation, for a trip length of approximately 75 hours with a highly professional crew created a "Band of Brothers" feeling that is difficult to explain. By the time I shut down the engines at the end of each trip I felt a sense of guilt that I didn't share with my wife and kids since I would already be looking forward to my next exhilarating mission.

My last flight in a C-133 as Aircraft Commander was on June 16, 1970. I had flown this controversial giant of the skies 4,671 hours and was looking forward to a safer way of continuing a career in aviation but would miss the Air Force. I was also hoping to diminish the anxiety I felt of being caught up in the clutches of the traitorous PGR almost every time I flew..

The C-133 was retired from active military service in 1971, but several were flown in civilian registration in Alaska. There were attempts to certify them in the lower 48 contiguous states, but the FAA stated that they did not meet the required airworthiness standards. However, the FAA in Alaska allowed them to fly under special restrictions for the airlifting of oversize cargo loads in support of the oil industry on the North Slope. According to reliable reports a C-133 was still flying out of the Anchorage International Airport as late as 2007.

Chapter Twelve --- Japanese Nihon YS-11

While waiting for the civilian aviation community to offer me a job, I took a position as a Cessna 150 flight instructor for a small airport operator in Dover, Delaware. This was quite a change from flying single-engine jets or 275,000-pound four-engine turboprop transports, but it provided some rewards. By not being away from home most of the time, I was able to build a stronger bond with my 18-year-old daughter, and ten-year-old son and able to give my wife a break from being both a mother and father, which was not possible when on active duty with the Air Force. I also enjoyed sharing my flying experiences with young pilots just starting out in aviation, but I was eager to fly bigger and faster aircraft and wondered how long it would be before I would be allowed to do so again.

In November 1970, the suspense was broken when I received a telephone call from Chuck Wenman, Vice President of IASCO, inquiring if I would be interested in flying a YS-11 turboprop transport for Japan Domestic Airlines (JDA), in Tokyo, Japan. He said that JDA was planning on hiring a group of experienced foreign pilots so Japanese captains could upgrade to DC-9s, and following their upgrade, the foreigners would stand a good chance of upgrading to jet aircraft as well. Chuck added that it was rumored that JDA would soon be absorbed by Japan Airlines (JAL) so it was possible I could be flying for them sometime in the future. I told Chuck that I was definitely interested and looked forward to the prospect of returning to Japan, as I had spent three years there when a pilot for the Air Force. He said, "I'll get back to you hopefully within a couple of days."

The next day, I received a telephone call from the FAA Air Carrier District Office in Burlingame, California, inquiring if I was interested in a position as a pilot inspector. I told them that I was, and they asked if I could be in their office at 9 a.m., November 16th for an interview. My response, "I'll be there." A couple days later I received a call from the FAA in Washington, DC inquiring if I would be interested in a position as a copilot on their flight inspection C-47s. I said that I would, and with that, the caller said they would get back to me. Things were starting to happen!

A few days later Chuck Wenman called and wanted to know if I could be in his office at 9 a.m. on November 16th to interview for a position as a captain with JDA. "I'll be there," I told Chuck. (This was the same date and time that I was scheduled for an interview with the FAA, also in Burlingamo, California, and knowing that the government is more flexible than the rigid Japanese, I called the FAA and requested that my interview be rescheduled for the afternoon of the 16th. They said no problem and rescheduled it for 2 p.m.)

My former squadron commander allowed me to occupy the jump seat on a C-133 flight to Travis AFB, California and after arriving I rented a car and obtained a room in the BOQ. Wearing my best business suit I checked in with an IASCO receptionist at 8:30 a.m. on November 16th. I was immediately impressed by the professional business like approach of the office, especially when I was addressed as Captain Martin. I was asked to have a seat and wait my turn to be called. There were several other well dressed men waiting, who I assumed were pilots also looking forward to a job interview, but I didn't know any of them.

While waiting, I reached into my flight bag and retrieved a book titled, Commercial Transports of The World, and started leafing through it. When Mr. Wenman called me and asked if I would be interested in flying a Japanese YS-11, I had no idea what type of aircraft he was referring to, so I visited the public library, checked out a book on transport aircraft and now had a basic understanding of it and where it was being operated. It was a Japanese-designed twin-engine turboprop, with a maximum takeoff weight of 54,000 lbs., carried 64 passengers and cruised at 300 mph. The first aircraft flew in 1962 and when production ended in 1973, 183 had been produced. In addition to being flown in Japan, it was operated by Piedmont Airlines in the U.S. and 11 other countries. It was later a very popular aircraft with all freight airlines and finally retired from passenger service in Japan in 2006. (See Photo No. 55.)

Precisely at 9 a.m. I was ushered into a conference room and asked to take a seat at a table facing Mr. Chuck Wenman, Captain Ogo (Chief Pilot for JDA) and a well dressed Japanese man who was an English-speaking representative from their personnel department. I was warmly greeted by all three, followed by Mr. Wenman asking me a series of questions relating to my background, education, knowledge of Japan and why I wanted to fly for JDA. During the interview, I noted that the two Japanese were reviewing copies of my job application, interspersed with the personnel representative interrupting to translate my answers into

Japanese for Captain Ogo, who up to this point had said nothing. About 20 minutes into the interview, Captain Ogo spoke up, and in fairly fluent English said, "Captain Martin, are you familiar with the Japanese Nihon YS-11?" "Yes, Sir," I said. I reached into my flight bag, pulled out my book on commercial transports, flipped it open to the tabbed section relating to the YS-11 and pointed to a picture of it in Piedmont Airlines markings. I then told Captain Ogo that I had nearly 4,700 hours in turboprop aircraft and was looking forward to flying the YS-11. I sensed that he was pleased with my answer as there was no follow-up.

The personnel official spoke up next stating that the starting salary for foreign captains would be $32,160 per year, plus a monthly tuition allowance of $650 for dependent children to attend an International School for grades K through 12. (This annual starting salary would be equal to $170,821 today.) He also pointed out that I would receive a per diem allowance of ten dollars per day when on trips, and that lodging (when on company overnights), ground transportation and uniforms would be furnished by the airline. Chuck Wenman added that the two-year contract would authorize 30 days vacation and 12 days sick leave per year, plus one annual round trip for myself and dependents, between Tokyo and a Japan Airlines station anywhere in the world.

I was then asked if this compensation schedule was satisfactory. I told Mr. Wenman that the proposed salary was very generous and I had a ten-year-old son who would benefit from the tuition allowance. The 30 minutes allocated for my interview was over and after a handshake from all three, and a slight bow from the Japanese, I was thanked for coming. As I rose to leave, Chuck Wenman told me that they were interviewing 30 potential candidates for 15 positions and I would be informed if I was one of the captains selected in about a week.

That afternoon I was interviewed for a position with the FAA less than a block away. Three FAA inspectors, Messrs. Henderson, Langon and White, conducted the meeting and were considerably more casual in their questioning than what I had experienced that morning at IASCO with the Japanese and Mr. Wenman. Two of the interviewers were former military pilots who seemed more interested in exchanging war stories than exploring my qualifications for a job with the FAA. After about two hours of casual discussion, I was thanked for coming, and told that if I was selected I would start out as a GS-11, with an annual salary of $15,000. (This was less than half of what a position with JDA would pay.)

I returned to Travis AFB, turned in my rental car and went to the Officers' Club for martinis and dinner. When at the bar I ran into Lloyd Tincher, a fellow C-133 pilot colleague from Travis. Lloyd told me that he had also attended two interviews that day. One for a position with JDA and the other with the FAA --- the same routine that I had gone through. We discussed our individual interviews, and discovered that the series of questions asked by the Japanese and IASCO were identical, along with the war stories with the FAA. Lloyd asked me how I responded to the question regarding the YS-11 as he didn't know much about it. When I told him how I reacted to that inquiry, he was impressed and thought it must have delighted the Japanese. We also talked about which position we would accept, if offered both. I said that this was a "no brainier," as I would take the job in Japan. Lloyd said that he would personally like to fly for the Japanese but his wife was against it, so he was hoping to be offered a job with the FAA. The next day I hitched a ride back to Dover on a C-133 that was commanded by a pilot I had checked out, and he let me fly it from the left seat for several hours.

On December 3rd I received a telegram from the FAA office in California, offering me a position as a pilot inspector. The message stated that I had 72 hours to decide if I would accept the offer. In the same time frame I was asked if I could attend a FAA job interview in Washington. These job offers put me in a quandary as I hadn't heard if I had been selected for a position with JDA, the position I preferred. I called Chuck Wenman, and inquired if the Japanese had provided him with the names of the captains they would invite to join their company. Chuck said that he hadn't heard anything so far, but expected to be informed shortly. I told him about my job offer with the FAA, which required a response within 72 hours, but I favored working for IASCO and the Japanese. He said he would call Tokyo to see if he could find out if I was one of the captains selected and call me back. The next day Chuck called and said that I was one of the captains JDA selected but not to tell any of the others. I chuckled at his request as I didn't know the other pilots interviewed, except Lloyd Tincher, and he didn't want a job in Japan anyway. Armed with this welcomed news, I sent a message to the FAA in California, declining their job offer, and canceled the job interview in Washington.

A couple days later I received a telegram from IASCO officially informing me that I was selected for a position as a captain with JDA in Tokyo, Japan. The message also stated that all administrative support would be handled by IASCO, while initial YS-11 qualification training would be provided by Piedmont Airlines. I was directed to proceed to their Training Center in Winston Salem, North Carolina, by presenting a copy of this message to any Piedmont ticket counter for a free travel pass. In addition, the instructional note stated that all foreign pilots assigned to JDA are required to coordinate personal requests and concerns with their respective YS-11 Chief Pilot, yet to be named.

On December 9, 1970 I and 14 other pilots were sitting in a classroom in Piedmont's Training Center, eager to begin the process of becoming YS-11 qualified pilots. My training colleagues ranged in age from 41 to 47 and most had military backgrounds. The transition training program, as contracted by the Japanese, would be composed of two weeks ground school and seven hours flight time in the actual aircraft. (Piedmont did not possess a YS-11 simulator.) The aircraft flight training would consist of four flights of three hours, with two students per session, thereby providing six hours of instruction. The seventh hour would be reserved for completing an ATP type rating flight check administered by a FAA inspector. I was impressed in the quality and eagerness of my new colleagues in absorbing the training presented, and equally delighted in the depth of knowledge of the Piedmont ground school instructors and in the quality of their training aids. It was quite a change from the military style of instruction. I didn't think that it was necessarily better, just more relaxed. I was proud to be associated with such an outstanding group of professional pilots. (See Photo No. 54.)

During the fourth day of ground school one of the instructors handed me a note requesting that I contact Chuck Wenman, the VP of IASCO. When I called him he told me that the Japanese and IASCO had selected me to represent the YS-11 captains as their Chief Pilot. This caught me by surprise as I was one of the youngest in the group, the most recent former military pilot and had not yet flown for a civilian airline. Chuck told me that the position was primarily administrative, as the Japanese will make all operational decisions, but they desire a Chief Pilot to turn to for disciplinary problems or contract dealings with IASCO. He then added that the Japanese prefer to deal with only one individual in these matters, versus coordinating with 15 different Gaijins (foreigners). He said that if I agreed to accept the position, I would receive an additional $540 per month ($297 when deducting IASCO's commission and taxes). I told Chuck to count me in, but requested that the manager of the Piedmont Training Department inform the rest of the pilots, so it wouldn't appear that I had sought the position on my own. He agreed to my request.

The next day as we were preparing to adjourn for the day, the Piedmont Training Department Manager entered the classroom and said that ho had an announcement to make. He said that he had just been informed by the VP of IASCO, Mr. Wenman, that Captain Lou Martin had been selected as Chief Pilot for the YS-11 Captains and all routine administrative questions or complaints should be directed to him. He ended his announcement with, "Congratulations, Captain Martin." A momentary hush fell over the group, and I tried to look as surprised as everyone else, as we stuffed our training manuals into our flight bags and prepared to head for our motel.

In the bar that evening, I was peppered with questions, like: What prompted the Japanese to select me as Chief Pilot? Did I know about the selection in advance? What authority, if any, did I have over the rest of the pilots?, etc. I thought it best to take a politician's approach in addressing their concerns and told them that I had no prior knowledge of who was going to be selected (a true statement), and that it was mostly a position of coordination so that the Japanese, when they wished to disseminate information, could do so by just dealing with one Gaijin. I also pointed out that I had spent three years in Japan and discovered that the Japanese were uncomfortable in addressing large groups of foreigners. (The pilots who had spent time in Japan agreed with me and at least for the time being my explanation seemed to satisfy their concerns.)

After two weeks of ground school we were split up into pairs and assigned to various Piedmont YS-11 domiciles, where a flight instructor would conduct flight training, followed by a FAA type rating flight check. I was teamed up with an affable pilot from Texas by the name of Bob Amon, who had flown KC-135s in the Air Force. After a few days off for Christmas, Bob and I reported to the Piedmont flight operations center in Norfolk, Virginia on Sunday, January 2, 1971.

Our flight instructor told us that the only YS-11s available for local training were aircraft that were used for passenger flights during the day, so our takeoff times would be around 2 or 3 a.m. He suggested we adjust our sleep patterns accordingly. My first flight in a YS-11 was on January 4th, with a takeoff time of 2 a.m. We flew training flights every night for the next four days and received our type rating flight check from FAA inspector, Lloyd M. Baxter, in the wee hours of January 9th. This was a most interesting checkout, as every flight was flown in instrument conditions, in the middle of the night, and usually in light icing. Our instructor would request radar vectors to an off-airways location, where

411

we would practice approaches to stalls, slow flight, steep turns and single-engine flight. We would then fly precision, non-precision and circling approaches (both two and single engine), missed approaches, V1 cuts (engine failure on takeoff) and no flap and normal landings. On most training flights it was not necessary to install an instrument hood to simulate weather conditions because we were flying in the clouds.

I found the YS-11 an easy airplane to fly and fortunately, possessed excellent night instrument lighting. Since we were flying empty airplanes, and in cold temperatures, we enjoyed excellent climb rates and single-engine performance. The cockpit had a comfortable jump seat, which allowed the pilot not flying to observe his colleague and learn from his mistakes, or expertise. Our instructor was well versed in the aircraft and by the time we had completed our second training flight (three hours of stick time each), stated that he didn't expect us to have any problem in obtaining a type rating in the allotted flight time of seven hours.

Following our second training flight we were informed that the JDA Chief Pilot, Captain Ogo, would be flying with us the following night, as he was visiting various Piedmont training sites to observe how his future Gaijin captains were doing in checking out in the YS-11. Knowing how the Japanese love Saki (strong rice wine), I purchased a bottle at the Norfolk Naval Base liquor store and thought I would surprise him with an unexpected treat after our early morning flight. Before I left my motel room for a 2:30 a.m. takeoff, I placed the bottle of Saki in my bathroom sink and allowed a slow trickle of warm water to flow over it. (The Japanese traditionally drink sake warm, but not hot.)

We landed in a snow storm around 5 a.m. and during our ride to the motel, I invited Captain Ogo and Bob Ammon to my room for a "nightcap" of Saki. Captain Oko's eyes popped wide open as he said, "You have Japanese Saki?" When I told him that I did and that it was sitting in my sink in warm water, he smiled widely (exposing two shining gold teeth) while stating, "That damn good idea, Ikimasho" (let's go).

It didn't take us long to finish off the bottle of Saki, and by the time Captain Ogo left for his own room we were good friends and slapping each other on the back as we exchanged stories about our flying and military backgrounds. I thought he must be in his early fifties and wondered if he was one of the pilots who bombed Pearl Harbor in 1941, but I didn't think it proper to ask my new boss if he had attacked my country so early in my employment career!

Later, when flying in Japan, I learned from my young Japanese copilots that Captain Ogo had indeed been a pilot in the Japanese military, and that ho was probably one of the pilots who bombed Pearl Harbor on December 7, 1941. Now, 30 years later, as I was in training to fly for his airline, he was observing me flying a Japanese YS-11 turboprop transport in the night skies of Virginia. I discovered later, that this was not an unusual circumstance as several senior Japanese JDA Captains that I would meet and fly with had been military pilots during the war and some had bombed Pearl Harbor, fought at Midway or even been members of Kamikaze Squadrons, but the war ended before they could launch.

After obtaining a U.S. YS-11 type rating, I was allowed to return to Dover, Delaware to await further instructions. Ten days later I received a certified mail package containing JAL tickets from New York to Tokyo, a copy of my employment contract and instructions to be in San Francisco in mid January to undergo a physical examination and obtain a Japanese Visa and work permit from the Japanese Consulate Office. The visit to the consulate office was accomplished without a hitch, leaving the satisfactory completion of a FAA First Class physical examination as the only item left to accomplish. After the physical exam we would standby for further instructions. Unfortunately our pay as captains would not start until we arrived in Japan but our motel room was paid for by the Japanese.

The physical examination was routine, with the exception of two additional items requested by the Japanese: one, was a check for stomach cancer through the use of an x-ray after drinking a large glass of liquid barium; the second, was an electroencephalograph, which records electrical signals generated by the brain from eight electrodes attached to the scalp. When undergoing this examination the technician instructed us to maintain a "blank mind," so as not to invalidate the test. (I thought that his requirement of maintaining a "blank mind" was a "no brainier" for a bunch of pilots.) We all passed the medical with the exception of Bucky Blair, who was diagnosed with a slight rupture in his groin. This problem was quickly corrected and all 15 pilots were declared qualified for duty.

Chuck Wenman, VP IASCO, requested I have lunch with him as there were a few things he wished to discuss regarding our assignment with JDA. Chuck told me that all pilots had completed training with Piedmont Airlines in the contracted flight time of seven hours except two. He said that Jack Spense and Dick Emery were not recommended for a FAA flight check after completing seven hours, so JDA authorized to pay for three additional hours. However, the additional three hours were absorbed in remedial flight training and didn't allow time for the FAA check, so JDA authorized two more hours.

Chuck wasn't inferring that this additional training for the two pilots would manifest itself into a problem when we were in Japan, but he wanted me to be aware of it. I told Chuck that I wasn't surprised in Jack Spence having a problem, as when we were attending ground school in Winston Salem, all the pilots were burning the midnight oil to learn as much as they could in the allotted time, except Jack, who in my opinion appeared to have spent too much of his free time in the motel bar.

Chuck also touched on my position as the YS-11 Chief Pilot. He said that the Japanese designated a foreign captain as Chief Pilot for each aircraft type foreigners flew, which included the B-727, DC-10 and DC-8. Part of my job was to help ensure cooperation and harmony between the Japanese and American pilots, as the difference in culture and basic philosophy is dramatically different. And in some cases, a lingering antipathy associated with WW II can occasionally crop up from either side. Chuck said that I was to work closely with Captains Jim Jack, president of IASCO, Chuck Smith, his assistant and Sid Joiner, IASCO's Chief Pilot who maintain an office in the JAL Headquarters building in Tokyo, and to keep them fully apprised of any potential problems. Chuck also pointed out that the JDA pilot's union voted unanimously against hiring foreign captains, but agreed to do so on a contractual trial basis for two years. But, when agreeing with the hiring of foreigners, they went on record stating that they would assume no responsibility for any problems or accidents resulting from introducing foreign pilots into their cockpits.

I told Chuck I would do my best in keeping the peace, and asked if I could ask him a question. "Absolutely," was his quick response. "I was wondering" I said, "why the Japanese selected me as Chief Pilot. I'm next to the youngest of the new captains, most recently retired from the military and have never flown for a civilian airline." Chuck smiled, while telling me it was a very interesting question, but he wasn't surprised in their decision. He said that when interviewing the 30 potential candidates, the Japanese had designed a list of identical questions that they were going to ask each one so they could establish a base line (not an unusual interviewing practice). When they asked the question, "Do you know what a YS-11 is?" I was the only one who responded with a clear informative answer, and in addition, I pulled out a book from my flight bag that was tabbed to the section pertaining to the YS-11. Also they were impressed in the fact that I had nearly 5,000 hours of turboprop flight time, had served three years in Japan with the Air Force, possessed a college degree, retired from the military as a Lt.Col., and was too young to have fought against Japan during WW II. He said these were some of the things the Japanese mentioned to him, when they submitted my name to Captain Jim Jack in Tokyo for his concurrence. I thanked Chuck for the lunch and his candid response to my question and returned to the motel.

We spent about ten days in California awaiting permission to proceed to Japan, and during this delay, I became more acquainted with my 14 pilot colleagues, and was very impressed and pleased to be allied with such a professional group. (See Photo 54.) A brief background of each follows:

Bob Ammon: Bob was from Texas and became a pilot with the U.S. Army Air Corps in 1944. He flew a variety of military aircraft, including 4,700 hours in the KC-135. After retiring from the Air Force he flew C-130s with Overseas National Airways. His total flight time was 12,000 hours and as previously stated was my "stick buddy" during flight training.

Bucky Blair: He was from Pennsylvania and started working at a local airport at age 14. He served two years in the U.S. Marines, flew for United Airlines, a charter company in Canada and had 16,700 hours flight time.

Dick Emery: Dick was from Lake Oswego, Oregon and a former military pilot, but was very quiet and didn't share much of his background with his fellow pilots.

Bob Frazier: Bob became a pilot with the U.S. Army Air Corps in 1945, flying both fighters and transports. He retired in 1970 with a total of 7,000 flight hours. He had an unusual side interest of postulating his belief in Christianity to anyone who would listen, including Japanese copilots.

Randy Hayes: Randy was from Tennessee and completed flight training with the U.S. Navy in 1950. He flew patrol bombers in the North Atlantic and was later stationed at Atsugi Air Base, Japan. After retiring from the Navy he flew ski-equipped C-130s in Antarctica. He had a college degree and 11,000 hours total flight time.

Bob MacClelland: Bob was a former U.S. Navy fighter pilot on the aircraft carrier Lexington that sailed into Tokyo Bay when the war ended in 1945. After retiring from the Navy he flew in Zambia and Alaska. He had 14,500 hours total flight time.

Mike Michaelis: Mike became a pilot with the U.S. Army Air Corps in 1944. He flew C-54s during the Berlin airlift and in 27 years as a military pilot had accumulated 16,000 hours flight time.

415

Frank Plonowski: Frank was from Connecticut and a former U.S. Air Force pilot who flew C-119 *Boxcars* in Japan and Europe. He retired from the Air Force in 1969 and flew C-130s in Alaska. Frank spoke English, Italian, French and Polish. His total flight time was 8,500 hours.

Penrod Rideout: A former Air Force pilot, Penrod listed his home as Santa Ana, California. After leaving the military he flew for several foreign airlines. His total flight time was 18,000 hours.

Dusty Rhodes: Dusty was from Georgia and at 38 was the youngest pilot in our group. He became a U.S. Marine Corps jet fighter pilot in 1954 flying F-9F *Panthers* and many other jet and propeller fighters. He also served in Japan and later qualified in the C-130 and landed in the South Pole. Dusty's total flight time was 8,000 hours.

Jack Spence: Jack was a former pilot in the U.S. Navy and had considerable experience in the C-130 before retiring.

Jim Treacy: Jim was from Massachusetts and entered the U.S. Navy in 1942. His 27 years in the Navy included flying both fighters and transports. He spent several assignments in Japan and was quite fluent in Japanese. Jim's total flight time was 10,000 hours.

Chris Weitzel: Chris was from New York and joined the U.S. Coast Guard in 1940, retiring as a Commander in 1969. He flew C-130s in the military and after retirement in Alaska. His total flight time was 10,000 hrs.

On February 3, 1971 my pilot colleagues and I were on a Japan Airlines DC-8 en route to Tokyo. After landing at Haneda Airport, we passed through the immigration checkpoint and moved on to customs. My colleagues in front of me passed through without a hitch, but when it became my turn things came to a dead stop! (When stationed in Japan six years earlier, I was active in shooting clay targets with both military and Japanese gun clubs. Hoping to continue with this hobby, I had packed a 12-gauge Browning over/under shotgun in my footlocker and naturally listed it on my customs declaration form.) When the Japanese custom agent looked at my customs form, I thought he was going to have a heart attack. "You have a 'boom-boom-gun' in your baggage?" he asked, in a tone of voice that inferred he was hoping I would say no, and that the statement on the form was a mistake! When I told him that I did have a "boom-boom-gun" in my footlocker he said, "*Chotto matte kudasai*" (wait a minute please) and called for his *kantoku* (supervisor). My colleagues, pissed off that I was holding up the line, moved to a different customs agent and were cleared on through without a problem.

A customs supervisor soon arrived, along with an armed policeman and an English interpreter who asked to see my shotgun. When I pulled it out from it's case they jumped back like they expected it to go off. Wearing white gloves, they carefully examined it while informing me, through an interpreter, that I could not bring it into Japan unless it was registered with the police and I possessed a gun handling permit. And since I did not have either, they would have to confiscate it and keep it locked up until I was able to produce the proper documents. (The interpreter, customs agent and policeman were very polite, when explaining this bureaucratic procedure, and seemed pleased when I told them that I fully understood what they must do.) I told them that when I was able to obtain the required documents, I would present it to them, but in the meantime I understood that they must keep it locked up. I apologized for any problem I may have caused, while explaining that my hobby, like many Japanese, was shooting clay targets, not people! They bowed in acknowledgment, and thanked me for being so cooperative.

They then spent 15 minutes in meticulous recording of the gun's dimensions, manufacturer and serial number, and filled out a detailed report in triplicate. They handed me the third copy, while stating that when I completed a gun handling course, and registered it with the police, I could return and redeem it. I thanked them for their patience and joined my colleagues who were waiting for me outside the terminal building, along with a group of JDA officials assembled to formally welcome us to Japan, which would include the customary practice of many PR photos.

I will explain the frustrating bureaucratic hurdles I had to go through to retrieve my boom-boom-gun in a later section.

We were warmly welcomed by Captain Ogo and other JDA officials and transported by bus to a hotel in downtown Yokohama. A Mr. Yamada, who spoke excellent English, was assigned as our company coordinator and informed us that we would not be involved with any duties for the next five days, except to be measured for uniforms, which would be ready by the time we started flying. We could utilize the time off recovering from jet lag, exploring Yokohama and searching for an apartment or house. We studied the classified section of the English edition of the Japan *Times,* which contained a listing of homes and apartments designed for rent to foreign tenants. I found a nice three-bedroom house in Nishinoya Naka-Ku, a suburb of Yokohama, that was owned by an American B-727 captain by the name of Joe Burke, who was married to a Japanese girl by the name of Kioko. Joe and Kioko were great people and we became good friends. I signed a two-year rental contract and arranged for Bob Ammon and Bob MacClelland to move in with me and share expenses until my family arrived in the summer of 1971.

JDA issued us a YS-11 pilot's manual (mostly in English), a company procedures manual (some of it in English), and a set of Jeppesen Manuals (100 percent in English). On February 8th, with manuals in-hand, we were enrolled in a two-week Foreign Pilot Ground School. Following satisfactory completion we would be administered a Japanese Civil Aviation Bureau (JCAB) written examination, which would authorize us to fly as observers in the jump seat of a YS-11. This would be followed by flying as copilots with a Japanese flight instructor in the left seat.

My first orientation flight in a jump seat was with Captain Fujimotto on February 18, 1971, on a flight from Tokyo to Oita, Kagoshima and return. Captain Fujimotto allowed me to make position reports and I experienced no problems in conversing with ATC personnel or company dispatchers. I figured that within the next day or so I would be flying as copilot, and soon thereafter as captain, since that was the position I was hired to fill. However, I underestimated the Japanese propensity of not making hasty decisions and moving like a tortoise in qualifying foreign pilots as captains. I flew 19 more flights and 20 hours in the jump seat before I was allowed to make a flight as copilot. My first flight in the right seat was with instructor pilot Captain Nakagawa, to Obihiro on March 2nd. A few days later I was administered a copilot flight check by Captain Sakaibara, (a Japanese instructor pilot who the young Japanese copilots said had bombed Pearl Harbor nearly 30 years earlier.)

On March 13th, I was administered a left seat check ride which would authorize me to fly Initial Operating Experience (IOE) flights as captain under the supervision of a Japanese flight instructor. I didn't know how long I would be required to fly these instructional flights, but on March 22nd, Captain Ogo contacted me and requested that I and three other foreign captains of my choosing proceed to their training base in Tokushima for a quick checkout, as he needed additional YS-11 captains for the April schedule. I selected Bob MacClelland, Bucky Blair, and Penrod Rideout as my companions for this "quasi" expeditious upgrade. The next day we were onboard a passenger flight to Tokushima Airport. (A shared Japanese military and civilian base close to Osaka.)

Casually dressed in sport shirts and trousers, we spent five days flying training missions in a YS-11 (JDA at the time did not possess a simulator). On the afternoon of the fifth day, our flight instructors had us assemble for a briefing on what to expect during our ATP flight check by a JCAB flight examiner the next day. They went over the standard flight maneuvers we would be required to perform, while emphasizing that when the government inspector entered the room, we would all stand up and not sit down until he did, and when receiving our check rides we must all wear our company uniforms. He noted an amazed look on my face, so he repeated the requirement that we wear our JDA uniforms during the government check ride! When I told him that we didn't have our uniforms with us, his chin dropped and his eyes popped, while stating, "Why you not have uniforms?" I told him that we were told to come to Takushima for training and in the U.S. we never wore uniforms during training. "But you are not in USA," he said, "and must wear uniforms for government check *lide*!" Shaking his head in frustration he made a telephone call to Tokyo!

After a couple minutes of excited conversation with his Tokyo superiors, he cupped his hand over the telephone and quipped, "Can we send company personnel to your homes in Tokyo to pickup your uniforms and *fry* them to Takushima?" I told him that this wouldn't work as we all lived in different locations and had the keys to our homes with us. He was back on the phone, and a few minutes later, with a disconcerting look, hung-up. He turned to us and asked, "Do you all have *brack* shoes?" Receiving a yes, his next question was, "Do you all have dark trousers?" Receiving another yes, he relaxed somewhat and color began to flow back into his ashen face. However, when he asked if we all had white shirts and *brack* ties, he slipped back into a mild state of depression when I said, "Sorry, but none of us have black ties or white shirts with us." There was a scurry of activity between our frustrated instructor and female clerks, as he began shouting instructions to them in Japanese. A couple minutes later several five-foot-tall female Japanese office workers, standing on chairs, started measuring our shoulders, neck, arm lengths and chest size with a centimeter tape measure, while an assistant recorded the measurements taken. With the recorded measurements in hand he rushed out the door and climbed into a waiting taxi.

A flight instructor then told us that the company was going to buy four white shirts and *brack* ties, which we must wear, along with our dark trousers, when we take our government check *lides* tomorrow morning. This will be your one-time uniform! He then, in a firm voice, said, "Captain

Martin, *prease* tell all Gajin captains that when they go for check *lide* with a High Government Examiner they must be in uniform." On March 29th, looking smart in our ad-lib uniforms, we all passed our JCAB flight checks and now held Japanese ATP Certificates with a YS-11 Type Rating.

The substitution of Ls for Rs in the above three paragraphs was intentional, but in no way was intended to insult the Japanese in their difficulty in correctly pronouncing words that have, as the first letter, an L or R. I just meant to add a little humor and present the episode as it appeared to us at the time. However, this satire will not be repeated.

My first official IOE flight with a Japanese instructor pilot in the right seat was on April 2, 1971. I would be required to fly a minimum of 25 hours of IOE followed by an initial line check administered by a JCAB flight examiner. Captain Ogo directed that all Gaijin captains would be required to complete two line checks, while Japanese captains were only required to complete the standard of one. In addition, we were required to commit to memory all pertinent airways information relating to the route that we would fly during the JCAB check. This remembrance of routine data included airways headings, minimum en route altitudes, frequencies of navigation radio stations, approach chart minimums and the names and height of prominent mountains (in both feet and meters). This seemingly superfluous requirement generated a lot of bitching by my fellow American pilots, but I spoke up in defense of the Japanese, stating that it was their airline and grumbling won't get the job done --- just do it!

I was the first foreign captain to complete 25 hours of IOE and scheduled for a JCAB line check with Mr. Matsushima (remember this name) on April 12, 1971. My initial line check was being watched closely by my colleagues, JDA supervisors, members of the Japanese pilot's union and IASCO managers. Everyone except me seemed to have their fingers crossed for a successful outcome. (Since taking my first flight check 26 years earlier, I adopted a mental attitude that check rides were my opportunity of demonstrating my extraordinary talents as a pilot. This approach may sound egotistical, and it may be, but it's a hell of a lot better than worrying that you might fail.) My copilot for the flight check would be our Japanese Chief Pilot, Captain Ogo.

The first route segment was from Tokyo to Obihiro, a city in the Northern Island of Hokkaido. Flying up the East Coast of Japan, at 15,000 feet in good weather, the flight was proceeding along smoothly

420

and I was able to answer all questions the "High Japanese Government Official" asked relating to radio frequencies, airways headings, minimum altitudes and a myriad of other facts I had committed to memory. Captain Ogo was making the required radio calls and performing the other duties expected of a copilot. Mr. Matsushima, sitting in the jump seat, engaged in a never-ending discussion (in Japanese) with Captain Ogo, except when he asked me questions in English. I had no idea what they were talking about, but would occasionally hear my name mentioned. (I figured as long as they were talking to each other, they wouldn't be pestering me with trivial questions, so I just kept hand flying the aircraft while striving to keep the heading within one degree of the desired course and the altitude within ten feet of our assigned altitude. (Japanese penchant for perfection demanded nothing less, even though the YS-11 didn't have autopilots.)

North of the city of Sendai, Mr. Matsushima tapped me on the shoulder, and said, "Captain Martin-san, tell me about that high snow-capped mountain about 25 miles west of our course." The name of it had escaped me, but I told him its height in both meters and feet. He asked me if I knew its name. When I told him that I couldn't recall the name, he shook his head, made a notation in his note pad and then resumed talking to Captain Ogo in Japanese, with the name Captain Martin-san now being mentioned more often. (See Photo No. 56 of author in YS-11.)

The weather at Obihiro was excellent, which would allow for a straight in visual approach, but Captain Ogo placed a navigation map in my windshield, instructed me to hold over the radio beacon, followed by flying a full non-precision NDB approach. I thought exposing our 64 passengers to an extra 20 minutes of circling maneuvers when the field was clearly visible was strange, but I just did what I was told! After an uneventful smooth "Martin landing," my Japanese leaders engaged in a lengthy discussion. I didn't understand what they were talking about, but English words, like approach, headings, air speed, Captain Martin, etc., were interjected in their discussion. Finally, Captain Ogo turned to me and said, "Mr. Matsushima wants to see another non-precision approach. So please fly a NDB approach at Kushiro Airport (our next passenger stop).

Apparently the next NDB approach, with a map blocking my view, was acceptable as there was little discussion after landing. After a tea and pee break we flew back to Obihiro, where I was allowed to make a visual approach, and 30 minutes later we were en route to Tokyo.

During the two and a half hour flight, along the East Coast of Japan, Captain Ogo and I took turns in eating our Obinto (box lunch), using chop

421

sticks, while sipping cups of hot o-cha (green tea). After lunch, I noted that Mr. Matsushima was slumped over in the jump seat and sound asleep, while Captain Ogo, sitting in the copilot's seat, would occasionally allow his head to drop while fighting off a cockpit siesta. Not wishing to disturb my Kantokus (supervisors), I made the required radio calls, kept us on course and altitude, while taking pleasure in the comforting solitude of not having to answer stupid questions and the pleasant hum of the Rolls Royce engines, which had lulled my cockpit colleagues into catching a sun-drenched afternoon "cat nap."

About 60 miles north of Tokyo I tuned the radio receiver to the Haneda Airport Automatic Terminal Information Service (ATIS) and nudged Captain Ogo, who quickly came alive and seemed refreshed after his siesta. The weather at Tokyo was reported as "severe clear" with radar vectors to a visual approach. Tokyo ATC cleared us to descend to 10,000 feet, with further descent as we were closer to the airport. Through hand signals, I called Captain Ogo's attention to the fact that our JCAB inspector, Mr. Matsushima, was sound asleep and questioned if I should wake him up. Ogo responded, by shaking his head **no** and displaying an OK signal with his thumb, meaning, "We should let him sleep." This was fine with me and to keep from disturbing him in performing his bureaucratic oversight responsibilities, I kept power reductions and altitude changes to a minimum and as smooth as possible.

As far as I was concerned, Mr. Matsushima's sleeping in the jump seat was upholding the tradition of many government flight inspectors I had met, be they JCAB or FAA, and I didn't wish to interfere!

Following radar vectors we were flying at 3,000 feet and ten miles from the airport, when approach control inquired if we had the airport in sight. When we stated that we did, they instructed us to contact the control tower for landing clearance. Captain Ogo switched to the tower radio frequency, which cleared us for a visual landing. I called, "gear down, approach flaps." The sound of flowing hydraulic fluid and the loud thump of the nose gear locking into the down position woke up our sleeping JCAB examiner. Shaking his head and rubbing his eyes, he engaged in a heated discussion with Captain Ogo. I didn't understand what they were talking about, but it was clear that it involved me and my initial line check.

Suddenly, Captain Ogo placed a map in my windshield (blocking my outside view), while stating, "Mr. Matsushima wants ILS approach." With my view of the runway blocked, I arrested my descent, while explaining to my "drowsy inspector" that I was in no position to fly an instrument approach as wo woro on a short final for a visual landing. I wasn't getting through to him and he and Captain Ogo were still talking in heated Japanese. Haneda Tower, observing our momentary level off, called and requested our intentions. I decided that I had enough of this bull shit, pulled down the map, told the tower we would land, reached over and placed the flaps to full down and got back on a proper visual glide slope. My two Japanese colleagues, obviously stunned, said nothing and I was sure I had busted my check ride, but at that point I didn't care. I just wanted to get the YS-11 and 64 passengers safely on the ground.

An uneventful landing followed, and except for routine taxi instructions from the control tower and the challenge and response when completing the After Landing and Engine Shutdown Checks, not a word was said. After the propellers stopped rotating and the passengers were deplaning, I turned to Mr. Matsushima and in a firm voice said, "Mr. Matsushima, if you wish to sleep, when administering an Initial JCAB Line Check, that's your business and I couldn't care less. However, when you placed a map in the windshield when I was on a visual short final, it jeopardized the safety of 64 passengers for whom I was responsible. Now, if you want me to fly an ILS, we can refuel this aircraft and I'll fly as many approaches as you wish." His response, "Check ride complete!" I knew enough to shut-up, and didn't say another word. The item relating to an ILS approach on my check flight report was rated satisfactory.

The next day I flew a training flight with a Japanese flight instructor from Tokyo to Hannimaki, Hachinohe and return to Tokyo. On April 15th, I flew the same route for my second JCAB required line check, with a High Government Official by the name of Mr. Miyoshi. I don't know if Matsushima and Miyoshi had discussed my first line check, but this flight was accomplished without any peculiar happenings and Inspector Miyoshi stayed awake the entire time! When we returned to Tokyo, I was now officially checked out as a JDA YS-11 captain and could fly passenger flights with a regular company assigned copilot in the right seat.

On April 20, 1971, with a backdrop of considerable "fanfare," I flew my first flight as captain with an all Japanese crew. I sensed considerable uneasiness on the part of the copilot and flight attendants, which, for them, was not unlike "stage fright." I did my best to calm their fears and before the flight was history the flight attendants seemed to accept the fact that a Gaijin captain could compete with, but not fully match, the exceptional pilot qualities of a Japanese pilot. However, it took some time before Japanese copilots shared their opinion.

My first flight as a JDA (solo) captain was a unique and interesting experience. After initialing the daily flight schedule roster, I wasn't able to ascertain who my copilot or flight attendants were as all crew names, except foreign pilots, were printed in Japanese. I moved down the dispatch counter until I found a copilot busily working on flight papers relating to my flight. When I located him he acknowledged my presence with a bow and a warm, "O-hayo Gozaimasu captain" (good morning). As he continued preparing the flight plan, navigation log and weight and balance for my signature, the dispatcher gave me a briefing, in Japanese/English, on the weather and aircraft status. However, before he endeavored to accomplish this mundane task he discreetly pulled out a large board from underneath his counter containing the picture and printed name of all 15 foreign pilots, thereby providing irrevocable evidence of to whom he was speaking. (This was necessary since in the eyes of our Japanese dispatchers all foreign captains looked alike!)

When everyone agreed that the flight could be dispatched safely, I signed the appropriate forms and the copilot and I proceeded to brief our cute mini-skirted flight attendants. As we approached them they all bowed politely and offered their individual "O-hayo Gozaimase," along with stating, "My name is Miss Tanaka" or "Miss Fujimoto", etc. We then gathered on opposite sides of a small table, that contained a cabin layout of a YS-11. This would be followed by the copilot briefing them (in Japanese) on the days flight. Most of the copilots were long-winded and when he would occasionally point to me I would nod my head, even though I didn't understand what he was talking about. At the conclusion of the briefing the flight attendants were required to position "magnet markers," representing the various emergency equipment carried in the cabin, in the proper location on a YS-11 cabin layout board. Following this we would all bow toward each other and walk to our respective aircraft.

Upon reaching the aircraft both pilots were required to perform a visual external walk around inspection, but naturally the captain always went first. However, this custom could present an Oriental face-saving problem, if a Japanese captain failed to note a safety of flight item, like a small inspection panel that was left open. It would not be proper for the copilot to just close it and move on, as this would reflect badly on the captain. He would stand next to the open panel and ask the captain, "Should this door be closed before we fly captain?" The captain, in an indignant tone of voice would say, "That door should be closed before flight, you should know that, so close it!" The copilot would click his heels and close the door, while stating, "Domo Arigato gazimous (thank you very much) captain. It was stupid of me not to know that and it is very obvious why you are the captain and I'm just a humble ignorant copilot."

My copilot on my first flight was a senior first officer who was close to upgrading to captain, moderately unfriendly and spoke very little English. He acted as if the hiring of foreign pilots would delay his upgrade to captain and he wasn't going to cooperate with me, or any other Gaijin pilot, when performing copilot duties. The company policy was that an altitude of 400 feet must be obtained after takeoff before initiating a turn. So when my altimeter registered 435 feet (400 feet AGL) I rolled into a shallow right bank. When I did my "non-smiling" copilot attempted to overpower me by attempting to roll the wings level while stating, "No turn below 400 feet!" I was not only shocked but pissed off in his effort to override me on the controls. I rolled the aircraft back into a right bank and as we were passing through 800 feet I glanced at his altimeter and noted that it was registering 30 feet less than mine. What this over-eager arrogant copilot had attempted to do on his first flight with a foreign captain was to override a control input when in his egotistical mind he thought had been initiated 30 feet below the stated minimum.

The rest of the flight was uneventful but I advised him to never attempt to override me on the controls again while pointing out that our altimeters were reading a difference of 30 feet (well within allowable tolerances). He complained to Captain Ogo that I was a difficult pilot to fly with and never wanted to fly with me again. (In spite of this rocky start every subsequent day was interesting and exciting and I considered myself fortunate to have been chosen for a flying job in Japan versus working for the FAA!)

Following my checkout my American colleagues were rapidly following in my foot steps and experiencing some of the same frustrations in the process. Our Japanese instructors, airline staff and JCAB examiners were extremely polite and compassionate during our extensive qualification program, but the differences in cultural philosophies and customs created situations that required sensible patience on the part of both parties. I found it necessary to caution some of my colleagues not to fight the system, but accept the fact that we were in Japan, working for a

Japanese Airline, and not flying for a company in New Jersey. Most accepted reality and worked hard to assimilate, but a few found it difficult to adopt the cultural tradition of the Japanese. One item that many Gaijin captains objected to was the requirement that Japanese copilots submit written reports on how well we transact with the crew on every flight. Several pilots requested that I pressure the company to eliminate this practice but I refused. I reminded them that it was a Japanese directive, was none of our concern and had no effect on our high salaries.

Captain Ogo called my attention to some examples of problems copilots experienced when flying with foreign captains, which in my mind were insignificant, but he requested that I counsel the pilots involved to be more understanding. Ogo added that several copilots had requested that they not be required to fly with foreign pilots but, due to crew scheduling demands, he told them that he could not honor their request. According to Ogo, most of their apprehension was based on a fear of not being able to speak English and not being able to work effectively with a foreigner. He said that many flight attendants expressed similar concerns.

This fear of making a mistake is a deep-rooted characteristic of the Japanese and was one of the most difficult obstacles to overcome in developing good working relationships. If an American pilot makes a mistake, he says, "What the hell," and moves on. A Japanese cannot do this as when he or she makes a mistake they feel that they have insulted their ancestors, and will be in a sullen mood for days afterwards!

In an attempt to smooth the waters, I sent a personal letter to Captain Ogo, apologizing for any misunderstanding on the part of the foreign captains and that we would work hard to ensure a close working relationship in the future. My letter was intended for Captain Ogo's eyes only, but he made copies of it and posted it on every bulletin board throughout the company. My American colleagues were incensed when they read it and accused me of embarrassing them and all foreign pilots worldwide. I thought their concerns were overblown, but I would have preferred that Captain Ogo had not published a personal expression of intended cooperation directed to him.

Captain Ogo requested that I and two other American captains meet with the President and staff members of the JDA Pilot's Union on April 30, 1971. (He emphasized that when we meet with them we should wear our uniforms.) I requested that Penrod Rideout and Bob MacClelland accompany me during this visit. When we arrived we were invited to take a seat on one side of a long table, while the President of the pilot's union and his two assistants sat on the other side.

We reached across the table and shook hands as two petite Japanese hostesses poured steaming cups of o-cha (green tea). In broken, but understandable English, the union President didn't hesitate in launching into the reason he wanted to meet with us. He said that the pilot's union had voted unanimously against hiring foreign captains, but after considerable discussion with company managers, they decided not to go on strike in opposition. He said that the company told them that to be able to expand their operation, and allow for senior Japanese captains to upgrade to DC-9s, it was necessary to hire foreign captains so they reluctantly agreed to a two-year trial period. If the first 15 foreigners were able to work well with Japanese copilots and flight attendants, they would consider hiring more in the future. However, he stressed that the pilot's union was adamant in disavowing any problems that having foreign pilots in the cockpit may create, or any accidents that there presence may cause. (I was surprised in hearing a Japanese speak about a perceived problem with such directness and clarity, and felt that it was obvious that he had thoroughly rehearsed his statement before the meeting.)

When he finished he asked if there were any questions. I said, "No, you made your point, and you can rest assured that we share the same goals. Safety is our foremost concern and we will strive to be productive members of JDA. Thanks for the o-cha." We shook hands and our ten-minute meeting was over. Walking to our waiting limousine, my two colleagues asked me what I thought about the meeting. I told them that in my mind, the pilot's union was worried about Gaijin pilots replacing low-time Japanese captains. Foreign pilots possessed between 10,000 to 20,000 hours flight time, while Japanese captains averaged around 5,000. Since JAL at the present time had more than 300 foreign pilots on their payroll, JDA didn't want the same fate to happen to their airline. Also, their concern for potential cockpit coordination problems was valid, as they hadn't flown with foreigners in the past, and consequently we would have to do our part in easing the tension.

Now that I was checked out as a captain and flying the line, I was enjoying two or three days off per week, so I thought it was time to rescue my "boom-boom-gun" from the airport customs office. I asked Mr. Hamada if Zeke Nakajima (our young official interpreter, who graduated from college with a degree in English) could accompany me in attending an all-day course in gun handling at a downtown police station. Mr. Hamada said, "No problem, Captain Martin. Have fun." Zeke and I met shortly before 8 a.m. at the designated police station and entered a large auditorium crammed with tables and chairs occupied by approximately 75 gun-handling applicants, (I noted that I was the only Gaijin). We took a seat in the rear, where I completed a two-page application form printed in broken English and Japanese. I submitted it to the proper officials and sat back to learn what the Japanese were going to teach me about a shotgun, albeit the information was to be presented in Japanese.

The lecture subject material was very basic and accompanied by large pictures and drawings. Instructors discussed the difference between the barrel and stock, how to insert shells, not to point it at anyone, etc. It was so basic that I didn't require Zeke to interpret the material covered. He sat next to me snoozing or doodling on a blank piece of paper. The morning session went from eight to twelve noon, with only one short pee break, before we broke for lunch. I bought Zeke lunch at a Sushi restaurant and at 1 p.m. we were back in class. Nakajima, with a full stomach, and no interest in shotguns, lowered his head and went to sleep. Even though I didn't understand Japanese, it was clear that the first hour of the afternoon session was devoted to a review of the morning material.

At around 2 p.m. instructors began passing out tests (all in Japanese), so I nudged Zeke awake and asked him to explain their contents. Yawning, he said that they were passing out exams. "I know that," I said, "but they are printed in Japanese, see if they have one in English!" He didn't think they did, but I persisted, so he spoke to one of the instructors and came back with an exam in "Pigeon English." The exam consisted of 25 multiple-choice questions, so basic that I could have answered them correctly when I was 14-years-old. I whipped through the exam in about 15 minutes and was about to turn it in when Zeke stopped me. He said that they had allowed 50 minutes to complete the exam so if I turned it in after only 15 minutes it would be considered an insult to the instructors. So I went back over it without changing a thing, and turned it in 25 minutes later. When all the exams were submitted, the applicants were excused and the chief instructor told us to be back in one hour when the test results would be announced.

When Zeke and I returned, the first thing that caught my eye was a list of ten names on the blackboard, with one of them being "Martin-San." I asked him why my name was listed on the blackboard, along with a group of Japanese names. His response, "Congratulations Captain Martin. You made 100 percent on the exam and you will receive your gun-handling certificate, along with the nine other men who made 100 percent before the remaining applicants receive theirs." Sure enough, the Chief Instructor read off nine Japanese names, and then Martin-San. We stood on the stage together as we were presented our diplomas and received a nice round of applause from our less fortunate gun-handling colleagues. With my official diploma in-hand, I was now ready for a visit to the police station in Yokohama, the next step in retrieving my shotgun from the customs office at the Tokyo International Airport.

A Yokohama police officer, after closely examining my gun-handling certificate and passport, issued a two-page document authorizing me to proceed to the airport to pick up my gun. An English speaking officer stressed that after retrieving it, I was to bring it directly to their office for inspection and registration. He also pointed out that I must pick it up within 72 hours or the authorization would become invalid. I presented my Japanese-issued police pickup authority to an airport customs agent and after a thorough check of my identification he retrieved the gun from storage, blew accumulated dust off the case, and made sure the serial number on the gun matched the number on my original receipt. However, before I could take it with me, I had to sign three different forms.

Back in the Yokohama Police Station, the gun was closely inspected by white-gloved officers, who measured its overall length with a centimeter tape measure and checked the breach and barrel openings with a micrometer. After informing them of the address where the gun would be stored, a head-and-shoulders picture was taken and a fold-out license (similar to a small passport) was issued. The polite, English-speaking police officer attending to my needs emphasized that the gun must be kept under lock and key when not in use and ammunition must be locked in a separate location. He cautioned that police officers would make periodic unannounced visits to my home to ensure that it was being properly stored. Two hours after entering the police station I was finally allowed to take my gun home. (I'm sure the NRA would welcome a similar procedure for registering shotguns be adopted in the United States.)

The next 60 days were very interesting, and tested my patience and ability of ensuring a smooth and productive working relationship between highly-experienced, self-assured American pilots and their somewhat shy, introverted Japanese copilots, disinclined to fly with Gaijin captains.

429

I will comment on a few problems brought to my attention by Captain Ogo but will withhold the names of the American captains involved.

A friend of mine, who I trained with, was accused of smacking copilot's knuckles with a pencil when he was unhappy with their cockpit coordination. Another captain agitated a copilot when he attempted to convert him to Christianity (less than one percent of the Japanese are Christians). He was on a weather hold that required he and his copilot to standby in the cockpit, so he decided to take advantage of the idle time by practicing his ministry. The copilot stated that he wasn't interested as his religion was Shintoism, but our evangelist captain tried to convince him that he was paying tribute to a heretic religion. To prove his point, he reached into his flight bag, pulled out a screw driver and removed a small wooden Shinto prayer board attached to the cockpit bulkhead. He then took out a jackknife and started whittling on it, while stating, "See this is a heathen object, I'm cutting it up and nothing is happening to me." Captain Ogo was livid when he heard about this and demanded that the captain apologize to the copilot and promise never to perform such a careless stupid act again. At first he was reluctant to atone for his actions, but after considerable pressure from me, he finally relented and expressed regret for his conduct and comments about a Japanese copilot's religion.

On another occasion, according to the copilot's report, an American captain was flying a NDB non-precision approach to the Hokkaido Obihiro Airport, but after descending to the Minimum Descent Altitude (MDA) they were still in snow showers and didn't have the airport in sight. The captain was about to execute a missed approach, when he thought he saw the asphalt runway through the low ragged ceiling. He called for landing flaps and started descending to what he thought was a runway. His copilot shouted that he was setting-up an approach for the black waters of the Obihiro River and refused to lower the flaps and attempted to advance the throttles for a missed approach. However, the captain insisted that what he had in sight was a runway, lowered the flaps himself, and continued his approach. However, after descending to about 200 feet, he realized his mistake and called for a go-around. But, by this time, he had pissed off his scared copilot to the point that he just sat there, with his hands in his lap, and refused to assist in the missed-approach procedure. The captain cleaned up the aircraft by himself and diverted to Chitose Airport. After landing his copilot headed for a telephone in one direction, while he headed for one in a different direction. They both called Tokyo and requested to be paired up with a different pilot. However, none were available, so they finished the day's schedule but their cockpit communication was limited to accomplishing the required checklist items. Captain Ogo contacted me and ordered the American captain and I to meet with him, the copilot and his flight commander to discuss the incident. After a long discussion, I finally persuaded the captain to apologize, but not until I threatened to recommend he be fired if he didn't.

Unfortunately, the same American captain allowed himself to create an additional problem that caused me to intercede, on his behalf, with the Japanese Chief Pilot once again. He was flying a trip up the West Coast of Japan, at around 15,000 feet, when he began encountering turbulent summer cumulus clouds. In attempting to provide a smooth ride for his passengers, he began deviating around and below them. However, his good intentions soon ran into trouble. The clouds became more numerous and bottomed out at around 2,000 feet above the Sea of Japan. In his quest for providing a comfortable ride (a commendable but ill-advised goal), he had descended to about 1,500 feet over the water without obtaining a clearance. He finally realized the errors of his ways and attempted to contact Tokyo radio, but he was now at such a low altitude that he couldn't establish radio contact.

In desperation he started making radio calls to any aircraft that could receive his transmission. An All Nippon Airlines B-727, flying at 35,000 feet, answered and offered assistance. He told the Japanese captain that he was flying a YS-11, over the Sea of Japan at 1,500 feet, and requested he contact Tokyo and obtain clearance for him to climb to his original assigned altitude of 15,000 feet. The ANA captain was naturally surprised in receiving such an unorthodox request from a JDA aircraft carrying passengers and grilled the captain as to why he was flying at such a low altitude and inquired if he was declaring an emergency!

The YS-11 American captain became agitated at the inquisition and in a curt manner told the Japanese captain to just relay his clearance request and he would explain everything to his Chief Pilot later. The Japanese captain relayed his request to Tokyo, who granted him a clearance to climb through the clouds to 15,000 feet, but requested a full report on why he had deviated from his original clearance. He turned on the seat belt sign, encountered moderate turbulence climbing through the clouds, but to his surprise broke out on top at 15,000 feet in smooth air.

A report on his unauthorized excursion over the Sea of Japan was forwarded to Captain Ogo by the B-727 Japanese captain, Tokyo ATC and his Japanese copilot. Once again the American captain and I were sitting before Captain Ogo and trying to explain his unorthodox behavior while promising that it wouldn't happen again.

Not long after this incident I received a call from Captain Ogo requesting that I check on why an American captain had not reported for flight duty in the last three days. He said that they hadn't received a call from him stating the reason for his absence and their attempts to contact him were unsuccessful. He was a likable soft-spoken colleague who always greeted his fellow American pilots with a firm handshake and a warm smile and lived in a BOQ room on the Yokohama Naval Base.

I visited his room, knocked on his door but didn't receive a response. However, I thought that he must be in as his car was parked out front so I knocked again, much louder! I heard some muffled sounds from inside and fearing that he may be sick, I knocked again. My third knock produced a guttural, "Who is it?" "It's Lou Martin. Open the door. I want to talk to you." I heard foot steps moving toward the door, along with the clink of bottles clearing a path. When the door opened, it was like a scene from the 1945 movie The Lost Weekend, starring Ray Milland. The smell of booze was overpowering and he was dressed in wrinkled underwear, had about a four-day growth of facial hair and the room was darkened by fully-closed window blinds. I hadn't been exposed to a similar situation and didn't know if I should show anger or pity. However, I did feel a sense of loyalty to a fellow military retiree and a colleague, who from past records was an excellent pilot.

I asked him to sit on the edge of the bed, opened up the window blinds, picked up several empty bottles and asked him if he knew what day it was. He wasn't sure, but did know that he had been on a drinking binge and had not made his flight schedule. He asked if that was the reason I was there. I told him that it was and that the Japanese wanted me to report back to them as to his physical condition. I asked him how long it had been since he had consumed a good meal but he couldn't remember. I got him to agree to take a shower and shave while I went to the Officers' Club to get him a sandwich. As I headed out the door, I noticed that all the liquor bottles were empty, so I felt confident he would keep his promise regarding a shower, shave and no more drinking.

When I returned, he was a new man, although squinting from the bright light shining in through the open blinds. As he wolfed down the sandwich, I told him that Captain Ogo wanted to see him in his office the next day, in uniform. As we talked he told me that he had an alcohol addiction problem before, but thought he had overcome it, but obviously he hadn't. Wo talked about what he should tell the Japanese, whether he should tell them the truth or just say he was sick. I told him that I wasn't an expert in this area, but did know that Japanese men often have a drinking problem and the company would probably be sympathetic to the truth. I left, stating that I would check back later that day to make sure he was OK.

He refrained from drinking that night and made his appointment with Captain Ogo the next morning. The Japanese were very compassionate and agreed to send him to a clinic to cure his drinking problem. And if he successfully completed the program, and passed a flight physical and flight check he would be returned to flight status. The Japanese paid all the expenses for the clinic, continued paying him his full salary and after he successfully completed the program was placed back on flight status. Following this incident he was a well-respected captain and didn't slip back into his old habits. I learned a lot from this experience, as my first reaction was that he should have been fired, since he violated his contract regarding the use of alcohol, but I was wrong! (This experience was very helpful when later in my aviation career I worked for the FAA.)

Japanese copilots reported that one of our captains was having difficulty in understanding radio calls and slow in responding to cockpit checklists. It was suspected that he may have a hearing problem, so Captain Ogo requested that I fly several trips with him by displacing his assigned copilot, who would move to the jump seat. After flying with him I was directed to submit a report on my observations. I flew with him on a turn-around flight to Hachinohe and on a flight to Obihiro, Kushiro and back to Tokyo, for a total of ten hours. My report to Captain Ogo was that he was an excellent pilot, but like the copilots reported, he missed several radio calls that were clear to me and the copilot in the jump seat and I concurred with the possibility of him having a hearing problem.

He was required to undergo a series of audiometer hearing tests, both in a local hospital and with a JCAB inspector in the cockpit. Following this he was required to wear a hearing aid, but was allowed to complete his initial two-year contract by flying between Tokyo and Osaka, where due to the large number of International flights, the English language proficiency of the Japanese ATC controllers was much better than controllers at small local airports. However, he was not offered a contract renewal.

I was also receiving complaints that American pilots were insulting Japanese limousine drivers by issuing brusque demands when requesting air conditioning temperature changes and departing their homes earlier than the scheduled pickup time. Requesting that the limousine driver lower the temperature should be made in a manner that would be perceived as a request, not an authoritarian demand. The driver's primary purpose is to insure his passenger's comfort and a direct command causes him to lose face, a sensitive issue in Japan. By leaving their homes before the scheduled pickup time also causes him to become uneasy, as an early departure will catch him in the process of dusting off his limousine while wearing working gloves. I told the pilots that if my pickup time was 6:30 a.m., I would observe the driver from a window and at around 6:28, when he has finished cleaning his limousine, is wearing his clean driving gloves, and standing by the limousine's rear door holding an English copy of the Japan *Times*, I walk out from my front door. If I left the house ten minutes earlier, I would screw up his ritualistic routine and ruin his entire day. Several American pilots thought my sensitivity concerns regarding limousine drivers were uncalled-for and merely supporting pointless Japanese customs. But I didn't know to what extent they thought I was fostering unessential concessions until sometime later.

There were other indications that several of my American colleagues were becoming unhappy with me as their Chief Pilot, but as I pointed out earlier, they were not aware of the "behind-the-scenes events" I was faced with in attempting to keep good relations between our Japanese employers and the foreign pilots. In many respects, they were just exercising the American penchant of bitching! (I was even accused of lying in regard to how much extra pay I received as Chief Pilot.) One of them said that I had stated that I only made an extra $297 per month, but when he checked the contract he discovered it was $540. When I told him that when you subtract IASCO's commission and taxes you will find it's $297, I'm sure he was unhappy, because I robbed him of a good bitching point, which he was sharing with other disgruntled American captains.

Several foreign captains also wanted me to complain to IASCO that the 15% contract commission fee deducted from our monthly salary was excessive and should be reduced. I refused to arbitrate stating that they signed the job contract like everyone else and without IASCO we wouldn't have a job. Some even requested that I attempt to have our annual JAL vacation tickets be upgraded to first class. I told them to forget it and consider themselves lucky in receiving a free economy class ticket for themselves and their family that wasn't limited to "space available."

In mid June, 1971, I received a disguised anonymous phone call informing me that the YS-11 American captains were meeting in the Yokohama Officers' Club, the following afternoon at 4 p.m. to elect a new Chief Pilot. Initially, I wondered how this could be possible, but a check of the flight schedule revealed that what my mystery caller had said was most likely true. Somehow, my colleagues had coordinated with the Japanese to have all Gaijin captains off the following day, except myself. I was scheduled for a turnaround flight to Hannimaki, arriving back in Tokyo around 3:45 p.m. (This would allow me time to make an unexpected attendance at the "Martin coup d'état meeting," even though I would be a little late.)

After landing I went next door to the IASCO's Tokyo Office and was pleased to find Captain Jim Jack in. I told his male secretary, Heinz, that I needed to talk to the boss on an important matter and was ushered into his office. (I had met with Captain Jack on several occasions before and we had developed a friendly, professional relationship.) As I entered, he rose, shook my hand and said, "Have a seat, Lou. What can I do for you?" When I told him about the clandestine meeting in the Yokohama Officers' Club to elect a new YS-11 Chief Pilot, he was furious, stating, "Who do those SOBs think they are? The Japanese are the ones who select their Foreign Chief Pilots, in concert with my advice and consent. We selected you to represent us and from the reports I receive from the Japanese they are well pleased with your performance." He then asked me if I was going to attend the meeting. I told him that I had my limousine driver waiting outside, and I was heading there as soon as I left his office. His response, "Good. When you go, I want you to get the names of the pilots who vote for your removal. I may just fire their ass for insubordination and violation of their contract." We shook hands and I left for Yokohama.

I told my limousine driver to wait in the Officers' Club parking lot as I wouldn't be long. Still in uniform and carrying my flight bag, I walked upstairs to the conference room being used for their meeting and walked in. Thirteen jaws dropped and silence filled the room! I pulled up a chair, slid it up to the table, sat down and said, "Sorry I'm late guys, but I had a flight to Hannimaki and got here as soon as I could. Would someone brief me on what I missed?"

No one volunteered to speak-up, but since Randy Hayes was sitting at the head of the table I assumed he was chairing the meeting, so I asked him to bring me up to-date. In a halting voice, he said that they had met to decide if they wanted a new Chief Pilot and 11 voted yes, one voted no and one abstained. "But you haven't counted my vote," I said. "We know how you would vote, Lou, so your vote wasn't important." Randy responded. "On the contrary, Randy, my vote is important and I think everyone should know that I had prior knowledge of this covert meeting, and before coming here I briefed Captain Jim Jack and he was mad as hell. He requested that I record the names of everyone who votes to have me replaced, as he may fire their ass for violating their contract. Now if you will provide me with the names of the 11 who voted yes, I'll pass it on to Captain Jack." There was long silence with no response!

I told the stunned group that I had no intention of resigning, and since we were all together there were a few things that had come to my attention that needed addressing. I pulled out a notepad from my flight bag and began reading from it, while instructing everyone to take notes. One-by-one they grabbed paper and pencil and began writing down my comments. (The items I discussed were routine subjects that I thought up during my 30-minute ride from the airport and could have been discussed anytime, but observing them taking notes I knew that I had won the battle.)   When I finished, I said that I was sorry I couldn't spend more time with them, as I was eager to get home for a shower, a cold beer and to prepare my report for Captain Jack. I picked up my flight bag and left!

The number of votes including mine totaled fourteen. Jack Spence, whose name you will hear again, was in the states to bring his wife Joyce back to Japan. I don't know for sure how he would have voted but assume he would have been swayed by the majority and also voted yes.

That night I received a phone call from Bob Ammon (my training partner in Norfolk, Virginia). Bob told me that my showing up at the meeting was a complete surprise and that Randy Hayes, who I correctly identified as the organizer, thought that since he had arranged with the Japanese for me to be flying I wouldn't be able to attend. I asked Bob how they were able to persuade the Japanese to allow all the American pilots, except me, to be off. He said that they told the schedulers that they were planning a surprise party for Captain Martin and therefore didn't want him to attend the meeting. (I guess this was fundamentally a true subterfuge, as they definitely wanted the outcome of the meeting to be a surprise!)

Bob Ammon told me that he was the one who voted no and Dusty Rhodes abstained. He said that many of our colleagues weren't aware of the nature of the meeting until after they arrived, but like a bunch of sheep they went along with the crowd. I asked Bob who they wanted as their new Chief Pilot and he said, "Bob MacClelland. However after you showed up, and told them that you had briefed Captain Jim Jack on their underhanded plan, their concerns switched from electing a new Chief Pilot to worrying about their own survival, and the discussion centered on that prospect until the meeting was adjourned."

The next day I visited Captain Jack, who, with a chuckle, said, "Tell me about the meeting yesterday, Lou. Do we have a new YS-11 Chief Pilot?" I told him about how I surprised them by showing up unexpected and telling them about my meeting with him before attending. Also about my switching the thrust of the meting by having them take notes on items I created on my way to Yokohama. I told him that I didn't think there would be any further problems so I didn't take names and no additional action on his part was required. He agreed, but told me that if there is any further attempts in dethroning his selected Chief Pilot to let him know. I agreed, but added that I didn't harbor any adverse feelings as they were all good pilots and doing a good job, and under the trying conditions we were exposed to, I considered their criticism a badge of honor.

As June 1971 was drawing to a close all American captains, except one, were checked out and flying the line with JDA assigned copilots, and resigned to the fact that I would continue as their Chief Pilot. The one exception was Jack Spence, who due to some problems in meeting accepted standards and an extended trip to the U.S. to pickup his wife was still flying IOE flights under the supervision of a Japanese flight instructor. I was relaxing in the dispatch office, awaiting an improvement in the weather for my flight, when Jack entered with a bottle of Coke in each hand. When he spied me sitting on a sofa reading the *Japan Times*, he shouted across the room, **"Hi Lou, how ya doing buddy?"** I walked over to say hello and with a big grin he offered me a Coke. As I drew closer, I thought I detected the smell of alcohol on his breath and asked him if he was OK. He seemed insulted that I would ask such a question. While we were talking, his Japanese flight instructor entered and he walked over to greet him. I thought his instructor might detect the odor of alcohol and cancel the flight, but he accepted his offer of a Coke, and after signing the dispatch release, they headed for their aircraft.

About an hour later my flight was canceled and I was released for the day. I walked next door to IASCO, found Captain Jack in, and reported my observations. I recommended that he consider firing Captain Spence for possible violation of our contract, since his rash behavior may damage our relationship with the Japanese, which was shaky at best. Captain Jack said that he understood my frustration, but since he was flying with a Japanese instructor, it was up to the Japanese to recommend any possible disciplinary action. Also, if he took action when the Japanese instructor wasn't concerned, it would cause him to lose face (good point). He told me to monitor the situation and keep him informed.

On July 3, 1971, I was enjoying a beer in my Yokohama home when I received a phone call from Captain Ogo. He told me that a YS-11 was missing on a flight from Sapporo to Hakodate. He feared for the worst but would continue to consider the aircraft missing until its estimated fuel onboard was exhausted or they found the aircraft. He said that the pilots were Captain Jack Spence in the left seat, instructor pilot Captain Hideyo Terada in the right seat, plus 64 Japanese passengers and two female flight attendants. Captain Ogo Suggested that I go over to Jack Spence's house and standby there for any further word. I asked him if Mrs. Spence had been informed that her husband was missing. He said no, as he was leaving that up to me.

My wife and I hurried over to Joyce Spence's house and as I drove up the driveway, I observed a swarm of reporters and photographers, looking like a "paparazzi" free-for-all, pounding on the front door and peering into the windows. As we walked toward the house I was peppered with questions in both Japanese and English. Reaching the front door, I identified myself to Joyce, who unlocked it and let us in. When entering I had to physically push back several reporters, who tried to follow us inside. Joyce was understandably hysterical, and throwing her arms around me said, "Something has happened to Jack, right?" My wife and I attempted to console her the best we could, and I told her everything I knew, while stressing that we shouldn't necessarily assume the worst, and that as soon as the company had more information they would call.

About 45 minutes later Captain Ogo called and informed me that the wreckage of the missing YS-11 was found in a heavily wooded area near the Kakodate airport and that all 68 people onboard were killed. I didn't have to tell Joyce the sad news as she knew from my facial expression that her husband was dead. In a whisper, she asked, "Did Jack suffer, or was he killed instantly?" I told her that he didn't suffer as he died instantly along with everyone else onboard. She accepted the sad news bravely, but her sobs were interspersed with the sound of reporters banging on the door and windows, demanding an interview. I knew that we had to get her away from this chaos, so I devised a plan that I thought would allow her to go to our house where she could lament in peace.

I opened the front door and, as expected, a horde of obnoxious reporters gathered around like a flock of vultures hoping to talk to Captain Spence's wife. To gain their attention, and entice the reporters congregated in the back of the house to come around to the front, I shouted, **"Attention everyone, Mrs. Spence is fixing her face and in a few minutes she will come out and answer questions for ten minutes, and ten minutes only, but she will only agree to this if you honor her request."** I noted everyone nodding their heads in agreement (which I knew they wouldn't keep) while photographers were getting their cameras ready. I then cracked the door and shouted, so everyone could hear, **"Five minutes Joyce. They agree to a ten minute interview and will leave after that."** This was my signal for my wife to sneak Joyce out the back door, grab a taxi and proceed to our house.

Five minutes later I told the unruly mob of reporters that I would go inside and bring out Mrs. Spence. When I entered the house I found it empty, so I knew that my plan had worked. I threw open the front door and allowed the mob of reporters to come inside, noting that even under these circumstances they removed their shoes before entering. When they found the house empty they knew they had been tricked, and soon left mumbling insults in my direction. Joyce later went to an undisclosed hotel and left for the U.S. a few days later, accompanying Jack's body.

The Japanese reaction to the accident was, "a guilty-by-association mentality." All 14 American YS-11 captains were immediately grounded and required to meet with JCAB inspector Mr. Matsushima. (Matsushima was the government inspector who fell asleep in the jump seat during my initial line check.) During the meeting we were grilled on what we thought may have caused the accident. We could offer no explanation, and Mr. Matsushima seemed upset when I stated that determining the cause of the accident would be the responsibility of a Japanese accident investigative team. His response, "Well, we had this other accident involving a foreign captain." Having no knowledge of what he was referring to, I asked him, "What accident?" He said, "A JAL Martin 202 flown by an American captain hit a mountain on Oshima Island in 1952, killing everyone onboard." (His reference to an accident, which occurred 19 years earlier, surprised us as it ignored numerous accidents, involving Japanese captains since.) During the discussion, Matsushima indicated that he may recommend to the Japanese Government that American YS-11 captains be restricted to flying into large airports only, and asked me what I thought of this suggestion. I told him that he might just as well recommend we all be fired, since restricting us to just a few large airports would brand us as second-rate pilots, and result in our being of little value to the airline! He seemed surprised by my direct response, but dropped the recommendation. However, before we were allowed to resume flying, we were required to take a JCAB administered written examination on landmarks, airport obstacles, weather minimums, airport approaches and cockpit coordination. (In addition, we were issued small Japanese/English dictionaries which were of little use as they were arranged for Japanese users since they were only printed in "Japanese to English.")

After resuming flight duties, I noted an increased scrutiny by dispatchers when signing our flight release and a hidden intolerant oversight on our activities by supervisors and copilots. However, this increased surveillance lessened somewhat after a Japanese Air Self Defense Force (JASDF) F-86F slammed into an All Nippon Airlines B-727 on July 30, 1971 (27 days after Jack Spence's accident), resulting in the crash of both aircraft and killing 164 passengers. Surprisingly, the fighter pilot ejected and landed safely, but was quickly arrested on suspicion of involuntary homicide, but later acquitted of all charges.

Ironically, before and after Jack Spence's accident Japanese pilots were involved in a series of accidents: a DC-8 crashed in New Delhi, India, killing 89; a DC-8 on a flight from London to Bombay, India crashed, killing 86 people, when the pilot mistook a small local airport for Bombay's Santa Cruz Airport; a DC-8 spun out of control when attempting a takeoff at Tokyo, injuring 16 passengers; a DC-8 crashed when taking off from Sheremetyevo Airport near Moscow, killing 61; a JDA B-727 ran off the runway at the Oita Airport and smashed into a concrete wall but fortunately there were no casualties; a YS-11 ran off the runway when landing during a rain storm at the Naha Airport in Okinawa and slammed into a water supply vehicle, which ruptured its fuel tanks, but there was no fire or injuries; a DC-8 spun out of control, and ran off the runway when attempting a rolling takeoff at Seoul, Korea, but encountered no injuries; a DC-8 ditched in the San Francisco Bay when attempting to land.

These series of accidents in aircraft flown by Japanese captains helped to remove the stigma of foreign pilots being incompetent and were instrumental in allowing foreign JAL captains to upgrade to B-747s and DC-10s, which in the past had been only flown by Japanese pilots.

The JDA YS-11 accident involving Jack Spence was determined to be pilot error. According to the report, the pilots, when still in the clouds, misjudged their distance from the airport and descended to the published Minimum Descent Altitude (MDA) too early. However, since Captain Spence was flying, with a Japanese instructor pilot in the right seat, it was difficult to lay total blame on him. But we were never allowed to forget the accredited Japanese premise, that if there had not been a foreign pilot in the cockpit, the accident would not have occurred.

With the hope of improving relations with the Japanese, I visited the Public Relations Department and requested they consider printing a "biographical snap-shot" of the foreign captains in their monthly news magazine. They agreed, providing I write the articles and provide the pictures that would accompany it. I interviewed each captain, and their families, took pictures, and for the next 14 issues a different captain was featured each month. These articles were well received by the Japanese, and many company pilots and flight attendants told me that they now had a better image of their Gaijin captains, and looked forward to each monthly issue like a "soap opera."

On July 20, 1972, I was scheduled for an annual line check administered by Captain Ebihara on a turnaround flight to Obihiro. My copilot for the outbound leg would be Captain Ishikawa, who would fly as captain on the return leg to complete his line check. I was looking forward to flying with Ebihara, as I had heard good things about him, and learned that he was a former Japanese Navy pilot who had reportedly flown combat missions during WW II. He was a trim, silver-haired, 53-year-old professional-looking airline captain, who carried himself with dignity, but spoke very little English. (Neither of us discussed his WW II experiences, but I must admit that I felt a little strange being administered a check ride by a former enemy, who was now my colleague.)

The takeoff from Tokyo was routine, and after retracting the landing gear and flaps we were flying in light rain showers and an overcast sky. Suddenly, the right engine fire light illuminated along with the loud alarm bell. I instructed my copilot to fly the aircraft, silenced the bell, checked the right engine instruments (which appeared normal), and as my copilot and check pilot watched, slowly retarded the right throttle. When it was slightly above the idle power position, the fire light went out. I then advanced it above this setting, and the fire light and bell returned. I once again retarded it to a position, where the fire light remained out and

441

turning to Captain Ebihara, stated that I suspected that our problem was a high pressure, high temperature, air leak and that I was not going to shutdown the engine, but would request an immediate return to Tokyo. I also told him that I was not going to declare an emergency, but just inform the control tower that we wished to land due a mechanical problem. He concurred with my decision. I then asked him if he would scan the engine, through a passenger window, to see if it appeared normal. He popped out of the jump seat, while stating "Hi" (Yes). He seemed excited, so I requested he put on his hat (a company requirement when visiting the cabin) and move slowly so as not to alarm the passengers.

The reason I decided not to declare an emergency, which would be a standard procedure in the U.S., was because I knew that paparazzi-type reporters monitor the control tower frequencies. And if I had declared an emergency, the next day's headline in the Japan Times would read, "Sixty-four passengers narrowly escaped death in a YS-11 flown by a foreign pilot when it made an emergency landing at Tokyo International Airport." I was sure Captain Ebihara understood my reasoning, but I wanted to get his concurrence, as I didn't wish to fail my line check.

As Captain Ebihara left the cockpit, I told the copilot that I had the controls and instructed him to request extended radar vectors to a final approach. He questioned the need for an extended pattern, until I reminded him that our present weight was greater than the maximum allowed landing weight, and it would be prudent to burn off some fuel before landing (a precaution that he hadn't thought of). Ebihara returned to the cockpit, reported the engine appeared normal and a routine extended ILS single-engine smooth landing was made.

We were parked next to a fully-serviced standby YS-11, and after transferring our passengers and baggage, we were back in the air 30 minutes later. The flight to Obihiro was routine, as well as the return flight to Tokyo when I flew as copilot for Captain Ishikawa. We gathered in the pilot's lounge over cups of tea, while Ebihara completed his check ride forms. The blocks requiring only a check mark were completed in an expeditious manner, but I noted that he was struggling when completing the narrative section that required written comments. I didn't wish to intervene as I knew he was doing his best to ensure his comments were recorded in English, so I just patiently kept on sipping my tea.

After several minutes of watching Ebihara agonizing over completing the comment section, he showed me what he had written and asked if it was acceptable. His printed statement read, "Captain Martin's performance, during an in-flight fire emergency, was yushu-na (excellent). He is one cool customer!" Without smiling, I told him that his remarks were much appreciated and very descriptive. He smiled and after I signed the form, I was in my Toyoto Crown limousine on my way home.

The check ride form containing blocks allowed the check pilot to rate our performance on a scale from 1 to 5, with five being superior. One of the blocks intended to infer initiative was labeled "Guts." Foreign pilots enjoyed ribbing each other in how we were rated on "Guts." The Japanese, sensitive to making a mistake, changed it to read "Initiative."

Following the rash of Japanese-piloted accidents, the stigma attached to the incompetence of foreign pilots gradually diminished and we were accepted as "roughly" equal to Japanese captains, but our copilots were still required to submit reports on how well we performed with the Japanese during each flight. This, so called "second-class" status bothered many of my American colleagues, but I believe I was successful in persuading them to ignore the inference and smile all the way to the bank. (Our annual salary in 1974 was $44,285, equal to $194,123 today.) Not bad wages for flying a two-engine 64-passenger turboprop transport for an airline now called Toa Domestic Airlines (TDA). (See Photo 55.)

After checking in for a flight (in the summer of 1972), the dispatcher, while exhibiting a big smile, greeted me with, "Congratulations, Captain Martin. You are very *yumei-na-hito (famous)."* I said that I didn't know what he meant by his comment, so he produced a copy of a Japanese aviation magazine, and opened it to a section containing a picture of me, in the cockpit of a YS-11, an in-flight photo of a Douglas C-133 *Cargomaster* and a three-page article. (I had no prior knowledge of any such write-up, and since it was printed in Japanese, I didn't understand its contents, other than the dispatcher's statement that it was complimentary.) I asked him if it would be possible to have it translateed into English and provide me with a copy. He said he would request a translation from the Public Relations Department, which should be available in a couple days. Three days later, the following translated article (exactly as it appeared) was in my mailbox.

"Dear Capt. Martin,   *10 July 1972*

I enclose the translation of the article which appeared in the July issue of the Japanese Sports Aviation Magazine. It was translated by Mr. K. Nakayama of Crew Training Department. We are very proud of you and this article will appear in the August issue of our company news bulletin.

Sincerely,   E. Nakajima, Public Relations Dept.

Excellent Flying Technique: Captain Martin, by Matsuoka Takeo.

There is a Gaijin [foreign] pilot named Martin with Toa Domestic Airlines. I fly TDA only between Haneda and Hanamaki and that is when I have business there, generally once a month. Probably only one out of five times of my trips, I find him as the pilot of my plane. Big as he is, I always get an impression that the center of gravity moved up forward on his YS-11 aircraft.

My business requires me to fly literally throughout Japan all round the year, by Japan Airlines today and maybe All Nippon Airways tomorrow. Quite naturally, I come to remember the name of the pilot of my airplane when his flying is good. It may be said that controllability of the aircraft depends on the type of aircraft. Whatever it may be, I would say that nobody can land as good as Captain Martin. His landing is so smooth that you rarely realize when the wheels touch down the ground. It is even a surprise to me that an airplane can be operated with a sense of such delicacy.

Take a DC-8 of Japan Airlines for example: It always land with a thump and a big shock to passengers. Sometimes, the shock is so awful to cause the oxygen masks to fall out. I had been thinking the shock is inevitable with the landing of a giant aircraft like the DC-8 until when I noticed its landing at Chitose Airport during winter was deliberate and smooth. I assume that the pilot was cautious because the runway was slippery due to snow.

I also say that the Boeing 727s or 737s of JAL or ANA generally make a smooth landing. And yet, nobody can match with Captain Martin's skill in landing. Then, what about the other YS-11 aircraft flown by different pilots? Again, they are no match for Captain Martin. Most of their landings give a big shock. Sometimes, the wheel rebounds after

444

touchdown, then the aircraft finally lands with a thump, or else, the aircraft swings left and right in a roll a moment after landing.

A majority of passengers of airlinero do not use airplane for their pleasure. Their purpose of riding airplane is to get to destination as quickly as possible. Most of time, they feel a comfort when their airplane finally made a touchdown at destination. Like driving a car, you do not get scared of riding a vehicle as long as you sit behind the steering wheel, but once in somebody else's car, you are grabbed by the sense of uneasiness, how much ever you trust in his driving. Speaking of myself, my fisted hands generally sweat at takeoff or landing, depending on how I feel that day.

Nevertheless, I feel no worries whatsoever when I am onboard Capt. Martin's plane. I can be pretty much confident that if a man uses such a care in making a landing, he must be much discreet and deliberate during takeoff or cruise. You can afford no better passenger services than presented by this.

Things about Captain Martin and his landings have become the topic of my recent conversation whenever I talk to people. One of those days, my American colleague, who just happened to be one of Captain Martin's passenger, came to me and said, 'I was right about him.'

I am taking another trip to Hanamaki next week. I am looking forward to the day when I probably can enjoy the ride with his excellent flying technique again."

Approaching the second year of my employment contract TDA supervisors were starting to realize that the American captains were well qualified and developing a reputation of being safe and reliable pilots. In fact, many Japanese copilots were now specifying a preference for flying with us, since they were able to make more takeoff and landings than with Japanese captains and improve their English language proficiency at the same time.

In late 1972, our two-year contracts were coming to an end and we were anxiously awaiting a decision on whether they would be extended. Captain Ogo called me at home and informed me that in concert with the pilot's union, they had decided to offer another two-year contract to 12 Gaijin captains. They were not offering to renew the contracts for Captains Emory and Ammon, and requested that I contact them to advise them of this decision. Not offering a contract renewal to Captain Emory came as no surprise, since for the past year he was on a medical waiver for a hearing deficiency and was only allowed to fly trips between Tokyo and Osaka. However, informing Bob Ammon was more difficult.

Bob and I were good friends and were teamed up together during our aircraft qualification training with Piedmont Airlines and had shared a house during our first six months in Japan. In addition, he was the only pilot who voted against me being fired as Chief Pilot, but unfortunately he had a temperament problem that Japanese copilots resented. (This character flaw had been brought to my attention on several occasions by Captain Ogo.) Bob was an excellent pilot, but rapping the knuckles of Japanese copilots with a pencil, for minor infractions, didn't sit well with their overly sensitive disposition. He was on a over-night flight to Sapporo when the contract extension news was released, and I called him to pass on the bad news. His response, "Well I'm not surprised, Lou, so to hell with them. I'll go back to selling cars in Texas." (I don't know how long Bob sold cars, but in 1977 I ran into him in Tehran, Iran, when he was flying a B-707 for a charter company in Saudi Arabia. See Photo No. 54.)

In 1972 senior Japanese YS-11 captains were in transitional training for the DC-9, and the Douglas Aircraft Company dispatched a group of American flight instructors, led by Dan Colburn, to Japan to assist in their upgrade. I was directed to conduct a one-week familiarization ground school, relating to procedures when flying in Japan, to these Douglas pilots and found them to be a friendly and a highly professional group. The fact that the Japanese trusted me to conduct their orientation training, was evidence that American captains were gaining acceptance as an integral part of their airline. It was a good feeling!

When the 1972 International Winter Olympics were held in Sapporo, February 3rd to the 13th, flights to this picturesque city were truly exciting. The main street of Sapporo was closed to vehicular traffic and international pedestrians, dressed in colorful winter garb, walked the main thoroughfare while displaying a friendly carnival appearance and speaking in a myriad of different languages. Naturally, hotel rooms were almost impossible to find, but working for the airline we had reserved rooms in the downtown five-star Sapporo Park Hotel.

On February 22nd, I was scheduled for a flight to Sapporo with an en route stop in Hachinohe. My copilot for the flight was a "Gaijin-friendly" young man by the name of Kato, along with two likable flight attendants, especially a Miss Chieko Hara, a senior flight attendant from Hachioji, a suburb of Tokyo. I was immediately impressed in the professional approach Miss Hara applied to her duties, and considered her the most competent of the flight attendants I had flown with since checking out as captain. Her perky character, nice warm smile and youthful fresh appearance made her passengers feel safe and comfortable. I noticed that she treated each one, especially the elderly passengers, with the considerate care expected of a member of your own family. When she brought me a cup of ocha (tea) in the cockpit, it was presented with a wide smile that exposed a cute dimple. (I decided that I wanted to get to know her better!) We landed at Sapporo at 8:40 p.m. and were not scheduled for a flight until 2:30 the following afternoon. (Photo No. 57.)

Japanese captains, on the first night of a flight schedule involving several days, would usually treat the crew to dinner and drinks. However, American captains didn't feel obligated to follow this custom. But influenced by the congenial spirit of the recent winter Olympics, and the fact that I had a very friendly crew, I invited them to join me for dinner and drinks at my expense. Miss Hara asked if my name indicated that I came from German descent. When I replied that my grandfather was German, she suggested we go to the famous German restaurant called the Loreley. So after changing clothes that's where we headed.

After a delicious German style dinner washed down with a bottle of Riesling Spatlese wine, we decided to visit a few night clubs to join in the jubilant merriment exhilarated by thousands of left-over international Olympic revelers. Every night spot was packed, but we did manage to enjoy a few night caps and a dance or two before heading back to our hotel. It was the most enjoyable layover I had experienced since joining the airline, and thanks to my American Express card I wouldn't have to pay for it until the following month. I was particularly thrilled in meeting Chieko and a mutual physical attraction appeared to have ignited between us. I felt that for the fifth time in my life I was once again smitten with an irresistible attraction for a pretty female, this time a Japanese.

The next day we flew two round trips to Hakodate, but were back in our hotel by 7 p.m. I invited Chieko to have dinner with me in the Sky View restaurant of the Park Hotel. She readily accepted and I made reservations for a candle-light table next to a large bay window overlooking downtown Sapporo, which due to the recent Winter Olympics was still lit up like a giant Christmas tree. The dinner and wine were exquisite and the view of the main streets of Sapporo, filled with gaily-dressed foreign visitors, was more entertaining than a fabricated

447

artificial floor show. Complementing the setting were large snow flakes, illuminated by colored spot lights, slowly drifting past our slanted bay window. I thought that perhaps these silver pointed flakes were specifically arranged by *Mother Nature* to enhance the romantic setting. When moisture on the glass tended to cloud the view, an attentive waiter quickly wiped it clean. (Hollywood, couldn't have contrived a more dreamlike scene!) After dinner, to mark the occasion, I presented Chieko with a small bottle of Je Reviens Worth French perfume I had purchased in the hotel's boutique. We then enjoyed sipping imported Cherry Heering, on the rocks, and some slow dancing to a small tuxedo-attired orchestra. The evening past very quickly and it was soon time to say goodnight. The next day we flew back to Tokyo and my exhilarating three-day trip was over, but I knew that I would see Chieko again, and I sensed that she felt the same way toward me.

My remaining tenure with TDA fell into a pattern of enjoying the life of a senior airline captain. I was flying about 70 hours per month, which provided approximately 12 days off. I was drawing a good salary, had access to the U.S. military clubs, BXs, commissaries and was free to ride my landlord's Honda motorcycles anytime I wished. I drove an air-conditioned Mazda sedan, joined various gun clubs (for the shooting of clay targets), and hoped that the job would last for another 18 years, when I would be forced to retire at age 60. (See Photos 58 and 59.)

Our TDA colleagues had finally accepted the American captains as near equals and didn't hold Captain Spence responsible for the fatal crash on July 3, 1971. They realized that there was a Japanese instructor pilot in the right seat who was the Pilot in Command. However, Japanese Government Bureaucrats continued to harbor thoughts that if there hadn't been a Gaijin in the cockpit, the accident would not have happened.

With the intent of making us feel welcome, senior Japanese pilots held a deferred welcome party in the ballroom of a prominent hotel for American captains and their families. After an excellent sit-down dinner I was asked to introduce each American pilot, along with a brief background and his home town in the U.S. In addition, in typical Japanese custom, we were presented with small gifts. It was an excellent party, but notably absent were representatives of the Japanese government and members of the recalcitrant pilot's union.

448

During my third year in Japan my relationship, and affection, for Chieko grew with each passing month, but we had to ensure that the airline was not aware that we were seeing each other. There was a policy that pilots and flight attendants not develop personal relationships, and since I was a foreigner the transgression would have been considered very serious. In spite of the potential problem, our meetings became more frequent. This newly-found feminine companionship came about at a time when the relationship between my wife and I had deteriorated into a platonic love alliance, even though we still respected each other as individuals. But I hungered for the sharing of outside activities that was not forthcoming at home but was provided in my relationship with Chieko.

We would frequently meet in downtown Tokyo, have dinner in the old *Sanno Hotel,* attend live theater shows, eat raw fish in Sushi bars, go sailing in Tokyo Bay and just enjoy being together and allowing our love for each other to grow. We didn't have very many flights together, but when we did we took full advantage of the opportunity. One flight we shared was a layover in Osaka, and we took a train to the ancient capital city of Kyoto, where we visited the Golden Pavilion of the Kinkakuji Temple, other famous landmarks and had tea in a unique Japanese tea house. We didn't know where the relationship would take us, but in keeping with the spirit of enjoying the "carefree" life of airline employees, we didn't give it much thought. I'm sure my wife was aware of my relationship with Chieko, but we never discussed it!

Chieko came from a very prominent family and was the eldest of three daughters, born to a Japanese WW II Army veteran working as a government civil servant in the justice department. It was no secret that he didn't approve of his daughter dating a Gaijin pilot, and because of this resentment, I never visited her home. (More on my relationship with Chieko in The Author's Footnote, on page 454.)

In 1973 TDA installed a YS-11 visual simulator, which eliminated the need for administering annual proficiency checks in the aircraft. However, Gaijin captains were never scheduled to fly together. When scheduled for a simulator flight check, a Japanese captain would be scheduled to fly at the same time and the check airman would direct that the Gaijin captain fly the first half of the four-hour period, while the Japanese captain flew as his copilot. Following a short pee break, we would reverse the roles and the Japanese captain would be administered his check.

The check airman, as expected, would concoct a series of abnormal and emergency problems designed to test the qualification and expertise of the pilot in the left seat (which would be the Gaijin during the first half of the period). When the Japanese captain moved to the left seat, the check airman would interject the identical scenario. Naturally, the Japanese pilot's performance, having had the opportunity of observing the mistakes made by the Gaijin, would be markedly better! This policy perpetuated the belief that Japanese pilots were superior to "ragtag" foreigners on temporary two-year contracts.

During my third year in Japan, we moved into a large house that was built around the turn of the century by a Dutch Sea Captain. Although spacious, it was expensive to cool during the hot humid summers and heat in the moderately cold winters. It was owned by an 80-year-old man from Portugal, who had been interned by the Japanese during the war. He had lived in Japan for many years and operated a very successful import/export business, but lost everything except the house we were renting. He and his daughter lived in a wing of the house and I enjoyed listening to his interesting anecdotes of life in Japan before and during the war. My son Michael attended an International School that was paid for by TDA, and my daughter Lynn attended Sophia University in Tokyo (International Division) for two years, and later transferred to the University of Guam, where she graduated with a BS degree.

When approaching my fourth year with TDA I thought that my tenure would continue for many more years, and that I may have an opportunity of upgrading to DC-9s, or transferring to JAL and check out in the B-727 or DC-8. However, the stigma of being associated with a group of foreign pilots, that had one member involved in a fatal accident, two not offered a contract renewal and occasional copilot criticism on several others, was a "millstone" around my neck that would not go away. Initially, TDA was planning on hiring a second group of foreign pilots, but this plan was quickly canceled after Jack Spence's accident. They had also planned on allowing a number of foreign pilots to upgrade to the DC-9, but, because of heavy government pressure, this plan was also abandoned.

Before our second two-year, contract was completed the Japanese Ministry of Transport publicly advised Toa Domestic Airlines to hire fewer foreign pilots. This written advisory was delivered to Mr. Goro Tominaga, President of TDA, by Transport Minister Kyoshiro Niwa. This government advisory could not be ignored, and it was obvious that I, and the 11 other

450

American YS-11 captains, could not expect to be working for the airline much longer. The directive, recommending the employment of fewer foreign pilots, was a typical oriental face-saving government mantra. It stated that, "Foreign pilots are not equipped to master the complicated knowledge required to fly in Japan, since many airports are located near high mountain ranges, where air turbulence can be expected, thunderstorms and lightning are often encountered and light aircraft increase the possibility of collisions." (Obviously, according to Japanese government nincompoops, foreign pilots were not qualified to meet these unique Japanese hazards.) The Transport Minister's memo went on to state, "To serve local Japanese routes, a pilot needs a very detailed knowledge of the local geography, and when a foreign captain mans the cockpit it is necessary that the company chooses, as his colleague, a Japanese copilot, or instructor pilot, who is fluent in English." The memo also directed that, "The company should spend less money on publicity and more on safety and to work closely with their bigger airline brothers, Japan Airlines and All Nippon Airways." (In Japan, when Big Brother speaks, the company listens!)

In the fall of 1974 the TDA Managing Director, Mr. M. Nakajima, called for a meeting with the 12 remaining American YS-11 captains, and presented a detailed briefing on the financial structure of the airline. He also mentioned the planned reduction in the number of aircraft and crews due to the oil crisis from the 1973 Yon-Kipper War, which resulted in a huge increase in the cost of aviation fuel. After speaking for an hour, and never mentioning the employment status of the American captains, I realized that he was caught up in the typical Japanese methodology of not wishing to be the bearer of bad news, so I thought I would help him out. "I have a question, Mr. Nakajima," I said. "Are you inferring that the contract with the American pilots will not be renewed in 1975?" Pleased that he didn't have to directly approach the subject himself, his answer was short and simple. "Unfortunately that is the case, Captain Martin. Thank you for asking." When I followed with a question regarding the date of our termination he said, "March 31, 1975." The company, in true Japanese thoughtfulness, was giving us six-months notice of employment termination. He added that if any American captain wished to leave before this date, they would be considered to have fulfilled their contract, and all bonuses and household shipping agreements would be honored.

It was apparent that the TDA Chief Pilot, Captain Ogo, did not wish to lose his small group of American captains, but as previously pointed out, he could not disregard a directive from the Japanese Minister of Transportation. In February 1975, the company sponsored an elaborate farewell party for the departing American pilots in conjunction with a welcoming party for the Douglas instructor pilots, at a swank "sit-on-the-floor" Japanese Ryoniya (restaurant). The festivities went on for hours, and sitting on the floor caused considerable leg stiffness, but the consuming of copious amounts of saki (rice wine) resulted in relaxing sore muscles. And for those who drank too much, it lessened the danger of injury when falling to the floor! During the height of the party the Japanese turned the event into a Karaoke session, and we were all required to contribute to "off-key," throat-clearing, entertainment. The singing was so bad that the only thing that prevented permanent damage to acoustic senses was the alcohol numbing of our musical appreciation sensitivity. The Japanese provided transportation, to and from the party, so other than an excruciating hangover, I arrived home safely.

Before the stated date of employment separation, about half of the American captains had found employment elsewhere and had left Japan. I hung on with the hope of being retained in Japan as a B-727 or DC-8 captain with JAL, and initially this prospect seemed feasible. Captain Jim Jack, the president of IASCO, told me that he would personally speak to the president of JAL, Mr. Shizuo Asada, and request that I be allowed to fly for JAL when my employment with TDA was terminated. However, his request was not honored. He said that Asada was sympathetic to his petition but was not able to grant it, stating three reasons: one, I was part of a group of 15 American pilots that experienced one member involved in a fatal accident, killing 64 passengers and two other members who were not offered a contract renewal; two, allowing me to upgrade from a twin-engine YS-11 turboprop, to a B-727 or DC-8, would cast dispersion on TDA Japanese captains who also wished to fly for JAL; third, the pilot's unions for both JAL and TDA would never approve my transfer.

My fate was sealed for any hope of continued employment in Japan. For nostalgic reasons, I requested that since I had flown the first flight in a YS-11 in April 1971, that I be allowed to fly the last flight commanded by a foreign pilot. My request was approved, and on March 30, 1975 I flew a turnaround flight to Hanamaki. My copilot for the flight was a Mr. Takehara, who said nothing about this being his last flight with a Gaijin pilot. I was also disappointed, when I turned in my post-flight paperwork to the dispatchers, as not a word was said in regard to this being the final

452

TDA flight by a foreign IASCO captain. I was left with the impression that many in the company were glad that the ghastly nightmare was over!

However, my spirits were lifted when I descended the stairs to my waiting limousine for my last ride home to Yokohama. Standing at the foot of the stairs was Chieko, who handed me a dozen roses, while stating, "Thank you, Captain Martin, for your service to our airline." Chieko, was no longer working for TDA, and since my employment was also over, it was no longer a concern if our relationship became common knowledge. I invited her to share my limousine to Yokohama, and we had dinner in *China Town* and drinks in Jimmy's Piano Bar. (A favorite hangout for airline pilots.) I dreaded the thought of leaving Japan, not only because I was leaving an enjoyable and well-paying job, but having to say farewell to Chieko, and not knowing when, and if, I would see her again. Once again, I was feeling a yearning for the company of a caring female and this time, the Japanese daughter of a prominent government civil servant who did not approve of our relationship. I wondered how this affair would end without hurting Chieko, her family, or my wife and kids. But I knew that I had found a person that I wanted to spend the rest of my life with, but how to make this a reality would be difficult. I remained in Japan until June to allow my son to finish the school year at the International School, but didn't have to worry about my daughter who was now living in Guam.

The day before our household goods were to be packed, I returned from a job search in Iran, and was dead tired. But there was no time to rest, as I had to spend the next day assisting the movers, and getting my family settled in temporary quarters in the Yokohama Navy Base. It was around 9 p.m. before these exhausting tasks were complete.

I was in dire need of sleep, but couldn't leave without saying good-bye to Chieko, and since I was leaving the next morning this was my last chance. I drove over to her apartment and through long hugs we said good-bye. As I prepared to leave she walked me to my car and through an open window we held hands. As I slowly drove off, our hands slowly separated, with the last contact being the tips of our index fingers. She stood in the road with tears in her eyes, while I blinked them back from mine. My feelings are best described in a refrain from a popular ballad:

"All my bags are packed and I'm ready to go, I'm already so lonesome I could die --- I'm leaving on a jet plane don't know when I'll be back again!"

453

Author's Footnote:

After leaving Japan, I realized how much I loved Chieko and couldn't wait to see her again. I spent three years flying as a civilian corporate pilot in Iran, and 19 years as a Safety Inspector for the FAA.

Chieko and I stayed in contact with each other, and I spent a couple days visiting her in January 1976 when on my way to Iran. (Which reinforced my desire to find a way that we could spend the rest of our lives together.) In January 1978, she also obtained a job in Tehran, and we were together once again, albeit, on the other side of the world. (This interesting epilogue is covered in my book, Wings Over Persia.) In 1980 she traveled to Napa, California where I was working as a Falcon jet flight instructor, and when I took a job with the FAA in New York, she joined me there. After chasing each other around the world for ten years, and defying pessimists, who said it would never happen, we were married in Valley Stream, New York on November 13, 1982. We presently reside in Apple Valley, Minnesota, but from 1992 to 1996 we lived in Frankfurt, Germany, where I was attached to the U.S. Consulate Office as the Operations Supervisor for the FAA International Field Office. In 1986, I took a trip to Japan to visit her father, who was dying from cancer. While on his death bed, I took his hand and told him (with Chieko translating) that he didn't have to worry about his daughter, as I loved her and would take good care of her. He feebly squeezed my hand and smiled. I think he finally accepted me as a son-in-law. He died shortly thereafter!

Chieko and I recently celebrated our 25th wedding anniversary when on a trip to Cairo, Egypt, and I give thanks every day for the circumstances that brought us together. She is a wonderful loving wife who makes every day one to look forward to. I try to reciprocate for her thoughtfulness and love, where I can, and one method I employ, which I recommend to other husbands is as follows: Since our retirement, Chieko likes to sleep-in, and by the time she wakes up I have already had my coffee, and read the newspaper. So when she rings a bell which sits on her night stand, I bring her a cup of coffee, the newspaper and a sliced banana garnished with ripe strawberries. The dividends, for this simple chore, are enormous!

454

Chapter Thirteen --- Wings Over Persia Encounters

Chapter Thirteen will contain excerpts from my book Wings Over Persia, that recount PGR Close Encounters I experienced when flying in Iran from 1976 to 1979. If you haven't read WOP, I highly recommend it, as you will find it intensely engaging, timely and educational. It's a pilot's true story of intrigue and adventure of flying in Iran before and during the revolution which overthrew the Shah (King), and allowed Ayatollah Khomeini to form an Islamic Theocracy. The Minnesota Aviation Hall of Fame (MAHOF) designated it the Best Aviation Writing by a Minnesotan for 2004. Their letter, notifying me of this award, stated, "Your book was exciting and personal, definitely the type of aviation writing we wish to honor and encourage with this annual award." (See Photos 80 and 81.)

Wings Over Persia may be reviewed on Amazon.com and Barnes & Noble.com. Autographed copies are available directly from the author.

My first flight in a Fokker F-27 *Friendship* was on a qualification training flight with Colonel Madnia, a pilot with the Imperial Iranian Air Force on February 19, 1976. The following day I flew another training flight with this colorful colonel and was issued an Iranian Air Transport Pilot Certificate (ATP), with a F-27 type rating. (See Photos No. 65 and 69.)

The Fokker F-27 Friendship is a twin-engine turboprop transport, with a 95 foot wingspan, 82 feet long, powered by two Rolls Royce Dart engines of 2,000 HP each, a maximum gross weight of 42,000 lbs., a seating capacity of 44, and cruises at 275 mph. It is an easy aircraft to fly and I was impressed by the nimble feel of its flight controls. It was more responsive than other turboprop aircraft I had flown.

My first Close Encounter with the PGR when operating in Iran occurred while taxiing out for takeoff at Tehran's Mehrabad Airport in an F-27. My aircraft was parked close to the Shah's private aircraft hangar, where his personal B-727, B-707 and *Falcon* Fan-jet were stored. The ramp space in front of his hangar was a restricted area and identified by a wide red semicircle "do-not-cross-line," and patrolled by armed guards 24 hours a day. Most of my departures required taxiing past this restricted zone, but because of a wide taxiway, infringement into it was normally not a problem. However, on this particular day, a parked Japan Airlines B-747 freighter was blocking part of the main taxiway, so it was necessary to taxi closer to the restricted area than I had in the past.

I taxied very slowly, figuring my left wing tip would come close to the red line, but not over it. However, in spite of my precaution I observed an Iranian military jeep speeding in my direction and came to an abrupt stop directly below my side cockpit window, causing me to also stop. An armed Iranian guard jumped out, pointed his M-16 assault rifle at my head and charged a live round into the firing chamber! My copilot said, "What should we do now captain?" "Stay calm, move slowly, and don't do anything stupid," was my response.

I instructed my copilot to call the control tower and inform them, in Farsi, that we were parked near the Shah's hangar and being held captive by an armed guard. I sat motionless, with an M-16 pointed directly at my head, for what seemed like a very long time, but soon an airport vehicle arrived, called off the over eager guard and waved us through the restricted area.

After landing at a secret Iranian Military base in the city of Chah Bahar, located near the Gulf of Oman and the border with Pakistan my crew and I were invited to have lunch with the civilian camp commander in his private dinning room and lounge. About 45 minutes after eating I started to experience severe stomach cramps, followed by a strong urge to go to the bathroom (WC). I made a mad dash down a long hallway, reaching it just in time. The toilet was a typical Iranian floor-level fixture with two porcelain foot pads designed for squatting. The room lacked air conditioning and with a large wide open window, the temperature was close to a humid 110 degrees. An overflowing sink resulted in the concrete floor being awash with water, greatly adding to the discomfort.

My stomach pains grew worse and were so painful that they caused me to double up in a fetal position on the wet floor. I laid there groaning in pain which increased severely if I attempted to straighten out my legs. I crawled over to the toilet opening and vomited until my body was completely dehydrated. I thought of attempting to seek help, but was too weak to cry out or stand up. With my pants down, and face hovering over a foul smelling floor-level toilet, I thought I was going to die on a hot wet floor of a putrid bathroom in Southeast Iran. The heat and pain induced a tranquilizing effect so strong that I passed out.

When I awoke, I noted that it had been about two hours since I had entered the WC, and although I was still suffering abdominal pains, I was able to straighton out my legs and stand up. My uniform shirt, trousers and underwear were soaking wet and it was obvious that no one had become concerned about me since the door remained locked. I stripped down to my birthday suit and spread out my clothes on a large bramble bush outside the window. The bush was in direct sunlight, and the high outside temperature and hot desert breeze was soon at work in drying my clothes. While my uniform was drying, I utilized the time by washing my face with cold water and doing mild bodily exercises. Although not completely recovered, I figured I wasn't ready for an undertaker, or the PGR. My clothes and underwear were soon dry enough to put on and I flew the aircraft back to Tehran.

The Chief Pilot informed me that a Pakistani submarine was making a good-will port call to Bandar Abbass, Iran, and he was dispatching a F-27 to fly its crew members to the city of Mashhad, where they would perform a Muslim pilgrimage in the local mosque. Mashhad is Iran's second largest city and located in Northeast Iran close to the Afghanistan border. It contains one of Islam's most revered Shiite Muslim mosques, as the body of Iman Reza, a noted Muslim martyr who died in 818 A.D. is entombed in this elaborate house of worship. After checking into a local hotel my two Iranian Navy copilots asked me if I had ever visited the Mashhad mosque. When I replied in the negative, they offered to take me there after we changed into civilian clothes.

The mosque is a huge gilded copper-domed structure that easily occupies an entire city block. It is protected by a high stone wall with Islamic security guards overseeing all visitors entering, as only men are allowed inside after removing their shoes. As an obvious infidel (non-believer), I was surprised that I was not challenged when visiting this most holy Muslim house of devotion, but naively assumed that my Iranian colleagues knew what they were doing and wouldn't lead me astray.

The interior walls and floors consisted of glittering ornamental tiles, along with a huge gold-encrusted sarcophagus in the center of a large doomed cupola. The mosque was filled to near capacity with male worshipers praying and reciting the Koran in a sort of hypnotic trance. Most men were dressed in long black robes, had full black beards and engaged in a slow-moving, tightly-packed, procession toward the sarcophagus of Iman Reza.

My copilots and I worked our way toward the rotunda, passing men touching and kissing the walls, with some, after coming in close proximity to Iman Reza's casket, so overcome with emotion that they were rolling on the floor, or beating bleeding heads against the walls. Most faces were drenched by tears trickling down through full beards, and a few were in such an emotional state that they had to be held up by friends. The sound of wailing and praying, that echoed off the walls and ceiling, produced a stereophonic, unearthly, hypnotic effect.

The activity I was observing was strange to my non-Muslim eyes and ears, yet I couldn't help but admire such vivid display of faith. It was obvious that everyone felt a deep sense of devotion to Allah (God) and were not ashamed of exhibiting this commitment in public.

I was standing off to one side, mesmerized by the religious scenes being played out around me, when I noticed a group of menacing-looking men encircling me and my companions. Through slow shuffling foot movements the circle was becoming smaller and soon formed a tight corral. The faces of this unhappy group were contorted with rage, as they shouted obvious insults regarding my presence. Their black piercing eyes, dilated with obvious hate, sent a clear message that I was not welcome. I sensed a serious concern on the part of my two copilots and when I asked them what was going on they told me not to speak, or make eye contact with any of the demonstrators, as they were outraged that an infidel had invaded the inner sanctum of one of their most holy mosques during the holy month of Ramadan.

I felt utterly helpless, as it appeared that the situation could turn ugly with the slightest provocation, and with a copilot on each arm we started a slow shuffle toward a nearby door. The circle of protesters, still shouting obscenities, moved along with us. When we reached the door I was literally pushed through it, and as it was closing, one of my copilots said, in an excited voice, "Wait here captain, out of sight, until we return with our shoes."

I breathed a sigh of relief in escaping the angry mob, inside the mosque, but soon learned that it was only a short reprieve from potential danger. I was standing in a small alcove, overlooking an open-air courtyard, and marching in unison around a half-darkened flowered garden were about 25 men wearing dirty white T-shirts and engaged in self-flagellation across their backs with small metal whips. Their whipping strokes were synchronized with a melodic muffled drum beat from a hidden source, and painful chants from the participants. Their backs were red with blood and when they passed my position they gave me a forbidding look I'll never forget. Hoping to escape their stares I flattened myself against the door, but I didn't wish to reenter the mosque.

As the marching mob was about to make their second pass, the door behind me opened and my two Iranian copilots appeared carrying our shoes. With backs bent in a slouch, we slowly worked our way around the courtyard and escaped through a side-door that fortunately opened onto a public street. After donning our shoes, we took a taxi to our hotel.

When we entered the hotel lobby, I was greeted by an Iranian Navy lieutenant commander, who had been a passenger on some of my previous flights. He extended a warm hand shake while stating, "Salam-u-Alaikum" (peace). He asked where I had been, and when I told him of my narrow escape in the Iman Reza Mosque, his face turned an ashen color. He called my two junior officer copilots to attention, and dressed them down mercilessly in Farsi. When he finished, they snapped him a salute and headed for their rooms.

After my copilots left, he told me that they had done a very foolish thing in taking me inside the mosque, especially during the holy month of Ramadan. He said that since I was an obvious infidel, I had exposed myself to the possibility of having my throat slit and my body thrown out into the street, where it would have lain until the following morning, or provided a midnight snack for wild dogs. He added that some Shiites living in the Mashad area are militant Islamic Fundamentalists who take writings in the Koran literally. Consequently, my visit to the Mosque could have been interpreted as a sin against Allah, and some radicals believe it is an honor to die for their religion and are following God's will when they kill infidel sinners. I felt I had escaped, once again, the clutches of the PGR in his recruitment attempt not directly related to flying.

During an early morning F-27 departure from Tehran, I was parked in the number one position for takeoff on runway 29 Right. After completing the "Before Takeoff Checklist" I contacted the control tower and requested departure clearance. The tower cleared me for takeoff without delay and as I started to taxi onto the runway, I directed my gaze toward the final approach area to ensure that there wasn't an aircraft about to land. Confirming that the approach zone was clear was difficult, as I was looking directly into a bright rising sun and a hazy sky. Because of the restricted visibility I slowed my taxi and shielding squinted eyes with a cupped hand, strained to view the approach end of the runway.

Suddenly, without warning, and no pre-landing radio calls, a Pan American B-747 jumbo jet emerged from the haze! I slammed on my brakes as the B-747 landed directly in front of my position. Had I not slowed my taxi to ensure the runway approach area was clear, and followed the tower's request for an expedited takeoff, my relatively small F-27 would have been squashed like a bug by the 600,000 pound *Jumbo* jet! Apparently, approach control authorized the B-747 to land without having the pilot switch to the tower radio frequency. If he had, I and the tower operator would have been aware of his presence on final approach. I wrote a detailed report regarding this incident, and presented it to my Iranian Chief Pilot, but I never received a response.

I was passing over the city of Shiraz at 20,000 feet, en route to the Persian Gulf Airport on Khark Island in a Fokker F-27 with a full load of passengers. My copilot was in the process of transmitting a position report, when suddenly, a Russian Tupolev TU-154, flying in the opposite direction, emerged from one of the cloud tops. It appeared to be flying at our altitude and on a direct collision course with our aircraft.

The sighting lasted only a split second and was gone as quickly as it had appeared, while missing our aircraft by mere feet. The sighting was so dramatic that I can close my eyes to this day and still see it. The TU-154 that nearly collided with us was operated by the Polish national airline LOT. The aircraft is very similar to a B-727, but has larger cabin windows, and the near-miss was so close that I could see passengers reading newspapers. My instinctive reaction, when I saw the aircraft emerge from the clouds, was to disconnect the auto pilot and take evasive action, but the event was over before I could move. The incident was so fleeting that my copilot never saw it.

I called Shiraz radio and requested the call sign of the other aircraft passing over Shiraz at my assigned altitude, but was told that they had no knowledge of any other aircraft. About one minute later a LOT pilot, with a heavy Polish accent, reported passing over Shiraz at 22,000 feet. (He may have been at 22,000 when he made his position report, but was unmistakably at my altitude of 20,000 feet earlier.)

I made a detailed report of the incident, submitted it to my Chief Pilot, but as usual never heard another word. (This near-miss could have resulted in a midair collision similar to the collision of a Russian TU-154 and an American B-757 over Germany in July 2002, that killed everyone onboard both aircraft.) The PGR wins some and loses some!

One summer day in 1977 I was requested to report to the Chief Pilot's office. As I entered, he closed the door and asked if I was interested in flying one of their all-black, unmarked F-27s, which contained long-range external fuel tanks (very unusual for this type aircraft), that were parked in an isolated fenced-in area of the ramp, and guarded 24 hours a day. When I responded that I was, he informed me that what he was about to reveal was secret and I was not to discuss it with any other pilot in the company, or anyone else in Iran. He insisted that I agree to his request before proceeding. I assured him I would remain silent.

He said that the two all-black F-27s were photo reconnaissance aircraft procured from the Fokker Aircraft Company on special order and that their cargo compartments contained "high-resolution" cameras that took pictures through discrete openings in the bottom of the fuselage. He added that the primary mission of these aircraft was the photo mapping of the Iran/Iraq border area, which the Iranian military wanted in the event of an armed conflict with Iraq. (Which came to fruition in 1980.) For public consumption, these aircraft were operated as "Geodetic Survey Flights."

His briefing continued by stating that these special flights were flown at 20,000 feet and could only be operated on cloudless days in calm winds, when ground visibility was not obscured by blowing sand, and obtaining both conditions was rare! (This explained the infrequent flying of these aircraft that I had noted in the past.) He stated that favorable conditions were expected the following morning and he was short a captain to fly one of them. He then handed me a briefing folder, marked secret, and requested I study it that evening. Before leaving his office, I mentioned that it was rumored that pilots flying these special missions receive double pay, and inquired if this was true. He acknowledged that it was!

I spent several hours reviewing the special flight folder and an Inertial Navigation Systems Manual, and felt I had a fair working knowledge of both when I turned out the lights around midnight and went to bed. As I drifted off to sleep, I looked forward to my next day's mission.

When I checked in with the dispatch center the next morning, it was apparent that my flight was something special. My flight briefing folder was in a closed binder and the dispatcher made sure we were in a secluded area when discussing the flight. My mission had me climbing to 20,000 feet and flying a series of concentric loops along the Iran/Iraq border. I was instructed that when conducting my Aircraft Preflight Inspection, I was not allowed to enter the cabin area and not to initiate discussions with the civilian personnel operating the cameras. The dispatcher, in his briefing, was emphatic in stating that I was not to cross the border into Iraq and if intercepted by Iraqi Mikoyan-Gurevich (Mig) jet fighters, to turn immediately to the East, away from the border. He added that several of their photo missions had been harassed by Iraqi fighters in the past, but so far none had been fired upon! After being cleared access to the aircraft I was again advised that my preflight would not allow me entrance to the rear of the aircraft, which was amplified by the existence of a thick curtain just a few feet behind the cockpit.

Takeoff was uneventful and I was soon level at 20,000 feet, in smooth air, and approaching the border with Iraq. Visibility was unlimited and ground markings were void of blowing sand. It appeared to be a beautiful day for taking pictures. A few minutes later I noted an amber light in the cockpit labeled, "Camera Doors Open" come on, so I knew that the crew in the back of the aircraft were starting to earn their pay. About four hours into a planned eight-hour mission, condensation trails from Iraqi jet fighters appeared in the western sky and came close enough that I could identify them as either Mig 15s or 21s. However, they didn't appear to be hostile but I took special measure to ensure that I was over Iranian territory. They soon headed west, but shortly thereafter another flight of fighters appeared. This flight leader seemed more aggressive and came uncomfortably close to my aircraft. However, this increased concern coincided with the completion of the mission and I returned to Tehran for an uneventful landing. I was credited with 16 hours flight time, for an eight-hour mission. (Not a bad day's work.)

In November 1978 I was directed to fly an F-27 to the Persian Gulf city of Bandar Abbass to transport Iranian Army electrical engineers to Tehran. They were going to take over the operation of the power generators that were being sabotaged by militant striking civilian government workers, sympathetic to the Islamic Fundamentalists attempting to overthrow the Shah. The flight was uneventful until I started my approach into Tehran's Mehrabad Airport. I was told by the control tower that I was not cleared to land and to set up a holding pattern south of the airport. After circling for about 30 minutes without receiving further instructions, I ordered my copilot to request clearance to land (in Farsi) and started flying toward the airport.

My copilot, when receiving a reply, also in Farsi, turned pale. When I asked him to translate the control tower's response, in a quivering voice, he said, "They said that if we continued our approach we would be shot down." Not wishing to become a casualty in their burgeoning internal revolution, I broke off my approach and diverted to an Iranian military base where I made an uneventful safe landing.

In November 1978, after returning to Tehran from a F-27 flight to the Persian Gulf, I was preparing to depart the company in my Volkswagen Beetle, when Fritz Grunt, a foreign pilot from Vienna, Austria, asked if he could ride into town with me. En route I asked him if he had any plans for dinner. When he said no, I suggested he join me for dinner at the Kansular Restaurant. Fritz said that he had heard other foreigners speak favorably about the Kansular, and since he had never been there, said that he would like to go. I suggested we make a short stop at my apartment first, which would allow me to telephone for a reservation, and while waiting we could enjoy a cold German beer.

The Kansular restaurant was very popular with foreigners and upper-class Iranians alike. Not only was the food excellent, but it served alcohol, had menus printed in English, baked fresh pita bread in a red-hot open oven right before your eyes and indigenous musicians and dancers entertained customers with authentic Middle East style music. The decorum was rich with Persian carpets, hand-made brass ornaments and was a great place to spend a couple hours.

I called the restaurant and requested reservations for 6 p.m. but the earliest that a table was available was seven. Even though this would require eating hurriedly, so as to be back in our apartments before the start of the mandatory 9 p.m. curfew, I accepted the reservation so Fritz could visit this unique ethnic restaurant. While waiting we drank several bottles of German beer and enthralled each other with stories (mostly true) about skiing and partying in Austria and Germany and didn't pay much attention to the passing of time. When I noticed the clock approaching seven, I was feeling the affects of the beer and didn't think it wise to drive the hectic streets of Tehran at night, since they were extremely dangerous even in the day time when stone sober. I suggested that we forget about going to the Kansular and burn a couple burgers in my apartment. Fritz agreed, and after a few more beers and a home-cooked hamburger dinner he left for his own apartment by taxi about 15 minutes before the curfew went into effect.

On the way to the airport the next morning, I stopped at a newsstand to buy a copy of the English edition of the Tehran *Kayhan* newspaper. The headline read, "**Several Foreigners Killed When Terrorists Bomb The Kansular Restaurant.**" The details of the attack stated that unknown terrorists had thrown a large bomb into the lobby of the restaurant, killing several foreigners waiting to be seated. The time of the attack was **7 p.m.!** Had Fritz and I kept our reservation appointment we would have been standing in the lobby, waiting to be seated, when the bomber struck and would most likely have been among the victims.

However, a friend of mine working in Iran was not as fortunate. Major Marty Berkowitz, an Air Force retired F-4 combat pilot, who was working in the city of Kerman, was murdered by Islamic Militants in the fall of 1978. I was leaving the U.S. Embassy in downtown Tehran when I met Marty on the street outside. I asked him what he was doing in Tehran and he told me that he had just returned from escorting his wife to the U.S. and would be joining her in six months, when he completed his two-year work contract. He said that he was returning to Kerman that afternoon and invited me to visit him the next time I was there.

Two days later I was shocked when I picked up a copy of the English edition of the *Kayhan* newspaper. The headline read, "**American Slain in Kerman!**" The article, accompanying the headline, told of a retired U.S. Air Force major, by the name of Marty Berkowitz, who was stabbed to death in the kitchen of his home in Kerman. The article stated that unknown assailants climbed the wall surrounding his house, by throwing a mattress over sections of broken glass, and stabbed him to death as he was preparing breakfast. (Marty's body was shipped to his wife, courtesy of the U.S. Embassy. Unfortunately he returned home to his wife sooner than he had planned and before completing his contract.)

After returning from a F-27 flight, I invited my Iranian copilot to my apartment for a beer and to view some snapshots. Within a few minutes my Iranian landlord was knocking on my door, and when I opened it he launched into a diatribe against me in Farsi. My copilot, acting as interpreter, told me that he was unhappy as he had observed a young female visiting my apartment {Chieko} whom he felt was not my wife, and in addition he noted numerous bottles of whiskey and wine in my kitchen.

He said that this type of behavior was in violation of the Koran and an insult to Allah. He demanded that the unmarried female not be allowod to visit my apartment, unless accompanied with other adults, and I get rid of my bottles of alcohol. I instructed my copilot to inform my landlord that activity in my apartment was my business and not a concern of his. He was obviously disappointed in my response and left in a mumbling rage.

When I opened the door to my apartment the next day, I was surprised to see my landlord cleaning the stove pipes to my naft (kerosene) space heater. He had removed the pipes from the wall, and was reinstalling them when I entered. It was my sense that he was surprised to see me, and without exchanging a word, or a nod, he left a few minutes later.

When the night air began cooling my apartment, I started a fire in the space heater, drank a couple bottles of beer and went to bed. Some hours later I awoke with a terrific headache and a bladder demanding attention. When I rolled out of bed, I was so dizzy that it was difficult to stand-up or walk. Relying on my experience of being exposed to hypoxia during aviation flight training, I knew that my body was being starved of oxygen and if I didn't do something fast, I would pass out. I staggered to the large French doors that opened onto an open-air balcony, opened them and stepped out into the clear cool night air. Within a few minutes my head began to clear and when feeling that I could walk with a steady gait, I reentered my apartment to investigate the cause of the problem.

The prime suspect was the space heater and upon inspection, I noted that the section of stove pipe, inserted into the wall, was slightly ajar. The gap was wide enough to allow odorless, poisonous, carbon monoxide fumes to enter my apartment. I turned off the space heater, and using a wet towel pushed the hot stove pipe firmly into the wall opening. I kept the windows open the rest of the night and gave thanks to Allah that the beers I drank just before retiring excited my bladder enough to cause me to wake-up. If I had not felt the need to relieve myself, I would still be sleeping. When I departed for work the next morning, I'm sure my landlord was surprised to see me still breathing. I don't think the misaligned stove pipe was an oversight, but I had no proof!

On November 5, 1978, when returning to Tehran from a flight to the Persian Gulf, I observed clouds of smoke rising up from many sections of the city. After landing, I discovered our company operations section in complete turmoil and was told that anti-government demonstrators were destroying Tehran and travel into the city was not recommended.

However, since I couldn't reach Chieko by telephone, and was concerned about my rial savings in an Iranian bank, I decided to drive into town.

I entered the Shahanshah (King of King) Expressway and headed toward the center of the city. The expressway is laid out in a valley, well below ground level, so my view of the downtown area was limited to distant skylines. However, I could see numerous plumes of smoke rising in the clear blue sky, but street level scenes were blocked by the steep sloping highway shoulders.

I exited the expressway on a familiar street, and as I crested the uphill exit my eyes bulged when I saw the pandemonium into which I had entered. An Iranian military truck was on its side and burning fiercely. Not far away an Army jeep was turned upside down and also on fire. Roving gangs of young demonstrators were bending steel road signs back and forth, until they broke off, and were using them as improvised crow bars to break open steel screens protecting shops and banks. From the buildings already broken into, they were removing desks, chairs, file cabinets and anything else not nailed down, and throwing them into roaring fires in the middle of the street. Motorists, like myself, who had driven into this chaos, formed a slow moving single file on the far side of the street, where the melee seemed less violent. I took off my airline blouse and threw it on the floor of my car, with the intent of preventing some young bearded Muslim radical, with eyes dilated with rage, of confusing me as a member of their hated military. Several demonstrators gave my Volkswagen a frightening curious once over, but I believe my Iranian license plates caused them to find mischief elsewhere, and moved on down the street.

I followed the slow moving line of cars, while anxiously looking for an opportunity of escaping onto a side street. After a slow drive of two long blocks, I began to hear the "rat-a-tat-tat" of machine gun fire and could see soldiers, wearing gas masks and armed with fixed bayonets, attempting to gain control of the crowd, with me right in the middle. Clouds of tear gas began drifting into the open windows of my Volkswagen, as I observed, through crying eyes, cars up ahead turning onto a side street. With a sigh of relief, I followed!

The sound of gun fire, and the din of shouting mobs, began receding in the distance as I drove through several blocks of narrow back roads, before safely reaching my apartment. With a chilled martini in hand I went to the top third-floor roof to observe, from a safe distance, the turmoil Tehran was going through. From my roof sanctuary I observed sections of the city going dark and could hear the sound of sporadic gun fire.

466

In 1976, Air Taxi purchased four retired FH-227s from Piedmont Airlines in Wilmington, North Carolina and assigned them to their subsidiary organization, The Air Service Company in the Southern Iranian oil capitol city of Abadan. I was sent to Abadan, on temporary assignment, and after a quick checkout was qualified as a FH-227 captain.

The FH-227 was built by the Fairchild Aircraft Company in Hagerstown, Maryland and is the American version of the Fokker F-27. It is similar in appearance to the Dutch model, but has many distinct differences. The fuselage is six feet longer, it is equipped with a Freon air conditioning system, has different propellers, the cockpit presentation is completely rearranged and has larger, more comfortable pilot seats, designed to accommodate the wide asses of American pilots. (See Photo No. 66.)

I enjoyed flying the FH-227, and preferred it over the F-27. Especially appealing was the Freon air conditioning system in the hot deserts of Southern Iran. It was a reliable aircraft, if operated properly, and during my time in Iran I only experienced one incident that is worth citing.

I was scheduled to fly an FH-227 from Tehran to Dubai in the United Arab Emirates, with an en route refueling/cargo stop in Shiraz. I dropped off about 30 passengers in Shiraz, and took on a maximum mixed load of cargo and passengers for Dubai. My takeoff was from runway 29 Right, which presents a rapidly rising mountain range west of the airport. Because of this high terrain a quick turn to the south (left) is required after becoming airborne.

My takeoff roll, due to the heavy gross weight and a field elevation of 5,000 feet, was long and slow, and just as I became airborne the tower operator advised me to use caution, and maintain the runway heading after takeoff, as a flight of four Iranian F-4 jet fighters were taking off on the parallel runway, 29 Left. This warning couldn't have come at a worse time! With a heavy gross weight, high ambient air temperatures and high field elevation, my ability to take evasive action to avoid the fighters and the high terrain was limited.

From past conversations with U.S. Air Force instructor pilot advisors, I knew that Iranian fighter pilots had a tendency of not looking out for other aircraft, or to put it another way, they had a tendency of "keeping their heads in the cockpit." I realized that the responsibility of avoiding a midair collision, and at the same time clearing the rapidly rising terrain, was mine. With one eye peering out the left window to observe the fighters, I focused my other eye on the nearby mountains, while striving to keep from going "cross-eyed."

While eyeballing the fighters, I signaled with my right hand and thumb for my copilot to retract the landing gear. I didn't feel or hear the gear come up and a quick glance at the instrument panel revealed the reason why. The "Nose gear not centered light" was illuminated, and for built-in safety reasons, the cockpit gear handle would be mechanically blocked, preventing movement to the up position.

The pilot's action to correct this condition is simple, but at this precise moment, I couldn't take the time to address it. I was busy eyeballing the Iranian jet fighters, converging on my left, and the mountains looming up straight ahead, while attempting to avoid both.

When the fighters disappeared to the south and I had skimmed over the high terrain, I was now able to devote attention to the nose gear problem. However, before I could address it, I felt and heard it retracting, even though the "Nose gear not centered light" was still on! (Retracting the landing gear, under this condition, was not good!) I asked my copilot, who was smiling with a look of self-esteem, what he had done to be able to retract the gear. With obvious pride, he told me that the reason he couldn't physically raise the cockpit landing gear retraction handle was that there was a small latch blocking it from moving. However, by using a pencil he was able to reach in behind it, move the latch out of the way, and then move the gear handle to the up position.

He noticed a look of shock on my face and asked if he had done something wrong. I said, "Mr. Irampour, you may have really screwed up this time when you overrode the built-in safety feature of the landing gear. The nose gear might be jammed in the up position and may not extend when we prepare to land at Dubai."

I engaged the autopilot and took out the aircraft flight manual for a little in-flight ground school. I explained to my confused colleague that there are times when taking off in cross winds that the nose gear might not be centered when becoming airborne. If this occurred, we would be alerted to this condition by a light in the cockpit. The corrective action was to move the nose wheel ground steering handle back and forth until the light went out. When it did, the latch blocking the movement of the cockpit gear handle would disappear and we would be able to retract the gear. If the light didn't go out, it was necessary to leave the gear extended and return to the airport and land. But, by him by-passing the safety feature, he may have retracted a nose gear that was not centored, and it might be jammed in the up position. If this occurred we will be forced to land on the main gear only and lower the aircraft down on its nose as gently as possible. Hearing this, he turned white with fright, while asking what I thought the Chief Pilot would say if we had to land with the nose gear jammed in the up position. I told him that I didn't think he would be very happy! The nose gear extended normally and an uneventful landing was made. Following this incident my errant Iranian colleague became a nose-gear expert and I frequently observed him sharing this expertise with fellow unenlightened copilots in the pilot's lounge.

The Chief Pilot had requested that I qualify in the Rockwell Turbo Commander 690A and the French Dassault *Falcon* 20 Fan jet, to provide back-up when Iranian captains qualified in these aircraft did not match demand. I had procrastinated in flying these smaller aircraft, as they were generally utilized on short-range VIP flights, and consequently generated modest flight hours for pay purposes. I preferred flying the larger F-27 or FH-227, which produced six to seven-hour daily missions. However, I felt obligated to acquiesce in company needs and agreed to check out in the Turbo Commander first and the *Falcon* Fan jet later.

The Rockwell Turbo Commander 690A is a six to nine passenger, twin engine, high wing, turboprop aircraft. It is powered by Garret Engines de-rated to around 800 hp, providing performance similar to most advanced World War II fighters. It climbs like a homesick angel to altitudes of 30,000 feet or higher, and cruises at 260 mph. Being pressurized, flights in the hot desert or high altitude, were in a shirt-sleeve environment. Air Taxi's Turbo Commanders were fully equipped with all the latest electronics, and even though the copilot's station was fully functional many flights were flown single pilot. (See Photo No. 67.)

After the standard self-study ground school program, I began flight training with the assistant Iranian Chief Pilot, Captain Samini, and after five hours of local training I was checked out as captain. My indecisiveness in flying the Turbo Commander was a mistake as it was a fun aircraft to fly. Performance and flight characteristics were very impressive and since it was equipped with an excellent autopilot and integrated flight management system, I soon found myself looking forward to being assigned missions in this nimble, light twin-engine, "near fighter." I experienced two instances in the 690A, which I consider suitable for inclusion in this book.

I flew a Turbo Commander to Khark Island in the Persian Gulf to provide administrative support for the Iranian Navy. When not flying I would be on standby status and free to lounge on the officers' white sandy beach or in their plush Officers' Club. I was returning from an uneventful flight to Tehran with a load of Iranian Navy officers when at touchdown the right main landing gear tire blew out. I tried desperately to keep the aircraft on the runway, but even when applying differential braking and reverse thrust, the aircraft ran off the right side of the runway and into a bed of crushed coral. Other than the blown tire, there was no damage to the aircraft, but there were a few anxious moments when the aircraft went racing toward open water. A large tractor was required to retrieve the aircraft, but after installing a new tire and a thorough inspection it was back in commission the next day.

The cause of the tire blowout was the frequent deposits of foreign material on the runway from construction trucks. I had complained about this hazard before, but my complaint was ignored. About two weeks later I experienced another Turbo Commander tire blowout, after landing at Khark Island, but this time I ran off the left side of the runway and, once again, came to an abrupt stop in crushed coral. However, when experiencing this incident my passenger was an Iranian Navy admiral, and he was so frightened by the experience that construction trucks depositing foreign debris on the runway was no longer a problem.

Soon after qualifying in the Turbo Commander I checked out in the DA-20 *Falcon* Fan-jet. My flight instructor was Captain Mohammad Mousavi, one of Air Taxi's high-time jet pilots. Mousavi had attended pilot training with the U.S. Air Force in the United States and flew F-4 jet fighters for several years with the Iranian Air Force. He and I quickly developed a professional warm relationship, so common among former military jet pilots.

The Falcon Dash 20 was manufactured by the Dassault Aircraft Company in Paris, France and operated by many corporations throughout the world. It cruises at 450 kts., carries up to eight passengers, has a range of about 1300 miles, and cost about $2,500 per hour to operate. (See Photo No. 68.)

I liked flying the *Falcon* and could understand why Pan American Airways and Japan Airlines used it in their advanced pilot training programs. Although relatively small in size, it flew like a large jet, and once you were settled down in its snug cockpit you could just as easily be flying a B-727, B-737 or DC-9.

Captain Mousavi seemed pleased in how quickly I grasped the basics of flying the *Falcon* and predicted a quick check-out. Reluctantly, he confessed that instructing Iranian pilots was often "nerve-racking" and sometimes even dangerous. An example of what he was faced with was illustrated one morning when we were walking toward an aircraft in preparation for my final training flight.

We heard a series of muffled explosions and when we discovered the source we couldn't believe our eyes. An Iranian captain was attempting to start the engines of a *Falcon* with the large "Day-Glow-Colored" plastic engine intake covers still installed. These covers are put in place when the aircraft is parked to prevent birds and other foreign objects from entering the engine. When an aircraft is being readied for flight they are removed, usually by maintenance personnel, but a pilot conducting an External Preflight Inspection would have to be blind, or stupid, not to note that they were still installed.

The pilots involved in this screw-up not only failed to ensure that the intake covers were removed, but persisted in attempting to start an engine being starved of air. The suction from the engine had caused the plastic cover to buckle inwards, thereby allowing some air to flow into the compressor section, but not enough for proper operation. The engine was experiencing violent explosive compressor stalls, with flames and smoke shooting out from the front and rear sections. Shaking our heads in disbelief, we continued to our aircraft and completed my DA-20 check-out. I was now qualified to fly all four aircraft operated by Air Taxi and would alternate from one aircraft type to another. I enjoyed flying a pure jet again and soon developed a reputation as a reliable *Falcon* fan-jet Captain and was being requested by name by several VIP passengers.

I was deadheading back to Tehran in a DA-20 being flown by two Iranian pilots who offered me a seat in the cabin, but I said I would be more comfortable in the jump seat. (I preferred the jump seat so I could keep an eye on my Iranian colleagues.) The flight was uneventful until we approached Tehran. During the descent we entered the cloud tops at 10,000 feet, and based on weather reports we could expect to break out in good weather after descending two or three thousand feet. However, to my surprise, and I'm sure to the Iranian pilots, we were still in the clouds when we leveled off at 8,000 feet (four thousand feet above the ground).

A few seconds later ATC cleared us to descend to 6,000 feet for an expedited ILS approach to runway 29 Right. Neither pilot had his instrument approach charts out, since it was standard practice for them to rely on memory when setting up their cockpit navigation equipment. However, in spite of their professed excellent recall, they were rushed when inserting the required data during a high speed diving dash to intercept the inbound course. In their haste to salvage a poorly planned approach, they became confused and flew right through it, at well over 200 knots, while maintaining a heading of northwest. Still in the clouds, we were heading toward the 10,000 foot Alborz Mountains, a few miles north of the airport at a high rate of speed.

I shouted to the pilots that we had flown through the inbound course and must make an immediate turn to the left. But they either didn't hear me, or were in such a muddled mental state of confusion that they had lost proper situation awareness. I didn't have time to figure out which, or engage in an argument, so I stood up, gripped a hold of the control column, and forced the aircraft into a left bank. We broke out of the clouds in a diving left turn, with the Alborz Mountains uncomfortably close on the right and the airport well off to our left. The pilots extended the speed brakes, lowered the landing gear and flaps, and through some abrupt maneuvering got the jet back on course and made an uneventful (albeit a little long and hot) landing. In discussing this approach with the pilots their only comment was "We trusted in Allah." (However, I think the PGR was close to recruiting a few more candidates, but lost the round to Allah.)

In late December 1978 I was dozing off in my apartment when I heard a loud speaker blaring out anti-Shah propaganda. I attempted to ignore the ear-shattering noise by covering my head with a pillow, when suddenly a long blast of machine gun fire erupted with such clarity that it sounded like it was in the next room. My bed vibrated from the concussions and my military training took over and I rolled out of bed and cowered on the cold floor. As quickly as it began, the firing stopped and along with it the blaring loudspeaker. Following this episode I decided it was time to leave Iran and with considerable difficulty was able to book a flight on a KLM flight to Amsterdam, abandoning my Volkswagen and months of unpaid salary, but thanks to Allah I left in one piece!

Chapter Fourteen --- Air Museum Encounters

Author's Note: *I thought it suitable to devote the last chapter and a postscript on some thoughtful reminiscences of a few unusual and captivating flying experiences, along with two close encounters, that occurred proximal to the end of my professional flying career.*

In the spring of 1988, I became a volunteer member of the Planes of Fame Air Museum at the Flying Cloud Airport in Eden Prairie, Minnesota. The museum was the brainchild of Bob Pond, a WW II Naval aviator and President of Advanced Machines, which he had built into a $100 "million-a-year" world-wide business. Bob began collecting WW II vintage aircraft in 1979 and ended up owning about 25, fully-restored, fighters, trainers and bombers. Planes of Fame was one of the few air museums in the world that not only maintained warbirds in flying condition, but took great pride in flying them at various air shows throughout the Midwest.

Pilots selected to fly these rare and expensive aircraft were hand-picked by Bob's Chief Pilot, Kermit LaQuey, and were easily recognized by their broad smiles, before and after, each time they had the opportunity of flying. Based on my extensive military and civilian flying experience, I had hoped to join the ranks of the air museum's warbird pilots, but knew that one doesn't become a volunteer one day and start flying these unique warbirds two days later. (See Photo of Kermit LaQuey on page No. 73.)

After joining the ranks of volunteers, I swept floors, cleaned bathrooms, sold tickets, directed traffic and performed many sorts of odd jobs. About three months after becoming a volunteer, Kermit called me aside and told me that he had been observing my eagerness in fostering the goals of the air museum, had reviewed my aviation resume and wanted to know if I would be interested in checking-out in the PT-17 *Sterman Kaydet* and help out in flying passenger hops. He also inquired, if at some later date, I would be interested in flying one of the air museum's warbirds. My answer was an emphatic, "Yes sir, I have been looking forward to it."

A few days later he checked me out in the PT-17 and the twin-engine Beechcraft *Barron* during a museum support mission to Bismarck, North

Dakota. This was followed by a check-out as copilot in the North American B-25 *Mitchel* by Randy Sohn on August 5th, and a recheck in the North American AT-6 *Texan* by Larry Daudt on September 2, 1988.

I say recheck, but it had been 39 years since I had flown a T-6, which was when I was an Air Force student pilot in 1949. I was surprised in how quickly I once again mastered the Terrible Texan, and Larry signed me off after only a one and a half-hour training flight.

Larry also checked me out in the single-engine Beechcraft *Bonanza*, of which the museum maintained two, that were used as support aircraft. Unless you are a pilot who loves flying, it may be difficult to grasp the joy in flying these exotic aircraft with someone else picking up the tab. The Planes of Fame Air Museum was heaven on earth for aviation buffs, young and old, and this enthusiasm was reflected in the spirit displayed in the eagerness of the volunteers, many of whom were WW II veterans, that worked and played together as a well-oiled organization.

I flew the PT-17 *Sterman* on passenger barnstorming flights almost every weekend, often flying as many as 15 flights per day. Flying passengers in a WW II primary trainer was so popular, that Bob Pond authorized Kermit to purchase a second one, a Navy N-2S. I was also actively flying the T-6 at air shows, as well as the Beechcraft support aircraft to locations sponsoring warbird flights. (See Photo No. 75.)

In the spring of 1990 Kermit mentioned that it was time he checked me out in one of the warbird fighters, and asked which one I would like to fly. I told him, "The FM-2 Grumman *Wildcat*." He seemed surprised, stating, "Most pilots shy away from the *Wildcat*, as it has a nasty habit of ground looping, you have to manually crank the gear up and down, and because of its narrow gear, it's a bitch to handle in a cross wind." I agreed with his assessment of the *Wildcat's* charms, but mentioned that I noted that when other warbirds were performing at airshows, it was often left sitting in the hangar, since there wasn't a pilot qualified to fly it. So, based on this reasoning, if I was checked out in the FM-2, I would have the opportunity of flying it to numerous airshows. He said that my logic was correct and if that was the fighter I wished to fly, to study the flight manual and he would check me out in this nimble single-seat fighter in the next week or so.

I studied the *Wildcat* flight manual, spent several hours sitting in its cockpit, and was eagerly awaiting Kermit's permisson to fly, when disaster struck! Kermit was showing his son-in-law around the museum on

474

Wednesday, July 19, 1990, when one of our mechanics asked him if he would like to fly a test hop in one of our two F-51 Mustang fighters. The aircraft had been experiencing a minor engine problem, but was now declared airworthy. Kermit said he would as it would provide him with the opportunity of giving his son-in-law a *Mustang* back-seat ride. Their wives were to wait for them at the museum, and after they landed, the four of them were planning on going out for lunch. Flying the other F-51 that day was Dick Rutan, who was acquiring "tail-dragger" time in preparation for flying Bob Pond's unique racer, designed by Dick's brother Burt.

About 30 minutes after Kermit and his son-in-law took-off, the police department in Carver County, received a telephone call from a farmer reporting a plane crash. From initial reports it appeared that an aircraft went out of control and nose-dived, at high speed, into a grove of trees on a farm north of Lake Waconia. The crash dug a large hole in the ground and scattered parts of the aircraft and bodies over a wide area. After Dick Rutan landed, and no contact could be established with Kermit, it was feared that his aircraft was the one that crashed. It wasn't long before our worst fears were discovered to be true.

Kermit and his son-in-law were killed instantly when their F-51 impacted the ground in a near vertical dive. Everyone at the Air Museum was shocked with disbelief, but none more so than Bob Pond. Kermit had been his friend and Chief Pilot for close to 30 years. In his shock and awe, he stated that warbird flying would be greatly reduced and there would be no more check-outs for new pilots. I placed my *Wildcat* flight manual in my desk drawer, but continued flying the open-cockpit *Stermans,* the T-6, and the Beechcraft *Bonanza* and *Barron.*

On April 2, 1991, I departed Flying Cloud Airport for Palm Springs, California, in *Bonanza* N1815G. Accompanying me were the Air Museum's Director, Jim Duffy, who would fly from the left seat, and Al Pike, a senior volunteer, who would occupy a passenger seat. As pilot in command and flight instructor, I would occupy the right seat. We planned en route refueling stops at McCook, Nebraska and Albuquerque, New Mexico. And after a night in Palm Springs, we would fly to the Mojave Airport to observe the roll-out of the *Pond Racer.*

The Pond Racer was a light-weight composite aircraft designed by Burt Rutan. Its mission was to break the unlimited speed record for propeller driven aircraft at the Reno air races. It was powered by two highly modified electromotive automobile racing engines. Initial flight testing was performed by Dick Rutan at the Mojave Airport, California, which uncovered problems in engine performance. Later flight tests were flown by veteran race pilot Rick Brickert, who unfortunately was killed when the aircraft caught fire and crashed during a qualifying run in Reno in 1993. The untimely death of Brickert was a tremendous loss to the warbird community. I had flown in air shows with Rick during his frequent visits to the Planes of Fame Air Museum's annual Memorial Day openings in Minnesota. There was no attempt to build a replacement, for the Pond Racer and the project was dropped. (See Photo No. 78.)

Our flight from Flying Cloud to McCook was flown in the clouds on an IFR flight plan. Jim Duffy, although not instrument rated, did a nice job of keeping the aircraft on course and altitude. This particular Beechcraft was equipped with a "throw-over" control yoke which allowed only one pilot at a time to fly the aircraft and I was pleased that not once during the flight was it necessary for me to take control. Jim flew it from takeoff to landing.

After filling the gas tanks and emptying our bladders, we filed an IFR flight plan for Albuquerque, New Mexico (AEG), via direct to Goodland, Kansas, and airways to AEG at 10,000 feet. The FAA Flight Service briefer stated that we would enter the clouds at 4,000 feet (1,500 feet above the airport) and since the tops were around 15,000 feet, we would be in the clouds at our cruising altitude of 10,000 feet. I asked the briefer about icing conditions, and he said he had no reports of aircraft experiencing ice and didn't forecast any for our route of flight.

Our takeoff and climb, with Jim still flying, was routine, although he was having a little trouble in maintaining heading and proper airspeed, due to light to moderate turbulence. However, his infractions were not serious enough for me to swing the control column to my side of the cockpit and fly the aircraft myself. (The best method for improving a pilot's skill level is to allow them to correct their own mistakes and improve in the process.) We were soon cruising along in the clouds at 10,000 feet, I adjusted the cabin heat to a comfortable level and we settled down for our three-hour flight to New Mexico. I sensed that Jim and Al were enjoying the experience of flying in the clouds, as it was a new adventure for them.

All this serenity came to an abrupt end, when a mixture of rime and clear ice began battering the aircraft. In a matter of minutes, the windshield was totally covered, and ice was rapidly building up on the leading edge of the wings. (I knew from experience that it was also building up on the tail surfaces at the same rate, but they were not visible from the cockpit.) Pitot heat was the only anti-icing equipment installed on the aircraft so our flight instruments were still functional, but our airspeed started dropping off precipitously. I shoved the throttle to maximum power and swung the control yoke over to my side of the cockpit and told Jim, **"I have control."**

It was possible that we had flown into an ice shower and if this was the case, we would soon fly through it, but If it was more than just a shower, we would have to do something fast as the ice was building up at such an alarming rate that it could force the aircraft into a dangerous stall. The sound of the ice pellets smashing into the aircraft was so loud that it was difficult to carry on a conversation and it showed no signs of dissipating. I pushed the nose over, slowly rolled the aircraft into a left bank and picked up a course to the southeast, away from high terrain. I switched the transponder to 7700 (emergency setting) and declared an emergency with the Denver Air Traffic Control Center.

Denver Center immediately responded and requested the nature of our problem. I told them that we were picking up ice at an alarming rate, that the aircraft was not equipped with deicing equipment and we needed to descend to an altitude above the freezing level without delay. They said that they had us on radar contact and the heading we were flying would take us east of Colby, Kansas, which had a reported ceiling of 2,000 feet (5,000 feet MSL). We broke out underneath the clouds at 5,000 feet and at 4,500 feet sheets of ice began breaking off from the aircraft. A few minutes later it was clear of ice, and rather than climb back up into the clouds, I canceled our IFR flight plan, and skimming over the ground, we continued on to Albuquerque, where Jim made a good strong crosswind landing. After refueling and draining our bladders we flew to Palm Springs, California and after enjoying martinis with anchovies (I prefer olives), and dinner in Bob Pond's 11-bathroom Pond de Rose Ranch, we flew to Mojave, Airport, the following morning. After three days in the desert we flew back to Flying Cloud, Minnesota, without incident.

On April 15, 1991, Jim Duffy and I were returning from Pensacola, Florida, in the same *Bonanza*. The flight was routine until about 40 miles south of Minneapolis. We were flying at 8,000 feet, in the clouds, when we started picking up clear ice at a very rapid and dangerous rate. I swung the control column to my side of the cockpit, declared an emergency with Minneapolis approach control, lowered the landing gear (to act as speed brakes) and entered a steep descent. We broke out of the clouds at 3,000 feet, where the accumulated ice quickly dissipated. Jim then flew the aircraft for an uneventful landing at Flying Cloud Airport.

Within the same time frame a Beechcraft Bonanza pilot reported picking up ice, declared an emergency, requested an immediate descent and radar vectors to the nearest airport. He reported that ice had completely covered his windshield, blocking out forward visibility and he would therefore have to make an emergency landing on instruments. He was provided radar vectors for an ILS approach to runway 30 at Airlake Airport. When seven miles out on final approach he reported that he was below the clouds, lowering his landing gear and flaps, and side slipping his aircraft so as to provide foreword visibility out of the side window. On short final, the aircraft stalled and crashed in an open filed killing the pilot. His mistake, after doing things right, was not flying below the clouds long enough for the accumulated ice to dissipate, and, not flying his ice-encrusted aircraft at an increased air speed on final approach. If he had done either he would have escaped the clutches of the PGR.

In May 1991, we were getting ready for our annual official opening of the air museum, a three-day extravaganza airshow during the Memorial Day weekend. It had been a year since we had lost Kermit LaQuey and I was hoping that the tremendous loss suffered by Bob Pond and the museum had somewhat withered. I sent a letter to Bob, stating how difficult it would be to face the new year without the guidance of a Chief Pilot, but he could rest assured that his pilots and volunteers would do everything that they could to ensure we enjoyed an accident-free season. In the letter, I mentioned that Kermit and I had discussed my checking out in the *Wildcat* shortly before he was killed and with his permission, I would like to proceed with what was previously approved. In a letter dated May 14, 1991, Bob approved my FM-2 check-out. His letter stated in part:

"Your FM-2 program sounds proper, Lou. I suggest that Randy Sohn be the one to brief you, as he would be most current. I am copying Jim Duffy and Larry Daudt on this matter as well, so they are aware of my approval and the manner in which you have laid out your safe approach in preparing yourself. Cordially, Robert J. Pond." (Sadly, Bob Pond, age 84, died suddenly on December 14, 2007, The aviation world lost a staunch supporter of maintaining valuable WW II warbirds in flying condition.)

The prospect of flying this famous WW II Grumman fighter gave me butterflies, a feeling I usually experienced whon preparing to fly a different type of a challenging aircraft. I had fantasized flying this famous navy fighter when it was first introduced to the U.S. Navy, and now 51 years later, I was about to realize this dream. (It appeared somebody up there liked me, but I diidn't think it was the PGR.) (See Photo No. 79.)

The Grumman Wildcat's original design was as a biplane, but was soon changed to a monoplane configuration. The prototype made its first flight on September 2, 1937, and the first production aircraft were delivered to the Navy in December 1940. The aircraft has a wing span of 38 feet, a length of 29 feet, a maximum weight of close to 9,000 lbs., a 1350 hp Pratt & Whitney engine, four or six .50 caliber machine guns and a maximum speed of around 320 mph at 34,000 feet. The FM-2 model I flew was the latest version delivered to the Navy in 1943.

On May 27, 1991 I made my first flight in the *Wildcat*. As I sat in the cockpit Randy Sohn knelt next to me on one wing and Steve Hinton on the other, while jointly briefing me on what to expect when flying this nimble, narrow-geared, single-seat Grumman fighter. A few minutes later they said, "Any questions, Lou?" Hearing none, they patted me on the back while stating, "Go fly, Lou. You will enjoy the *Wildcat*."

The engine started with short bursts of flame and smoke belching out from the two exhaust stacks on either side of the aircraft and was soon producing a rhythmic rumble at 1,000 rpm. I contacted Flying Cloud ground control, stating, "*Wildcat* 201, ready for taxi." Clearance was forthcoming and while taxiing to runway 09 Right, I checked the operation of the tail wheel locking mechanism, an important and critical requirement on this narrow gear fighter, as it was designed to land on straight-deck aircraft carriers, pointed directly into the wind and utilizing a tail hook for stopping. Therefore being able to lock the tail wheel during takeoffs and landings on concrete runways, subject to crosswinds, was essential.

Parked in the number one position for takeoff, I performed an engine run-up and had to press down hard on the brake pedals to keep the aircraft from creeping forward during the check of the dual magneto system. (The brakes on the Wildcat are "shoe and drum" not unlike those installed on 1930s Model A Fords.) The smooth and throbbing sound of nine cylinders, eager to demonstrate their ability of producing 1350 roaring horse power, didn't permit me to linger very long before requesting takeoff clearance from the tower.

When lined up on the runway, I checked that the cowl flaps were in a half-open position (and not obstructing air flow to the rudder), and that the tail wheel was locked. I pushed the throttle to 30 inches of manifold pressure, released the brakes and advanced it to 44 inches and 2,600 rpm. I had preset a considerable amount of right rudder trim to offset the anticipated torque, but when the engine came up to full power, I had to apply hard right rudder to keep the aircraft on the runway center line. I hadn't rolled more than a few feet before I was able to raise the tail and now had a clear view of the runway, which had been blocked by the big round nose. The thunderous roar of the engine, just a few feet in front of me, sent shivers up my spine and my skin crawled with "goose bumps." The exhilaration I felt, when sitting behind exploding horsepower, must have been similar to what the jockey of "Sea Biscuit" felt when his eager mount burst out from the starting gate. I don't think there is any thrill that a pilot can experience that can compare with making a takeoff in a high-powered WW II fighter, with the canopy open, on a hot summer day. I'm sure there was a smile on my face that reached from ear-to-ear.

Being void of guns, ammunition, bombs, external fuel tanks and heavy armor plating, the aircraft leaped off the ground in a matter of seconds. I reduced the power to 40 inches of manifold pressure and 2,500 rpm, followed by a further reduction to 33/23, and established a 2,500 feet per minute rate of climb at 125 kts. I then tightened the throttle friction knob, took a hold of the control stick with my left hand, unlocked the landing gear crank with my right hand and started cranking up the gear (which would require 29 turns). During the cranking operation, I paid special care not to produce fore and aft movements of the control stick, as I had heard that many *Wildcat* pilots allow their aircraft to go through up and down oscillations when cranking up the gear. After about 25 revolutions, the cranking movement stiffened, and following Randy's recommendation, I pushed slightly forward on the control stick, inducing a slight negative G load, and the gear locked in the up position with the ease of "a fresh Krispy Kreme doughnut."

After the landing gear was retracted, I allowed the airspeed to increase to 185 kts and climbed to 8,500 feet. As the airspeed increased, I noted that the wind noise, with the canopy fully open, was extremely loud. When half-open it produced a hurricane-like howl, and when fully closed the engine heat made the cockpit very hot, so I decided to leave it open.

When level, I set the power at 29/1900 which produced a comfortable 190 kts indicated airspeed. I re-trimmed the rudder and elevator trim controls and the aircraft flew hands off. (I didn't have to touch the aileron trim.) The sound of the engine running at 1900 rpm reminded me of an old Ford tractor, but I love the sound of engines so it was music to my ears.

I performed a series of stalls, with the gear and flaps retracted and with them extended. The aircraft stalled at around 58 kts, with no tendency of falling off in either direction. I performed a couple high speed dives and noted that with the canopy open the wind noise and buffet was discomforting at speeds above 225 knots. I closed the canopy, performed additional high speed dives, lazy-eights, aileron rolls, loops and four G banks. My first attempt at an aileron roll ended up in nothing more than a steep turn, because I mistakenly expected a roll rate, with little control stick pressure, similar to the jet fighters I had flown. However, when I realized that the *Wildcat* was a brute force aircraft without boost controls, I laid into the controls with a grunt and a fart, and it performed like the nimble fighter it was. I was sure that a 22-year-old U.S. Marine pilot, with a Japanese zero on his ass, would have no problem in mustering the strength to perform every aerobatic maneuver in the book without the grunts and farts required of a 62-year-old pilot like myself.

After about 45 minutes of becoming comfortable with the aircraft I figured I was ready to try a landing. I initiated a 360 degree overhead approach at 200 knots, reduced the throttle to idle, flipped the flap handle to the down position, set the propeller control to full RPM, turned on the electric fuel booster pump, checked that the tail wheel was locked, and when the airspeed dropped to around 130 knots, unlocked the gear handle and cranked it down. (It was much easier to crank down than up, but I noted that I scratched my bare right forearm in several places. In future flights I will ensure that the right sleeve of my flying suit is rolled down.) I flew the final approach at around 90 kts and flared for a three-point smooth "Martin" landing at around 80. Touchdown and roll out was similar to a T-6, with the exception that the landing gear struts had a habit of settling at different ground speeds, giving the impression of a flat tire, until both struts had settled and the aircraft was level.

Randy Sohn and Steve Hinton thought my approach and landing was OK, and after refueling I departed for Mankato to shoot takeoffs and landings, with air work en route. Before the day was over, I had flown the *Wildcat* three hours, made about ten takeoffs and landings, and felt like it was my personal airplane and was ready to take on a flock of Japanese zeros, but none were to be found in the skies over Minnesota in 1991.

For the remainder of the year, and most of 1992, I enjoyed a retired pilot's dream. I was actively flying the *Wildcat,* the T-6, the open-cockpit *Stermans,* occasional flights in the B-25 *Mitchel,* the air museum's support aircraft, the T-34 *Mentor* and maintaining currency with the FAA in the B-747. I even made a takeoff and landing, from the left seat, in a B-17 *Flying Fortress* with Randy Sohn. However, the aircraft that provided the most kicks per gallon of gas was the *Wildcat.* However, the extremely narrow gear during crosswind conditions was always a challenge.

I was landing on runway 32 at the St. Paul downtown airport in a 12 to 15 knot crosswind from the West, which was of some concern, but I had mastered similar wind conditions in the past. When on final approach, I "crabbed" into the wind, and when on short final dropped the left wing and fed in right rudder to keep the aircraft tracking straight down the runway. I executed a smooth three-point touchdown, but even with full left aileron and right rudder, the left wing began to rise to an uncomfortable level. I wasn't able to keep the aircraft on the runway and it scooted into a field of high grass and performed a head-snapping 360 degree "ground-loop." Fortunately the grassy field was free of parked aircraft or drainage ditches and I didn't strike any runway lights or drag a wing tip. Observing my departure from the runway, the control tower operator inquired if I needed any assistance. I replied that the only damage was to my ego and requested permission to taxi to the parking ramp.

The prime suspect in not being able to keep the aircraft on the runway was a sheared tail wheel locking pin, because I had double-checked that the tail-wheel locking control lever was in the "locked" position prior to landing. When we raised the tail wheel off the ground we discovered that the tail wheel would swivel freely, regardless of the position of the tail wheel locking control lever in the cockpit. After installing a new locking pin the FM-2 was back in commission.

When flying out of St. Paul, my airshow mission was a "mock shoot-down" of a T-6 modified to simulate a *Kate* Japanese torpedo bomber and several low passes over the airport. When turning onto a four-mile final, for a low high speed pass, the control tower operator said that I was cleared to follow an F-16 jet fighter, three miles ahead. I was indicating 200 kts and somewhat surprised that I was flying at the same speed as the jet. I then realized, that because of airport speed restrictions, the F-16 was flying his low level pass at only 200 kts.

I went to maximum continuous power, entered a dive and was soon indicating 260 kts and rapidly gaining on the F-10. As the F-16 passed over the crowd line, I was right on his ass, and as he pulled up I stayed with him for a few seconds. According to the airshow announcer, Tom Lymburn, the sight of an F-16 being overtaken by a WW II prop fighter was a great crowd-pleasing event, even if only for a few brief seconds.

When flying the *Wildcat* back to Flying Cloud, I encountered our Beechcraft *Bonanza* being flown by Larry Daudt and Sue Lymburn. I reversed course and did a Barrel Roll around their aircraft. Later Planes of Fame volunteers painted a *Kate* bomber, an F-16 and a *Bonanza* on the side of the *Wildcat*. Two more and I would have been an Ace!

In October 1992 I was transferred to Frankfurt, Germany as the Operations Unit Supervisor for the FAA International Field Office. It was a very interesting and demanding assignment, which provided frequent trips throughout Europe. During one of my two trips to Moscow I was permitted to visit the Russian Military Air Museum, which contains many extremely rare and unusual aircraft. Living in Germany was great, but it limited my flying of warbirds to my infrequent visits to Minneapolis for B-747 recurrent training or during short vacation trips. But I intended to make each visit as productive as the museum director, Jim Duffy, would allow. One such memorable opportunity occurred in 1995.

I flew the FM-2 *Wildcat* to Newton, Iowa, on Friday, June 23rd to be in position to participate in the weekend "Newton Air Fair." This warbird mission should have been a unforgettable event, which it was, but not for the reasons I had anticipated. After landing, Larry Daudt, who had flown an F-51 to Newton earlier, asked if I had locked the tail wheel before landing. (The reason he was asking was that he noticed it rotating freely when I was on final approach.) I told him that I double-checked that the cockpit tail wheel locking control lever was in the locked position, but since he observed it swinging freely, I suspected another sheared locking pin. We jacked up the aircraft's tail, and sure enough, the pin had fractured. Fortunately, the winds were calm so I had no problem in keeping the aircraft on the runway. Had there been a notable crosswind, I probably would have run off the side of the runway and smashed into a row of aircraft parked on either side! A local machinist produced a new pin in his machine shop and the aircraft was soon ready for flight.

The second surprise relates to the Des Moines FAA Office which left a painful ache and a professional disappointment in the conduct of the agency. Saturday morning, June 24th, the warbird pilots who would participate in the Newton Air Fair assembled for the standard airshow briefing. The FAA monitor, when inspecting pilot and medical certificates made note that my Class II Medical had reverted to a Class III, and was therefore restricted to non-commercial privileges. But, when I told him that I was a non-paid warbird volunteer, and would obviously not be carrying paying passengers in my single-seat *Wildcat* fighter, he said, "I have no problem with your certificates, Mr. Martin." He also told a private pilot, flying a T-6 from Minneapolis, that since he was also a non-paid volunteer, he didn't have any problem with his certificates either. He never discussed the legitimacy of my qualifications again, in spite of the fact that we saw each other several times during the day, including his visit to the FM-2, where I allowed him to sit in the cockpit and answered his questions relating to the neat single-engine Grumman fighter.

The following day, Sunday, June 25th, a different FAA Inspector was the air show monitor. At the conclusion of the pilot's briefing he was asked by the airshow boss, Mr. Doug Rozendaal, if he wished to inspect pilot and medical certificates. His response, "No, they were inspected yesterday, by the other FAA inspector, who said they were all OK." After participating in the Air Fare I flew the *Wildcat* in formation with Larry Daudt in a *Mustang* and Blake Middleton in a *Hellcat* back to Minneapolis. Two days later I returned to Frankfurt, Germany to resume my mundane job of shuffling papers and answering the telephone.

On July 24th, I received a certified letter, from the Des Moines, FAA Office, informing me that I was under investigation for a violation of Federal Aviation Regulations. The letter stated, "It was determined that you received compensation during the Newton Air Fair. At the time, your medical certificate was invalid for commercial pilot privileges. Operations of this type are contrary to the Federal Aviation Regulations." (The thought ran through my mind about the mindless harassment Bob Hover experienced, at the hands of overzealous FAA inspectors, who were now directing their wrath at me, with an obvious "gotcha mentality.")

Based on my 15 years of working for the FAA, it was patently apparent that the procedures followed in this alleged violation were in conflict with established procedures, chief among them was that two different FAA inspectors had, in front of witnesses, stated that my pilot and medical certificates were valid! I placed an international phone call to the Des

Moines FSDO Operations Supervisor and explained my objections regarding the violation. But he adhered to the bureaucratic party line by accusing me of accepting compensation in the form of being able to fly a valuable warbird, the free use of a motel room, local transportation and having the aircraft serviced with gas at no expense. In spite of my objections, he said that there was nothing he could do as all the information collected relating to the violation had been submitted to the FAA Central Region. I asked him if his inspectors had informed him that when inspecting my pilot and medical certificates they stated that they found no discrepancies. He said, "No, but I will talk to them."

Later that month I received a letter dated July 18, 1995, signed by the Des Moines FAA Office Manager, stating that I had violated the Federal Aviation Regulations and my airman's records would reflect this violation. I elevated my complaint to the Manager of the FAA Central Region, but like his subordinates, he wasn't interested in facts and took no action.

Having access to the FAA computer data base, I discovered that the Des Moines FSDO had filed a similar violation against the T-6 *Texan* private pilot, who had been told that his certificates were also valid. I contacted him and requested the circumstances surrounding his violation along with a promise of anonymity. He told me that a FAA inspector from the Des Moines office had contacted him and apologized for involving him in a violation, but they were after that FAA guy {me} flying the *Wildcat,* and he was just in the wrong place at the wrong time.

The picture was now clear! I had heard scuttlebutt that FAA Headquarters personnel had considered my association with the Planes of Fame Air Museum a conflict of interest, and that I should discontinue in such folly. I disagreed with their premise as I felt that I was adhering to the FAA's mission of fostering aviation. I had utilized my position, as a FAA inspector and flight instructor, in issuing Letters of Authorization (LOAs), administered Biennial Flight Reviews (BFRs), checked out pilots in the PT-17, AT-6, and T-34, wrote an Operations Manual, flew support missions in the *Bonanza* and *Barron* and the *Wildcat* and T-6 at airshows, all of which were on my days off and without compensation. I told these concerned "plutocrats" that what I did on my free time should not be of any concern to them, as I was fostering aviation, developing a higher respect for the FAA, not guilty of any impropriety and enjoying myself in the process. However, it is my belief that they didn't agree and found a way to fight back by coercing an amicable field inspector to slap me with a violation. When I wrote to the Des Moines Office stating that I was a victim of a discriminatory finding since other warbird pilots, under similar conditions, were judged to be in full compliance, they responded by stating, "Your case was handled no differently than any other violation brought to our attention. We investigate the circumstances surrounding the violation, interview persons having knowledge of the incident, create an evidence file, and after a thorough review, arrive at a decision."

On May 3, 1996, I sent a "Registered Letter, Return Receipt," to the FAA stating, "Pursuant to the Freedom of Information Act, 5 U.S.C. 552, I hereby request a copy of the records pertaining to my violation." Several weeks later I received the following answer. "Our office has no records on file regarding your request." (This may have been a true statement, as the records were probably stored in a different office.) I continued to fly warbirds, but not in the Des Moines FSDO area of responsibility.

In reviewing the FAA Data Base I discovered that the same office that filed a violation against me considered CAF pilots holding Private Pilot Certificates and Third Class Medicals to be in full compliance during air shows in Clarinda and Dubuque, Iowa. Their rationale for not filing a violation was: "The pilots were volunteers and received no compensation." (This decision was less than 60 days after they filed a violation against me for flying a warbird under identical conditions.)

However, the die was cast and the FAA wasn't going to back off. Unfortunately, this was a typical "cover-up philosophy" by supervisors that seems to permeate a small number of FAA offices. The agency is staffed with many outstanding professionals and it always mystified me why some supervisors would never admit to mistakes. They would do almost anything in defending their flawed actions. Ethical decision making is not an inherent trait exhibited by many FAA supervisors and this characteristic is an insult to the majority of the excellent inspectors I had the pleasure of working with during my 19 years of service. The reasons I included this unpleasant encounter were: one, I thought it was a story that should be told; two, it may help other warbird pilots in avoiding a similar problem. (My mistake was not asking the Inspector, "eyeball-to-eyeball" in front of a witness, "Are you going to file a violation?")

The approach taken by FAA supervisors in the U.S. was far different from managers in Frankfurt, Germany. An official office visit in 1994 stated in part: "Mr. Martin is a 'straight shooter' and a good communicator. You always know where you stand with Lou. He is seen as a manager who is not afraid to go out into the field and get his hands dirty. He is a

*proactive, people oriented manager, who likes to get things done. I ou is
very relaxed, confident and sure of himself. He wants you to take the
initiative. He has a good sense of humor and is a pleasure to work with."*

In August 1995, when on vacation in the U.S., I spent many enjoyable
days flying warbirds. One flight in the *Wildcat* was truly memorable. Bob
Pond asked me to fly it to Sioux Falls, S.D. for the dedication ceremony of
the Jo Foss Airport. After arriving, General Foss met the aircraft, put his
arm around my shoulders and announced to the waiting crowd that I was
the pilot who flew his beloved *Wildcat* in for the dedication ceremony.

That night I parked it next to an open hangar being used for a banquet.
Spotlights illuminated the aircraft and I enjoyed showing his daughter and
grandkids the airplane that made their father and grandfather famous. I
flew it back to Minneapolis the next day and when passing over Mankato,
I danced amongst the clouds with loops, aileron rolls, Cuban eights, and
high G pullouts. Ten minutes was about all I could take in rringing the
aircraft out and soon realized that I was no longer 22-years-old. I leveled
off at 6,000 feet, opened the canopy and landed at Flying Cloud Airport in
a cool rain. By the time I taxied to the parking ramp it was raining quite
hard and when I climbed out of the cockpit, the ground crew didn't know if
I was wet with sweat or rain, which I'm sure was a combination of both.

*Joe Foss was a famous WW II Marine pilot who flew Wildcats from
Henderson Field, Guadacanal Island in 1942. He was 27-years-old and
considered, by many, too old to fly fighters. But he proved them wrong by
shooting down 26 Japanese aircraft. For his outstanding heroism he was
awarded the Medal of Honor. Sadly, in November 2001, when wearing his
Medal, he was prevented from getting on a civilian airliner because some
overzealous airport security person thought that its sharp edges might be
used as a weapon by the 86-year-old man to hijack the aircraft. This
ridiculous blunder was later resolved and he was allowed to fly. Joe Foss
died on January 1, 2003 at age 87. I was proud to have known him and
participated in the dedication of the Joe Foss Airport.*

On May 29, 1992 the Air Museum observed a 50-year observance of
the WW II air war over Guadalcanal, which was fought mostly by Marine
Corps pilots in *Wildcat* fighters. I had the privilege of flying the FM-2 as
some of these famous pilots looked on, and had them shake my hand in
thanks for putting on a good show. That night I attended a party at Bob

Pond's Lake Minnetonka estate and persuaded four Medal of Honor pilots to sign the back of my Wildcat LOA, they were: Joe Foss 26 kills, Jeff DeBlanc 8, Robert Galer 14, and James Swett 15. I treasure this momento, and it hangs on my "heroes" wall in our family room.

The one close encounter I experienced when flying for the air museum was in a PT-17 in August 1990. Bob Pond's secretary, Pat Duryee, called me and said that Bob would like me to check out his personal pilot, Jowell Nachtigal, in the Stearman. I had recently administered a single-engine commercial pilot check to Jowell in my Cessna 150 and found him to be an excellent pilot so I willingly accepted the assignment.

With Jowell flying from the rear cockpit we proceeded to a private grass runway near Lake Waconia, and began shooting touch-and-go wheel landings. Jowell was doing a nice job so I told him to make a series of "tail-low" three pointers. When at about 100 feet, on short final, I thought I spotted something on the runway. I kicked in right rudder, yawing the aircraft to the right, and observed a vehicle parked in the middle of the runway with a man standing next to it shaking his fist! I shoved the throttle full forward, pulled back on the stick and barely avoided crashing into it. As we roared overhead I observed him running to escape what appeared to be an impending collision. If I hadn't yawed the aircraft, to ensure the runway was clear, we would have smashed directly into the parked car and ended up in a big fireball. It was apparent that the owner didn't want us shooting landings on his airport but sought a stupid and dangerous way, of making his point known. I informed the Minneapolis FAA Office about our "Close Encounter" but they werent interested since it was a private facility. (I had thought that the PGR had given up on me, but obviously he was still hoping to add me to his long list of victories.)

I will end this book by commenting on my last flight in one of my favorite aircraft. In December 1998, I was flying as an FAA observer on a Northwest Airlines B-747, with Captain Terry Marsh (now retired) as the instructor pilot. Terry was allowing new copilots to make familiarization landings at the Duluth International Airport. After completing his mission, he made a full-stop landing and when clear of the runway, turned to me and said, "Lou, I hear that your retiring next month, so why don't you fly the aircraft back to Minneapolis and show these young kids how a FAA inspector flies." I flew the *Jumbo* Jet back to MSP. However, I believe Terry, sitting in the right seat, had his eyes closed the entire time. After my smooth "Martin" landing Terry said, "Can I open my eyes now, Lou?"

Epilogue

In 1942, at age 14, I was a Western Union delivery boy in Ladysmith, Wisconsin. This was a critical year in the war against the Axis Powers and the U.S. Government and American Military servicemen engaged in this conflict relied on telegrams to keep their families informed. The majority of them pertained to soldiers coming home on leave, being promoted or similar good news. However, there were others that did not bring joy, as they informed loved ones that their sons or husbands were killed, missing or prisoners of war. When I would pick up these telegrams from the lady telegrapher, she would inform me of the nature of the message and not to expect a tip or wait for a reply when I delivered them.

I would hop on my *Flyer* bicycle and slowly peddle toward the family that was to receive the unhappy news. I figured that if I took my time in delivering it, I could extend the time they would have before receiving such sad tidings. When arriving at my destination I would gently knock on the door and when it opened, hand the telegram to the family member standing before me (usually a woman). I sensed that whoever answered the door that they could tell, from my facial expression, that the telegram was not a happy one. They would rip it open, read the contents and collapse in subdued sobs. With tears streaming down my cheeks, I would leave, climb on my bike and peddle home. This was an emotional experience for a 14-year-old boy and it made me realize how fragile life is!

During WW II family members were informed of the death of loved ones by an impersonal telegram. Fortunately, this practice is no longer used. Family members are now notified of this terrible loss by a personal visit from an officer and a chaplain, not a 14-year-old boy on a bicycle.

The first time I flew across the Pacific Ocean it seemed extremely vast, but at age 24 the world itself seemed large. However, by the time I was in my 40s I had crossed it so many times that its immensity had diminished to the size of a large lake. I think this phenomenon is analogous to life itself. When I was in my 20s every year seemed to drag on forever, and I felt that I was immortal and didn't give much thought about tomorrow. (I adopted the attitude, expressed by Scarlett O'Hara in the movie *Gone*

With the Wind, when she said, "I'll think about that tomorrow.") However, by the time I reached my 70s, time seemed to rush by in a blur, and tomorrows arrived with such rapidity that this philosophy of intellective procrastination was no longer an option.

I believe that the perception of time, moving at a "fast-forward-pace," is a natural dogma of growing old, since you're closer to the end of life than the beginning and supposedly "getting ready to meet the saints." Another possible rationale for this perceived phenomena is that at age 20 a year is 5% of your life, but at age 70 it's only 1.5%, so it's a natural subliminal feeling that the years race by at such an alarming rate. Also, at age 20, the days remaining to reach a life expectancy of 82 (my father's age when he died) are 22,630, so it's no big deal to waste a few lying on a beach or watching too much TV. However, at age 79, the days remaining to reach 82 are only 1,095, so each one becomes more precious. One thing is certain, when Mother Nature and Father Time join forces they become a formidable foe and it's very difficult to defeat their insidious assaults.

I was asked by a young friend on my last birthday, "Lou, what's it like being a 79-year-old pilot?" I responded by stating, "I don't know, this is the first time that I've been 79. Ask me that question when I turn 80 and I may be able to give you a good answer. But, I'll say this, every year of my life has been interesting and challenging, so I don't expect the remaining years to be any different." An interesting paradox is that no one aspires to die young, but dreads the thought of growing old. As for me, I prefer being a healthy active 79-year-old "live pilot" than a 22-year-old "dead one", who was snared by the PGR very early in his flying career!

When traveling down life's meandering highway it would be great if we could see the many different forks in the road that lie ahead, but we know this isn't possible. However, the roads already traveled, be they bumpy or smooth, are clearly "high-lighted" in our memory "hard drive" and provide interesting anecdotes for aspiring authors. Recording some of the more interesting ones in my life was my goal in writing this book.

When I received my Pilot's Certificate at age 17, I was eager to move into adulthood and become a part of the world of aviation and didn't give much thought to the various forks in the road that life would present. My approach was, "If I was enjoying myself, and there was adventure to be had, go for it." I have already talked about many of these adventures, but with the risk of boring my readers, I'm going to reflect on a few more.

My formative life of growing up in a small Northern Wisconsin town during the economic depression seemed harsh and unfair at the time, but in retrospect it provided the foundation for meeting unseen obstacles in adult life. Being the ninth member of ten siblings prepared me for accepting --- what many of my colleagues consider hardships --- as nothing more than bumps in the road of life and easily conquered. The fact that I had to earn my own spending money, even at a very young age, created a desire to make my own way without depending on others.

It is my belief that persons of my generation are often accused of inflating the hardships experienced during The Great Economic Depression of the 1930s, especially by people who hadn't lived through them. But I can assure you that reading or talking about these difficult times, in a comfortable chair, with a full stomach, does not adequately describe the tragedy of the times. The 2005 movie, Cinderella Man, starring Russell Crowe and Renee Zellweger, presents "in graphic detail" the scourge Americans went through during this dark period.

My 22 years in the Air Force (1948-1970) were extremely exciting and passed far too quickly, and there is very little that I would change, even if I had the opportunity of doing so. These were years with an inexhaustible reserve of youthful exuberance, which allowed burning the "candle-of-life" at both ends, without giving much thought about tomorrow. My attitude was, "Why follow a more reserved pace, when I may not live to use banked energy." As a military pilot, I held the feeling "real or not" that life could be cut short at any time and that I should live life at its fullest! Strange as it may sound I was not concerned about being personally caught-up in the PGR's web, however, I did worry about the pain and aggravation my demise would be for my wife and kids, and worried about them having the financial resources to "get-by" without my monthly pay check. I experienced similar concerns for my wife Chieko, when I flew 50-year-old WW II warbirds. Fortunately this potential problem never occurred! One aspect that made my military career so exciting was that I served during some of the best years for following a military career. I had the opportunity of serving with and learning from WW II veterans, spent ten years overseas, flew both transports and single-engine jets, never went hungry, earned a college degree, was never awarded a Purple Heart and was rapidly promoted to the respectable rank of lieutenant colonel.

I have great empathy for men and women following a military career today as they have to be ever-cognizant of being politically correct in everything they do, and constantly alert to criticism from lawyers and the

ACLU. Our military academies are frequently criticized for sexual abuse against female students, but what can we expect when we billet healthy and virile 19-year-old male and females in adjoining rooms. The military is no place for "Social Engineering." Their job is to break things and kill or capture our enemies, and anything short of fulfilling this goal is unacceptable. I have the greatest respect for our men and women presently serving in our military, but I believe their job would be easier and more productive if we would discard some of our PC concepts.

After my retirement from the Air Force, I flew as a captain for Japan Domestic Airlines (1970-1975), and was paid $194,000 a year (in today's dollars) for flying 70 hours per month. My time in Japan allowed my daughter to graduate from the University of Guam, followed by obtaining a Master's Degree in Pacific Studies from the University of Hawaii, and my son attending an International School in Japan, where he was exposed to schoolmates from around the world. This exposure, to different cultures, languages and people, provided them with the foundation for success in their adult life. Also, when in Japan, I met and later married my wife Chieko, who has made everyday a pleasure beyond belief, and makes me wish I had some magic dust to slow down the fast pace of time.

When my job in Japan ended, I was able to secure a unique position of flying as a charter pilot in the Shah's Iran (1976 to 1979). This period in my life was not only financially rewarding, but was the most interesting and challenging flying job I held. I was exposed to an area of the world that was, and is, an interesting and critically important newsworthy region, and provided me with the fodder for writing my award-winning book, *Wings Over Persia.* My tenure in Iran also allowed Chieko to break free from the shackles binding her to Japan and also obtain a job in Tehran. If we had not been able to be together in Iran, free from the encumbrances of my family and her Japanese parents, I doubt if we would have found the courage and ability of overcoming cultural barriers and obtain happiness in marriage. (See Photos 62, 63, 64, 71 and 72).

When returning from Iran, I took a job in Napa, California, as a *Falcon* Fan-jet flight instructor, and was soon joined by Chieko, who was now in a position to freely move about the world without worrying about her strong ties to Japan. When I accepted a job with the FAA in New York, she went with me and we were married on November 13, 1982, ending ten years of courtship and chasing each other around the world. Happiness is spending the rest of my life with someone I love and pray that *Mother Nature* and *Father Time* are kind to me in future years.

I spent the next 19 years working for the FAA and found the position rewarding, challenging, but sometimes frustrating. It was rewarding from the stand-point that I was hired as a GS-11, and six years later was a GS-15. It was also rewarding in that from 1992 to 1996 I was attached to the U.S. Consulate Office in Frankfurt, Germany, which allowed Chieko and I to travel throughout Europe on Diplomatic Passports, to live in a large apartment (at no expense), and to ski most of the major down hill slopes in Germany, Switzerland and Austria. (See Photo No. 70). Another memorable event was that my retirement luncheon in the Minneapolis Fort Snelling Officers' Club in December 1998 was attended by many high ranking Northwest Airlines officials and ten years later NWA pilots still come-up, shake my hand, and wish me well. It was also challenging in that I was personally responsible for the certification of many "start-up" airlines when assigned to the New York Office, and having oversight responsibility for the merger of Northwest and Republic Airlines.

However, there were times that my position with the FAA was frustrating in that some supervisors and higher headquarters personnel had a propensity for accepting mediocrity within the ranks of the inspectors. This acceptance of poor performance required that the "hard-core" productive members (which were the majority) carry the load for their "dead-wood" colleagues, as discharging incompetent employees was nearly impossible. I attempted to fire an unqualified inspector but couldn't overcome his appeals so in disgust, I approved his transfer to FAA Headquarters in Washington, DC where incompetence is not a handicap. In another incident Pan American Airlines fired a captain after he failed three successive aircraft upgrade flight checks. He applied for a position with our office but my supervisor rejected his application. However, he applied for a job with a different FAA office and was hired as a pilot safety inspector in spite of our negative recommendations. Another irritant was the agency's constant endeavor to increase the number of minorities by pushing them into supervisory positions before they were ready. This practice was not fair to them or the employees they supervised.

When I retired from the FAA in January 1999, I submitted a three-page letter to the FAA Administrator, outlining observations that I thought would be helpful. One area of concern I elucidated on was the easy access a hijacker or terrorist would have in gaining entrance to the cockpits of U.S. passenger aircraft. I pointed out that all a potential hijacker had to do was obtain a seat in first class and wait until the flight attendant opened the cockpit door to take coffee to the pilots, or when a pilot left the cockpit to use the lavatory. I also pointed out that some airlines employed a "discreet" cockpit door knock, which authorizes the flight engineer to unlock the door from the inside and a potential hijacker could easily be made aware of this secret knock by sitting in the front of the aircraft. I suggested that a possible solution, although expensive, would be to provide double cockpit doors. As a potential overseas problem, I pointed out that foreign airlines frequently fly with their cockpit doors open. I did not receive a response to my letter, which was sent two years before the 9/11/01 terrorist attacks on the WTC and the Pentagon. However, it may be disingenuous to direct my criticism solely at the FAA. I believe the same frustrations could be said about any government agency that seems to grow immeasurably with each new administration. When the 9/11 National Commission on Terrorist Attacks Upon the United States was formed, I sent a copy of the letter I sent to the FAA in 1999, to the Commission Chairman, but once again my comments went unanswered.

In July 2005, my son, who flies for a U.S. airline, was "deadheading" in uniform from Salt Lake City to Los Angeles. He secured a seat in the cabin and after takeoff the lead flight attendant said that she wished to speak with him. She was concerned about five black-turbaned male passengers, with long shaggy beards, and dressed in full-length Islamic-style robes. Because of their strange appearance she requested a printout of their travel itinerary, and discovered that they had flown from Pakistan, Bangkok, Taipei, New York and Salt Lake City, without making a lay-over stop, had been traveling for 40 straight hours and didn't check any baggage. She told him that she had been a flight attendant for 20 years and this was the most concerned she had ever been regarding suspicious looking passengers, especially since they numbered five, the same number that hijacked three of the aircraft on 9/11/01.

According to the flight attendant, the captain requested that my son stand next to the cockpit door for the remainder of the flight and that she was going to position two galley carts in the aisle "as a possible barrier" and that the seat-belt sign was to be left on. However, her announcement that all passengers must remain seated was ignored by the five suspicious passengers, who stood in the aisle while engaging in Muslim praying bows of touching their foreheads on the floor, while chanting to Allah. The flight landed at LAX without incident and the suspect passengers were allowed to go their merry way, without anyone questioning their strange behavior. I sent a detailed report of the incident, including times, dates, flight numbers, etc. to the Secretary of Homeland

Security, but received no response. Why these passengers were not questioned, or charged with interfering with a crew member, is a mystery. (I guess airline officials feared an ACLU lawsuit if they raised the issue.)

I'm not implying that our government leaders are inept or don't have the best interest of the country in mind, but I am inferring that our government has grown to such an unwieldy size that the left hand doesn't know what the right hand is doing. A case in point would be in trying to understand the thousands of pages of instructions published by the IRS, deciphering the Government's Medicare Prescription Drug Program, reviewing the catastrophe surrounding Hurricane Katrina, the UN oil-for-food program, the Vietnam and Iraq wars and the undocumented immigration problem. I believe these are mere examples of what lies ahead if our politicians continue to expand our already "out-of-control" bloated government.

Author's Final Note: I thought that when I retired from professional flying the PGR would give up on me, but I was wrong! Following a visit to Owatonna, Minnesota, I was flying back to Minneapolis with an overfly of Stanton Airport (the home port of the Minnesota Soaring Club). Approaching Stanton at 3,500 feet, I switched to their radio frequency to decide if it would be feasible to land and make a glider flight. I made a visual check for airborne gliders and observed none but noted a long line of gliders on the ground waiting to be launched so I decided to continue on toward Minneapolis. I momentarily directed my attention inside the cockpit to change radio frequencies and when I again looked up there was a *Schleicher* ASK-21 glider, slightly above, but heading directly at me. We missed colliding "head-on" by about 85 feet. The near-miss was so fleeting that I didn't have time to initiate evasive action. I don't believe the glider pilot saw my aircraft approaching as I was in his "blind-spot" directly below his nose. As we passed the thought ran through my mind of how shocking it would have been for my wife and family to be informed that I was killed in a mid-air collision. I was with her when she was informed that her mother had suddenly died and was able to hold her in my arms and comfort her, but I wouldn't be with her this time. When investigators would sift through the wreckage of my C-150 they would find copies of my book *Close Encounters with the Pilot's Grim Reaper (a tragic irony)*. As I laid in bed next to my wife that evening it was difficult to erase the image of the glider I almost collided with and how terrible she would feel to have the space next to her empty for the rest of her life. The PGR never sleeps and cockpit complacency is his "siren-call" to strike.

495

Glossary

Angle of attack -------------------The angle at which the relative airflow meets the airfoil (wings).

ATIS------------------------------Automatic Terminal Information System that provides weather and other related information to pilots.

ATP-------------------------------Highest level of pilot's certificate.

Compressor stall-----------------A jet engine that is starved of sufficient air flow to sustain combustion.

Cuban Eight maneuver---------A loop where on the down-side the aircraft rolls upright and completes a loop in the opposite direction.

Deadheading--------------------Crew member flying as a non-member of the assigned crew.

DME------------------------------Onboard electronic equipment which measures distance to a station.

Dutch Roll-----------------------A roll/yaw phenomenon that is usually associated with high speed swept-wing jet aircraft. It can be confusing and fatal.

Feathered propeller------------Causing the propeller blade to streamline to the relative air flow (minimum drag).

Flux-gate compass------------Electronic magnetic compass which provides heading information to RMI.

Immelman----------------------A half loop with rolling upright on top.

ITO--------------------------------Takeoff by reference to instruments only.

Manifold pressure--------------Barometric pressure in engine cylinders measured in inches of mercury.

MDA------------------------------Minimum descent altitude allowed during a non-precision approach to an airport.

Propeller P factor---------------An aerodynamic effect that causes aircraft manufactured in the U.S. to yaw to the left when operated at high power and low speed. (takeoff and climb.)

Ram air generator--------------Electrical generator driven by airflow.

Ramadan------------------------Month when devout Muslims do not drink, eat or engage in sex from sunrise to sunset.

RMI------------------------------Remote magnetic indicator in the cockpit which provides heading information.

Safe single-engine speed------The minimum speed to fly a multi-engine aircraft with engine(s) inoperative.

Seat of pants--------------------Flying an aircraft by natural instincts only.

Skeet shooting-------------------Shooting clay targets with a shotgun.

Space-available seat-----------Allowed to occupy a passenger seat without displacing a revenue passenger.

Split S maneuver----------------Rolling the aircraft inverted and completing the bottom half of a loop to level flight.

Stall------------------------------When the aircraft wings can no longer provide sufficient lift to support the weight of the aircraft. A stall occurs when the Angle of Attack is too great.

Tail wheel aircraft--------------Aircraft that is equipped with wheel or skid on aircraft tail.

Tailspin--------------------------An aircraft spiraling down in a tight circle after stalling. It is sometimes very difficult to recover from this phenomenon depending on the aircraft and pilot skill.

Three-point landing------------Landing on the main gear and tail wheel at the same time (most difficult landing).

Triangulation fix-----------------Determining the relative position of an aircraft by two or more radio stations.

UHF radio-----------------------Ultra High Frequency radio, normally used in military aircraft.

VHF radio------------------------Very High Frequency radio, used by both military and civilian aircraft.

Index

Playing golf in Thailand, 288
Plymouth afterburner, 206
PMB assignment, 270
Popped rivets on F-100, 316
Power off stall in C-133, 333
Promoted to captain, 173
promoted to major, 269
PRT failure in C-119G, 168
PT-17 close encounter, 488
Pubic hair crabs, 60
Publicity articles on Gaijins, 439

Q
Qui Nhon, Vietnam, 367

R
Rats in C-133 at Midway, 380
Reporting to Dover AFB, 320
Restriction on flying the Alps, 183
Returning to Japan in 1976, 297
Returning to U.S. in 1957, 185
RF-101 crew and F-100, 311
Rhine Main Gateway Gardens, 69
Rickshaw race in Japan, 129
RMI failure in C-133, 381
Rope & pulley ride, 14

S
Saigon Majestic Hotel, 279
Salt Lake City to LAX incident, 379
Sanno Hotel, Tokyo, 134
Security inspection Misawa, 315
Selling off-base in Japan, 301
Sgt. Battleson in Mitchel, 227
Sgt. Thomas in Misawa, 274
Shooting Germans in Germany, 59
Sick Capt. Alexander, 350, 359
Simulator check in YS-11, 449
Sioux Falls, Iowa & Joe Foss, 486

Ski trip to Switzerland, 374
Skiing in Japan, 302
Small arms flt. to Vietnam, 356
Snap-shot on Pacific bases, 350
Spence accident in YS-11, 438
Spence & Emery extra time, 414
St. Lawrence Sea-way flt., 192
Stag Bar in Misawa, 267
Stripteaser incident, 276
Sunday drive in Japan, 277
Swimming in Athens Bay, 181

T
T-6 ITO accident in Waco, TX., 38
T-33 accident in Georgia, 234
T-33 initial checkout, 222
T-33 crash at Niagara Falls, 197
T-33 night flight odyssey, 238
T-34 Mentor, 41, 42, 43
T-39 initial checkout, 307
T-39 flight to Saigon, 308
T-6 Texan description, 30
TDY to South Vietnam, 278
Teenage years in Wisconsin, 10
Terrorist attack 9/11/01, 235
Tet Offensive battle in 68, 394
Three eng. C-133 landing, 342
Three stops to Vietnam, 352
Tiger Moth flight, 155
Tire blow-outs in 690, 470
Tour in Germany ending, 99
Towing Delmar targets, 225
Trip home in 1950, 76
Trip to Reno 1966, 373
Turbo-Commander 690, 469
Twenty-seven C-82s in-flt, 83
Two-year contract renewal, 445
Typhoon evacuation, 342
Typical YS-11 flight, 424

U

Upgraded to C-133 pilot flight examiner, 358

V

Vietnam war tax exemption, 374
Volk Field, Wis. flight in T-33, 229
Wake Island description, 351
Walter Cronkite's comment on war, 394
Washer/dryer in off-base housing in Japan, 264
Weslar's wild ride in Niagara Falls, 201
West Point of The Air movie and book, 13, 219
Wiesbaden nymphomaniac, 68
Wiesbaden Germany Rod & Gun Club, 58
Wild Boar hunt in Germany, 59
Wildcat initial checkout, 478
Wildcat flying at St. Paul, 482
Wildcat Letter of Authorization, 487
Willys sedan in Germany, 93
Winter Olympics in Japan 1972, 446

Y

YS-11 in Japan and U.S., 419
YS-11 training at Piedmont Aviation, 410
YS-11 IOE flight in Japan, 420

Printed in the United States
By Bookmasters